eighth edition

Latin
for AMERICANS

Now in its eighth edition!

Latin for Americans continues to offer a solid approach to teaching the Latin language and Roman culture, and also includes many contemporary new features.

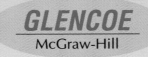

GLENCOE
McGraw-Hill

goes beyond the basics to create interest and excitement in the classroom with

- Active use of Latin through a new focus on **group and paired activities**
- Fascinating insights into **Roman civilization** and its influence on the modern world
- Lots of **colorful** photographs and art reproductions
- **Stimulating reading** including stories in Latin and reading selections from authors such as Ovid, Pliny, Vergil and Julius Caesar. . .

Students discover a world of words

The eighth edition of **Latin for Americans** features user-friendly presentations on Latin grammar and structure and an increased focus on vocabulary. Therefore, students are able to read passages in Latin more easily. Their command of English vocabulary will continue to grow!

Unit XI

Greek Myths and Roman History

Although the Romans had their own stories and traditions surrounding their gods, many stories were also borrowed or adapted from the Greek. In this scene, Perseus is seen slaying the dragon that threatens Andromeda, an Ethiopian princess whose mother had boasted that Andromeda was more beautiful than the Nereids. This enraged Neptune, who sent a sea monster to ravage Ethiopia. The only recourse was to sacrifice Andromeda, so she was chained to a cliff. Perseus saw her, rescued her, and killed the monster, who was then turned into the world's first coral.

Alinari/Art Resource, NY

351

8th Edition

Latin for Americans 8th edition is a result of valuable insights and feedback from Latin instructors nationwide

New Features for Levels 1 & 2

- Colorful photographs and beautiful art reproductions with an attractive design add visual interest to each unit.
- Concise, logical presentations of Latin structure enable students to grasp concepts more easily.
- New vocabulary and derivative sections help to expand students' English vocabulary.
- Group and paired activities encourage critical thinking and creativity.
- New and updated readings in English provide students with a knowledge of Roman civilization's influence upon the modern world.
- Complete and concise review of Level 1 eases students' transition into Level 2.
- Expanded vocabulary and word studies increase students' confidence in both English and Latin.

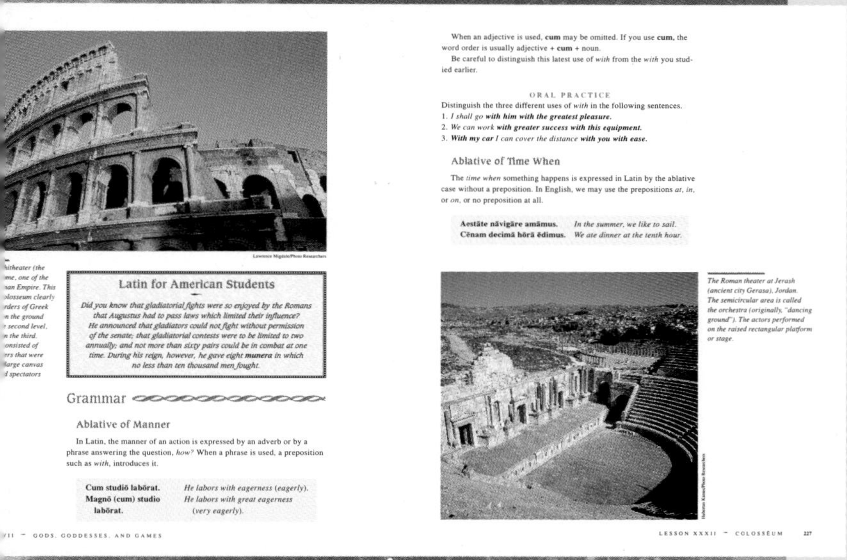

Lawrence Migdale/Photo Researchers

...hitheater (the ...me, one of the ...nan Empire. This ...olosseum clearly ...rders of Greek ...n the ground ...e second level, ...n the third. ...onsisted of ...ers that were ...large canvas ...d spectators

Latin for American Students

Did you know that gladiatorial fights were so enjoyed by the Romans that Augustus had to pass laws which limited their influence? He announced that gladiators could not fight without permission of the senate; that gladiatorial contests were to be limited to two annually; and not more than sixty pairs could be in combat at one time. During his reign, however, he gave eight ***munera*** *in which no less than ten thousand men fought.*

Grammar

Ablative of Manner

In Latin, the manner of an action is expressed by an adverb or by a phrase answering the question, *how?* When a phrase is used, a preposition such as *with*, introduces it.

Cum studiō labōrat.	*He labors with eagerness (eagerly).*
Magnō (cum) studio labōrat.	*He labors with great eagerness (very eagerly).*

...II — GODS, GODDESSES, AND GAMES

When an adjective is used, **cum** may be omitted. If you use **cum,** the word order is usually adjective + **cum** + noun.

Be careful to distinguish this latest use of *with* from the *with* you studied earlier.

ORAL PRACTICE

Distinguish the three different uses of *with* in the following sentences.

1. *I shall go* ***with him with the greatest pleasure.***
2. *We can work* ***with greater success with this equipment.***
3. ***With my car*** *I can cover the distance* ***with you with ease.***

Ablative of Time When

The *time when* something happens is expressed in Latin by the ablative case without a preposition. In English, we may use the prepositions *at, in,* or *on*, or no preposition at all.

Aestāte nāvigāre amāmus.	*In the summer, we like to sail.*
Cēnam decimā hōrā ēdimus.	*We ate dinner at the tenth hour.*

The Roman theater at Jerash (ancient city Gerasa), Jordan. The semicircular area is called the orchestra (originally, "dancing ground"). The actors performed on the raised rectangular platform or stage.

Hubertus Kanus/Photo Researchers

LESSON XXXII — COLOSSĒUM 227

New Features for Level 3

- Colorful and attractive design with new photographs and illustrations enhances content and supply visual interest.
- Focus on Latin literature by authors including Pliny, Cicero, Aulus Gellius, and Ovid gives students an overview of Roman literary heritage.
- Expanded vocabulary and word studies increase students' confidence in both English and Latin.

Available for Levels 1, 2, & 3

NEW! Teacher's Annotated Edition

Teachers will find everything they need for class preparation in this all-in-one Teacher's Annotated Edition. On every page teachers will find the following items:

- Answer Keys for all exercises
- Teaching suggestions and notes
- Pre- and post-reading activities
- Bell Ringer Reviews

The Teacher's Manual located in the front of the book contains sample lesson plans, English translations for all readings, project ideas, cooperative learning activities, and a bibliography of supplementary sources.

Available for Levels 1 & 2

Student Workbook

Provides additional practice through a variety of exercises. Revised to correspond to the updated student text. A **Teacher's Annotated Edition Workbook** is also available and provides answer keys for all the exercises.

Progress Tests

Includes a test for each unit—measuring reading comprehension, vocabulary, syntax, and cultural knowledge. Answer key available for teachers.

Audiocassette Program

Revised recordings of stories and reading selections from the main text cued with Latin music.

NEW! Art and Map Transparencies

Contains colorful, easy-to-use art reproductions and maps of the ancient Roman World. A perfect tool for sparking interest and generating discussion!

Crossword Puzzle Booklet

Contains a Latin puzzle with answer key for each vocabulary lesson—an entertaining way to reinforce and review newly-acquired vocabulary.

Latin for Americans - Level 1

Student Edition	0-02-640912-
Teacher's Annotated Edition	0-02-640915-
Workbook, PE	0-02-640916-
Workbook, TAE	0-02-640917-
Progress Tests	0-02-640918-
Audio Cassettes	0-02-640919-
Crossword Puzzle Booklet	0-02-646024-
Color Transparencies	0-02-646025-

Latin for Americans - Level 2

Student Edition	0-02-640913-
Teacher's Annotated Edition	0-02-640923-
Workbook, PE	0-02-640924-
Workbook, TAE	0-02-640925-
Progress Tests	0-02-640926-
Audio Cassettes	0-02-640927-
Crossword Puzzle Booklet	0-02-646026-
Color Transparencies	0-02-646027-

Latin for Americans - Level 3

Student Edition	0-02-640914-
Teacher's Annotated Edition	0-02-640945-
Teacher's Resource Guide	0-02-640946-

For more information, contact your nea[r] regional office or call 1-800-334-7344

1. Northeast Region
Glencoe/McGraw-Hill
15 Trafalgar Square #201
Nashua, NH 03063-1968
Phone: 603-880-4701
Phone: 800-424-3451
Fax: 603-595-0204

2. Mid-Atlantic Region
Glencoe/McGraw-Hill
P.O. Box 458
Hightstown, NJ 08520-0458
Phone: 609-426-5560
Phone: 800-553-7515
Fax: 609-426-7063

3. Atlantic-Southeast Region
Glencoe/McGraw-Hill
Brookside Park
One Harbison Way, Suite 101
Columbia, SC 29212
Phone: 803-732-2365
Phone: 800-731-2365
Fax: 803-732-4582

4. Southeast Region
Glencoe/McGraw-Hill
6510 Jimmy Carter Boulevard
Norcross, GA 30071
Phone: 770-446-7493
Phone: 800-982-3992
Fax: 770-446-2356

5. Mid-America Region
Glencoe/McGraw-Hill
936 Eastwind Drive
Westerville, OH 43081
Phone: 614-890-1111
Phone: 800-848-1567
Fax: 614-899-4905

6. Great Lakes Region
Glencoe/McGraw-Hill
846 East Algonquin Road
Schaumburg, IL 60173
Phone: 708-397-8448
Phone: 800-762-4876
Fax: 708-397-9472

7. Mid-Continent Region
Glencoe/McGraw-Hill
846 East Algonquin Road
Schaumburg, IL 60173
Phone: 708-397-8448
Phone: 800-762-4876
Fax: 708-397-9472

8. Southwest Region
Glencoe/McGraw-Hill
320 Westway Place, Suite 550
Arlington, TX 76018
Phone: 817-784-2113
Phone: 800-828-5096
Fax: 817-784-2116

9. Texas Region
Glencoe/McGraw-Hill
320 Westway Place, Suite 550
Arlington, TX 76018
Phone: 817-784-2100
Phone: 800-828-5096
Fax: 817-784-2116

10. Western Region
Glencoe/McGraw-Hill
709 E. Riverpark Lane, Suite 15C
Boise, ID 83706
Phone: 208-368-0300
Phone: 800-452-6126
Fax: 208-368-0303
Includes Alaska

11. California Region
Glencoe/McGraw-Hill
15319 Chatsworth Street
P. O. Box 9609
Mission Hills, CA 91346
Phone: 818-898-1391
Phone: 800-423-9534
Fax: 818-898-3864
Includes Hawaii

Glencoe Catholic School Region
Glencoe/McGraw-Hill
25 Crescent Street, 1st Floor
Stamford, CT 06906
Phone: 203-964-9109
Phone: 800-551-8766
Fax: 203-967-3108

Canada
McGraw-Hill Ryerson Ltd.
300 Water Street
Whitby, Ontario
L1N 9B6, Canada
Phone: 905-430-5088
Fax: 905-430-5194

International
The McGraw-Hill Companies
International Marketing
1221 Avenue of the Americas
28th Floor
New York, NY 10020
Phone: 212-512-3641
Fax: 212-512-2186

DoDDS and Pacific Territories
McGraw-Hill School
Publishing Company
600 Delran Parkway
Delran, NJ 08075
Phone: 609-764-4586
Fax: 609-764-4587

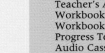

FL 91232-6

GLENCOE
McGraw-Hill

Teacher's Manual

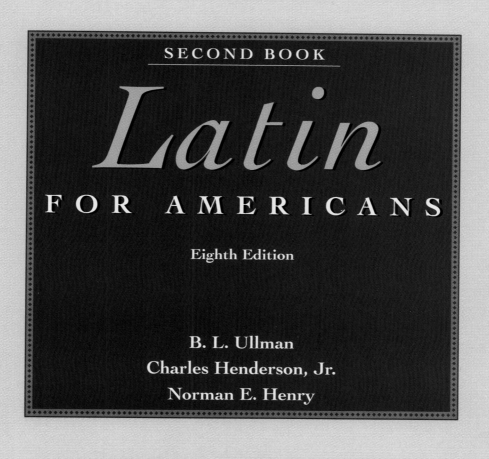

SECOND BOOK

Latin FOR AMERICANS

Eighth Edition

B. L. Ullman
Charles Henderson, Jr.
Norman E. Henry

GLENCOE
McGraw-Hill

New York, New York   Columbus, Ohio   Mission Hills, California   Peoria, Illinois

Glencoe/McGraw-Hill

A Division of The ***McGraw-Hill*** *Companies*

Send all inquiries to:
Glencoe/McGraw-Hill
15319 Chatsworth Street
P.O. Box 9609
Mission Hills, CA 91346-9609

ISBN 0-02-640923-2 (Teacher's Annotated Edition)

Printed in the United States of America

1 2 3 4 5 6 7 8 9 10 RRDW 00 99 98 97 96

Contents

Second-Year Latin TM–4

Sources of Supplementary Teaching Materials TM–5

Latin to English TM–6

Second-Year Latin

The suggested teaching procedure for *Latin for Americans, Second Book* is generally the same as that for the *First Book*, except that by now students are expected to know a minimum of forms, syntax, and vocabulary and to use this minimum to get meaning quickly out of Latin sentences and paragraphs.

The *Second Book* contains far more reading material than can be taught slowly and carefully, in the traditional fashion, in one year. There are two reasons for this. First, the abundance of material gives greater freedom of choice. Some teachers are less interested —or not interested at all—in some reading material; others may like the same readings that the first group rejects. On the other hand, a certain amount of conformity, without regimentation, is desirable. This book permits such conformity without sacrifice of individual choice because forms, syntax, and vocabulary are constantly repeated in the units. For teachers who like to have a lesson plan presented to lessen the demand on their time, some suggestions are made in the Introduction, p. xi of the *Second Book*. These suggestions are elaborated in the following paragraphs.

Second, the large amount of reading material encourages you to get your students to read more rapidly and thus to cover more ground. Of course, when unfamiliar English constructions such as the subjunctive are introduced, you should proceed slowly enough to ensure that the students get a thorough understanding of them, using the explanations and examples in the book as well as the practice drills and the translation exercises. Your own experience contributes much also.

The amount of time you devote to Unit I will vary according to what the class remembers from the first year. A good class can read the stories in Lessons I and IX in one or two weeks. A less advanced class will take longer. It is difficult to get away from the slow pace to which first-year students too easily become accustomed, but they must learn to read Latin rapidly. If the class can read the material with comprehension, do not linger at this stage over the finer grammatical points. Just as important, the teacher must learn to speed up. Unit I can be omitted entirely if the review does not appear to be necessary, or if the material does not appeal to you or the class.

Unit II (Lessons X to XXVI) will take longer than Unit I because the subjunctive and other new forms and constructions are introduced. Yet, here again be careful of excessive slowness. The stories are no more difficult than those in Unit I, except for the new forms and syntax, and the secret is to keep the students *reading Latin* first and foremost.

Since Unit III is largely based on a review of the grammar in Unit II, it ought to be possible to cover many of the lessons rapidly. Units II and III contain the basic lessons for the first semester.

Unit IV can be omitted very easily, as far as grammar is concerned, though it prepares for Caesar by emphasizing Caesarian constructions and phraseology. Unless you have a particular fondness for this unit, or plenty of time, it would be advisable to omit it or read only a few selections at sight.

Units V to VII give the most interesting parts of Caesar's *Gallic War*. In most cases, it seems best not to begin Caesar until the second semester.

For some teachers whether or not to "stick with Caesar," and how much Caesar to cover, can be a painful decision. Here are some considerations on both sides.

Pro Caesar: Julius Caesar was unquestionably a great man. His career, were it not so well attested, would be a legend, and his personality is a constant source of fascination. Students know his name beyond that of all other Romans. The narrative of the *Gallic War* is action-packed and can easily be made to come alive. Caesar's style is relatively simple (though less simple than is often claimed) and of remarkable purity and uniformity, so that after mastery of a limited vocabulary and relatively few grammatical constructions, students can move fairly rapidly. Since Caesar is a standard second-year author, students share an educational experience with a great many others of their age and joins a still greater number of their elders who have also laid down stern commands to Ariovistus, bridged the Rhine, and brought Vercingetorix to his knees. And, to mention a very small point, the Caesar students meet their colleagues in various local and state competitions at no disadvantage. There is also the likelihood that if students do not study Caesar in high school, even if they go on in Latin, they will not meet the *Gallic War* until graduate school—perhaps not even then. There are at hand many attractive teaching aids to supplement the classwork (Shakespeare's *Julius Caesar* and Shaw's *Caesar and Cleopatra*, to mention just two). Finally, you as the teacher have probably studied Caesar and may have already worked an effective program, so that change simply for the sake of novelty may not be worth the risk of destroying a successful method.

Contra Caesar: Great as Caesar was, his ruthless drive to win and wield power has made him a symbol of absolutism, something repugnant to the ideals of American democracy. And while the fact of his bloody conquest of a free Gallic nation cannot and should not be suppressed, neither should aggression be extolled, particularly when its motives so often seem to be personal glory and gain. If the narrative is not put in a proper historical perspective, and if some attention is not paid to the overall military and political strategy, the *Commentaries* can become nothing more than a series of disconnected and monotonous battles that tell very little of Rome itself. Girls in particular find it hard to keep their interest up through the many forced marches, camp pitchings, and other accounts of military life; boys and girls alike will soon lose interest if each page of the text is made into a grammatical battleground. Although Caesar is a traditional second-year author, he has not always been one (Ovid, Nepos, Eutropius, Livy, Phaedrus, the Vulgate, and medieval authors have all shared the burden), and one of the main reasons for Caesar's preeminence in the second year is that he can be and has been used as a gold mine of grammar. But the very consistency and impersonality of his style make it unique; and to devote a whole year to Caesar is perhaps to specialize too early and to deprive students of that general basis in Latin that will serve them well with every author.

One sure criterion remains: if free to do so, teachers who have had no success with Caesar, with whatever approach, should change, and change without qualms of conscience. *Latin for Americans, Second Book*, offers plenty of material for deviation from the normal program.

Unit VIII, through the intimate glimpses of "human Romans" given in Pliny's *Letters*, may have a strong influence on those who are fascinated by the sameness of human nature over the centuries. It is intended for rapid reading, preferably at sight.

A mere glance at Unit IX will give students a faint idea of the richness of Latin literature and the length of time it persisted. It can give no idea of the vast number of books written in Latin during the last 2200 years and still in existence. Here again it is up to you to choose what you prefer. No part of it is in any sense required reading.

Unit X is for those teachers who like to give their students a taste of the Ovid and Vergil to come in the third or fourth year, and to whet their appetites for more.

Sources of Supplementary Teaching Materials

General Background (Biography, Daily life, Literature, etc.)

Adcock, F. E., *Roman Art of War Under the Republic*. New York: Barnes and Noble, 1970.

Balson, J. P. V. D., *Roman Women: Their History and Habits*. Greenwood Press, 1975.

Barrow, Reginald H., *The Romans*. Penguin, 1975. Paperback.

Collingwood, R. G. and Richmond, Ian, *The Archaeology of Roman Britain*. Methuen, Inc., 1969.

Hadas, Moses, *A History of Latin Literature*. New York: Columbia University Press, 1952.

Hadas, Moses, *A History of Rome from Its Origins to 529 A.D*. Peter Smith.

Mellersh, H. E., *Imperial Rome*. Harper and Row, 1964.

Oxford Classical Dictionary. New York: Oxford University Press, 1970.

Parker, Henry D., *Roman Legions*. New York: Barnes and Noble, 1971 reprint.

Pomeroy, Sarah B., *Goddesses, Whores, Wives and Slaves: Women in Classical Antiquity*. Schoken Books, 1975.

Quennell, C. H., *Everyday Life in Roman and Anglo-Saxon Times*. David and Charles, 1969.

Richmond, I. A., *Roman Britain*. Penguin, 1978. Paperback.

Classical Heritage

Bolgar, R. R., *The Classical Heritage and Its Beneficiaries*. New York: Cambridge University Press, 1977.

Hamilton, Edith, *The Roman Way*. Avon, 1973.

Highet, Gilbert, *Classical Tradition: Greek and Roman Influences on Western Literature*. New York: Oxford University Press (Galaxy Paperback), 1957.

Thomson, J. A. K., *The Greek Tradition*. Appel. 1971.

Thomson, J. A. K., *Shakespeare and the Classics*. R. West, 1979.

Art and Archaeology

Deiss, Joseph, Jay, *Herculaneum: Italy's Buried Treasure*. Harper & Row, 1985.

Pallottino, Massimo, *The Etruscans*. (Illus.) Penguin, 1978, Paperback.

Robertson, Martin, *Greek Painting*. Rizzoli International, 1979. Paperback.
Toynbee, J. M. C., *Animals in Roman Life and Art*. (Aspects of Greek and Roman Life Series.). (Illus.). Cornell University Press, 1973.
Toynbee, J. M. C., *Roman Historical Portraits*. (Aspects of Greek and Roman Life Series.). (Illus.). Cornell University Press, 1978.

Fiction

Anderson, Paul L., *For Freedom and for Gaul*. Quality Library, 1931.
Anderson, Paul L., *Slave of Catiline*. Biblo and Tannen. Reprinted 1967.
Anderson, Paul L., *Swords of the North*. Biblo and Tannen. Reprinted 1967.
Anderson, Paul L., *With the Eagles*. Biblo and Tannen. Reprinted 1967.
Wells, Reuben F., *With Caesar's Legions*. Biblo and Tannen. Reprinted 1962.
Williams, John, *Augustus*. Penguin, 1979. Paperback.

Reference

Dictionaries and Grammars

Allen, J. H., and Greenough, J. B., *New Latin Grammar*. Caratzas Brothers, 1971.
Bennett, C. E., *New Latin Grammar*. Boston: Allyn & Bacon. Reprinted 1967.
Cassell's New Compact Latin-English, English-Latin Dictionary. New York: Macmillan Publishing Co., 1977.
Hale, W. G. and Buck, C. D., *A Latin Grammar*. University of Alabama Press, 1966. Paperback.
Oxford Latin Dictionary. New York: Oxford University Press, 1983.
Palmer, L. R., *The Latin Language*. Humanities, 1961. An introduction to Latin philology.
Smith, William, *Dictionary of Greek and Roman Antiquities*. 2 Vols. Longwood Press, 1977 reprint.
Smith, William, *Dictionary of Greek and Roman Biography and Mythology*. 3 Vols. New York: Amsco School Publications Inc. Reprint of 1890.

Geography and Topography

Smith, William, ed., *Dictionary of Greek and Roman Geography*. 2 Vols. Amsco Schools Publications Inc. Reprint of 1873.

Mythology

Hamilton, Edith, *Mythology*. New York: New American Library, 1971. Paperback.
Sabin, F. E., *Classical Myths That Live Today*. Morristown: Silver Burdett, 1957. Junior High Level. Has good bibliography for projects.
Schwab, Gustav, *Gods and Heroes*. New York: Pantheon, 1977. Paperback.

Word Study and Derivatives

Green, Amsel, *Word Clues*. New York: Harper and Row, 1983. High school workbook. Requires no knowledge of classical grammar.
Greenough, J. B., and Kittredge, G. L., *Words and Their Ways in English Speech*. New York: The Macmillan Co., 1980.
Pei, Mario, *The Story of Language*. Rev. ed. New York: New American Library. Paperback.
Skeat, Walter W., *A Concise Etymological Dictionary of the English Language*. New York: Oxford University Press, 1911 reprint. Old but reliable.

Latin to English

p. 2. Pūblius and Secunda

SECUNDA: Where were you, Publius?

PUBLIUS: I was in the Roman Forum, Secunda.

SECUNDA: Whom did you see there, Publius?

PUBLIUS: I saw our father and Augustus, the chief of state, the one who established the peace. Haven't you heard about this peace? It is called the "Pāx Augusta" by a grateful people.

SECUNDA: If Augustus is chief of state, is our father, Publius Caecilius Rufus, chief of the family?

PUBLIUS: That's so; however he isn't called chief but master of the house. Our mother Fulvia is the mistress of the house.

SECUNDA: What does the master of the house do?

PUBLIUS: He governs the whole household—both children and slaves. He also worships the family gods and alone conducts all business affairs. The father's authority, which is called "patria potestās" by us Romans, is very great. If he desires to put to death a slave or a son, he has the power. But you must not be scared, for at the present time no Roman fathers have that desire. Our father is good, not harsh. We love him and all the slaves love him.

SECUNDA: Where is Father now?

PUBLIUS: He is conducting public business in the Forum; he once was a soldier. He is a distinguished noble. But what did you do today, Secunda?

SECUNDA: I was with our older sister Caecilia. She talked about our mother's duties. Mother is the mistress of the female slaves and directs their work. She is always consulted by our father, for she is educated and alert. After that Mother taught me, for girls are not sent to school. Mother taught me about events [*deeds*[1]] which she remembered and about famous men whom she knows herself and those about whom she has read in books.

PUBLIUS: Good. What else did Mother teach [you]?

SECUNDA: She taught me about our father. Father obtained the "iūs trium līberōrum" [*right of three children*] because he has three children, me and you and Caecilia. This right has been granted by Augustus because in few noble families are there many children at the present time, and because Augustus wants the number of best citizens to be larger. But, Publius, you who are already grown-up [*a man*], what are you going to do now?

PUBLIUS: I have finished [my] studies in our school; I am getting ready to sail soon to Greece, where there are famous schools.

SECUNDA: Oh, lucky you. I want to sail to Greece too.

PUBLIUS: Today I am turning over other things in my mind, for tomorrow the best day [of all] will be here.

SECUNDA: What's that?

PUBLIUS: If you are [*will be*] a good girl, you'll soon find out.

---

[1] Words in italic type within [ ] are the literal translation of the Latin, given especially where the construction may be obscure. Words in roman type with [ ] are explanatory, added for the sake of clearness.

p. 11. A New Cousin

It was [day]light: Publius ran headlong to his father Publius Caecilius and greeted him [*paid him his respects*].

"Why are you in a hurry?" [his] father asked.

"Don't you remember? The time has come when Quintus Furius will be one of us [*ours*]."

Quintus Furius was the firm friend of Publius. The family of Quintus was humble. His father had six children but not much money. Marcus Caecilius, the brother of Publius Caecilius, Publius' father, had much money but no children.

"Don't you wish to adopt a son?" Publius had said to Marcus.

"Certainly," Marcus replied. All Romans desired to have sons, because sons preserved the name of the family, worshiped the gods of the family, [and] strengthened the "patria potestās." Adoptions among the Romans were numerous. Many famous Romans were adopted. The youngest son of Lucius Aemilius Paulus was adopted by Publius Cornelius Scipio, son of the famous leader, and was afterwards called Publius Cornelius Scipio Aemilianus Africanus. Augustus himself had been adopted by Gaius Julius Caesar, and the entire name which he took was Gaius Julius Caesar Octavianus Augustus.

Publius had brought Quintus Furius to [see] Marcus Caecilius.

"Quintus is a lad of great spirit. I desire to adopt him," said Marcus. "He will live with my family, but he will often see his father, mother, brothers, [and] sisters."

This had been satisfactory [*pleasing*] to the father of Quintus, and now the time had come [*was present*]. Many clients were already coming to Publius Caecilius and were paying their respects. [In company] with the clients and his son, Caecilius proceeded to the Forum and came to the praetor's building. Quintus Furius, his father, Marcus Caecilius [and] friends were already present. Quintus Furius was wearing a new toga.

The praetor explained the conditions of adoption.

"I free my son Quintus from my paternal power," the father of Quintus said three times.

Then Marcus Caecilius said, "He is now my son."

"He is now your son," said the praetor. "He is now in your power. His name is no longer Quintus Furius, but Marcus Caecilius Furianus."

All paid their respects to the new Furianus and to Marcus Caecilius; then they went away.

"Now you are our Furianus," Publius said to Furianus.

"I thank you," replied Furianus, and departed with his new father. You will hear more about Furianus and Publius.

p. 17. The Women Have Their Say

Fulvia, Publius' mother, with his sisters, Caecilia and Secunda, was waiting for Publius and Rufus.

"It's hard to be always waiting," exclaimed Secunda. "We wait for the men, we do nothing ourselves. The life of boys and men is more agreeable. They go to school, to the Forum, to the public places. But Rome does not like [*is unfriendly to*] girls."

"What? Doesn't Rome always remember famous Roman women?" asked Caecilia.

"It's true," were Fulvia's words. "Who does not remember Veturia, who saved Rome? Coriolanus, Veturia's son, had proposed a law which was not pleasing to the citizens [*state*]. And so his enemies drove Coriolanus out [*put C. to flight*], and he fled to the Volscians, the foes of the Romans. Made leader of the Volscians, he came to the gates of Rome and prepared to seize the city. Veturia with other distinguished Roman women proceeded to Coriolanus' camp and begged for peace. Coriolanus, affected by his mother's words, said, 'Mother, you have saved Rome.' "

"And what Roman has not been deeply moved by the deeds of Cloelia?" said Caecilia. "[Though] a captive, she fled from the camp of the Etruscans, enemies of the Romans, and swam across the river."

"In those times it was easier to win fame because the Romans were carrying on war," said Secunda. "But now there is peace. What can women do in [time of] peace?"

"Many things!" replied Caecilia. "Have not the Vestal Virgins often saved Rome by their sacred services, when the gods were unfriendly? And who will not remember the good Livia?"

"But they do not go to the Forum."

"Wasn't Laelia able to make excellent speeches?" asked Fulvia. "Didn't Hortensia plead the case of the Roman women in the Forum? In the civil war the triumvirs ordered the Roman women to give money. But Hortensia said in the Forum: 'Why ought we to give money? We have no influence in the state. If the enemy comes [*will come*], we shall give you money, but never will we give aid in support of a civil war.' By these words the triumvirs were compelled to yield.

"In the schools Roman boys read and hear about these and about Cornelia, Claudia, Lucretia, Tuccia, and even about our own Caecilia Metella, and they will always read and hear [about them] as long as Rome will endure. Good Roman women protect the state. When dangers [*will*] come, they will always be ready."

p. 22. Days with Books and Writers

In the beautiful temple of Apollo, which Augustus had vowed [while] at war and afterward completed on the Palatine Hill, there was a public library where many books, both Greek and Latin, were kept. Publius and Furianus often remained there a long time. Often they used to walk through the part of the city in which were the shops of the booksellers. In front of the shops hung books written by both new and well-known authors. In the shops the slaves of the booksellers were always copying books. The large shop of the Sosii was the most attractive [*pleasing*] to Furianus and Publius.

Once Publius Ovidius Naso, a poet popular with [*pleasing to*] the Romans at that time, prepared to give a reading [*read his poems*]. Publius Caecilius Rufus, Publius' father, knew a friend of the poet; and so Rufus with his friend and with his son and Furianus proceeded to the house in which Ovid lived. Great was the interest of Publius and Furianus, for they had seen and unrolled many poems of Ovid in the shop of the Sosii, and had often longed to see Ovid himself. On the way Rufus and his friend were saying many things about poets.

"Ovid is the best poet," the friend exclaimed. "When men have forgotten [*will have placed aside from the memory*] the names of all the other poets who are now [living], the name of Ovid will endure."

"He is good, but he is not better than Virgil and Horace, whom we used to hear [as] boys. Rome has neither seen nor heard better [poets] than they were," Rufus said.

"To be sure, he has not written the *Aeneid* [or] the *Secular Hymn*; the *Amores* and other books of his are pleasing, [but] they are not outstanding. But I have heard many things about his new book, which is called the *Metamorphoses* [Transformations]."

"Has Augustus seen that book?"

"That I do not know. Ovid, however, does not seem to be popular with [*very pleasing to*] Augustus. Augustus remembers Horace and Virgil."

They had come to the house in which Ovid was living, and Ovid was already reciting his new book. He read a poem about Orpheus and his wife. Publius and Furianus listened with great interest. After the poem had been read, they slowly departed from the house.

"He certainly is a poet!" were Publius' words.

p. 26. The Laws of the Twelve Tables

Once the following words were being recited by Publius, [while] Secunda, his little sister, was listening: "Against a foreigner the right [in property shall be] everlasting."

Secunda was going to ask Publius about these words, but he had gone away to the Forum. Therefore Rufus, her father, was sought out by Secunda. Upon finding Rufus [*Rufus having been found*], Secunda asked:

"What is [the meaning of] 'Against a foreigner the right [in property shall be] everlasting?' I heard Publius saying these [words]."

Her father explained: "These are words chosen from the Laws of the Twelve Tables, which have always been committed to memory by all Roman boys ever since [*from the time that*] they were written."

"At what time were they written?"

"During the first years of the state, when the Decemvirs were in [*had*] power. For a long time the laws of the Romans, preserved [only] in men's memories, were unwritten. But written laws were sought by the Roman people because many serious wrongs had been suffered [*received*] by men who did not know [*not knowing*] the words of the laws. After the advice of the most famous men of the state had been sought, this method was found to be best: three famous men were sent to Greece, where they became acquainted with the laws of the Greeks. Others were sent to Hermodorus, a Greek living in Italy. Even now the statue of Hermodorus, erected by the Romans, stands in the Comitium. Then the highest power of the state was given to ten men, who were directed to write down the Roman laws. When these men, [with] Appius Claudius [as] chairman, [had] labored a long while, the great work was completed. The laws, written on twelve tablets, were placed in the Forum. There they were seen by all during many years, and there they are seen now."

"I have often seen them. But what are those laws?"

"There are many—about penalties, about wrongs, about families, about a father's authority, about debts, about roads, about tombs—about Roman justice. Many other laws were afterwards proposed, but the Roman power was established by the Laws of the Twelve Tables. When those laws [*will*] have been lost, then the power of Rome will be [*will have been*] lost; as long as they remain [*they remaining*], Rome will be eternal."

p. 32. The Senate in Session

Publius came through the door, at which his mother Fulvia had been waiting for a long time.

"Where have you been?" asked Fulvia. "You are late."

"I went to the Curia Julia [Senate House] with Father," replied Publius. "I think that Father will come soon. I was standing in the Comitium, near the Senate House. Since the door was not shut [*the door not being closed*], I heard and saw many things. Many senators, among whom I saw the most famous [men] of the state, came together through the streets to the Senate House. When these were already in their seats [*who already sitting*], the consuls came in, then Augustus himself. After the sacrifice it was announced that the omens were favorable. Then Augustus read many long letters."

"About what?"

"I could not hear because many boys were standing near the door, pushing the men and shouting. Who do you think scattered them?—Furianus did it! He told the boys that Augustus, the chief of state, was consulting the senators about important matters; that the gods had been invoked and were present; that [by] shouting the boys were doing wrong to the gods; that they would pay the penalty—these and many other things [he said]. In what way I did not see, but he compelled the boys to go away. He has a loud voice; I think that the boys feared him. Augustus was by this time asking, 'What letters do you have?' and he ordered the senators to read the letters. When all the letters had been read [*all the letters having been read*], the consul made a speech, [stating] that many famous Romans had been overpowered and killed by slaves; that to others aid had not been given by slaves; that this was wrong; that the slaves of a murdered Roman citizen ought to be arrested and tortured and then put to death."

"What were the opinions like [*of what sort*]?"

"Almost all the senators felt that the plan of the consul would be good; a few thought that it would be cruel. Augustus announced that the majority of the senators were in favor of the proposal of the consul."

"What was your father's opinion?"

"He did not make a long speech, and I was unable to hear it; but I think that he voted on the side of the consul. After they had given their opinions, Augustus said, 'I do not detain you,' and all the senators left the Senate House."

p. 38. Holidays

By this time the month of March had come—formerly the first of the new year among the Romans. All the Caecilii and their slaves were decked out [*conspicuous*] in new clothes. Business was assigned to no one, because the duties of the whole state had been laid aside on account of the holidays. Publius and Furianus made their way through the Forum among many people, some hastening toward the temple, others standing [about], all wearing new clothes. While Publius and Furianus were looking at the decorated buildings, it was reported through the Forum that the Vestal Virgins had carefully put out the fire of Vesta, and had already collected wood for a new fire. Two men were standing near Publius; one said to the other, "It is well. With that fire remaining always, Rome cannot be conquered."

Now voices could be heard: "The Salii! The Salii are coming!"

Through the streets they came, armed and carrying shields. One of the shields was said to have fallen from heaven in ancient times. The Romans, not wishing this sacred [token] to be carried off, had ordered a clever man to make others like it. And so no one now was able to recognize that sacred shield. The Salii were running, displaying the shields which they carried. It was the duty of these [priests] to drive evils from the Roman gates.

There were other very ancient festivals, many in number and varying in character and importance: the Cerealia and the Parilia (or Palilia), the latter [*the festival*] of shepherds, whose goddess was Pales, the former of farmers, who worshiped Ceres; the Latin festival, when all the Latins used to worship Jupiter on the Alban Mount; the Consualia, when swift-footed horses [*swift in foot*] raced in the Circus [Maximus]; the Lupercalia, when two men would run through the streets laughing and striking all the women whom they saw; the Parentalia, when the tombs of all Rome were decorated; and others. The priests alone could remember them all, but Publius and the other Roman boys remembered many, because, with their studies over [*stopped*], they were able to play.

p. 44. Superstitions

Once Rufus, while going to the Forum on [*to*] business, looked at the sky and saw three birds on the right [*part*].

"It's a sign!" he said. "Fortune will be friendly to my business."

So it happened: his business came out well; therefore Rufus always thought that the birds had brought good luck to that transaction [*business*].

Most of the Romans were always looking for signs and omens—in the sky, on the ground, in the rivers. They thought that the gods themselves often came to men when they were buried in sleep and warned them. Many Romans sought advice from the gods in the temples; they would even sleep there. Those who were not well would consult Aesculapius in this way; but all thought that Apollo was the most useful of the gods to men on account of his oracles [*answers*]. These oracles, very numerous but not often very clear, were given through his priests.

Rufus, in worshiping the family gods, always said the same words, always performed the same sacred duties in the same way, with the family looking on. It was thought that if the gods were not invoked in this way, the family would suffer the severest punishment [*pay the greatest penalty*].

Even the dead were worshiped by the Romans [*the Romans worshiped*] with care, because they thought that these could very easily and swiftly come to their friends who were still [*remaining*] on earth and frighten them; and that the dead, if burial was not granted, were compelled to spend many years in severe toil, performing a hard journey through all lands.

At a time of great danger gods and dead men were said to have come into the very streets. After the battle of [Lake] Regillus, Castor and Pollux were reported to have come into the Forum. When Caesar was killed, dead men and the strangest animals were seen in the streets—most serious omens, which were thought to show that fortune would be cruel toward Caesar's enemies.

At that time [men] believed that fortune was more important and sacred than [they do] now. Men to whom she had long been kind were more pleasing to the gods (so they thought) than those to whom she had been unfriendly. All soldiers fought more bravely and fiercely under the leader who was dear to fortune—and for that reason conquered more frequently.

The Romans, fearing evils, seem foolish to us; but do we not ourselves at the present time do or hear many [things] of the same sort?

p. 49. The Big Show

From the remotest streets, from the Forum, from the top of the Aventine and the Caelian Hills, from all parts of Rome men were going toward the gladiatorial schools. On the next day Augustus was going to give very important gladiatorial shows; now a free dinner was being given to the gladiators in the schools, and many Romans, hurrying to them [i.e., to the schools], were going to look at the gladiators. Publius and Furianus ran with great eagerness through the streets. After looking at the first gladiators, Publius exclaimed, "These games will be better than all others; these are the finest gladiators that I have seen."

Now the day of the games arrived. The amphitheater was filled with people. Publius was sitting with Furianus in the lower part. A man next to Publius said that Augustus had provided two thousand gladiators for these games. Publius, remembering the conspiracy of Spartacus, hoped that there would be no danger to Rome; but Augustus himself was present, and Publius knew that his power was very great.

There advanced into the arena a great many gladiators, resplendent in their varied armor. Amid the shouts of the spectators they advanced with firm step toward Augustus and greeted him [*paid their respects to him*].

"Do you see those ten [fellows] who are wearing armor of the same kind?" Furianus asked.

"[Yes], I see [them]. I think that they are captives, sent from Farther Gaul. They look fierce, but don't you think that those seven Ethiopians will fight better? But who is that fellow? [Is that] Veturius, a Roman citizen, [whom] I see in the arena?"

"Yes, it really is he. That most infamous fellow was condemned because he had killed his father and a friend."

First, eight pairs of slaves of the same race, Spanish, came forward; but they fought less fiercely than the people expected and withdrew from the arena with everyone jeering. After that, ten Thracians fought better with ten Britons. One of the Britons, who was strong and fought very well, pleased the spectators. This man, after being defeated with very great difficulty by a Thracian, was not killed and was freed because of the cries of the people. Then men fought with animals, and animals with [other] animals. Finally Veturius [was] brought in alone, [and] a fierce lion was sent into the arena. The lion was wounded by Veturius, but it killed him.

Shows of this sort now seem very cruel; but they very greatly strengthened the influence of Augustus, because they were very pleasing to the Roman people.

p. 58. The Farewell Dinner

On one occasion [*once*] the house of a noble Roman family, the Caecilian, was in the greatest confusion. Publius, the son of Publius Caecilius Rufus, and Furianus, the adopted son of Marcus Caecilius, had long had in mind to sail to Greece and hear the famous Greek philosophers; and now they had fixed upon the next day for their departure. It was the ninth hour—the dinner hour. The dinner had been prepared in the atrium of the house, not in the dining room, because only a few were going to be present. The men came from the baths into the atrium, where the women were waiting.

Rufus gave a signal with his hands and called out: "Let dinner be served."

As the men reclined and the women took their seats, their sandals were laid aside, and a table was carried into the atrium by slaves. After the table had been put in place, water and napkins were given to all.

The first part of the dinner, the first course, was brought into the atrium—eggs and lettuce; then grape juice. After the water and napkins had been passed around again, the dinner itself was brought in. The food was good, resembling ours. Throughout the dinner many things were said about Greece and the Greeks.

Great was the interest of Publius and Furianus, because they were about to go to Greece and the time for departure was at hand. But Rufus spoke seriously to Marcus: "They have decided to go to a country new to them. Let us wish that they will live a worthy life." "Let them always remember that they are Romans," replied Marcus. "Let them not act unjustly —then they will live a worthy life."

"Let the Greek slave be heard," cried Publius.

"And let him sing a Greek song," said Furianus.

After the slave sang a song, Rufus said: "Now let us keep silent [*let us favor with our tongues*] and worship the gods."

When the household gods were placed upon the table, Rufus put food and wine near them. As all stood, silence was observed. Then, after the Lares had been removed with great care, the dessert [*second table*] was brought into the atrium—cakes and fruits. After the dinner had been finished from beginning to end [*from the egg to the apples*], Rufus said, "Let the slave Davus come in." This [slave] stood on his hands, then on his head, and did many other [stunts].

But now it was time to leave. The slaves were ordered to fetch the sandals, and all departed in deep silence.

p. 64. On the Way

The day was now here. The baggage and slaves being ready, the whole family left the house and proceeded on foot from the city to the Capena Gate, because, on account of the narrow streets, there were no buses within the city. Near the gate Publius and Furianus and the slaves climbed into a coach drawn by four horses, while his [Publius'] mother and sisters wept and all shouted "Farewell!"

Leaving the gate, they proceeded along the Appian Way, which now descended to a small river. Then a level road stretched for many miles through the fields. Publius said to Furianus: "Let us stop to see the tomb of our famous relative Caecilia Metella."

They saw many other tombs, among which that of Messala Corvinus was noteworthy. They saw the Sacred Plain of the Horatii, where the Horatii had fought with the Curiatii in ancient times.

Afterwards they came to the Pontine Marshes, across which sailors were getting ready to carry many persons in a small boat during the early hours of the night. "We ought to hurry," Furianus said, "so as to get into the boat, for many others wish to get in." There was great danger on account of the number of those getting in. "That's quite [*already*] enough!" those who had found a place on the boat shouted; "let's go on so that we won't all be killed." At last the sailors set sail and all are glad. But on account of the mosquitoes and frogs no one was able to sleep. Besides, a sailor was singing about his absent sweetheart [*friend*]. Two angry men [i.e., passengers] who wanted to throw the sailor into the water were held back by other sailors [*Other sailors held back two angry men, etc.*] At last they reached land during the seventh hour of the night but many remained on the boat until the eighth or tenth hour.

Then Publius said: "Let's go more quickly so as not to lose our lives in these terrible marshes and so that we may spend the fourth night in the villa of a guest-friend of my father's." This done, they came to the forum of Capua, the last city on the Appian Way, on the sixth day.

What happened in this city? You will read about this on another day.

p. 68. An Adventure

At this time Capua was a very magnificent and beautiful city, the largest of all in this part of Italy. Situated in a very level location, it had very good wide streets. So as to see the city, Furianus and Publius decided to remain one day. A man who saw them said: "So as to see everything properly [*well*] today, you ought to have a guide. I will show you everything; then I will give you a very good dinner; for better food you will find in no [other] city." The boys accepted the aid of the guide. But after showing them a few buildings the man snatched money from Publius' hand [while they were] in a narrow street and ran away. But on hearing the shouts of the boys two soldiers arrested the rascal [*bad man*].

And so the boys gratefully left Capua. They now journeyed over wooded mountains [*mountains and woods*], and the road was bad. Furianus said to Publius, "Let's hold tight to the bus so as not to be thrown out." In these regions no guest-friends of Rufus lived; and so they were forced to go to an inn, called "At [the Sign of] the Elephant," to spend one night. But the inn was dirty, and it was not easy to sleep. The next day they saw armed men on the road; but the slaves took arms, and the men ran off. Then a violent storm arose, and they hastened toward a deserted villa so as not to be overtaken by the storm. Finally, on the fourteenth day, they arrived at the gates of Brundisium. In this place they left the coach and speedily sought a ship so that they might not be delayed and might sail as quickly as possible to Greece. But the pilot said, "There is a terrible storm on the sea now. Let us remain in this place today so as not to run into danger." And so, after sending letters to the family, Publius and Furianus stayed at [the house of] a guest-friend.

p. 73. Sight-Seeing at Brundisium

Publius and Furianus stayed at Brundisium for a long time so as to sail across the sea without danger. During this time they took in the sights of [*explored*] the city. For in this city there were many famous places. Many [persons] came to this port to sail for Greece and Asia—merchants, generals, armies, [and] messengers carrying letters.

Furianus said to Publius: "This is a famous city. Don't you remember that Cicero, when driven into exile, came here [*to this place*] so that a ship might take him to Greece? One friend received him in his grief [*grieving*], and he could never thank him enough. But after Cicero was recalled from exile and came to Brundisium on the birthday of the colony itself, all the citizens received him with the greatest rejoicing."

Then Publius said: "You are right [*you speak rightly*]. Afterwards Pompey gathered his forces in this town in order to flee across the sea. Caesar hurried to the town to intercept him. But without ships he was unable to stop him. Let's go to the harbor and with our own eyes look at the place where Caesar tried to block the mouth of the harbor." "Fine," replied Furianus. And so the two friends first went to an elevated place so as to see the whole region. Then they went down from the elevated place and looked at the harbor itself. Where the harbor was narrowest, Caesar had placed barriers [*works*] and rafts, but Pompey, so as not to be shut in, had burst the barriers with his ships and escaped.

"Certainly this city has seen many famous deeds, and has endured many serious disasters," said Publius.

p. 78. A Letter from Athens

Publius sends heartiest greetings to his father, mother, and sisters. If you are in good health, it is well; I am well. At present I'm feeling fine; but I haven't felt well all the time. For on leaving Brundisium after a long delay, after our little ship sailed out into the wide sea, such a storm blew up that I thought that the high waves would wreck our ship. Furianus, however, said, "The sailors are so capable that they will easily save the ship." But I replied: "I can't stand this any longer. Let's hurry below [*into the lower part*] so as to get [some] sleep there and let's hope for a clear sky."

We went below. The ship was pitching about so much that death was hoped for by all; but after a long day and a longer night we arrived at the Greek city Dyrrachium. We traveled over such bad roads through Greece that we were almost worn out. Through deserted towns, through untilled fields, through cities crushed by civil wars, we made our way. At last we arrived at the famous city [of] Athens, a city which is so beautiful that all the things that have been written about it do not say enough. The Agora, which is the forum of Athens, and the Acropolis, resembling the Roman Capitol, are so splendid that they are not praised enough. But in my next letter I shall write more about the city. Now you are eager to hear about [our] studies.

When we approached the gate of Athens, we saw many wearing the scholastic garb and calling with such loud shouts that we stopped and looked at them in silence. "Aren't you looking for the school of Philip?" "Aren't you looking for the school of Lycurgus?" and other things they shouted. "We are on our way to the school of Enchorio, the rhetorician," we said. Then we were abandoned by some and seized by others. We were led to a small building, and the door was shut. We remained there so long that we thought that they were never going to return. Finally we were set free so that we might not become thoroughly frightened, and conducted to dinner by them amid laughter [*laughing*], after which we were made sport of in all sorts of ways. Then, after being taken to the baths, we received the robe of a scholar. The next day we were enrolled as [*added to the number of*] students of Enchorio, who seems agreeable. Tomorrow we shall begin our studies. We are living with a Greek family near the Agora.

You see that all is well. We shall write often and expect letters frequently. Good-by.

p. 82. A Gossipy Letter from Rome

Marcus Caecilius to his [son] Furianus. You asked, "How [*what*] is the government doing?" The consuls for the next year have been elected—Lepidus and Taurus. The former is a favorite of Augustus. His ancestors were Sulla and Pompey, [the latter] Caesar's personal enemy, but Augustus so wants harmony that he can forget [*put aside the remembrance of*] things of this sort.

This news will be much more serious: Corellius, the tribune, has now been dead ten days. All his friends had had the hope that, sick [as he was], he would live a few days longer, so as to be able to see his brother who was hurrying from Gaul; but this was not to be [*permitted*]. The funeral was a notable one—an oration delivered before the house, a long procession, buglers, very many wax masks, a funeral pyre many feet high (but there were so many persons present that it was difficult to see the pyre), a splendid tomb.

Ovid, the poet, exiled from the city to a foreign town, has now for almost two years been writing pleading letters to Augustus, but the latter is unmoved. Moreover, the silence of Augustus is such that no one can find out the reason for Ovid's punishment. Ovid has published a new book, which I shall buy and send to you so that you can read it.

Do you know Calpurnius, who has so much money that one house cannot hold it—the fellow who quickly buys buildings after they have started to burn, then, putting out the fire with the aid of trained slaves, repairs them? He has bought a large farm. For many days now I have desired to buy a small farm that I may be a farmer in my leisure [hours]. I have found a beautiful farm among the Sabines, which is not many miles away from that of Horace, the poet. What do you think about it?

All days are about alike. I get up; after listening to clients, I proceed to the Forum either to hear decisions or to attend the senate; I have lunch; I take a nap; I exercise; I go to the baths of Agrippa and there I see friends. Then it's dinner, then rest. This I do every day. What is my Furianus doing?

p. 86. Alma Mater

When Publius and Furianus were traveling to Athens, they saw many Romans on the way. A few days after they reached Athens, they saw many more Romans. For a great many other Romans of the same age had come to this distinguished city to hear the Greek philosophers and rhetoricians. So famous were those who had taught in this city for many years that many pupils came to them from every land.

When the two friends had been in the city a few days and had listened to many teachers, Furianus said to Publius: "Don't you think that our teacher Enchorio is keen and the best of all [of them]?" "[Yes], you are right," replied his friend. "I am glad that [*because*] our fathers picked him out. I don't despise the rest, to be sure, but he certainly is the best. When he made a speech, I was affected in a remarkable way. Besides, those things which he teaches are very useful to Romans. For Romans make speeches in the Forum and in the senate." Then Furianus said: "Those things which the philosophers teach also are useful for living [*that we may live*] a good life. To be sure, we are Romans, and it is very useful for Romans to be able to make speeches. But we are also men, and a good life is more useful than a good speech."

After these and other things had been said by our two friends about philosophers and rhetoricians, Furianus finally said: "We agree that Enchorio is very good. Let us be glad, therefore, that we are in his school. Long live the school of Enchorio!"

p. 91. Athens the Beautiful

A little later Publius sent his father and mother a letter, in which many wonderful things were related about the city of Athens.

"When we [*had*] reached this city," he wrote, "we desired as soon as possible to see the Parthenon, the temple of Minerva. It stands on a hill which is called the Acropolis. This hill's gates, the name of which is the Propylaea, are so beautiful that we stood a long while looking [at them] on that occasion. Near the Propylaea is a little temple in which there is a statue of Victory made without wings. When we [*had*] asked about this, the reply was: 'The goddess Victory was made in this fashion so that she might not depart from the city.' It has often been said that the Parthenon is the most beautiful of all buildings; when we went through the Propylaea and came to the Parthenon itself, we could understand this. In it is the statue of Athena, taller than six men. The goddess herself is made out of ivory; her robe and armor, of gold. So remarkable is it that no one can look upon it unmoved, no one can forget it [*put aside the memory of it*]. When we had seen the Parthenon, we proceeded to another temple of Athena, in the porch of which are statues of maidens. When we left the Acropolis, we went down to the Agora. There we saw, among others, a building erected by Caesar and Augustus.

"When we had been in the city many days and had been able to find many other famous places every day, the following seemed the finest: the Stadium, the Olympieum, the largest temple of Greece, [and] the Academy, which is a mile from the city, and in which famous philosophers teach. The time is so short and we have been so tired that we have not yet attended the plays held in the theater; however, we have seen the theater and think that it is very beautiful.

"But the city is so large that all the magnificent places and buildings have not yet been found by us. But we shall seek them out soon as possible and write about them."

When the letter had been read, Rufus related many other [stories] about Athens, so pleasing that finally Secunda said, "Oh! Why am I not a boy! I want to go to that beautiful city right away!"

p. 97. A Request for Funds

Publius sends heartiest greetings to his father, mother, and sisters. If you are in good health, it is well. I'm well. I was very glad to get [*with great gladness I got*] your letter today, which you wrote twenty-five days ago. After I read the letter, I gave it to Furianus to read. When we had talked about Rome and our friends, Furianus said that Rome was a long way off. But we are happy, for we have friends here, and the city is very beautiful.

Our life is so quiet that I have almost nothing to write [*I can write*]. But yet there is one matter about which it is necessary to write. Father, can you send [some] money right away [*without delay*]? I am sorry that it is necessary to write this, but it is not my fault. For everything in this city is so dear that almost all my money has been spent. My teacher Enchorio is so friendly that many think that I am his son, not his pupil. I am with him whole days and often a part of the night; for he often dines with me. At these times he talks so well on many subjects that I hear many useful things. For this reason I often invite him to dinner. In this way my money is soon spent.

For another reason, too, I must have money. When Enchorio had talked much about the [various] parts of Greece, I asked him about Delphi. He replied that everyone ought to see Delphi with his own eyes. Therefore we wish to set out as quickly as we can to see that place. Enchorio has promised to go with us and to show and explain everything [to us]. I believe he knows everything. He speaks so well that he has a wonderful influence over all his pupils [*has affected them in a wonderful manner*]. Good-by.

p. 101. A Wedding

While Publius was studying in Greece, a most welcome ceremony was taking place at Rome—the wedding of Caecilia, Publius' sister, and Marcus Junius Vorenus. A few months before, when the Caecilii and the Junii with their friends had entered the [reception] hall of Rufus, Vorenus' father had stood with his son before Rufus and Caecilia and had asked Rufus: "Do you promise your daughter to my son [as his] wife?" Rufus had replied: "I do [*promise*]." Then Vorenus had given Caecilia a ring, and Caecilia [had given] Vorenus a handsome slave, and their fathers had arranged with each other about the dowry—how much Rufus intended to give, in what manner the money could be provided.

Finally the wedding day was at hand. The day before Caecilia had offered gifts to the Lares; now at sunrise, after the omens had been pronounced most favorable, she was being got ready for the wedding by her mother, and her girl friends were talking with her. Her mother put a bridal veil and then a wreath upon Caecilia's head.

"I wonder what my brother is doing," said Caecilia, "and what he will think when the news about me reaches him."

Now Caecilia descended with her mother and her friends to the decorated atrium, where Rufus and the priest were waiting. When Vorenus and his friends had entered the atrium, the matron [of honor] joined the hands of Caecilia and Vorenus and Caecilia said, "Ubi tū Gāius, ego Gāia." Now they sat down, and the priest invoked the gods (especially Juno). Then all shouted, "Good luck! I hope that all things will turn out well for you and that your lives will be long!"

"No longer is she ours," said Rufus to Vorenus, "but yours."

At the ninth hour a sumptuous dinner was brought in, and Rufus announced, "Let us refresh ourselves with food." All admired the beautiful bride.

In the evening everybody went to the street. There, while her mother wept and held Caecilia back, the others arranged the procession. Suddenly Vorenus carried Caecilia off, and the procession started, the friends singing, laughing, and shouting "Talassiō!" When they reached the door of Vorenus' house, Caecilia decorated it. After Vorenus carried his wife through the door, Caecilia again said, "Ubi tū Gāius, ego Gāia." In the atrium Vorenus gave the new matron fire and water. On the following day another dinner was given, when Caecilia sacrificed to the gods. Her family was no longer Caecilian but Junian.

p. 106. The Trip to Delphi

His father had furnished money to Publius so that he and Furianus might go to Delphi. When the appointed day had come, they went to Enchorio, who had promised to go with them. And so these three with some slaves left the city of Athens.

Why did they wish to see Delphi? Because this place was, so to speak, the temple of all Greece. Here [*in this place*] was a noted oracle of Apollo. Many came from all parts of the earth to consult the oracle. Besides, the place itself was—and is—very beautiful.

So our friends traveled over the sacred road which led to the famous city of Eleusis, and from that city they proceeded to another famous city, Thebes. When, after a few days, they came to the end of their journey, they were filled with joy and admiration. For the city, situated at the foot of Mount Parnassus, was very beautiful. It had the form of a very large theater. On one side were high rocks; on the other side, trees, a river, and a second mountain.

After admiring all these a long time, they came to the famous Castalian spring. All who consulted the oracle would bathe themselves in the water of this spring. This spring was sacred to Apollo and the Muses.

Then our travelers saw some buildings which were called treasuries. Certain Greek states built these on account of some victory. A Greek author has said that the Cnidians built a treasury, not on account of success [*things well done*] in battle, but to show off their wealth. In these buildings and in other parts of the city there were three thousand statues.

After seeing these buildings, they entered the temple of Apollo and immediately caught sight of the sayings of the Seven Wise Men of Greece, inscribed in large letters: "Know thyself," "Nothing in excess," and others. But they could not enter the oracle itself because the oracle was so sacred that few entered it.

Therefore they returned to the spring, and, after admiring it and the rocks and the trees and the sky a second time, they went off at evening to dinner.

p. 112. Totalitarianism and Democracy

One day Publius and Furianus were talking with [some] other young men about Sparta and Athens. "Surely everyone must grant that the ancient Spartans were the bravest of all [men]," one of the Greeks said; "don't you remember Leonidas, who with three hundred [fellow] citizens fought so bravely at Thermopylae? Eagerly [*with eager spirit*] he urged his men on to that battle in which they were going to die."

"I don't deny what you say," the other said, "but the Athenians too were brave. The Spartans were brave, to be sure, but they did not have other good qualities [*virtues*]. That ancient leader of theirs, Lycurgus, should be blamed for the severity of their laws."

Then Furianus asked what Publius thought. "I grant that the Athenians are better," he replied. "Spartan boys had to live a hard life. At the age of seven they left their mothers to be trained for war. They prepared their own meals out of very poor foods, for the Spartans believed that hunger was the best seasoning for food. The boys were beaten with whips, while their fathers urged them to be patient [*to patience*], so that they might learn to endure pain."

"Even worse was the life of the people whom the Spartans conquered," said one young Athenian. "Not only did they become slaves, but they had to suffer many wrongs. They were secretly watched by some [guards]. The slave who had the facial expression of a free man was put to death. All the slaves had to wear slaves' clothing. They were beaten daily so that they would remember that they were slaves."

"I don't deny that the life of the slave was very unhappy," said Furianus, "but worst of all was that of the Spartans themselves. Even in peace [time] they always lived in camp. Liberty was unknown to them. Everything had to be done for the fatherland; yet the fatherland did nothing for the people. 'Prō bonō pūblicō' [*for the public good*] meant 'for the good of the state,' not 'for the good of the citizens.' "

"You're right [*You tell the truth*]," said the Athenian. "Let us remember the words of the noble Pericles, who said that the government of the Athenians was in the hands of the many, not of the few; that public service was the reward for outstanding citizens of all classes; that all had equal rights. To the Athenians liberty was very precious; so they were not angry if others did what they liked. Their boys lived in peace and were not always trained for war. Yet they fought and died eagerly in war. They cultivated the liberal arts; and so their city was the school of Greece."

"That's true," said Publius; "even now this city is the school, not only of Greece but of the world. Athens has given us very beautiful statues, outstanding buildings, [and] excellent books. I hope that all nations will always be like Athens, not like Sparta."

p. 116. Athletics and Patriotism

One day Publius and Furianus left school in company with two young Greeks. It happened that, while walking through the streets, they saw a statue of a man running, made by the famous Myron. And so they stopped to look at it.

"The Greeks always like runners [*running men*], don't they?" asked Publius.

"If one runs very swiftly," replied one of the Greeks, "he is the most popular man of his own city; if one wins in the Olympic Games, he is the idol [*most beloved man*] of all Greece. Those games, which are ancient and well-known, are held in honor of [*to*] Jupiter this very year in the city of Olympia, and four years later they will be held again. Men from all the cities of Greece go to this city to contend there. Permission to compete is not given a man who acts in an unworthy manner or has done a wrong. The victors receive wreaths, statues, and poems."

"Haven't I heard about a man who in a time of great danger ran a long distance?" asked Furianus.

"It was Philippides," replied the other of the Greeks. "He had to carry a message. The leaders of the Persians, advancing into Greece with many thousands of soldiers, descended into the plain which is called Marathon. The Athenians decided that a man named [*certain*] Philippides should go to the city of the Spartans to seek aid. Although this city was about one hundred and fifty miles away, he arrived there on the second day and urged them to send aid. The Spartans, however, decided not to go on account of the holidays. Therefore the Athenians alone had to drive out the cruel Persians, and Greece was saved. After this battle the same messenger Philippides ran swiftly to the city of Athens, but after he arrived in the city shouting 'Victory!' he died suddenly."

"The Greeks are brave," said Publius, after they had left their Greek friends. "Don't you wonder how it happens that they have not conquered the Romans?"

p. 120. National Heroes

Publius and Furianus often talked with the two young Greeks about famous men. To Publius it was especially pleasing to hear about the Greek Demosthenes —he who as a boy had had a very weak voice, but who had trained it by speaking on the seashore, by shouting while he ran, [and] by speaking while he had something in his mouth; and who finally had reached first place among all orators. "He alone was better than Cicero and deserves to be praised and held in honor even by Romans," Publius once said.

Furianus spoke about military affairs and told of the deeds of Caesar, Scipio, Pompey, [and] Marius. But one of the Greeks said: "My favorite [*to me the most pleasing*] of the Greek commanders is Themistocles. At a time of the greatest danger, he made the authority of Athens supreme by means of her ships, fortified Athens most securely, [and] finally drove the army of the Persians out of Greece."

"Many Romans resemble Greeks," said Publius one day. "Virgil, the famous Roman poet, who wrote a poem about the Trojans and the founding of Rome, is like Homer, who wrote about the Trojan War. Moreover, Numa, who in ancient times gave the Romans laws which he [*had*] received from the gods, is like Solon, who made laws to restore Athens."

"But what Roman is equal to the Greek philosophers?" asked the other of the Greeks. "Cicero, Lucretius, he who wrote about atoms and the origin of men and things, other Roman philosophers—these came to Greece for the purpose of hearing and learning. Who does not remember Socrates, who taught boys by asking questions and trained them for righteous living [and] who always worked hard to drive out evil and point out the good; who was put to death on account of his opinions?"

"But what Greek is equal to our Augustus?" replied Furianus. "Pericles, to be sure, was remarkable—he beautified Athens, increased the influence of the city, [and] ruled in peace. Augustus, however, has not only beautified and enlarged Rome—the city which he received made of brick he now leaves [made] of marble—but now he rules all lands in peace [and] with wisdom [and] justice."

And the two Greeks granted that Augustus was a remarkable [man].

p. 125. A Visit to the Academy

Publius and Furianus often liked to [*it was pleasing to*] walk through the city of Athens and listen to men of the greatest importance pleading cases. Often, however, it seemed more pleasant to leave the city and retire to a beautiful and peaceful place, the Academy, to read [*for the sake of reading*].

One day they were making their way there slowly, carrying books of poems.

"How many worthy Romans have walked over this very road!—Romans who afterwards became very famous—you so that you may become a renowned general, I an orator."

Now they were standing among the trees of the Academy. These were young but already tall.

"How tall the trees are getting!" said Publius. "I heard some Athenians say that in a few years these will be as tall as those old [ones]. For Sulla, who cut them down in order that implements of war might be made from the timber, despised beautiful things. Statues, to be sure, he carried away from Greece; but this he did in order to bring back much loot to the city of Rome."

Now under a tall tree they read the books which they had brought with them. Then Furianus said, "I like best of all [*it is most pleasing to me*] to come to this place to read [*for the sake of reading*] the poems of Horace, because here Horace himself used to read and write poems. Horace, who was a man with a small, plump figure, was opposed to war—most unlike Sulla. When news of war was received, he was not disturbed. Brutus alone was able to induce him (I often wonder how) to become a military tribune and to go off to war. When Brutus and Cassius were defeated near the city of Philippi, Horace had to leave his shield behind (do you remember?), and he himself fled. Afterwards he was chosen as a friend by Augustus, against whom he had borne arms, and he became a very well-known poet."

"Here I am often reminded of the philosophers," said Publius; "of Plato, who first taught here; of Aristotle, who instructed King Alexander; of Carneades, who could make splendid speeches, now in favor of justice, now against it."

Suddenly two Greeks approached. Having been informed by these that a famous orator was going to plead a case in the Agora, and the time was near, Publius and Furianus quickly closed [*rolled up*] their books and, delaying no longer, left the Academy.

p. 128. Athens and Rome

Furianus sends greetings to his father. You ask in what ways Rome and Athens differ from each other and which of the two cities I like better [*more*]. For me, at least, it is difficult to answer. Rome is my native land and for this reason is very dear to me. You don't want me to criticize Rome and the Romans, do you? I have already written about the magnificent buildings which we have seen here. But Rome has beautiful buildings, too. Roman streets are certainly better. Everything here is dirtier—the streets, the private houses, the people. There are no sewers. Some

Roman ought to be sent here to construct sewers. The water is so bad that many die. Doesn't some Roman wish to build an aqueduct here? However, when I catch sight of the Acropolis, then this city seems to be the most beautiful of all, and I no longer remember the more disagreeable things.

So much [*this*] about the city itself; now I wish to say some things about the people. I grant that the Greeks have many virtues, but these are not the Roman virtues. Our people are brave and prudent, they work very hard and rule very well. On the other hand, the Greeks are the best philosophers, rhetoricians, poets, and doctors, and they build the finest temples and make the most beautiful statues.

I have many Greek friends, and so I am unwilling to criticize all Greeks. But I am fonder of [*are dearer to me*] the Romans. The bad faith of the Greeks is well known; and yet I do not deny that the Greeks talk of Roman bad faith. It makes a difference whether you are a Roman or a Greek. Thus all peoples despise others. Don't we also talk about Punic treachery? But it is true that in Greek shops cheating is more common than in Roman [ones].

Although there are many slaves in Italy, I have never seen so many slaves as in this city. Everything is done by slaves; for the citizens themselves do not work.

But the condition of women is especially different. Greek women do not have the same liberty as Roman women. With us, married women are honored, but not here. Husbands want their wives to see nothing, to hear nothing, and to ask no questions. But yet the girls whom I have seen have been pretty.

p. 132. The Homecoming

At last the day arrived when [*on which*], after completing their studies, Publius and Furianus were to leave Athens [*Athens was to be left behind by P. and F.*].

"I envy those who live, now in Greece, now in Italy," said Furianus, wishing to see Rome, unwilling, however, to desert Athens.

After being informed by a merchant that the roads were good, they decided [*persuaded themselves*] to start out without delay. Upon receiving the report that bandits were molesting travelers, they armed their slaves [*the slaves having been armed*] to furnish [*be for*] protection to the baggage, and made the trip through Greece. The sea being calm, they sailed into the harbor of Brundisium without mishap, and there they remained two days because [there were] some things they wanted to see: the place where Augustus had received the name of Caesar, and the building in which Virgil had died after he returned from Greece. This was so agreeable to Publius that he was unwilling to depart. Furianus, however, said, "Don't you wish to see your home as soon as possible?"

"Yes, I do!" replied Publius. And so they set out as quickly as they could.

Great was the joy of the Caecilian family upon the return in the evening of the two weary young men. At sunrise the clients came, and almost the entire day the atrium was filled with clients and friends paying their respects. Afterwards the Caecilii went to the Campus Martius to the beautiful baths of Agrippa. There, while talking with other friends, they exercised and bathed.

The next day, on being asked what he wished to do, Publius said that he wanted to go to the Circus. His father replied that no [*not*] circus games, but stage plays were being given that day; that a poet too was going to read his poems. Publius said that he didn't want to hear that unknown poet; that stage performances, however, pleased him and that he wanted to see them.

The play, written by Plautus about ghosts, was delightful. Then a ballet dancer, portraying Augustus' victories, danced so well that the enthusiastic people shouted, ran toward the dancer, and threw money. Even Augustus gave him a wreath, to receive which was the greatest honor for a ballet dancer. When the games were over, they all returned through the Forum.

Publius and Furianus now entered upon the life of Roman citizens. Publius was made a quaestor, and prepared to pass through the entire course of offices. Furianus, having been made a military tribune, was sent to the aid of a general who had been surrounded by the enemy, and acted so bravely that he became a general. And so Publius and Furianus by their lives both preserved and increased the great influence of the Caecilian family.

p. 141. A Latin Play: Bulla

Characters

Aelia, *a little Roman girl*
Laneis, *a female slave*
Damyx, **Thoa** } *the wives of bandits*
Quintus Aelius Fronto, *a Roman, the father of Aelia*

The Place: In the town of Paestum, before a temple.

(*From the right side approach Fronto, Aelia, and Laneis.*)

LANEIS: Aelia! Your golden bulla! I don't see it. Has it been lost?

AELIA: Look! It's not lost—it's under my tunic.

LANEIS: How frightened I was! You must [*it is necessary for you to*] always guard it carefully, because it will guard you from evils.

FRONTO: This is the temple. Aelia, I want you to remain here with Laneis. I shall ask the gods to give us a successful journey. Laneis, stay with Aelia, because great dangers are near.

LANEIS: Yes, yes. I'll stay. (*Fronto goes into the temple.*)

AELIA: When shall we go home, Laneis?

LANEIS: Whenever the gods will be willing to give us a successful journey. But isn't the town of Paestum beautiful? Isn't Titurius, your father's guest-friend, always good to us while we stay in this town?

AELIA: Yes; and I like Titurius very much, but—

LANEIS: He has many slaves—my work here is light. Don't you want the work of your Laneis to be light?

AELIA: But I want to see my mother. I haven't seen her for a long time now. (*They now sit down in front of the temple.*)

LANEIS: How hot the day is! I'm used up.

AELIA: Laneis, when will Father know that the journey will be successful?

LANEIS: Whenever the omens are favorable [*will be good*].

AELIA: Oh! (*Laneis prepares to go to sleep.*) Laneis, don't you want to see Rome again?

LANEIS: What? Yes, yes.

AELIA: I shall do many things. First, I shall greet Mother. Then I shall tell all my friends many things about Paestum, about Titurius, and about the trip. Not one of my friends has made such a long journey. How they will admire me! (*Laneis is now asleep.*) Then I shall give my friends all those presents which I have bought for them—it will be fine.

(*Damyx and Thoa approach from the left side.*)

DAMYX: Do you see that [child]?

AELIA: I shall go through the streets, and look at all the new buildings.

THOA: She's beautiful. And she seems clever. Let's kidnap her.

AELIA: I shall make new dresses for my dolls.—

DAMYX: But we must act with great care. There's a slave woman [with her].

THOA: She's sleeping. (*Aelia sees Thoa and Damyx. She goes forward to look at them.*)

DAMYX: You're a pretty girl. Don't you want to take a walk with us? We shall show you many very nice things.

AELIA: I don't want to. Father told me to stay here.

THOA: Oho! You're a good girl. But we shall not go far away. We shall return in a short time. Besides, we shall give you a pretty present.

AELIA: I will not go.

DAMYX (*to Thoa*): What shall we do?

THOA (*to Aelia*): If you will come with us, we shall teach you many nice things.

AELIA: Mother teaches me many things. What can you teach me?

THOA: We shall teach you how you can always get a lot of money without work. Then you will always be able to buy everything which you desire.

AELIA: I will not go with you. You are thieves.

DAMYX: We are not thieves, but Furies. Do you hear? If you don't go with us willingly, we'll force you to go.

THOA: And if you [*will*] cry out, we'll kill you.

AELIA: I'm not afraid of you.

DAMYX: Why?

AELIA: Furies are evil, and evil things can't hurt me.

THOA: Why?

AELIA: My bulla protects me from all evils. (*She shows the bulla.*)

DAMYX: Look!

THOA: It's gold. (*Both Damyx and Thoa attempt to seize the bulla at the same time; they fight with each other.*)

DAMYX AND THOA: Ouch—ouch! (*Laneis stirs.*)

THOA: Sh-hush! The slave is stirring. We shall be caught.

DAMYX: Let's run. (*They go out quickly toward the left side.*)

LANEIS: Aelia!

AELIA: I'm here, Laneis.

LANEIS: I almost went to sleep. The day is very hot. (*Fronto comes from the temple.*)

Fronto: Aelia! Laneis! The omens are very favorable. The gods grant us a successful journey. We shall start this very day.

AELIA: Goody, goody!

FRONTO: And what was my Aelia doing?

AELIA: I saw two Furies.

FRONTO AND LANEIS: What?

AELIA: Yes. They wanted me to go with them. They tried to injure me. They were evil–but my bulla saved me.

FRONTO (*in a low voice*): What is she saying, Laneis?

LANEIS (*in a low voice*): It's nothing. The day is hot, and the girl, worn out, was sleeping. These things she saw in her sleep; now she thinks it all is real.

FRONTO: I understand. Let's go, Aelia. Let's forget the Furies, and prepare [*ourselves*] for the journey.

AELIA: Yes. But I shall always love my bulla, because it defended me from the Furies.

LANEIS: Right. (*Fronto and Laneis laugh. All go out to the right side.*)

p. 148. Early Kings of Rome

The Roman Empire begins with Romulus, who built a small city on the Palatine Hill. After founding the state, which he called Rome from his own name, he did these things: he received a great number of neighbors into his state and chose a hundred of the older men, whom he called senators because they were old men. He did everything in accordance with their advice.

After the death of Romulus, Numa Pompilius was chosen king. He added no part to Rome, to be sure, but aided the state no less than Romulus; for he established laws and customs for the Romans, who because of their habit of [fighting] battles, were considered half-civilized by [their] neighbors. He divided the year into ten months and founded many sacred rites and temples at Rome.

He was succeeded by Tullus Hostilius. When the latter was king, the Romans carried on war with the Albans. By chance in the two armies there were triplet brothers, alike both in age and strength. The Horatii were Romans; the Curiatii, Albans. The kings arranged with them to fight alone for their country and army.

At the appointed time they armed themselves [*took their arms*]. The three Albans were wounded and two Romans were killed. By chance the third Roman was untouched; alone he was not equal to the three Curiatii, but against them singly he was bold. Therefore in order to fight with them one at a time he ran away. Then looking back, he saw them pursuing at long intervals; one was not far from him. He returned to him with great fury; and while the Alban army shouted to the Curiatii to lend aid to their brother, Horatius, after killing his enemy, was already seeking a second contest and killed the second Curiatius. And now one remained on each side, but they were equal neither in confidence nor in strength. After the third Curiatius also had been killed, the Romans received Horatius with joy.

The sister of Horatius had been betrothed to one of the Curiatii. When Horatius approached the city, his sister saw him wearing the cloak of Curiatius which she herself had made. Because she wept, her brother killed her. "Go to your betrothed," he said, "having forgotten your dead brothers and your one living brother, having forgotten your country. So may every Roman woman perish who will mourn for an enemy."

p. 152. Out Go the Kings

After Hostilius, Ancus Martius took up the [reins of] government, then Tarquinius Priscus. He built the Circus at Rome. He established the Roman Games. He likewise conquered the Sabines. He built walls and sewers. He erected the Capitol.

In that time a wonderful thing occurred. The boy Servius Tullius was the king's slave. On the head of this boy as he slept there appeared a flame in the sight of many. When someone brought water to put it out, he was restrained by the queen, who forbade that the boy be disturbed. Then with [the departure of] sleep the flame also departed. Then the queen said secretly to the king: "Tarquin, do you see this boy, humble as he is? He will be the glory of our reign and a protection for us; let us be kind to him and train him in good arts." This was done and the boy became a distinguished man. When a husband was sought for Tarquin's daughter, no Roman could be compared with Tullius, and the king said that he preferred to betroth his daughter to him. After Tarquin's death, Servius, who had been a slave, was made king.

Tullius added to the city three hills, the Quirinal, the Viminal, and the Esquiline; he constructed trenches around a wall. He was the first who held a census of all [the people], [something] which up to this time had not been known [anywhere] in the world. Under him, now that all had been enrolled in the census, Rome had eighty-four thousand citizens.

Lucius Tarquinius Superbus, son of Tarquinius Priscus, murdered Tullius and ruled at Rome. When his son had wronged [*visited with wrong*] Lucretia, a most noble matron, and she had told her husband and her father and her friends about the wrong, she [*Lucretia*] killed herself before them all. For this reason Lucius Junius Brutus aroused the people against Tarquin. Afterwards the army too deserted him. After ruling twenty-five years, he fled with his wife and children. Seven kings had reigned two hundred and forty-four years. The death of a brave woman freed the state, for after this two consuls, who held the power for a year at a time, were elected by the people.

p. 156. How Brutus Got His Name

Now a second story about Brutus should be told. While Tarquin, the last of the Roman kings, was building the temple of Jupiter at Rome, a terrifying omen was seen: a snake, slipping out of a column, filled the heart of the king with anxious cares. And so he sent his two sons to Delphi to consult the oracle. Lucius Junius joined [*was added to*] them as a companion. He had deliberately feigned stupidity, in allowing himself and his possessions to become the spoils of the king [*for booty to the king*], and also did not object to the nickname Brutus [*stupid*] given him by Tarquin, so that, hiding under that name, he, the [famous] liberator of the Roman people, might bide his time. At this time then, he was taken to Delphi by the Tarquins, the sons of the king, more [*truly*] as a laughingstock than as a companion. After they arrived there and carried out the commands of their father, the young men were seized with the desire [*the desire entered the young men's hearts*] to inquire to which of them the Roman kingdom would come. They hear the reply [given back] from the bottom [of the cave]: "Young men, the one of you who first kisses his mother will have the supreme power at Rome." The Tarquins entrust to chance which of them would kiss his mother first when they returned to their country, [but] Brutus, thinking that the response of oracle had another meaning, as if he had stumbled and fallen, touched the earth with a kiss, because she [i.e., the earth] is the common mother of all mortals. And thus it turned out: after the flight of Tarquin and his sons, Brutus obtained the power at Rome.

p. 159. How "Lefty" Scaevola Got His Name

Tarquin, with the help of Porsena, king of the Etruscans, made war upon the Romans in order to recover his kingdom. At that time Horatius Cocles defended the bridge and saved Rome. The city was then being besieged by Porsena, and there was a lack of grain. Porsena hoped to capture [*that he would capture*] the city by remaining encamped. Then Gaius Mucius determined to go into the enemy's camp. So as not to be brought back through [some] chance by Roman soldiers, he went to the senate. "I wish to cross the Tiber, senators," said he, "and go into the enemy's camp. I have resolved upon [*have fixed in my mind*] a great deed, with the help of the gods." The senators approved. With a sword concealed within his clothing, he started out. When he got there, he took his place in a crowd of the enemy near the king's tribunal. There, as it happened, pay was being given out to the soldiers, and the king's secretary, who was very much like the king in dress, was very busy [*doing many things*]. Mucius did not know Porsena and was unwilling to ask [which was he], for fear that he might reveal who he himself was; and so he killed the secretary, whom he supposed to be the king, instead of the king. Then after he had made a way for himself with his sword through the terrified enemy, the king's soldiers seized him and dragged him back. Standing before the king's tribunal, even then in the midst of such danger [a man] more to be feared than fearing, he said, "I am a Roman citizen; they call me Gaius Mucius. I wanted to kill an enemy, but I know how to die. Nor am I the only one who holds these feelings toward you. No army, no battle need be feared by you; the decision will be between you alone and individual [enemies]." Then the king, moved by anger and alarmed by the danger at the same time, ordered fire to be placed around him so that Mucius might be compelled at once to reveal the plot. But Mucius said, "Look you that you may learn how cheap the body is to those who see great glory," and he thrust his right hand into a fire which had been built for a sacrifice. The king, admiring such courage, let Mucius go free. Afterwards the name Scaevola was given to this Mucius because he had lost his right hand.

p. 163. The Plebeians Go On Strike

A short time after the expulsion of the kings, civil war arose between the senators and the common people on account of debt. Many of the latter said that while fighting within the enemy's borders for liberty and power, they had been oppressed by citizens at home, and that the freedom of the people was safer in [time of] war among the enemy than in [time of] peace among citizens. One man, who had been a brave soldier in the Sabine war, said, "In my absence my farm was ruined, my house burned, and a tax levied. It was necessary for me to incur debt. Afterwards I lost the farm and was thrown into chains by [my] creditors." When they heard this, the crowd demanded that the senate be called. After the senate had been summoned, it was reported that the Volscians were on their way to attack the city. All [classes] put aside their hostility and fought, and the enemy were defeated. But after the war the senate did nothing with regard to the common people. Then another war arose. The consuls read [out] the names of the citizens. When no one responded to his name, everybody said that their liberty ought to be restored [to them] before arms are given [them], so that they might fight for their native land and their fellow citizens, not for masters. The dictator promised the people better conditions after the war. But when the war was over nothing was done.

Then the people withdrew to the Sacred Mount. This hill is three miles from the city across the river Anio. The senators decided to send Menenius Agrippa to the people. He told this story:

"Once upon a time all the rest of the parts of the human body were angry because through their care, their toil, everything was sought for the stomach, which did nothing itself. They took an oath together that the hands should not carry food to the mouth, nor the mouth receive it, nor the teeth chew it up. While they wished to beat the stomach in this way, the [other] members themselves almost died. From this it appeared that the stomach was no more nourished [by them] than it nourished [the rest]." When Menenius had shown how the discord of the body was like the wrath of the people, peace was made on this condition, that tribunes of the people should be elected and that no patrician should be permitted to hold that office. The tribunes received authority to give assistance against the consuls.

p. 167. Extra! Rome Captured by the Gauls

The Gauls, attracted by the sweet fruits and especially by the wine of Italy, crossed the Alps and advanced against the Romans. But although the Romans while fighting with neighboring peoples had often appointed a dictator, at this time they sought no extraordinary power or aid. The speed of the enemy brought to the Romans a great deal of fear. Near the Allia River the Romans were defeated. Most of them fled to the city of Veii; they sent no guard to Rome. Others made their way to Rome and fled to the citadel without even closing the gates of the city. So easily had the Romans been defeated that at first the Gauls halted in surprise, fearing a trap. Then they advanced toward the city. Although the cavalry had reported that the gates of the city had not been closed [and] that there were no soldiers on the walls, fearing a plot [under cover of the] night, they pitched their camp between Rome and the river Anio.

Since there was no hope of defending the city, the Romans decided that the youth capable of bearing arms, together with the women and children, should withdraw to the citadel and Capitol. There, after collecting grain, they prepared to defend gods and men and the Roman name.

The old men, however, resolved upon death, preferred to wait for the enemy's approach in their houses. Those who had held offices, clothed in their most resplendent robes, sat on ivory chairs within [*in the midst of*] their homes. The next day the Gauls entered the city and hurried to [secure] loot. Full of reverence they gazed upon the men sitting [there], who, because of their clothing and their grandeur and their seriousness, seemed just like gods. When the Gauls, having turned toward them sitting [there] as if to statues, stopped, one of the old men with his ivory staff struck a Gaul who was stroking his [i.e., the old man's] beard. This was the beginning of the massacre. The rest were killed in their homes. After the massacre of the leaders, no one was spared, the buildings were plundered, and torches applied. But not yet did the Gauls try to capture the citadel.

p. 171. Rome Sweet Home

The citadel and the Capitol were in great danger. For the Gauls made their way to the top [of the Capitoline Hill] so silently at night that they not only deceived the guards but did not even arouse the dogs. They did not deceive the geese, which, being sacred to Juno, the Romans, though in the greatest need of food, nevertheless had not killed. This fact saved the Romans [*was to the Romans for safety*]; for by their cackling Marcus Manlius was awakened, and, seizing his arms, he called the rest to arms. The latter easily pushed the Gauls down.

But afterwards not only food but also hope failed. Then the military tribunes were instructed [*the task was given to*] to make peace. The matter was arranged, and a thousand pounds of gold was fixed as the price. Unfair weights were brought by the Gauls and when a Roman tribune rejected [them], a sword was added to the weight by a Gaul and a cry intolerable to Romans was heard, "Woe to the vanquished!"

But gods and men prevented the Romans from being ransomed. For before all the gold had been weighed out, Camillus, who in his absence had been elected dictator a second time, arrived. He ordered the Gauls to withdraw and commanded them to prepare for battle. He ordered his own men to redeem their country with steel, not with gold. The Gauls rush upon the Romans but are defeated; their camp is taken; not even a messenger [to report] the battle is left.

But now the people wished to abandon the ruins of Rome and move to the city of Veii. Camillus delivered a vigorous speech and stirred them:

"Does not this land which we call mother hold you back? For my part, when my country comes to my mind, I think of all these things: the hills and the plains and the Tiber and this sky beneath which I was born and brought up. Not without reason did gods and men choose this place for founding a city, near the sea, in the midst of the districts of Italy. The very size of the city, so new, [serves as] proof. No one city, not the Volscians united with the Aequians, not all Etruria is your equal in war. Here is the Capitol, which the god said would be the capital [*head*] of the empire. Here are the fires of Vesta, here the shields sent down from heaven, here all the gods will be propitious if you remain."

p. 175. Torquatus, or Courage and Discipline

The Gauls were fighting against the Romans. One of the Gauls who excelled the rest in strength and size and courage came forward and called out in a very loud voice: "If anyone wants to fight with me, let him step forward." Everybody refused on account of his size and his savage appearance. Then the Gaul began to jeer and to stick out his tongue. Then Titus Manlius, a Roman soldier, stepped forward and faced the Gaul. The Gaul, who had two large swords, held his shield before him and waited; Manlius struck the [Gaul's] shield with his own and drove the Gaul from his position. In this way he got under the Gaul's sword and with his own small sword killed him. He took off his collar [of gold] and placed it upon his own neck. From this act he and his descendants were called the Torquati.

After Torquatus was made consul, war was undertaken against the Latins. The Latins were like the Romans in language, customs, style of arms, and military practices. Therefore Torquatus and the other consul determined to fight with the greatest care, and they ordered that no one should engage in skirmishes [*fight outside the ranks*] with the enemy.

By chance, among the others who had been sent out to scout and forage, Titus Manlius, the consul's son, made his way out to the enemy's camp. When he saw a Latin horseman, he forgot his father's order and began to fight with the enemy. When the consul heard this, he at once ordered the soldiers to be called together. Then he said to his son, "Since you have respected neither the consul's command nor your father's authority and have fought in a skirmish with the enemy and have broken military discipline, by reason of which the Roman state has endured up to this day, I shall be a sad but wholesome example for our posterity. I, at any rate, am moved by love for my children and your courage; but if there is any of my blood in you, you too will wish to restore military discipline by your own punishment." On saying this, he ordered his son to be put to death at once.

After this the Latins were defeated in a great battle.

p. 178. The Punic Wars

In the First Punic War the Romans for the first time fought and defeated an enemy on the sea. And no victory was more pleasing to the Romans, because, invincible on land, they were by this time also very powerful on the sea. After Sicily was captured and Corsica and Sardinia were ruined, the war was carried over to Africa. The defeated Carthaginians asked the Romans for peace. At that time Regulus, the general of the Romans, persuaded the senate not to make peace with the Carthaginians. Finally the consul Catulus set out with three hundred ships for Sicily; the Carthaginians fitted out four hundred ships against him. Never was a battle fought on the sea with such large forces. The Carthaginians were defeated.

The Second Punic War was started against the Romans by Hannibal. With a large army he crossed the Alps. After several minor victories, Hannibal defeated the Romans most decisively at Lake Trasumennus.

In Rome at the first news of the battle, the people rushed in great terror to the Forum. The women asked everybody what the fate of the army was. Finally the praetor said, "We have been defeated in a great battle." On the following days an almost larger crowd of women than of men stood at the gates, awaiting either some one of their relatives or news about them. One woman, they say, suddenly meeting her uninjured son at the very gate, died in his arms; while sitting at home another [woman], they say, to whom her son's death had been falsely reported, died for joy at the first sight of her returning son.

The next year the Romans, defeated by Hannibal, suffered an even greater loss near Cannae. Many states of Italy revolted to the Carthaginians. Still this fact did not move the Romans [to the point] that mention of peace was ever made among them. They made soldiers [of] their slaves, [a thing] which had never been done before. Hannibal sent to Carthage three pecks of gold rings which he had taken from the hands of dead Roman knights.

Still after many years the Romans defeated Hannibal.

p. 182. The Romans Give Liberty to the Greeks

After the Punic War there followed the Macedonian [War], which the Romans undertook against King Philip to free the Greek states. Titus Quinctius Flamininus was sent against Philip and conducted the campaign successfully. He went to Corinth to proclaim the terms of peace there at the Isthmian Games. Everybody had sat down for the show, and the announcer, as was the custom, moved to the center and, after calling for silence with a trumpet, announced that the Roman senate and the commander Quinctius told all the people of Greece to be free. After the words of the announcer had been heard, no one could really believe that he had heard correctly. Then such a cheer arose that it was readily apparent that of all blessings none was more pleasing to the crowd than liberty. One said to another that here was [one] nation that waged wars at its own expense, trouble, and danger for the freedom of others.

Two years later, when Quinctius was on the point of starting for Italy, he advised the Greeks as follows: "Consult [with one another] for [the sake of] harmony. No king or tyrant will be strong enough [to prevail] against you if you agree. By your own vigilance preserve your freedom, which has been restored by foreign arms, so that the Roman people may know that liberty has been given to those who are worthy [of it]." When they heard these words, so like those of a parent, for [very] joy tears flowed from [the eyes of] all, so that they overcame Quinctius too while he was speaking.

p. 186. Civil War

In the consulship of the orator Marcus Tullius Cicero and of Gaius Antonius, Lucius Sergius Catiline, a man of very noble family, along with certain men who were famous, to be sure, but rash, conspired to destroy the country. He was driven out of the city by Cicero. His accomplices were arrested and put to death. Catiline himself was defeated in battle and killed.

But Cicero did not free the Romans from the fear of civil war. Gaius Julius Caesar, who is said by some to have aided Catiline, became consul. Gaul and Illyricum, with ten legions, were assigned to him. In nine years he brought almost the whole of Gaul under the power of the Roman people. Soon he made war upon the Britons, to whom not even the name of the Romans was known before his day. After defeating these and receiving hostages, he forced them to pay tribute. He attacked the Germans across the Rhine and defeated them in battles.

Caesar, returning as victor from Gaul, began to demand a second consulship. When the senate refused, he advanced against his country with an army.

Then he crossed over into Greece and fought against Pompey. In the first battle he was defeated, but escaped because, with night coming on, Pompey did not wish to pursue. Caesar said that Pompey did not know how to conquer, and that on that day only could he have been defeated.

Then they fought in Thessaly near Pharsalus. Never before had larger Roman forces assembled in one place nor had they had better leaders. At last Pompey was defeated and went to Alexandria in order to receive reinforcements from the king of Egypt. But the king murdered Pompey and sent his head to Caesar. Caesar is said to have shed tears on seeing the head of so great a man, once his son-in-law. Caesar gave the kingdom of Egypt to Cleopatra.

After bringing the civil wars throughout the whole earth to an end, Caesar returned to Rome. He began to act contrary to the practice of Roman liberty. When in accordance with his own wishes he assigned offices which were previously bestowed by the people, and did other kinglike things, a conspiracy was formed against him by sixty or more senators and Roman knights, the leaders of whom were Gaius Cassius and the two Brutuses. And so when Caesar came into the senate on the Ides of March [March 15], he received twenty-three wounds and died.

p. 190. Pāx Rōmāna

Octavian, the grandson of Caesar, had been adopted by Caesar and was afterwards called Augustus. He was a young man of outstanding appearance [*and*] with a calm expression. After Caesar's death the consulship was given to Octavian, a youth of twenty years. Not long after in company with Mark Antony he set out against Brutus and Cassius, who had killed Caesar. Near Philippi, a city of Macedonia, Brutus and Cassius were defeated and killed.

Divorcing the sister of Caesar Augustus, Antony married Cleopatra, queen of Egypt. Then he started a great civil war, urged on by his wife Cleopatra, who desired to rule in the city [i.e., Rome] too. Near Actium, which is a place in Epirus, he was defeated by Augustus in a famous naval battle, after which he fled to Egypt, and, despairing of his situation, he committed suicide. Cleopatra let an asp bite her [*applied an asp to herself*] and died from its poison. Egypt was added to the Roman Empire by Augustus.

By establishing the Roman peace Augustus freed the Romans from the fear of war. From that year on he had exclusive control of the state for forty-four years. He was buried in the Campus Martius, a man who through his services, at least, was thought to be like a god. For no one was either more successful in war or more moderate in peace. The Scythians and Indians, to whom not even the name of the Romans had previously been known, sent gifts and ambassadors to him.

He built very many public works at Rome and often urged the other leading men to beautify the city with monuments, either new or restored. He divided the area of the city into fourteen wards. He established watchmen [to guard] against fires. He repaired the streets and temples. The calendar [*year*] which had been corrected [*reduced to order*] by Julius Caesar but had later been neglected, he restored again to its former accuracy. The month Sextilis he called August from his own name.

p. 195. Roman Scandals

About Nero many notorious [stories] were related. Nero was an emperor of uncommon extravagance, so much so that he bathed in perfumes and fished with golden nets. He wore no garment twice. He always traveled with a thousand or more wagons. The shoes of his mules were made of silver. He built a house from the Palatine Hill to the Esquiline Hill, which he called his Golden [House]. In its entrance was placed a statue of Nero one hundred and twenty feet high. There were lakes, buildings, fields, and forests with a multitude of animals of every sort. In other parts everything was covered with gold and adorned with gems. When he was dedicating this house, he said: "At last I have begun to live like a human being."

He also danced and sang on the stage. He went to Greece in order to sing there. While he was singing, no one was permitted to leave the theater. Many became weary of listening and applauding, and, since the town gates had been closed, either leaped down from the wall by stealth or, feigning death, were carried out in a funeral procession. Upon returning to Italy he did not relax his enthusiasm. For the sake of saving his voice he never addressed soldiers or did anything unless a singing teacher stood near to warn him to spare himself and to hold a handkerchief to his mouth.

He killed his brother, wife, sister, and mother. He set the city of Rome on fire that he might see a spectacle like the burning of ancient Troy. He is said to have killed a large part of the senate.

Finally he was judged [to be] an enemy by the senate. When he was being sought for punishment, he fled and killed himself. With him the whole family of Augustus became extinct.

p. 206. The Wicked Uncle

Once upon a time in Thessaly there were two brothers, one of whom was called Aeson, the other Pelias. At first Aeson had held the royal power; but after a few years Pelias, led on by the desire for power, not only drove his brother out, but even planned to kill Jason, Aeson's son. But some of Aeson's friends determined to save the boy from [any] such danger. In the night, therefore, they took Jason away from the city and, when they returned to the king on the following day, they reported to him that the boy had died. When Pelias heard this, he presented an appearance of grief and asked what the cause of his death was. But since they well knew that his grief was feigned, they invented a story about the boy's death.

After a short time Pelias, fearing that he would lose his power, sent a friend to Delphi to consult the oracle. The latter, therefore, proceeded to Delphi as quickly as possible and indicated for what reason he had come. The oracle warned Pelias that, if anyone should come wearing one shoe, he should be aware of him. After a few years it happened that Pelias was going to hold a great sacrifice. On the appointed day a large number of people came together from everywhere; among others Jason also came, who had lived from boyhood with a centaur. But while he was on his way [*make the journey*], he lost one shoe in crossing a river.

p. 208. The Golden Fleece and the Building of the Argo

Therefore Jason arrived at the palace with one foot bare. When Pelias saw him, he was at once filled with fear; for he realized that this was the man whom the oracle had indicated. Therefore he formed this plan. There was a king named [*by name*] Aeetes, who at that time held the kingdom of Colchis. To him had been entrusted the golden fleece which Phrixus had once left there. Therefore Pelias determined to assign Jason the task of getting [*that he should get*] this fleece; for, since it was an undertaking of great danger, he hoped that Jason [*he*] would perish on the way. So he summoned Jason and showed what he wanted done. But Jason, although he realized that the undertaking was very difficult, gladly undertook the task.

Since Colchis was many days' travel from that place, Jason was unwilling to go alone. Therefore he sent messengers in all directions to explain the reason for the journey and to report the day appointed for assembling. In the meantime he gave Argus the job of building [*to build*] a ship. In these matters about ten days were spent; for Argus showed such industry that he did not stop work even at night. For transporting a large number of men the ship was a little wider than those which we are accustomed to use.

p. 210. Dinner Under Difficulties

Meanwhile the day which Jason had appointed through the messengers was approaching, and from all parts of Greece many men were assembling from every direction. Now it has been handed down [by tradition] that among this number were Hercules, Orpheus, Castor, and many others whose names are very familiar. From these Jason selected to the number of fifty those who he thought would be most ready to undergo all dangers. Then, after waiting a few days so as to provide the means for all emergencies, he launched the ship and, finding the weather suitable for sailing, set sail.

After this the Argonauts sailed directly [*held their course*] to Thrace and there they landed. When they asked [*of*] the inhabitants who held the royal power in that region, they were informed that a certain Phineus was then king. They learned that he was blind and was being punished [*visited with punishment*] because he had once treated his sons very cruelly [*had shown himself very cruel toward*]. The character of his punishment was this: Jupiter had sent some dreadful-looking monsters, which had the heads of maidens, [and] the bodies of birds. These birds, which were called Harpies, caused the greatest annoyance to Phineus; for every time he reclined [at table], they would come and immediately carry off the food [which had been] served. As a result, Phineus almost died of hunger.

p. 213. Two Good Turns

Matters therefore were in this state when the Argonauts landed. Now as soon as Phineus heard that they had landed in his country, he was very glad. For he did not doubt that the Argonauts would help him. So he sent a messenger to the ship to invite Jason and his companions to the palace. When they arrived there, Phineus promised that he would give great rewards if they found a remedy. The Argonauts willingly undertook the task and took their places at the table [*reclined*] with the king; but as soon as the dinner was served, the Harpies tried to carry off the food. At first the Argonauts attacked the birds with their swords; but when they saw that this did not help, Zetes and Calais, who were provided with wings, rose in the air so as to attack them from above. When the Harpies observed this, they were frightened and fled at once, nor did they ever return afterwards.

After this was done, Phineus, in order to show his gratitude for such kindness, explained to Jason how [*in what manner*] he could avoid the Symplegades. Now the Symplegades were two rocks of huge size. These were floating in the sea a short distance [apart], and if anything came between them [*into the middle space*], they would rush together with incredible swiftness. Jason weighed anchor and set sail, and soon drew near the Symplegades. Then standing on the prow, he released a dove. She flew straight through between the rocks [*middle space*], and before the rocks clashed together, escaped, merely losing her tail. Then the rocks drew back on both sides; but before they could rush together again, the Argonauts rowed [*strove with the oars*] with all their might and brought the ship through.

p. 215. A Risky Job

After a short time had elapsed, the Argonauts came to the river Phasis, which was in the country of the Colchians. When they had disembarked there, they immediately went to King Aeetes and demanded of him that the golden fleece be delivered to them. He became angry and for a long time said that he would not give up the fleece. Finally, however, because he knew that Jason had not undertaken this task without the aid of the gods, he promised that he would give up the fleece, if Jason would perform two very difficult tasks; and when Jason said he was ready to undergo any danger, he explained what he wanted done. First, two horrible-looking bulls, which emitted flames from their mouths, were to be yoked; then, when they were yoked, a field was to be plowed, and the teeth of a dragon were to be sown. When Jason heard this, he undertook the task, so as not to lose this opportunity of accomplishing his mission.

But Medea, the king's daughter, loved Jason, and when she heard that he was to undergo such great danger, she did not like it [*took it hard*]. For she realized that her father had proposed this task with this very design, that Jason should die. Since this was so, Medea (who had a perfect knowledge of medicine) formed this plan. At midnight she secretly left the city and gathered certain herbs; from these she prepared an ointment which by its virtue would nourish the body and strengthen the muscles. This done, she gave the ointment to Jason; besides, she directed that on the day on which the above-mentioned tasks were to be performed, he should anoint his body and armor. Although Jason excelled almost all men in size and strength of body, he nevertheless thought that this advice should not be disregarded.

p. 217. Sowing the Dragon's Teeth

When the day came which the king had appointed for plowing the field, Jason with his companions went at daybreak to the designated place. There he found a huge stable in which the bulls had been penned; then, after opening the doors, he dragged the bulls into the light, and with the greatest difficulty placed the yoke upon [them]. Then, with everybody looking on, Jason began to plow the field. In this he displayed such industry that he finished the whole job before noon. After this was done, he went to the place where the king was sitting and asked for the dragon's teeth; when he received them, he scattered them in the field. Now the nature of these teeth was such that, in the place where they had been scattered, armed men were produced in a miraculous way.

Therefore, after sowing all the teeth in the field, Jason, overcome with weariness, went to sleep [*gave himself over to rest*] until those men should be produced. He slept a few hours; toward evening, however, he was suddenly aroused from sleep and learned that the matter had turned out just as had been predicted; for in all parts of the field men of huge stature, armed with swords and helmets, were miraculously springing up out of the ground. On discovering this, Jason thought that the advice which Medea had given should not be disregarded. So he threw a huge stone into the midst of the men. From every direction they rushed to the spot, and since every one wished to have this stone for himself, a violent dispute began. Soon they drew their swords and began to fight with one another, and after most [of them] had been killed in this way, the rest, weakened by wounds, were killed by Jason without trouble.

p. 219. Jason Gets the Fleece

But when King Aeetes learned that Jason had accomplished the appointed task, he was very angry; for he realized that Medea had given help to Jason [*him*]. And Medea, realizing that she was in great danger, determined to seek safety in flight. So after making all preparations for flight, at midnight she escaped with her brother Absyrtus and went as quickly as she could to the place where the Argo had been beached [*drawn up*]. When she got there, she threw herself at Jason's feet, and with many tears begged him not to leave her in such great danger. He gladly received her and urged her not to fear her father's anger. Besides, he promised that he would carry her away in his ship as soon as he could.

The next day at daybreak, Jason with his companions launched the ship and, finding suitable weather, hurriedly rowed [*hurried with oars*] to the place where Medea told them the fleece was hidden. When they got there, Jason landed and himself hurried into the forest with Medea. After he had gone into the forest a few miles, he saw hanging on [*from*] a tree the fleece which he was looking for. But to carry this off was a matter of the greatest difficulty; for not only had the place itself been excellently fortified both by nature and by artificial means, but a horrible-looking dragon also was guarding the tree. Then Medea, who, as we have pointed out above, had very great knowledge of medicine, infected [saturated] with poison a branch which she had torn from a near-by tree. This done, she approached the place and with the poison sprinkled the dragon, which, with open jaws, was awaiting her coming; then, while the dragon, overcome by drowsiness, was sleeping, Jason snatched the golden fleece from the tree and withdrew with Medea as quickly as possible.

p. 221. Escape Through Murder

After Jason and Medea, carrying the golden fleece, had arrived at the ship, all reembarked without delay and set sail during the first watch. But when King Aeetes learned that his daughter had not only gone to the Argonauts but had even aided in carrying off the fleece, he ordered a warship to be launched as quickly as possible and pursued the fugitives [*those fleeing*]. The Argonauts rowed with all their might; but since the ship in which they were sailing was of huge size, they were not able to proceed with the same speed as the Colchians. As a result, they were almost captured by the pursuing Colchians. But when

Medea saw in what a plight matters were, she formed an unspeakable plan.

There was on the ship of the Argonauts a son of King Aeetes named Absyrtus, whom Medea had taken with her on fleeing, as we have shown above. Medea determined to kill this boy so that, by scattering his limbs in the sea, she might hinder the speed of the Colchians; for she knew that Aeetes, when he had seen the parts of his son's body, would not pursue farther. Nor was she mistaken in her expectation. As soon as Aeetes saw the parts of the body, he ordered the ship to be stopped for the purpose of collecting them. However, while this was being done, the Argonauts soon drew out of sight of their foes; and they did not stop their flight [*cease to flee*] until they reached the Po river.

Finally, after many perils, Jason reached the same place from which he had once started. Then having disembarked, he immediately went to King Pelias and, showing him the golden fleece, demanded that the kingdom be delivered to him. Pelias at first made no reply but remained silent for a long time in the same gloomy attitude; finally he spoke as follows: "You see that I am already weak from age, and my last day is certainly near. Let it be permitted me, therefore, as long as I live, to hold this power; but when at last I shall die, you shall succeed me [*coming into my place*]." Influenced by this talk, Jason replied that he would do what the king [*he*] asked.

p. 224. Boiled Mutton

Upon learning these facts, Medea, drawn by a desire for royal power, decided to cause the king's death [*bring death to the king*] by treachery. She went to the king's daughters and spoke as follows: "You see that your father is already weak from age and is not strong enough to stand the hard work of ruling. Do you wish him to become young again?" Then the daughters of the king replied [*thus*]: "This can't be done, can it? For what old man [*who from an old man*] ever became a young man?" But Medea replied: "You know that I have a perfect knowledge of medicine. Therefore I shall now show you how this can be done." After saying this, she killed a ram which was already weak from age, placed the parts of its body in a bronze kettle, put fire under it, and poured certain herbs into the water. Then she sang a magic song. Soon the ram leaped out of the kettle and, with strength renewed, went running through the fields.

While the king's daughters looked at this wonderful thing in amazement, Medea spoke as follows: "You see how powerful the medicine is. Therefore, if you wish to restore your father to youth, you will yourselves do what I have done. Put your father's body in the kettle; I shall furnish the magic herbs." When they heard this [*this was heard*], the king's daughters thought that the advice which Medea had given should not be disregarded. Therefore they killed their father Pelias and threw the parts of his body into the kettle. But Medea did not give [them] the same herbs as she herself had used. And so after they had waited a long time in vain, they realized that their father was really dead. By these acts Medea hoped that she with her husband would receive the royal power; but when the citizens learned in what manner Pelias had perished, they drove Jason and Medea from the kingdom and made Acastus king.

p. 226. Death and More Death

After this Jason and Medea came to the city of Corinth, in [*of*] which city at that time Creon held the royal power. Now Creon had one daughter, named Glauce. When Jason saw her, he determined to divorce his wife Medea so that he might marry Glauce. But when Medea realized what he had in mind, she was thoroughly enraged and declared with an oath that she would avenge such a wrong. So she formed this plan. She prepared a robe woven with the greatest skill; this she infected with a poison whose potency was such that, if anyone put on that robe, his body would be burned as with fire. This done, she sent the robe to Glauce. But Glauce, suspecting no evil, gladly accepted the gift and, woman-like, without delay put on the new garment.

At once Glauce felt severe pain all over her body and a little later, filled with the greatest agony, she died. Then Medea, driven on by madness, killed her own sons and decided to flee from that country. She prayed the Sun to bring her aid in such danger. And the Sun, influenced by these prayers, sent a chariot to which there had been yoked dragons provided with wings. Medea got in the chariot, and so, carried through the air, arrived safely at the city of Athens. But Jason, after a short time, was killed in a remarkable manner. For one day he was sleeping under the shadow of his ship, which had been drawn up on shore. But the ship suddenly falling toward that side where Jason was lying, crushed the unfortunate man.

p. 240. A Geography Lesson

I, 1. Gaul, as a whole is divided into three parts, one of which is inhabited by the Belgians, another by the Aquitanians, and the third by those who in their own language are called Celts, in ours [i.e., Latin] Gauls. All these differ from one another [*among themselves*] in respect to language, customs, and laws. The Garonne river separates the Gauls from the Aquitanians; the Marne and the Seine separate them from the Belgians.

Of all these [peoples] the bravest are the Belgians, for the reason that they are farthest away from the civilization and refinement of the Province, and merchants very rarely [*least often*] visit them and introduce those things which tend to weaken courage. They are the nearest to the Germans who live across the Rhine, with whom they are always waging war. And for this reason the Helvetians too surpass the rest of the Gauls in courage, because they fight with the Germans in almost daily battles, when they either keep them from their [*own*] territory or themselves wage war in the Germans' [*their*] territory.

One part of this territory [*of these*], which the Gauls hold, begins at [*takes its beginning from*] the river Rhone; it is bounded by the Garonne river, the ocean, and the territory of the Belgians; it also touches the river Rhine on the side of the Sequanians and the Helvetians; it slopes to the north. The [territory of] the Belgians begins at the extreme borders of Gaul, extends to the lower part of the river Rhine, and faces toward the north and east. Aquitania extends from the Garonne river to the Pyrenees mountains and that part of the ocean which is near Spain; it faces the northwest [*looks between the setting of the sun and the north*].

p. 244. An Entire Nation Emigrates

I, 2. Among the Helvetians by far the most distinguished and the richest was Orgetorix. During the consulship of Marcus Messala and Marcus Piso, this man, influenced by a desire for royal power, formed a conspiracy among the nobles [*of the nobility*], and persuaded the citizens to leave their country with all their forces.

He persuaded them the more easily [to] this [course] because the Helvetians are confined on all sides by the character of the country: on one side by the river Rhine, very wide and deep, which separates the Helvetian country from the Germans; on the second side by the Jura range, extremely high, which is between the Sequanians and the Helvetians; on the third side by Lake Geneva and the river Rhone, which separates our [i.e., the Roman] province from the Helvetians.

As a result of these things it happened that they roamed less widely and could less easily make war upon their neighbors; and for this reason, [being] men fond of fighting, they were filled with great discontent. Moreover in proportion to their population [*multitude of men*] and fame in war and bravery, they thought that they had too small a country [*narrow borders*], which extended in length two hundred and forty miles, in width one hundred and eighty miles.

3. Moved by these considerations and stirred [to action] by the influence of Orgetorix, they determined to make ready those things which had to do with their departure, to buy up as large a number of beasts of burden and carts as possible, to sow as much grain [*to make the greatest sowings*] as possible, so that there might be [*might supply*] plenty of grain on the journey, and to establish peace and friendship with the nearest states. They thought that two years' time was sufficient for completing these preparations; [consequently] by statute they fixed their departure for the third year.

Orgetorix was chosen to carry out these plans. He took upon himself the embassy to the states. On this journey he persuaded Casticus, a Sequanian, to seize in his [*own*] state the royal power which his father had previously held; and he likewise persuaded Dumnorix, a Haeduan, Diviciacus' brother, who at that time held the chief power in the state and was greatly acceptable to the common people, to attempt the same thing, and he gave him his own daughter in marriage. He said that he himself was going to hold the control of his own state.

p. 248. A Mysterious Death and a Bonfire

I, 4. This plot was reported to the Helvetians. In accordance with their customs, they forced Orgetorix to plead his case in chains. If condemned, he was doomed to [*it was necessary that he*] be burned [alive] [*with fire*].

On the appointed day Orgetorix gathered from everywhere all his household, about ten thousand men, for the trial, and he brought all his vassals, of whom he had a large number, to the same place; through these he escaped and did not [*that he might not*] plead his case.

When the state, aroused because of this act, attempted by means of arms to enforce its right, and the magistrates were mobilizing a large body of men from the farms, Orgetorix died. However, the Helvetians think that he killed himself.

5. After his death the Helvetians nevertheless attempted to do what they had decided upon, [namely] to leave their country. When at last they thought that they were ready for this undertaking, they burned all their towns, about twelve in number, about four hundred villages, and the rest of their private buildings. All their grain, except what they were going to take with them, they burned up so that, with the hope of return home removed, they might be more ready to undergo all dangers.

They persuaded the Rauraci and the Tulingi and the Latobrigi, their neighbors, to burn up their towns and villages and start out along with them. The Boii, who had lived across the Rhine and had crossed into the Norican country and were besieging Noreia, they received [*to themselves*] as allies.

6. There were in all two routes by which they could go out from home: the one through the Sequanians, narrow and difficult, between the Jura range and the river Rhone, where carts could scarcely be drawn one at a time; besides, a very high mountain overhung it [i.e., commanded it] so that very few could easily stop [them]; the other [route] through our province, far easier and more convenient, because the Rhone flows between the territory of the Helvetians and the Allobroges, who lately had been reduced to peace, and this is crossed in several places by fording. The farthest town of the Allobroges and [the one] nearest to the borders of the Helvetians is Geneva.

From this town a bridge reached across to [the country of] the Helvetians. They thought that they would either persuade the Allobroges or compel them by force to allow them to pass through their territory. Having provided everything for their departure, they appointed a day on which all were to assemble on the bank of the Rhone. This day was March 28, in the consulship of Lucius Piso and Aulus Gabinius.

p. 252. Caesar Says: "You Shall Not Pass"

I, 7. When it had been reported to Caesar that they were trying to march through our province, he hastened to depart from the city and hurried by as rapid marches as he could to Farther Gaul and arrived in the vicinity of Geneva. He levied upon the whole province as large as a number of soldiers as possible (there was in all only one legion in Farther Gaul), and the bridge which was at Geneva he ordered to be broken down.

When the Helvetians were informed of his arrival, they sent the most distinguished men of their state to him as envoys, who should say that they intended, without any mischief, to journey through the Province. Caesar told the envoys that he would take time to consider.

8. Meanwhile from Lake Geneva, which flows into the river Rhone, to the Jura range, which separates the Sequanians from the Helvetians, for [a distance of] nineteen miles he constructs a rampart sixteen feet in height and a trench. This work completed, he stations garrisons at intervals, and builds forts so that he can stop them if they try to cross.

When that day which he had arranged with the envoys came, and the envoys returned to him, he said that in accordance with the custom and precedents of the Roman people, he could not give to anyone the [right of] way through the Province; and, if they should attempt to use force, he indicated that he would stop them. Disappointed in this hope, some of the Helvetians attempted to break through by boats joined together and many rafts, others by fording [*at the fords of*] the Rhone where the depth of the river was the least, sometimes in the daytime, more frequently at night. But being repulsed by the strength of our works and by the rally of our soldiers and their missiles, they gave up this attempt.

p. 256. The Harder Way

I, 9. There was left only the way through the Sequanians, by which, because of its narrowness, they could not go if the Sequanians were unwilling. When they were unable to persuade the latter by their own influence, they sent envoys to Dumnorix the Haeduan, that he might obtain the request from the Sequanians. Dumnorix, owing to his popularity and gifts, was very powerful among the Sequanians and was friendly to the Helvetians, because he had married the daughter of Orgetorix from that state; and influenced by a desire for royal power, he was eager for a revolution and wanted to have as many states as possible under obligations to himself [*bound by his kindness*]. He therefore undertook the mission and obtained the request from the Sequanians that they allow the Helvetians to pass through the territory, and he caused them to exchange hostages: the Sequanians gave hostages, [agreeing] not to keep the Helvetians from their journey; the Helvetians, that they would cross without [doing] harm.

10. It was reported to Caesar that the Helvetians intended [*have in mind*] to march through the land of the Sequanians and the Haeduans to the territory of the Santoni, who are not far from the territory of the

Tolosates, a state which is in the Province. Caesar realized that it would be very hazardous [*with great danger*] to the Province for warlike men, enemies of the Roman people, to seize these places which were unprotected and especially fertile. For these reasons he put general Titus Labienus in charge of the fortifications that he had made. He himself hurried to Italy by rapid marches and enlisted two legions there, and led from winter quarters the three which were wintering about Aquileia, and with these five legions he hastened to go by the shortest road over the Alps into Farther Gaul.

p. 257. Developing Word Sense

1. In all human affairs custom is powerful.
2. The fear of death is powerful; more powerful still is the love of glory.
3. Diviciacus was very influential because of his popularity; Dumnorix had very little power because of his youth.
4. How powerful Lady Luck is in war!
5. The Helvetians were not powerful in cavalry [warfare].
6. Caesar will realize what the undefeated Germans can [do], i.e., how strong they are.

p. 260. The Gauls Appeal to Caesar

I, 11. The Helvetians had already led their forces through the pass and the territory of the Sequanians and had arrived in the territory of the Haeduans and were destroying their fields. Since the Haeduans could not protect themselves and their possessions from them, they sent envoys to Caesar to ask for help. At the same time the Ambarri, kinsmen of the Haeduans, informed Caesar that their lands had been destroyed and they could not easily hold off the attack of the enemy from their towns. Likewise the Allobroges, who had villages and possessions beyond the Rhone, fled to Caesar and pointed out that they had nothing left but the soil of their land. Influenced by these reports, Caesar decided that he must not wait until all the property of his allies should be destroyed and the Helvetians should arrive in [the territory of] the Santoni.

12. The Saône is a river which flows with incredible smoothness through the territories of the Haeduans and the Sequanians into the Rhone. This the Helvetians were crossing with rafts and boats joined together. Through scouts Caesar was informed that the Helvetians had already led three-fourths of the troops across the river, but that one-fourth remained on this side of the Saône river. Therefore during the third watch he set out from camp with three legions and came up to that part which had not yet crossed the river.

Attacking these while burdened, he cut a great part of them to pieces; the rest took to flight and hid in the neighboring forests. This canton was called Tigurinus; for the entire Helvetian state is divided into four parts or cantons. This particular [*one*] canton, after going from home, within the memory of our fathers had killed the consul Lucius Cassius and had sent his army under the yoke.

Thus either by chance or by the design of the immortal gods, that part of the Helvetian state which had inflicted a notable disaster on the Roman people was the first to pay the penalty. In this Caesar avenged not only public but also personal wrongs; for the Tigurini had killed general Lucius Piso, grandfather of Caesar's father-in-law, in the same battle as Cassius.

13. After fighting this battle, he built a bridge over the Saône so as to be able to follow the rest of the Helvetian troops and in this way led his army across. The Helvetians were frightened by this sudden arrival, on realizing that he had done in one day what they themselves had done with the greatest difficulty in twenty days, [namely] to cross the river, and sent envoys to him.

p. 264. A Surprise That Failed

I, 21. On the same day, on being informed by scouts that the enemy had encamped at the foot of a mountain eight miles from his camp, he sent scouts to find out what the character of the mountain was and what sort of ascent there was on the other side. It was reported that the ascent was easy. During the third watch [i.e., after midnight] he ordered general Titus Labienus, with two legions and those as guides who knew the road, to climb the highest ridge of the hill; he explained his plan. He himself during the fourth watch hurried toward the enemy by the same road by which they had gone and sent all the cavalry ahead [*before him*]. Publius Considius, who was considered very skillful in military matters and had been in the army of Lucius Sulla and afterwards in [that] of Marcus Crassus, was sent forward with scouts.

22. At dawn, when the top of the mountain was held by Labienus and [Caesar] himself was not more than a mile and a half from the enemy's camp and (as he found out later from prisoners) neither his coming nor [that] of Labienus had been discovered, Considius, with his horse at full speed, rushed up to him. He said that the mountain which he had wished [*to be*] seized by Labienus was held by the enemy; that he knew this from the Gallic arms and ornaments. Caesar withdrew his troops to the nearest hill and formed a battle line. He had commanded Labienus not to begin battle, unless his [i.e., Caesar's] forces should be seen near the camp of the enemy, in order that the attack might be made upon the enemy from all sides at once. Therefore Labienus, having seized the mountain, was waiting for our men and holding off from battle. Finally late in the day Caesar learned through scouts both that the mountain was held by his own men and that the Helvetians had broken camp and that Considius, panic-stricken, had reported to him as seen what he had not seen. On that day he followed the enemy at the usual [*at which he was accustomed*] interval and pitched camp three miles from their camp.

p. 267. The Fight Is On

I, 23. The next day, because only two days remained until [*when*] it was necessary to distribute grain to the army, and because he was distant from Bibracte, by far the greatest and richest town of the Aedui, not more than eighteen miles away, he thought that he should provide for supples [*of grain*]. Therefore he turned away from the Helvetians and hastened to go to Bibracte. This town, by far the largest of the Haeduans, was not more than eighteen miles away. This move was reported to the enemy by deserters from Lucius Aemilius, an officer of Gallic cavalry. The Helvetians, either because they thought that the Romans, being panic-stricken, were retreating from them or because they felt sure that they [i.e., the Romans] could be cut off from a supply of grain, changed their plan, turned around, and began to pursue and harass our men at the rear.

24. After he noticed this, Caesar led his forces up the nearest hill and sent the cavalry to hold back the attack of the enemy. He himself in the meantime drew up a triple line of battle [composed] of the four veteran legions halfway up the hill. On the top of the ridge, he stationed the two legions which he had enlisted most recently in Nearer Gaul and all the allied troops [that] he might fill the whole mountain with men. Meanwhile, he ordered the baggage to be gathered into one place and this place to be fortified by those who had taken their position in the upper line. The Helvetians, following with all their wagons, gathered their baggage into one place; the men themselves, in very dense formation, hurled back our cavalry and advanced from below against our first line.

25. Caesar first removed [*his own horse having been removed*] his own horse, then those of all [the officers] from sight in order that, by making the danger of all equal, he might take away the hope of flight. Having addressed his men, he began battle. The soldiers threw their javelins from their higher position and easily broke through the phalanx of the enemy, it having been dispersed, they charged upon them with their swords. The Gauls were greatly hindered [*it was a great hindrance to the Gauls*] in fighting [by the fact] that when several of their shields were pierced and fastened together by a single volley [*blow*] of javelins, when the iron had bent itself in, they could neither pull them out nor fight very well with the left hand hampered; so that many since their arms had been tossed about for a long time, let go their shields from their hands and fought with their bodies unprotected.

p. 271. The Helvetians Surrender

I, 26. So they fought, with a doubtful battle, long and fiercely. When they could no longer withstand the rushes of our men, the one [division of the enemy] retreated to the mountain, as they had begun, the other gathered about their baggage and wagons. For during this whole battle, although the fighting lasted from the seventh hour [i.e., noon] till evening, no one was able to see an enemy in retreat. Even until late at night they fought near the baggage, because [the enemy] had put their wagons in the way as a barricade and from their higher position kept throwing their weapons at our men as they advanced, and some among the wagons kept thrusting up their spears and wounding our men. After the fighting had lasted a long time, our men gained possession of the baggage and the camp. There the daughter of Orgetorix and one of his sons were captured. About one hundred and thirty thousand men survived this battle, and they kept on the march incessantly that whole night. On the fourth day they arrived in the territory of the Lingones, since our men, having delayed three days both on account of the wounds of the soldiers and on account of the burial of the dead, had not been able to follow them. Caesar sent letters and messengers to the Lingones [telling them] that they should not help them with grain or anything else who if they did assist them, he [Caesar] would have them in the same place as the Helvetians [were]. He himself, after three days had intervened, began to follow them with all his forces.

27. The Helvetians, forced by lack of all provisions, sent envoys to him about a surrender. When these [*had*] met him on the march and cast themselves at his feet and wept and begged for peace, and he ordered them to wait for his arrival in that place where they then were. After Caesar arrived there, he demanded hostages, their arms, and the slaves who had deserted to them. While these were being hunted up and collected, as night came on, about six thousand men of the canton which is called Verbigenus, either panic-stricken or led on by the hope of safety, came out of the Helvetians' camp early in the night and hurried toward the Rhine and the territory of the Germans.

p. 274. The Price of Peace

I, 28. When Caesar learned [*knew*] this, he commanded those through whose territory they had gone to hunt them out and bring them back; when they were brought back, he treated them as enemies; after the hostages, arms, and deserters had been handed over, he received all the rest in surrender.

He ordered the Helvetians, Tulingi, and Latobrigi to return to their own territories, from which they had departed; and because they had lost all their crops and there was nothing at home with which to satisfy their hunger, he commanded the Allobroges to furnish them a supply of grain; he ordered them [i.e., the Helvetians] to rebuild the towns and villages which they had burned. He did it especially for this reason, because he did not wish the place from which the Helvetians had gone to be unoccupied, so that the Germans, who live beyond the Rhine, might not, on account of the fertility of the fields, cross from their territory into the territory of the Helvetians and be neighbors to the Province of Gaul and the Allobroges. As to the Boii, because they were [men] of outstanding courage, the Haeduans wished to settle them in their own territory; Caesar allowed this. They [i.e., the Hadeuans] gave them lands and afterwards received them into the same terms of justice and liberty as they themselves [enjoyed].

29. In the camp of the Helvetians records were found, written in Greek letters, and were brought to Caesar; in these an itemized account had been made, [showing] what number had gone from home of those who were able to bear arms, and likewise [the number of] boys, old men, and women. The sum total of these accounts was two hundred and sixty-three thousand Helvetians, thirty-six thousand Tulingi, fourteen thousand Latobrigi, twenty-three thousand Rauraci, and thirty-two thousand Boii; of those who were able to bear arms, there were about ninety-two thousand. The total of all was about three hundred and sixty-eight thousand. A census of those who returned home was taken, as Caesar had commanded, and the number was found [to be] one hundred and ten thousand.

p. 277. The German Threat

I, 31. Assembly of all Gaul was called. After this assembly had been dismissed, the same leaders of the states who had been [there] before, returned to Caesar and begged that they be allowed to talk [*discuss*] with him privately [and] secretly about their own safety and that of all. Diviciacus the Haeduan spoke in their behalf:

"There are two factions in all Gaul; the leadership of one of these is held by the Haeduans, that of the other by the Arvernians. After these had been [*were*] fighting with each other for many years for the leadership, it happened that the Germans were hired to come in [*summoned for pay*] by the Arvernians and Sequanians. Of these [Germans] about fifteen thousand crossed the Rhine at first; after the wild and uncivilized men had begun to like the lands, civilization, and wealth of the Gauls, more were brought over; at the present time there are in Gaul about [*to the number of*] one hundred and twenty thousand. With these the Haeduans and their partisans have fought [*with arms*] again and again; defeated, they have suffered great disaster and have lost all their nobles, all the senate, and all the knights.

"But a worse [thing] has happened to the victorious Sequanians than to the conquered Haeduans, because Ariovistus, the king of the Germans, has settled in their territory and taken possession of a third of the Sequanian land, which is the best of all Gaul, and now he is ordering the Sequanians to withdraw from a second third, because, a few months ago, twenty-four thousand of the Harudes came to him, and room is being provided for them. In a few years all the Gauls will be driven from the confines of Gaul and all the Germans will cross the Rhine; for the Gallic land should not be compared with that of the Germans nor our mode of living with theirs [*this mode...with that,* i.e., the German is inferior].

"Moreover, Ariovistus, having once defeated the forces of the Gauls in battle, rules arrogantly and cruelly, demands as hostages the children of all the noblest men, and inflicts all kinds of cruelties upon them, if anything has not been done at his nod or according to his wish. The man is barbarous and hot-tempered; we cannot endure his rule any longer. You, either because of your influence and the recent victory of your army or by the name of the Roman people, can prevent a larger number of Germans from being brought over the Rhine, and you can protect all Gaul from the injustice of Ariovistus."

p. 281. Caesar Promises to Support the Gauls

I, 33. Upon learning these things, Caesar encouraged [*the spirits of*] the Gauls in a talk and promised that this matter would receive his attention [*be of concern to him*]: [saying] that he had great hope that Ariovistus, induced by his [i.e., Caesar's] personal favor and influence, would put an end to his acts of injustice. Having delivered this address, he dismissed the conference. And many things spurred him on to think that he ought to consider and undertake this matter: especially the fact that he saw that the Haeduans, often called brothers and kinsmen of the Roman people by the senate, were held in slavery under [*of*] the Germans and he knew that their hostages were in the hands of [*with*] Ariovistus and the Sequanians; and he thought that this was most disgraceful to him and the state in view of the [*in such a*] great empire of the Roman people. Besides, he saw that it was dangerous to the Roman people for the Germans gradually to form the habit of crossing the Rhine and for a great number of them to come into Gaul. He thought that the savage and uncivilized people, after seizing all Gaul, would come out into the Province and from there hurry to Italy, especially since [only] the Rhone separated the Sequanians from our province; he thought he ought to meet this situation as promptly as possible. Besides, Ariovistus himself has assumed such arrogance that he seemed unbearable.

34. Therefore he decided to send envoys to Ariovistus to demand of him that he should select some place midway between them for a conference, [stating] that he wished to talk with him about business of state and matters very important to [*of*] both. To this embassy Ariovistus replied:

"If I needed anything from Caesar, I should have come to him; if he wishes anything of me, he ought to come to me. Besides, I neither dare to come into those parts of Gaul which Caesar holds without an army nor can I get an army together into one place without supplies and much trouble. Furthermore, it seems strange to me what business either Caesar or in fact the Roman people has in my [part of] Gaul, which I conquered in war."

p. 285. Ariovistus' Defiant Stand

I, 36. To this [i.e., Caesar's ultimatum] Ariovistus replied:

"It is the right of war for conquerors to rule the conquered as they wish; likewise the Roman people are accustomed to rule their subject [*the conquered*], not according to another's direction, but according to their own judgment. If I do not direct the Roman people how to exercise [*use*] their right, I ought not to be interfered with in my rights by the Roman people. [As for] the Haeduans, since they have tried their fortune in war and have engaged in battle [*arms*] and have been defeated, they have become tributary to me. Caesar, who by his coming makes my revenues [*taxes*] less, is doing great wrong. I will not return the hostages to the Haeduans, [*but*] I shall not wage war unjustly either upon them or upon their allies, if they will abide by that which has been agreed upon and will pay tribute every year; if they do not do this, the name of brothers of the Roman people will not help [*will be far from*] them. As to the fact that Caesar declares that he will not overlook the wrongs of the Haeduans, no one contends with me without being destroyed [*his own destruction*]. Whenever he wishes, let him come on; he will discover what undefeated Germans, thoroughly trained in arms, who have not entered a house for fourteen years, can accomplish by their valor."

38. When he had advanced a three days' journey, it was reported to him that Ariovistus was hurrying with all his forces to seize Besançon, which is the largest town of the Sequanians, and had made a three days' journey from his own territory. Caesar hurried there by forced marches by night and day and, after seizing the town, established a garrison there.

42. On learning of Caesar's arrival Ariovistus sent envoys to him: [to say] that, as far as he was concerned, that might be done which Caesar had previously requested about a conference, since he had come nearer and he thought he could do this without danger. Caesar did not reject the condition and thought that Ariovistus was beginning to return to sanity.

p. 297. The First Battle of the Atlantic

III, 14. When, after capturing several of their towns, Caesar realized that such labor was spent in vain, [*and*] that the flight of the enemy could not be checked by taking their towns, and that they could not be injured, he decided that he must await the fleet. As soon as it arrived and was sighted by the enemy, about two hundred and twenty of their ships, fully ready and provided with every kind of equipment, sailed out of the harbor and took their station opposite our vessels; and it was not quite clear to Brutus, who commanded the fleet, or to the military tribunes and centurions, to each of whom a ship had been assigned, what they should do or what plan of battle they should adopt. For they knew that [the enemy's vessels] could not be injured by ramming [*with the beak*]; besides, even though towers had been erected, nevertheless the high sterns [*height of*] on the native ships overtopped these, so that from the lower level missiles could not be thrown easily enough and those thrown by the Gauls fell with [all] the greater force. One device prepared by our men was very useful [*to great advantage*]–pointed hooks set in and fastened to long poles, in shape not unlike wall hooks. Whenever the ropes which bound the sail yards to the masts were caught by these and pulled in, the ship was driven forward with oars, and [the ropes] were severed. When these ropes were cut away, the sail yards necessarily fell down; so that, since all hope in the case of the Gallic ships depended on their sails and rigging and these were torn away, all control of the ships was at once lost. The rest of the contest depended on valor, in which our soldiers easily excelled, and the more so because the engagement took place in sight of Caesar and the entire army, so that no deed a little braver [than usual] could escape notice; for all the hills and higher places, from which there was a near view down upon the sea, were occupied by the army.

p. 300. A Decisive Victory

III, 15. After the sail yards had been torn down (as we have said), whenever two or [*and*] three ships had surrounded each [Gallic vessel], the soldiers would hasten with the greatest energy to board the enemy's ships. After the barbarians noticed that this was taking place, since many of their vessels had been captured and no remedy for it was found, they hastened to seek safety in flight. And just when their vessels had headed in that direction in which the wind was blowing, suddenly there was so great a calm that they were unable to move from the spot. This circumstance, at any rate, was exceedingly opportune for finishing the business; for our men pursued and captured them one by one, so that very few out of all the number reached land [and that, too,] because of the coming on of night, the fighting going on from about the fourth hour until sunset.

16. By this battle the war with the Veneti and the whole seacoast was brought to a close. For not only had all the young men, even all those of more advanced age who had any intelligence or rank, assembled there, but they had also collected in the one place all the ships they had anywhere; when these were lost, the rest did not have [a place] where they could take refuge or means whereby they could defend their towns. They accordingly surrendered themselves and all their possessions to Caesar. Caesar decided that punishment ought to be inflicted all the more severely upon these [people] in order that for the future the rights of ambassadors would be more carefully respected by the barbarians. And so, after putting to death all the senate, he sold the rest as slaves [*under the crown*].

19. So at the same time Sabinus was informed about the naval battle and Caesar about Sabinus' victory; and all the states at once surrendered to Titurius. For just as the spirits of the Gauls are eager and ready to take up wars, just so their mental character is yielding and not at all firm [*resisting*] in enduring disasters.

p. 303. Description of the Suebi

IV, 1. In the following winter, which was the year that Gnaeus Pompey and Marcus Crassus were the consuls, the German Usipites and Likewise the Tencteri with a great number of men crossed the river Rhine, not far from the sea into which the Rhine flows. The reason for their crossing was that, having been harassed for several years by the Suebi, they were [now] being hard pressed in war and were being kept from tilling the soil.

The nation of the Suebi is by far the largest and most warlike of all the Germans. They are said to have a hundred cantons, from each of which they lead yearly a thousand armed men beyond their borders for the purpose of war. The rest, who have remained at home, support themselves and the others. The latter in turn are again in arms the next year, the former stay at home. In this way neither agriculture nor the theory and practice of war is neglected. But no private land exists among them, nor are they permitted to remain in one place longer than a year for the purpose of cultivating the soil. They do not live much on grain, but the most part on milk and cattle, and they are much given to hunting; this manner of living—

because of the kind of food, daily exercise, and freedom of life (for they are accustomed from boyhood to no duty or training and do nothing at all contrary to their wishes)—both increases their strength and makes them men of vast size of body. And they have developed such hardihood [*have brought themselves to this habit*] that, [although they live] in a very cold country, not only do they not have any clothing except skins, on account of whose scantiness a large part of the body is bare, but they even bathe in the rivers.

p. 306. The Bridging of the Rhine

IV, 12. In that battle seventy-four of our horsemen were killed; among these a very brave man, Piso the Aquitanian, descended from a very illustrious family, whose grandfather had held the royal power in his state and had been called a friend by our senate. When this [Piso] went to the aid of his brother who had been cut off by the enemy, he rescued him from danger; he himself was thrown from his wounded horse but resisted most gallantly as long as he could; when he was surrounded and fell after receiving many wounds, his brother, who had already withdrawn from the fight, noticed this at a distance, spurred on this horse, rushed upon the enemy, and was killed.

16. The German war being ended, Caesar for many reasons decided that he ought to cross the Rhine. The best of these [reasons] was that, since he saw the Germans were so easily induced to come into Gaul, he wanted them to fear for their own possessions too, when they realized that an army of the Roman people both could and dared cross the Rhine.

17. For these reasons which we have mentioned Caesar had decided to cross the Rhine; but to cross by means of boats he neither thought quite safe, nor considered [it] in accord with his own dignity or [that] of the Roman people. Therefore, although the greatest difficulty in building a bridge was presented on account of the width, swiftness, and depth of the river, nevertheless he thought that he must make the effort or else not take his army across.

p. 309. Scarcity of Information about Britain

IV, 20. Only a small part of the summer [being] left, although in these parts the winters are early [for Gaul as a whole faces the north], Caesar nevertheless hurriedly started for Britain, because he realized that in almost all the wars with the Gauls reinforcements were furnished our enemies from that quarter; and, if there should not be sufficient time to carry on war, still he thought it would be of great service to him if he merely approached the island, observed the character of its people, and became acquainted with its localities, harbors, and approaches, all of which were for the most part unknown to the Gauls. For nobody except traders goes there without good reason, and even they know nothing except the seacoast and those districts which are opposite Gaul. And so, although he called to him traders from everywhere, he was able to discover neither what the size of the island was, nor what or how powerful were the nations inhabiting it, no what skill in war they possessed, nor what customs they observed, nor what harbors were suitable for a rather large number of ships.

21. In order to discover these things before making his attempt, Caesar [*he*] sent Gaius Volusenus ahead with a warship, thinking him a suitable [person]. He told him to investigate everything and return to him as soon as possible. He himself set out with all his forces for [the land of] the Morini, because from there the passage to Britain was shortest. He ordered the ships from all the neighboring regions and the fleet, which he had built the preceding summer for the Venetan war, to assemble at this point. In the meantime, after his plan had been discovered and reported to the Britons by traders, envoys from several states of that island came to him, to promise to give hostages and submit to the rule of the Roman people. After listening to them, he made generous promises and urged them to continue in that attitude; [then] he sent them back home. Along with them he sent Commius, whom he himself, after subduing the Atrebatians, had set up as king there, whose courage and intelligence he approved, [*and*] whom he believed to be loyal to him, and whose influence was considered great in these regions. He directed him to visit whatever states he could, to urge them to remain loyal to [*follow the faith of*] the Roman people, and to announce that [Caesar] himself would quickly come there. After examining the country as far as opportunity could be given to one who did not dare to disembark and entrust himself to the natives. Volusenus returned to Caesar the fifth day and reported what he had observed there.

p. 312. Midnight Sailing

IV, 23. Having made these arrangements, he found the weather suitable for sailing and set sail about the third watch; he told the cavalry to proceed to the farther port and embark and follow him. While they [*had*] carried out his order a little too slowly, he himself reached Britain and the first ships about the fourth hour of the day and there he caught sight of the armed forces of the enemy drawn up on all the hills. Thinking this place by no means suitable for disembarking, he waited at anchor till the ninth hour for the rest of the ships to arrive there. Meanwhile he called together his generals and military tribunes and made known what he had learned from Volusenus and what he wanted done. He then dismissed them, and finding both the wind and the tide favorable at the same time, he gave the signal, weighed anchor, and proceeding about seven miles from that place, stationed his ships off an open and level shore.

24. But the barbarians, perceiving the design of the Romans, sent ahead their cavalry and chariot fighters, and following closely with the rest of their forces, they kept preventing our men from disembarking. There was the greatest difficulty [in landing] for these reasons, because our ships, on account of their great size, could not be stationed except in deep water; furthermore, our soldiers, being ignorant of the place, their hands impeded, and weighed down [as they were] with the big heavy burden of their arms, had at the same time to leap down from the ships and stand in the waves and fight with the enemy; while the Britons, either on dry ground or advancing [only] a little way into the water, with their entire bodies [*all parts of the body*] free, on thoroughly familiar ground, boldly threw their weapons and spurred on their trained horses. Alarmed by these circumstances and altogether unacquainted with this style of fighting, our men did not display the same spirit and eagerness which they usually showed in battles on land.

25. When Caesar observed this, he ordered the warships, the sight of which was less familiar to the barbarians, to be withdrawn a little way from the transports and driven forward with the oars and stationed on the exposed flank of the enemy and [he ordered that] the enemy be dislodged and driven back from that point with slings, arrows, and artillery. This move was of great service to our men. For the barbarians, alarmed by the shape of the ships, the motion of the oars, and the strange kind of artillery, halted and retreated a little. But while our soldiers were hesitating, chiefly on account of the depth of the sea, the one who carried the eagle of the tenth legion, praying to the gods that his act might turn out well for his legion, said, "Jump down, comrades, unless you wish to betray your eagle to the enemy; I certainly shall perform my duty to the state and the commander." After he [*had*] said this in a loud voice, he jumped down from the ship and began to carry the eagle toward the enemy. Then our men, urging one another not to commit such a disgrace, jumped down from the ship in a body. When the men on the nearest ships saw them, they likewise followed and approached the enemy.

p. 315. Difficult Fighting

IV, 26. Both sides fought fiercely. Our men, however, were thrown into great confusion because they could neither keep their ranks nor find firm footing nor keep up with their standards, and one from one vessel, another from another would join whatever standard he met. But the enemy knew all the shallow places, and whenever from the shore they observed any [soldiers] disembarking one by one, they would spur on their horses and attack them while impeded, and several would surround a few, while other threw their weapons at our main body on the exposed flank. When Caesar [*had*] noticed this, he ordered the boats belonging to [*of*] the warships, and also the patrol craft to be filled with soldiers, and these he sent as a relief to those who he noticed were hard pressed. As soon as our men stood on dry ground, and all their comrades had followed them, they made an attack upon the enemy and put them to flight; but they could not pursue them farther because the cavalry had not been able to hold their course and reach the island. This one thing was lacking for Caesar's former luck.

27. As soon as the enemy, defeated in battle, recovered from their flight, they at once sent ambassadors to Caesar about peace. Along with these ambassadors came Commius the Atrebatian, who, [as] we pointed out above, had been sent on ahead into Britain by Caesar. After he got off the ship, they [the enemy] had seized him and thrown him into chains, although he was bringing Caesar's instructions to them as an envoy [*in the manner of a speaker*]. Then after the battle was fought, they sent him back, and in seeking peace they placed the blame for this act upon the common people, and begged that they be pardoned for their lack of sense. Caesar, complaining that they had made war without cause after they had sent envoys to the continent and voluntarily sought peace of him, stated that he pardoned their lack of sense; he demanded hostages. A part of these they gave at once; a part which had been sent for from more distant places they said that they would give in a few days. Meanwhile they ordered their people to go back to their fields, and the chiefs began to assemble from every quarter and entrust themselves and their states to Caesar.

p. 318. Storm and Tide Cause Trouble

IV, 28. Peace was established by these means, and on the fourth day after [the main body] arrived in Britain, the eighteen vessels mentioned above, which carried the cavalry, set sail from the upper port before a gentle wind. When they were drawing near to Britain and were seen from our camp, so violent a storm suddenly arose that not one of them could hold its course, but some were carried back to the same point from which they [*had*] started; others with great danger to themselves were driven to the lower part of the island, which is nearer the west. Nevertheless, when after anchoring they were filling with water, they of necessity put out to sea in the face of the night and made for the continent.

29. The same night it happened that the moon was full, a time which usually causes very high tides in the ocean, and this fact was unknown to our men. Thus at the same time the tide began to fill the warships, by which Caesar had arranged for the army to be transported and which he had drawn up on dry land, and the storm began to wreck the transports which were held at anchor, nor was any chance of controlling or helping them offered our men. Since a great many ships had been wrecked and the rest were useless for sailing, a great panic arose through the whole army. For there were no other ships by which they could be carried back, and everything which was needed for repairing ships was lacking; and as it was clear to all that they should pass the winter in Gaul, grain had not been provided in these places against the winter.

30. When these facts became known, the chiefs of Britain, who had assembled after the battle in order to do those things which Caesar had ordered, conferred with one another. Realizing that the Romans lacked cavalry, ships, and grain, and becoming aware of the small number of the soldiers from the small size of the camp—which was even smaller for the reason that Caesar had brought his legions over without baggage—they thought it best to renew hostilities, cut our men off from grain and supplies, and prolong the struggle into the winter; for they were confident that if these [Romans] were conquered or cut off from return, no one thereafter would cross over into Britain to make war. Therefore, starting their conspiracy again, they began to withdraw, a few at a time, from the camp and to bring their men back secretly from the fields.

p. 321. New Difficulties

IV, 31. But although Caesar had not yet learned their plans, nevertheless both from the accident to his ships and the fact that they had ceased to give hostages, he was beginning to suspect that that would occur which [actually] happened. He therefore provided resources for all emergencies. For he brought grain daily from the fields into the camp, and used the timber and bronze of those vessels which had been most seriously damaged in repairing the rest, and whatever was of use for that purpose he ordered brought from the continent. And so, since the work was carried on with the utmost energy by the soldiers, though twelve vessels had been lost, he made it possible to sail well enough in the others.

34. Caesar brought aid at a most opportune time to our men, who were greatly alarmed by these doings. For at his coming the enemy halted, and our men recovered from their fear. After this, thinking that the time was unsuitable for attacking the enemy and beginning battle, he remained in a favorable position and, after a short time had intervened, led the legions back to camp. While these things were going on and all of our men were busy, the rest [of the Britons] who were in the country districts [*fields*] withdrew. For several days in succession storms followed, which both kept our men in camp and restrained the enemy from battle. In the meantime the natives sent messengers out in all directions and reported to their [people] the small number of our soldiers and pointed out how great an opportunity was afforded for securing plunder and freeing themselves forever, if they should drive the Romans from the camp. By this means they quickly collected a large force of infantry and cavalry and came toward the camp.

36. Ambassadors sent by the enemy came to Caesar about peace. Caesar doubled for them the number of hostages which he had previously demanded and ordered them to be brought to the continent. He himself, on finding the weather suitable, set sail a little after midnight; all these vessels arrived safely at the continent; but two of the transports were unable to reach the same ports as the rest and were carried a little farther down [the coast].

p. 325. Britain and Its People

V, 12. The interior part of Britain is inhabited by those who say themselves that they originated on the island; the part near the sea [is inhabited] by those who crossed over from Belgium for the sake of plunder and waging war (almost all of these are called by [the same] names of states as those from which they originated and from which they migrated to this place), and after the invasion they remained there and began to till the fields. The population is beyond estimate; their houses [stand] very close together and are almost exactly like those of the Gauls; the number of cattle is great. They use either bronze or gold money or, instead of money, iron bars tested according to a fixed weight. Tin is produced there in the inland regions; in the regions along the sea, iron,but the supply of it is meager; the bronze they use is imported. There is timber of every kind as in Gaul, except beech and fir. They do not consider it right to eat hare, chicken, and goose; yet they raise them for pastime and pleasure. The climate [*places*] is more temperate than in Gaul, the cold seasons being milder.

13. The island is three-cornered in shape, and one side of it is opposite Gaul. The one corner of this side, which is in Kent, where almost all vessels from Gaul land, faces toward the east; the lower [corner], toward the south. This side extends about five hundred miles. A second [side] lies toward Spain and the west; on this side is Ireland, an island less than half as large as Britain (as it is thought), but at the same distance as it is from Gaul to Britain. In midchannel there is an island which is called Man; besides, several smaller islands are thought to lie opposite; concerning these islands some have written that about [the time of] the winter solstice it is night for thirty successive days. We learned nothing about this, except that by accurate measurements with a water glass we saw that the nights were shorter than on the continent. The length of this side, as their opinion goes, is seven hundred miles. The third side faces the north, and no land lies opposite this part; but an angle of this side faces principally toward Germany. This [side] is supposed to be eight hundred miles in length. Thus the whole island is two thousand miles in circumference.

14. By far the most civilized of all these [peoples] are those who inhabit Kent (a district which lies entirely along the coast), nor do they differ much from the Gallic manner of life. The majority of those who live in the interior do not plant crops but live on milk and meat and are clothed in skins. But all the Britons stain themselves with woad, which produces a blue color, and for this reason they have a more terrible appearance in battle; and they let their hair grow long.

p. 330. Two Rival Heroes

V, 44. In this legion there were two very valiant men, centurions, who were already approaching first rank, Titus Pullo and Lucius Vorenus. These men used to have continual disputes with each other as to which should be preferred to the other, and every year they used to quarrel over promotion. One of them, Pullo, while the fighting was the fiercest before the fortifications, said,

"Why do you hesitate, Vorenus, or what chance of proving your valor are you looking for? This day shall decide our quarrels."

Saying this, he advanced beyond the fortifications and rushed upon that part of the enemy which seemed to be the thickest. Then Vorenus did not remain inside the rampart either, but fearing every one's opinion, he followed him closely. When only a short distance remained [between him and the enemy], Pullo threw his javelin at the enemy and pierced one of the crowd as he ran forward; run through and rendered senseless as he was, the enemy protected him with their shields and all threw their weapons at Pullo and gave him no chance to advance. Pullo's shield was pierced and a dart was driven into his sword belt. This accident turned aside his scabbard and delayed his [*right*] hand when he tried to draw his sword, and the enemy surrounded him while [thus] hindered. His rival Vorenus ran to his aid and rescued him in his distress. The whole crowd immediately turned from Pullo to Vorenus. Vorenus got into action with his sword; he killed one and drove back the rest a little; [*while he was*] pressing on too eagerly, he stumbled [*thrown down*] into a hollow and fell. When he in turn was surrounded, Pullo brought him aid, and, after killing many, both retired unharmed within the fortifications in great glory. In the contest Fortune dealt with each in such a way that the one rival helped and saved the other, nor could it be determined which seemed superior to the other in valor.

45. There was one Nervian in camp, by name Vertico, born of an honorable family, who had fled to Cicero and had shown his loyalty to him. He persuaded a slave with the hope of freedom and large rewards to carry a letter to Caesar. This he carried out bound inside a javelin, and moving about as a Gaul among Gauls without any suspicion, he made his way to Caesar. From him Caesar learned about the dangers of Cicero and his legion.

p. 333. A Coded Message and a Clever Trick

V, 48. Caesar advanced by forced marches into the lands of the Nervii. There he learned from prisoners what was taking place at Cicero's [camp] and in how great danger the situation was. Then he persuaded one of the Gallic horsemen with large rewards to deliver a letter to Cicero. This he sent written in Greek characters, so that, if the letter were intercepted, our plans would not be discovered by the enemy. He instructed him, if he could not approach [the camp], to throw his dart with the letter fastened to it, inside the fortifications of the camp. In the letter he wrote that he had started with his legions and would be there quickly; he urged him to maintain his former courage. The Gaul, fearing danger, threw the dart as he had been instructed. By chance it stuck fast to a tower and was not noticed by our men for two days, but on the third day it was seen by a soldier; it was delivered to Cicero. After reading it through, he read it aloud before an assembly of his soldiers and filled them all with the greatest joy. Then the smoke of fires was seen at a distance, a fact which dispelled all doubt about the arrival of the legions.

52. Fearing to pursue too far, because woods and swamps intervened, with all his force intact, he reached Cicero the same day. He marvelled at the towers which had been erected, the [movable] sheds and the fortifications of the enemy; when the legion was drawn up [for review], he discovered that not one soldier in ten was left without a wound. From all these facts he judged with what danger and courage matters had been conducted. He commended Cicero for his services and the legion [also]; he called up individually the centurions and the tribunes of the soldiers, whose courage, upon Cicero's testimony, he discovered to have been extraordinary.

p. 338. Gallic Leaders

VI, 11. Since we have arrived at this point, it does not seem out of place to make a statement about the customs of Gaul and Germany and [to state] how these nations differ from each other. In Gaul, not only in all states and in all districts and divisions, but even in almost every single home, there are factions, and of these factions those are the leaders who in the estimation of the Gauls are believed to have the greatest influence, so that to their [*whose*] decision and judgment the management of all affairs and policies is referred.

12. When Caesar came into Gaul, the leaders of the one faction were the Haeduans, of the other the Sequanians. Since the latter were less powerful of themselves, because from ancient times the highest power rested [*was*] with the Haeduans and their clientships were extensive, the Sequanians had attached to themselves the Germans and Ariovistus and had won them over by great sacrifices and promises. But after fighting several successful battles and killing all the nobles of the Haeduans, they had increased so much in power that they transferred from the Haeduans a great part of their vassals and received from them the sons of the leaders as hostages and compelled them as a people to take an oath that they would form no plot against the Sequanians. [Other results were that] they kept a part of the neighboring land, which they had seized by force, and obtained the leadership of all Gaul. Influenced by this need, Diviciacus had gone to the senate in Rome to seek aid, [but] had returned without accomplishing his mission. At the coming of Caesar a complete change had been brought about: the hostages were returned to the Haeduans, their former clientships were restored and new one secured through Caesar, because those who had attached themselves to the Haeduans' friendship saw that they were enjoying better terms and a more just rule, and their influence and honor were extended in all other respects; and the Sequanians had lost their leadership. The Remi had succeeded to their position; because it was understood that these equaled [the Haeduans] in influence with Caesar, those who on account of oldtime enmities could not possibly unite with the Haeduans attached themselves in clientship to the Remi. These the Remi guarded carefully; thus they retained their new and suddenly acquired influence. At that time matters were in such a situation that the Haeduans were regarded as by far the leaders, [and] the Remi held second place in influence.

p. 341. The Druids

VI, 13. Throughout Gaul there are two classes of those persons who are of some account and importance. For the common people are regarded almost as slaves, who dare do nothing of themselves and are admitted to no council. The majority, whenever they become oppressed with debt or the heavy burden of taxes or the injustice of more powerful men, bind themselves in servitude to the nobles; and these have over them precisely the same rights as masters over slaves. But of these two classes the one consists of druids, the other of knights. The former attend to divine matters, perform sacrifices, public and private, and interpret religious questions. A great number of young men flock to them for [*the sake of*] instruction, and the druids are in great honor among the Gauls. For they render decisions in almost all disputes, public and private; and if any crime has been committed, if murder has been done, or if there is a dispute about an inheritance or about boundaries, they likewise decide it; they fix rewards and penalties; if any person or people does not abide by their decision, they exclude [such] from the sacrifices. This penalty is the severest [known] among them. Those who have thus been banned are numbered among the impious and wicked, all keep away from them, avoid their approach and conversation with them so as not to receive some harm from the contact, nor is justice accorded them when they seek it, nor any honor shared. Now over all these druids there presides one man, who holds supreme authority among them. When he dies, either he is succeeded by whichever of the rest excels in rank, or, if several are of equal rank, [the successor] is chosen by vote of the druids; sometimes they even fight with arms for the leadership. At a fixed time of the year they hold a session in a sacred spot in the land of the Carnutes, a district which is regarded as the center of entire Gaul; at this place all who have disputes assemble from everywhere and obey the druids' decisions and judgments. The system [of druidism] is thought to have been invented in Britain and to have been brought from there into Gaul; and now those who wish to study this subject more thoroughly generally proceed to that place for instruction.

p. 344. Druids and Knights

VI, 14. The druids, according to custom [*are accustomed to be*], are exempt from war, nor do they pay taxes along with the rest. Attracted by these great privileges, many of their own accord assemble for training; and many are sent by parents and relatives. They are said to learn by heart there [i.e., in the druidical schools] a large number of verses. And so some remain in training twenty years. Nor do they think it proper to commit these principles to writing, although in almost all other matters, in their public and private accounts, they employ Greek characters. This [course] they seem to me to have decided upon for two reasons: [*because*] they neither want their doctrine to become public nor those who study [it] to pay less attention to the memory through their reliance upon writing—because it generally happens in the case of most men that, in their dependence on writing, they relax their zeal for learning thoroughly and their memorizing. They want to prove this [doctrine] especially, that souls do not perish but pass after death from one [body] to another; and by this [belief] they think men are particularly aroused to courage if the fear of death is disregarded. They also discuss and transmit to the young men many [beliefs] about the stars and their motion, about the size of the universe and of the earth, about the nature of things, and about the might and power of the immortal gods.

15. The other class consists of the knights. Whenever there is need or some war breaks out (and before Caesar's coming this used to happen almost every year, that they either inflicted injuries themselves or warded off injuries inflicted by others), all of these engage in war, and [in proportion] as each of them is most prominent because of birth or wealth, so has he the most retainers and vassals about him. This is the only influence and power they recognize.

p. 347. Religion

VI, 16. The nation of the Gauls as a whole is greatly devoted to religious observances; and for this reason those who are afflicted with more serious diseases and those who are involved in battles and dangers, either sacrifice men as victims or vow that they will sacrifice them, and they employ the druids [as] ministers for these sacrifices, for they think that, unless the life of a man is paid for the life of a man, the immortal gods cannot be appeased; and they have publicly instituted sacrifices of the same sort. Others have likenesses [of the human form] of huge size, whose parts, woven with twigs, they fill with living men; these they set on fire and the men perish, enveloped in flame. The punishment of those who have been caught in theft or highway robbery or some crime, they think is more acceptable to the immortal gods; but whenever a supply of this sort fails, they even resort to the sacrifice of the innocent.

17. Of the gods they chiefly worship Mercury. There are numerous images of him; they say that he is the inventor of all the arts, that he is the guide for their travels and journeys; they think that he exerts the greatest influence over the acquisition of money and commercial transactions; after him they worship Apollo, Mars, Jupiter, and Minerva. They hold about the same belief about these as other peoples: that Apollo wards off diseases, that Minerva teaches the elements of the arts and crafts, that Jupiter holds the sovereign power of the gods, that Mars controls wars.

To the latter, whenever they have decided to engage in battle, they generally vow whatever they may take in war; when they win, they sacrifice the animals which they have captured; the remaining spoils they collect in one place. In many states one may see heaps of these spoils piled up in consecrated spots.

18. All the Gauls state that they are descended from Father Dis and they say that this [tradition] has been handed down by the druids. For this reason they determine all periods of time, not by the number of days but of nights; they observe birthdays and the first days [*beginnings*] of the months and years in such a way that the day follows the night [of the holiday].

p. 349. Marriages and Funerals; Censorship

VI, 19. Husbands, after making an estimate, combine with the dowries from their own possessions as much property as they have received from their wives by way of dowry. An account of all this money is jointly kept and the income saved; whichever survives, to this one reverts the portion of both along with the income of the intervening time. Husbands have the power of life and death over their wives just as over their children; and when the master of a house of somewhat noble rank dies, his relatives assemble and if there is anything suspicious about his death, they hold an examination of the wives as is done in the case of slaves, and if [their guilt] is detected they put them to death, torturing them with fire and every form of torment. The funerals, considering the civilization of the Gauls, are magnificent; and all objects which they think were dear to the [dead while] living they place on the fire, even living creatures; and a little before our time slaves and vassals who it was known had been chosen by them, were burned together with [their masters], after the regular rites had been completed.

20. Those states which are thought to manage their government more effectively have it ordained by law that, if anyone has heard anything about the government from his neighbors by rumor and gossip, he shall report it to a magistrate and not share it with anyone else, because it has been discovered that frequently rash and ignorant men are frightened by false reports and impelled to crime and take counsel about the most important matters. The magistrates conceal whatever seems best, and give out to the people whatever they have concluded is of advantage. It is not permissible to speak about a public matter except in [*through*] the council.

p. 351. Description of the Germans

VI, 21. The Germans differ greatly from this mode [of living]. For they neither have druids to preside over divine matters nor do they pay attention to sacrifices. They consider in the number of the gods only those whom they see and by whose resources they are clearly aided, the Sun, Vulcan [i.e., the god of fire], and the Moon; the rest they have never even heard of. Their whole life consists in hunting and military pursuits; from childhood they devote themselves to toil and hardship.

22. They are not interested in the tilling of the soil, and the greater part of their food consists of milk, cheese, and meat. No one has a fixed amount of land or boundaries of his own; but the magistrates and chiefs assign for a single year to families and groups of kinsmen as much land and in such a place as they think best, and the year after they compel them to go somewhere else. They assign many reasons for this practice: that, captivated by fixed habits [of life], they may not give up their interest in warfare for agriculture; that they may not become anxious to gain extensive lands and that the more powerful may not drive the lower classes from their possessions; that no desire for money may arise, from which factions and dissensions spring; that they may keep the common people in contentment, when everybody sees that his own wealth is made equal to [that of] the most powerful.

23. It is the greatest distinction for their states to have solitudes as wide as possible about them, by laying waste their frontiers. They think that it is a sign of courage that their neighbors are driven from their farms and retire and that nobody dares to settle near them. At the same time they think that they will be safer for this reason, if the fear of a sudden invasion is removed. Whenever a state fights either a defensive or an offensive war, magistrates are chosen to have charge of this war and to hold the power of life and death. In peace there is no common magistrate, but the chiefs of the districts and cantons pronounce judgment among their people and settle disputes. Robberies which are committed outside the boundaries of any state involve no dishonor, and they declare that these are made for the purpose of training their youth and reducing laziness. They do not think it right to injure a guest; those who for any reason have come to them they shield from injury and hold inviolable, and the homes of all are open to them, and their food is shared [with them].

p. 354. The Hercynian Forest and Its Animals

VI, 25. The breadth of the Hercynian forest is a nine days' journey for one unencumbered; for in no other way can it be determined, and [its inhabitants] know no [system of] measuring roads. Many kinds of wild animals evidently are found there which have not been seen in any other places; and of those which differ most from all others and seem worthy of mention there are the following.

26. There is an ox in the shape of a stag, from the middle of whose forehead a single horn stands out between the ears, higher and straighter than those horns which are known to us. From its tip hands, as it were, and branches spread out widely [i.e. branching antlers spread out like a hand]. The characteristics of the female and male are the same, the shape and size of their horns [are] the same.

27. There are likewise [animals] which are called elk. Their shape and the spotted appearance of their skins are quite similar to [those of] goats; but they excel them a little in size, and their horns [have] a broken appearance [*are broken in respect to horns*], and they have legs without joints; they do not lie down to rest and if they meet with an accident and fall, they cannot raise themselves up. Trees serve them as resting places [*beds*]; they lean against these and reclining in this way just a little they take their rest. Whenever hunters have observed by their tracks where they are in the habit of resorting, they either undermine all the trees in that place at the roots or they cut into them only far enough so that the appearance of standing [trees] is still left. When [the elk] lean against these according to their habit, they throw the weakened trees over with their weight and fall down themselves along with them.

28. There is a third kind, consisting of those [animals] which are called buffaloes. In size they are a little below [that of] elephants, and of the appearance, color, and shape of a bull. Great is their strength and great their speed; they spare neither man nor beast which they have [once] caught sight of. ([The natives] capture and kill them by means of pits. With this [kind of] work the young men harden themselves and by this style of hunting they keep in training; and those who kill the largest number of them receive great praise when they bring the horns into a public place to serve as proof.) But they cannot become accustomed to men even when caught very young. The spread, shape, and appearance of their horns differ widely from the horns of our oxen. These [horns] they collect and cover with silver at the edges and use them as cups at their most sumptuous feasts.

p. 357. Vercingetorix Takes Charge

VII, 4. By a similar plan Vercingetorix, son of Celtillus, an Arvernian, a young man of great influence, whose father had held the leadership of all Gaul and had been put to death by the government for the reason that he was aiming at royal power, called together his vassals and easily stirred them up. When his plan became known, people rushed to arms. He was restrained by his uncle and the other leaders, who did not think that this chance should be taken; he was expelled from the town of Gergovia. Still he did not give up and in the farming country held a levy of the needy and desperate. After collecting this band, he brought over to his way of thinking all the people in the state whom he approached; he urged them to take arms for the freedom of all; and after collecting large forces, he expelled his opponents from the state, by whom he had been ejected a short time before. He was proclaimed king by his men. He sent committees in every direction; he begged them to remain loyal. He quickly attached to himself all those who border on the ocean; by the consent of all the supreme command was offered to him. After this power was conferred, he demanded hostages from all these states, ordered a fixed number of soldiers to be brought to him quickly, decided how many arms each state should produce at home and by what time; he was particularly eager for cavalry. To his great thoroughness he added exceedingly severe control; those who hesitated he brought over by the severity of his punishment. For if a major crime had been committed, he put [the culprits] to death by fire and all [sorts of] torture; for lighter offenses [*reasons*] he cut off their ears or dug out an eye and [then] sent them home so as to be an object lesson to the rest and to scare others by the severity of the punishment.

8. Although the Cévennes Mountains, which separate the Arverni from the Helvii, at the worst season of the year blocked the road with very deep snow, he nevertheless pushed aside the snow, which was six feet high, and in this way opened up the roads and after great effort [on the part] of the soldiers he came to the territory of the Arverni. These being caught by surprise, for they thought that they were protected by the Cévennes as by a wall, and not even for a man [who was] all alone had paths ever been open at that time of year, he gave orders to the cavalry to scatter as widely as they could so as to instill the greatest [possible] fear in the enemy.

p. 360. Roman Spirit

VII, 17. Although the army was experiencing the greatest difficulty in getting supplies, so much so that for many days the soldiers were without grain and avoided extreme hunger [only] by driving in cattle from the more distant villages, yet not a word was heard from them unworthy of the dignity of the Roman people and their previous victories. Besides, when Caesar addressed each legion [while] at its work and stated that he would abandon the siege if they were suffering too severely from want, they all begged him not to do so, [saying] that they had served for several years under his command in such a way that they suffered no disgrace and never gave up with their objective unattained; that they would regard this as a disgrace if they should abandon the siege after once commencing it; that it was better to endure every [form of] suffering than not to avenge the Roman citizens who had perished through the treachery of the Gauls.

57. While these things were taking place in Caesar's army, Labienus started with four legions for Lutecia. This is a town of the Parisii, situated on an island of the river Seine. When his arrival was discovered by the enemy, large forces assembled from the neighboring states. The supreme command was entrusted to Camulogenus, an Aulercan. When he [*had*] observed that there was a continuous marsh which flowed into the Seine and made that whole country largely impassable, he encamped there.

p. 363. The Siege of Alesia

VII, 69. The town itself was on the top of a hill in a very high location so that it did not seem possible to capture it except by siege. In front of the town a plain about three miles long stretched out; on all the other sides, [beyond] a small space in between, hills surrounded the town. Below the wall (and all this part of the hill faced east) the Gallic troops had filled the entire space and built a trench and a wall six feet high. The circuit of the fortification which was set up by the Romans extended ten miles. Camps were pitched at convenient places and twenty-three forts were placed there; in these, outposts were placed in the daytime so that no sally [from the town] could be made all of a sudden; these same forts were held by strong garrisons at night.

76. In previous years in Britain Caesar had employed the faithful and efficient aid of Commius; in return for these services he had directed that his state should be free from tribute, and he had restored its rights and laws and had assigned the Morini to [Commius] himself. So strong, however, was the agreement of entire Gaul to claim its liberty and to recover its former renown in war that [the Gauls] were moved neither by kindnesses nor by the remembrance of friendship, and all lent their efforts to this war with [their whole] heart and resources. After they had collected eight thousand cavalry and about two hundred and fifty thousand infantry, these [forces] were reviewed in the country of the Haeduans, and officers were appointed. Eager and full of confidence, all start out for Alesia; nor was there one of all [that number] who thought that merely the sight of so large a number could be endured [by the Romans], especially in a battle on two fronts, when [those within] would sally forth from the town and fight, [and] on the outside such large forces of cavalry and infantry would be seen.

p. 366. A Horrible Suggestion

VII, 77. But those who were being besieged in Alesia, when the day on which they had expected reinforcements from their countrymen had passed, and all the grain had been used up, not knowing what was going on among the Haeduans, called together a council and went into consultation about the outcome of their fortunes. Various opinions were expressed among them, some of which favored surrender, others a sally while they had the strength; [but] the speech of Critognatus should not, it seems [to me], be passed over, in view of its remarkable and unspeakable cruelty.

This man was born of a most eminent family among the Arvernians and was considered [a man] of great influence.

"I am going to say nothing," said he, "about the opinion of those who call the basest slavery by the name of surrender, and I think that they should neither be regarded as citizens nor invited to the council. Let my speech deal with those who favor a sally; in whose suggestion, by your general agreement, there seems to linger a remembrance of your former courage. That is faintheartedness on your part, not courage, to be unable to endure lack [of food] for a short while. [Men] who would voluntarily offer themselves to death are more easily found than those who endure suffering patiently. And I might approve this view (so much does their high position weigh with me), if I saw that no sacrifice other than [that of] our lives would be made; but in adopting a plan let us consider all Gaul, which we have roused to our aid. What do you think will be the spirit of our relatives and kinsmen, when eighty thousand men have been killed in one spot, if they are forced to fight a decisive battle almost upon our dead bodies? Do not deprive of your aid those who for the sake of your safety have disregarded their own danger; nor through your folly and rashness or weakness of resolution ruin all Gaul and subject it to lasting slavery.

"What, then, is my plan? To do what our forefathers did in the war with the Cimbri and Teutons, [a war] by no means equal [to this]; when driven into their towns and pinched by a similar lack [of food], they supported life with the bodies of those who by reason of age seemed useless for war, and they did not surrender to the enemy. And if we did not have a precedent for such a course, I should nevertheless consider it a most noble thing for [such a precedent] to be established and handed down to posterity for the sake of liberty. For what likeness was there [between] that war [and this]? The Cimbri, after plundering Gaul and inflicting great loss, withdrew at last from our borders, at any rate, and sought other lands; they left us our rights, laws, farm lands, and liberty. But as for the Romans, what else do they seek or what do they want except, influenced by envy, to settle in the lands and states of those whom they have learned by reputation to be noble and powerful in war, and to impose upon them lasting slavery? For they never have waged wars on any other terms. But if you do not know what is going on among distant nations, consider the neighboring [part of] Gaul which, reduced to a province, with its rights and laws completely changed, has been made subject to authority and crushed in perpetual slavery!"

p. 369. Innocent Victims of War

VII, 78. After [different] opinions had been expressed, they decided that those who through sickness or age were useless for war should depart from the town, and that they should try anything before they resorted to the suggestion of Critognatus; yet that plan was to be used if the situation required it and the reinforcements delayed, rather than that they should submit to any terms of surrender or peace. The Mandubii, who had taken them into their town, were forced to leave with their children and wives. When these [people] reached the fortifications of the Romans, with tears and all sorts of entreaties they begged them to receive them as slaves and help them with food. But Caesar, stationing guards on the rampart, prevented them from being admitted.

79. Meanwhile Commius and the rest of the leaders, to whom the supreme command had been entrusted, arrived with all their forces in the neighborhood of Alesia, and seizing an outer hill, encamped not more than a mile from our fortifications. The next day they led their cavalry out of camp and filled all that plain which extended three miles in length; and leading their infantry forces a little aside from this place, they stationed them on the higher points. There was a view from the town of Alesia over the plain. Upon seeing these reinforcements, they [i.e., the besieged Gauls] rushed up; they congratulated one another, and the hearts of all were stirred to joy. So they led out their forces, took up their position before the town, and prepared themselves for a sally and all emergencies.

82. While the Gauls were farther away from our fortification, they had more success by reason of the number of their weapons; after they came up nearer, they either impaled themselves unexpectedly upon the spurs or, falling into wolfholes, were pierced or were struck by wall javelins from rampart and towers and perished. After they had received many wounds from all directions without breaking through the fortification at any point, since daylight was approaching, they feared that they might be surrounded on the exposed flank by a sortie from the upper camps and so retreated to their comrades. But those within, while bringing out those [devices] which had been prepared by Vercingetorix for a sally, filled up the first trenches; having delayed too long in performing these tasks, they discovered that their [comrades] had withdrawn before they [even] got near our fortifications. So they returned to the town without accomplishing their purpose.

p. 372. Near Disaster Followed by Victory

VII, 88. When his arrival had been discovered from the color of his cloak, a color which he had been in the habit of employing as a distinguishing mark in battles, and when the troops of cavalry and the cohorts which he had ordered to follow him had been seen, as these slopes were visible from the heights, the enemy began battle. A shout is raised on both sides and the shout is answered from the rampart and all the fortifications. Our men, dropping their javelins, carry on the struggle with their swords. Suddenly

[Caesar's] cavalry comes into sight behind the [enemy's] backs; other cohorts approach. The enemy turn their backs; the cavalry meets them as they flee; great slaughter follows. Seventy-four military standards are brought to Caesar; only a few out of the large number retire uninjured to camp. [Those besieged], observing from the town the slaughter and flights of their countrymen [and] despairing of their own safety, withdrew their forces from the fortifications. At once, upon hearing of this defeat, the Gauls fled from their camp. And if the soldiers had not become exhausted by the frequent giving of relief and their hard work of the whole day, all the forces of the enemy might have been destroyed. The cavalry, which had been sent out after midnight, overtook the rear; a great number were captured and killed; the rest after the flight scattered to their states.

89. The next day Vercingetorix called a council and pointed out that he had undertaken this war, not for his own advantage but for the common liberty; and since they must yield to fortune, [he declared] that he offered himself to them for either purpose, whether they wished to satisfy the Romans with his death or to deliver him alive. Envoys were sent to Caesar with regard to these matters. He ordered their arms to be surrendered [and] their chieftains brought forward. He himself sat down within the fortifications in front of his camp; there the leaders were brought before him. Vercingetorix was given up; their arms were thrown down. After reserving the Haeduans and the Arvernians [to see] whether he might regain their states through them, he distributed the rest of the prisoners among his entire army, [giving] one to each [soldier] as loot.

90. When the accomplishments of this year were made known at Rome through Caesar's dispatches, a thanksgiving of twenty days was decreed.

p. 374. Word Studies

One scholar has ingeniously translated **tollendum** as "immortalized," i.e., both "exalted" and "made no longer a mortal." Other possibilities: "elevated to the skies," "fixed up for good," "polished up and off," "given the full treatment."

p. 376. A Latin Play: Caesar the Dictātor

Characters

Gaius Julius Caesar	**An aedile**
Babidus, *an aging secretary*	**Bubulo,** *brother of Caesar's baker*
Fronto, *a young secretary*	**Syphax,** *a pearl dealer*
Marcus Terentius Varro	**Calpurnia,** *wife of Caesar*
Sosigenes, *astronomer*	**Rhoda,** *a slave*
Marcus Flavius, *a friend of Sosigenes*	
First *and* **Second Senator**	

(*Enter Babidus and Fronto. They carry tablets, books, and styli.*)

BABIDUS: Put the books down, Fronto.

FRONTO: Will many visitors be here today?

BABIDUS: Yes [*many*]. The entire country is [*for*] a concern of the dictator Caesar.

FRONTO: He works more than a slave.

BABIDUS: I'm often scared about [*for*] him. He works all the time; he does not eat [*take food*]. He does not enjoy very good health. Sometimes he even faints.

FRONTO: I heard a rumor in town—that Caesar wants to be king.

BABIDUS: Nonsense! Caesar wants to establish peace, harmony, and tranquillity in the city and the world.

FRONTO: He certainly names the candidates for the offices.

BABIDUS: He names some, the people name others. However, the old [form of] government is dead.

FRONTO: Are the books properly prepared? I recall that Caesar once put his secretary Philemon to death.

BABIDUS: Philemon was an unspeakable [criminal]. A slave of Caesar, he promised Caesar's enemies that he would kill his master with poison. You are neither a criminal nor a slave. Don't be afraid.

FRONTO: Listen! Caesar is coming.

(*Enter Gaius Julius Caesar.*)

CAESAR: Greetings.

BABIDUS AND FRONTO: Greetings, General.

CAESAR: First, the records of the senate and the people. Are they ready?

FRONTO: There you are, General. (*Hands Caesar a book, which Caesar reads.*)

CAESAR: Good! Well written! Now let's turn our attention to my commentaries on the Civil War.

BABIDUS: There you are, Caesar. (*Hands Caesar a book.*)

CAESAR: I want to add a few words.

BABIDUS: I'm ready. (*Babidus sits down; he gets ready to take shorthand notes. Exit Fronto.*)

CAESAR (*dictates*): "Caesar, abandoning everything [else], thought that he ought to pursue Pompey into whatever regions he retreated, so that he [Pompey] could not again assemble other forces and renew the war."

BABIDUS: It is written down.

CAESAR: Has my letter to Marcus Cicero, which I dictated yesterday, been written? (*Enter Fronto.*)

BABIDUS: There you are, Caesar. (*Hands Caesar the letter.*)

CAESAR: Change the letters. Write D for A, and so on.

Babidus: I understand.

FRONTO: Visitors are here, General.

CAESAR: Have Varro come in. (*Exit Fronto; he then enters with Varro.*) Greetings, Varro.

VARRO: Greetings, General.

CAESAR: Varro, you are a scholar. I have it in mind to build a very large library, Greek and Latin. It will be a public library. I want to make you director of the library.

VARRO: Me?

CAESAR: You, of course.

VARRO: But I was a general of Pompey, your enemy.

CAESAR: Don't fear, Varro. I am a dictator but not the kind of dictator that Sulla was [*such a dictator as*]. Proscription lists of lives and property are not to Caesar's taste.

VARRO: General, how can I thank you?

CAESAR: No need to speak about thanks. You will be a very good library director. Good-by, Varro.

VARRO: May the gods [make this] turn out well! Good-by. [*Exit.*]

CAESAR: Have the astronomers come in. (*Exit Fronto. He enters with Sosigenes and Flavius.*) Greetings, Sosigenes and Flavius.

SOSIGENES AND FLAVIUS: Greetings, General.

CAESAR: What have you accomplished?

SOSIGENES: In our opinion, the year should be made to agree with the path of the sun. The year must be three hundred and sixty-five days [long]; one day must also be inserted every fourth year.

CAESAR: You are on the right track, at least in my opinion.

FLAVIUS: If it pleases Caesar, have Caesar's birth month, now Quinctilis, called July.

CAESAR: On this point let's talk later. Meanwhile, continue as you have begun. Good-by.

SOSIGENES AND FLAVIUS: Good-by, General. (*Exeunt.*)

CAESAR: Have the senators come in now. (*Exit Fronto. He comes in with the senators.*) Greetings.

SENATORS: Greetings, Caesar.

CAESAR: What's on your minds?

FIRST SENATOR: We are much worried [*there are great cares to us*], Caesar. We have heard that without the senate's authorization you are sending Roman soldiers throughout the world to kings so as to help them out; that out of public funds you are building fine buildings [*decorating with public works*] [in] cities in Asia, Greece, Spain, and Gaul.

SECOND SENATOR: You have bestowed citizenship on physicians, grammarians, and others. You have enrolled in the senate semicivilized Gauls. Your soldiers have entered the homes of citizens and carried off food. You yourself annulled the marriage of Roman citizens.

FIRST SENATOR: Evil rumors are spreading throughout the city. What are you doing, Caesar?

CAESAR: I am the dictator. I am restoring the government, ruined by war.

SECOND SENATOR: You are destroying the government, Caesar.

CAESAR: All will be well. Don't stir up my anger. Farewell, friends.

SENATORS: Good-by, Caesar. (*Exeunt.*)

CAESAR: Let's turn our attention to pleasanter matters. Have the aedile come in. (*Exit Fronto. He enters with the aedile.*) Greetings.

AEDILE: Greetings, General. Everything is ready, as you ordered—the show of gladiators, the hunt, the sea battle, the stage plays, the circus games.

CAESAR: Good.

AEDILE: The shows will be the greatest of all.

CAESAR: Well done. I thank you.

AEDILE: I am honored to help Caesar. Good-by.

CAESAR: Good-by. (*Exit Aedile. Enter Rhoda. She carries food and letters. She hands the letters to Babidus.*)

RHODA: The mistress begs that master will take food.

CAESAR: Go away, go away! (*Exit Rhoda, taking the food.*) What letters are those?

BABIDUS: The building contractor has written about the Julian Forum, about the new temple, and about the statue of your horse.

CAESAR: Yes, yes.

BABIDUS: Another man has written about building a new road, about digging [a canal through] the Isthmus [of Corinth], and about draining the Pontine marshes.

CAESAR: Give me this letter.

BABIDUS: A veteran thanks you for the loot, the slaves, and the farm which you gave him. A poor Roman thanks you on receiving gold and grain.

CAESAR: That letter I shall read in a moment. Who is waiting in the hall?

FRONTO: A big fellow—Bubulo. And a pearl dealer.

CAESAR: Bubulo?

FRONTO: The brother of your baker.

CAESAR: What's he want? Have him in. (*Exit Fronto. He enters with Bubulo.*)

BUBULO: General Caesar, I implore you, I implore you!

CAESAR: What do you want?

BUBULO: Free my brother, your baker, [who has been] thrown into chains.

CAESAR: He gave me one [kind of] bread in my dining room and a different [kind] to my friends.

BUBULO: But you are Caesar.

CAESAR: My friends and I will have the same food. But your brother has by now paid the penalty. I will free him. (*He writes on a tablet; he hands the tablet to Bubulo.*)

BUBULO: Oh, may the gods love you, Caesar! (*Exit. Caesar laughs.*)

CAESAR: Have Syphax the pearl dealer come in. (*Exit Fronto. He comes in with Syphax.*)

SYPHAX: Hail, General. I have a pearl—a very large one. (*He shows the pearl to Caesar.*)

CAESAR: What are you talking about? This pearl is not large. (*Enter Calpurnia.*) This pearl is small. I want the queen of pearls—for my wife.

CALPURNIA: What's that I hear?

CAESAR: Calpurnia!

CALPURNIA: Show me the pearl.—It is very beautiful.

CAESAR: Do you like it? I wanted to give you a bigger one.

CALPURNIA: Of course I like it. It is beautiful—and big enough.

CAESAR: It will be yours. (*He speaks to the secretaries.*) Take care of all [the details].

SYPHAX: Thank you, General. [*Exit, with the secretaries.*]

CALPURNIA: I wish you would take care of yourself as well as [you do] of me!

CAESAR: I am well.

CALPURNIA: You refuse food; you don't get enough rest; even in sleep you often are terrified.

CAESAR: It's nothing.

CALPURNIA: You are giving your life for the state. The omens too are bad.

CAESAR: Omens do not scare me. (*Enter Babidus. He gives the pearl to Caesar.*)

There! To my most beautiful wife I give a most beautiful gem. Now let's go to lunch.

(*Exeunt Caesar and Calpurnia, the Babidus.*)

p. 383. The Eruption of Vesuvius

You ask that I write to you about my uncle's death so that you may transmit it to posterity. I thank you; for I see that undying glory has been promised his death. Although he himself wrote very many works and ones that will endure, yet the immortality of your [books] will add much to the immortality of his [*books*]. Happy do I consider those to whom it has been given by the blessings of the gods either to do [things] worthy of being written about or to write [things] worthy of being read, but most happy those to whom both [have been given]. My uncle will be among the latter [*these*], because of both his own books and yours.

He was at Misenum. At about the seventh hour [i.e., shortly after noon] my mother pointed out to him a cloud of unusual size and appearance. He climbed to a place from which this marvel could be viewed to the best advantage. The cloud was rising from Mount Vesuvius. It had the shape of a pine tree.

He ordered ships to be got ready; he gave me the privilege of going [with him]. I replied that I preferred to study. Then he received a letter from a woman who was alarmed by the danger. He embarked so that he might carry aid not only to that woman but to many [others]. He hastened to that place from which others were fleeing and held his course straight toward the danger, so free from fear that he took notes on all that he saw.

Now thicker ashes were falling upon the ships, now pumice stones also and black stones. When the pilot warned him to turn back, he said. "Fortune aids the brave." When he came to the shore, he saw a friend. He reassured the man, who was frightened. Then he went to the bath and afterwards to dinner, either cheerful or appearing [*similar to*] cheerful.

Meanwhile from Mount Vesuvius they saw very broad flames. So that the other might not be alarmed, [my uncle] said that they were fires left by farmers. Then he went to bed [*gave himself to rest*]. But shortly afterwards the slaves aroused him so that escape might not be cut off on account of the ashes. The house seemed to be moved by frequent tremors, now this way, now that. And so it seemed best to go out upon the shore. They placed cushions upon their heads. But [my uncle] lay down, called for water, and drank it. Then he rose and immediately collapsed. The rest fled. On the following day his body was found untouched. He was more like [one who was] sleeping than one who was dead.

Meanwhile at Misenum my mother and I—but [this has] nothing [to do] with history, and you did not want anything other than to know about his death. Therefore I shall close.

p. 384. Flight from Disaster

You say that, influenced by the letter which I wrote to you concerning my uncle's death, you desire to learn what fears and experiences I went through. "Though my mind shudders to remember, I will begin."

After my uncle had gone, I [*myself*] devoted the rest of the time to my studies. Then [came] the bath, dinner, and a short sleep. Earthquakes had been going on for many days before. But that night they increased to such an extent that everything seemed not to be moving but to be turning upside down. My mother and I went out into the courtyard of the house and sat down. I am in doubt whether I should call it firmness or lack of sense (for I was [only] seventeen years old), but I asked for a book of Titus Livy and read it.

It was now the first hour of the day. Great and certain was the fear of destruction. Then at last we decided to leave the town. Many follow us. After getting outside [the town] we stop. There we experience many astonishing things, many frightful things. For the wagons which we had ordered to be brought out, although on an entirely level plain, were rolling about in opposite directions. From the other side a black and alarming cloud appeared. A little later that cloud descended upon the earth. Then my mother begs, urges, commands me to flee. She said: "You can [flee, but] I, burdened with years and weight, shall die happily if I shall not be the cause of your death." But I declare that I will not be safe except with her. Then I force her to go on ahead. She obeys reluctantly. Ashes are already [beginning to] fall. Then [there is] night, not like one without a moon, but like one within closed rooms when the light has been put out. The shrieks of women are heard, the wails of infants, the shouts of men. Some were seeking parents with their voices; others, their children; others, their wives; and by their voices they were recognizing them. Some because of their fear of death prayed for death. Many lifted their hands to the gods; more said that there were no longer any gods and that this was everlasting and final night. The ashes [became] thick and heavy. Rising again and again, we shook them off so that the weight would not injure us. I can say that in all the [*so great*] danger I did not utter a groan. Finally the cloud departed. Then [there was] real daylight. Everything had been changed and covered with deep ashes as if with snow.

p. 386. The Secret of Success

You wonder how my uncle, a busy man, was able to write so many books. You will wonder more if you [*will*] know that he pleaded cases, lived fifty-five years, and that the time in between was burdened by most important duties and by the friendship of emperors. But his genius was keen, his zeal incredible. In winter he began to study at the seventh hour of the night. He was [a man] of very ready sleep, which sometimes came and went even in the midst of his studies. Before daylight he would go to Vespasian, the emperor (for he too would make use of the nights), then to his appointed task. After returning to his home, he would devote the remaining time to his studies. After a light meal, in summer he would often lie in the sun, a book would be read [to him], and he would take notes. He used to say that no book was so bad that it was not useful in some respect. After the sun [bath] he generally bathed in cold water; then he slept a little bit. Then he would study until dinnertime as if [it were] another day.

I remember that one of his friends, when a reader had pronounced some words badly, called him back and made him recite them again. My uncle said to him, "You understood him, didn't you?" When he did not deny it, [my uncle said] "Why did you call him back? We have lost ten verses in this way."

Even while he bathed he would listen to a slave reading. On a journey, free, as it were, from other cares, he had leisure for this one thing; at his side there was a slave with book and writing tablets, whose hands were protected in winter by gloves, so that no time for study might be lost. He thought that all time which was not given to studies was lost.

p. 387. How to Keep Young

Spurinna, though an old man, does everything in order. At the second hour he calls for his shoes, walks three miles, and he does not exercise his mind less than his body. If friends are present, conversation is indulged in; if they are not, a book is read [to him] while he walks. Then he sits down, and [there is] a book again or conversation. Then he climbs into his carriage with his wife or some friend. After covering seven miles he again walks a mile, and again sits down. When the hour for the bath is announced (it is, by the way, the ninth in winter, the eighth in summer), he takes a walk in the sun. Then he plays ball vigorously [*and*] for a long while; for by this kind of exercise too he fights [*with*] old age. He is seventy-seven years old, but the vigor of his ears and his eyes and his body is still unimpaired.

p. 387. The Good Die Young

I write these [lines] to you filled with sorrow, for the younger daughter of our Fundanus is dead. I have never seen anything more charming or lovable than that girl. She had not yet completed her thirteenth year, but already she had the good sense of an old woman, the dignity of a matron, and yet the sweetness of a girl. How she clung to her father's neck! How lovingly and modestly she embraced us, her father's friends! How she loved her teachers! How eagerly, how intelligently she read! How sparingly she played! With what patience, with what courage also she bore her last illness! She obeyed the doctors, she cheered her sister and her father, and kept herself up by her strength of will. This strength was broken neither by the length of her illness nor by the fear of death. And so she has left us more and greater reasons for grief. She had already been betrothed to an excellent young man; already the wedding day had been chosen; we had already been invited.

I cannot express in words how great a wound I received in my heart when I heard Fundanus himself giving orders that that money which he had intended to spend on clothes and gems be spent for ointments and perfumes. He has lost a daughter who resembled him no less in character than in features [*reproduced his character no less than his features*].

p. 389. A Ghost Story

At Athens there was a large house [*but*] with a bad reputation. In the silence of the night the sound of chains was heard, farther away at first, then very near. Thereupon a ghost appeared, an old man with shaggy hair. He was wearing chains. Then there were bad nights for those who lived there; death followed. The house was deserted and left to that ghost. It was advertised nevertheless, but no one wished either to buy or to rent it.

There came to Athens the philosopher Athenodorus; he read the sign, and after hearing the price, asked why it was so cheap. He found out everything, but in spite of that, rented it. When night came, he called for writing tablets, a stylus, and a light; he dismissed all his slaves, and he himself directed his thought, his eyes, and his hand to writing so that his mind might not invent fears. At first there is silence; then chains are heard. He does not raise his eyes. Then the sound of chains increases; it comes nearer. Now it is heard at the threshold, now within the threshold. He looks around and sees the ghost. It was standing and beckoning with its finger like [one] calling. But the philosopher again gives himself up to his studies. Again the sound of chains is heard. He again looks around at the ghost beckoning [to him]. Without delay he takes up the light and follows. After the ghost has turned aside into the courtyard of the house, it leaves him; he places a mark at the spot. The next day the philosopher goes to the magistrates and advises them to order that place dug up. Bones are found and chains. These are collected and buried. Never afterwards was a ghost seen in that building.

p. 389. Don't Be a Harsh Father

A man was scolding his son because he bought horses and dogs a little too extravagantly. I said to him: "Say you, did you never do [anything] that could be criticized by your father? Do you not do even now what your son, if he were your father, would criticize with equal severity?"

Reminded by an example of great severity I have written this to you so that you too will not handle your son too severely and harshly. Consider both that he is a boy and that you were one [once] and that you are a human being and the father of a human being.

p. 390. Graded Friendship Is Degraded Friendship

It is too long [a story] to look back [into the question] how it happened that I dined at the house of a man [who], as it appeared to him, was magnificent and careful, but, as it seemed to me, was mean and extravagant. For he served rich foods to himself and a few friends, cheap foods to the rest. The wine too he had divided into three grades in small bottles, not that there might be a chance of choosing but that there might not be the right of refusing, one grade for himself and us, another for his lesser friends (for he has friends of different degrees), another for his freedmen and ours. The man who was reclining next to me noticed this and asked whether I approved. I said no. "What about yourself then?" he said. "What practice do you follow?" "I put the same before everybody; for I invite them to dine, not to be insulted [*insults*], and those persons whom I have treated as equals at table I treat as equals in everything." "Even the freedmen?" "Yes: for then I consider them friends, not freedmen." He said: "Does it cost you a great deal?" "Not at all." "How can it be done?" "Because my freedmen don't drink the same wine I drink, but I drink the same wine my freedmen drink."

p. 390. Wanted, A Teacher

What more pleasing thing could you have asked of me than that I look for a teacher for your brother's children? For thanks to you [*through your kindness*], I return to school and resume, as it were, that most delightful time of life. I sit among the young men, as I used to do, and I even discover how much influence I have among them as a result of my studies. For on a recent occasion they were joking with one another: I entered, silence fell. This does them more credit than it does me [*pertains to their praise*].

When I [*shall*] have heard all the professors, I shall write what I think about each. For I owe you, I owe your brother's memory, this loyalty, this interest, especially in so important a matter.

p. 391. A Courageous Wife

Paetus, the husband of Arria, was sick, and his son also was sick. The son died. She arranged for his funeral in such a way that her husband did not know of it. Whenever she would enter his bedroom, she would say that their son was alive and even better, and often when her husband would ask her how the boy was doing she would reply to him, "He has slept well and taken food." Then, when tears overcame her, she would go out. Then she would give way to her grief. With composed looks she would return.

Paetus with Scribonianus had stirred up a revolt in Illyricum against Claudius. Scribonianus was killed, and Paetus was dragged off to Rome. He was about to embark; Arria begged the soldiers that she be put on board, too. "You are going to give my husband, a man of consular rank," said she, "some slaves from whose hands he may take food, clothing, and shoes. I alone shall do all these things." When this request was denied, she hired a small boat and followed the large vessel.

After they arrived at Rome, she drew a sword, drove it into her heart, drew it out, gave it to her husband, and added a remark immortal and almost divine: "Paetus, it doesn't hurt."

p. 392. Two Love Letters

Never have I complained more about my business, which has not permitted me to follow you as you start out for Campania for your health. For I wish to be with you now especially that I may see with my own eyes what strength you have gained. Both your absence and your sickness scare me. I fear everything; I imagine everything, especially those things which I fear the most. And so I ask you to write one or even two letters each day. I shall be without anxiety while I read, and I shall immediately fear after I [*shall*] have read. Good-by.

You write that you are greatly affected by my absence and have only one comfort, [namely] that you have my books in place of me. It is nice that you miss me. I read your letters and take them in my hands again and again as if new. Write as often as possible. Good-by.

p. 392. A Fish Story

In Africa there is a colony very close to the sea. Here people of all ages are filled with an interest in fishing, sailing, and also swimming, especially the boys, who have the time and are eager to play. For these, to swim the farthest is glory and [a mark of] excellence; he is the winner who has left the shore and the other swimmers the farthest behind. One boy, bolder [than the rest], made for a more remote point. A dolphin meets [him], and now it precedes the boy, now it follows [him]; then it takes him upon its back [*comes up from under*], sets him down; again it takes him up and carries the frightened boy first into deep water, then turns toward the shore and brings him back to land.

Everybody rushes up; they look upon the boy as if a prodigy; they ask [him questions] and listen to him. The next day the boys swim again; again the dolphin comes to the boy. He flees with the rest. The dolphin, as if calling him back, leaps up and dives. This it does several days. Finally the boys approach, call it, and even touch it. Their boldness increases. Above all, the boy who first had experience with it swims up to it, leaps upon its back, and is carried [out] and back. He thinks that he is liked, and he himself likes [the dolphin]. Neither fears, neither is feared.

All the officials came to [view] the spectacle, and by their arrival and [continued] stay the little state was being ruined because of the unusual expenses. Later the place itself began to lose its quiet. It was decided to kill the dolphin, which everybody was coming to see [*to see which*].

p. 393. Advice to a Provincial Governor

Consider that you have been sent to the province of Achaia, that true Greece, in which culture, literature, and even crops are believed to have been discovered first; that you have been sent to men [who are] really men, to freemen really free, who through their excellence and merits have held on to the rights given them by nature. Respect their ancient glory. Let their antiquity and great deeds be [held] in high honor by you. Keep before your eyes [the fact that] this is the land which has sent us our rights, which has given laws not to the vanquished but to those asking for them, that it is Athens which you are visiting, and Sparta which you are ruling. Love can do more than fear to obtain what you want.

p. 394. A Humane Master

Illnesses, deaths too, of my slaves have overcome me. There are two comforts, not equal to such grief: the one, the privilege of setting them free (for I seem not to have utterly lost those whom I have lost after they are free); the other, because I permit my slaves too to make wills, as it were. They give and ask in these what they wish; I obey as ordered. They divide, give, bequeath, only within the house; for the house is, as it were, a commonwealth and state for the slaves.

I am not unaware that others call misfortunes of this sort nothing more than loss. Perhaps they are great and wise, as they consider [*seem to*] themselves; they are not human beings. For a human being ought to be affected by grief.

I have said more about these things perhaps than I ought, but less than I wanted. For there is also a sort of pleasure in grieving.

p. 395. A Busy Holiday

I spent this entire time among my writing tablets and books in the most pleasing quiet. "How," you say, "could you do it in the city?" Circus games were [going on], a kind of show by which I am attracted least of all. There is nothing new, nothing different, nothing which it is not enough to have seen once. I marvel that so many thousands of men so childishly desire to see again and again horses running and men standing in chariots. They are not attracted by the swiftness of the horses or by the skill of the men. They favor the cloth, it's the cloth that they love. If during the race itself this color should be transferred to that side, that color to this side, their enthusiasm and favor will be transferred, and immediately they will abandon those charioteers and those horses which they know from far off, and whose names they shout. Such great popularity, such influence is there in one worthless tunic, not only in the case of the crowd, but in the eyes of some important men. I take some pleasure [from the fact] that I am not captivated by this pleasure. I invest my leisure in literature during these days which others waste. Good-by.

p. 398. Ennius

Oh Titus Tatius, tyrant, you yourself produced so great [misfortunes] for yourself.

The Roman state stands firm on [*because of*] old-fashioned customs and men.

p. 400. The Boastful Soldier

ARTOTROGUS. I remember one hundred and fifty in Cilicia, one hundred in Scythia-robber-land, thirty Sardinians, sixty Macedonians—that is the number of men whom you—killed in one day.

PYRGOPOLINICES. How large a total of men is that?

AR. Seven thousand.

PY. It ought to be that many. You have the calculation right.

AR. What about that time in Cappadocia, where you would have killed five hundred at once, with one blow, if your sword had not been dull? Why should I tell you what all mortals know: that you, Pyrgopolinices, are [*live*] unique on earth, in courage, good looks, and unsurpassable deeds? All the women love you, and not without reason, since you are so handsome; for example, those women who yesterday caught me by the coat.

PY. What did they say to you?

AR. They kept asking: "Is this fellow Achilles?" "No, but he is his brother," I said.

p. 401. Knowledge Produces a Tranquil Mind

It is sweet, when the winds are stirring up the waters on the great sea, to watch from the shore the great struggle of another; not because it is a gratifying pleasure that anyone is in difficulty, but since it is sweet to see from what troubles you yourself are free. Yet there is nothing sweeter than to hold those lofty regions well-fortified by the serene learning of the philosophers, whence you can look down and see others everywhere going astray and in their wandering [vainly] seeking the [right] way of life, contesting with their mental powers, rivaling [each other] in nobility, struggling night and day with surpassing labor to rise to the highest wealth and gain possession of [material] things. Oh pitiable minds of men, oh blind hearts!

Nothing can be created from nothing. There exist atoms [*bodies*] and void.

Thus the sum total of things is constantly renewed, and mortals live in turn with each other. Some races grow great, others are diminished, and in a brief space of time the generations of living beings are changed, and pass on the lamp of life like [relay] runners.

p. 402. Cornelius Nepos

Phocion the Athenian often commanded armies and received the highest civil offices, but nevertheless he is much better known on account of his private life than on account of the glory of his military record. For he was always poor, although he might have been very rich because of the offices bestowed upon him and the vast powers which were given him by the people. When he rejected the large gifts of money offered [to him] by envoys of King Philip, the envoys said: "If you yourself do not want these [gifts], still you ought to look out for your children, for whom it will be difficult in the midst of extreme poverty to maintain their father's [*so*] great reputation." "If [my children] will be like me," said he to them, "this same little farm which has brought me to this position will support them; if they are going to be unlike me, I don't want their extravagance fostered and increased by money."

p. 402. "Poor Little Sparrow"

Mourn, O Venuses and Cupids and all the handsome men there are! My sweetheart's sparrow is dead, the sparrow, my sweetheart's pet, which she loved more than her own eyes; for it was sweet as honey, and knew its [mistress] as well as the girl knew her [own] mother, nor did it move from her lap, but hopping around now here, now there, it would chirp constantly to its mistress alone. It is now passing along the shadowy road to that place from which they say that no one returns. But bad luck to you, evil shades of Orcus, which devour all things beautiful; you have robbed me of such a beautiful sparrow. O woeful deed! Oh, poor little sparrow! Through your doing my sweetheart's dear little eyes are now swollen and red with weeping.

p. 404. Counting Kisses

Let us live, my Lesbia, and let us love, and let us count at one penny all the gossip of the too-strict old fuddy-duddies. Suns can set and rise again; [but] when once our brief light has set, we must sleep one long everlasting night. Give me a thousand kisses, then a hundred, then another thousand, then a second hundred, then still another thousand, then a hundred. Then when we have kissed [*made*] many thousand kisses, we will mix them all up, so that we may not know [their total], and no malicious fellow can cast the evil eye, when he knows that there are so many kisses.

p. 405. The Regulation of War

In a republic the rights of war must be preserved most of all. For there are two ways of deciding [matters], the one through discussion, the other through force. The former is characteristic of man; the latter, of beasts. Therefore we must not resort to force and war unless we are not permitted to make use of discussion. Wars must be undertaken, to be sure, so that we may live in peace without injustice; but after the victory those are to be spared who were not cruel in war, as our forefathers even received into citizenship the Tusculans, the Volscians, and the Sabines. But Carthage they destroyed completely; and Corinth too [and that I hardly approve], but I believe that they did it so that the very site might not encourage [the inhabitants] to make war. For a peace which will involve no treachery is always to be aimed at. But those who, after laying aside their arms, flee to the protection of generals are to be received. In this, justice has been greatly fostered among our [people]. No war is justified except either one which is waged if restitution of [stolen] property is sought, or [one which] has been declared beforehand. But let war be undertaken in such a way that nothing except peace may seem to be sought.

p. 406. Good Citizenship

No [other] place ought to be sweeter to you than your country.

Of all our associations none is more important, none dearer than that which exists between the republic and each one of us. Parents are dear, children, relatives, friends, [are] dear, but all the affections of all [these] are bound up in one's country alone, for [the sake of] which no patriot would hesitate to seek death. Therefore the ferocity of those who have attacked their country with every crime and [who] are and have been busy in its destruction is [all] the more detestable.

It is the special duty of a magistrate to realize that he represents the state and ought to maintain its dignity, preserve its laws, administer justice, and bear in mind those things which have been committed to his trust.

Furthermore, the private individual ought to live with [his fellow] citizens on just and equal terms, and in public affairs [he ought] to desire those things which are peaceful and honorable; for such a one we are accustomed to regard and call a good citizen.

If it does not seem best that all should have the same amount of money, if the natural capacities of all cannot be the same, surely the rights of those who are citizens in the same republic ought to be equal.

The mind and the soul and the wisdom and the judgment of a state depend upon its laws. As our bodies cannot use their members without the mind, so the state cannot function [*use its parts*] without law.

The foundation of justice is good faith.

p. 406. Quotations from Cicero

1. Other nations can endure slavery; the characteristic mark of the Roman people is freedom.
2. Beware, senators, lest in your hope of an immediate peace you lose a lasting peace.
3. Let arms yield to the toga.
4. Great is the force of custom.
5. O what times, O what customs!
6. Equals associate most easily with equals.
7. Let the safety of the people be the supreme law.

p. 407. The Good Old Days of Early Rome

Therefore at home and abroad good morals were cultivated; there was the greatest harmony and the least avarice; justice and equity prevailed among them less [*no more*] due to laws than to nature. The citizens took out their quarrels, discords, and hatreds on [*with*] their enemies, and with their fellow-citizens they vied in [*about*] valor. In their entreaties to the gods they were lavish, at home they were sparing, toward their friends they were faithful. With these two arts, boldness in war and justice when peace had come about, they provided for themselves and their state. Of these things I have these very great proofs, [*in that*] in war punishment was more often inflicted on those who had fought against an enemy contrary to orders [*command*] and on those who left the battle too slowly when recalled, than on those who had dared to desert their standards or retreat when repulsed; and [*in that*] in peace, however, they exercised their authority more by kindness than by fear, and when wrong had been done them they preferred to forgive rather than avenge [it].

p. 408. Publilius Syrus

1. Expect from others that which you have done to another.
2. Another's [possessions] please us, [while] ours please others more.
3. Debt is bitter slavery to a free man.
4. A woman either loves or hates; there is no third course.
5. A greedy man is himself the cause of his own wretchedness.
6. A greedy man does nothing right, except when he dies.
7. He conquers twice who conquers himself in [the hour of] victory.
8. An interesting companion on the road is as good as a carriage.
9. He to whom more is allowed than is fair wants more than is allowed.
10. Harmony becomes more precious through discord.
11. To escape from desire is to conquer a kingdom.
12. Even a single hair casts [*has*] its shadow.
13. He gives twice to a poor [man] who gives quickly.
14. By governing badly the greatest government is lost.
15. The beginnings of the greatest things are of necessity very little things.
16. The villainy of a few is the misfortune of many.
17. The timid [man] sees even dangers which do not exist.
18. Whatever is done with courage is done with glory.
19. Even the thorn is pleasing from which a rose is seen.
20. The foolish fear fortune, the wise put up with it.
21. Fortune [first] makes a fool [of the one] whom she wishes to destroy.
22. In a foolish man silence is [taken] for wisdom.

p. 409. Cato and the Women

Amid the cares of great wars there occurred a little thing but [one] which developed into a great struggle. In the midst of the Punic War a law had been passed that no woman should have more than half an ounce of gold or wear clothing of various colors or ride in a carriage within the city. After the war the women wanted this law repealed. Neither by the influence nor by the command of their husbands could they be restrained; they blocked all the streets of the city; they even dared to approach the consuls. But the consul Marcus Porcius Cato, made a speech as follows: "If each one of us in the case of his own wife, fellow citizens, had begun to hold on to the rights of the husband, we should have less trouble with all the women. Because we have not restrained them individually, we are afraid of them all. Our forefathers wanted women to attend to no business, not even private, without their parents or brothers or husbands; we, if it please the gods, are now even permitting them to seize the government. When this stronghold has been taken by assault, what will they not attempt? If you [*will*] allow them to be equal to their husbands, do you believe that they are going to be endurable to you? As soon as they have begun to be [your] equals, they will be [your] superiors. No law is entirely satisfactory to all; this only is asked, whether it is beneficial to the majority." Then one of the tribunes spoke against the law, and the law was repealed. The women had won.

p. 410. Horace

1. Remember amid difficulties to keep the mind calm.
2. The golden mean.
3. Seize the [present] day.
4. Care follows upon growing wealth.
5. There is a mean in [all] things.
6. Whatever it is impossible [*wrong*] to correct becomes lighter with patience.
7. Poor amid great wealth.
8. Nothing is hard for mortals.
9. Life has given nothing to mortals without great toil.
10. Leave the rest to the gods.
11. A rare bird.
12. To tell the truth laughing.
13. Brave men lived before Agamemnon.

p. 411. Sulpicia

My hateful birthday is here
And I have to spend it in the hateful country, with Cerinthus,
What could be nicer than the city?
Is a farmhouse and a frigid river in the Arretinan field fit for a girl?
Now, Messalla, so anxious about me, relax,
Journeys are often inconveniently timed
Even if taken away, I leave behind here my heart and soul,
Since I am not allowed to control my life.
Do you know that the troubles of the journey
have been carried away from your girl's sad spirit?
I can now spend my birthday in Rome.
Let us all celebrate this day, which comes by chance so unexpectedly for you.

p. 412. Ovid and Roman Elegy

If, however, there remains something of us besides a name and a shade, Tibullus will be in the Elysian Fields. Come to meet him, learned Catullus, along with your friend Calvus, your youthful temples crowned with ivy. Your shade, [Tibullus], is their companion. If there is somehow any shade of the body, you, refined Tibullus, are among [*have increased the number of*] the blessed [dead]. Peaceful bones, I pray, rest safely in your urn, and may the earth be not heavy on your ashes.

p. 413. The Wolf and the Lamb

A wolf and a lamb had come to the same river; the wolf stood upstream [*above*], the lamb far below. Then the wolf, forced by hunger, brought up a pretext for a quarrel. "Why," he said, "did you make the water muddy for me when I was drinking?" The lamb was scared and replied: "How can I do this, wolf? The water runs down from you to me." Defeated by the force of truth, he said: "Six months ago you swore at me." The lamb replied: "I wasn't born [then]." "Of course [it was] your father [who] swore at me," the wolf said. And so he grabbed [the lamb] and tore him to pieces though he did not deserve to die [*in an unjust death*].

This fable was written for those people who make up pretexts and mistreat innocent persons.

p. 413. The Greedy Dog

He who goes after someone else's property deservedly loses his own. While a dog was carrying meat as he swam across a river, he saw his reflection in the water, and thinking it was another piece of meat [*prize*] being carried by another dog, he wanted to grab it; but being greedy he was deceived and dropped the food he held in his mouth; but he could not reach the food which he was after.

p. 414. Sour Grapes

Forced by hunger, a fox was trying to get a bunch of grapes on a lofty arbor, leaping with all his might. When he could not reach them, he said as he departed, "They are not ripe yet; I don't want to take sour grapes."

Those who by their words make light of what they cannot do ought to apply this moral to themselves.

p. 414. Damon and Pythias

When Dionysius, king of Syracuse, wished to put to death Pythias the philosopher, the latter begged Dionysius to allow him to go home in order to settle his affairs. His friend was Damon. So great was the friendship between Damon and Pythias that Damon did not hesitate to give himself to the king [as] bail for the return of the other [i.e., Pythias]. When the appointed day drew near and Pythias did not return, everyone condemned Damon's stupidity. But he said that he had no fears about his friend's word. At the appointed hour Pythias came. Dionysius, admiring the spirit of both, remitted the punishment and asked them to receive him as a partner in their friendship.

p. 414. A Costly Joke

When Publius Scipio Nasica as a young man was a candidate for [*seeking*] the aedileship, after the manner of candidates he clasped a farmer's hand, hardened with work in the fields. As a joke he asked the farmer whether he was in the habit of walking on his hands. This remark, overheard by the bystanders, was carried to the people and was the cause of Scipio's defeat. For all the farmers, thinking that their poverty was being ridiculed by him, showed their anger at his jest.

p. 415. Seneca

1. A great thing it is to know when to speak and when to keep silent [*the times of speech and of silence*].
2. The greatest remedy for anger is delay.
3. Vice does not exist in things, but in the mind itself.
4. I have not been born for one corner alone; my country is this whole universe.
5. All art is an imitation of nature.
6. It is best to endure what you cannot cure.
7. Leisure without books is death.
8. Let him who has done a kindness keep silent; let him tell [of it] who has received it.
9. If you wish to be loved, love.
10. Wherever there is a human being, there is an opportunity for kindness.

p. 415. Petronius

His secretary read off as if from the city newspaper: "Today on the estate at Cumae, which belongs to Trimalchio, there were born thirty [slave] boys and forty girls; five hundred thousand pecks of wheat were stored [*transferred*] in the barn; five hundred oxen were broken in. On the same day: ten million sesterces which could not be invested were transferred to the vault. On the same day: there was a fire in the Pompeian Gardens." "What?" said Trimalchio, "When were the Pompeian Gardens bought for me?" "In the preceding year," said the secretary, "and therefore they have not yet been entered [*come*] in the account book." Trimalchio said, "Unless I hear about whatever estates are bought for me within six months I forbid them to be entered in my accounts."

p. 417. Quintilian

Above all, [his] nurses' language ought not be faulty. Chrysippus hoped that they [i.e., the nurses] be philosophers if it were possible [*to be done*]; certainly, as far as circumstances might permit, he wanted the best to be chosen. And in their case undoubtedly the first consideration is, to be sure, their morals; nevertheless, they should speak correctly also. The boy will hear them first, and he will try to form his words by imitating them. Further [*and*], we are by nature most tenacious of those things which we learned when our minds were unformed, and those very things stick the more stubbornly according as they are the worse. For good things are easily changed for the worse; but will you ever turn vices into virtues? He [the future orator] should, therefore, not accustom himself, not even during the time when he is an infant, to language which must be unlearned.

But in his parents I could wish there be the greatest possible amount of learning; and I am not only speaking about fathers, for we know that their mother Cornelia contributed much to the eloquence of the Gracchi. Her very refined style has been handed down to posterity too in her letters; and Laelia, daughter of Gaius, is said to have reproduced her father's correctness in her own speaking; and a speech of Hortensia, the daughter of Quintus, is [still] read. However, not even those who did not happen to get an education themselves [*to whom it did not happen,* etc.] should have less care in teaching their children; but let them be on this very account all the more diligent about [all] the other details.

p. 418. Martial

1. Why don't I send you my books, Pontilianus? So that you won't send me yours, Pontilianus.
2. You are alike difficult, easy, pleasant, and disagreeable. I can live neither with you nor without you.
3. You wish to marry Priscus: I do not wonder, Paula; you are wise. Priscus does not want to marry you: he also is wise.
4. You inquire why I am unwilling to marry a rich wife? I will not be given in marriage to my wife. Let the wife, Priscus, be inferior to her husband; in no other way do woman and man become equals.
5. The book which you recite, Fidentinus, is mine, but when you recite it badly, it begins to be yours.
6. Since you are alike and well-matched in [your mode of] life, the worst of wives and the worst of husbands, I wonder that you are not well suited [to each other].

p. 419. Tacitus

Already, in fact, [Agricola] was educating the sons of the chieftains in the liberal arts and advancing the quick mental talents of the Britains over the [plodding] studies of the Gauls, so that those who recently were rejecting the Roman language were [now] eager for rhetoric. From that point on our clothing also was fashionable [*an honor*] and the toga was common. Little by little they descended [*it was descended*] to the enticements of vice, porticoes, and baths, and the luxury of banquets. And among the inexperienced [natives] this was called "culture," when [actually] it was part of their servitude.

p. 420. Juvenal

1. Honesty is praised and shivers.
2. Bread and circus games.
3. No wicked person [is] happy.
4. Who will watch the watchmen themselves?
5. A sound mind in a sound body.

p. 420. A Lesson in Voting

Fabricius was a man of great fame and great deeds. Publius Cornelius Rufinus was a good and brave general and skilled in military tactics, but he was grasping. Fabricius did not approve of him and was opposed [*unfriendly*] to him on account of his character. But when at a very difficult time for the state consuls were to be elected and Rufinus was seeking the consulship and his rivals were not experienced in war, Fabricius put forth every effort [*worked with great effort*] to have the consulship go to Rufinus. To some people who expressed surprise at this [*thing*], he said, "I prefer to be robbed by a citizen rather than to be sold by an enemy." Marcus Cicero reports that this was said, not to others, but to Rufinus himself, when the latter thanked Fabricius for his help.

Fabricius when censor expelled this Rufinus from the senate on account of his extravagance after Rufinus had twice been consul and dictator.

p. 421. Androclus and the Lion

In the Circus Maximus, a hunt was being presented before the people. Many were the wild beasts there, but beyond all others one lion by the great size of its body had focused the minds and eyes of all upon it.

Among many others a slave had been brought in for a fight with the wild beasts. The name of this slave was Androclus. When the lion saw him at a distance, it at once stopped as if in amazement and then as if recognizing him gently approached the man. Then like [*after the manner of*] a dog it wagged its tail and gently licked the man's hands with its tongue. Androclus, frightened at first, now looked at the lion. Then, apparently recognizing the lion, the man seemed to be filled with joy.

At this strange sight, great shouts were raised by [*of*] the people. Caesar called Androclus and asked the reason why this very ferocious lion had spared only him. Then Androclus told a marvelous tale.

"When my master was governing the province of Africa," he said, "I was forced to run away after having been unjustly beaten. I cam upon a remote cave and entered it. Not long afterwards this lion, wounded in one foot and groaning [*uttering groans*] from pain, came to the same cave. At the first sight of the lion, to be sure, I was frightened; but after the lion came in and saw me, it approached gently and seemed to stretch out its paw to me as if [*for the purpose of*] asking for help. Then I removed a large thorn sticking in its foot, and squeezed out the pus. Then after placing its foot in my hands, it took a nap. From that day on for three years the lion and I lived in the same cave. The lion would bring me parts of wild beasts, which I would roast in the sun, not having the means of [making] fire. But finally I left the cave and, on being caught by soldiers, was brought from Africa to Rome to my master. He at once sent me to the wild beasts. But I realize that this lion, which also was captured later, is showing his gratitude to me."

That was the story of Androclus. At the request of everybody, he was let go, and the lion was presented to him. Afterwards Androclus and the lion, tied by a strap, used to go around among the taverns. Androclus received money; the lion, flowers. Everybody said, "This is the lion [which was] the man's host; this is the man [who was] the lion's doctor."

p. 422. Miscellaneous Quotations

1. Divine nature has given the fields; human skill has built the cities.[1]
2. By harmony small republics grow; by discord the greatest fall.
3. There is a god within us.
4. It is right to be taught even by an enemy.
5. You will proceed most safely by the middle course.
6. Fear of a foreigner is the greatest bond for harmony.
7. (He said) that in a free state the tongue and mind are free.
8. They condemn what they do not understand.
9. Everything strange is [regarded] as grand.
10. Virtue is its own reward, to be sure.
11. Death makes all things equal.
12. You make a virtue out of necessity.
13. Great is the truth and it prevails.
14. Whoever desires peace, let him prepare for war.
15. No one suffers punishment for his thoughts.
16. The rules of justice are these: to live honorably, not to injure another, and to grant to each his due.
17. The study of literature is a wonderful thing because, in the first place, it cleanses the character of men; second, it gives charm to speech.
18. Necessity knows [*has*] no law.
19. Of two evils, the lesser is always to be chosen.
20. O how swiftly passes the glory of the world!
21. Knowledge itself is power.
22. I think, therefore I am.
23. He snatched the lightning from the sky, then scepters from tyrants.
24. Crocodile tears.
25. Clothes make the man.
26. Make haste slowly.
27. Don't tell all that you know; don't believe all that you hear; don't write all that you do; don't do all that you can.

---

[1] Cf. "God made the country, and man made the town."

p. 423. Teaching School

You therefore dealt with me so that I was persuaded to go to Rome and [*rather*] teach there what I was teaching at Carthage. I did not want to go to Rome because [*on this account, that*] I was promised greater profits and greater dignity by my friends who were urging this [course] (although these things too influenced my mind at the time), but the greatest and almost sole cause was that I heard that their [i.e., in Rome] the young men studied more peaceably and were restrained by the discipline from boldly breaking into the school. By contrast, at Carthage the license of the pupils is intemperate: they burst in shamelessly and disturb the class.

p. 424. A Palace Full of Tricks

In Constantinople next to the palace there is a house of remarkable size and beauty. A tree made of bronze but covered with gold stood in front of the emperor's throne, [a tree] whose branches were filled with gilded bronze birds, which uttered the sounds of various [kinds of] birds. Now the emperor's throne had been skillfully constructed in this fashion, that now it seemed low, then higher, finally very high. Gilded lions (it is uncertain whether they were made of bronze or wood) guarded the throne; these beat the floor [*earth*] with their tails and, opening their mouths, let out a roar.

I was escorted into the presence of the emperor. Although on my arrival the lions roared and the birds sang, I was not struck by fear, since those [persons] who knew all about it [*knew everything well*] had informed me. Flat on my face [*prone*] I did homage to [*worshiped*] the emperor, then raised my head; earlier I saw him in a chair [*sitting*] raised up [only] a little distance from the floor, now I looked up at him, wearing different clothes, sitting near the ceiling of the house. I could not imagine how it was done, unless perhaps he was lifted up by a hydraulic machine.

p. 425. The Norse Discovery of America

The king of Denmark said that in that ocean an island had been found which is called Winland for the reason that vines grow there spontaneously which produce the best wine. Adalbert, a priest of blessed memory, also told us that some noblemen had sailed to the north to explore the ocean. On leaving Britain and icy Iceland they suddenly were swallowed up in a fog which eyes could hardly penetrate. Then on getting away from the danger of fog they reached an island protected by very high cliffs. Here they landed to look at [*for the sake of seeing*] the regions and found men hiding at noon in underground caves; in front of the entrances to these lay a vast number of gold dishes. So they took the part that they could lift and joyfully rowed back to their ships, when all of a sudden they saw men of amazing height coming [toward them]. By these one of the comrades was seized; the rest, however, escaped danger.

p. 428. This Crazy World

This crazy world offers false joys which disappear and vanish like the lilies of the field. Worldly things, a worthless life destroy real rewards; for they drive souls to Hell and submerge them [there].

p. 428. Spring Song

Look, pleasant, longed-for spring brings back joy. The purple meadow is in flower, the sun makes everything bright. Let sadness [*sad things*] depart at once. Summer is coming back, now the fierceness of winter is passing away.

p. 428. In the Tavern

1. When we are in the tavern, we do not worry what the ground is [like] but hurry off to the game [of dice], over which we work hard. What's going on in the tavern, where money serves as a waiter [i.e., brings service], that is what to ask about [*there is need of being asked about*]; so let what I say be listened to.
2. Some play, some drink, some live indiscreetly. But of those who spend their time in the tavern, some of them are stripped [i.e., lose everything], others win clothing [*are clothed*] there, some put on sacks. There no one fears death, but they cast lots for wine.

p. 429. Stābat Māter

1. The grieving mother stood in tears beside the cross while her son hung [there]. The sword pierced her heart, groaning and sad and grieving.
3. Who is the man who would not weep if he saw the mother of Christ in such torture? Who would not be saddened at beholding the loyal mother grieving with her son?
5. Loyal mother, fount of love, make me feel the power of sorrow so that I may grieve with you, make my heart burn with love for [*in loving*] Christ the Lord, so that I may please him.
10. Have me guarded by the cross, protected by the death of Christ, cherished by grace. When the body dies, have the glory of paradise bestowed upon my soul.

p. 429. Diēs Īrae

1. The day of wrath, that day will crumble [our] age [i.e., life on earth] in ashes, [as] testified to by David and the Sibyl.
2. What a shaking there will be when the judge will come and will completely destroy everything!
3. The trumpet emitting its marvelous sound over the tombs of [all] regions will bring in everyone before the throne.
4. Death and nature will be amazed when [all] creatures rise to answer [God] rendering judgment.
5. The book that is written will be brought out, in which is contained all that by which the world is judged.
11. Judge of just vengeance, grant the boon of remission [of sins] before the day of reckoning.
18. That tearful day on which will rise from the ashes.
19. Man as a defendant to be judged, spare him, O Lord.
20. Pious Lord Jesus, give them rest.

p. 431. The "Hanging Tree"

A man [who was] in tears said to all his neighbors: "Alas, alas! I have in my garden an unlucky tree, on which my first wife hanged herself, later my second, now the third, and I am filled with grief." One of his neighbors said, "I am surprised that you have shed tears amid such good luck. Give me, please [*I ask you*], three sprouts of that tree, because I want to distribute them among my neighbors so that we may have trees for our wives to hang themselves on."

p. 431. Petrarch

From my very boyhood, when others devoted themselves to Aesop, I read Cicero's books. And at that age, to be sure, I could understand nothing; some fine-sounding words alone attracted me.

I afterwards formed various friendships, because there took place a great influx of people from every region to the place in which I was. When friends were leaving and would ask me what I wished sent from their country, I used to reply to them that [I wanted] nothing but the books of Cicero. And often I sent letters, often money, not only throughout Italy, where I was better known, but [also] throughout France and Germany and clear to Spain and Britain. I even sent to Greece, and from the place from which I expected [to receive] Cicero, I obtained Homer. "Labor conquers everything," said Virgil. With much enthusiasm and much care I collected many books. In my eyes Cicero alone was wise. Concerning him Quintilian said: "Let him hope well of himself whom Cicero will please."

Later, when I had arrived at Liège, I found two of Cicero's orations; one I copied in my own hand, the other a friend copied. And—you'll laugh at this—[*that you may laugh*] it was most difficult in so fine a city to find some ink (and that nearly yellow).

About the books of the *Republic,* to be sure, I had come to despair and looked for the treatise *On Consolation,* [but] did not find it. With my own hand I copied a large book of his letters, though my health at the time was bad [*against it*]; but my great love for the work and my joy and the desire to possess it outweighed my sickness. This book, in order that it might always be at hand, I used to place near the door.

p. 433. The Shrewd Priest

There was a country priest [who was] very rich. When his dog, [who was] dear to him, died, he buried it in the cemetery. The bishop learned of this and, casting his thoughts on the priest's money, called the priest to him for punishment. The priest, who knew the bishop's mind quite well, went to the bishop, taking fifty gold pieces with him. The bishop, vehemently criticizing the burial of the dog, ordered the priest to be carried off to prison. This shrewd man [i.e., the priest] said: "Father, if you knew how much good sense the dog had, you would not wonder if he deserved burial among human beings. For he was more than human, both in life and especially in death." "What in the world is this?" said the bishop. "Making a will at the end of this life," said the priest, "and knowing about your poverty, he left fifty gold pieces to you in his will; these I have brought with me." Then the bishop, approving of both the will and the burial, accepted the money and freed the priest.

p. 433. An Alarm Clock

I don't mind that you are gladly using the clock brought to you from my library, so that you can be awakened at whatever hour you wish. Only let it not call you away from sleep too early. For I want you first of all to take care of your health. As to the plan of your studies, I suggest nothing to you, at least for the present, except one thing: see that in the letters you send me you copy Cicero more carefully and imitate more closely his manner of writing, his words, rhythm, and dignity. If you do this, I will consider that you have accomplished everything. Best regards to your teacher. Good-by. 1554, Rome.

p. 426. Hildegard von Bingen

Patriarchs and Prophets

We are the roots, and you, the boughs,
fruits of the living eye,
and we grew up in its shadow.

Humility

I, Humility, queen of the Virtues, say:
come to me, you Virtues,
    and I'll give you the skill
to seek and find the drachma that is lost
and to crown her who perseveres blissfully.

Discretion

I am Discretion,
    light and moderator of all creatures–
the impartiality of God, that Adam
    drove away by acting wantonly.

Mercy

How bitter in human minds is
    the harshness that does not soften
and mercifully ease pain!
I want to reach out my hand to all who suffer.

p. 438. The Flood—Deucalion and Pyrrha

Now there was no difference between land and sea. Everything was water, and the sea even lacked a shore. One man grabs a hill-top; another sits in a curved boat and plies oars [*there*] where he recently had ploughed. One man sails over his crops, or the top of his submerged farmhouse; another [*this*] man catches a fish in the top of an elm. If chance brings it [about], an anchor catches in a green meadow or curved ships scrape the vineyards lying below; and, where just now the graceful goats cropped the grass, there now unshapely seals rest their bodies. The sea-nymphs gaze in amazement at the groves and cities and homes beneath the water, and the dolphins take over the forests and run into the tall branches and bump against the tossing oaks. The wolf swims amid the sheep; the flood carries along the tawny lions and [*the flood carries along*] tigers.

The goddess was moved and gave this response: "Depart from the temple, cover your heads, loosen your girt-up clothes, and throw behind your backs the bones of your great mother." For a long time they were dumfounded, but Pyrrha first broke the silence [*with her voice*] and refused to obey the commands of the goddess. She asks with trembling words [*mouth*] that [Themis] forgive her [*grant her pardon*], but [*and*] she is afraid to offend her mother's ghost by throwing her bones about. Then the son of Prometheus calms the daughter of Epimetheus with soft words, and says, "Either I am mistaken [*my skill is faulty*], or oracles are holy and urge no sin [upon us]. The earth is our great mother; I think that the 'bones' are meant to be the stones in the body of the earth; these [are what] we are ordered to throw behind our backs."

Although the Titan's daughter was affected by her husband's interpretation, her hope was nevertheless doubtful, so distrustful were they both of the heavenly advice. But what will it hurt to try? They leave, cover their heads, loosen their tunics, and hurl the stones, as ordered, behind their footprints. The stones (who would believe this if antiquity were not a witness?) began to lose their hardness and to soften their stiffness, and gradually to take on shape as they were softened. And in a brief space of time, by the power of the gods, the stones tossed by the hands of the man took on the appearance of men, and from the cast of the woman, woman was refashioned. Hence we are a hard race, used to toil, and we give proof of what we have come from [*the origin whence we were born*].

p. 441. Echo and Narcissus

Echo still had a body, she was not a [mere] voice; and yet, although talkative, she had no other use of speech than she now has, [namely] the power to repeat [only] the last of many words. Therefore when she saw Narcissus wandering over the trackless countryside and fell in love [with him], she followed his footsteps secretly, and the more she follows, the hotter the flame [with which] she glows. O how often she wanted to approach with endearing words and to use tender entreaties! Nature prevents this nor does it permit her to begin; but, a thing which it does permit, she is ready to await sounds to which she may give back her own words.

By chance the lad, separated from his faithful band of companions, had called out, "Is there anyone here?" and Echo had answered "Here!" He is amazed and when he casts a glance around in all directions, with a loud voice he shouts "Come!"; she calls him as he calls [*calling*]. He looks back and, when no one comes, he shouts again, "Why do you flee from me?" and receives in answer the same number of words as he uttered. He persists and, deceived by the echo of her answering voice, he cries, "Here let us meet," and Echo, never to answer another sound more gladly, repeated, "Let us meet," and she suits the action to [*favors*] her words, and coming out from the wood, she advanced to throw her arms about the neck she longs [to embrace]. He flees and as he flees he cries: "Keep your hands from embraces. May I die before you have a chance at me." She repeated nothing except "you have a chance at me."

Spurned, Echo hides in forests and, ashamed, hides her face among the leaves, and ever since she lives in lonely caves. But yet her love clings to her and grows by reason of her grief at his refusal, and wakeful cares waste her wretched body, and emaciation contracts her skin and all the strength of her body passes off into the air. Only her voice and bones are left—[now merely] her voice remains; her bones they say took on the shape of stone. Therefore she lurks in forests and is seen on no mountain, [but] she is heard by all, for sound is the [only thing] which lives in her.

p. 443. Perseus and Atlas

Atlas had a thousand flocks and as many herds wandered over the grassy plains, and no neighbors hemmed in his land. The leaves on [one of his] trees, gleaming with shining gold, concealed branches of gold and apples of gold. "My friend," said Perseus to him, "if the boast of noble birth moves you, Jupiter is my father [*founder of my line*]; or if you are an admirer of deeds, you will admire ours. I seek hospitality and rest." But Atlas was mindful of an old prophecy (Parnassian Themis had given this prophecy): "The time will come, Atlas, when your tree will be robbed of its gold, and a son of Jupiter will get the glory for this loot." Fearing this, Atlas had enclosed his orchard with solid mountains and had caused it to be guarded by a huge dragon, and he shut out all strangers from his borders. To Perseus, too, he said: "Go far away, so that Jupiter and the glory of the deeds which you falsely claim may not be of no help to you [*be far from you*]." He adds violence to his threats and with his hands attempts to drive away [Perseus], who holds back, trying to mingle brave with gentle words. Being inferior in strength (for who could be equal to the strength of Atlas?), he said: "Well, since my friendship is of little value to you, accept a gift," and turning his face away, he held out on his left side the foul head of Medusa. Atlas became a mountain, as huge as he had been [in life]; for his beard and hair change into forests, his shoulders and hands become ridges; what was formerly his head becomes the peak on a very high mountain. His bones become stone; then increasing in every direction, he grew to an immense size (thus, O gods, you have willed), and the whole heaven with its many stars rested on him.

p. 444. Orpheus and Eurydice

"All things we owe to you, and tough we stay a little [while], sooner or later we hasten to the one abode. Here we all come, this is our final home, and you hold the longest sway over the human race. She too will be within your power when of ripe age she has completed her allotted years; instead of a gift we ask only for the [temporary] enjoyment [of life]. But if the fates deny this boon for my wife, I have resolved that I do not want to return; rejoice in the death of two." As he spoke these words and struck the strings, accompanying his words, the bloodless spirits wept. Thracian Orpheus received her and at the same time [accepted] this condition, that he should not turn back his eyes until he had gone out from the valleys of the lower world [*of Avernus*], or else the gift would be void. They pursued the ascending path through voiceless silence, steep, dark, and thick with gloomy mist. And now they were not far from the margin of the upper earth. Fearing that she might fail and eager to see her, he lovingly turned his eyes; and immediately she slipped back and, stretching out her arms, eager to be embraced and to embrace, unhappily caught nothing except the empty [*yielding*] breezes.

p. 445. Pygmalion

Meanwhile he successfully carved the snow-white ivory with wonderful art and gave it a beauty in which no woman could be born, and fell in love with his own work. The appearance is that of a real maiden, one you could believe was alive and which, if modesty did not prevent, would move, so artfully does its art lie hidden. Pygmalion gazes in wonder and drinks into his breast the fires of love for the body he has fashioned. Often he touches [*moves his hands toward*] his work, testing [to see] whether it was a real body or ivory; no longer does he admit it is ivory. He gives her kisses and imagines that they are returned; he speaks [to her] and holds her, and believes that his fingers sink into her limbs when he touches them; and he is afraid lest a bruise appear [*come*] on the limbs he has pressed. And now he uses caresses, now he brings presents to her—presents that delight girls, shells and smooth pebbles and tiny birds and flowers of a thousand colors and lilies and colored balls and the Heliades' [amber] tears that fell from trees. He also dresses her limbs in clothes, and gives her gems for her fingers, and a long necklace for her neck.

The holiday sacred to Venus and celebrated throughout all Cyprus had arrived, and the incense was smoking, when, having performed his sacrifice, Pygmalion stood at the altar and timidly said, "If, gods, you can give everything, may my wife, I pray, be"—not daring to say "my ivory maiden"—"like my ivory maiden." When he returned he saw the statue of his girl and, lying on the couch, he kissed it. It seems to grow warm. She was alive [*a body*]! When he touched them with his thumb, the veins beat, and the maiden felt the kisses he had given her and blushed.

p. 448. Aeneid Book I

I sing of the arms and the man who first came from the shores of Troy to Italy and the coast of Lavinium, a fugitive by fate. Much had he been tossed about on land and sea by the violence of the gods because of the unforgetting anger of cruel Juno; much too had he suffered in war also until he could found a city and bring his gods into Latium. From this source [sprang] the Latin race, the Alban fathers, and the walls of lofty Rome.

"Aeneas will wage a mighty war in Italy and will crush fierce nations and set up a life [*customs*] and [build] a wall for his men. But the boy Ascanius, to whom the cognomen Iulus is now given, will build strong walls for [*with great strength fortify*] Alba Longa. Romulus will [next] take over the nation and will build the walls of Mars, and will call [the people] Romans from his own name. I set no bounds for their state nor any time [limit]; I have given them power without end. Even the harsh Juno, who now wearies sea and land and sky with her fears, will change her plans for the better and with me will care for the Romans as lords of the world and as the toga-clad nation. [Julius] Caesar [i.e., Augustus] will be born, a Trojan of illustrious origin, to bound his empire by the Ocean, his glory by the stars, Julius, a name descended from the great Iulus. Then, when wars have been abandoned, the ages will become gentle. Venerable Faith and Vesta, Romulus with his brother Remus will dispense [*say*] justice; the horrible gates of war will be closed with tight joints of [*and*] iron; impious Madness sitting within [the temple] on top of his cruel arms, [his hands] bound with a hundred hard knots behind his back, will rage, a frightful [object] with his bloody mouth."

p. 450. Book IV

But the queen, for a long time stricken by powerful love, feeds the wound in her veins and is seized by an unseen passion [*fire*]. The great manliness of the man and the nobility of his race run back and forth in her mind. His features and his words remain fixed in her heart, and her love grants no peaceful sleep to her limbs. The next day [*following*] Dawn was lighting the earth with Apollo's lamp and had moved away the damp darkness from the heavens when Dido, insane [as she was], addressed her sympathetic sister in these words: "Sister Anna, what dreams frighten me, kept in suspense! What strange guest is this who has come to our home, what a man he shows himself in his looks; how strong he is in courage and in arms! For my part, I believe—and my belief is not unfounded—that his is the race of the gods. [Only] ignoble souls are revealed by fear. Alas, by what [evil] fates has he been tossed about! What wars endured [by him] did he tell about!"

But Aeneas, confused at the sight of him, became silent. His hair stood on end in awe, and his voice stuck in his throat. He is eager to flee and to abandon this sweet land, astounded by the strong warning and command of the gods. Alas, what should he do? With what sort of speech should he now dare to approach the raging queen? How should he begin [*what beginnings should he make*]?

But the queen sensed the trick (who could deceive one who is in love?) and first noted the moves that were about to take place, fearing everything, [even if] safe. These same tales wicked Rumor brought to her in her rage, that the fleet was being fitted out and that a voyage was being made ready. Finally, without waiting for him to speak [*voluntarily*], she addresses Aeneas in these words: "Did you even expect, faithless [Aeneas], that you could conceal so great a wrong and leave my country without saying a word? Does not our love keep you [here] nor the pledge that you once gave nor [the thought that] Dido will die a cruel death?"

But the pious Aeneas, though he longed to alleviate her grief [*her grieving*] by consoling her and to remove her worries by words, and though he groaned a great deal and his heart was overcome by deep love, yet he carried out the instructions of the gods and returned to his ships. Then the Trojans really get to work and drag down the lofty ships all along the [*from the entire*] beach.

p. 451. Book VI

He was praying in these words and was holding the altar when the prophetess began to speak as follows: "Sprung from the blood of gods, Trojan son of Anchises, the descent to Hades is easy (the door of dark Pluto is open night and day): but to retrace one's steps and to come out to the air above, that is a task, that is hard work. Only few, those whom a friendly Jupiter has loved or whose glowing courage has carried them aloft to the sky, those descended from the gods, have been able [to do so]."

In the dark of the lonely night they went through the shadows and through the vacant halls of Pluto and his empty kingdom, just as one goes [*as is the way*] in the woods by the stingy light of the flickering moon, when Jupiter has concealed the sky in shadows and black night has taken the color from things. In front of the entrance itself and at the beginning of the [*first*] jaws of Orcus, Grief and avenging Worries placed their couches, and pale Diseases live there and gloomy Old Age and Fear and Starvation, urging to do wrong, and ugly Need, shapes horrible to look at, and Death and Trouble, then Sleep, blood brother of Death, and wicked Joys of the heart, and on the threshold facing [them], death-dealing War and the ironbound chambers of the Furies and mad Discord.

"Now turn both your eyes in this direction, look at this race, [*and*] your Romans; here is Caesar and all the descendants of Iulus who will come up to the great vault of heaven. This is the man, this is the one whom you often hear promised you, Augustus Caesar, son of the divine [Julius], who once again will establish a Golden Age in Latium in the lands once ruled by Saturn. He will advance the empire beyond the Garamantes and Indians (there lies a land beyond the stars, beyond the path of the sun in his annual course, where heaven-carrying Atlas holds the revolving sky [*turns the sky*] on his shoulder, the sky studded with glowing stars)."

"Others will mould life-like statues of bronze more delicately (so at least I believe), they will draw forth living features from marble; they will plead cases better and they will mark with the rod the movements of the sky and will tell of the rising stars. You, Roman, remember to rule the nations with your power (these will be your arts) and to make peace customary [*to impose custom upon peace*], to spare the humbled, and to crush the proud in war."

There are two gates of sleep; one of these is said to be of horn, through which a ready exit is granted true dreams, the other made of gleaming white ivory [*gleaming with white ivory*], but the spirits send false dreams to the [open] sky. With these words Anchises then [and] there addressed his son and the Sibyl with him and let them out by the ivory gate. Aeneas makes his way to the ships and sees his comrades again. Then he proceeds straight along the shore to the harbor of Caieta. The anchor is cast from the prow; the sterns settle [*stand*] on the beach.

p. 453. Quotations from Vergil

1. Perhaps even these things it will some day be a pleasure to recall.
2. Here is my home, this my country.
3. A mind conscious of right.
4. We cannot all [do] all things.
5. Fear gave wings to his feet.
6. Whereof I was no small part.
7. One safety the vanquished have, to hope for no safety.
8. A fickle and changeable thing ever [is] woman.

SECOND BOOK

Latin

FOR AMERICANS

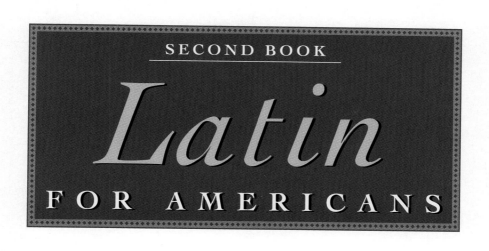

Teacher's Annotated Edition

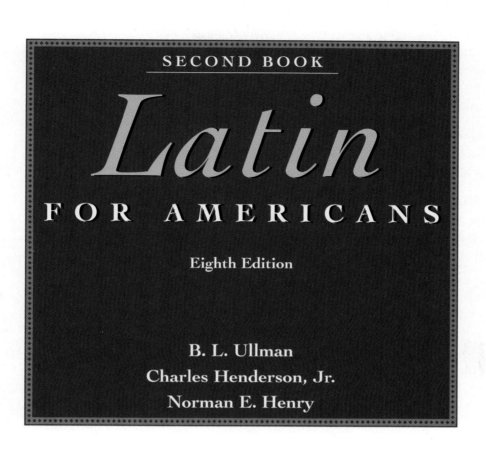

SECOND BOOK

Latin FOR AMERICANS

Eighth Edition

B. L. Ullman
Charles Henderson, Jr.
Norman E. Henry

GLENCOE
McGraw-Hill

New York, New York   Columbus, Ohio   Mission Hills, California   Peoria, Illinois

About the Authors

B. L. Ullman enjoyed a distinguished career of teaching and scholarship at the Universities of Pittsburgh, Iowa, Chicago, and North Carolina. An authority on all aspects of the Roman world, ancient, medieval, and Renaissance, he was also a pioneer in modern methods of teaching elementary Latin.

Charles Henderson, Jr. collaborated with Professor Ullman in the previous revisions of this book. He has taught at New York University, the University of North Carolina, and at Smith College.

Norman E. Henry, collaborator with Professor Ullman in earlier editions of the *Latin for Americans* series, taught for many years at the Peabody High School, Pittsburgh, and contributed material that has been tested in high school classrooms.

Glencoe/McGraw-Hill

A Division of The ***McGraw-Hill*** *Companies*

Send all inquiries to:
Glencoe/McGraw-Hill
15319 Chatsworth Street
P.O. Box 9609
Mission Hills, CA 91346-9609

ISBN 0-02-640913-5 (Student Text)

Printed in the United States of America

1 2 3 4 5 6 7 8 9 10 RRDW 00 99 98 97 96

ISBN 0-02-640923-2 (Teacher's Annotated Edition)

1 2 3 4 5 6 7 8 9 10 RRDW 00 99 98 97 96

Acknowledgements

The editors would like to thank the following individuals for their assistance in this revision of Latin for Americans:

Nancy Seltz
Walnut Hills High School
Cincinnati, Ohio

Ron Tetrick
Kokomo High School
Kokomo, Indiana

Carolyn Beach White
Columbus School for Girls
Columbus, Ohio

Front cover:

Giovanni Paolo Panini, *Interior of the Pantheon, Rome,* c. 1734, Samuel H. Kress Collection, © 1995 Board of Trustees, National Gallery of Art, Washington, D.C., oil on canvas, 1.283 x .991 (50 1/2 x 39); framed: 1.441 x 1.143 (56 3/4 x 45)

This painting is typical of those commissioned by 18th century sight-seeing noblemen to bring home as a souvenir of the Italian part of their "grand tour" of Europe. Rome was a major destination of all educated travellers, who realized their debt to the Roman heritage, its language and its achievements in literature, architecture, science, and the arts.

The most famous and best preserved ancient building in Rome is the Pantheon. (See also page 35.) The original building was built in 27 B.C. by Agrippa, son-in-law of Augustus Caesar. Because of fire and earthquakes, it was rebuilt and altered a number of times, but its original design and purpose remained. The building, with its great dome and round opening at its crown (the oculus), may have first served as a temple to the seven planetary divinities and then to all the gods ("Pantheon" in Greek). Later, in 609, it was made into a church dedicated to the Christian martyrs of the first three centuries. Still later in the 16th century, it served as the burial place of notable artists such as Raphael, while in the 19th century the Italian kings were buried there.

Throughout the centuries, people have marvelled at the Pantheon's interior—its order, proportion, and the sense of calm. For 2,000 years, it has served a spiritual use and has been a major reminder of Rome's contribution to civilization. Just to the right of its great bronze doors, there is a marble plaque that sums up the building. The inscription, first placed on the wall in 1632 reads:

PANTHEON
AEDIFICIUM TOTO TERRARUM ORBE
CELEBERRIUM

The Pantheon
The Most Celebrated Edifice
In the Whole World

Title page:

Brian Blake/Photo Researchers

While Greek political influence waned in the first two centuries B.C., Greek cultural influence remained as strong as ever. The Romans took on Greek culture as their own and spread what can be called Greco-Roman thought and art throughout the then-known world. This Temple of Jupiter in Tunisia is one of the hundreds of temples the Romans built in honor of their gods. It was dedicated to Jupiter, who in the Greek religion was Zeus.

Cartography: Mapping Specialists Limited, pp. 136-137, p. 194, pp. 228-229
Electronic Enhancement: Paul Mirto, p. 197, p. 205, p. 253, p. 364

Contents

Introduction xi

Unit I—A Roman Family

Lesson I: Pūblius and Secunda 2
Form Review (Nouns and Adjectives, Verbs); Syntax Review (Nominative, Accusative, Ablative of *Place Where,* Ablative of *Time When,* Agreement of Adjectives, Apposition); Reading Strategies

Lesson II: A New Cousin 11
Form Review (Nouns, Adjectives); Syntax Review (Ablative of Accompaniment, Dative); Reading Strategies

Lesson III: The Women Have Their Say 17
Form Review; Syntax Review (The Ablative of Means, The Infinitive Used as Subject and Object)

Lesson IV: Days with Books and Writers 22
Form Review

Lesson V: The Laws of the Twelve Tables 26
Form Review (The Passive Voice, Participles); Syntax Review (Perfect Participles Used as Adjectives and Nouns, Participles Used as Clauses, Ablative Absolute, Ablative of Agent)

Lesson VI: The Senate in Session 32
Form Review (Infinitives, Relative Pronouns and Interrogative Pronouns and Adjectives); Syntax Review (Tenses of the Infinitive, Indirect Statement, Relative Pronouns)

Lesson VII: Holidays 38
Form Review (Irregular Adjectives, The Demonstratives *Hic* and *Ille,* The Verb *Possum*); Syntax Review (Ablative of Respect, Use of *Mille* and *Milia*)

Lesson VIII: Superstitions 44
Form Review (The Declensions of *Is, Īdem,* and *Ipse,* Comparison of Regular Adjectives and Adverbs); Syntax Review (Comparison of Adjectives and Adverbs, Dative with Adjectives)

Lesson IX: The Big Show 49
Form Review (Comparison of Irregular Adjectives, Comparison of Irregular Adverbs); Syntax Review (The Uses of the Ablative)

Unit II—Two Roman Students in Athens

Lesson X: The Farewell Dinner 58
Review of the Fourth Declension; Subjunctive Mood; Hortatory and Jussive Subjunctive

Lesson XI: On the Way 64
Purpose Clauses with *Ut* and *Nē*

Lesson XII: An Adventure 68
Imperfect Subjunctive; The Imperfect Subjunctive of *Sum;* Tense Sequence in Purpose Clauses

Lesson XIII: Sight-Seeing at Brundisium 73
Conjugation of *Ferō*

Lesson XIV: A Letter from Athens 78
Result Clauses with *Ut* and *Ut nōn;* Summary of Purpose and Result Clauses

Lesson XV: A Gossipy Letter from Rome 82
Review of the Fifth Declension; Subjunctive of *Sum* and *Possum*

Lesson XVI: Alma Mater 86
Pluperfect Active Subjunctive; Time Clauses: *Ubi, Postquam, Cum*

Lesson XVII: Athens the Beautiful 91
Perfect and Pluperfect Subjunctive; Summary of Sequence of Tenses

Lesson XVIII: A Request for Funds 97
Deponent Verbs

Lesson XIX: A Wedding 101
Personal Pronouns; Reflexive Pronouns; Indirect Questions

Lesson XX: The Trip to Delphi 106
Indefinite Pronouns and Adjectives; The Seven Wise Men of Greece

Lesson XXI: Totalitarianism and Democracy 113
Formation and Use of the Future Passive Participle

Lesson XXII: Athletics and Patriotism 116
Indirect Commands

Lesson XXIII: National Heroes 120
The Gerund; Use of the Gerund and the Gerundive

Lesson XXIV: A Visit to the Academy 125
Conjugation of *Fīō*

Lesson XXV: Athens and Rome 128
Conjugation of *Volō* and *Nōlō*

Lesson XXVI: The Homecoming 132
The Dative with Special Verbs; The Datives of Reference and Purpose

Our Heritage: Greeks and Romans 138

Unit II Review 141
A Latin Play: *Bulla*

Unit III—Livy

A Great Historian 146

Lesson XXVII: Early Kings of Rome 148
The Dative with Compounds

Lesson XXVIII: Out Go the Kings 152
The Conjugation of *Mālō;* The Locative Case

Lesson XXIX: How Brutus Got His Name 156
Review: Future Passive Participle and Gerund

Lesson XXX: How "Lefty" (Scaevola) Got His Name 159
The Subjunctive after Verbs of Fearing; Latin Sentence Structure

Lesson XXXI: The Plebeians Go On Strike 163
Impersonal Verbs

Lesson XXXII: Extra! Rome Captured by the Gauls 167
Genitive of the Whole; More about *Cum* Clauses

Lesson XXXIII: Rome Sweet Home 171
Omission of *Sum*

Lesson XXXIV: Torquatus, or Courage and Discipline 175
Indirect Command; The Indefinite *Quis, Aliquis,* and *Quīdam*

Lesson XXXV: The Punic Wars 178
The Relative as Connective; *Place to Which*

Lesson XXXVI: The Romans Give Liberty to the Greeks 182
The Imperative; *Quisque* and *Quisquam*

Lesson XXXVII: Civil War 186
Ablative of Separation

Lesson XXXVIII: Pāx Rōmāna 190
Description; Ablative of Degree of Difference; *Etiam* and *Quoque; Quidem*

Lesson XXXIX: Roman Scandals 195
Relative Purpose Clauses

Our Heritage: The Roman Empire 199

Unit IV—The Argonauts

The Story of the Golden Fleece 204
The Argonauts and Latin Grammar

Lesson XL: The Wicked Uncle 207

Lesson XLI: The Golden Fleece and the Building of the Argo 208

Lesson XLII: Dinner Under Difficulties 210

Lesson XLIII: Two Good Turns 213

Lesson XLIV: A Risky Job 215

Lesson XLV: Sowing the Dragon's Teeth 217

Lesson XLVI: Jason Gets the Fleece 219

Lesson XLVII: Escape Through Murder 221

Lesson XLVIII: Boiled Mutton 224

Lesson XLIX: Death and More Death 226

Unit V—Dē Bellō Gallicō I

Julius Caesar 232

Caesar's Army 236

Lesson L: A Geography Lesson 240

Lesson LI: An Entire Nation Emigrates 244

Lesson LII: A Mysterious Death and a Bonfire 248

Lesson LIII: Caesar Says: "You Shall Not Pass" 252

Lesson LIV: The Harder Way 256

Lesson LV: The Gauls Appeal to Caesar 260
The Dative of Possession; The Subjunctive in Anticipatory Clauses

Lesson LVI: A Surprise That Failed 264

Lesson LVII: The Fight Is On 267
Causal Clauses with *Quod* and *Quoniam*
Lesson LVIII: The Helvetian Surrender 271
Lesson LIX: The Price of Peace 274
Lesson LX: The German Threat 277
Lesson LXI: Caesar Promises to Support the Gauls 281
Lesson LXII: Ariovistus' Defiant Stand 285
Our Heritage: The Gallic Conquest and Its Effect on the World 290

Unit VI—Dē Bellō Gallicō II-V

Summary of Book II–Caesar's *Gallic War* 294
Lesson LXIII: The First Battle on the Atlantic 297
Lesson LXIV: A Decisive Victory 300
Lesson LXV: Description of the Suebi 303
Lesson LXVI: The Bridging of the Rhine 306
Lesson LXVII: Scarcity of Information about Britain 309
Lesson LXVIII: Midnight Sailing 312
Lesson LXIX: Difficult Fighting 315
Lesson LXX: Storm and Tide Cause Trouble 318
Lesson LXXI: New Difficulties 321
Our Heritage: Caesar's Invasions of Britain 324
Lesson LXXII: Britain and Its People 325
Lesson LXXII: Two Rival Heroes 330
Lesson LXXIV: A Coded Message and a Clever Trick 333

Unit VII—Dē Bellō Gallicō VI-VII

Lesson LXXV: Gallic Leaders 338
Lesson LXXVI: The Druids 341
Lesson LXXVII: Druids and Knights 344
Lesson LXXVIII: Religion 347
Lesson LXXIX: Marriages and Funerals; Censorship 349
Lesson LXXX: Description of the Germans 351
Lesson LXXXI: The Hercynian Forest and Its Animals 354
Lesson LXXXII: Vercingetorix Takes Charge 357
Lesson LXXXIII: Roman Spirit 360
Lesson LXXXIV: The Siege of Alesia 363
Lesson LXXV: A Horrible Suggestion 366
Lesson LXCXXVI: Innocent Victims of War 369
Lesson LXXXVII: Near Disaster Followed by Victory 372

Our Heritage: Vercingetorix and Alesia 375
A Latin Play: Caesar Dictator 376

Unit VIII—The Letters of Pliny

An Ancient Letter Writer–382; The Eruption of Vesuvius–383; Flight from Disaster–384; The Secret of Success–386; How to Keep Young–387; The Good Die Young–387; A Ghost Story–389; Don't Be a Harsh Father–389; Graded Friendship Is Degraded Friendship–390; Wanted, A Teacher–390; A Courageous Wife–391; Two Love Letters–392; A Fish Story–392; Advice to a Provincial Governor–393; A Humane Master–394; A Busy Holiday–395

Unit IX—Latin Literature

Ennius–398; Plautus and Terence–399; Lucretius–400; Cornelius Nepos–402; Catullus–402; Cicero–404; Sallust–407; Publilius Syrus–408; Livy–409; Horace–410; Sulpicia–411; Ovid and Roman Elegy–412; Phaedrus–413; Valerius Maximus–414; Seneca–415; Petronius–415; Quintilian–417; Martial–418; Tacitus–419; Juvenal–420; Aulus Gellius–420; Miscellaneous Quotations–422; Augustine– 423; Liutprand–424; Adam of Bremen–425; Hildegard von Bingen–426; From the *Carmina Burana*–428; Iacopone of Todi–429; Thomas of Celano–429; From *Gesta Romanorum*–431; Petrarch–431; Poggio–433; Pietro Bembo–433

Unit X—Ovid and Vergil

Reading Latin Verse 436

Ovid's *Metamorphoses* 438
The Flood: Deucalion and Pyrrha–438; Echo and Narcissus–441; Perseus and Atlas–443; Orpheus and Eurydice–444; Pygmalion–445

Vergil's *Aeneid* 446
Book I–448; Book IV–450; Book VI–451

Quotations from Vergil 453

Appendix 454

Vocabulary

Latin–English 489
English–Latin 517

Subject Index 523

Grammar/Vocabulary Index 528

Maps

Imperium Romanum 136-137
Italia 194
Gallia 228-229

Introduction

In content, theme, and organization, this edition of *Latin for Americans, Second Book* retains the emphasis earlier editions have placed upon American ideals and their classical background. The textbook makes comparisons between ancient and modern ways of life, builds upon English vocabulary-building through the study of Latin roots, and provides thorough and yet simple explanations of the similarities and differences between English and Latin grammar. The reading selections are often accompanied by exercises intended to help the student analyze the real sense of what is being said, to develop a feeling for the variety of meanings possible in many Latin words, depending upon the context, and to instill the confidence to use the full resources of his or her own English vocabulary.

It is not intended that all the Latin readings be completed by every class. The first three units present virtually all the essentials of second-year grammar, and the teacher should feel a certain freedom thereafter in matching the readings to the interests and abilities of the class. The wealth of material provides an ample choice for both regular classwork and for additional assignments to the better students. The reading in Caesar can well be postponed until the second semester, and there should be no need to feel that it must all be done. The work of two new female authors has been introduced in this edition: Sulpicia and Hildegard von Bingen. Numerous full-color photos replace those found in earlier editions, providing visual appeal and reinforcement to the reading topics.

The revised *Workbook,* authored by Donald Peet and Marcia Stille, offers a wealth of supplemental practice. The *Progress Tests* and a set of cassette tapes rerecorded with new voices are equally usable with this revision.

A.K.G., Berlin/SuperStock, Inc.

Unit I

A Roman Family

UNIT OBJECTIVES

To review the endings of all five declensions; To review the declensions of adjectives; To review the present and perfect system active and passive of all regular verbs and **sum** and **possum**; To review the case uses; To review formation and uses of the infinitive, including indirect statement; To review participles and the ablative absolute; To review relative pronouns and interrogative pronouns and adjectives; To review irregular adjectives; To review all demonstratives and the emphatic **ipse**; To review the regular and irregular comparison of adjectives and adverbs

Daily life inside the home of Cornelius Rufus in Pompeii. The boy is using a conch shell to blow his sailboat across the ***impluvium*** *(pool). A female servant sets out a bowl of fruit and a male servant sorts through several books. Meanwhile, the* ***dominus*** *discusses something with another servant while his wife speaks with her maidservants. Notice that the bottoms of the pillars are painted red to help hide fingerprints.*

LESSON OBJECTIVES
To review the endings of first and second declension nouns and adjectives; To review the present system indicative active of the first and second conjugations; To review the present system of **sum**; To review the following constructions: nominative (subject and predicate nominative), accusative (direct object), ablative *(place where, time when),* agreement of adjectives, apposition

STUDY TOPICS
Augustus and his attempts to reform Roman domestic life

LESSON I
Pūblius and Secunda

SECUNDA: Ubi fuistī, Pūblī?

PŪBLIUS: In Forō Rōmānō fuī, Secunda.

SECUNDA: Quem ibi vīdistī, Pūblī?

PŪBLIUS: Patrem nostrum et Augustum, prīncipem cīvitātis, vīdī, illum quī pācem cōnstituit. Nōnne dē hāc pāce audīvistī? "Pāx Augusta"[1] ā populō grātō appellātur.

SECUNDA: Sī Augustus prīnceps cīvitātis est, estne pater noster, P. Caecilius Rūfus, prīnceps familiae?

PŪBLIUS: Ita est; nōn autem prīnceps sed paterfamiliās[2] appellātur. Māter nostra Fulvia māterfamiliās[2] est.

SECUNDA: Quid facit paterfamiliās?

PŪBLIUS: Ille tōtam familiam regit—et līberōs et servōs. Etiam deōs familiae colit et sōlus omnia negōtia gerit. Auctōritās patris, quae ā nōbīs Rōmānīs "patria[3] potestās" appellātur, maxima est. Sī servum aut fīlium interficere cupit, potestātem habet. Sed nōn timēre dēbēs, nam hōc tempore nūllī patrēs Rōmānī id cupiunt. Pater noster bonus, nōn dūrus est. Nōs eum amāmus et omnēs servī eum amant.

SECUNDA: Ubi nunc pater est?

PŪBLIUS: In Forō negōtia pūblica gerit; quondam mīles fuit. Nōbilis et īnsignis est. Sed quid tū hodiē fēcistī, Secunda?

SECUNDA: Cum sorōre nostrā maiōre Caeciliā eram. Ea dē officiīs mātris nostrae verba fēcit. Māter domina servārum est et labōrem eārum regit. Ā patre nostrō semper cōnsulitur, nam docta ācrisque est. Posteā māter mē docuit, nam puellae nōn in lūdum mittuntur. Māter mē docuit dē factīs quae memoriā tenuit et dē hominibus clārīs quōs ipsa nōvit et dē eīs dē quibus in librīs lēgit.

PŪBLIUS: Bene. Quid aliud māter docuit?

---

[1] Named after the emperor Augustus who brought about a long period of peace after many years of civil war.

[2] The second part of the word is an old genitive form; *paterfamilias* and *materfamilias* are used in English.

[3] Adjective: *the father's power*

Scala/Art Resource, NY

SECUNDA: Dē patre nostrō docuit. Pater "iūs trium līberōrum"[4] obtinuit, quod trēs līberōs habet, mē et tē et Caeciliam. Hoc iūs ab Augustō datum est quod in paucīs nōbilibus familiīs hōc tempore multī līberī sunt, et quod Augustus maiōrem esse numerum optimōrum cīvium Rōmānōrum cupit. Sed tū, Pūblī, quī iam vir es, quid nunc faciēs?

PŪBLIUS: Studia in lūdō nostrō perfēcī; iam in Graeciam, ubi clārae scholae sunt, nāvigāre parō.

SECUNDA: Ōh, fēlīx tū. Ego quoque in Graeciam nāvigāre cupiō.

PŪBLIUS: Hodiē alia in mente volvō, nam crās optimus diēs aderit.

SECUNDA: Quid est hoc?

PŪBLIUS: Sī bona puella eris, iam cognōscēs.

All official business was conducted in the Roman Forum. After receiving his ***clientes*** *in the morning, a Roman* ***patronus*** *would go on to the Forum to meet with his business or political colleagues.*

SUGGESTION
After this dialogue has been read, have two students take the parts and read them aloud in class.

QUESTIONS

1. What legal right did a Roman father have?
2. What was the name of Secunda's father?
3. Whom did the Romans include under "family"?
4. Describe Fulvia's household duties.
5. Compare and contrast Roman and American family life.

ADDITIONAL QUESTIONS
What does Publius and Secunda's father do? How many children are there in the family? What are Publius' plans for the future?

[4] Fathers having three children were exempted from certain taxes and were given preference in official positions. Compare modern income tax exemptions for married couples with children.

Grammar

Form Review

Nouns and Adjectives

Review the following models of the endings for first and second declension nouns and adjectives. Remember that almost all first declension nouns are feminine (exceptions are **agricola, nauta, pirata, poēta**). Second declension nouns are either masculine (nominative in **–us** or **–r**) or neuter (nominative in **–um**).

SUGGESTION
Provide students with several nouns to practice an oral drill on endings; start with a noun alone, then do an adjective plus noun.

FIRST DECLENSION		SECOND DECLENSION	
SINGULAR	PLURAL	SINGULAR	PLURAL
vi**a**	vi**ae**	serv**us**	serv**ī**
vi**ae**	vi**ārum**	serv**ī**	serv**ōrum**
vi**ae**	vi**īs**	serv**ō**	serv**īs**
vi**am**	vi**ās**	serv**um**	serv**ōs**
vi**ā**	vi**īs**	serv**ō**	serv**īs**

SECOND DECLENSION		SECOND DECLENSION		SECOND DECLENSION	
SING.	PLUR.	SING.	PLUR.	SING.	PLUR.
age**r**	agr**ī**	puer	puer**ī**	sign**um**	sign**a**
agr**ī**	agr**ōrum**	puer**ī**	puer**ōrum**	sign**ī**	sign**ōrum**
agr**ō**	agr**īs**	puer**ō**	puer**īs**	sign**ō**	sign**īs**
agr**um**	agr**ōs**	puer**um**	puer**ōs**	sign**um**	sign**a**
agr**ō**	agr**īs**	puer**ō**	puer**īs**	sign**ō**	sign**īs**

WORKBOOK
Assign Ex. A on nouns and adjectives.

FIRST AND SECOND DECLENSIONS		
	SINGULAR	
magn**us**	magn**a**	magn**um**
magn**ī**	magn**ae**	magn**ī**
magn**ō**	magn**ae**	magn**ō**
magn**um**	magn**am**	magn**um**
magn**ō**	magn**ā**	magn**ō**
	PLURAL	
magn**ī**	magn**ae**	magn**a**
magn**ōrum**	magn**ārum**	magn**ōrum**
magn**īs**	magn**īs**	magn**īs**
magn**ōs**	magn**ās**	magn**a**
magn**īs**	magn**īs**	magn**īs**

NOTĀ·BENE

Remember that the vocative is the same as the nominative except for nouns in –us, *whose vocative is* –e (serve) *and nouns in* –ius, *whose vocative ends in* –ī (fīlī).

Verbs

The present, imperfect, and future tenses comprise the present system because they are all formed from the present stem of the verb. To find the present stem, drop the **–re** from the present infinitive (second principal part), add the tense sign (if necessary), and the personal ending.

SUGGESTION
Assign each student a verb and a tense and have him or her write it on the board. Students can work in pairs, while one dictates, the other writes.

PRESENT		IMPERFECT	
port**ō**	doce**ō**	portā**bam**	docē**bam**
portā**s**	docē**s**	portā**bās**	docē**bās**
porta**t**	doce**t**	portā**bat**	docē**bat**
portā**mus**	docē**mus**	portā**bāmus**	docē**bāmus**
portā**tis**	docē**tis**	portā**bātis**	docē**bātis**
porta**nt**	doce**nt**	portā**bant**	docē**bant**

FUTURE	
portā**bō**	docē**bō**
portā**bis**	docē**bis**
portā**bit**	docē**bit**
portā**bimus**	docē**bimus**
portā**bitis**	docē**bitis**
portā**bunt**	docē**bunt**

*The **ātrium** of the House of the Faun at Pompeii. Typically, the **ātrium** had a funnel-shaped roof designed so that rainwater would drain into the **impluvium** (shallow pool) in the foreground. The water would then be stored in a cistern for household purposes. In the distance, you can see the **peristylum**, or open area, at the rear of the house, where there was usually a garden and a fountain. The basic design of the Roman house can still be seen today in Italy and throughout Europe in former Roman provinces.*

Scala/Art Resource, NY

The present, imperfect, and future of **sum** are formed irregularly.

PRESENT		IMPERFECT		FUTURE	
sum	sum**us**	er**am**	er**āmus**	er**ō**	er**imus**
es	es**tis**	er**ās**	er**ātis**	er**is**	er**itis**
est	su**nt**	er**at**	er**ant**	er**it**	er**unt**

WORKBOOK
Assign Ex. B on verb forms.

ORAL PRACTICE

1. Decline **agricola līber, officium dūrum**.
2. Tell the form(s) of **servō, paucīs, optimōrum, familiā, fīlī, fīliae, fīliī, virī, līberōs, negōtiīs**.
3. Give the second person singular of **obtineō** and the third person plural of **nāvigō** in the present, imperfect, and future indicative active.

CASSETTE
Do Unit I, Drill 1, Ex. A on subjects and verbs.

Syntax Review

Nominative: Subject and Predicate Nominative

The subject of a conjugated verb is in the nominative case. A noun or adjective used in the predicate after a linking verb is in the nominative case.

Mīles cum hostibus pugnat.	*The soldier is fighting with the enemy.*
Sardinia īnsula est.	*Sardinia is an island.*

NOTE
You may want to remind students that the subject of an infinitive is in the accusative.

Accusative: Direct Object

The direct object of a transitive verb is in the accusative.

Magister līberōs laudāvit.	*The teacher praised the children.*
Fēminae aquam portant.	*The women are carrying the water.*

SUGGESTION
If you have students keep a notebook, they should allot one page to each case; new uses can be added easily and reviewed efficiently.

Ablative of *Place Where*

The ablative case with the preposition **in** or **sub** is used to indicate *where* something is or is happening. Sometimes the preposition is omitted, especially in poetry.

Gentēs in prōvinciā in īnsulā habitant.	*The people live in a province on an island.*
Canēs sub arbōre sunt.	*The dogs are under the tree.*

Ablative of *Time When*

The ablative without a preposition is used to express *time when* or *within which*.

Hieme animalia dormiunt.	*In the winter, the animals sleep.*
Paucīs diēbus pervenient.	*Within a few days, they will arrive.*

Agreement of Adjectives

Adjectives agree in gender, number, and case with the nouns they modify.

Beātus nauta ad Ītaliam nāvigāvit.	*The happy sailor sailed to Italy.*
Flūmen celere multōs piscēs habuit.	*The swift river had many fish.*

Apposition

Appositives agree in case. You may want to supply *as* when you are translating.

Rūfus dux factus est.	*Rufus was made leader.*
Servus magister dēlēctus est.	*The slave was chosen as teacher.*

WORKBOOK
Assign Ex. C on syntax.

SuperStock, Inc.

Servants and children gather around the community well to exchange news as well as to retrieve fresh water that they carry home in metal or earthenware jugs. Note that the bottoms of the pillars here, as in the houses, are painted to keep them from looking dirty.

ANSWERS
1. Illō/Eō tempore servī dominōs dūrōs saepe habēbant. 2. Nōnne cupis dē Pūbliō, fīliō Rūfī, audīre? 3. Māter fīliās et pater fīliōs docēbat. 4. Rūfus dē officiīs līberōrum et servōrum Fulviam cōnsulēbat. 5. Paucī erant līberī in multīs familiīs Rōmānīs tempore Augustī.

TRANSLATION

1. The slaves at that time often had harsh masters.
2. Do you not wish to hear about Publius, son of Rufus?
3. The mother taught the daughters and the father, the sons.
4. Rufus consulted Fulvia about the duties of the children and slaves.
5. There were few children in many Roman families in the time of Augustus.

Vocabulary Review

The following words should already be familiar. Remember that it is important to learn not only the meaning, but also the essential facts about each word: for nouns, this means the genitive and gender; for adjectives, all three nominative forms; for verbs, the principal parts; and for prepositions, the case. Try to think of an English derivative for each vocabulary word.

Nouns

fīlius
līberī
negōtium
officium
populus
servus
vir

Adjectives

dūrus
paucī

Verbs

appellō
doceō
habeō
nāvigō
obtineō
teneō
timeō

NOTE
The Workbook contains a list of vocabulary familiar to students. You may want to review all or parts of the vocabulary in class or assign it for homework. Students may see some of these words on the test, even though they have not been officially reviewed.

Word Studies

Many English words in the singular retain the exact form of the Latin original, even though the meaning may have changed: *arena, radius, victor, impetus, species.* Many even retain the Latin ending in the plural.

Other English words preserve only the Latin base: *duct, legion, long, tend, timid.* Others preserve the Latin base plus silent *–e; mode, grave, produce, dire.* Still others show a minor change of spelling in the base: *boon* (**bonus**), *example* (**exemplum**), *pair* (**pār**), *obtain* (**obtineō**).

Give two more examples of each of the four types of derivatives presented above. The next stage will be to review the prefixes and suffixes commonly attached to the bases of Latin words.

Reading Strategies

When you read or listen to English you naturally take in the words as they come. So it is in Latin. When Romans were conversing they understood each other as the words were spoken. They did not stop to look first for the subject, then for the verb; that would have been impossible! In reading as in speaking they understood the meaning of the words in their Latin order. *And you should try to do the same.*

SUGGESTION
After you have reviewed this section with students, reread the story so students will become more familiar with phrasing and word groups.

Pūblius, hīs rēbus impulsus, litterās longās prīmā nocte ad patrem amīcī mittit.

Just take the words as they come; at the same time, try to see what words belong together in phrases:

Pūblius: The ending shows that it is nominative singular—for this reason it is probably the subject. In English, it will probably come first.

hīs rēbus: These words seem to go together (demonstrative and noun) and are either dative or ablative plural. You have to wait until you read more of the sentence, however, before their meaning will be clear.

impulsus: This word, which is nominative singular masculine, looks like "impulse," which comes from the Latin verb meaning "impel." It must agree with **Pūblius,** since it has the same gender, number, and case. The punctuation shows that **hīs rēbus** depends upon it; the latter is therefore the ablative of means. The sentence so far reads: "Publius, impelled by these things (facts)."

litterās longās: These words clearly belong together, both being in the same case, number, and gender. They are in the accusative plural and must be the direct object of some verb or else the subject of an infinitive—we cannot tell which until we go on.

prīmā nocte: the long **a** in **prīmā** shows that it is ablative singular in agreement with **nocte.** The latter suggests "nocturnal" but is a noun. The phrase, therefore, probably means "on the first night"—or could it possibly mean "at the first (part of) the night"?

ad patrem amīcī: The sense seems clear as it stands: "to the father of (his) friend," for **ad** always is followed by the accusative and **patrem** must be its object; **amīcī** is genitive singular and evidently depends upon **patrem.**

mittit: At last the sense of the whole passage is clear! **Mittit** is the verb and it agrees with the first word, **Pūblius,** for it is third person singular. Now it is evident that **litterās longās** is the direct object of **mittit.** All the words seem to fall into line and make sense just as they stand.

You may notice, as you go over the words with the thought of the whole sentence more or less clearly in mind, that the first meaning of a word is not always the best, and that the general sense of the passage (i.e., the context) helps you decide the exact meaning to be given to each word. The complete sentence reads as follows:

Publius, urged by these considerations, sends a long letter in the evening to the father of his friend.

LESSON II

A New Cousin

LESSON OBJECTIVES
To review the endings for third declension nouns (including **i**-stems) and adjectives;
To review the ablative of accompaniment and the dative of indirect object

Lūx erat: Pūblius praeceps ad patrem P. Caecilium cucurrit et eī salūtem dīxit.

"Cūr properās?" pater rogāvit.

"Nōnne memoriā tenēs? Tempus adest quō Q. Fūrius erit noster."

Q. Fūrius amīcus firmus Pūblī erat. Familia Quīntī humilis fuit. Pater eius sex līberōs sed pecūniam nōn magnam habuit. M. Caecilius, frāter P. Caecilī, magnam pecūniam sed nūllōs līberōs habuit.

"Nōnne cupis fīlium adoptāre?" Pūblius Mārcō dīxerat.

"Certē," respondit Mārcus. Omnēs Rōmānī fīliōs habēre cupiēbant, quod fīliī nōmen familiae servābant, deōs familiae colēbant, "patriam potestātem" cōnfirmābant. Multae erant adoptiōnēs inter Rōmānōs. Multī clārī Rōmānī adoptātī sunt. Fīlius minimus L. Aemilī Paulī ā P. Cornēliō Scīpiōne, fīliō ducis clārī, adoptātus est, et posteā P. Cornēlius Scīpiō Aemiliānus Āfricānus appellābātur. Augustus[1] ipse ā C. Iūliō Caesare adoptātus erat, et nōmen tōtum quod sūmpsit erat C. Iūlius Caesar Octāviānus Augustus.

Pūblius Q. Fūrium ad M. Caecilium dūxerat.

"Quīntus puer magnī animī est. Eum adoptāre cupiō," dīxit Mārcus. "Cum meā familiā habitābit, sed saepe patrem, mātrem, frātrēs, sorōrēs vidēbit."

Id grātum patrī Quīntī fuerat, et nunc tempus aderat. Multī clientēs ad P. Caecilium iam veniēbant et salūtem dīcēbant. Cum clientibus et fīliō Caecilius in Forum prōcessit et ad aedificium praetōris accessit. Q. Fūrius, pater eius, M. Caecilius, amīcī iam aderant. Q. Fūrius novam togam gerēbat.

Praetor condiciōnēs adoptiōnis prōposuit.

"Quīntum, fīlium meum, ā patriā potestāte meā līberō," pater Quīntī ter dīxit.

Tum M. Caecilius dīxit, "Meus fīlius nunc est."

"Tuus fīlius nunc est," praetor dīxit. "In tuā potestāte nunc est. Nōmen nōn iam Q. Fūrius est, sed M. Caecilius Fūriānus."

STUDY TOPIC
Patria potestas

The family unit was very important in Roman society. If a family had no sons, they frequently adopted a son from a family with several in order to pass on the family name. Many famous Romans, including Augustus Caesar, were adopted.

Ronald Sheridan/Ancient Art & Architecture Collection

[1] An honorary surname (the "revered" or "reverend"), conferred by the Roman Senate upon Octavian when he became emperor.

Omnēs Fūriānō novō et M. Caeciliō salūtem dīxērunt; tum discessērunt.

"Nunc noster Fūriānus es," Pūblius Fūriānō dīxit.

"Tibi grātiās agō," Fūriānus respondit, et cum patre novō discessit. Plūra dē Fūriānō et dē Pūbliō audiētis.

ADDITIONAL QUESTIONS
Why did the Romans want to have sons? Whom did Julius Caesar adopt? What was Quintus Furius wearing?

QUESTIONS

1. Who adopted Quintus and why?
2. Where did the adoption take place?
3. What was the name of Publius' uncle?

Grammar

Form Review

SUGGESTION
Do a quick oral drill using first a noun alone, then a noun and adjective.

Nouns

Third declension nouns are characterized by **–is** in the genitive singular. They can be regular masculine, feminine, neuter, or **i**–stem masculine, feminine, or neuter. Both the masculine and the feminine, whether regular or **i**–stem, are declined alike.

REGULAR NOUNS

MASCULINE		FEMININE		NEUTER	
SING.	PLUR.	SING.	PLUR.	SING.	PLUR.
mīles	mīlit**ēs**	lēx	lēg**ēs**	corpus	corpor**a**
mīlit**is**	mīlit**um**	lēg**is**	lēg**um**	corpor**is**	corpor**um**
mīlit**ī**	mīlit**ibus**	lēg**ī**	lēg**ibus**	corpor**ī**	corpor**ibus**
mīlit**em**	mīlit**ēs**	lēg**em**	lēg**ēs**	corpus	corpor**a**
mīlit**e**	mīlit**ibus**	lēg**e**	lēg**ibus**	corpor**e**	corpor**ibus**

I–STEM NOUNS

MASCULINE AND FEMININE		NEUTER	
SINGULAR	PLURAL	SINGULAR	PLURAL
cīv**is**	cīv**ēs**	mar**e**	mar**ia**
cīv**is**	cīv**ium**	mar**is**	mar**ium**
cīv**ī**	cīv**ibus**	mar**ī**	mar**ibus**
cīv**em**	cīv**ēs**	mar**e**	mar**ia**
cīv**e**	cīv**ibus**	mar**ī**	mar**ibus**

NOTĀ·BENE

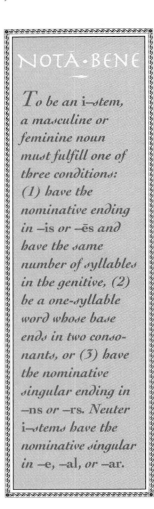

To be an i–*stem, a masculine or feminine noun must fulfill one of three conditions: (1) have the nominative ending in* –is *or* –ēs *and have the same number of syllables in the genitive, (2) be a one-syllable word whose base ends in two consonants, or (3) have the nominative singular ending in* –ns *or* –rs. *Neuter* i–*stems have the nominative singular in* –e, –al, *or* –ar.

Adjectives

Third declension adjectives fall into one of three categories, based on the number of endings they have in the nominative singular. Third declension adjectives are declined like **i–**stems.

THREE ENDINGS

SINGULAR			PLURAL		
ācer	ācr**is**	ācr**e**	ācr**ēs**	ācr**ēs**	ācr**ia**
ācr**is**	ācr**is**	ācr**is**	ācr**ium**	ācr**ium**	ācr**ium**
ācr**ī**	ācr**ī**	ācr**ī**	ācr**ibus**	ācr**ibus**	ācr**ibus**
ācr**em**	ācr**em**	ācr**e**	ācr**ēs**	ācr**ēs**	ācr**ia**
ācr**ī**	ācr**ī**	ācr**ī**	ācr**ibus**	ācr**ibus**	ācr**ibus**

TWO ENDINGS

SINGULAR		PLURAL	
M AND F	N	M AND F	N
fort**is**	fort**e**	fort**ēs**	fort**ia**
fort**is**	fort**is**	fort**ium**	fort**ium**
fort**ī**	fort**ī**	fort**ibus**	fort**ibus**
fort**em**	fort**e**	fort**ēs**	fort**ia**
fort**ī**	fort**ī**	fort**ibus**	fort**ibus**

ONE ENDING

SINGULAR		PLURAL	
M AND F	N	M AND F	N
pār	pār	par**ēs**	par**ia**
par**is**	par**is**	par**ium**	par**ium**
par**ī**	par**ī**	par**ibus**	par**ibus**
par**em**	par	par**ēs**	par**ia**
par**ī**	par**ī**	par**ibus**	par**ibus**

WORKBOOK
Assign Ex. A, B to practice nouns and adjectives.

NOTE
A review of comparatives will be done later. If you wish, you may mention here that comparatives are declined like a third declension non-**i**-stem, but it is probably better to reacquire these endings before alluding to the exceptions.

NOTE
If you want your students to know the alternate forms of the third declension nouns and adjectives, you may introduce them here or have students refer to the Appendix.

ORAL PRACTICE

1. Decline **frāter humilis, potestās nostra.**
2. Give the form of **condiciōnēs, patrī, sorōrum, omnium, fīlium, salūte, togīs, nōminibus, mātrum, ducēs.**

CASSETTE
Do Unit I, Drill 2, Ex. A, B, C to practice the first three declensions.

Nimatallah/Art Resource, NY

A wall painting from an Etruscan tomb at Tarquinia, northwest of Rome, shows dancers performing to the accompaniment of lyres and flutes. The Etruscans, precursors of the Romans, taught them many aspects of painting, dance, and architecture.

WORKBOOK
Assign Ex. C to review verbs and practice syntax.

Syntax Review

Ablative of Accompaniment

Accompaniment is expressed by the ablative with the preposition **cum**. When **cum** is used with a personal, reflexive, or relative pronoun, it is attached to the end of the pronoun.

Anna cum matre suā ambulābat.	*Anna was walking with her mother.*
Possumne tēcum venīre?	*Can I come with you?*

Dative: Indirect Object

The indirect object of a verb is in the dative. It is used with verbs of giving, showing, telling, reporting, etc. and in English is often preceded by *to* or *for*.

Magister librum puellae dedit.	*The teacher gave the book to the girl.*
Mōnstrā praemium mihi.	*Show me the reward.*

TRANSLATION

1. Who came to the Forum with Publius?
2. A new name is given to the humble boy.
3. I shall tell everything (*neut. plur.*) to my father and mother.
4. Publius proceeds to the leader with his father and Marcus.

ANSWERS
1. Quis ad Forum cum Pūbliō vēnit? 2. Nōmen novum puerō humilī datur. 3. Omnia patrī meō et mātrī dīcam. 4. Pūblius ad ducem cum patre suō et Marcō prōcēdit.

Vocabulary Review

Nouns

condiciō	**māter**	**salūs**
dux	**nōmen**	**soror**
frāter	**pater**	**toga**
lūx	**potestās**	

Adjectives

humilis **omnis**

Verbs

respondeō **rogō** **servō**

Word Studies

Review the prefixes **ab–**, **dē–**, **ex–**, and **sē–** in the Appendix, noting that each has a basic "from" meaning.

Select the proper form of each prefix and define its English derivative: **(ab)** *–rogate, –vert, –tain;* **(dē)** *–duct, –cease, –scribe;* **(ex)** *–tract, –vent;* **(sē)** *–parate, –cede.*

Reading Strategies

Reading Latin as Latin implies acquaintance with a certain number of Latin words. We shall assume that at the beginning of the second year you know all the ordinary prepositions and conjunctions and several hundred of the most common nouns, adjectives, adverbs, and verbs that occurred almost every day in your first year work.

In your reading you will discover many new words. Your first impulse may be to turn at once to the Vocabulary at the end of the book for the meaning, but that always takes time and should be done only if other methods fail. There are three easier and better ways of getting at the meaning of a new word. Sometimes just one of them, more often a combination of two or of all three of them, makes it possible for you to get the meaning of the word. Try all three before you turn to the Vocabulary:

1. Think of an English derivative from the Latin word (about sixty percent of our English words come from Latin). The English derivative, if the same part of speech as the Latin original, will at least serve as a stopgap until you can find a synonym that may suit the sense better.
2. If you can think of no related English word, try to recall a related Latin word; for example, **amīcitia** suggests **amīcus,** which you already know.
3. If no related English or Latin word suggests itself, guess at the meaning from the context and later check your guess by looking up the word in the Vocabulary.

Children, especially boys, were taught to read from an early age. Of course, Roman books were not bound as ours are today, but rather written on long sheets of papyrus that were rolled into a scroll.

Erich Lessing/Art Resource, NY

LESSON III

The Women Have Their Say

LESSON OBJECTIVES
To review the present, imperfect, and future of the third and fourth conjugations; To review the ablative of means; To review the infinitive used as subject and as a complementary infinitive

Fulvia, māter Pūblī, cum sorōribus eius, Caeciliā et Secundā, Pūblium Rūfumque exspectābat.

"Dūrum est semper exspectāre," Secunda clāmāvit. "Virōs exspectāmus, nihil ipsae agimus. Vīta puerōrum et virōrum grātior est. In lūdum, in Forum, in loca pūblica prōcēdunt. Sed Rōma puellīs inimīca est."

"Quid? Nōnne Rōma clārās mulierēs Rōmānās semper memoriā tenet?" rogāvit Caecilia.

"Vērum est," erant verba Fulviae. "Quis Veturiam, quae Rōmam servāvit, memoriā nōn tenet? Coriolānus, fīlius Veturiae, lēgem prōposuerat, quae cīvitātī nōn grāta erat. Itaque inimīcī Coriolānum in fugam dedērunt, et is ad Volscōs, hostēs Rōmānōrum, fūgit. Dux Volscōrum factus, ad portās Rōmae veniēbat et urbem occupāre parābat. Veturia cum aliīs ēgregiīs mulieribus Rōmānīs ad castra Coriolānī prōcessit pācemque petīvit. Coriolānus, verbīs mātris affectus, dīxit, 'Māter, Rōmam servāvistī.' "

"Et quī Rōmānus factīs Cloeliae nōn permōtus est?" dīxit Caecilia. "Captīva, ex castrīs Etrūscōrum, hostium Rōmānōrum, fūgit et trāns flūmen trānāvit."

"Eīs temporibus facilius erat fāmam merēre quod Rōmānī bellum gerēbant," dīxit Secunda. "Sed nunc pāx est. Quid mulierēs in pāce efficere possunt?"

"Multa!" respondit Caecilia. "Nōnne Virginēs Vestālēs officiīs sacrīs saepe Rōmam servāvērunt, deīs inimīcīs?[1] Et quis nōn Līviam[2] bonam memoriā tenēbit?"

"Sed in Forum nōn prōcēdunt."

"Nōnne Laelia ōrātiōnēs ēgregiās facere poterat?" Fulvia rogāvit. "Nōnne Hortēnsia causam Rōmānārum in Forō ēgit? In bellō cīvīlī triumvirī[3] mulierēs Rōmānās pecūniam dare iussērunt. Sed Hortēnsia in Forō dīxit: 'Cūr nōs

---

1 *when the gods were unfriendly (*ablative absolute)
2 *Livia,* wife of Augustus
3 *triumvirs,* a board of three officials

Northwind Picture Archives

Although men are mentioned more frequently in Roman literature and in everyday life, the influence of many women, especially the Vestal Virgins, cannot be overstated. They had enormous prestige. Chosen by lot from patrician families and inducted between the ages of six and ten, Vestals served for 30 years. In this engraving, the Vestal Virgins tend the sacred fire, one of their chief duties. They were to ensure that it never went out.

pecūniam dare dēbēmus? Nūllam auctōritātem in cīvitāte habēmus. Sī hostēs venient, pecūniam vōbīs dabimus, sed numquam prō cīvīlī bellō auxilium dabimus.' Hīs verbīs triumvirī concēdere coāctī sunt.

"Puerī Rōmānī dē hīs et dē Cornēliā, Claudiā, Lucrētiā, Tucciā, ipsā Caeciliā Metellā nostrā in lūdīs legunt audiuntque, et semper legent audientque dum Rōma manēbit. Mulierēs Rōmānae bonae cīvitātem mūniunt. Ubi perīcula venient, parātae semper erunt."

QUESTIONS

1. What did Cloelia do?
2. Who was Veturia's son?
3. Why did Coriolanus flee?
4. To what did Hortensia object?
5. What light does this story shed upon the status of women in Rome?

ADDITIONAL QUESTIONS
Why does Secunda think that boys and men have a better life than women? What things can women do in time of peace? Did Roman boys read about famous women? Why or why not?

Grammar

Form Review

Like the present system of first and second conjugation verbs, the present, imperfect, and future of third, third **–io**, and fourth conjugations are formed by starting with the present stem and adding the tense sign (if any) and the personal endings.

	PRESENT	
pōn**ō**	capi**ō**	mūni**ō**
pōn**is**	cap**is**	mūn**īs**
pōn**it**	cap**it**	mūn**it**
pōn**imus**	cap**imus**	mūn**īmus**
pōn**itis**	cap**itis**	mūn**ītis**
pōn**unt**	cap**iunt**	mūn**iunt**
	IMPERFECT	
ponē**bam**	capi**ēbam**	mūni**ēbam**
ponē**bās**	capi**ēbās**	mūni**ēbās**
ponē**bat**	capi**ēbat**	mūni**ēbat**
ponē**bāmus**	capi**ēbāmus**	mūni**ēbāmus**
ponē**bātis**	capi**ēbātis**	mūni**ēbātis**
ponē**bant**	capi**ēbant**	mūni**ēbant**
	FUTURE	
pōn**am**	capi**am**	mūni**am**
pōn**ēs**	capi**ēs**	mūni**ēs**
pōn**et**	capi**et**	mūni**et**
pōn**ēmus**	capi**ēmus**	mūni**ēmus**
pōn**ētis**	capi**ētis**	mūni**ētis**
pōn**ent**	capi**ent**	mūni**ent**

NOTE
Remind students that third **–iō** verbs retain the **–i** found in the first principal part even though the **–i** is not in the infinitive.

SUGGESTION
Do a quick drill with three to four verbs to establish the endings in students' minds. Then have them work in pairs, one writing at the blackboard and one dictating forms as you give them a verb and tense.

ORAL PRACTICE

1. Conjugate **fugiō** and **veniō** in the present, imperfect, and future indicative active.
2. Give the second singular of **gerō** and the first plural of **audiō** in the present, imperfect, and future indicative active.
3. Decline **magna cīvitās.**

WORKBOOK
Assign Ex. A to review verb forms.

Giraudon/Art Resource, NY

Livia Drusilla (58 B.C. - A.D. 29) was the second wife of the emperor Augustus. She was also the mother of Tiberius, Augustus' successor. During Augustus' reign, she became his esteemed counselor and ran his domestic life with integrity and grace.

Syntax Review

The Ablative of Means

The means or instrument by which something is done is expressed by the ablative without a preposition.

Mīlitem gladiō interfēcit.	*He killed the soldier with a sword.*
Id litterīs nūntiāvērunt.	*They announced it in a letter.*

The Infinitive Used as Subject and Object

Although the infinitive is a verb, it it sometimes used as the subject of a conjugated verb, generally the verb *to be*. In this case it is called a verbal noun and is singular and neuter.

Natāre facile est.	*It is easy to swim./To swim is easy.*
Esse grātum bonum est.	*To be pleasant is good.*

The infinitive is often used to complete the meaning of certain verbs that cannot stand alone. When it is used this way, it is called a complementary infinitive.

Adesse nōn potest.	*He is not able to be here.*
Excēdere mox debēmus.	*We ought to leave soon.*

TRANSLATION

1. Can girls in these times win fame by good deeds?
2. Coriolanus did not occupy the city with his troops.
3. It was not easy for many Roman women at that time to earn money.
4. Will the men order the women to give money or will Hortensia's words compel the men to yield?

SUGGESTION
Go back over the story and have students find all instances of the ablatives of means, *time when*, and accompaniment.

WORKBOOK
Assign Ex. B, C to review infinitives and the ablative of means.

ANSWERS
1. Puellaene hīs temporibus fāmam factīs bonīs merēre possunt? 2. Coriōlanus urbem (cum) copiīs suīs nōn occupāvit. 3. Eō/illō tempore nōn erat facile multīs fēminīs/mulieribus Rōmānīs pecūniam merēre. 4. Iubēbuntne virī feminas/mulierēs pecūniam dāre aut verba Hortēnsiae virōs concēdere cōgent?

PHOTRI/AISA

Women were responsible for the early education of their children, especially their daughters. They also got together to plan parties or celebrations. This scene of a Roman domestic interior is an early 19th century reconstruction. It portrays women's domestic activities.

Vocabulary Review

Nouns

cīvitās	**fuga**	**pāx**

Adjectives

ēgregius	**facilis**

Verbs

afficiō	**faciō**	**mūniō**
agō	**fugiō**	**occupō**
cōgō	**gerō**	**veniō**
dō	**iubeō**	

Word Studies

Review the prefixes **ad–**, **in–**, and **con–**, noting carefully that assimilation may take place, depending upon the initial sound of the base to which the prefix is attached.

Define **admoveō, inveniō, confundō, commoveō;** *accede, impel, inquire, comprehend.*

Apply the proper form of the prefix and define the resulting English compound: **(ad)** *–similate, –gressive, –sent, –tribute;* **(in)** *–duce, –pede, –vert;* **(con)** *–fection, –lect, –mission, –rupt.*

LESSON OBJECTIVE
To review the perfect, pluperfect, and future perfect of all conjugations and **sum**

LESSON IV

Days with Books and Writers

[1] *hung*

STUDY TOPICS
Books and libraries

In pulchrō templō Apollinis, quod Augustus in bellō vōverat et posteā in Palātīnō cōnfēcerat, erat bibliothēca pūblica ubi multī librī, et Graecī et Latīnī, continēbantur. Ibi Pūblius et Fūriānus saepe diū manēbant. Saepe per partem urbis in quā librāriōrum tabernae erant ambulābant. Prō tabernīs pendēbant[1] librī ab auctōribus et novīs et nōtīs scrīptī. In tabernīs servī librāriōrum semper librōs dēscrībēbant. Magna taberna Sosiōrum grātissima Fūriānō Pūbliōque erat.

Quondam P. Ovidius Nāsō, poēta Rōmānīs eō tempore grātus, carmina legere parāvit. P. Caecilius Rūfus, pater Pūblī, amīcum poētae nōverat; itaque Rūfus cum amīcō et cum fīliō Fūriānōque ad aedificium in quō Ovidius habitāvit prōcessit. Magnum erat studium Pūblī et Fūriānī; multa enim carmina Ovidī in tabernā Sosiōrum vīderant et explicāverant, et saepe Ovidium ipsum vidēre cupīverant. In viā Rūfus amīcusque multa dē poētīs dīcēbant.

"Ovidius poēta optimus est," amīcus clāmāvit. "Ubi hominēs nōmina omnium aliōrum poētārum quī nunc sunt ex memoriā dēposuerint, nōmen Ovidī remanēbit."

"Bonus est, sed nōn est melior quam Vergilius et Horātius, quōs puerī audiēbāmus. Meliōrēs quam illī erant Rōma neque vīdit neque audīvit," dīxit Rūfus.

"Certē, certē, *Aeneidem*,[1] *Carmen Saeculāre*[2] nōn scrīpsit; *Amōrēs* et aliī librī eius grātī, nōn ēgregiī sunt. Sed multa dē novō librō eius, quī *Metamorphōsēs*[3] appellātur, audīvī."

"Augustusne eum librum vīdit?"

"Id nōn sciō. Ovidius autem Augustō nōn grātissimus esse vidētur. Augustus Horātium et Vergilium memoriā tenet."

---

[1] *The Aeneid*, an epic poem by Vergil
[2] *The Secular Hymn*, a poem by Horace written for Secular (i.e., Century) Games
[3] "Transformations," a long poem dealing with supernatural changes, or miracles, from the creation of the world out of chaos to the fabled transformation of Julius Caesar into a star

Ad aedificium in quō Ovidius habitābat vēnerant, et Ovidius iam librum novum recitābat. Carmen dē Orpheō et uxōre eius lēgit. Pūblius et Fūriānus magnō cum studiō audīvērunt. Carmine lēctō, ex aedificiō tardē excessērunt.

"Poēta certē est!" erant verba Pūblī.

QUESTIONS

1. In what library did Publius read?
2. Where else did he see many books?
3. How did he come to appreciate Ovid's *Metamorphoses?*
4. Which poets did Augustus prefer?

Scala/Art Resource, NY

Augustus was the first emperor in the Julio-Claudian line. The adopted son of Julius Caesar, he understood well the importance of propaganda. He encouraged the leading writers and poets of his day, especially Vergil and Horace, to glorify Rome's and Augustus' achievements in their works.

Grammar

Form Review

The perfect, pluperfect, and future perfect tenses make up the perfect system. For all conjugations, these tenses are formed by dropping the **–i** from the third principal part (which gives you the perfect stem), then adding a tense sign if necessary and the personal endings.

		PERFECT		
portāv**ī**	docu**ī**	posu**ī**	cēp**ī**	mūnīv**ī**
portāv**istī**	docu**istī**	posu**istī**	cēp**isti**	mūnīv**istī**
portāv**it**	docu**it**	posu**it**	cēp**it**	mūnīv**it**
portāv**imus**	docu**imus**	posu**imus**	cēp**imus**	mūnīv**imus**
portāv**istis**	docu**istis**	posu**istis**	cēp**istis**	mūnīv**istis**
portāv**ērunt**	docu**ērunt**	posu**ērunt**	cēp**ērunt**	mūnīv**ērunt**
		PLUPERFECT		
portāv**eram**	docu**eram**	posu**eram**	cēp**eram**	mūnīv**eram**
portāv**erās**	docu**erās**	posu**erās**	cēp**erās**	mūnīv**erās**
portāv**erat**	docu**erat**	posu**erat**	cēp**erat**	mūnīv**erat**
portāv**erāmus**	docu**erāmus**	posu**erāmus**	cēp**erāmus**	mūnīv**erāmus**
portāv**erātis**	docu**erātis**	posu**erātis**	cēp**erātis**	mūnīv**erātis**
portāv**erant**	docu**erant**	posu**erant**	cēp**erant**	mūnīv**erant**
		FUTURE PERFECT		
portāv**erō**	docu**erō**	posu**erō**	cēp**erō**	mūnīv**erō**
portāv**eris**	docu**eris**	posu**eris**	cēp**eris**	mūnīv**eris**
portāv**erit**	docu**erit**	posu**erit**	cēp**erit**	mūnīv**erit**
portāv**erimus**	docu**erimus**	posu**erimus**	cēp**erimus**	mūnīv**erimus**
portāv**eritis**	docu**eritis**	posu**eritis**	cēp**eritis**	mūnīv**eritis**
portāv**erint**	docu**erint**	posu**erint**	cēp**erint**	mūnīv**erint**

NOTE
The story of Orpheus and Eurydice is in Unit X.

ADDITIONAL QUESTIONS
In what languages were the books written? What were the titles of some famous works and who wrote them?

WORKBOOK
Assign Ex. A to review the perfect system.

NOTĀ·BENE

The personal endings in the perfect tense are different from all others.

The perfect, pluperfect, and future perfect of **sum** *are formed regularly.*

PERFECT		PLUPERFECT		FUTURE PERFECT	
fuī	fu**imus**	fu**eram**	fu**erāmus**	fu**erō**	fu**erimus**
fu**istī**	fu**istis**	fu**erās**	fu**erātis**	fu**eris**	fu**eritis**
fu**it**	fu**ērunt**	fu**erat**	fu**erant**	fu**erit**	fu**erint**

ORAL PRACTICE

1. Conjugate **videō** and **occupō** in the perfect indicative active.
2. Give the third person singular of **dīcō** and the third plural of **veniō** in all tenses of the indicative active.

TRANSLATION

1. Augustus completed a beautiful temple of Apollo on the Palatine.
2. Publius had read many books written by Greek and Latin authors.
3. Publius had read many poems of Ovid but had not seen the poet himself.
4. "Ovid is certainly a good poet," said Publius to his father, "but Rome will always remember Vergil."

SUGGESTION
Now that students have reviewed all tenses of the indicative, have them do a brief synopsis on the board, working in pairs, e.g., **dīcō** in 3rd sing, **moneō** in 1st pl, **veniō** in 2nd pl.

ANSWERS
1. Augustus templum pulchrum Apollinis in Palātīnō cōnfēcit. 2. Pūblius multōs librōs scrīptōs ab auctoribus Graecīs et Latīnīs lēgerat. 3. Pūblius multa carmina Ovidī lēgerat sed poetam ipsum non viderat. 4. "Ovidius bonus poēta certē est," Pūblius patrī suō dīxit, "sed Rōma Vergilium semper memoriā tenēbit."

Giraudon/Art Resource, NY

Publius Vergilius Maro, or simply Vergil, was one of Rome's finest poets. His first works include the ***Eclogues****, ten poems praised for their beautiful and charming descriptions of pastoral landscapes; the* ***Georgics****, a poem in four books dedicated to the art of farming; and the* ***Aeneid****, an epic poem that tells of the wanderings of Aeneas and the founding of Rome.*

Vocabulary Review

WORKBOOK
Assign Ex. B, C to review prepositions.

NOTE
Have students identify **pars** as an **i**-stem.

Nouns

amīcus
auctor
homō
pars

Adjectives

grātus
novus

Verbs

clāmō
cōnficiō
contineō
cupiō
dīcō
maneō
nōscō
scrībō
videō, videor

Adverb

autem

Word Studies

Review the prefixes **re–, prō–, sub–** in the Appendix. Only **sub–** is assimilated. **Re–** adds a *d* before vowels and before forms of **dō**.

Define according to the prefix: **recēdō, redigō, reddō, redūcō, prōmoveō, prōpellō, succēdō, sustineō;** *recession, refer, proclaim, provide, subtract.*

Use the proper form of the prefix **sub–:** *–ficient, –ject, –cession, –gest, –port.*

Explain by derivation: *resurrection, cogent, remain, subvention, refugee, affection, repatriation, resumption.*

LESSON OBJECTIVES
To review the passive voice (formation) of all conjugations; To review the formation and use of participles; To review the ablative absolute and the ablative of agent

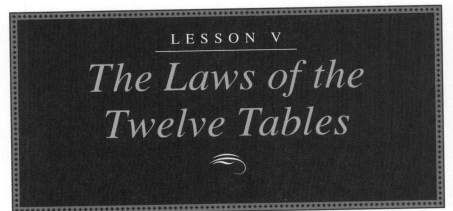

LESSON V
The Laws of the Twelve Tables

STUDY TOPIC
Many interesting fragments of the Twelve Tables can be found in E. H. Warmington's, *Remains of Old Latin,* Vol. III (Loeb Classical Library), London and Cambridge, MA, 1957.

Quondam haec verba ā Pūbliō recitābantur, Secundā, sorōre parvā, audiente: "Adversus hostem aeterna auctōritās."[1]

Dē hīs verbīs Secunda Pūblium rogātūra erat, sed hic in Forum excesserat. Itaque Rūfus pater ā Secundā petītus est. Rūfō inventō, Secunda rogāvit: "Quid est 'Adversus hostem aeterna auctōritās'? Pūblium haec dīcentem audīvī."

Pater explicāvit: "Haec sunt verba dē Lēgibus Duodecim Tabulārum lēcta, quae ab omnibus puerīs Rōmānīs memoriae semper mandātae sunt, ab eō tempore quō scrīptae sunt."

"Quō tempore scrīptae sunt?"

"Prīmīs annīs cīvitātis, ubi Decemvirī potestātem habuērunt. Diū lēgēs Rōmānōrum, memoriā hominum retentae, nōn scrīptae erant. Sed ā populō Rōmānō scrīptae lēgēs petītae sunt, quod multae gravēs iniūriae ab hominibus verba lēgum nōn scientibus acceptae erant. Cōnsiliō clārissimōrum hominum cīvitātis petītō, hic modus, optimus inventus est: trēs virī clārī in Graeciam missī sunt, ubi lēgēs Graecōrum cognōvērunt. Aliī ad Hermodōrum, Graecum in Italiā habitantem, missī sunt. Etiam nunc statua Hermodōrī, ā Rōmānīs posita, in Comitiō stat. Tum summa potestās cīvitātis decem virīs data est, quī iussī sunt lēgēs Rōmānās dēscrībere. Ubi hī virī, Appiō Claudiō prīncipe, diū labōrāvērunt, magnum opus cōnfectum est. Lēgēs, in tabulīs duodecim scrīptae, in Forō positae sunt. Ibi ab omnibus per multōs annōs vīsae sunt, et ibi nunc videntur."

"Eās saepe vīdī. Sed quae sunt illae lēgēs?"

"Multae sunt—dē poenīs, dē iniūriīs, dē familiīs, dē patriā potestāte, dē dēbitīs, dē viīs, dē sepulchrīs—dē iūre Rōmānō. Multae aliae lēgēs posteā lātae[1] sunt, sed Lēgibus Duodecim Tabulārum potestās Rōmāna cōnfirmāta est. Ubi illae lēgēs āmissae erunt, tum potestās Rōmae āmissa erit; illīs manentibus, Rōma aeterna erit."

[1] *proposed*

---

[1] *Against a foreigner the right* (*in property shall be*) *everlasting;* e.g., a Roman citizen could obtain legal possession of public land by settling on it, a foreigner could not.

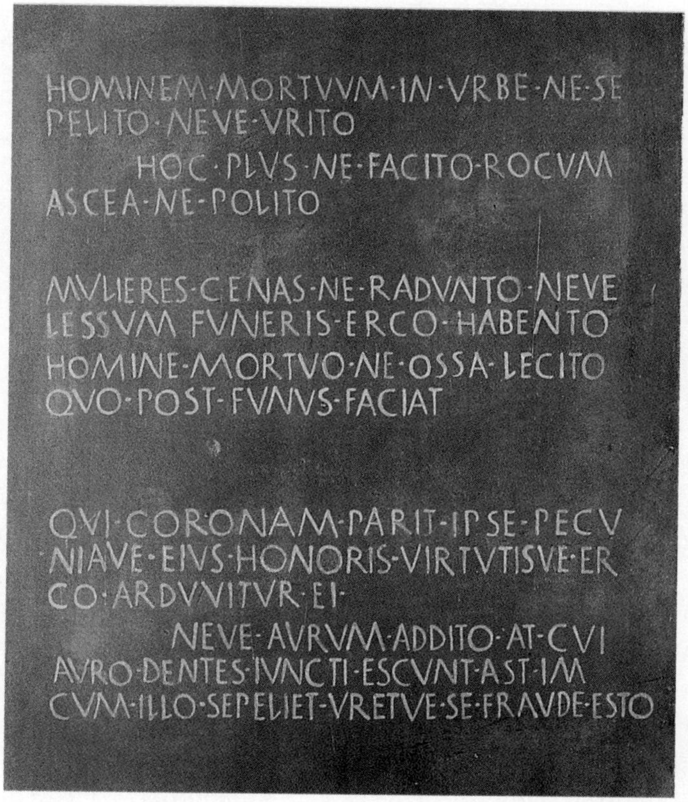
HOMINEM·MORTVVM·IN·VRBE·NE·SE
PELITO·NEVE·VRITO
HOC·PLVS·NE·FACITO·ROGVM
ASCEA·NE·POLITO
MVLIERES·GENAS·NE·RADVNTO·NEVE
LESSVM·FVNERIS·ERGO·HABENTO
HOMINE·MORTVO·NE·OSSA·LEGITO
QVO·POST·FVNVS·FACIAT
QVI·CORONAM·PARIT·IPSE·PECV
NIAVE·EIVS·HONORIS·VIRTVTISVE·ER
GO·ARDVVITVR·EI·
NEVE·AVRVM·ADDITO·AT·CVI
AVRO·DENTES·IVNCTI·ESCVNT·AST·IM
CVM·ILLO·SEPELIET·VRETVE·SE·FRAVDE·ESTO

Archivio e Studio Folco Quilici

Tablets containing the Laws of the Twelve Tables. They were first put together in the 5th century B.C. They include important information on the rules of court procedure (lawsuits, witnesses, etc.), property (wills, protection), crimes, rights, damage, the relationship between a ***patronus*** *and his* ***clientes****, the disposal of the dead, as well as rules against bewitching crops or making incantations.*

QUESTIONS

1. What were the Twelve Tables?
2. What is meant by squatter's rights?
3. Who was the most important of the Decemvirs?
4. Compare the origin of the Twelve Tables with that of the United States Constitution.

ADDITIONAL QUESTIONS
Who was Hermodorus? Who were the Decemvirs? What are some of the topics that are discussed in the Twelve Tables?

Grammar

Form Review

The Passive Voice

The passive voice is used to indicate that the action of the verb is being received by the subject, rather than being done by the subject. The present system is formed from the present stem. A different set of personal endings is used.

SUGGESTION
Have students work in pairs to produce a full synopsis, active and passive, as quickly and as accurately as possible.

		PRESENT		
port**or**	doce**or**	pōn**or**	capi**or**	mūni**or**
portā**ris**	docē**ris**	pōne**ris**	cape**ris**	mūnī**ris**
portā**tur**	docē**tur**	pōni**tur**	capi**tur**	mūnī**tur**
portā**mur**	docē**mur**	pōni**mur**	capi**mur**	mūnī**mur**
portā**minī**	docē**minī**	pōni**minī**	capi**minī**	mūnī**minī**
port**antur**	doc**entur**	pōn**untur**	capi**untur**	mūni**untur**
		IMPERFECT		
portā**bar**	docē**bar**	pōnē**bar**	capiē**bar**	mūniē**bar**
portā**bāris**	docē**bāris**	pōnē**bāris**	capiē**bāris**	mūniē**bāris**
portā**bātur**	docē**bātur**	pōnē**bātur**	capiē**bātur**	mūniē**bātur**
portā**bāmur**	docē**bāmur**	pōnē**bāmur**	capiē**bāmur**	mūniē**bāmur**
portā**bāminī**	docē**bāminī**	pōnē**bāminī**	capiē**bāminī**	mūniē**bāminī**
portā**bantur**	docē**bantur**	pōnē**bantur**	capiē**bantur**	mūniē**bantur**
		FUTURE		
portā**bor**	docē**bor**	pōn**ar**	capi**ar**	mūni**ar**
portā**beris**	docē**beris**	pōn**ēris**	capi**ēris**	mūni**ēris**
portā**bitur**	docē**bitur**	pōn**ētur**	capi**ētur**	mūni**ētur**
portā**bimur**	docē**bimur**	pōn**ēmur**	capi**ēmur**	mūni**ēmur**
portā**biminī**	docē**biminī**	pōn**ēminī**	capi**ēminī**	mūni**ēminī**
portā**buntur**	docē**buntur**	pōn**entur**	capi**entur**	mūni**entur**

The perfect system passives of all verbs are formed by using the fourth principal part (perfect passive participle) plus a conjugated form of **sum**.

WORKBOOK
Assign Ex. A to review the passive voice.

CASSETTE
Do Unit I, Drill 3, Ex. A to practice the present and perfect; Ex. B to practice the present and imperfect; Ex. C to practice the future; and Ex. D to practice the perfect and pluperfect.

PERFECT	PLUPERFECT	FUTURE PERFECT
portāt**us, –a, –um** sum	doct**us, –a, –um** eram	posit**us, –a, –um** erō
portāt**us, –a, –um** es	doct**us, –a, –um** erās	posit**us, –a, –um** eris
portāt**us, –a, –um** est	doct**us, –a, –um** erat	posit**us, –a, –um** erit
portāt**ī, –ae, –a** sumus	doct**ī, –ae, –a** erāmus	posit**ī, –ae, –a** erimus
portāt**ī, –ae, –a** estis	doct**ī, –ae, –a** eratis	posit**ī, –ae, –a** eritis
portāt**ī, –ae, –a** sunt	doct**ī, –ae, –a** erant	posit**ī, –ae, –a** erunt

Participles

SUGGESTION
Remind students that participles are used much more commonly in Latin than in English.

There are four participles in Latin: present active, perfect passive, future active, and future passive. The future passive participle will be discussed in Lesson XXI.

The present participle is formed from the present stem and is declined like a third declension **i–**stem; the perfect participle is the fourth principle part; and the future participle is formed by dropping the **–us** from the perfect passive participle and adding **–ūrus**.

PRESENT ACTIVE	PERFECT PASSIVE	FUTURE ACTIVE
port**āns**	portāt**us**	portāt**ūrus**
doc**ēns**	doct**us**	doct**ūrus**
pōn**ens**	posit**us**	posit**ūrus**
capi**ēns**	capt**us**	capt**ūrus**
mūni**ēns**	mūnīt**us**	mūnīt**ūrus**

NOTA · BENE

Participles are verbal adjectives and must agree with the noun they modify, whether it is stated or understood, in gender, number, and case.

ORAL PRACTICE

1. Conjugate **āmittō** in the present passive, **inveniō** in the future passive, and **mandō** in the perfect passive.
2. Give the third singular of **āmittō** and the third plural of **cōnficiō** in the six passive tenses of the indicative.
3. Form and translate the participles of **pōnō, dō, videō.**
4. Give in Latin: *having been said* (acc. sing. neut.); *recognizing* (dat. plur.); *going to entrust* (gen. sing. fem.); *standing* (nom. plur. fem.); *having been sent* (abl. sing. neut.)

WORKBOOK
Assign Ex. B to review participles.

Syntax Review

Perfect Participles Used as Adjectives and Nouns

Perfect passive participles are often used simply as adjectives.

Mīlitēs parātī sunt.	*The soldiers are prepared/ready.*

They can also be used as nouns.

Factum celeriter confectum est.	*The deed (done thing) was finished quickly.*

Participles Used as Clauses

A participle can often be a one-word substitute for a whole clause introduced by *who, which, when, after, since, because, although,* or *if* in English.

Līberōs ludentēs spectāvī.	*I watched the children who were playing.*
Librum lectum eī dedistī.	*After you read the book, you gave it to him.*

Ablative Absolute

This commonly used construction in Latin is a combination of two words in the ablative: a noun plus a noun, a noun plus an adjective, or a noun plus a participle. The words must not be grammatically connected to the rest of the sentence.

Marcō patre, sententia facta est.	*Since Marcus was the father, the decision was made.*
Flūmine altō, līberī terrēbant.	*Because the river was deep, the children were afraid.*
Urbe oppugnātā, fugere constituimus.	*After the city was attacked, we decided to flee.*

Ablative of Agent

The ablative is used with the preposition **ā** or **ab** after a passive verb to show the person (or animal) by whom something is done.

Ab equīs portābāmur.	*We were being carried by the horses.*
Ā nuntiō dictī sumus.	*We were told by the messenger.*

Archivio e Studio Folco Quilici

Since the Roman Forum was the area where business was transacted and political speeches were made, it was fitting that the Laws of the Twelve Tables would be displayed here for all to see and use as a reference. That way, plebeians were assured of fairness. Prominent in the photo is the Senate House (the Curia) and near it the Arch of Septimius Severus.

TRANSLATION

1. Secunda heard Publius reciting strange words.
2. Having found her father, Secunda asked about the words (which she had) heard.
3. Her father said: "The words (which you have) heard were selected from the laws."
4. "These words were written on tablets under the direction of Appius Claudius."
5. "These laws, placed in the Forum, can be seen by all Romans. While they remain,[2] we shall be free."

ANSWERS
1. Secunda Pūblium recitantem verba nova audīvit. 2. Patre inventō, Secunda dē verbīs audītīs rogāvit. 3. Pater eius dīxit, "Verba audīta dē lēgibus lēcta (dēlēcta) sunt." 4. "Haec verba in tabulīs scrīpta sunt, Appiō Claudiō prīncipe/duce. 5. "Hae lēgēs positae in Forō ab omnibus Rōmānīs vidērī possunt. Hīs manentibus, līberī erimus."

Vocabulary Review

Nouns

annus
auctōritās
iūs
lēx
modus
opus
prīnceps

PRESENTATION
Choose a noun and an adjective from this list for a quick oral declension drill. Verify orally that students can produce all the essential facts.

Adjectives

gravis
hostis

Verbs

āmittō
audiō
cognōscō
inveniō
mandō
mittō
petō
pōnō
sciō
stō

Adverb

ubi

Word Studies

Review the prefixes **in–** (*negative*), **dis–**, **per–** in the Appendix. All three may be assimilated. **Per–**, like **con–**, may have the intensive meaning "very," or "thoroughly." Define according to the prefix: **inimīcus, impius, dispōnō, diffundō, perficiō, perlegō;** *inaudible, independent, disperse, permission.*

Select the proper form of each prefix: **(in)** *–legal, –proper, –responsible;* **(dis)** *–gest, –vert, –claim;* **(per)** *–manent, –turb, –lucid.* Explain by derivation: *imperfect, incognito, command, differ, invisible, ignoble.*

---

[2] Use ablative absolute.

LESSON OBJECTIVES
To review the formation and uses of infinitives of all conjugations; To review relative pronouns

LESSON VI

The Senate in Session

Pūblius per iānuam vēnit, ad quam Fulvia māter diū exspectāverat.

"Ubi fuistī?" Fulvia rogāvit. "Tardus es."

"Ad Cūriam Iūliam cum patre prōcessī," Pūblius respondit. "Putō patrem iam ventūrum esse. In Comitiō, ad Cūriam, stābam. Iānuā nōn clausā, multa audīvī et vīdī. Multī patrēs,[1] inter quōs clārissimōs cīvitātis vīdī, per viās in Cūriam convēnērunt. Quibus iam sedentibus, cōnsulēs accessērunt, tum Augustus ipse. Post sacrificium nūntiātum est ōmina bona esse. Tum Augustus litterās multās et longās lēgit."

"Dē quō?"

"Audīre nōn poteram, quod multī puerī ad iānuam stābant, virōs prementēs et clāmantēs. Quem putās eōs dīmīsisse? Fūriānus hoc fēcit! Puerīs dīxit Augustum, prīncipem cīvitātis, patrēs dē gravibus rēbus cōnsulere; deōs vocātōs esse et adesse; eōs puerōs clāmantēs deīs iniūriam facere; eōs poenam datūrōs esse—haec et multa alia. Quō modō, nōn vīdī; sed coēgit puerōs discēdere. Magnam vōcem habet; puerōs eum timuisse putō. Augustus iam rogābat, 'Quās litterās habētis?' et patrēs litterās legere iubēbat. Litterīs omnibus lēctīs, cōnsul verba fēcit: multōs Rōmānōs clārōs ā servīs oppressōs et interfectōs esse; aliīs auxilium ā servīs nōn datum esse; hoc malum esse; servōs cīvis Rōmānī interfectī prehendī et torquērī dēbēre et tum interficī."

"Cuius modī erant sententiae?"

"Paene omnēs patrēs sēnsērunt cōnsilium cōnsulis bonum futūrum esse; paucī putāvērunt dūrum futūrum esse. Augustus nūntiāvit maiōrem partem patrum cōnsilium cōnsulis probāre."

"Quae erat sententia patris tuī?"

"Verba multa nōn fēcit, et ea audīre nōn poteram; sed putō eum in parte cōnsulis sēnsisse. Sententiīs datīs, Augustus dīxit: 'Nihil[2] vōs teneō,' et omnēs patrēs ex Cūriā discessērunt."

[1] *senators*
[2] *not*

STUDY TOPIC
Qualifications for membership in the **Senatus** and **Equester Ordo**

QUESTIONS

1. What did Furianus do?
2. What was the consul's motion?
3. In what way was the meeting of the senate opened?
4. Compare the Roman senate with that of the United States senate.

ADDITIONAL QUESTIONS
What did Augustus do after the sacrifice? Why couldn't Publius hear everything? What was the big issue that was brought before the Senate?

Robert E. Bright/Photo Researchers

Roman Senators wielded much power. It was before the Senate that legal cases were argued. They met in the Curia. (See photo and caption on page 30.)

Grammar

Form Review

Infinitives

Infinitives have three tenses—present, perfect, and future, and two voices—active and passive. There is no future passive infinitive.

PRESENT ACTIVE

The present active infinitive is the second principal part.

portāre **docēre** **pōnere** **capere** **mūnīre**

PRESENT PASSIVE

To form the present passive infinitive, the first, second, and fourth conjugations change the **–e** of the present active infinitive to **–ī**. Third conjugation verbs change **–ere** to **–ī**.

portārī **docērī** **pōnī** **capī** **mūnīrī**

PERFECT ACTIVE

The perfect active infinitive is formed by adding **–isse** to the perfect stem.

portāvisse **docuisse** **posuisse** **cēpisse** **mūnīvisse**

PERFECT PASSIVE

To form the perfect passive infinitive, use the perfect passive participle (fourth principal part) plus **esse**.

portātus, –a, –um esse	**doctus, –a, –um esse**
positus, –a, –um esse	**captus, –a, –um esse**
mūnītus, –a, –um esse	

FUTURE ACTIVE

To form the future active infinitive, use the perfect passive participle, drop the **–us**, and add **–ūrus** plus **esse**.

portātūrus, –a, –um esse	**doctūrus, –a, –um esse**
positūrus, –a, –um esse	**captūrus, –a, –um esse**
mūnītūrus, –a, –um esse	

The infinitives of **sum** are as follows:

PRESENT ACTIVE	**esse**
PERFECT PASSIVE	**fuisse**
FUTURE ACTIVE	**futūrus, –a, –um esse**

Relative Pronouns and Interrogative Pronouns and Adjectives

The relative pronoun and the interrogative adjective are declined as follows.

NOTE
Remind students that the purpose of an interrogative is to ask questions. Have them make up some simple questions in class and work with a partner to answer them (in English), e.g., **Quis est dux patriae nostrae? Cuius liber est? Quī diēs est?**

SINGULAR			PLURAL		
M	F	N	M	F	N
quī	quae	quod	quī	quae	quae
cuius	cuius	cuius	quōrum	quārum	quōrum
cui	cui	cui	quibus	quibus	quibus
quem	quam	quod	quōs	quās	quae
quō	quā	quō	quibus	quibus	quibus

Vanni/Art Resource, NY

*Exterior of the Pantheon. The inscription says, "Marcus Agrippa, son of Lucius, having been consul three times, built it." (**M . AGRIPPA . L . F. COS . TERTIUM . FECIT**). Note the great dome which holds the crown or oculus, the round opening which lets the light into the building. The Pantheon was probably a temple to all the gods before it was converted into a church in* A.D. *609. (See copyright page for more information.)*

The interrogative pronoun is declined as follows in the singular. The plural is declined the same as **quī**.

M+F	N
quis	quid
cuius	cuius
cui	cui
quem	quid
quō	quō

WORKBOOK
Assign Ex. C to review **quī** and **quis**.

ORAL PRACTICE

1. Give the present infinitive, active and passive, of **sentiō, cōgō,** and **appellō;** the future infinitive active of **accēdō, exspectō,** and **respondeō;** the perfect infinitive, active and passive, of **afficiō, nūntiō,** and **probō.**
2. Give the Latin for *whose* (plur.); *whom?* (fem. sing.); *to whom* (masc. sing.); *what?* (nom. sing.); *who?* (fem. sing.); *by whom* (plur.); *whose?* (masc. sing.); *to whom?* (plur.); *by whom* (fem. sing.); *what?* (acc. sing.).

CASSETTE
Do Unit I, Drill 4, Ex. A to review indirect statements.

NOTĀ·BENE

Notice that the actions are happening at the same time, not necessarily in the present, although a present infinitive is used.

SUGGESTION
Review many simple sentences until students are comfortable with the concept of *same time, time before,* and *time after.*

WORKBOOK
Assign Ex. A to review infinitives.

WORKBOOK
Assign Ex. B to review indirect statement.

CASSETTE
Do Unit I, Drill 5, Ex. B to review questions.

NOTĀ·BENE

Remember that the subject of the infinitive is always in the accusative.

Syntax Review

Tenses of the Infinitive

You know that the infinitive has three tenses—present, perfect, and future. The *present infinitive* is used to indicate that the action of the infinitive is occurring at the same time as that of the main verb.

Sciō tē pugnāre.	*I know that you are fighting.*
Scīvī tē pugnāre.	*I knew that you were fighting.*

The *perfect infinitive* is used to indicate that the action of the infinitive happened before that of the main verb.

Sciō tē pugnāvisse.	*I know that you were fighting.*
Scīvī tē pugnāvisse.	*I knew that you had fought.*

The *future infinitive* is used to indicate that the action of the infinitive happened after that of the main verb.

Sciō tē pugnātūrum esse.	*I know that you will fight.*
Scīvī tē pugnātūrum esse.	*I knew that you would fight.*

Indirect Statement

Indirect statements retell (indirectly) someone else's words. In Latin, this is done by using the infinitive after a verb of *saying, knowing, telling, hearing, perceiving,* etc. The preceding sentences are all in indirect statement because they are reporting the words that were once a direct quote, "You are fighting."

Dixit Caesarem magnum ducem esse.	*He said that Caesar was a great leader.*

Relative Pronouns

Relative pronouns are used to join two sentences or clauses. The relative pronoun must agree with its antecedent in gender and number, but takes its case from its own clause. In Latin, a relative pronoun can be used at the beginning of a sentence to refer to the thought of the preceding sentence. Generally, in English, this is translated by using a demonstrative.

Est nauta quem vīdī.	*He is the sailor whom I saw.*
Quā dē causā, excessī.	*For this reason, I left.*

TRANSLATION

1. Publius had heard that the consuls would come to the Forum.
2. The consul reported that many Romans were being killed by slaves.
3. Fulvia asked: "Did your father feel that the consul's opinion was good?"
4. Fulvia did not know that Publius had been with her father in the Forum.

NOTĀ·BENE

Occasionally, the antecedent is omitted in Latin, and sometimes it represents an entire clause. In this case, the pronoun is best translated by a thing which.

ANSWERS
1. Pūblius cōnsulēs in Forum ventūrōs esse audīverat.
2. Cōnsul nūntiāvit multōs Rōmānōs ā servīs interficī.
3. Fulvia rogāvit: "Sēnsitne pater tuus cōnsulis sententiam esse bonam?" 4. Fulvia nōn scīvit Pūblium cum patre in Forō fuisse.

Vocabulary Review

Nouns

auxilium
consilium
poena
sententia
vōx

Adjective

tardus

Verbs

accēdō
adsum
claudō
dēbeō
dīmittō
exspectō
interficiō
nūntiō
opprimō
premō
probō
putō
sentiō
vocō

Word Studies

The suffix **–ia** and its various combinations **(–cia, –tia, –antia, –entia)** form many nouns in Latin. Note the way they change in English.

LATIN	ENGLISH
–ia	*–y* (usually)
–tia (or **–cia**)	*–ce*
–antia	*–ance, –ancy*
–entia	*–ence, –ency*

Give the English forms of **glōria, prōvincia, iniūria, clēmentia, cōnstantia, Germānia, iūstitia.**

What are the Latin words from which come *memory, providence, science, Thessaly, audience, instance*?

LESSON OBJECTIVES
To review the formation of irregular adjectives; To review the declension of **hic** and **ille**; To review the conjugation of **possum**; To review the ablative of respect

LESSON VII
Holidays

STUDY TOPICS
Salii, Vesta; read parts of Ovid's *Fasti* to learn about the variety of Roman festivals

Mēnsis Mārtius iam aderat—ōlim prīmus novī annī inter Rōmānōs. Omnēs Caeciliī servīque eōrum vestibus novīs īnsignēs erant. Negōtium nūllī hominī mandābātur, quod mūnera tōtīus cīvitātis ob fēriās dēposita erant. Pūblius Fūriānusque per Forum prōcēdēbant inter multōs hominēs, aliōs ad templum properantēs, aliōs stantēs, omnēs vestēs novās gerentēs. Pūbliō et Fūriānō[1] aedificia adōrnāta spectantibus,[1] per Forum nūntiātum est Vestālēs Virginēs ignem Vestae cum cūrā exstīnxisse māteriamque ad novum ignem iam collēgisse. Duo virī ad Pūblium stābant; alter alterī dīxit, "Bonum est. Illō igne semper manente, Rōma superārī nōn potest."

Nunc vōcēs audīrī poterant: "Saliī! Saliī veniunt!"

Illī per viās veniēbant, armātī et ancīlia ferentēs. Ūnum ex ancīlibus temporibus antīquīs dē caelō cecidisse dictum est. Rōmānī, nōn cupientēs hoc sacrum rapī, iusserant virum callidum alia huic similia facere. Itaque nēmō illud sacrum ancīle nunc cognōscere poterat. Saliī currēbant, ancīlia quae ferēbant ostendentēs. Officium hōrum erat mala ē portīs Rōmānīs expellere.

Aliae antīquissimae fēriae erant multae numerō, variae nātūrā et auctōritāte: Cereālia et Parīlia (vel Palīlia), hae fēriae pāstōrum, quōrum dea Palēs erat, illae agricolārum, quī Cererem colēbant; fēriae Latīnae, ubi omnēs Latīnī Iovem in monte Albānō colēbant; Cōnsuālia, ubi equī pede celerēs in Circō currēbant; Lupercālia, ubi duo virī per viās currēbant, rīdentēs et omnēs fēminās quās vidēbant verberantēs; Parentālia, ubi sepulchra tōtīus Rōmae adōrnābantur; et aliae. Pontificēs sōlī illās omnēs memoriā tenēre potuērunt, sed Pūblius aliīque puerī Rōmānī multās memoriā tenuērunt, quod, studiīs intermissīs, lūdere potuērunt.

QUESTIONS

ADDITIONAL QUESTIONS
What had been the first month of the year for the Romans? Who worked on the holiday? What did people wear on the holiday? Who were the Salii?

1. What did the Vestal Virgins do on March 1st?
2. What three festivals had something to do with the food supply?
3. What method was adopted of preventing the theft of the sacred shield?

---

[1] Ablative absolute

The Bettmann Archive

Roman festivals frequently included a parade or procession. Often the celebrants would march to the temple of a particular god or goddess, bringing offerings and gifts. The New Year, the Saturnalia, and the Lupercalia were joyous celebrations for all. This painting is a 19th century reconstruction of such a festival.

Grammar

Form Review

Irregular Adjectives

There are a few groups of irregular adjectives in Latin. Their declensions are as follows.

M	F	N	M+F	N
ūnus	ūna	ūnum	trēs	tria
ūnīus	ūnīus	ūnīus	trium	trium
ūnī	ūnī	ūnī	tribus	tribus
ūnum	ūnam	ūnum	trēs	tria
ūnō	ūnā	ūnō	tribus	tribus

M	F	N		
duo	duae	duo	mīlle	mīlia
duōrum	duārum	duōrum	mīlle	mīlium
duōbus	duābus	duōbus	mīlle	mīlibus
duōs	duās	duo	mīlle	mīlia
duōbus	duābus	duōbus	mīlle	mīlibus

NOTE
You might tell students that **duo** and **ambo** are the only two words left over from the old "dual" form that was used for things that naturally came in twos.

Adjectives that are declined like **ūnus** are: **alius, alter, ūllus, nūllus, sōlus, tōtus, uter, uterque,** and **neuter**. The plurals are regular. **Ambō** is declined like **duo**.

WORKBOOK
Assign Ex. A to review irregular adjectives.

The Demonstratives *Hic* and *Ille*

The demonstratives **hic** *(this)* and **ille** *(that)* have irregular declensions.

WORKBOOK
Assign Ex. B to review **hic** and **ille**.

M	F	N	M	F	N
hic	haec	hoc	ille	illa	illud
huius	huius	huius	illīus	illīus	illīus
huic	huic	huic	illī	illī	illī
hunc	hanc	hoc	illum	illam	illud
hōc	hāc	hōc	illō	illā	illō
hī	hae	haec	illī	illae	illa
hōrum	hārum	hōrum	illiōrum	illārum	illōrum
hīs	hīs	hīs	illīs	illīs	illīs
hōs	hās	haec	illōs	illās	illa
hīs	hīs	hīs	illīs	illīs	illīs

The verb *Possum*

The verb **possum** is a compound of **sum** and many of its forms are similar. Remember that **possum** is generally followed by a complementary infinitive.

WORKBOOK
Assign Ex. C to review **possum**.

PRESENT	IMPERFECT	FUTURE
pos**sum**	pot**eram**	pot**erō**
pot**es**	pot**erās**	pot**eris**
pot**est**	pot**erat**	pot**erit**
pos**sumus**	pot**erāmus**	pot**erimus**
pot**estis**	pot**erātis**	pot**eritis**
pos**sunt**	pot**erant**	pot**erunt**
PERFECT	PLUPERFECT	FUTURE PERFECT
potu**ī**	potu**eram**	potu**erō**
potu**istī**	potu**erās**	potu**eris**
potu**it**	potu**erat**	potu**eris**
potu**imus**	potu**erāmus**	potu**erimus**
potu**istis**	potu**erātis**	potu**eritis**
potu**ērunt**	potu**erant**	potu**erint**

C. M. Dixon

Not only adults, but children took part in various celebrations and processions during the year. This wall painting from Ostia is from the late imperial period.

ORAL PRACTICE

1. Decline **hoc mūnus, alius nūntius, illa lēx.**
2. Give the third singular of **possum** in all tenses of the indicative.
3. Give all the participles and infinitives of **ostendō** and **exspectō.**
4. Give the third plural of **lūdō** in all tenses of the indicative, active and passive.

Syntax Review

Ablative of Respect

The ablative of respect, with no preposition, tells how a certain statement applies.

SUGGESTION
Have students do a quick review of all the ablatives they have reviewed thus far.

Magister me sapientiā superat.	*The teacher surpasses me in wisdom.*
Qui exercitus fortior virtute est?	*Which army is stronger in courage?*

Use of *Mille* and *Milia*

Mille is an indeclinable adjective; **milia** is a neuter **i–stem** noun that is followed by the genitive.

Mille milites urbem oppugnaverunt.	*A thousand soldiers attacked the city.*
Milia militum urbem oppugnaverunt.	*Thousands of soldiers attacked the city.*

TRANSLATION

ANSWERS
1. Feriae Rōmānae novae natūrā et multae numerō fuērunt. 2. Eīs temporibus negōtium tōtius populī semper depositum est. 3. Aliī ad Forum properābant, aliī ad templa celeriter procēdēbant. 4. Illī aedificia adōrnāta spectābant, hī deōs colēbant.

1. Roman holidays were strange in nature and many in number.
2. At these times the business of the entire people was always laid aside.
3. Some hastened to the Forum; others quickly proceeded to the temples.
4. The former looked at the decorated buildings; the latter worshiped the gods.

Ronald Sheridan/Ancient Art & Architecture Collection

Behind the House of the Vestal Virgins in the Roman Forum was a beautiful garden. In addition to ensuring that the sacred fire never went out, the Vestals tended the garden. The three pillars in the background are part of the Temple of Venus and Rome.

Vocabulary Review

Nouns

mēnsis
mūnus
numerus
pēs

NOTE
Have students identify **mēnsis** as an **i–**stem.

Adjectives

alius
alter
celer
nūllus
similis
tōtus

Verbs

cadō
currō
expellō
lūdō
ostendō
possum
properō
rapiō
spectō

Adverb

semper

Word Studies

Review the suffixes **–tās** (*–ty*), **–or** (*–or*), and **–iō** (*–ion*). (See the Appendix.)

Give the English forms of **nōbilitās, gravitās, condiciō, vocātiō.**

What are the Latin words from which are derived *utility, facility, paucity, production, retention?*

Give and define, according to their derivation, four English words formed by adding the suffix *–or* to the present base of Latin verbs which you have studied, and four others formed by adding this suffix to the stem of the perfect participle.

Give five English words formed by adding the suffix *–ion* to Latin verbs and five formed by adding the suffix *–ty* to Latin adjectives.

LESSON OBJECTIVES
To review the declensions of **is, īdem,** and **ipse**; To review the comparison of regular adjectives and adverbs; To review the dative with adjectives

STUDY TOPIC
Oracles, prophecies

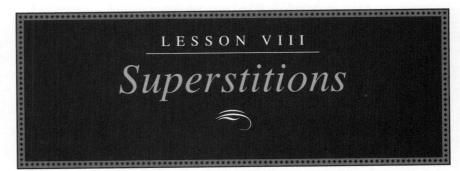

LESSON VIII

Superstitions

Quondam Rūfus, in Forum ad negōtium prōcēdēns, caelum spectāvit avēsque trēs in dextrā parte vīdit.

"Signum est!" dīxit. "Fortūna negōtiō meō amīca erit."

Ita accidit: negōtium bene ēvēnit; itaque Rūfus semper putāvit avēs fortūnam bonam eī negōtiō dedisse.

Plūrimī Rōmānī signa et ōmina semper exspectābant—in caelō, in terrā, in flūminibus. Putābant deōs ipsōs ad hominēs somnō oppressōs saepe accēdere et eōs monēre. Multī Rōmānī in templīs cōnsilium ā deīs petēbant; etiam ibi somnum capiēbant. Eī quī nōn valēbant Aesculāpium hōc modō cōnsulēbant; sed omnēs Apollinem hominibus ūtilissimum deōrum esse ob respōnsa eius putābant. Haec respōnsa plūrima, sed nōn saepe clārissima,[1] per pontificēs eius dabantur.

Rūfus, deōs familiae colēns, eadem verba semper dīcēbat, eadem mūnera sacra eōdem modō semper efficiēbat, familiā spectante. Putābātur, deīs nōn ita vocātīs, familiam gravissimam poenam datūram esse.

Etiam mortuōs Rōmānī cum cūrā colēbant, quod putābant hōs facillimē et celerrimē ad amīcōs in terrā manentēs venīre posse et eōs terrēre; et mortuōs, sepultūrā nōn datā, per omnēs terrās iter dūrum facientēs, multōs annōs in labōre gravī agere cōgī.

Tempore magnī perīculī deī et virī mortuī in viās ipsās vēnisse dictī sunt. Post pugnam Rēgillēnsem[2] Castor Polluxque in Forum vēnisse nūntiābantur. Caesare interfectō, virī mortuī et novissima animālia in viīs vidēbantur—ōmina gravissima, quae mōnstrāre putābantur fortūnam inimīcīs Caesaris dūram futūram esse.

Eō tempore fortūnam graviōrem et sacriōrem esse crēdēbant quam nunc. Virī quibus haec diū bona fuerat grātiōrēs deīs erant (ita putābant) quam eī quibus inimīca fuerat. Omnēs mīlitēs fortius et ācrius sub duce quī fortūnae grātus erat pugnābant—et ob eam causam saepius vincēbant.

Rōmānī, mala timentēs, stultī nōbīs videntur; sed nōnne ipsī multa eiusdem generis nunc facimus vel audīmus?

---

[1] The responses of the oracles were often so worded that they could be interpreted in two exactly opposite ways. So they were always right!

[2] The victory of the Romans *at Lake Regillus,* 498 B.C.

One of the Laws of the Twelve Tables decreed that cemeteries had to be built outside the city limits. As a result, they were usually placed along the main highways near the city, as is this family tomb on the Via Appia.

QUESTIONS

1. How does the belief in dreams among the Romans and among people today differ?
2. How does the belief in ghosts among the Romans and among people today differ?
3. How does the belief differ among the Romans and among people today that some persons are naturally lucky?

ADDITIONAL QUESTIONS
What did Rufus see on his way to the Forum? Was it a good or a bad omen? Where did the Romans look for signs? What did Rufus do when worshiping the family gods? What strange thing happened at Lake Regillus? What appeared after Caesar was assassinated?

Grammar

Form Review

The Declensions of *Is, Īdem,* and *Ipse*

The demonstratives **is** *(he, she, it, this, that)* and **īdem** *(the same, likewise)* and the emphatic **ipse** *(himself, herself, itself, the very)* are declined as follows:

	SINGULAR			PLURAL	
is	ea	id	eī	eae	ea
eius	eius	eius	eōrum	eārum	eōrum
eī	eī	eī	eīs	eīs	eīs
eum	eam	id	eōs	eās	ea
eō	eā	eō	eīs	eīs	eīs

	SINGULAR			PLURAL	
īdem	eadem	idem	eīdem	eaedem	eadem
eiusdem	eiusdem	eiusdem	eōrundem	eārundem	eōrundem
eīdem	eīdem	eīdem	eīsdem	eīsdem	eīsdem
eundem	eandem	idem	eōsdem	eāsdem	eadem
eōdem	eādem	eōdem	eīsdem	eīsdem	eīsdem

	SINGULAR			PLURAL	
ipse	ipsa	ipsum	ipsī	ipsae	ipsa
ipsīus	ipsīus	ipsīus	ipsōrum	ipsārum	ipsōrum
ipsī	ipsī	ipsī	ipsīs	ipsīs	ipsīs
ipsum	ipsam	ipsum	ipsōs	ipsās	ipsa
ipsō	ipsā	ipsō	ipsīs	ipsīs	ipsīs

SUGGESTION
Remind students that **is, ea, id** is also used for the third personal pronoun as well as for *this* and *that* when a distinction is not being made between two things.

WORKBOOK
Assign Ex. A to review **is, īdem,** and **ipse**.

NOTE
Point out that the neuter comparative adjective and the comparative adverb look similar.

WORKBOOK
Assign Ex. B to review the comparison of adjectives and adverbs.

NOTA·BENE

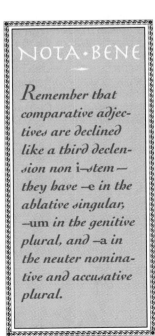

Remember that comparative adjectives are declined like a third declension non i–stem — they have –e *in the ablative singular,* –um *in the genitive plural, and* –a *in the neuter nominative and accusative plural.*

Comparison of Regular Adjectives and Adverbs

Adverbs formed from first and second declension adjectives add **–ē** to the base. Adverbs formed from third declension adjectives add **–iter** to the base. The comparative adjectives add **–ior** *(m., f.)* and **–ius** *(n.)* to the base and the comparative adverbs add **–ius**. The superlative adjectives add **–issimus (–rimus, –limus)** to the base and the superlative adverbs add **–ē** to the base of the superlative adjective.

POSITIVE		COMPARATIVE		SUPERLATIVE	
ADJECTIVE	ADVERB	ADJECTIVE	ADVERB	ADJECTIVE	ADVERB
alt**us**	alt**ē**	alt**ior**	alt**ius**	alt**issimus**	alt**issimē**
fort**is**	fort**iter**	fort**ior**	fort**ius**	fort**issimus**	fort**issimē**
līber	līber**ē**	līber**ior**	līber**ius**	līber**rimus**	līber**rimē**
ācer	ācr**iter**	ācr**ior**	ācr**ius**	ācer**rimus**	ācer**rimē**
facil**is**	facil**e**	facil**ior**	facil**ius**	facil**limus**	facil**limē**

Adjectives in **–er** are like **ācer** or **līber**. Other adjectives that are compared like **facilis** are **difficilis, similis, dissimilis, gracilis,** and **humilis,** but their positive degree adverbs vary (and are not used in this book).

ORAL PRACTICE

1. Decline **idem iter, ipsa lēx.**
2. Give the forms of **ipsī, eius, illud, eundem, ipsō, eī, haec, id, hoc, ipsīus.**
3. Compare **ūtilis, celer, tardus, humilis, clārus; grātē, ācriter, amīcē, facile, graviter.**

NOTA·BENE

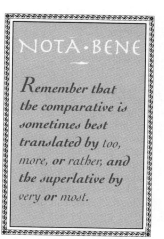

Remember that the comparative is sometimes best translated by too, more, *or* rather, *and the superlative by* very *or* most.

SUPERSTITION

Syntax Review

Comparison of Adjectives and Adverbs

To join the two words that are being compared, you use **quam** *(than).* Remember that the two things being compared must be in the same case.

Ego celerius quam tū currō.	*I run more swiftly than you.*
Hic puer altior quam ille est.	*This boy is taller than that one.*

Quam is also used with superlative adverbs to express *as ... as possible.*

Quam fortissimē pugnābimus.	*We shall fight as bravely as possible.*
Ea quam celerrimē aderit.	*She will be here as quickly as possible.*

WORKBOOK
Assign Ex. C to review the dative with adjectives.

ANSWERS
1. Rōmānī dē signīs deōs ipsōs cōnsulēbant. 2. Putāvērunt Fortūnam esse deam aliīs amīcam, aliīs inimīcam.
3. Mīlitēs sub duce cui Fortūna amīcissima erat fortius pugnābant. 4. Caesare interfectō, novissima ōmina eiusdem generis vīsa sunt.

Ronald Sheridan/Ancient Art & Architecture Collection

The goddess Fortuna represented fate with all its unknown factors. A golden statuette of Fortuna was always in the bedroom of the emperor. She is often depicted with a wheel, a ship's rudder or prow, or a cornucopia.

Dative with Adjectives

The dative is used after certain adjectives that are often followed by *to* or *for* in English. These adjectives include: **amicus, idoneus, par, proximus, similis, utilis,** and their opposites. Others will be identified in the Vocabulary sections as they appear in the reading selections.

Anna tibi par virtūte est.	*Anna is equal to you in courage.*
Rōmānī nōbīs inimīcī sunt.	*The Romans are unfriendly to us.*

TRANSLATION

1. The Romans consulted the gods themselves about signs.
2. They thought that Fortune was a goddess friendly to some, unfriendly to others.
3. Soldiers fought more bravely under a leader to whom fortune was most friendly.
4. When[3] Caesar was killed, very strange omens of the same kind were seen.

Vocabulary Review

Nouns

flūmen	**iter**	**signum**
genus	**mīles**	

Adjectives

ācer	**inimīcus**	**ūtilis**

Verbs

accidō	**efficiō**	**valeō**
capiō	**moneō**	**vincō**
cōnsulō	**terreō**	

Word Studies

Review the prefixes **inter–, ob–, ante–, trāns–** in the Appendix.

Define according to the prefix: **intercipiō, occurrō, oppugnō, antecēdō, trānsmittō, trādūcō;** *intercede, interscholastic, opposition, antedate, transcription, transportation.*

Select the proper form of **ob–:** *–casion, –fer, –ject, –lige, –press.*

Explain by derivation *admonition, deterrent, invalid, public utility.*

[3] Use ablative absolute.

LESSON IX

The Big Show

LESSON OBJECTIVES
To review the comparison of irregular adjectives and adverbs;
To review the eight uses of the ablative covered in Lessons I-VIII

STUDY TOPIC
Gladiators, the Circus Maximus

Ex extrēmīs viīs, ē Forō, dē summō monte Aventīnō et dē Caeliō, ex omnibus partibus Rōmae hominēs ad lūdōs gladiātōriōs[1] prōcēdēbant. Proximō diē Augustus maxima mūnera gladiātōria datūrus erat; nunc gladiātōribus cēna lībera in lūdīs dabātur, et multī Rōmānī, ad hōs properantēs, gladiātōrēs spectātūrī erant. Pūblius et Fūriānus magnō studiō per viās cucurrērunt. Gladiātōribus prīmīs spectātīs, Pūblius clāmāvit, "Haec mūnera meliōra quam omnia alia erunt; hī sunt optimī gladiātōrēs quōs vīdī."

Nunc diēs mūnerum aderat. Amphitheātrum hominibus complētum est. In īnferiōre parte Pūblius cum Fūriānō sedēbat. Vir Pūbliō proximus dīxit Augustum duo mīlia gladiātōrum ad haec mūnera parāvisse. Pūblius, coniūrātiōnem Spartacī memoriā tenēns, spērāvit nūllum perīculum Rōmae futūrum esse; sed Augustus ipse aderat, et Pūblius scīvit illīus potestātem maximam esse.

In arēnam prōcēdēbant plūrimī gladiātōrēs, armīs variīs īnsignēs. Firmō pede inter clāmōrēs spectantium ad Augustum accessērunt et eī salūtem dīxērunt.

"Vidēsne illōs decem quī arma eiusdem generis gerunt?" rogāvit Fūriānus.

"Videō. Putō eōs esse captīvōs, ex ulteriōre Galliā missōs. Ācrēs videntur, sed nōnne putās illōs septem Aethiopēs melius pugnātūrōs esse? Sed quis est ille? Veturiumne, cīvem Rōmānum, in arēnā videō?"

"Ipse est. Pessimus ille homō damnātus est, quod patrem et amīcum interfēcerat."

Prīmum octō paria servōrum eiusdem gentis, Hispānae, prōcessērunt; sed minus ācriter pugnāvērunt quam populus exspectābat et, omnibus irrīdentibus, ex arēnā discessērunt. Posteā decem Thrācēs cum decem Britannīs melius pugnāvērunt. Ūnus ē Britannīs, quī valēbat et optimē pugnābat, spectantibus grātus erat. Hic, ā Thrāce difficillimē superātus, nōn interfectus est et clāmōribus populī līberātus est. Tum hominēs cum animālibus, animālia cum animālibus pugnāvērunt. Tandem Veturiō sōlō adductō, leō ācer in arēnam missus est. Leō ā Veturiō vulnerātus est, sed hunc interfēcit.

Mūnera huius modī nunc crūdēlissima videntur; sed auctōritātem Augustī plūrimum cōnfirmāvērunt, quod populō Rōmānō maximē grāta erant.

[1] *gladiatorial (training) schools*

Ronald Sheridan/Ancient Art & Architecture Collection

An emperor, probably Theodosius I (A.D. 378-395), holding a victor's laurel crown and flanked by two princes, presides over the games. The frieze is part of the base of an obelisk in Istanbul, Turkey.

ADDITIONAL QUESTIONS
Where did the Romans go to see the gladiators before the games? Where were the fights held? How many gladiators were going to fight? What were some of the gladiators wearing? What important person was going to be present at these games?

QUESTIONS

1. Why did Veturius fight?
2. What three kinds of fights were there at the Roman games?
3. What six nationalities were represented among the gladiators?

Grammar

Form Review

Comparison of Irregular Adjectives

In Latin as in English, some commonly used adjectives and adverbs are compared irregularly. You must simply memorize them. Notice that some adjectives are lacking certain degrees. All but **plus** are declined regularly.

POSITIVE	COMPARATIVE	SUPERLATIVE
bon**us**	mel**ior**	opt**imus**
mal**us**	pe**ior**	pess**imus**
magn**us**	ma**ior**	max**imus**
parv**us**	min**or**	min**imus**
mult**us**	—, plūs	plūr**imus**
mult**ī**	plur**ēs**	plūr**imī**
īnfer**us**	īnfer**ior**	īnf**imus** *or* **īmus**
super**us**	super**ior**	suprē**mus** *or* sum**mus**
—	exter**ior**	extr**ēmus**
—	inter**ior**	int**imus**
—	pr**ior**	prī**mus**
—	prop**ior**	prox**imus**
—	ulter**ior**	ult**imus**
senex	sen**ior**	—

SUGGESTION
Drill each set orally in class. Students will learn them better as groups of three rather than over 50 separate words.

Comparison of Irregular Adverbs

The irregular adverbs are as follows. Remember that adverbs do not decline.

POSITIVE	COMPARATIVE	SUPERLATIVE
ben**e**	mel**ius**	opt**imē**
mal**e**	pe**ius**	pess**imē**
magnopere	mag**is**	max**imē**
—	min**us**	min**imē**
mult**um**	plūs	plūr**imum**
mult**ī**	plūr**ēs**	plūr**imī**
diū	diūt**ius**	diūt**issimē**
prop**e**	prop**ius**	prox**imē**
saep**e**	saep**ius**	saep**issimē**

WORKBOOK
Assign Ex. A to review the comparison of irregular adjectives and adverbs.

ORAL PRACTICE

1. Compare **multus, malus, dūrus, parvus, ācer.**
2. Compare **bene, magis, līberē, multum, celeriter.**
3. Give the positive of **optimus, minimus, humillimus;** the comparative of **minimē, bonus, ācerrimus;** the superlative of **magnus, facilius, graviter.**

WORKBOOK
Assign the Unit Review as an excellent overall review of vocabulary and syntax.

Syntax Review

SUGGESTION
Have students think of sentences in English that contain each of these constructions. Do not translate them into Latin, but ask students whether or not a preposition would be used (in Latin), and if so, which one.

The Uses of the Ablative

You know that the ablative, with or without a preposition, is used to express several different things in Latin. Let's review them here.

Ablative of *Place Where*

The ablative case with the preposition **in** or **sub** is used to indicate *where* something is or is happening. Sometimes the preposition is omitted, especially in poetry.

Hostēs in Galliā sunt.	*The enemy are in Gaul.*
Neptūnus sub marī habitat.	*Neptune lives under the sea.*

Ablative of *Time When*

The ablative without a preposition is used to express *time when* or *within which.*

Aestāte natāre amō.	*In the summer, I like to swim.*
Paucīs horīs cēnam edent.	*Within a few hours, we shall eat dinner.*

Ablative of Accompaniment

Accompaniment is expressed by the ablative with the preposition **cum**. When **cum** is used with a personal, reflexive, or relative pronoun, it is attached to the end of the pronoun.

Rūfus cum equō venit.	*Rufus is coming with the horse.*
Quis est cum patre tuō?	*Who is with your father?*

The Ablative of Means

The means or instrument by which something is done is expressed by the ablative without a preposition.

Nova litterīs mē mīsit.	*He sent me the news in a letter.*
Frumentum carrō portāvērunt.	*They carried the grain with a wagon.*

Ablative Absolute

This commonly used construction in Latin is a combination of two words in the ablative: a noun plus a noun, a noun plus an adjective, or a noun plus a participle. The words must not be grammatically connected to the rest of the sentence.

Caesare dūce, omina bona erant.	*With Caesar as leader, the omens were good.*
Campō latissimō, diūtissimē laborāvimus.	*Because the field was very wide, we worked for a very long time.*
Carrō fractō, excēdere nōn potuērunt.	*Since the wagon was broken, they were unable to leave.*

Ablative of Agent

The ablative is used with the preposition **ā** or **ab** after a passive verb to show the person (or animal) by whom something is done.

Ā magistrō doctī sunt.	*We were taught by a teacher.*
Ā mīlite vulnerātus est.	*He was wounded by a soldier.*

Ablative of Respect

The ablative of respect, with no preposition, tells how a certain statement applies.

SEF/Art Resource, NY

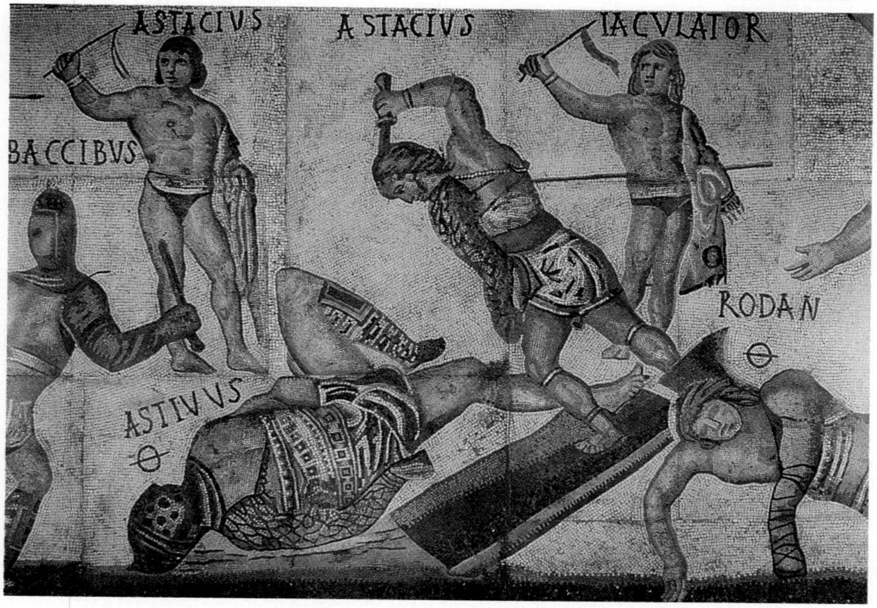

A mosaic in Rome honors several gladiators. The Romans appreciated a good game. Clearly, each of these gladiators excelled for a different reason: some have little or no armor, others appear well protected.

Equus mē celeritāte superat.	*The horse surpasses me in speed.*
Quae patria maior virtūte est?	*Which country is greater in courage?*

WORKBOOK
Assign Ex. B to review uses of the ablative.

ANSWERS
1. Nōnne putās haec munera crūdēlissima fuisse? 2. Multī captīvī et servī, Rōmānīs spectantibus, in arēnā interfectī sunt. 3. In lūdīs gladiātōriīs erant plūrimī hominēs missī ex extrēmīs/ultimīs partibus Galliae. 4. Ad haec mūnera multa mīlia optimōrum cīvium maximō studiō properābant. 5. Illīs temporibus, damnātī saepe cum gladiātoribus pugnābant et ab hīs interficiēbantur.

SUGGESTION
Verify that students can supply all essential facts for all the review vocabulary in Unit I (Lessons I-IX). You may want to make a game out of it.

NOTE
Have students identify **civis**, **gēns**, and **mons** as **i**–stems.

GAME
Using all the vocabulary in Unit I have students write out a list of 10 words together with a number and case (nouns), gender, number, and case (adjectives), or person, number, tense, and voice (verbs)—with the answers for a homework assignment. [e.g., **genus**—abl. pl.; **celer**—dat. sing. masc.; **vincō**—2nd. pl. fut. pass]. Each student asks one of the things on her/his list to a student on the other team until all words are exhausted. Each team with a correct response the first time wins a point. No one gets "out." This serves as a good form review for everyone.

Ablative of Comparison

When the two nouns or pronouns you are comparing are in the nominative or accusative, you may omit **quam** and put the second noun or pronoun in the ablative.

Hoc flūmen altius illō.	*This river is deeper than that (one).*
Equus meus melior tuō.	*My horse is better than yours.*

TRANSLATION

1. Do you not think that these shows were very cruel?
2. Many prisoners and slaves were killed in the arena (while) Romans looked on.
3. In the gladiatorial schools were very many men sent from the farthest parts of Gaul.
4. To these shows many thousands of the best citizens hurried with the greatest eagerness.
5. In those times condemned (men) often fought with the gladiators and were killed by them.

Vocabulary Review

In addition to the following words, be sure you know the meanings of the irregular adjectives and adverbs presented in this lesson.

Nouns

arma	**diēs**	**mōns**
cīvis	**gēns**	**perīculum**

Adjective

pār

Verbs

addūcō **cōnfirmō** **spērō**

SUGGESTION
A game to review the irregular comparisons by themselves, perhaps using flashcards, would be helpful to students.

Adverb

ācriter

Word Studies

The spelling of English words is often made easier by considering the Latin words from which they come.

The Latin double consonant is usually kept in English, except at the end of a word: *expelled,* but *expel* (from **pellō**). Give five additional examples.

As assimilation of prefixes often caused a doubling of consonants, it is frequently possible to obtain help in spelling by analyzing the word. Compare *de–ference* and *dif–ference, ac–com–modate* and *re–com–mend.* Give five additional examples in English.

Gianni Tortoli/Photo Researchers

Sports and spectacles were important not only in Rome but also in the provinces. The remains of this Roman amphitheater in El Djem, Tunisia indicate that it was a substantial size. Built in A.D. 238 by the emperor Gordiano, it had 35,000 seats. It has been partially dismantled over the centuries to build the Arab city around it.

Unit II

Two Roman Students in Athens

UNIT OBJECTIVES

To review the fourth and fifth declensions; To learn the formation of the present subjunctive (active and passive) of all conjugations and **sum, possum**; To learn the imperfect, perfect, and pluperfect subjunctive, active and passive; To learn the hortatory/jussive subjunctive; To learn purpose and result clauses; To learn the sequence of tenses; To learn the verb **ferō**; To learn the ablative of degree of difference; To learn time clauses with **ubi, postquam, cum**; To learn deponent verbs; To review personal and reflexive pronouns; To learn indirect question; To learn indefinite pronouns; To learn the conjugation of **eō**; To learn the formation and use of the future passive participle (gerundive); To learn noun clauses with the subjunctive; To learn the formation and use of the gerund; To learn the conjugation of **fiō**; To learn predicate nominatives and adjectives after certain passive verbs; To learn the conjugations of **volō** and **nolō**; To learn the dative with special verbs; To learn the datives of reference and purpose

George Grigoriou/Tony Stone Images

The Acropolis in Athens is the ancient hill upon which the Greeks built their most famous monument to civilization, the Parthenon, which we see here. The Propylaea, or entrance to the Acropolis, is to the left.

LESSON OBJECTIVES
To review the fourth declension; To learn the formation of the present subjunctive; To learn the hortatory/jussive subjunctive

LESSON X

The Farewell Dinner

STUDY TOPICS
Foods, meals, Roman house

Quondam domus nōbilis familiae Rōmānae, Caeciliae, maximē perturbābātur. Pūblius, fīlius P. Caecilī Rūfī, et Fūriānus, fīlius adoptātus M. Caecilī, diū in animō habuerant ad Graeciam nāvigāre et clārōs philosophōs Graecōs audīre; et nunc proximum diem exituī cōnstituerant. Nōna hōra fuit—hōra cēnae. Cēna in ātriō domūs, nōn in trīclīniō, parāta erat, quod adfutūrī erant paucī. In ātrium, in quō mulierēs exspectābant, ē balneīs vēnērunt virī.

Rūfus manibus signum dedit et clāmāvit: "Cēna pōnātur."

Virīs accumbentibus[1] et mulieribus sedentibus, soleae sunt dēpositae, et mēnsa ā servīs in ātrium portāta est. Mēnsā positā, aqua et mappae[1] omnibus datae sunt.

Prīma pars cēnae, prōmulsis,[2] in ātrium allāta est[3]—ōva et lactūca;[4] tum mulsum.[5] Aquā et mappīs iterum datīs, cēna ipsa allāta est. Cibus bonus erat, nostrō similis. Per cēnam multa dē Graeciā et Graecīs dicta sunt.

Magnum erat studium Pūblī et Fūriānī, quod in Graeciam prōcessūrī erant et tempus exitūs aderat. Sed Rūfus verba gravia Mārcō dīxit: "In terram illīs novam prōcēdere cōnstituērunt. Cupiāmus eōs vītam dignam āctūrōs esse." "Semper memoriā teneant sē Rōmānōs esse," respondit Mārcus. "Nē iniūstē faciant—tum vītam dignam agent."

"Servus Graecus audiātur," clāmāvit Pūblius.

"Et Graecum carmen canat," dīxit Fūriānus.

Postquam servus carmen cecinit, Rūfus dīxit: "Nunc linguīs faveāmus,[2] et deōs colāmus."

Ubi Larēs in mēnsā positī sunt, Rūfus cibum et vīnum ad eōs posuit. Omnibus stantibus, silentium factum est. Tum, Laribus magnā cūrā remōtīs, secunda mēnsa[3] in ātrium portāta est—dulcia et frūctūs. Cēnā

[1] *napkins*
[2] *first course*
[3] *was brought in*
[4] *eggs and lettuce*
[5] *grape juice*

---

1 The men *reclined* on couches, resting on their left elbows.
2 Literally, "let us favor with our tongues," i.e., by refraining from evil words; therefore, *let us keep silent*.
3 As the dessert was brought in on a separate table, **secunda mēnsa** came to mean *dessert*.

Ronald Sheridan/Ancient Art & Architecture Collection

perfectā "ab ōvō usque ad māla,"[4] Rūfus dīxit, "Servus Dāvus veniat." Ille in manibus, tum in capite stetit, et multa alia fēcit.

Sed nunc erat tempus discēdere. Servī soleās parāre iussī sunt, et omnēs magnō silentiō discessērunt.

At this family dinner, the whole family is eating together, including the children. When this course is done, servants will remove the table top and replace it with the next course.

QUESTIONS

1. Where was the dinner?
2. Who stood on his head?
3. Who sang a Greek song?
4. What was the last course?
5. Who did not recline at the table?

ADDITIONAL QUESTIONS

What was the reason for the dinner? Where are Publius and Furianus going? What do they plan to do there? What foods were served? What did Rufus do between the dinner and the dessert?

Grammar

Review of the Fourth Declension

Fourth declension nouns can be recognized by the **–u** in the endings.

[4] A proverbial expression which came to mean *from beginning to end* (cf. "from soup to nuts"), from the Roman practice of beginning a dinner with *eggs* and ending with *apples* or other fruits.

SINGULAR	PLURAL	SINGULAR	PLURAL
cās**us**	cās**ūs**	corn**ū**	corn**ua**
cās**ūs**	cās**uum**	corn**us**	corn**uum**
cās**uī**	cās**ibus**	corn**ū**	corn**ibus**
cās**um**	cās**ūs**	corn**ū**	corn**ua**
cās**ū**	cās**ibus**	corn**ū**	corn**ibus**

NOTĀ • BENE

Most fourth declension nouns are masculine; the chief exceptions are **manus** *and* **domus**, *which are feminine. The only neuter used in this textbook is* **cornu.**

ORAL PRACTICE

Decline **exitus ipse, illa manus.**

SUGGESTION
Do a quick drill with a fourth declension noun from the vocabulary, then do another with a noun and an adjective.

Subjunctive Mood

The subjunctive is a mood. Other moods you have studied are the indicative and the imperative. The subjunctive is used to express several things in Latin, although its use in English is primarily limited to expressing ideas that are not facts.

The subjunctive has four tenses: present, imperfect, perfect, and pluperfect—and two voices, active and passive. We will just work with the present subjunctive, active and passive, in this lesson.

To form the present subjunctive, you need to make a vowel change in the present stem; then you add the personal endings that you already know.

WORKBOOK
Assign Ex. A to review the fourth declension.

NOTE
Point out that a true command can only be in the second person; thus the hortatory/jussive subjunctive is not a true command but rather a strong suggestion.

WORKBOOK
Assign Ex. B for an overview of the indicative, imperative, and subjunctive and to practice subjunctive forms.

PRESENT ACTIVE				
port**em**	doce**am**	pōn**am**	capi**am**	mūnī**am**
port**ēs**	doce**ās**	pōn**ās**	capi**ās**	mūnī**ās**
port**et**	doce**at**	pōn**at**	capi**at**	mūnī**at**
port**ēmus**	doce**āmus**	pōn**āmus**	capi**āmus**	mūnī**āmus**
port**ētis**	doce**ātis**	pōn**ātis**	capi**ātis**	mūnī**ātis**
port**ent**	doce**ant**	pōn**ant**	capi**ant**	mūnī**ant**

SUGGESTION
Do several oral drills with verbs from all conjugations. You may want to use the current vocabulary and then add others.

PRESENT PASSIVE				
port**er**	doce**ar**	pōn**ar**	capi**ar**	mūnī**ar**
port**ēris**	doce**āris**	pōn**āris**	capi**āris**	mūnī**āris**
port**ētur**	doce**ātur**	pōn**ātur**	capi**ātur**	mūnī**ātur**
port**ēmur**	doce**āmur**	pōn**āmur**	capi**āmur**	mūnī**āmur**
port**ēminī**	doce**āminī**	pōn**āminī**	capi**āminī**	mūnī**āminī**
port**entur**	doce**antur**	pōn**antur**	capi**antur**	mūnī**antur**

Notice that the **–a** of the first conjugation becomes **–e**; the **–e** of the second conjugation becomes **–ea**, the **–e** of the third becomes **–a** and the **–ī** of the fourth and third **–iō** verbs becomes **–ia**. If you remember the phrase "w**e** b**ea**t **a** l**ia**r," you will always remember the order of the vowel changes.

ORAL PRACTICE

Give the present subjunctive, active and passive, of **laudō** in the first singular; of **perficiō** in the first plural; of **colō** in the second singular; of **cōnstituō** in the second plural; of **teneō** in the third singular; and of **audiō** in the third plural.

Hortatory and Jussive Subjunctive

A command or imperative in the first or third person is expressed in Latin by the *hortatory or jussive* subjunctive. We translate it into English using *Let*.

Cōpiās moneāmus.	*Let us warn the troops.*
Mīlitēs urbem oppugnent.	*Let the soldiers attack the city.*

SUGGESTION
Find all examples of the hortatory/jussive subjunctive in the story.

C. M. Dixon

Reclining at the dinner table was a city custom not always followed in the countryside or in the provinces, as shown in this relief from Germany.

To make a sentence negative, you use **nē** instead of **nōn**.

Nē captivos spectēmus.	*Let us not look at the captives.*
Nē mala faciat.	*Let him not do evil.*

WORKBOOK
Assign Ex. C to practice the hortatory/jussive subjunctive.

CASSETTE
Do Unit II, Drill 1 to practice the hortatory/ jussive subjunctive.

ANSWERS
1. Dē exitū Pūblī Fūriānīque audiāmus. 2. Magna cēna parāta est, per quam pater Pūblī verba fēcit. 3. Tum pater dīxit, "Puer meus semper memoriā teneat Rōmānōs esse fortēs." 4. "Vītam dignam in Graeciā agat; pius maneat et domum deōsque memoriā teneat."

SUGGESTION
The more students learn to think in terms of derivatives, the faster their English and Latin vocabularies will grow. It is worthwhile to spend time having them think of (and verify in a dictionary, if need be) as many derivatives in English and related Latin words as possible.

ORAL PRACTICE

Translate the following phrases into Latin: *let us praise, let him not fear, let them read, let us not flee, let him hear, let them not seize.*

TRANSLATION

1. Let us hear about the departure of Publius and Furianus.
2. A great dinner was prepared, during which Publius' father spoke.
3. Then the father said, "Let my boy always remember that Romans are brave."
4. "Let him live a worthy life in Greece; let him remain dutiful and remember home and the gods."

Vocabulary

Nouns

ātrium, ātrī, *n. atrium, hall* (atrium)
balneum, -ī, *n. bath* (balneology)
cibus, -ī, *m. food*
domus, -ūs, *f. home, house* (dome, domicile)
exitus, -ūs, *m. outcome, departure* (exit)
fructus, -ūs, *m. fruit* (fructify, fructose)
manus, -ūs, *f. hand* (manual, manufacture)
silentium, -tī, *n. silence*
solea, -ae, *f. sandal, shoe* (sole, solely)
trīclīnium, -nī, *n. dining room*

Adjectives

dignus, -a, -um, *worthy* (dignify, dignitary)
nōnus, -a, -um, *ninth*

Verbs

colō, -ere, coluī, cultus, *cultivate, inhabit, worship*

cōnstituō, -ere, -stituī, -stitūtus, *determine* (constituent, constitute)

perficiō, -ere, -fēcī, -fectus, *finish* (perfect, perfecto)

perturbō, -āre, āvī, ātus, *disturb, throw into confusion* (perturb, perturbation)

Adverb

maximē, *very greatly, especially*

Word Studies

In Latin, when a prefix is added to a word, as **in** to **capiō,** or **con** to **teneō,** the root vowel is often changed. This change is carried over into English.

1. Short **–a–** and short **–e–** before any single consonant except **–r–** usually become short **–i–.**
2. Short **–a–** before two consonants usually becomes short **–e–.**
3. The diphthong **–ae–** usually becomes long **–ī–,** and **–au–** becomes long **–ū–.**

Prefix	+	*Word*	=	*New Word*	(*English*)
in	+	**capiō**	=	**incipiō**	(incipient)
ex	+	**faciō**	=	**efficiō**	(efficient)
con	+	**teneō**	=	**contineō**	(continent)
in	+	**aequus**	=	**inīquus**	(iniquity)
ex	+	**claudō**	=	**exclūdō**	(exclude)

Give some additional examples of these rules by using different prefixes with the Latin words above; give also the English derivatives. Apply these rules to **agō, cadō, caedō, damnō, habeō,** and **statuō,** and give English derivatives. Not all the prefixes can be attached to each of these words.

LESSON OBJECTIVE
To learn purpose clauses with **ut** and **nē**

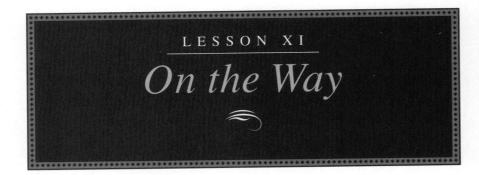

LESSON XI
On the Way

STUDY TOPIC
Travel

NOTE
Point out that **Valēte** is the imperative of **valeō**.

[1] *relative*
[2] *mosquitoes*

SUGGESTION
Review various uses of the ablative as they appear in the reading.

Nunc diēs aderat. Impedīmentīs et servīs parātīs, familia tōta domum relīquit et ex urbe ad portam Capēnam pedibus prōcessit, quod ob viās angustās nūllae raedae in urbe erant. Ad portam Pūblius et Fūriānus et servī in raedam, quattuor equīs trāctam, ascendērunt, mātre et sorōribus flentibus et omnibus "Valēte!" clāmantibus.

Portā relīctā, in Appiā Viā prōcessērunt, quae iam ad flūmen parvum dēscendēbat. Tum via plāna multa mīlia passuum per agrōs tetendit. Pūblius Fūriānō dīxit, "Cōnsistāmus ut sepulchrum clārae nostrae cognātae,[1] Caeciliae Metellae, videāmus." Multa alia sepulchra vīdērunt, inter quae īnsigne erat id Messālae Corvīnī. Vīdērunt Campum Sacrum Horātiōrum, ubi Horātiī cum Cūriātiīs temporibus antīquīs pugnāverant.

Posteā ad palūdēs Pomptīnās vēnērunt, trāns quās nautae nāvigiō parvō prīmīs hōrīs noctis multōs hominēs trānsportāre parābant. "Properāre dēbēmus," Fūriānus dīxit, "ut in nāvigium ascendāmus, nam multī aliī ascendere cupiunt." Ob numerum ascendentium magnum perīculum erat. "Iam satis est!" eī clāmāvērunt quī in nāvigiō locum invēnerant; "prōcēdāmus nē omnēs occīdāmur." Tandem nautae nāvigium solvunt et omnēs gaudent. Sed ob culicēs[2] et rānās nēmō dormīre poterat. Praetereā nauta dē amīcā suā absentī cantābat. Duōs hominēs īrātōs nautam in aquam ēicere cupientēs aliī nautae retinuērunt. Tandem septimā hōrā noctis ad terram accessērunt sed plūrimī in nāvigiō ad hōram octāvam vel decimam mānsērunt.

Tum Pūblius dīxit, "Celerius prōcēdāmus nē in hīs palūdibus pessimīs vītam āmittāmus et ut noctem quārtam in vīllā hospitis patris meī agāmus." Hōc factō, sextō diē in forum Capuae, ultimae urbis Appiae Viae, pervēnērunt. Quid in hāc urbe accidit? Aliō diē dē hōc legētis.

ADDITIONAL QUESTIONS
By what means did the family arrive at the Capena Gate? What had happened on the Sacred Plain of the Horatii? Why did the boys have trouble sleeping on the boat? What is special about Capua?

QUESTIONS

1. Where was the tomb of Caecilia Metella?
2. How many days did the boys take for this part of the journey?
3. Why did the two men want to throw the sailor into the water?
4. Compare traffic problems and restrictions in Rome and in our cities.

E. Streichan/SuperStock, Inc.

The tomb of Caecilia Metella can be seen along the Appian Way. The Metellus family was well regarded in ancient Rome and produced a long and distinguished line of military generals. Caecilia was the daughter of Quintus Caeciliius Metellus Creticus, who subdued Crete in 68-66 B.C. She was also the wife of Crassus.

Grammar

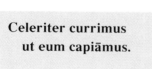

Purpose Clauses with *Ut* and *Nē*

Latin uses the subjunctive to express purpose; in English, the infinitive or any one of several phrases are generally used. In Latin, the conjunction **ut** is used to introduce the purpose clause; if the clause is negative, you use **nē**.

Celeriter currimus ut eum capiāmus.	*We run fast to catch him.* *We run fast in order to catch him.* *We run fast so as to catch him.* *We run fast for the purpose of catching him.* *We run fast that we may catch him.* *We run fast so that we may catch him.*
Celerius currit nē capiatur.	*He runs faster so as not to be caught.* *He runs faster in order that he may not be caught.* *He runs faster that he may not be caught.* *He runs faster so that he may not be caught.*

SUGGESTION
Point out that "in order to" can almost always be inserted in English to determine whether or not a sentence has a purpose clause.

WORKBOOK
Assign Ex. B to practice expressing purpose.

CASSETTE
Do Unit II, Drill 2 to practice purpose clauses.

ANSWERS
1. Nautane cantat ut rānās terreat? 2. Properā, Fūriāne, nē relinquāris. 3. Pūblius properābit ut ad Graeciam prōcēdat. 4. Nē mātrem flentem videāmus nōn exspectābimus. 5. Saepe cōnsistāmus ut loca clāra ad viam videāmus.

ORAL PRACTICE

Find all examples of purpose clauses in the lesson's reading. Try to translate them in a variety of ways.

TRANSLATION

1. Is the sailor singing to scare the frogs?
2. Hurry, Furianus, in order not to be left behind.
3. Publius will hurry in order to proceed to Greece.
4. So as not to see Mother weeping, we will not wait.
5. Let us often stop to see famous places near the road.

Vocabulary

Nouns

facultās, -tātis, *f. faculty; (pl.) means*
palūs, palūdis, *f. swamp* (paludal)
rana, -ae, *f. frog*

Adjectives

antīquus, -a, -um, *ancient* (antique, antiquate)
decimus, -a, -um, *tenth* (decimal, decimate)
octāvus, -a, -um, *eighth* (octave, octet)
quartus, -a, -um, *fourth* (quarter, quartet)
septimus, -a, -um, *seventh*
sextus, -a, -um, *sixth* (sextant, sextet)

WORKBOOK
Assign Ex. A to review Roman numerals and cardinal and ordinal numbers.

Verbs

dēdūcō, -ere, dēdūxī, dēductus, *lead* (deduct, deduction)
dēscendō, -ere, dēscendī, dēscēnsus, *descend* (descendant, descender)
fleō, flēre, flēvī, flētus, *weep (for)*
tendō, -ere, tetendī, tentus, *stretch, go* (tendency, tendon)

Conjunctions

nē, *(so) that . . . not*
ut, *(in order) that, so that*

ARCHIV/Photo Researchers

Roman biremes (with two banks of oars) were fairly common in ancient Rome. Notice how protected the rowers are. Smaller boats with just one bank of rowers worked well for coastal trips.

Word Studies

From the following English words derive the Latin ordinal numerals (*first,* etc.) and arrange them in the proper order: *tertiary, quintuplet, noon, quartet, secondary, octave, primary, decimal.*

Give the Latin cardinal numerals (*one,* etc.) for the following Spanish cardinal numerals: *tres, cinco, siete, dos, ciento, nueve, cuatro, ocho, seis, diez.*

LESSON OBJECTIVES
To learn the formation of the imperfect subjunctive; To learn sequence of tenses in purpose clauses

LESSON XII
An Adventure

Capua hōc tempore urbs amplissima atque pulcherrima erat, maxima omnium in hāc parte Italiae. In plānissimō locō posita, viās lātās optimāsque habuit. Ut urbem vidērent, Fūriānus Pūbliusque ūnum diem manēre cōnstituērunt. Homō quīdam[1] eōs vidēns dīxit: "Ut omnia bene hodiē videātis ducem habēre dēbētis. Ego vōbīs omnia mōnstrābō; deinde vōbīs optimam cēnam dabō; meliōrem enim cibum in nūllā urbe inveniētis." Puerī auxilium ducis accēpērunt. Sed paucīs aedificiīs mōnstrātīs, homō in viā angustā pecūniam ex manū Pūblī rapuit et fūgit. Sed clāmōre puerōrum audītō, duo mīlitēs hominem pessimum comprehendērunt.

Itaque puerī grātō animō Capuam relīquērunt. Iter nunc per montēs et silvās faciēbant, et via mala erat. Fūriānus Pūbliō dīxit, "Raedae adhaereāmus, nē ēiciāmur." In hīs regiōnibus nūllī hospitēs Rūfī habitāvērunt; itaque in caupōnam,[2] appellātam "Ad[3] Elephantum," accēdere coāctī sunt, ut noctem ūnam agerent. Sed caupōna sordida erat, neque dormīre facile erat. Proximō diē hominēs armātōs in viā vīdērunt; sed servī arma cēpērunt, et hominēs fūgērunt. Deinde maxima tempestās commōta est, et ad vīllam dēsertam properāvērunt nē tempestāte opprimerentur. Tandem, quārtō decimō diē, ad portās Brundisī pervēnērunt. In hōc locō raedam relīquērunt nāvemque celeriter petīvērunt, nē morā impedīrentur et ut quam mātūrissimē ad Graeciam veherentur. Sed gubernātor dīxit, "Magna nunc tempestās in marī est. In hōc locō hodiē maneāmus, nē perīculum suscipiāmus." Itaque, litterīs ad familiam missīs, Pūblius et Fūriānus apud[4] hospitem mānsērunt.

[1] *a*
[2] *inn*
[3] *At (the Sign of)*
[4] *at (the house of)*

STUDY TOPIC
Inns

NOTE
In ancient times, Capua was much more important than Naples and in the early Republic, more important than Rome.

QUESTIONS

1. What happened to the boys in Capua?
2. How long did they stay in Capua? Why?
3. How many days did the whole journey take?

ADDITIONAL QUESTIONS
What was Capua like? What means of transportation did they use to get through the mountains? What was the inn like? Where did they go during the storm? Where did they stay in Brundisium?

Michael Holford

Roman inkpot and pen date from the 1st century A.D. Originally, the inkpot had a hinged lid. With the attached chain, travelers could easily take their writing implements with them to correspond with those at home. In Roman times, ink was made from a pouch in the body of the cuttlefish.

Grammar

Imperfect Subjunctive

The imperfect subjunctive of verbs of all conjugations, regular and irregular, is formed by adding the personal endings to the present active infinitive.[1]

IMPERFECT ACTIVE				
portā**rem**	docē**rem**	pōne**rem**	cape**rem**	mūnī**rem**
portā**rēs**	docē**rēs**	pōne**rēs**	cape**rēs**	mūnī**rēs**
portā**ret**	docē**ret**	pōne**ret**	cape**ret**	mūnī**ret**
portā**rēmus**	docē**rēmus**	pōne**rēmus**	cape**rēmus**	mūnī**rēmus**
portā**rētis**	docē**rētis**	pōne**rētis**	cape**rētis**	mūnī**rētis**
portā**rent**	docē**rent**	pōne**rent**	cape**rent**	mūnī**rent**
IMPERFECT PASSIVE				
portā**rer**	docē**rer**	pōne**rer**	cape**rer**	mūnī**rer**
portā**rēris**	docē**rēris**	pōne**rēris**	cape**rēris**	mūnī**rēris**
portā**rētur**	docē**rētur**	pōne**rētur**	cape**rētur**	mūnī**rētur**
portā**rēmur**	docē**rēmur**	pōne**rēmur**	cape**rēmur**	mūnī**rēmur**
portā**rēminī**	docē**rēminī**	pōne**rēminī**	cape**rēminī**	mūnī**rēminī**
portā**rentur**	docē**rentur**	**pōnerentur**	cape**rentur**	**mūnīrentur**

[1] The **–e–** before the ending is long except before final **–m, –r, –t, –nt,** and **–ntur.**

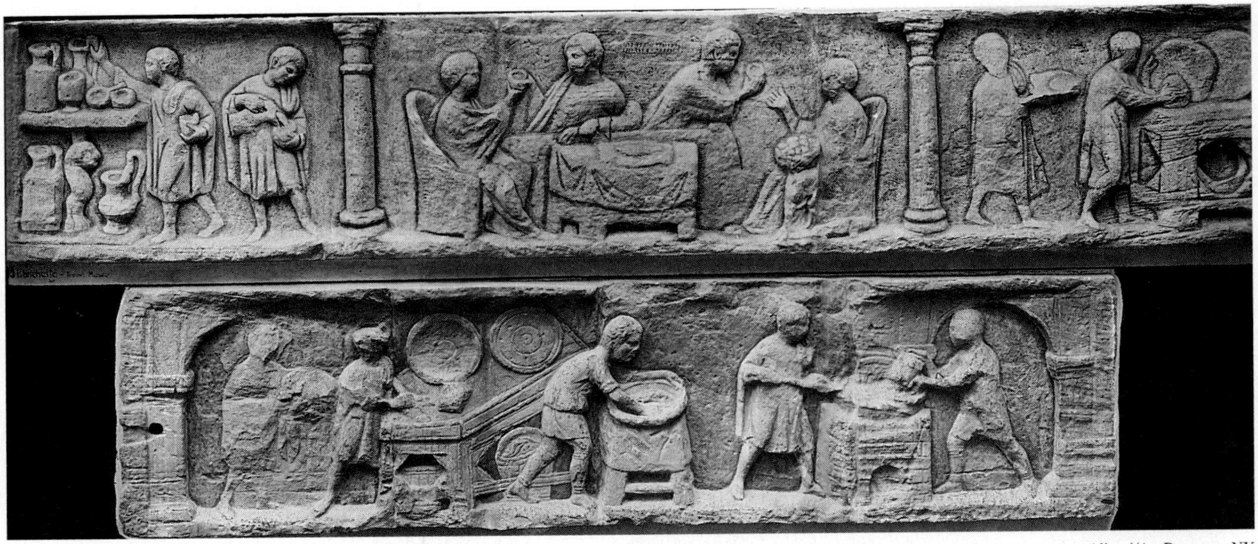

Alinari/Art Resource, NY

These friezes show scenes of food and dining preparation for a Roman family in the provinces. Whether at home or at an inn, daily tasks, often performed by slaves, included shopping, cooking, serving, and cleaning up.

NOTE
The present subjunctive of **sum** (and **possum**) will be covered in Lesson XV. Point out that the imperfect subjunctive of **possum** is regular, **possem**, etc.

WORKBOOK
Assign Ex. A to practice forming the imperfect subjunctive.

SUGGESTION
You may want to introduce the terms "primary sequence" and "secondary sequence" here.

The Imperfect Subjunctive of *Sum*

The imperfect subjunctive of **sum** is formed regularly.

essem	essēmus
essēs	essētis
esset	essent

ORAL PRACTICE

1. Conjugate **vehō** in the present and imperfect subjunctive active; **terreō** in the present and imperfect subjunctive passive.
2. Give the forms of **flēmus, cōnstituātur, dēscenderētis, perficiēmus, sentīrētur, possētis, cōnfirmārēmur, accident, valētis, opprimātur.**

Tense Sequence in Purpose Clauses

Since the subjunctive has no future tense in Latin, the only tenses that can be used in the dependent purpose clause are present and imperfect.

If the verb in the main clause is present, future, or future perfect, you use the present subjunctive in the subordinate clause.

Venīmus ut tē videāmus.	*We are coming to see you.*
Aderit ut tē audiat.	*He will be here so that he might hear you.*

If the verb in the main clause is in the past (imperfect, perfect, or pluperfect), use the imperfect subjunctive in the dependent clause.

Vēnimus ut tē vidērēmus.	*We came to see you.*
Aderat ut tē audīret.	*He was here in order to hear you.*

WORKBOOK
Assign Ex. B to practice sequence of tenses.

TRANSLATION

1. They remained one day to see Capua.
2. So as not to lose their money, they left Capua.
3. They sought fresh horses so as not to be hindered by the bad roads.
4. They hurried (on) to spend the night in the villa of a guest-friend.
5. They hurried to the ship in order to sail to Greece and not spend another night in Italy.

ANSWERS
1. Diem ūnum mānsērunt ut Capuam vidērent. 2. Nē pecūniam āmitterent Capuam relīquērunt. 3. Equōs integrōs petīvērunt nē itineribus/viīs malīs impedīrentur. 4. Properābant ut noctem in vīllā hospitis agerent. 5. Ad nāvem properāvērunt ut ad Graeciam nāvigārent et nē in Italiā alteram noctem agerent.

North Wind Picture Archives

A very elaborate Roman traveling carriage. Notice that the horses are harnessed four abreast, rather than two and two. Certainly whoever owned this carriage was going to travel in style.

Vocabulary

Nouns

aedificium, -cī, *n. building* (edification, edify)
hospes, -pitis, *m. guest, guest-friend, host* (hospice, hospital)
mora, -ae, *f. delay* (moratorium)
raeda, -ae, *f. carriage, bus*
tempestās, -tātis, *f. storm* (tempest, tempestuous)
vīlla, -ae, *f. farmhouse, villa*

Adjectives

amplus, -a, -um, *great, magnificent*	(ample, amplify)
angustus, -a, -um, *narrow*	(anguish)
sordidus, -a, -um, *dirty, mean*	(sordid)

Verbs

adhaereō, -ēre, adhaesī, adhaesus, *stick (to)*	(adhere, adhesive)
ēiciō, -ere, ēiēcī, ēiectus, *throw (out), stick out, expel*	(eject, ejectment)
vehō, -ere, vexī, vectus, *carry*	(vector)

Adverbs

deinde, *then*
hodiē, *today*
mātūrē, *soon*

Conjunction

enim, *for (never first word)*

Word Studies

The following suffixes have no sharply defined meanings, but if you know them you can recognize many English derivatives: **–ium** (English *–e* or *–y*), **–tium** (English *–ce*), **–men** (English *–men, –min, –me*), **–tūs** (English *–tue*).

Give the English form of **studium, officium, aedificium, sacrificium, spatium, volūmen, crīmen, virtūs.**

What must be the Latin words from which are derived *silence, commerce, remedy, prodigy, culmin*(*ate*), *lumin*(*ous*), *crimin*(*al*)?

Explain by derivation *amplifier, descendant, immature, manual, moratorium, vehicle.*

LESSON XIII

Sight-Seeing at Brundisium

LESSON OBJECTIVE
To learn the conjugation of **ferō**

Pūblius et Fūriānus Brundisī[1] diū mānsērunt ut sine perīculō trāns mare nāvigārent. Hōc tempore urbem explōrāvērunt. Namque in hāc urbe multa loca clāra erant. Multī ad hunc portum vēnērunt ut ad Graeciam Asiamque nāvigārent—mercātōrēs, imperātōrēs, exercitūs, nūntiī litterās ferentēs.

Fūriānus Pūbliō dīxit: "Haec urbs clāra est. Nōnne memoriā tenēs Cicerōnem in exsilium ēiectum ad hunc locum vēnisse ut nāvis eum ad Graeciam ferret? Ūnus amīcus eum dolentem excēpit, cui numquam satis grātiās agere poterat. Sed posteāquam Cicerō ex exsiliō revocātus Brundisium[2] diē nātālī colōniae ipsīus vēnit, omnēs cīvēs cum maximō gaudiō eum excēpērunt."

Tum Pūblius dīxit: "Rēctē dīcis. Posteā in hōc oppidō Pompeius cōpiās collēgit ut trāns mare fugeret. Caesar ad oppidum properāvit ut eum interclūderet. Sed sine nāvibus eum retinēre nōn poterat. Prōcēdāmus ad portum et propriīs oculīs spectēmus locum in quō Caesar exitūs portūs impedīre temptāvit." "Bene," respondit Fūriānus. Itaque duo amīcī prīmum ad locum ēditum prōcessērunt ut tōtam regiōnem vidērent. Deinde dē locō ēditō dēscendērunt et portum ipsum spectāvērunt. Quā parte[3] portus angustissimus erat Caesar opera et ratēs collocāverat, sed Pompeius, nē interclūderētur, nāvibus opera rūperat et fūgerat.

"Certē haec urbs multa clāra facta vīdit et multōs et gravēs cāsūs tulit," inquit Pūblius.

[1] *at Brundisium*
[2] *to Brundisium*
[3] *where* (literally, *in which part*)

STUDY TOPICS
Brundisium, navigation

QUESTIONS

1. Why did Caesar hurry to Brundisium?
2. What did Publius and Furianus see?
3. Why did many people go to Brundisium?

ADDITIONAL QUESTIONS
Why did the boys stay for a while in Brundisium? What is the connection between Brundisium and Cicero? Who burst through the rafts so as not to be caught?

G. Tortoli/Ancient Art & Architecture Collection

The Appian Way began in Rome and originally ended in Capua. It was eventually extended to Brundisium, on the southeast coast of Italy. This original Roman column marks the end of the Appian Way at Brundisium.

SUGGESTION
Point out to students that there are really very few irregular verbs in Latin—this is their third (after **sum** and **possum**).

Grammar

Conjugation of *Ferō*

The indicative of **ferō** is irregular in the present tense only; in all other tenses it is conjugated like a verb of the third conjugation. Its principal parts, however, require memorization. They are **ferō, ferre, tulī, lātus.**

ACTIVE		PASSIVE	
ferō	**ferimus**	**feror**	**ferimur**
fers	**fertis**	**ferrīs**	**feriminī**
fert	**ferunt**	**fertur**	**feruntur**

The infinitives, active and passive, are **ferre** and **ferrī**. The imperative is **fer**. The other forms of **ferō** are as follows (the first person singular is given):

	ACTIVE	PASSIVE
IMPERFECT	ferēbam	ferēbar
FUTURE	feram	ferar
PERFECT	tulī	lātus sum
PLUPERFECT	tuleram	lātus eram
FUTURE PERFECT	tulerō	lātus erō

SUGGESTION
Drill this verb orally every day for several days, since it is so important; point out that **ferō** is frequently compounded.

Like many other important Latin verbs, **ferō** has several meanings, including *bear, carry, bring, receive, report, propose*. You will have to decide which one is best in your translations.

WORKBOOK
Assign Ex. A and B to practice **ferō**.

WORKBOOK
Assign Ex. C to review and practice formation of the present and imperfect subjunctive of all conjugations.

ORAL PRACTICE

1. Give the third singular of **ferō** in all tenses of the indicative, active and passive, and in the present and imperfect subjunctive, active and passive.
2. Give all the infinitives and participles of **ferō.**
3. Conjugate in the present and imperfect subjunctive, active and passive: **colligō, cōnfirmō, dēbeō.**
4. Tell the form of **dolent, excipiāmur, nūntiētur, ferrētis, properent, rumperet, cōnstituantur, perficient, moneāminī, occupās.**

Mosaics were used to decorate not only homes but business offices. This mosaic comes from an office building that housed the representatives of Roman and overseas shipping and trading companies.

PHOTRI/INDEX

ANSWERS
1. Pūblius et amīcus ad portum prōcessērunt ut ad Graeciam nāvigārent. 2. "Properēmus nē relinquāmur," dīxit Pūblius. 3. Amīcus eius respondit, "Ad locum ēditum prōcēdāmus ut tōtam regiōnem videāmus." 4. Caesar hunc portum impedīvit nē nāvēs Pompeī fugerent.

TRANSLATION

1. Publius and his friend proceeded toward the harbor to sail to Greece.
2. "Let us hurry (on) so that we shall not be left behind," said Publius.
3. His friend replied, "Let us proceed to an elevated place to see the whole region."
4. Caesar obstructed this harbor in order that Pompey's ships might not escape.

Vocabulary

Nouns

exsilium, -lī, *n. exile*
mercātor, -ōris, *m. merchant*
oculus, -ī, *m. eye* (ocular, oculist)
portus, -ūs, *m. harbor* (port)
ratis, -is, *f. raft*

Adjectives

ēditus, -a, -um, *elevated*
proprius, -a, -um, *(one's) own, characteristic of* (proper, property)

Verbs

colligō, -ere, -lēgī, -lēctus, *collect* (collection)
doleō, -ēre, doluī, dolitūrus, *grieve* (dolor)
excipiō, -ere, excēpī, exceptus, *receive* (except, exception)
ferō, ferre, tulī, lātus, *bear, carry* (fertile, fertility)
rumpō, -ere, rūpī, ruptus, *break* (interrupt, interruption)

Conjunctions

namque, *for*
posteāquam, *after*

Adverbs

rectē, *rightly*
satis, *enough, rather* (satisfaction, satisfy)

Aesculapius was the god of medicine. He was also the son of Apollo and Coronis, a young woman from Thessaly. Aesculapius was taught the art of healing by the wise centaur, Chiron. In this Greek relief from the 4th century B.C., Aesculapius treats a patient.

Ronald Sheridan/Ancient Art & Architecture Collection

C. M. Dixon

This funerary slab shows that the person buried within was a surgeon. Notice the surgical instruments and the serpent, the revered symbol of medicine.

Word Studies

Physicians make use of Latin words and phrases every day. The science of anatomy, with which all physicians must be familiar, uses a large number of Latin terms. In writing prescriptions, physicians use Latin constantly, and druggists must be able to understand it. The symbol ℞ at the top of a prescription stands for **recipe,** *take.*[1] Other examples are: **aq(ua) pur(a),** pure water; **aq(ua) dest(illata),** *distilled water;* **t(er) i(n) d(ie),** *three times a day;* **cap(iat),** *let him take;* **gtt.** (abbreviation of **guttae**), *drops;* **sig(na),** *write;* **stat(im),** *at once;* **a(nte) c(ibum),** *before meals;* **p(ost) c(ibum),** *after meals;* **det(ur),** *let it be given.*

Explain *condolence, corruption, dilated, inoculate, oculist, rupture.*

[1] The stroke through the R is a sign of abbreviation, like our period.

LESSON OBJECTIVES
To learn result clauses with **ut** and **ut nōn**; To review the characteristics of purpose and result clauses

STUDY TOPIC
The topography of Athens

LESSON XIV
A Letter from Athens

Pūblius patrī et mātrī et sorōribus suīs s. p. d.[1] Sī valētis, bene est; valeō. Nunc valeō; sed nōn semper valuī. Namque Brundisiō post longam moram relīctō, posteāquam nāvis parva in mare lātum prōcessit, tanta tempestās commōta est ut putārem undās altās nāvem frāctūrās esse. Fūriānus autem dīxit, "Nautae ita perītī sunt ut nāvem facile servent." Sed ego respondī: "Hoc nōn iam ferre possum. In īnferiōrem partem properēmus ut ibi somnum capiāmus et clārum caelum spērēmus."

Dēscendimus. Nāvis ita volvēbātur ut mors ab omnibus spērārētur; sed post diem longum et noctem longiōrem ad urbem Graecam Dyrrachium pervēnimus. Viīs tam malīs iter per Graeciam fēcimus ut paene cōnficerēmur. Per oppida dēserta, per agrōs nōn cultōs, per urbēs bellīs cīvīlibus oppressās prōcessimus. Tandem ad clāram urbem Athēnās pervēnimus, quae est forum Athēnārum, et Acropolis, Capitōliō Rōmānō similis, ita ēgregiae sunt ut nōn satis laudentur. Sed in proximīs litterīs plūs dē urbe scrībam. Nunc dē studiīs audīre cupitis.

Ubi ad portam Athēnārum accessimus,[2] vīdimus multōs vestem scholasticam gerentēs et tantīs clāmōribus vocantēs ut cōnsisterēmus et cum silentiō eōs spectārēmus. "Nōnne petitis scholam Philippī?" "Nōnne petitis scholam Lycurgī?" et alia clāmābant. "Ad scholam Enchōriōnis rhētoris prōcēdimus," dīximus. Deinde ab aliīs relīctī sumus, ab aliīs prehēnsī. In aedificium parvum ductī sumus, et iānua clausa est. Tam diū ibi mānsimus ut putārēmus illōs numquam reversūrōs esse. Tandem līberātī sumus nē perterrērēmur et ab illīs rīdentibus ad cēnam ductī sumus, post quam omnibus modīs lūdificātī sumus. Tum ad balnea ductī vestem scholasticam accēpimus. Posterō diē ad numerum scholasticōrum Enchōriōnis, quī grātus vidētur, ascrīptī sumus. Crās studia incipiēmus. Cum Graecā familiā ad Agoram habitāmus.

Vidētis omnia bona esse. Saepe scrībēmus et saepe litterās exspectābimus. Valēte.

---

[1] **salūtem plūrimam dīcit,** *sends heartiest greetings.* These words are regularly abbreviated.

[2] The following description of student life in Athens is based on that given by Libanius in the fourth century A.D., but it is not improbable that it is substantially correct for the age of Augustus.

Ronald Sheridan/Ancient Art & Architecture Collection

The Agora, or marketplace, of Athens has been partially excavated. Located just northwest of the Acropolis, it was a large public space on either side of the sacred way. The Painted Stoa, discovered in 1981, was decorated with paintings by Polygnotus and Micon done in the 5th century B.C.

QUESTIONS

1. Why wasn't Publius well?
2. What was the Agora of Athens?
3. Where did Publius live in Athens?
4. What did Publius see on entering the city?

ADDITIONAL QUESTIONS
Where did the boys go so that Publius might feel better? How were the roads in Greece? What did the students do to Publius and Furianus?

Grammar

Result Clauses with *Ut* and *Ut nōn*

A result clause is a subordinate clause used to express an action that results from the action of the main verb. In Latin, the result clause is introduced by the conjunction **ut**; for a negative, use **ut nōn**. The verb is in the subjunctive, following the rules for the sequence of tenses.

Tam celeriter cucurrit ut nōn eum caperēmus.	*He ran so fast that we did not catch him.*
Flūmen tam altum est ut nāvēs maximae urbem perveniant.	*The river is so deep that the biggest ships arrive at the city.*

SUGGESTION
Have students find all examples of result clauses (and purpose clauses) in the reading.

SUGGESTION
Point out that you can nearly always insert the words *as a result* after the *so/such* etc. to introduce the subordinate result clause.

NOTĀ·BENE

Usually, one of the following words appears in the main clause. If you do not know any of them, check the vocabulary.

ita
sic
talis
tam
tantus, –a, –um
tot

Summary of Purpose and Result Clauses

Purpose Clauses

1. Subjunctive.
2. Introduced by **ut,** negative **nē.**

Result Clauses

1. Subjunctive
2. Usually prepared for by **ita, tam,** etc.
3. Introduced by **ut,** negative **ut nōn.**

SUGGESTION
Have students contrast with English usage: an infinitive, the indicative with the auxiliary verbs *may* or *might*, no introductory word, a phrase such as *(in order) that.*

SUGGESTION
Have students contrast with English usage: the indicative, a preparation word such as *so*, introduced by *that.*

TRANSLATION

1. We hurried into a building in order not to see the storm.
2. The storm on the sea was so great that all were frightened.
3. The waves were so high that the ship did not easily proceed.
4. Leaving the ship behind, we hurried toward the city (of) Athens.
5. This city is so adorned with beautiful buildings that it is praised by all.

WORKBOOK
Assign Ex. A and B to practice purpose and result clauses.

ANSWERS
1. In aedificium properāvimus/contendimus nē tempestātem vidērēmus. 2. Tempestās in marī tanta fuit ut omnēs terrērentur. 3. Undae tam altae fuērunt ut nāvis nōn facile prōcēderet. 4. Nāvī relīctā, ad urbem Athēnās properāvimus. 5. Haec urbs aedificiīs pulchrīs ita adōrnāta est ut ab omnibus laudētur.

NOTE
Have students identify **mors** and **vestis** as **i–stems**.

Vocabulary

Nouns

clāmor, -ōris, *m. shout* (clamor, clamorous)
forum, -ī, *n. marketplace, Forum (at Rome)*
mors, mortis, *f. death* (mortal, mortality)
vestis, -is, *f. clothing* (vest)

Adjectives

perītus, -a, -um, *skilled*
posterus, -a, -um, *following* (posterior, posterity)
tantus, -a, -um, *so great, so much, so large*

Verbs

perterreō, -ēre, -terruī, -territus, *scare thoroughly, alarm*
prehendō, -ere, -hendī, -hensus, *seize* (prehensile)
relinquō, -ere, relīquī, relictus, *leave (behind), abandon* (relinquish, relinquishment)

Adverbs

ita, *so, in such a way, thus*
paene, *almost*
saepe, *often*
sīc, *so, thus*
tālis, *such*
tam, *so*
tot, *so many*

Word Studies

Difficulties of English spelling due to silent or weakly sounded letters or to other causes are often cleared up by examination of the Latin. Give the Latin originals of the following words: *ascension, assign, comparative, conscience, consensus, debt, deficit, desperation, doubt, laboratory, receipt, reign, repetition, separate.*

Derivatives of compounds of **capiō** have *ei: rec**ei**ve, dec**ei**ve, conc**ei**ve, perc**ei**ve.* Explain by derivation *apprehension, penultimate, posterity, vestments.*

Vanni/Art Resource, NY

Caryatid is a term for an architectural support that is wholly or partly in human form. The Porch of Maidens, on the south face of the Erechtheum on the Acropolis, was done in 421-413 B.C. The porch was a great inspiration to the Romans, who made best use of the style at Hadrian's Villa at Tivoli.

LESSON OBJECTIVES
To review the fifth declension; To learn the present subjunctive of **sum** and **possum**; To learn the ablative of degree of difference

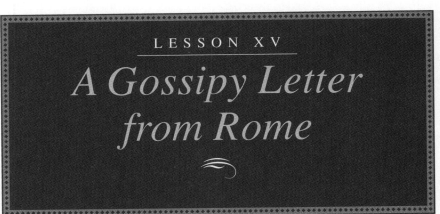

LESSON XV
A Gossipy Letter from Rome

STUDY TOPICS
The **Vigiles** (fire brigade); funeral rites

M. Caecilius Fūriānō suō. Rogāvistī, "Quid agit rēs pūblica?" Cōnsulēs proximī annī creatī sunt—Lepidus et Taurus. Ille Augustō cārus est. Maiōrēs eius erant Sulla et Pompeius, Caesaris inimīcus, sed Augustus tam concordiam cupit ut memoriam rērum eius modī dēpōnere possit.

Hic nūntius multō gravior erit: Corellius, tribūnus, iam[1] decem diēs mortuus est. Omnēs amīcī eius spem habuerant eum aegrum paucīs diēbus diūtius vīctūrum esse, ut frātrem, ex Galliā properantem, vidēre posset; sed hoc nōn permissum est. Fūnus īnsigne erat—ōrātiō ante domum habita, pompa longa, cornicinēs,[1] plūrimae imāginēs,[2] rogus[2] multōs pedēs altus (sed tot hominēs aderant ut difficile esset rogum vidēre), sepulchrum ēgregium.

Ovidius poēta, ex urbe ad oppidum barbarum expulsus, iam paene duōs annōs litterās supplicēs ad Augustum scrībit, sed hic nōn commovētur. Augustī autem silentium tantum est ut nēmō causam poenae Ovidī cognōscere possit. Ovidius librum novum ēdidit, quem emam et mittam ut legere possīs.

Nōvistīne Calpurnium, quī tantam pecūniam habet ut domus ūna eam capere nōn possit—illum quī aedificia incēnsa celeriter emit, tum, igne operā servōrum exercitōrum[3] exstīnctō, reficit? Agrum magnum ēmit. Multōs diēs iam cupiō agrum parvum emere, ut agricola in ōtiō sim. Pulchrum agrum in Sabīnīs, quī nōn multīs mīlibus passuum ab eō Horātī poētae abest, invēnī. Quid dē hōc putās?

Diēs omnēs paene similēs sunt. Surgō; clientibus audītīs, in Forum prōcēdō, ut aut iūdicia audīre possim aut senātuī adsim; prandium[4] capiō; dormiō; exerceor;[5] in thermās Agrippae prōcēdō, et ibi amīcōs videō. Tum est cēna, tum quiēs. Haec cotīdiē agimus. Quid agit Fūriānus meus?

[1] *buglers,* i.e., a band
[2] *funeral pyre*
[3] Not from **exercitus,** *army!*
[4] *lunch*
[5] *train myself, exercise*

---

[1] The present tense is used with **iam** where the English idiom calls for the present perfect: *has now been dead.*

[2] *wax masks* of ancestors who had held high public office. These were kept in a special room in the house and served as a portrait gallery. At funerals they were worn by hired mourners, so that it seemed as if all of a man's great ancestors were at his funeral.

Brian Blake/Photo Researchers

A visit to the baths was a frequent daily ritual, especially for well-to-do Romans, even far from home. These baths at Bath, England, were built around magnificent natural springs in A.D. 44. The upper gallery with busts of famous Romans was added in the 18th century. Bath is still today one of Britain's spas.

QUESTIONS

1. Where was Ovid?
2. Why was he punished?
3. Of whom was Augustus fond?
4. Where was Corellius' brother?

ADDITIONAL QUESTIONS
How often are consuls elected? Who are the consuls for next year? What happened to Corellius? What does Marcus want to buy? Describe a typical day for Marcus.

WORKBOOK
Assign Ex. A to review the fifth declension.

Grammar

Review of the Fifth Declension

There are relatively few words in the fifth declension, but two, such as **rēs** and **diēs**, are very common and must be memorized. All nouns in the fifth declension are feminine, except **diēs**, which is usually masculine.

SINGULAR	PLURAL	SINGULAR	PLURAL
diēs	diēs	rēs	rēs
diēī	diē**rum**	reī	rē**rum**
diēī	diē**bus**	reī	rē**bus**
diem	diēs	rem	rēs
diē	diē**bus**	rē	rē**bus**

Subjunctive of *Sum* and *Possum*

The present subjunctive of **sum** and **possum** has **–ī–** as its mood sign:

sim	s**īmus**	poss**im**	poss**īmus**
s**īs**	s**ītis**	poss**īs**	poss**ītis**
s**it**	s**int**	poss**it**	poss**int**

ORAL PRACTICE

1. Decline **ipsa rēs pūblica, multī diēs.**
2. Give the second singular of **sum** and the second plural of **possum** in all tenses of the indicative and in the present and imperfect subjunctive.
3. Tell the forms of **sumus, erunt, potuistī, posset, fuērunt, possint, esset, poterō, posse, fuerāmus.**

Ablative of Degree of Difference

The ablative without a preposition is used with comparatives and with **ante** and **post** to express the degree or measure of difference between two things.

Vīlla mea multō maior est quam tua.	*My house is much larger (larger by much) than yours.*
Paucīs post hōrīs puellam parvam invēnimus.	*A few hours later (after by a few hours) we found the little girl.*

TRANSLATION

1. Consuls were elected a few days before.
2. Ovid was banished to a town which was many miles away.
3. For two years Marcus had desired to buy a small farm so that he might be a farmer.
4. For many months Calpurnius had been setting buildings on fire so that he could buy them.

SUGGESTION
Have students work in pairs to produce a complete synopsis on the board of **sum** and **possum** in all persons and numbers, indicative and subjunctive. You may want to add **ferō** also, as a review.

NOTE
Remind students that the imperfect subjunctive of these verbs is regular: **essem, possem,** etc.

WORKBOOK
Assign Ex. B to practice the subjunctive of **sum** and **possum**.

CASSETTE
Do Unit II, Drill 3, Ex. A to practice the present subjunctive and Ex. B to practice the imperfect subjunctive.

SUGGESTION
Have students find all examples of the ablative of degree of difference in the reading. You may also want to review accusative of extent of space.

WORKBOOK
Assign Ex. C to practice the ablative of degree of difference.

ANSWERS
1. Cōnsulēs paucīs ante diēbus creātī sunt. 2. Ovidius ad oppidum quod multīs mīlibus passuum aberat expulsus est. 3. Duōs annōs Mārcus agrum parvum emere cupīverat ut agricola esset. 4. Multōs mēnsēs Calpurnius aedificia incenderat ut ea emere posset.

Vocabulary

Nouns

cliēns, -entis, *m. client* (clientele)
cōnsul, -ulis, *m. consul* (consulate)
ignis, -is, *m. fire* (ignite, ignition)
maiōrēs, -um, *m. pl. ancestors*
opera, -ae, *f. work, effort*
quiēs, -ētis, *f. rest* (quiescence, quiescent)
rēs, reī, *f. thing, matter, affair* (res gestae)
spēs, speī, *f. hope*

Adjectives

aeger, aegra, aegrum, *sick*
mortuus, -a, -um, *dead, having died* (mortuary)

Verbs

emō, -ere, ēmī, emptus, *take, buy*
incendō, -ere, incendī, incensus, *set on fire, burn* (incinerate, incinerator)
reficiō, -ere, refēcī, refectus, *repair* (refect, refectory)
surgō, -ere, surrexi, surrecturus, *rise* (resurrection, surge)
vīvo, -ere, vixi, victus, *live* (vivacious, vivid)

Adverb

cotīdiē, *daily* (quotidian)

Word Studies

For meaning and use of **prae–** (*pre–*), **contrā–** (*contra–, counter–*), **bene–** (*bene–*), **male–** (*male–*), see the Appendix. Define according to the prefix: *prevent, premonition, predict, preclude, prerequisite, counter-irritant, contradict, counterrevolutionary, benefactor, benediction, malefactor, malediction.*

What is the difference between a modern consul and an ancient Roman consul?

Explain *ignition, incendiary, refectory.*

Scala/Art Resource, NY

Ovid was born in 43 B.C., just a year after the assassination of Julius Caesar. Though his father had wanted him to pursue a political life, Ovid was drawn to the literary circles in Rome and very early on established himself as a major player in the poetry scene. He had a loyal following before the age of 20 and by the time he was 30 was considered Rome's leading poet.

NOTE
Have students identify **cliēns** and **ignis** as **i–**stems.

LESSON OBJECTIVES
To learn the pluperfect active subjunctive of all conjugations; To learn time clauses with **ubi, postquam, cum**

LESSON XVI
Alma Mater

[1] *to Athens*

STUDY TOPIC
Greek and Roman education

Cum Pūblius Fūriānusque Athēnās[1] iter facerent, multōs Rōmānōs in viā vīdērunt. Paucīs diēbus postquam Athēnās[1] pervēnērunt, multō plūrēs Rōmānōs vīdērunt. Namque plūrimī aliī Rōmānī eiusdem aetātis ad hanc urbem īnsignem vēnerant ut philosophōs rhētorēsque Graecōs audīrent. Tam clārī erant illī quī multōs annōs in hāc urbe docuerant ut multī discipulī ad eōs ex omnibus terrīs venīrent.

Cum amīcī duo paucōs diēs in urbe fuissent et multōs magistrōs audīvissent, Fūriānus Pūbliō dīxit: "Nōnne exīstimās magistrum nostrum Enchōriōnem acūtum et optimum omnium esse?" "Rēctē dīcis," respondit amīcus. "Gaudeō quod patrēs nostrī eum ēlēgērunt. Cēterōs quidem nōn contemnō, sed ille certē optimus est. Eō ōrātiōnem habente, mīrō modō affectus sum. Praetereā ea quae ille docet Rōmānīs ūtilissima sunt. Nam Rōmānī in forō senātūque ōrātiōnēs habent." Tum Fūriānus dīxit: "Etiam ea quae philosophī docent ūtilia sunt ut vītam bonam agāmus. Rōmānī quidem sumus, et Rōmānīs ūtilissimum est ōrātiōnēs habēre posse. Sed etiam hominēs sumus, et vīta bona ūtilior est quam ōrātiō bona."

Cum haec aliaque ab amīcīs duōbus nostrīs dē philosophīs rhētoribusque dicta essent, tandem Fūriānus dīxit: "Cōnsentīmus Enchōriōnem optimum esse. Gaudeāmus igitur quod in eius scholā sumus. Vīvat schola Enchōriōnis!"

ADDITIONAL QUESTIONS
Whom did Publius and Furianus see on their way to Athens? Which school did they attend? What did the boys think of their teacher?

QUESTIONS

1. Why was Publius glad?
2. What was useful to the Romans?
3. Why did many Romans go to Athens?
4. What is more useful than a good speech?

Young men used to gather around their favorite orator or philosopher to learn the fine art of rhetoric. This mosaic from the 1st century depicts several students clustered around their teacher, the great Plato.

Scala/Art Resource, NY

Grammar

Pluperfect Active Subjunctive

The pluperfect active subjunctive for all verbs, regular and irregular, is formed by adding the personal endings to the perfect active infinitive.

PLUPERFECT ACTIVE

portā**vissem**	docu**issem**	posu**issem**	cēp**issem**	mūnī**vissem**
portā**vissēs**	docu**issēs**	posu**issēs**	cēp**issēs**	mūnī**vissēs**
portā**visset**	docu**isset**	posu**isset**	cēp**isset**	mūnī**visset**
portā**vissēmus**	docu**issēmus**	posu**issēmus**	cēp**issēmus**	mūnī**vissēmus**
portā**vissētis**	docu**issētis**	posu**issētis**	cēp**issētis**	mūnī**vissētis**
portā**vissent**	docu**issent**	posu**issent**	cēp**issent**	mūnī**vissent**

SUGGESTION
Drill this tense orally with verbs from all conjugations, and include **sum, possum, ferō**.

ORAL PRACTICE

Conjugate the following verbs in the pluperfect active subjunctive: **incendō, cōnsentiō, possum.**

WORKBOOK
Assign Ex. A to practice the present, imperfect, and pluperfect subjunctive.

NOTE
Cum clauses are difficult for most students. Practice several sentences on the board; also remind students that it is less important that they be able to go from English to Latin than it is to recognize **cum** clauses in real Latin so they can translate them properly.

SUGGESTION
Have students find and translate all the **cum** clauses in the reading.

NOTĀ·BENE

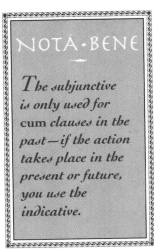

The subjunctive is only used for cum *clauses in the past—if the action takes place in the present or future, you use the indicative.*

WORKBOOK
Assign Ex. B to practice **cum** clauses.

ANSWERS
1. Pūblius, cum iter cum amīcō faceret, multōs virōs īnsignēs vīdit. 2. Paucīs post diēbus, amīcī duo ad pulcherrimam urbem Graeciae pervēnērunt. 3. Cum omnēs magistrōs vīdissent et audīvissent, suum magistrum optimum esse dīxērunt. 4. Postquam in urbe diū fuērunt, patrēs suōs sapientissimē ēlēgisse consensērunt.

Time Clauses: *Ubi, Postquam, Cum*

The conjunctions **ubi, postquam,** and **cum** are regularly used in Latin to express time clauses in the past. They are generally translated as *when, since,* or *although* in English. When simply establishing the time that something took place, **ubi**, **postquam**, and **cum** are followed by the perfect indicative.

Cum puerī in Graeciā erant, Lepidus consul creatus est.	*When the boys were in Greece, Lepidus was made consul.*
Postquam urbem vidērunt, ē Brundisiō excessērunt.	*After they saw the city, they left Brundisium.*

When a **cum** clause is expressing the circumstances under which or around which the action of the main verb has taken place, you use the imperfect or pluperfect subjunctive.

Cum puerōs Athēnās iter facerent, multōs Rōmānōs vidērunt.	*When the boys were on their way to Athens, they saw many Romans.*
Cum primum consensissent, pugnāre constituērunt.	*Although they had agreed at first, they decided to fight.*

TRANSLATION

1. When Publius was traveling with his friend, he saw many noted men.
2. A few days later the two friends arrived at (**ad**) the most beautiful city of Greece.
3. When they had seen and heard all the teachers, they said that their own teacher was the best.
4. After they had been[1] in the city for a long time, they agreed that their fathers had chosen most wisely.

[1] Use perfect indicative.

Vocabulary

Nouns

aetās, -tātis, *f. age, time of life*
fidēs, -eī, *f. trust, protection* (fidelity)

Adjectives

acūtus, -a, -um, *sharp* (acute, acuteness)
cēterī, -ae, -a, *the other(s)*
īnsignis, -e, *noted* (insignia, insignificant)
mīrus, -a, -um, *wonderful*

Verbs

cōnsentiō, -īre, -sēnsī, -sēnsus, *agree* (consensus, consent)
contemnō, -ere, -tempsī, -temptus, *despise* (contempt, contemptuous)
ēligō, -ere, ēlēgī, ēlēctus, *pick out* (elect, election)
exīstimō, -āre, -āvī, -ātus, *think*
gaudeō, -ēre, —, gāvīsus, *rejoice, be glad* (gaudery, gaudy)
perveniō, -īre, -vēnī, -ventūrus, *arrive (at), come (through)*

Adverbs

igitur, *therefore*
praetereā, *besides*
quidem, *at least, to be sure (follows emphasized word)*

Conjunction

cum, *when, since, although*

Word Studies

Most of our musical terms come from Italian and thus ultimately from Latin. Explain the following, all derived from Latin words used in this book: *accelerando* **(celer)**, *allegro* **(alacer)**, *alto, cantabile, cantata, con amore, contralto, crescendo, da capo* **(dē capite)**, *diminuendo* **(minuō)**, *duet, finale, forte, fortissimo, libretto, mezzoforte* **(medius)**, *octave, opus, piano, quintet, ritardando* **(tardus)**, *sextet, solo, sonata, soprano* **(super)**, *tempo, trio, vivace.*

Young women were taught the fine arts of needlework and music. This wall painting from Pompeii shows a young lady playing the cithara, an ancient stringed instrument resembling a lyre.

LESSON XVII

Athens the Beautiful

LESSON OBJECTIVES
To learn the perfect active and the perfect and pluperfect passive subjunctives; To review the sequence of tenses with the subjunctive

Paulō post[1] Pūblius litterās ad patrem mātremque mīsit, in quibus multa mīra dē urbe Athēnīs nārrāta sunt.

"Cum ad hanc urbem accessissēmus," scrīpsit, "cupīvimus quam prīmum Parthenōnem, templum Minervae, vidēre. In monte stat quī Acropolis appellātur. Huius montis portae, quārum nōmen est Propylaea, tam pulchrae sunt ut eō tempore diū spectantēs steterīmus. Ad Propylaea est templum parvum in quō est statua Victōriae sine ālīs facta. Cum dē hāc rogāvissēmus, respōnsum est: 'Dea Victōria ita facta est nē ab urbe discēderet.' Saepe dictum est Parthenōnem pulcherrimum esse omnium aedificiōrum; cum per Propylaea prōcessissēmus et ad Parthenōnem ipsum vēnissēmus, hoc intellegere poterāmus. In eō est statua Athēnae, altior quam sex virī. Dea ipsa ex ebore[2] facta est, vestis et arma ex aurō. Ita īnsignis est ut nēmō eam nōn permōtus spectāre possit, nēmō memoriam eius dēpōnere possit. Cum Parthenōnem vīdissēmus, ad aliud templum Athēnae prōcessimus, in porticū cuius sunt statuae virginum. Cum Acropolis relīcta esset, in Agoram dēscendimus. Ibi, inter alia, aedificium ā Caesare Augustōque factum vīdimus.

"Cum in urbe multōs diēs fuissēmus, et cotīdiē multa alia clāra loca invenīre potuissēmus, haec optima vīsa sunt: Stadium; Olympiēum, maximum templum Graeciae; Acadēmia, quae mīlle passibus ab urbe abest et in quā clārī philosophī docent. Tempus tam breve est et nōs tam dēfessī sumus ut lūdīs in theātrō habitīs nōndum adfuerīmus; theātrum autem vīdimus, et exīstimāmus id pulcherrimum esse.

"Sed urbs tanta est ut nōndum omnia loca aedificiaque amplissima ā nōbīs inventa sint. Sed quam prīmum ea petēmus et dē eīs scrībēmus."

Cum litterae lēctae essent, Rūfus multa alia dē Athēnīs tam grāta nārrāvit ut tandem Secunda dīceret, "Ōh! Cūr puer nōn sum! Ad eam urbem pulchram statim prōcēdere cupiō!"

[1] adverb
[2] *ivory*

STUDY TOPIC
The Acropolis

QUESTIONS

1. Of what material was the statue of Athena made?
2. What other places did Publius visit?
3. What did Publius want to see as soon as possible?
4. Why was the statue of Victory made without wings?

ADDITIONAL QUESTIONS
What is the Parthenon? Where is the Acropolis? How big was the statue of Athena? Did the boys attend the theater? Why not? What was Secunda's reaction?

From this angle, you can see the Propylaea, or entrance to the Acropolis at Athens. In the distance is the Temple of Athena Nike.

Vanni/Art Resource, NY

Grammar

Perfect Active and Perfect and Pluperfect Passive Subjunctive

The perfect active subjunctive looks very much like the future perfect indicative, except for the first person singular.

PERFECT ACTIVE				
portāv**erim**	docu**erim**	posu**erim**	cēp**erim**	mūnīv**erim**
portāv**erīs**	docu**erīs**	posu**erīs**	cēp**erīs**	mūnīv**erīs**
portāv**erit**	docu**erit**	posu**erit**	cēp**erit**	mūnīv**erit**
portāv**erīmus**	docu**erīmus**	posu**erīmus**	cēp**erīmus**	mūnīv**erīmus**
portāv**erītis**	docu**erītis**	posu**erītis**	cēp**erītis**	mūnīv**erītis**
portāv**erint**	docu**erint**	posu**erint**	cēp**erint**	mūnīv**erint**

For the passive voice of both the perfect and pluperfect subjunctive, use the perfect passive participle with the present or imperfect subjunctive of **sum**. Verbs of the first three conjugations are shown as models; the others are formed the same way.

PERFECT PASSIVE		
portātus, –a, –um sim	doctus, –a, –um sim	positus, –a, –um sim
portātus, –a, –um sīs	doctus, –a, –um sīs	positus, –a, –um sīs
portātus, –a, –um sit	doctus, –a, –um sit	positus, –a, –um sit
portātī, –ae, –a sīmus	doctī, –ae, –a sīmus	positī, –ae, –a sīmus
portātī, –ae, –a sītis	doctī, –ae, –a sītis	positī, –ae, –a sītis
portātī, –ae, –a sint	docti, –ae, –a sint	positī, –ae, –a sint

SUGGESTION
Choose a few verbs from the third **–io** and fourth conjugations to verify that students can follow the model.

PLUPERFECT PASSIVE		
portātus, –a, –um essem	doctus, –a, –um essem	positus, –a, –um essem
portātus, –a, –um essēs	doctus, –a, –um essēs	positus, –a, –um essēs
portātus, –a, –um esset	doctus, –a, –um esset	positus, –a, –um esset
portātī, –ae, –a essēmus	doctī, –ae, –a essēmus	positī, –ae, –a essēmus
portātī, –ae, –a essētis	doctī, –ae, –a essētis	positī, –ae, –a essētis
portātī, –ae, –a essent	doctī, –ae, –a essent	positī, –ae, –a essent

WORKBOOK
Assign Ex. A to practice perfect and pluperfect subjunctive.

Erich Lessing/Art Resource, NY

This statue of the goddess Victory, or Nike, was probably sculpted to commemorate a great naval victory by a Greek king. This figure, from Samothrace, is quite massive and has a very powerful effect. It was created around 190 B.C. and is now in the Louvre in Paris.

NOTĀ·BENE

The perfect subjunctive, like the perfect indicative, states an act as finished from the present point of view; *while the pluperfect subjunctive, like the pluperfect indicative, represents an act as finished from the* past point of view.

SUGGESTION
Have students work in pairs at the board to write a full synopsis, indicative and subjunctive, active and passive of a variety of verbs.

CASSETTE
Do Unit II, Drill 3, Ex. C and D to practice the perfect subjunctive and the pluperfect subjunctive.

WORKBOOK
Assign Ex. B to practice sequence of tenses.

NOTE
You may want to point out that the sequence of tenses with the subjunctive is not unlike that for the infinitives in indirect statement; the basic difference being that there is no future tense in the subjunctive.

ORAL PRACTICE

1. Give the first singular of **intellegō**, the second singular of **ferō**, the third singular of **līberō**, and the third plural of **reficiō** in all tenses of the subjunctive, active and passive.
2. Tell the form of **prehendātur, cōnsēnsisset, contemnī, contempsī, potuerīs, incēnsus sit, dolērent, ruptī essent, vexissēmus, exīstimārem, sītis.**

Summary of Sequence of Tenses

As you know, *sequence of tenses* is the term used to describe the relationship between the main verb and the subjunctive verb in the subordinate clause. There are two sequences, primary and secondary.

Primary sequence means that the main verb is in the present, future, or future perfect. The present subjuctive is used if the action in the subordinate clause is going on at the same time as or after the main verb. The perfect subjunctive is used if the action in the subordinate clause happened before the main verb.

MAIN VERB	SUBORDINATE VERB
present	present subjunctive (same time or time after)
future	perfect subjunctive (time before)
future perfect	

Secondary sequence means that the main verb is in the imperfect, perfect, or plurperfect. The imperfect subjunctive is used if the action in the subordinate clause is going on at the same time or after the main verb. The pluperfect subjunctive is used if the action in the subordinate clause happened before the main verb.

MAIN VERB	SUBORDINATE VERB
imperfect	present subjunctive (same time or time after)
perfect	perfect subjunctive (time before)
pluperfect	

The Bettmann Archive

The Olympeium, in Athens, is one of the largest Greek temples known. It was built by the emperor Hadrian in the 2nd century A.D. Note the majestic height of the Corinthian columns.

TRANSLATION

1. When Publius had been in the city a few days, he sent a letter to his father.
2. When Publius' sister had read his long letter, she asked many things about Athens.
3. The city was so large that he had not been able to see all the famous places.
4. A little later, when he stood before the Parthenon, he exclaimed, "This is the most beautiful of all temples!"

ANSWERS
1. Cum Pūblius paucōs diēs in urbe fuisset, litterās ad patrem mīsit. 2. Cum soror Pūblī litterās longās eius lēgisset, multa dē Athēnīs rogāvit. 3. Urbs tanta fuit ut omnia clāra loca vidēre nōn potuisset. 4. Paulō post, cum ante Parthenōnem stāret, clāmāvit, "Hoc est pulcherrimum omnium templōrum!"

Vocabulary

Nouns

ala, -ae, *f. wing* (alate)
aurum, -ī, *n. gold* (auric)
passus, -ūs, *m. step, pace;*
mīlle passūs, *mile*
porticus, ūs, *f. colonnade* (portico)
rūmor, -ōris, *m. rumor* (rumormonger)
statua, -ae, *f. statue* (statuesque, statuette)

WORKBOOK
Assign Ex. C to review the constructions with **mille/milia**.

Adjectives

dēfessus, -a, -um, *tired*
potēns, potentis (gen.), *powerful* (potent, potential)

Verbs

intellegō, -ere, -lēxī, -lēctus, *realize, understand* (intelligent, intelligible)
narrō, 1,[1] *tell, relate* (narrate, narrative)
pācō, 1, *pacify, subdue*

Adverbs

diū, *long*
nōndum, *not yet*
prīmum, *first* (prime, primeval)
quam prīmum, *as soon as possible*
statim, *at once, immediately*

Word Studies

For the meaning and use of **–ilis**, (*–ile, –il*), **–bilis** (*–ble, –able, –ible*), **–āris** (*–ar*), **–ārius** (*–ary*), see the Appendix. Give the English forms of **agilis, fertilis, memorābilis, possibilis, volūbilis, particulāris, necessārius.**

What are the Latin words from which are derived *facile, docile, delectable, defensible, fragile, noble, popular, primary?* Find five other examples of each of the suffixes *–ble* (*–able, –ible*), *–ar,* and *–ary* in English words derived from Latin words already studied.

---

[1] From now on verbs of the first conjugation whose principal parts are regular (i.e., like **portō**) will be indicated by the figure 1.

LESSON XVIII

A Request for Funds

LESSON OBJECTIVE
To learn deponent verbs

Pūblius patrī et mātrī et sorōribus suīs s. p. d. Sī valētis, bene est; valeō. Cum magnō gaudiō litterās vestrās hodiē accēpī, quās ante vīgintī quīnque diēs[1] scrīpsistis. Cum litterās lēgissem, Fūriānō eās dedī ut legeret. Cum dē Rōmā et amīcīs nostrīs locūtī essēmus, Fūriānus dīxit Rōmam longē abesse. Sed fēlīcēs sumus, nam amīcōs hīc[2] habēmus, et urbs pulcherrima est.

Vīta nostra tam quiēta est ut paene nihil scrībere possim. Sed tamen ūna rēs est dē quā scrībere necesse est. Potesne, pater, sine morā pecūniam mittere? Doleō quod haec scrībere necesse est, sed nōn est mea culpa. Omnia enim in hāc urbe tam cāra sunt ut paene tōta pecūnia mea cōnsūmpta sit. Enchōriō magister tam amīcus est ut multī mē fīlium, nōn discipulum eius esse arbitrentur. Sum tōtōs diēs cum eō et saepe noctis partem; nam mēcum saepe cēnat. Hīs temporibus dē multīs rēbus ita bene loquitur ut multa ūtilia audiam. Ob hanc causam eum saepe ad cēnam vocō. Hōc modō pecūnia celeriter cōnsūmitur.

Etiam ob aliam causam pecūniam habēre necesse est. Cum ab Enchōriōne multa dē partibus Graeciae dicta essent, dē Delphīs eum rogāvī. Ille respondit omnēs Delphōs propriīs oculīs vidēre dēbēre. Itaque quam celerrimē proficīscī cupimus ut illum locum videāmus. Enchōriō pollicitus est nōbīscum proficīscī et omnia mōnstrāre atque explicāre. Arbitror eum omnia scīre. Ita bene verba facit ut omnēs discipulōs mīrō modō affēcerit. Valēte.

[1] *twenty-five days ago* (literally, *before twenty-five days*)
[2] *here*

STUDY TOPIC
Letters, writing instruments/means

QUESTIONS

1. Why was Publius happy?
2. What trip did he plan to take?
3. Whom did he often invite to dinner?
4. How long did it take his father's letter to reach Publius?

ADDITIONAL QUESTIONS
Why is Publius out of money? Is his life very busy? Who seems to know everything?

Ancient Roman coinage often commemorated various exploits or buildings erected by the emperor. These coins, from 60-44 B.C. illustrate some of the special moments in Caesar's life. Do you know why the elephant was significant?

Boltin Picture Library

Grammar

Deponent Verbs

NOTE
Point out that there are about 40 deponent verbs—a fairly complete list is given in Ex. A of the workbook for this lesson.

Some Latin verbs are *active* in meaning but *passive* in form. They are called *deponents,* because they have *put away* **(dēpōnō)** their active forms. Deponent verbs are conjugated throughout the indicative and subjunctive like the passive of regular verbs of the four conjugations.

arbitror	*I think*
loquuntur	*they talk*

Some of the participles and infinitives of deponent verbs, however, are active in both form and meaning. The present and future participles and the future infinitive (formed from the future participle) are active in both form and meaning. The perfect participle, while passive in form, is active in meaning.

PARTICIPLES		**FORM**	**MEANING**
PRESENT	**arbitrāns,** *thinking*	active	active
PERFECT	**arbitrātus,** *having thought*	passive	active
FUTURE	**arbitrātūrus,** *going to think*	active	active
INFINITIVES			
PRESENT	**arbitrārī,** *to think*	passive	active
PERFECT	**arbitrātus esse,** *to have thought*	passive	active
FUTURE	**arbitrātūrus esse,** *to be going to think*	active	active

ORAL PRACTICE

1. Give and translate the third singular of **proficīscor** and the third plural of **polliceor** in all tenses of the indicative.
2. Give the second singular of **arbitror** and the second plural of **loquor** in all tenses of the subjunctive.
3. Give all the participles of **proficīscor** and the infinitives of **loquor.**

TRANSLATION

1. When Publius had spent all his money, he sent a letter to his father.
2. He said that his teacher spoke so well that he often invited him to dinner.
3. He wrote that his teacher had promised to set out with him **(sēcum)** to see Delphi.
4. Publius was with him almost night and day, and many thought that he was the teacher's son.

WORKBOOK
Assign Ex. A and B to practice deponent verbs.

ANSWERS
1. Publius, cum omnem pecūniam cōnsūmpsit, litterās ad patrem mīsit. 2. Dīxit magistrum suum tam bene loquī ut saepe eum ad cēnam vocāret. 3. Scrīpsit magistrum sēcum proficīscī pollicitum esse ut Delphōs vidēret. 4. Pūblius paene noctem diemque cum eō erat, et multī arbitrātī sunt eum fīlium magistrī esse.

NOTE
You may want to use these sentences to review sequence of tenses and indirect statement.

Delphi, a city in central Greece, is where Apollo killed the Python and founded the most famous center for prophesy in the ancient world. Here you can find the ***omphalos****, or beehive-shaped stone that indicated the center of the earth.*

G. Barone/SuperStock, Inc.

Vocabulary

Adjectives

fēlīx, fēlīcis (gen.), *happy, fortunate, successful, lucky* (felicific)
necesse, *necessary (indeclinable)*
quiētus, -a, -um, *quiet* (quietude)
totidem, *the same number (indeclinable)*
vīgintī, *twenty (indeclinable)*

Verbs

arbitror, arbitrārī, arbitrātus,[1] *think* (arbitrate, arbitration)
cōnsūmō, -ere, -sūmpsī, -sūmptus, *use up, spend* (consume, consumption)
loquor, loquī, locūtus, *talk* (loquacious, soliloquy)
polliceor, pollicērī, pollicitus, *promise*
proficīscor, proficīscī, profectus, *set out, start*
sollicitō, 1, *stir up* (solicitate, solicitor)
versō, 1, *turn over; (passive) live* (verso)

Adverb

longē, *far*

Word Studies

Here are a few scientific terms: *antenna* in Latin means "sail yard"; carbon is from **carbō**, "coal"; *detector* **(dē, tegō)**; *deterrent* **(dē, terreō)**; *exhaust* **(ex, hauriō)**; *flux* **(fluō)**; *neutron* **(neuter)**; *nucleus, nuclear, thermonuclear* (**nucleus, nux;** *thermo–* is from a Greek word meaning "heat") *operational* **(opus)**; *radar, radiation, ray* (**radius,** "ray"); *rotate* (**rota,** "wheel"); *sensor* **(sentio)**; *vehicle* **(vehō)**.

---

[1] In this book the principal parts of deponent verbs are given as present indicative, present infinitive, and perfect participle: **arbitror, arbitrārī, arbitrātus.** Regular deponent verbs of the first conjugation will be indicated by the figure 1 in the vocabularies.

LESSON XIX
A Wedding

LESSON OBJECTIVES
To review personal and reflexive pronouns; To learn indirect question

STUDY TOPIC
Marriage ceremonies

Pūbliō in Graeciā studente, rēs grātissima Rōmae[1] agēbātur—nūptiae Caeciliae, sorōris Pūblī, et M. Iūnī Vorēnī. Paucīs mēnsibus ante Caeciliīs Iūniīsque in ātrium Rūfī cum amīcīs ingressīs, pater Vorēnī cum fīliō prō Rūfō et Caeciliā cōnstiterat Rūfumque rogāverat: "Spondēsne fīliam tuam fīliō meō uxōrem?"[2] Rūfus responderat: "Spondeō." Tum Vorēnus Caeciliae ānulum,[3] Caecilia Vorēnō pulchrum servum dederat, et patrēs inter sē dē dōte[4] ēgerant—quantum Rūfus in animō habēret dare, quō modō pecūnia parārī posset.

Tandem diēs nūptiārum aderat. Prīdiē Caecilia mūnera Laribus dederat;[1] nunc, sōle oriente, ōminibus optimīs nūntiātīs, ā mātre ad nūptiās parābātur, et cum eā amīcae loquēbantur. Māter flammeum[5] et deinde corōnam in caput Caeciliae posuit.

"Mīror quid frāter meus agat," dīxit Caecilia, "et quid arbitrātūrus sit, nūntiō dē mē allātō."

Nunc Caecilia cum mātre amīcīsque in ātrium adōrnātum dēscendit, ubi Rūfus et pontifex exspectābant. Cum Vorēnus et amīcī in ātrium ingressī essent, prōnuba[2] manūs Caeciliae et Vorēnī iūnxit, et Caecilia dīxit, "Ubi tū Gāius, ego Gāia."[3] Eīs nunc sedentibus, pontifex deōs (maximē Iūnōnem) vocāvit. Deinde omnēs "Fēlīciter!" clāmāvērunt. "Spērō vōbīs omnia bona futūra esse, vītam vestram longam!"

"Nōn iam nostra est," Rūfus Vorēnō dīxit, "sed tua."

Nōnā hōrā cēna maxima allāta est, et Rūfus nūntiāvit, "Nōs cibō reficiāmus." Omnēs uxōrem pulchram mīrātī sunt.

Vesperī omnēs in viam sē recēpērunt. Ibi, mātre flente et Caeciliam retinente, aliī pompam parāvērunt. Subitō Vorēnus Caeciliam rapuit, et pompa profecta est, amīcīs canentibus, rīdentibus, "Talassiō!"[4] clāmantibus. Cum

[1] *at Rome*
[2] *(as) wife*
[3] *ring*
[4] *dowry*
[5] *bridal veil* (flame-colored)

Just as today, weddings were a special day in the lives of Romans. The bride and groom ate a special cake. Then there was a procession to the bride's new home, where her husband was waiting for her. After a ceremony, the groom carried his bride over the threshold. This husband and wife are depicted on a sarcophagus in Rome.

Nimatallah/Art Resource, NY

[1] On the eve of her marriage, the Roman girl dedicated her toys and childish garments to the household gods.
[2] The *matron* who attended the bride.
[3] An old formula, equivalent to "Where you go, I will go."
[4] An ancient marriage cry, the meaning of which is unknown.

ad iānuam domūs Vorēnī accessissent, Caecilia eam adōrnāvit. Postquam Vorēnus uxōrem per iānuam portāvit,[5] Caecilia iterum dīxit, "Ubi tu Gāius, ego Gāia." In ātriō Vorēnus mātrōnae novae ignem aquamque dedit.[6] Posterō diē cēna altera data est, ubi Caecilia deīs sacrificāvit. Familia eius nōn iam Caecilia, sed Iūnia erat.

ADDITIONAL QUESTIONS
What did Vorenus give to Caecilia? What did Caecilia do first on her wedding day? What did she wear? What did Vorenus give to Caecilia after they entered the house?

QUESTIONS

1. What did the priest do?
2. What did the matron do?
3. By whom was a slave given?

Grammar

Form Review

Personal Pronouns

The personal pronouns for the first and second persons are as follows. The third person personal pronoun is **is, ea, id,** which was reviewed earlier. If you do not remember the declension, refer to Lesson VIII.

WORKBOOK
Assign Ex. A to review personal and reflexive pronouns.

SINGULAR	PLURAL	SINGULAR	PLURAL
ego	nōs	tū	vōs
meī	nostrum (nostrī)	tuī	vestrum (vestrī)
mihi	nōbīs	tibi	vōbīs
mē	nōs	tē	vōs
mē	nōbīs	tē	vōbīs

Reflexive Pronouns

The reflexive pronouns for the first and second persons are the same as the personal pronouns, except that there is no nominative. Since a reflexive refers back to the nominative, it can't be one.

SINGULAR	PLURAL
suī	suī
sibi	sibi
sē (sēsē)	sē (sēsē)
sē (sēsē)	sē (sēsē)

[5] So that she might not stumble on the threshold—an unlucky omen.
[6] With these gifts, symbols of the essentials of domestic life, the bride becomes the mistress of the house.

ORAL PRACTICE

1. Give and translate the dative singular and plural of **ego, tū, is, suī;** give the ablative singular and plural of the same.
2. Conjugate reflexively and translate the present and perfect tenses of **ego mē moneō, tū tē monēs,** etc.
3. Give the third singular of **sē contemnere** in all tenses of the indicative and subjunctive.

Indirect Questions

An indirect question in Latin includes an interrogative word and a verb of asking, knowing, saying, perceiving, etc. The verb in the indirect question is in the subjunctive, following the rule for sequence of tenses. Compare the following direct and indirect questions.

"Ubi id invēnistī?"	*Where did you find it?*
Mē rōgāvit ubi id invēnissēs.	*He asked me where you had found it.*

SUGGESTION
Have students make up simple direct questions (in English), then change them to indirect questions (also in English). When they become more comfortable with finding the question word and determining the correct sequence of tenses, do the same thing in Latin.

Ronald Sheridan/Ancient Art & Architecture Collection

In this 2nd century A.D. *relief you can see the priest officiating at the wedding ceremony. Notice that the bride and groom have joined their hands.*

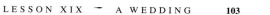

NOTĀ·BENE

If the indirect question has a yes/no answer, it is introduced by **num. Rogavit num id invenissem.** He asked if I had found it.

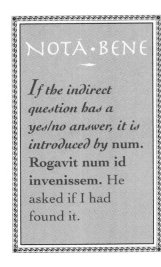

NOTE
Remind students that there is a big difference between indirect statement, which uses an infinitive, and indirect question, which uses the subjunctive. Finding the question word is the key.

WORKBOOK
Assign Ex. B to practice indirect question.

CASSETTE
Do Unit II, Drill 4 to practice indirect questions and sequence of tenses.

SUGGESTION
Before students translate these sentences, have them identify the question word and the appropriate sequence.

ANSWERS
1. Caecilia mīrābātur quid Pūblius dē nuptiīs putāret. 2. Amīcae eam rogāvērunt quantum pecūniae (quanta pecūnia) darētur. 3. Sē rogābat ubi (quō in locō) Pūblius tum (eō tempore) esset et quid faceret/ageret. 4. Cum pompa profecta esset, amīcī sē rogāvērunt quō modō Vorēnus et Caecilia ingrederentur/ingressūrī essent.

In this case, **ubi** is the question word after a verb of asking, knowing, etc. It is in the secondary sequence, so the pluperfect subjunctive is used. To review the sequence of tenses, study the following sentences, paying attention to the clocks.

I Time: 3 P.M. Place: Schoolroom *you*

Rogō quid faciās.
I ask (now) what you are doing (now).

Rogō quid fēcerīs.
I ask (now) what you did (earlier).

Rogāvī quid facerēs.
I asked (then) what you were doing (then).

Rogāvī quid fēcissēs.
I asked (then) what you had done (earlier).

TRANSLATION

1. Caecilia wondered what Publius thought about the wedding.
2. Her (girl) friends asked her how much money was being given.
3. She kept asking herself where Publius then was and what he was doing.
4. When the procession had started, the friends asked themselves how Vorenus and Caecilia would enter.

Vocabulary

Nouns

pontifex, pontificis, *m. priest* (pontiff, pontificate)
sōl, sōlis, *m. sun* (solar, solarium)
uxor, -ōris, *f. wife* (uxorial, uxorious)
vesper, -erī, *m. evening;* (vespers, vespertine)
vesperī, *in the evening*

Adjectives

plērīque, -aeque, -aque, *most*
quantus, -a, -um, *how great, how much* (quantity, quantum)

Verbs

canō, -ere, cecinī, cantus, *sing, tell (about)* (cant, cantabile)
experior, experīrī, expertus, *try* (experience, experiment)
ingredior, ingredī, ingressus, *step into, enter* (ingredient)
mīror, 1, *wonder, admire*
orior, orīrī, ortus, *rise*
spondeo, -ēre, spopondi, sponsus, *promise, engage* (respond, response)
studeō, -ēre, studuī, —, *be eager (for), study* (student, studious)

Adverbs

paulisper, *for a little while*
prīdiē, *on the day before*
subito, *suddenly*

Word Studies

The base ending of the Latin present participle (**–ant, –ent, –ient,** according to conjugation) is used as a suffix in English. All English words derived from the first conjugation have **–ant**; most of those derived from the other conjugations have **–ent**; but some derived through the French have **–ant**. Give examples.

The addition of **–ia** to the base ending of the present participle gives a suffix **–antia, –entia (–ance, –ence, –ancy, –ency)**. The same rule for spelling which was given above holds true. Give samples.

Explain *ingredient, loquacity, miracle, orient, quantity, soliloquy, solstice, uxoricide, vespers.*

LESSON OBJECTIVES
To learn the indefinite pronouns and adjectives; To learn the conjugation of **eō**

LESSON XX
The Trip to Delphi

Pater Pūbliō pecūniam praebuerat ut is et Fūriānus Delphōs[1] īrent. Cum diēs cōnstitūtus adesset, ad Enchōriōnem iērunt, quī pollicitus erat cum eīs īre. Itaque hī trēs cum servīs aliquibus ex urbe Athēnīs exiērunt.

Cūr cupīvērunt Delphōs vidēre? Quod hic locus erat, ut ita dīcam,[2] templum tōtīus Graeciae. In hōc locō erat īnsigne ōrāculum Apollinis. Multī ex omnibus partibus terrae vēnērunt ut ōrāculum cōnsulerent. Praetereā locus ipse pulcherrimus erat—et est.

Itaque amīcī nostrī duo per sacram viam eunt quae ad urbem clāram Eleusim dūcit et ex illā urbe ad aliam urbem clāram, Thēbās, prōcēdunt. Cum post paucōs diēs ad fīnem itineris vēnissent, gaudiō et admīrātiōne complētī sunt. Namque urbs sub monte Parnassō posita pulcherrima erat. Fōrmam maximī theātrī habēbat. Ab[3] ūnā parte erant saxa alta; ab alterā, arborēs et flūmen et alter mōns.

Haec omnia diū mīrātī ad fontem īnsignem Castalium vēnērunt. Omnēs quī ōrāculum cōnsulēbant aquā huius fontis sē lavābant. Hic fōns Apollinī Mūsīsque sacer erat.

Tum viātōrēs nostrī aedificia aliqua cōnspexērunt quae thēsaurī[4] appellāta sunt. Haec cīvitātēs quaedam Graecae propter victōriam aliquam aedificāvērunt. Auctor quīdam Graecus dīxit Cnidiōs nōn ob rēs in proeliō bene gestās thēsaurum aedificāvisse sed ut opēs suās ostenderent. In hīs aedificiīs et in aliīs partibus urbis erant tria mīlia statuārum.

Hīs aedificiīs vīsīs, templum Apollinis ingressī statim sententiās[5] septem sapientium Graecōrum litterīs magnīs īnscrīptās cōnspexērunt: "Cognōsce tē ipsum," "nē quid nimis,"[6] et cētera. Sed in ōrāculum ipsum ingredī nōn potuērunt, quod ōrāculum tam sacrum erat ut paucī ingrederentur.

Itaque ad fontem rediērunt et eum et saxa et arborēs et caelum iterum mīrātī ad cēnam vesperī discessērunt.

QUESTIONS

1. What spring did the boys see?
2. What cities did they see after they left Athens?
3. Why did the Greek states erect buildings at Delphi?
4. What mottoes did the boys see in the temple of Apollo?

[1] *to Delphi*
[2] *so to speak* (literally, *to say (it) so*)
[3] *on*
[4] *treasuries*
[5] *sayings*
[6] *nothing in excess*

STUDY TOPICS
Delphi; Delphic Oracle

SUGGESTION
Tell students that **Delphi** is declined like a second declension masculine plural noun, though it is translated in the singular. It takes a plural verb.

NOTE
There is a selection (in English) at the end of this lesson on the Seven Wise Men of Greece.

SUGGESTION
Ask students to think of famous or wise sayings by poets, writers, philosophers, or politicians today.

ADDITIONAL QUESTIONS
Who went on the trip? How long did it take to get there? Describe the physical layout of the city. Why was the spring important?

Vanni/Art Resource, NY

The Treasury of the Athenians at Delphi was where the Athenians housed their trophies and offerings to Apollo. It dates from the late 6th century B.C.

Grammar

Indefinite Pronouns and Adjectives

Indefinite pronouns and adjectives refer to persons and things in an indefinite way. They are usually translated as *someone* or *something*. There are three levels of indefinite pronouns and adjectives.

Quīdam means a *certain or definite someone or something*; someone or something I know of.

Quendam vīdī quī tē esse magnum dīxit.	*I saw someone who said you were great.*

SUGGESTION
Point out that although all three are indefinite, there are levels of indefiniteness, just as there are in English.

The declension is similar to **quī** with a **–dam** as a suffix. The pronoun and the adjective are declined the same EXCEPT in the neuter nominative and accusative singular which is **quiddam** for the pronoun. The adjective declension is as follows:

SUGGESTION
Remind students of the declensions of **quis/quid** and **quī/quae/quod**. Point out the similarities and differences.

SINGULAR			PLURAL		
M	F	N	M	F	N
quīdam	quaedam	quoddam	quīdam	quaedam	quaedam
cuiusdam	cuiusdam	cuiusdam	quōrundam	quārundam	quōrundam
cuidam	cuidam	cuidam	quibusdam	quibusdam	quibusdam
quendam	quandam	quoddam	quōsdam	quāsdam	quaedam
quōdam	quādam	quōdam	quibusdam	quibusdam	quibusdam

Aliquis, which is a compound of **quis**, means someone or something—I don't know who; someone/something or other. It is less definite than **quidam**.

Puto aliquem ibi habitare.	*I think that someone lives here.*

The pronoun is declined like **quis** with an **ali-** as a prefix EXCEPT in the neuter nominative and accusative plural, which is **aliqua**; the adjective is declined much like **qui**, as follows:

NOTĀ·BENE

Notice that the feminine nominative singular is not exactly like quī.

SINGULAR			PLURAL		
M	F	N	M	F	N
aliqui	aliqua	aliquod	aliquī	aliquae	aliqua
alicuius	alicuius	alicuius	aliquōrum	aliquārum	aliquōrum
alicui	alicuī	alicui	aliquibus	aliquibus	aliquibus
aliquem	aliquam	aliquod	aliquōs	aliquās	aliqua
aliquō	aliquā	aliquo	aliquibus	aliquibus	aliquibus

WORKBOOK
Assign Ex. A to practice indefinite adjectives.

Quis, the indefinite pronoun (declined like the interrogative **quis** EXCEPT in the nominative singular feminine and neuter nominative and accusative plural, which is **qua**) is the least definite of all. It means *some* or *any*, and it is only used after **sī, nisi, num, and nē**.

Sī quis me vidit, timēbitur.	*If anyone sees me, he will be frightened.*
Curram nē quis mē videat.	*I shall run so that no one sees me.*

Conjugation of *Eō*

The verb **eō**, *go,* is irregular in the present, future, and perfect tenses:

Boltin Picture Library

The Temple of Apollo contains the ancient home of the Delphic Oracle, who was consulted by Oedipus, Socrates, and many others. Two maxims are inscribed on the walls of the temple, "Know Thyself" and "Nothing in Excess."

NOTE
Point out that **eo**, like other important verbs, is frequently compounded. Some of the compounds of **eō** are transitive (**adeō, trānseō**) and therefore have passive forms (which are regular: **adeor**, etc.).

PRESENT		FUTURE		PERFECT	
eō	**īmus**	**ībō**	**ībimus**	**iī**	**iimus**
īs	**ītis**	**ībis**	**ībitis**	**iīstī**	**īstis**
it	**eunt**	**ībit**	**ībunt**	**iit**	**iērunt**

NOTA·BENE

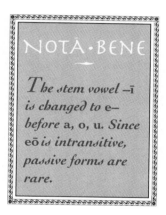

The stem vowel –ī *is changed to* e– *before* a, o, u. *Since* eō *is intransitive, passive forms are rare.*

The principal parts of **eo** are **eo, ire, ivi, iturus**. Although the present subjunctive is conjugated regularly, it has an irregular stem and the present participle has a stem change in the genitive.

PRESENT SUBJUNCTIVE		PRESENT PARTICIPLE
eam	eāmus	iēns, euntis
eās	eātis	
eat	eant	

WORKBOOK
Assign Ex. B to practice the forms of **eō**.

ORAL PRACTICE

1. Decline **duo oculī, trēs arborēs, mīlle cōnsulēs, duo mīlia vīllārum.**
2. Give the third singular of **eō**, the first plural of **exeō**, and the third plural of **redeō** in all tenses of the active indicative and subjunctive.

TRANSLATION

1. Some often returned to see the place and to consult the oracle.
2. Delphi was so famous that many thousands of people went to see it.
3. This beautiful place was called by some the temple of entire Greece.
4. Publius got money from his father in order to go to the city (of) Delphi.
5. If any one desired to consult the oracle about a certain matter, do you know what he did first?

ANSWERS
1. Aliquī saepe redībant ut locum vidērent et ōrāculum cōnsulerent. 2. Delphī tam clārī erant ut multa mīlia populōrum īrent ut eōs vidērent. 3. Hic locus pulcher ab nōn nūllīs templum totīus Graeciae appellātus est. 4. Pūblius ā patre pecūniam parāvit ut ad urbem Delphōs īret. 5. Scīsne quid prīmum fēcerit sī quis ōrāculum dē quādam rē cōnsulere cupiēbat?

Vocabulary

Nouns

arbor, -oris, *f. tree* (arboreal, arboretum)
caelum, -ī, *n. sky*
fōns, fontis, *m. spring* (font)
gaudium, gaudī, *n. joy* (gaudery, gaudy)
ops, opis, *f. aid; (pl.) wealth*
ōrāculum, -ī, *oracle, prophesy* (oracular)
saxum, -ī, *n. rock*

Pronouns

aliquis, aliquid, *some(one), any*
quīdam, quaedam, quiddam, *certain (one)*

Adjectives

aliquī, aliqua, aliquod, *some(one), any*
quīdam, quaedam, quoddam, *certain (one)*

Verbs

compleō, -ēre, -ēvī, -ētus, *fill, cover, complete* (completion)
eō, īre, iī, itūrus, *go*
exeō, exīre, exiī, exitūrus, *go out (from), go forth* (exit)
praebeō, -ēre, -uī, -itus, *furnish*
redeō, -īre, rediī, reditūrus, *go back, return*

Prepositions

ob (+ acc.), *because of, on account of* (obscure, obstruct)
propter (+ acc.), *because of, on account of*

Word Studies

Here are some legal phrases in English:

Supersedeas, *(I command that) you suspend (proceedings).*

Ne exeat, *Let him not go out (of the jurisdiction of the court).*

Caveat emptor, *Let the buyer beware* (for he buys at his own risk).

Scire facias, *(I demand that) you cause to know (why a certain court action should not be carried out).*

Habeas corpus, *(I command that) you have the body (of a certain person brought into court),* a writ issued by a judge to see whether a person is justly imprisoned.

Look up the meanings of **mandamus, nunc pro tunc, post mortem, prima facie, pro bono publico**.

The Seven Wise Men of Greece

A common practice of the scholars of antiquity was the drawing up of lists (called *canons*) of persons considered outstanding in their fields. Thus there have been preserved for us lists of "The Ten Attic Orators," "The Nine Lyric Poets," and "The Seven Wise Men." Here is one version of the names of the Seven Wise Men, with one of the sayings each is supposed to have made famous. Many of these men were politicians or poets, as well as philosophers. All of them lived between 620 and 550 B.C.

Cleobulus of Rhodes	*"Moderation is the chief good"*
Periander of Corinth	*"Forethought in all things"*
Pittacus of Mytilene	*"Know your opportunity"*
Bias of Priene	*"Too many workers spoil the work"*
Thales of Miletus	*"To go bond brings ruin"*
Chilon of Sparta	*"Know thyself"*
Solon of Athens	*"Nothing in excess"*

SUGGESTION
Have students do some research on one or more of these people.

Ronald Sheridan/Ancient Art & Architecture Collection

In addition to attending school, young Romans learned the art of oratory, or speech-making, by listening to famous speakers and trying to imitate them.

LESSON OBJECTIVE
To learn the formation and use of the future passive participle (gerundive)

LESSON XXI
Totalitarianism and Democracy

STUDY TOPICS
Democracy; Plutarch's *Life* of Lycurgus

Quōdam diē Pūblius Fūriānusque cum aliīs adulēscentibus dē Spartā Athēnīsque loquēbantur. "Certē omnibus concēdendum est Spartānōs antīquōs omnium fortissimōs fuisse," ūnus ē Graecīs dīxit; "nōnne Leōnidam memoriā tenēs, quī cum CCC cīvibus apud Thermopylās[1] tam fortiter pugnāvit? Alacrī animō suōs ad id proelium hortātus est quō peritūrī erant."

"Ea quae dīcis nōn negō," alter dīxit, "sed Athēniēnsēs quoque fortēs fuērunt. Fortēs quidem Spartānī fuērunt sed aliās virtūtēs nōn habuērunt. Lycurgus,[2] dux ille antīquus, ob sevēritātem lēgum accūsandus est.

Deinde Fūriānus rogāvit quid Pūblius arbitrārētur. "Concēdō Athēniēnsēs meliōrēs esse," hic respondit. "Vīta dūra puerīs Spartānīs agenda erat. Septem annōs nātī[1] mātrēs relinquēbant ut ad bellum instituerentur. Cēnās ipsī parābant ex pessimīs cibīs, nam Spartānī crēdēbant famem optimum condīmentum cibī esse. Puerī flagellīs caesī sunt, patribus ad patientiam hortantibus, ut dolōrem ferre discerent."

"Etiam peior," quīdam adulēscēns Athēniēnsis dīxit, "erat vīta eōrum quōs Spartānī vīcērunt. Nōn sōlum servī factī sunt sed multae iniūriae eīs ferendae erant. Ā quibusdam sēcrētō observābantur. Ille servus quī faciem hominis līberī habuit occīsus est. Vestis servīlis omnibus servīs gerenda erat. Cotīdiē caesī sunt ut memoriā tenērent sē servōs esse."

"Nōn negō vītam servōrum miserrimam esse," Fūriānus dīxit, "sed pessima erat vīta Spartānōrum ipsōrum. Etiam in pāce semper in castrīs habitābant. Lībertās eīs nōn nōta fuit. Omnia prō patriā facienda erant; nihil tamen patria prō populō fēcit. 'Prō bonō pūblicō' significāvit 'prō bonō reī pūblicae,' nōn 'prō bonō cīvium.' "

"Vērum dīcis," Athēniēnsis dīxit. "Memoriā teneāmus verba nōbilis Periclis, quī dīxit rem pūblicam Athēniēnsium in manibus plūrimōrum, nōn paucōrum, esse; cīvibus ēgregiīs omnium generum mūnera pūblica

[1] *at the age of seven* (literally, *born seven years*)

Pericles, 495-429 B.C., was a major political leader in Athens during a time when Athenian culture and military power were at their height. Among other things, he initiated a great public building program that included the Parthenon.

C. M. Dixon

[1] *at Thermop´ylae*, a mountain pass in Greece

[2] *Lycur´gus*, the king who was supposed to have originated the Spartan way of life

praemia esse; iūra paria omnibus esse. Athēniēnsibus lībertās cārissima fuit; itaque illī nōn īrātī fuērunt sī aliī fēcērunt id quod amāvērunt. Puerī eōrum in pāce vīxērunt nec ad bellum semper īnstitūtī sunt. Alacrī tamen animō in bellō pugnāvērunt et periērunt. Artēs līberālēs coluērunt; itaque eōrum urbs schola Graeciae fuit."

"Vērum est," Pūblius dīxit; "etiam nunc haec urbs schola est, nōn sōlum Graeciae sed orbis terrārum. Athēnae statuās pulcherrimās, aedificia ēgregia, librōs optimōs nōbīs dedērunt. Spērō omnēs gentēs semper Athēnīs, nōn Spartae, similēs futūrās esse."

QUESTIONS

1. Who died at Thermopylae?
2. In what way were Spartan slaves worse off than any others?
3. What did the Athenians consider to be of highest importance?

ADDITIONAL QUESTIONS
Who was Leonidas? Who had a harder life, Athenians or Spartans? What was the childhood of Spartan boys like? Who was Pericles?

Grammar

Formation and Use of the Future Passive Participle

The *future passive participle*, often called the *gerundive*, is formed by adding **–ndus, –a, –um** to the present stem of any verb. In the case of **–iō** verbs add **–endus**. The stem vowel is shortened before **–nd–**.

portandus, –a, –um	*to be carried*
docendus, –a, –um	*to be taught*
ponendus, –a, –um	*to be put*
capiendus, –a, –um	*to be taken*
mūniendus, –a, –um	*to be built*

The future passive participle is often used with a form of **sum** as a predicate adjective to express obligation or necessity. In English, we insert the words *must, had to, ought to,* etc. The person upon whom the obligation rests is in the dative; this is called the dative of agent. This construction is sometimes called the passive periphrastic.

SUGGESTION
Have students practice all the different possible translations with some simple sentences on the board.

Hic liber legendus est.	*This book is to be read.*
	This book has to be read.
	This book must be read.
	This book ought to be read.
Hic liber tibi legendus est.	*This book must be read by you.*
	You must read this book.

SUGGESTION
Have students find all the examples of passive periphrastics in the reading and translate.

NOTE
Remind students that the ablative of agent uses the preposition **ā** or **ab** after a passive verb.

A Roman mosaic shows a skeleton pointing to the Greek motto **gnothi sauton**, *which in Latin is* **cognosce te ipsum.** *The point here is that life is short.*

The Bettmann Archive

WORKBOOK
Assign Ex. A, B to practice forming and using the gerundive.

ORAL PRACTICE

Give the future passive participle of **caedō**, **negō**, **compleō**, and **excipiō**.

TRANSLATION

ANSWERS
1. Puerīne semper ad bellum īnstituendī sunt? 2. Quid prō patriā nōbīs faciendum est? 3. Pūblius rogāvit cūr Lycurgus nōbīs accūsandus est. 4. Cūr cēna ā puellīs ipsīs paranda erat?

1. Must boys always be trained for war?
2. What ought to be done by us for our country?
3. Publius asked why Lycurgus had to be blamed by us.
4. Why did dinner have to be prepared by the girls themselves?

Vocabulary

Nouns

NOTE
Have students identify **adulescēns** and **famēs** as **i**–*stems.*

adulēscēns, -entis, *m. young man*	(adolescence, adolescent)
famēs, -is (abl. **fame**), *f. hunger*	(famine, famish)
flagellum, -ī, *n. whip*	(flagellate)

Adjective

alacer, -cris, -cre, *eager*	(alacrity)

Verbs

adeō, adīre, adiī, aditūrus, *go to, approach* (adit)

caedō, -ere, cecīdī, caesus, *cut, beat, kill* (caesura)

concēdō, -ere, -cessī, -cessūrus, *withdraw, grant* (concede)

discō, -ere, didicī, —, *learn*

hortor, 1, *urge, encourage*

instituō, -ere, instituī, institūtus, *establish, train* (institute, institution)

negō, 1, *deny, say . . . not* (negate, negation)

pereō, -īre, -iī, -itūrus, *perish*

significō, 1, *mean* (signify, significant)

Adverbs

fortiter, *bravely*

prōtinus, *immediately*

quoque, *too (follows the word it emphasizes)*

Word Studies

Spanish is so much like Latin that it is easy for those who know Latin to recognize hundreds of Spanish words, especially if you know a few simple principles. Spanish nouns are usually not derived from the Latin nominative but from a common form made from the other cases.

If you remember that the final letters and syllables are often lost in Spanish, you can give the Latin for *alto, ánimo, ceder, constituir, dar, fácil, gente, libro, orden, responder.*

If you know that double consonants become single, you can give the Latin from which are derived *aceptar, común, difícil, efecto.*

If you know that *e* often becomes *ie*, and *o* becomes *ue*, you can give the Latin for *bien, ciento, cierto, tierra; bueno, cuerpo, fuerte, muerte, nuestro, puerto.*

Since *c* and *q* sometimes become *g*, and *t* becomes *d*, what must be the Latin words from which are derived *agua, amigo, edad, libertad, madera, madre, padre, todo*?

Since *li* becomes *j*, and *ct* becomes *ch*, from what Latin words are the following derived: *ajeno, consejo, dicho, mejor, noche, ocho?*

LESSON OBJECTIVES
To learn indirect commands;
To learn substantive clauses of result

LESSON XXII

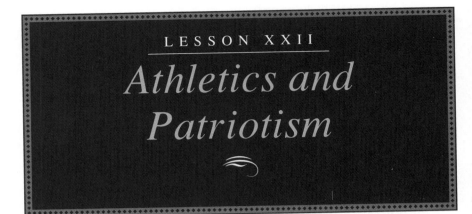

Athletics and Patriotism

STUDY TOPICS
Athletics; the Olympic Games

Athletics and fitness were not only important parts of a man's daily workout ritual, but they also provided great entertainment. Boxing has been popular for hundreds of years; in fact, it was one of the original Olympic sports. The gloves used then are not quite like those used today, however.

Scala/Art Resource, NY

Quōdam diē Pūblius et Fūriānus ē scholā cum duōbus adulēscentibus Graecīs exiērunt. Accidit ut per viās gradientēs statuam virī currentis, ā clārō Myrōne[1] factam, cōnspicerent. Itaque cōnstitērunt ut eam spectārent.

"Nōnne Graecī semper virōs currentēs amant?" Pūblius quaesīvit.

"Sī quis celerrimē currit," respondit ūnus ē Graecīs, "cārissimus urbis suae est; et sī quis in lūdīs Olympicīs vincit, cārissimus est tōtīus Graeciae. Illī lūdī, quī antīquī et īnsignēs sunt, Iovī in urbe Olympiā hōc ipsō annō habentur et post quattuor annōs iterum habēbuntur. Ad hanc urbem virī ex omnibus urbibus Graeciae eunt ut ibi contendant. Virō sē nōn dignō modō gerentī, virō quī fraudem fēcit, nōn permittitur ut contendat. Victōrēs corōnās, statuās, carmina accipiunt."

"Nōnne audīvī dē quōdam virō quī tempore magnī perīculī longē cucurrit?" Fūriānus quaesīvit.

"Philippidēs[2] erat," respondit alter ē Graecīs. "Nūntius eī portandus erat. Ducēs Persārum, cum multīs mīlibus mīlitum in Graeciam prōgressī, ad campum quī Marathōn appellātur dēscendērunt. Athēniēnsēs cōnstituērunt ut Philippidēs quīdam ad urben Spartānōrum īret ut auxilium peteret. Etsī haec urbs circiter centum quīnquāgintā mīlia passuum aberat, ille secundō diē ad eam pervēnit et eōs hortātus est ut auxilium mitterent. Spartānī autem ob fēriās cōnstituērunt nē īrent. Itaque Athēniēnsibus sōlīs Persae dūrī expellendī erant, et Graecia servāta est. Post hoc proelium īdem nūntius Philippidēs ad urbem Athēnās celeriter cucurrit sed posteāquam in urbem pervēnit 'Victōria!' clāmāns subitō mortuus est."[3]

"Graecī fortēs sunt," dīxit Pūblius, amīcīs suīs Graecīs relīctīs. "Nōnne mīrāris quō modō accidat ut Rōmānōs nōn vīcerint?"

1 *Myron*, a Greek sculptor
2 In Greek the name seems to have been Pheidippides.
3 The marathon race of today is so named because its length (about 26 miles) equals the distance which Philippides ran from Marathon to Athens.

QUESTIONS

1. What did Philippides do?
2. What were the prizes for the winners at the Olympic Games?
3. How do these prizes compare to today's Olympians?

ADDITIONAL QUESTIONS
What did Publius and Furianus see that caused them to stop? What kind of people are allowed to compete? How far was Sparta from Athens? What happened to Philippides?

Grammar

Indirect Commands

Indirect commands, sometimes called substantive clauses of purpose, follow verbs of asking (**rogō, petō,** etc.), ordering (**mandō, imperō,** etc.), advising (**moneo, persuadeō,** etc.). They are followed by **ut** or **nē** and the subjunctive following the sequence of tenses. The verb that is used to ask, order, or advise takes one of the following three cases:

SUGGESTION
Do a quick review of indirect statement, indirect question, and the sequence of tenses.

imperō, mandō, and **persuadeō** take the *dative*:

Mihi imperāvit ut librum legerem.	*He ordered me to read the book.*

moneō, ōrō, and **rogō** take the *accusative:*

Mē rogāvit ut librum legerem.	*He asked me to read the book.*

petō, quaerō, and **postulō** take the *ablative* with the preposition **ā** or **ab**:

Ā mē petīvit ut librum legerem.	*He asked me to read the book.*

NOTE
Point out that this is not an exhaustive list of verbs, but a sample.

Noun Clause of Result

Verbs that mean to *happen* (such as **accīdō**) or to *cause* or *effect* or *bring about* (**efficiō**) are followed by **ut** or **ut nōn** and the subjunctive, following the sequence of tenses.

Accīdit ut exercitus oppugnāret.	*It happened that the army attacked.*
Effēcērunt ut hostēs fugerent.	*They caused the enemy to flee.*

WORKBOOK
Assign Ex. A to practice indirect command.

SUGGESTION
Review result clauses, telling students that what they know are adverbial result clauses whereas these are noun result clauses.

WORKBOOK
Assign Ex. B to practice substantive result clauses.

In ancient times, women were not allowed to participate in the Olympic games. The modern games, which began in 1896, allowed women to compete beginning in 1900. Today, women athletes train just as hard as their male counterparts.

Bill Ross/Westlight

ANSWERS
1. Nūntiusne rogāvit nē Spartānī auxilium mitterent? 2. Celeritāte (suā) effēcit ut Persae vincerentur. 3. Nūntius ad urbem a Graecīs mittendus erat. 4. Graecī constituunt ut dux victus poenam det.

TRANSLATION

1. Did the messenger ask the Spartans[4] not to send aid?
2. By his speed he caused the Persians[4] to be defeated.
3. A messenger had to be sent to the city by the Greeks.
4. The Greeks determine that the defeated general should pay the penalty.

Vocabulary

Nouns

campus, -ī, *m. plain*	(campus)
fraus, fraudis, *f. fraud, wrong*	(fraudulence, fraudulent)
tumultus, -us, *m. uproar*	(tumult, tumultuous)

[4] In Latin this will be the subject of the verb in the subordinate clause.

Adjective

īnferior, -ius, *lower, inferior* (inferiority)

Verbs

adorior, adorīrī, adortus, *rise up to, attack*
gradior, gradī, gressus, *walk* (grade, gradient)
ōrō, 1, *beg, ask, pray (for), plead* (oration, oratory)
perspiciō, -ere, -spexī, -spectus, *see (clearly)* (perspicacious, perspicuous)
postulō, 1, *demand* (postulant, postulate)
prōgredior, prōgredī, prōgressus, *step forward, advance* (progress, progression)
quaerō, -ere, quaesīvī, quaesītus, *seek, inquire* (query)

Adverbs

circiter, *about*
itaque, *and so, therefore*

Conjunction

etsī, although

Word Studies

For the meaning and use of the suffixes **–ānus** *(–an, –ane, –ain)*, **–ālis** *(–al)*, **–icus** *(–ic)*, **–īlis** *(–ile, –il)*, **–īvus** *(–ive)*, **–ōsus** *(–ous, –ose)*, see the Appendix. Give the English forms of **hūmānus, urbānus, mortālis, cīvicus, virīlis, āctīvus, cūriōsus, bellicōsus.**

What must be the Latin words from which are derived *meridian, certain, liberal, classic, passive, morose*? Give three other examples of each of the above suffixes in English words.

Frequently several suffixes are used together in the same word. Sometimes these are joined together so closely that we think of them as one suffix. Particularly common is the attachment of noun suffixes to adjectives to form nouns, and vice versa: *simil–ari–ty, hum–ani–ty, fert–ili–ty, act–ivi–ty*. Sometimes several adjective suffixes are used together: *republ–ic–an*.

Out of the Latin participle **nātus** we make the noun *nat–ion*, then the adjective *nat–ion–al*, then the verb *nat–ion–al–ize*, then the noun *nat–ion–al–iza–tion*. Sometimes even more suffixes are used.

LESSON OBJECTIVE
To learn the formation of the gerund and the uses of the gerund and gerundive

STUDY TOPICS
Any of the famous Greeks or Romans mentioned in the reading: Demosthenes, Cicero, Caesar, Scipio, Pompey, Marius, Themistocles, Vergil, Homer, Numa, Solon, Lucretius, Socrates, Augustus, Pericles.

LESSON XXIII
National Heroes

Dē virīs clārīs Pūblius et Fūriānus saepe cum adulēscentibus duōbus Graecīs loquēbantur. Pūbliō maximē grātum erat dē Graecō Dēmosthene audīre—quī puer vōcem pessimam habuerat, sed quī eam exercuerat loquendō ad lītus maris, clāmandō dum currit,[1] prōnūntiandō dum aliquid in ōre habet;[1] et quī tandem prīmum locum inter omnēs ōrātōrēs attigerat. "Ille sōlus melior quam Cicerō erat et etiam Rōmānīs laudandus et in honōre habendus est," quondam dīxit Pūblius.

Fūriānus dē rēbus mīlitāribus locūtus est factaque Caesaris, Scīpiōnis, Pompeī, Marī nārrāvit. Sed ūnus ē Graecīs dīxit: "Mihi grātissimus imperātōrum Graecōrum est Themistoclēs. Tempore maximī perīculī, auctōritātem Athēnārum nāvibus summam fēcit, Athēnās optimē mūnīvit, Persārum exercitum tandem ē Graeciā expulit."

"Multī Rōmānī Graecīs similēs sunt," quōdam diē Pūblius dīxit. "Vergilius, clārissimus poēta Rōmānus, quī carmen dē Troiānīs et dē Rōmā cōnstituendā scrīpsit, similis Homērō est, quī dē bellō Troiānō scrīpsit. Numa autem, quī temporibus antīquīs lēgēs quās ā deīs accēperat Rōmānīs dedit, similis Solōnī est, quī lēgēs fēcit ad Athēnās reficiendās."

"At quī Rōmānus philosophīs Graecīs pār est?" alter ē Graecīs quaesīvit. "Cicerō, Lucrētius, quī dē atomīs et dē orīgine hominum rērumque scrīpsit, aliī philosophī Rōmānī—hī ad Graeciam audiendī et discendī causā vēnērunt. Quis Sōcratem memoriā nōn tenet, quī puerōs interrogandō docēbat et eōs ad bene vīvendum īnstituēbat; quī malī[2] expellendī et bonī[2] mōnstrandī grātiā semper labōrābat; quī ob sententiās suās occīsus est?"

"At quī Graecus Augustō nostrō pār est?" respondit Fūriānus. "Periclēs quidem īnsignis erat—Athēnās adōrnāvit, auctōritātem urbis auxit, pāce regēbat. Augustus autem nōn sōlum Rōmam adōrnāvit auxitque—urbem quam ex latere factam accēpit nunc marmoream relinquit—sed nunc omnēs terrās pāce, sapientiā, iūstitiā regit."

Et duo Graecī concessērunt Augustum īnsignem esse.

---

[1] In English the past tense is used.
[2] Neuter noun forms: *evil, good*

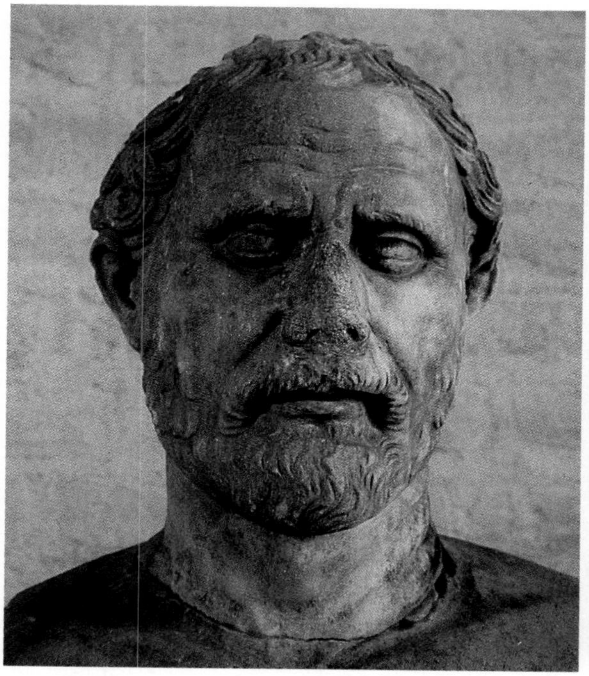

Ronald Sheridan/Ancient Art & Architecture Collection

Demosthenes was the greatest orator of ancient Greece. Tradition has it that he practiced his delivery by putting pebbles in his mouth and by carefully studying the masters. He had an explosive and exciting style.

Ronald Sheridan/Ancient Art & Architecture Collection

The blind poet Homer is credited with being the author of two of the earliest and finest examples of epic poetry. It is likely that he lived in the Ionian part of Greece in the 8th or 9th century B.C.

QUESTIONS

1. Who beautified Rome?
2. What Greek was like Vergil?
3. What Roman was like Solon?
4. What was (and is) the Socratic method of teaching?

ADDITIONAL QUESTIONS
How did Demosthenes learn to speak? What did Themistocles do? Who codified the laws? Who wrote about atoms and the origin of man? How did the Greeks feel about Augustus?

Grammar

The Gerund

The gerund corresponds to the English verbal noun in *–ing*, as in *We learn to do by* ***doing***. It is formed by adding **–ndī, –ndō, –ndum, –ndō** to the present stem of any verb.[3] It is declined in the singular only, in all cases except the nominative. For the nominative constructions of the English verbal noun, Latin uses the present active infinitive:

Vidēre est crēdere.	*Seeing is believing.*

[3] Add **–endī**, etc., in **–iō** verbs.

Note these differences between the gerund and the future passive participle:

GERUND	FUTURE PASSIVE PARTICIPLE
1. Is a *verbal noun.*	1. Is a *verbal adjective.*
2. Has only four endings (**–ī, –ō, –um, –ō**).	2. Has thirty forms (**–us, –a, –um,** etc.).
3. Is always *active* (translate "–ing").	3. Is always *passive* (translate "to be –ed," "must be –ed").
4. Never agrees with anything.	4. Always agrees with a noun or pronoun.

SUGGESTION
Tell students that in English, an **agenda** is a list of things that *must be done* (gerundive from **agō**) and a **modus operandi** is a way of *operating* (gerund of **operor**).

ORAL PRACTICE

1. Give the gerunds of **laudō, moneō, fugio, regō, audiō.**
2. Decline the gerunds of **nārrō** and **pōnō**, and the future passive participles of **capiō** and **exigō.**

WORKBOOK
Assign Ex. A to practice gerunds and to learn about supines.

Uses of the Gerund and the Gerundive

- Since the gerund is a noun, it may have typical noun constructions, such as object of a preposition or ablative of means.

Celeriter currendō pervēnit.	*He arrived quickly by running.*
Copiās ad pugnandum collēgit.	*He gathered the troops for fighting.*

SUGGESTION
Review all the ways students have in Latin to express purpose: a relative purpose clause, the future active participle, the gerundive construction with **causā**, the gerundive construction with **ad**.

- Since the gerund is a noun, it usually does not take a direct object. Instead, use the gerundive, modifying the noun.

Carmen dē Romā constituendā scrīpsit.	*He wrote a poem about founding Rome.*

- The gerund or the gerundive is used with the preposition **ad** (plus the accusative) to express purpose.

Hostēs pervēnērunt ad praedam petendam.	*The enemy arrived looking for loot.*

- The gerund or the gerundive is used with **causā** or **grātiā** (plus the genitive) to express purpose. Both **causā** and **grātiā** can be translated as *for the sake of.*

Hostēs pervēnērunt praedae petendae causā.	*The enemy arrived looking for loot.*
Hostēs pervēnērunt praedae petendae grātiā.	*The enemy arrived looking for loot.*

TRANSLATION

Translate the words in italics, using the gerund or the gerundive, as the case may be:

1. He sat down *to read.*
2. We felt the joy *of giving.*
3. I have come *to tell a story.*
4. This is not time *for talking.*
5. He gained fame *by writing.*
6. He sat down *to read a book.*
7. We felt the joy *of giving money.*
8. He gained fame *by writing books.*
9. He leaned forward *for-the-sake-of seeing.*
10. He leaned forward *for-the-sake-of seeing the man.*

Archivio e Studio Folco Quilici

A copy of the ***Discus Thrower****, or* ***Discobolus****, by the Greek sculptor Myron (5th century B.C.), noted for his ability to portray figures in action. Unfortunately, the original bronze statue has been lost.*

Vocabulary

Nouns

exercitus, -ūs, *m. army* (exercise, exercitation)
honor, -ōris, *m. honor* (honorable, honorary)
imperātor, -ōris, *m. commander, general* (emperor)
later, lateris, *m. brick, tile* (laterite)
lītus, lītoris, *n. shore* (littoral)
orīgo, originis, *f. origin*

Verbs

attingō, -ere, attigī, attāctus, *touch, reach*
augeō, -ēre, auxī, auctus, *increase, enlarge, make grow* (augment, augur)
dēcertō, 1, *fight (it out)*
interrogō, 1, *ask, question* (interrogate, interrogation)
occīdo, -ere, occīdi, occīsus, *kill*
prōnūntiō, 1, *recite* (pronounce, pronunciation)

SUGGESTION
Have students find and translate all examples of the gerund and gerundive in the reading.

WORKBOOK
Assign Ex. B to practice different ways of expressing purpose.

ANSWERS
1. Ad legendum. 2. Dandī. 3. Ad fābulam nārrandam. 4. Loquendō. 5. Scrībendō. 6. Ad librum legendum. 7. Pecūniae dandae. 8. Librīs scrībendīs. 9. Videndī causā/grātiā. 10. Virī/Hominis videndī causā/grātiā.

Adverbs

audācter, *boldly* (audacious, audacity)
sōlum, *only* (sole, solely)

Conjunction

at, *but*

Word Studies

Animis opibusque parati, *Prepared in spirit and resources* (motto of the state of South Carolina).

Qui transtulit sustinet, *(God) who transported (us here) sustains (us)* (motto of the state of Connecticut).

Crescit eundo, *It grows by going (forward)* (motto of the state of New Mexico, from the Roman poet Lucretius).

Si quaeris peninsulam amoenam, circumspice, *If you are seeking a pleasant peninsula, look about you* (motto of the state of Michigan).

Find the Latin words for which the following abbreviations stand and their meanings: **etc., et al., s.v., ult., prox., e.g., A.B., A.M., S.B., LL.D**

Art Resource, NY

This painting by Raphael (1483-1520), called ***School of Athens****, shows Plato and Aristotle in a discussion surrounded by their followers, who listen intently to every word.*

LESSON XXIV

A Visit to the Academy

LESSON OBJECTIVES
To learn the conjugation of **fīō**;
To learn about predicate nouns and adjectives after certain passive verbs

STUDY TOPICS
Plato, the Academy

Saepe Pūbliō et Fūriānō grātum erat per urbem Athēnās ambulāre et virōs maximae auctōritātis causās ōrantēs audīre. Saepe autem grātius vidēbātur urbem relinquere sēque ad locum pulchrum et quiētum, Acadēmiam, legendī grātiā recipere.

Quōdam diē eō tardē prōcēdēbant, librōs carminum ferentēs.

"Quot Rōmānī dignī per hanc ipsam viam ambulāvērunt!—Rōmānī quī posteā clārissimī factī sunt," dīxit Pūblius. "Nōs quoque in studiīs dīligentēs sīmus ut clārī fīāmus—tū ut dux īnsignis fīās, ego ōrātor."

Nunc inter arborēs Acadēmiae stābant. Hae erant novae sed iam altae.

"Quā magnitūdine arborēs fīunt!" Pūblius dīxit. "Audīvī quōsdam Athēniēnsēs dīcere hās paucīs annīs tam altās quam illās antīquās futūrās esse. Nam Sulla, quī illās cecīdit ut ē māteriā īnstrūmenta bellī fierent, rēs pulchrās contempsit. Statuās quidem ē Graeciā tulit; hoc autem fēcit ut magnam praedam in urbem Rōmam referret."

Nunc sub arbore altā librōs quōs sēcum tulerant legunt. Tum Fūriānus dīxit, "Mihi grātissimum est ad hunc locum venīre carminum Horātī legendōrum causā, quod hīc Horātius ipse carmina legēbat et scrībēbat. Horātius, quī vir corpore parvō et rotundō erat, bellō erat inimīcus—Sullae dissimillimus. Nūntiō bellī allātō, nōn perturbātus est. Brūtus[1] sōlus eum permovēre potuit (saepe mīror quō modō) ut tribūnus mīlitāris fieret et ad bellum proficīscerētur. Brūtō et Cassiō ad urbem Philippōs victīs, Horātiō scūtum relinquendum fuit (memoriāne tenēs?) ipseque fūgit. Posteā ab Augustō, contrā quem arma tulerat, amīcus dēlēctus est, et nōtissimus poēta factus est."

"Hīc saepe dē philosophīs admoneor," dīxit Pūblius; "de Platōne, quī prīmus hīc docuit; dē Aristotele, quī rēgem Alexandrum īnstituit; dē Carneade, quī nunc prō iūstitiā, nunc contrā eam, verba īnsignia facere potuit."

1 Brutus, together with Cassius and others, had killed Caesar and fled from Rome, pursued by Antony, Caesar's friend, and Octavian, Caesar's nephew, later called Augustus.

Subitō accessērunt duo Graecī. Ab hīs certiōrēs factī rhētorem clārum causam in Agorā ōrātūrum esse et tempus adesse, Pūblius et Fūriānus librōs celeriter volvērunt et nōn iam morātī ex Acadēmiā exiērunt.

QUESTIONS

1. Against whom did Horace fight?
2. How was Horace different from Sulla?
3. What did Sulla do in the Academy?

ADDITIONAL QUESTIONS
What does Publius want to be? What does he think Furianus will be? What was Horace built like? What happened to Horace's shield? Where did the boys hurry off to?

NOTE
Point out that this is virtually the opposite of deponent verbs.

SUGGESTION
Have students find all examples of this construction in the story.

WORKBOOK
Assign Ex. A, B to practice **fīō** and the idiom **certior fīō**.

Grammar

Conjugation of *Fīō*

Faciō has no passive in the present, imperfect, or future tenses. To express *be made, be done, become* in these tenses, the Romans used the irregular verb, **fīō**, which, although it is for the most part active in form, has passive meanings:

INDICATIVE			SUBJUNCTIVE	
PRESENT	IMPERFECT	FUTURE	PRESENT	IMPERFECT
fīō	fīēbam	fīam	fīam	fierem
fīs	fīēbās	fīēs	fīās	fierēs
fit	fīēbat	fīet	fīat	fieret
fīmus	fīēbāmus	fīēmus	fīāmus	fierēmus
fītis	fīēbātis	fīētis	fīātis	fierētis
fīunt	fīēbant	fīent	fīant	fierent

The imperatives are regular: **fī, fīte**.

The verb **fīō** as well as some other passive forms, such as **appellor** *(be called)* and **dēligor** *(be selected, chosen)* are often used with a predicate noun or adjective.

Imperātor fīet.	*He will be made commander.*
Dūcēs dēlectī sunt.	*They were chosen leaders.*
Anna appellor.	*I am called Anna.*

NOTĀ·BENE

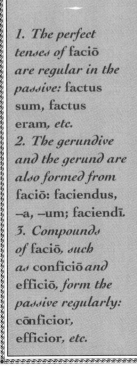

1. The perfect tenses of faciō *are regular in the passive:* factus sum, factus eram, *etc.*
2. The gerundive and the gerund are also formed from faciō: faciendus, –a, –um; faciendī.
3. Compounds of faciō, *such as* conficiō *and* efficiō, *form the passive regularly:* cōnficior, efficior, *etc.*

TRANSLATION

1. Horace, who had borne arms against Augustus, became a noted poet.
2. "Let us strive to become men of the greatest influence," said Publius to Furianus.
3. "Leaving the city behind, let us retire to the Academy, carrying our books with us."
4. Sulla, who had come to Greece for the sake of waging war, carried back many beautiful things.

Vocabulary

Nouns

aditus, -ūs, *m. approach, access*

carmen, -minis, *n. song, poem*

contumēlia, -ae, *f. insult* (contumelious, contumely)

magnitūdō, -dinis, *f. greatness, size* (magnitude)

scūtum, -ī, *n. shield* (escudo, escutcheon)

tribūnus, -ī, *m. tribune* (tribunal, tribunate)

Adjectives

dīligēns, (gen.) **-entis,** *careful* (diligence, diligent)

quot, *how many; as (many as) (indeclinable)* (quote, quotient)

Verbs

admoneō, -ēre, admonuī, admonitus, *remind, advise* (admonish, admonition)

dēligō, -ere, dēlēgī, dēlēctus, *select*

fīō, fierī, —, (factus), *be made, become;* **certior fīō,** *be informed* (fact, factitious)

moror, 1, *delay* (moratorium)

perturbō, 1, *disturb* (perturb, perturbation)

referō, referre, rettulī, relātus, *bring back* (refer, referendum)

Adverb

eō, *there*

Word Studies

For the meaning and use of **circum–** *(circum–)* and **super–** *(super–, sur–)*, see the Appendix. Define according to the prefix: *circumscribe, circumference, circuit, supervise, survive.*

Prefixes often have intensive force; this is especially true of **con–, ex–, ob–, per–: cōnficiō,** *"do up," do thoroughly*; **efficiō,** *make out, complete*; **occīdō,** *cut up, kill*; **perficiō,** *do through and through, finish.* Define according to the intensive use of the prefix: *complement, commotion, conserve, experience, emotion, extensive, obtain, persist, permanent.*

Explain *fiat, gradual, inquisitive, interrogation, littoral, perturbation, progressive.*

Giraudon/Art Resource, NY

Sulla, after defeating Mithradates VI of Anatolia, returned to Rome. Supported by the aristocratic families in Rome, he took over the government and succeeded in making himself dictator from 82-81 B.C. There were many massacres that followed. After serving as consul from 81-80 B.C., he retired.

ANSWERS
1. Horātius, quī arma contrā Augustum tulerat, nōtus/īnsignis poēta factus est. 2. "Contendāmus ut virī maximae auctōritātis fīāmus," dīxit Pūblius Fūriānō. 3. "Urbe relīctā, ad Acadēmiam nōs recipiāmus, ferentēs nōbīscum librōs nostrōs." 4. Sulla, quī ad Graeciam bellī gerendī causā vēnerat, multās pulchrās rēs rettulit.

LESSON OBJECTIVE
To learn the conjugations of **volō** and **nōlō**

LESSON XXV

Athens and Rome

[1] *from each other*
[2] *sewers*
[3] *longer*
[4] *the more disagreeable things*
[5] *whether*

STUDY TOPIC
Values of the Greeks and Romans

Fūriānus patrī s. p. d. Quaeris quibus modīs Rōma et Athēnae inter sē[1] differant et utram urbem magis amem. Mihi quidem respondēre difficile est. Rōma patria mea est et ob eam rem mihi cārissima est. Num vīs mē Rōmam et Rōmānōs accūsāre? Iam dē aedificiīs amplissimīs quae hīc vīdimus scrīpsī. Sed Rōma quoque aedificia pulchra habet. Viae Rōmānae certē meliōrēs sunt. Omnia sordidiōra hīc sunt—viae, aedificia prīvāta, hominēs. Nūllae cloāca[2] sunt. Aliquis Rōmānus hūc mittendus est ad cloācās faciendās. Aqua ita mala est ut multī pereant. Nōnne vult aliquis Rōmānus aquaeductum hīc facere?[1] Cum autem Acropolim cōnspiciō, tum haec urbs pulcherrima omnium esse vidētur, neque iam[3] peiōra[4] memoriā teneō.

Haec dē urbe ipsā; nunc dē populō quaedam dīcere volō. Concēdō Graecōs multās virtūtēs habēre, sed hae nōn sunt virtūtēs Rōmānae. Nostrī sunt fortēs atque prūdentēs, maximē labōrant et optimē regunt. Graecī autem optimī philosophī, rhētorēs, poētae, medicī sunt et optima templa pulcherrimāsque statuās faciunt.

Multōs amīcōs Graecōs habeō; itaque nōlō omnēs Graecōs accūsāre. Sed Rōmānī mihi cāriōrēs sunt. Perfidia Graecōrum nōta est; quamquam nōn negō Graecōs loquī dē perfidiā Rōmānā. Interest utrum[5] Rōmānus an Graecus sīs. Ita omnēs populī aliōs contemnunt. Nōnne nōs loquimur etiam dē Pūnicā perfidiā? Sed vērum est in tabernīs Graecīs fraudēs frequentiōrēs esse quam in Rōmānīs.

NOTE
Point out that this sentence is a double indirect question (with **utrum** and **an**).

Etsī multī servī in Italiā sunt, numquam tot servōs vīdī quot in hāc urbe. Omnia ā servīs fīunt; cīvēs enim ipsī nōn labōrant.

Maximē autem condiciō mulierum differt. Mulierēs Graecae nōn habent eandem lībertātem quam Rōmānae. Apud nōs mātrōnae in honōre sunt, sed nōn hīc. Virī volunt uxōrēs nihil vidēre, nihil audīre, nihil quaerere. Sed tamen puellae quās vīdī pulchrae fuērunt.

[1] This was actually done later at the Emperor Hadrian's expense.

Giraudon/Art Resource, NY

Like the Romans, Greek women went to a community well to bring water back home. Publius and Furianus, however, thought the quality of the Greek water was not up to Roman standards.

QUESTIONS

1. Did the Greeks or the Romans have better roads? Why?
2. Did Rome or Athens have a better water supply? Why?
3. Which city had better doctors? Which had more slaves? Why?

ADDITIONAL QUESTIONS
Where are things dirtier? Where is cheating more common? What do Greek citizens do?

Grammar

Conjugation of *Volō* and *Nōlō*

The present indicative and subjunctive of both **volō** and **nōlō** are irregular. The other tenses are formed regularly. There is no passive.

PRESENT INDICATIVE		PRESENT SUBJUNCTIVE	
volō	nōlō	velim	nōlim
vīs	nōn vīs	velīs	nōlīs
vult	nōn vult	velit	nōlit
volumus	nōlumus	velīmus	nōlīmus
vultis	nōn vultis	velītis	nōlītis
volunt	nōlunt	velint	nōlint

SUGGESTION
Take a few moments to review, by doing synopses on the board, all the irregular verbs thus far: **sum, possum, ferō, eō, fīō, nōlō, volō**.

NOTE
Tell students there is only one irregular verb left to learn, **malō** in Lesson XXVII.

WORKBOOK
Assign Ex. A to practice **nōlō** and **volō**.

Although **volō** has no imperative, the imperative of **nōlō** plus the present infinitive is used to form negative commands in Latin.

Nōlī eō īre.	*Do not go there!*
Nōlīte eī audīre.	*Don't listen to him!*

WORKBOOK
Assign Ex. B to negative imperatives with **nōlō**.

ORAL PRACTICE

1. Give the second singular of **volō** and the third plural of **nōlō** in all tenses of the indicative and subjunctive.
2. Conjugate the following verbs in all tenses of the indicative and subjunctive, giving the first singular of the first verb, the second singular of the second verb, etc.: **prōgredior, sum, ferō, fīō, possum, eō.**

ANSWERS
1. Vīsne scīre utram urbem magis amem? 2. Mihi difficillimum est dīcere, quod tam dissimilēs sunt. 3. Graecōs accūsāre nōlō, sed labōrāre nōlle videntur. 4. Semper autem dīcere voluī Graecōs nōbīs omnibus artibus praestāre.

TRANSLATION

1. Do you wish to know which city (of the two) I like more?
2. It is very difficult for me to say, because they are so unlike.
3. I don't wish to criticize the Greeks, but they do not seem to be willing to work.
4. I have always been willing, however, to say that the Greeks excel us in all the arts.

Ronald Sheridan/Ancient Art & Architecture Collection

Roman married women enjoyed far more liberty than did their Greek counterparts. Roman men thought very highly of their wives and many wives acted as their husbands' advisors.

Vocabulary

Nouns

mulier, mulieris, *f. woman* (muliebrity)
perfidia, -ae, *f. treachery* (perfidious, perfidy)

Adjectives

prūdēns, (gen.) **prūdentis,** *sensible* (prudent, prudential)
uter, utra, utrum, *which (of two)*

Verbs

differō, differre, distulī, dīlātus, *differ* (difference, differential)
interest, *it makes a difference*
nōlō, nōlle, nōluī, —, *not want* (nolo contendere)
volō, velle, voluī, —, *want, wish* (volition, volitive)

Adverbs

hīc, *here* (hic jacet)
hūc, *to this side, here*
num, *introduces question expecting negative answer*
sīc, *so, thus*

Conjunctions

an, *or*
num, *whether*
quamquam, *although*

Word Studies

per se, *by itself*
bona fide, *in good faith*
in re, *in the matter (of)*
nolens volens, *willy-nilly*
Deo volente, *God willing*
me iudice, *in my judgment*
Pax vobiscum, *Peace (be) with you!*
sui generis, *of its own kind,* i.e., *unique*
sine die, *without a day (being set)*; used for adjournment by a parliamentary body
Fiat panis, *Let there be bread*; motto of the Food and Agriculture Organization of the United Nations.

LESSON OBJECTIVES
To learn the dative with special verbs; To learn the datives of reference and purpose (and double dative)

STUDY TOPIC
Roman Drama

LESSON XXVI
The Homecoming

Tandem diēs aderat quō, studiīs perfectīs, Athēnae Pūbliō Fūriānōque relinquendae erant.

"Illīs invideō quī nunc in Graeciā, nunc in Italiā habitant," dīxit Fūriānus, volēns Rōmam vidēre, nōlēns tamen Athēnās dēserere.

Certiōrēs autem ā mercātōre factī viās bonās esse, sibi persuāsērunt ut sine morā proficīscerentur. Nūntiō allātō latrōnēs viātōribus nocēre, servīs armātīs ut praesidiō impedīmentīs essent, per Graeciam iter fēcērunt. Marī quiētō, in portum Brundisī sine cāsū nāvigāvērunt, et ibi duōs diēs mānsērunt, quod quaedam vidēre volēbant: locum ubi Augustus nōmen Caesaris accēperat, et aedificium in quō Vergilius mortuus erat postquam ē Graeciā rediit. Hoc tam grātum Pūbliō erat ut discēdere nōllet. Fūriānus autem dīxit, "Nōnne dēsīderās quam prīmum domum tuam vidēre?"

"Dēsīderō!"[1] respondit Pūblius. Itaque quam celerrimē profectī sunt.

Magnum erat gaudium familiae Caeciliae, adulēscentibus duōbus dēfessīs vesperī reversīs. Sōle oriente, clientēs vēnērunt, et paene tōtum diem ātrium clientibus et amīcīs salūtem dīcentibus complētum est. Posteā Caeciliī ad Campum Mārtium in pulchrās thermās Agrippae iērunt. Ibi cum aliīs amīcīs locūtī, sē exercuērunt et lāvērunt.

Proximō diē, rogātus quid facere vellet, Pūblius dīxit sē velle in Circum īre. Pater respondit nōn circēnsēs lūdōs, sed scaenicōs eō diē darī; quendam poētam quoque carmina sua lēctūrum esse. Pūblius dīxit sē nōlle istum poētam ignōtum audīre; lūdōs autem scaenicōs sibi placēre et eōs vidēre velle.

Fābula, ā Plautō dē lārvīs scrīpta, grāta erat. Tum pantomīmus[1] victōriās Augustī exprimēns tam bene saltāvit ut populus alacer clāmāret, ad pantomīmum curreret, pecūniam iaceret. Etiam Augustus eī corōnam dedit, quam accipere maximō honōrī pantomīmō erat. Lūdīs perfectīs, omnēs per Forum reversī sunt.

[1] *pantomime, ballet dancer*

[1] *Yes* was often expressed in conversation by repeating the verb.

C. M. Dixon

Mosaic by Dioskorides of Samos showing masked actors in a play. The Romans loved the comedies of Plautus, which were enjoyed by the plebeians as well as the patricians.

Pūblius et Fūriānus nunc vītam cīvium Rōmānōrum iniērunt. Pūblius quaestor creātus est, perque tōtum cursum honōrum īre parāvit. Fūriānus, tribūnus mīlitum factus, auxiliō ducī ab hostibus circumventō missus est, sēque tam fortiter gessit ut lēgātus fieret. Itaque et Pūblius et Fūriānus vītā suā magnam auctōritātem familiae Caeciliae et servāvērunt et auxērunt.

QUESTIONS

1. Whom did Furianus envy?
2. To whom did Augustus give a wreath?
3. What did Publius and Furianus do after their return to Rome?

ADDITIONAL QUESTIONS
How did Publius and Furianus feel about leaving Greece? What was the purpose of the slaves during the trip? How long did they remain in Brundisium? How was the dancer received?

Grammar

The Dative with Special Verbs

With some verbs, such as **imperō, permittō,** and **persuādeō,** an indirect personal object (dative) is used in addition to a subordinate **ut** clause as a direct object. The **ut** clause is in the subjunctive following the sequence of tenses.

WORKBOOK
Assign Ex. A to practice the dative with special verbs.

Eī imperō ut urbem circumveniat.	*I order him to surround the city.*
Eīs persuāsimus ut hīc manērent.	*We persuaded them to remain here.*

A few other verbs are followed by the dative, but not by an **ut** clause. These verbs include **invideō, noceō,** and **placeō**.

Saxa līberīs nocuērunt.	*The rocks injured the children.*
Voluērunt nōbīs placēre.	*They wished to please us.*

The Datives of Reference and Purpose

First, the dative case alone, like several other constructions you have seen, can be used to express purpose.

SUGGESTION
Have students find and translate all examples of the dative of purpose, dative of reference, and double dative in the story.

Locum scholae dēlēgit.	*He chose a place for the school.*

The dative of reference is used to indicate the person concerned or referred to.

Līberī bonī mihi esse volunt.	*The children want to be good for me.*

These two functions of the dative, when used together, are often called the double dative. This often happens after a form of **sum**.

WORKBOOK
Assign Ex. B to practice datives of purpose, reference, and double datives.

Mīlitēs praesidiō urbī erant.	*The soldiers served as a garrison to the city.*
Puella auxiliō matrī erat.	*The girl was a help to her mother.*

ANSWERS
1. Certiōrēs factī sunt latrōnēs viātōribus nocēre. 2. Fūriānus autem Pūbliō persuāsit ut quam prīmum proficīscerētur. 3. Praesidiō sibi et impedīmentīs servōs armāvērunt. 4. Eīs placuit iterum domum vidēre, et dīxērunt sē velle quam celerrimē iter facere.

TRANSLATION

1. They were informed that bandits were molesting travelers.
2. Furianus, however, persuaded Publius to start as soon as possible.
3. They armed the slaves as a protection for themselves and the baggage.
4. It was pleasing to them to see home again, and they said that they wanted to make the journey as swiftly as possible.

Vocabulary

Nouns

cāsus, -ūs, *m. chance, misfortune*	(case, casual)
lēgātus, -ī, *m. envoy, general*	(legate, legation)
poēta, -ae, *m. poet*	(poetic, poetry)
quaestor, -ōris, *m. quaestor, treasury official*	

NOTE
Point out that **poēta** is one of the few first declension nouns that is masculine.

Verbs

circumveniō, -īre, -vēnī, -ventus, *surround*	(circumvent)
dēdō, dēdere, dēdidī, dēditus, *surrender*	
dēsīdero, 1, *long for*	(desirable, desire)
ineō, inīre, iniī, initūrus, *enter upon*	(initial)
noceō, -ēre, nocuī, nocitūrus, *do harm to, injure*	(nocent, nocuous)
perfero, -ferre, -tuli, -lātus, *endure*	
persuādeo, -ēre, -suāsī, -suāsūrus, *persuade*	(persuasion, persuasive)
placeō, -ēre, placuī, placitūrus, *please*	(placate, placater)
revertō, -ere, revertī, reversus, *(sometimes deponent) turn back, return*	(reversion, revert)

WORKBOOK
Assign Unit II Review to review the names of famous people.

Word Studies

For the meaning and use of **–tūdō** *(–tude)*, **–mentum** *(–ment)*, **–ūra** *(–ure)*, **–faciō, –ficō** *(–fy)*, see the Appendix. Give the English forms of **multitūdō, servitūdō, argūmentum, agricultūra, pictūra**.

What must be the Latin words from which are derived *altitude, solitude, instrument, moment, conjecture*?

Give three other examples of each of the above suffixes in English words.

Explain *casualty, circumvent, imprudence, initiative, innocent, legation.*

From your knowledge of the basic verbs, assign a meaning to these Latin nouns: **arbitrātus, cāsus, cōnsēnsus, cursus, flētus, gressus, habitus, impulsus, ingressus, intellectus, monitus, reditus, status.**

CASSETTE
Do Unit II, Drill 5, which includes true/false questions on the content of the reading, *The Homecoming.* It is a good drill for oral comprehension.

OCEANUS ATLANTICUS
MARE GERMANICUM
MARE SUEV
HIBERNIA
BRITANNIA
Eboracum
Londinium
Saxones
Albis
Rhenus
GERMANIA
GERMANIA
Belgae
Remi
Sequana
Matrona
Lutetia
Liger
GALLIA
Celtae
Genua
Lugdunum
Helvetii
ALPES
RAETIA
NORICUM
PANNONIA
Garunna
AQUITANIA
Rhodanus
Mediolanum
Padus
Genua
Rubico
ILLYRICUM
PYRENAEI
Narbo
Massilia
Numantia
Hiberus
HISPANIA
Tagus
LUSITANIA
Tarraco
CORSICA
Roma
Ostia
ITALIA
Saguntum
Anas
Cannae
Neapolis
Pompeii
Dyrrachi
Taren
Corduba
Gades
BALEARES
SARDINIA
Nova Carthago
MARE
Utica
Carthago
Zama
SICILIA
Aetna
Syracusae
MAURETANIA
NUMIDIA
AFRICA
MELITA
Thapsus
ATLAS
MED
Leptis Magna
Roman Walls
Roman Territory 264 B.C. Before Punic Wars
Added Territory 238-201 B.C. After First and Second Punic Wars
Added Territory 133 B.C.
Added Territory 44 B.C. Death of Caesar
Added Territory 14 A.D. Death of Augustus
Added Territory Second Century A.D.
20°
10°
0°
10°
50°
40°
30°
0°
10°

IMPERIUM ROMANUM
30°
40°
50°
60°
50°
40°
30°
SARMATIA
Tanais
SCYTHIA
DACIA
Danuvius
MOESIA
THRACIA
PONTUS EUXINUS
MARE CASPIUM
CAUCASUS
DONIA
Phillipi
Thessalonica
Byzantium
Bosporus
BITHYNIA
PONTUS
ARMENIA
GALATIA
Troia
Pharsalus
ASIA
Mare
Aegaeum
Corinthus
Athenae
CIA
Sparta
CAPPADOCIA
PARTHIA
ASSYRIA
MESOPOTAMIA
PAMPHYLIA
CILICIA
LYCIA
Antiochia
RHODUS
Euphrates
Palmyra
PHOENICIA
SYRIA
Tigris
CRETA
CYPRUS
Damascus
Babylon
RANEUM
Tyrus
PALAESTINA
Hierosolyma
Cyrene
Alexandria
ARABIA
AEGYPTUS
Nilus
Scale of Miles
0 100 200 300 400 500
30°
40°
50°

Our Heritage

GREEKS AND ROMANS

Although we may sometimes think of the civilizations of the Greeks and Romans as identical, the Roman people differed in many respects from the Greeks. The languages of the two peoples were about as different as French and German today.

The Greek cities and states retained their independence for a long time and each contributed to Greek civilization, although Athens played a more prominent part than the rest. The Greeks excelled in philosophy, science, mathematics, art, and literature.

The Greeks developed their civilization earlier than the Romans. The fifth and fourth centuries B.C. mark the high point of Athenian culture. At that time Rome was still a struggling small town, but gradually it extended its influence, first over Italy, then over the rest of what was then the civilized world. The Romans were a practical people, with a genius for both law and government.

The earliest important contact of the Romans with Greek culture was an indirect one, through the Etruscans. This mysterious people who lived north of Rome borrowed a number of things from the Greeks, such as the alphabet, forms of architecture, and some religious practices, and transmitted them to the Romans. Later the Romans met Greek culture directly as they moved south to the Greek colonies in Italy and Sicily. In the second century B.C. Greece itself came under Roman rule which directly inspired the influence of Greek culture and customs. The poet Horace noted: **Graecia capta ferum victōrem cēpit et artēs Intulit agrestī Latiō ...**

Captured Greece took captive its fierce conqueror by bringing the arts to rustic Latium.

Though Greece was defeated by Roman arms, uncivilized Rome was conquered by Greek art. The Romans began to develop art and literature in imitation of the Greek but usually added the stamp of their own individuality. So Vergil, inspired by Homer, produced a masterpiece quite like Homer's. Greek architecture was imitated, but one can always tell a Roman building from a Greek building. The Romans generally preferred the Corinthian style and, unlike the Greeks, often placed their temples and other buildings on a high base. The round temple with dome is distinctly Roman. Greek sculpture attained a beauty never since equaled, but the Romans excelled in making realistic portrait statues. The Greeks were superior in mathematics, especially geometry (the name of their greatest geometrician, Euclid, still is a synonym for geometry); the Romans developed applied mathematics, such as surveying and engineering.

For a thousand years after the fall of the Roman Empire, Greek thought and art were preserved in western Europe only through Latin literature and tradition. The civilization of western Europe, and therefore of the United States, was developed from this Roman tradition, with its Greek borrowings. Just as the Romans had been inspired by Greek culture, so now the world was imbued with the Greco-Roman. Then, through the interest created by the praise of Greek literature found in the works of Roman writers, Greek began to be studied again during the Renaissance and the world supplemented its huge Roman inheritance by direct borrowing from the Greeks.

Nimatallah/Art Resource, NY

An Etruscan tomb painting at Tarquinia depicts a lyre player. Notice the two birds in the tree at the left, charmed by the music of the player.

So it has come about that two such different peoples as the Greeks and Romans have, through Roman hospitality to Greek ideas, transmitted to us a joint Greco-Roman civilization. But it must be said that without Rome, Greek culture might not have been preserved at all or at least the modern world would not have been prepared to appreciate and welcome it.

Your mission, Romans, is to govern the peoples [of the Empire] (these will be your arts) and to make peace a habit. Treat subject peoples gently but be ruthless to the overbearing.

Vergil, the great poet who describes Rome's ideals, stated that others (meaning the Greeks) were better sculptors, orators, astronomers, but:

Tū regere imperiō populōs, Rōmāne, mementō. (Hae tibi erunt artēs) pācīque impōnere mōrem, Parcere subiectīs et dēbellāre superbōs.

QUESTIONS

1. What do we owe to the Greeks? To the Romans?
2. Which modern nations are more like the Greeks than the Romans? Which are more like the Romans?

The Greek Temple of Neptune (Hera) at Paestum, in southern Italy. It is the best preserved and most handsome of the Doric temples. It was built in the 5th century B.C.

Ronald Sheridan/Ancient Art & Architecture Collection

Unit II Review
LESSONS X-XXVI

A Latin Play

Bulla

Persōnae

Aelia, parva puella Rōmāna
Lāneis, serva
Q. Aelius Frontō, Rōmānus, pater Aeliae
Damyx, **Thoa** } uxōrēs latrōnum

LOCUS: In oppidō Paestō, ante templum. *(Ē dextrā parte accēdunt Frontō, Aelia, Lāneis.)*

LĀNEIS: Aelia! Bulla tua aurea! Eam nōn videō. Estne āmissa?

AELIA: Ecce! Nōn āmissa est—sub tunicā est.

LĀNEIS: Quam[1] terrēbar! Necesse est tē eam semper dīligenter servāre, quod tē ē malīs servābit.

FRONTŌ: Hoc est templum. Aelia, volō tē cum Lāneide hīc remanēre. Ego deōs ōrābō ut nōbīs iter fēlīx dent. Lāneis, manē cum Aeliā, quod magna perīcula adsunt.

LĀNEIS: Ita, ita. Manēbō. *(Frontō in templum it.)*

AELIA: Quandō domum[2] ībimus, Lāneis?

LĀNEIS: Quandō deī iter fēlīx nōbīs dare volent. Nōnne autem Paestum pulchrum oppidum est? Nōnne Titūrius, hospes patris tuī, nōbīs in hōc oppidō manentibus semper bonus est?

AELIA: Ita; et Titūrium maximē amō, sed—

LĀNEIS: Multōs servōs habet—labor meus hīc levis est. Nōnne vīs labōrem Lāneidis tuae levem esse?

AELIA: Sed mātrem vidēre volō. Iam diū eam nōn videō. *(Ante templum nunc cōnsīdunt.)*

LĀNEIS: Quam calidus est diēs! Cōnfecta sum.

AELIA: Lāneis, quandō pater sciet iter fēlīx futūrum esse?

LĀNEIS: Quandō ōmina bona erunt.

AELIA: Ōh! *(Lāneis dormīre parat.)* Lāneis, nōnne cupis Rōmam rūrsus vidēre?

LĀNEIS: Quid? Ita, ita.

[1] *how*
[2] *home*

Unit II Review
LESSONS X-XXVI

AELIA: Multa agam. Prīmum mātrī salūtem dīcam. Tum omnibus amīcīs multa dē Paestō, dē Titūriō, dē itinere nārrābō. Nūlla ex amīcīs meīs iter tam longum fēcit. Quam mē mīrābuntur! *(Lāneis nunc dormit.)* Tum omnia illa dōna quae prō amīcīs ēmī eīs dabō—bene erit. *(Ē sinistrā parte accēdunt Damyx et Thoa.)*

DAMYX: Vidēsne illam?

AELIA: Per viās ībō, et omnia aedificia nova spectābō.

THOA: Pulchra est. Et callida vidētur. Eam rapiāmus.

AELIA: Prō pūpīs[3] meīs novās vestēs faciam.—

DAMYX: Cum magnā autem cūrā agere dēbēmus. Serva adest.

THOA: Illa dormit. *(Aelia Thoam et Damycem videt. Prōcēdit ut eās spectet.)*

DAMYX: Puella pulchra es. Nōnne vīs nōbīscum ambulāre? Multa grātissima tibi mōnstrābimus.

AELIA: Nōlō. Pater iussit mē hīc remanēre.

THOA: Oho! Bona puella es. Nōs autem nōn longē prōcēdēmus. Brevī tempore revertēmur. Praetereā dōnum pulchrum dabimus.

AELIA: Nōn ībō.

DAMYX: *(Thoae)*: Quid faciēmus?

THOA: *(Aeliae)*: Sī nōbīscum veniēs, tē multa grāta docēbimus.

[3] *dolls*

Scala/Art Resource, NY

Servants not only ran the household but helped and protected their masters. The servant on the left is pouring liquid in a bowl for her mistress. The servant on the far right brings a tray of food for her.

Unit II Review
LESSONS X-XXVI

AELIA: Māter mē multa docet. Quid vōs mē docēre potestis?

THOA: Docēbimus quō modō magnam pecūniam sine labōre semper parāre possīs. Tum semper poteris emere omnia quae cupis.

AELIA: Vōbīscum nōn ībō. Fūrēs[4] estis.

[4] *thieves*

DAMYX: Nōn fūrēs, sed Furiae sumus. Audīsne? Sī nōbīscum libenter nōn ībis, tē īre cōgēmus.

THOA: Et sī clāmābis, tē interficiēmus.

AELIA: Vōs nōn timeō.

DAMYX: Quid?

AELIA: Furiae malae sunt, et malae rēs mihi nocēre nōn possunt.

THOA: Cūr?

AELIA: Ex omnibus malīs mē servat bulla. *(Bullam mōnstrat.)*

DAMYX: Ecce!

THOA: Aurea est. *(Eōdem tempore et Damyx et Thoa bullam rapere cōnantur; inter sē pugnant.)*

DAMYX ET THOA: Au—au! *(Lāneis sē movet.)*

THOA: S—st! Serva sē movet. Prehendēmur.

DAMYX: Fugiāmus. *(In sinistram partem celeriter exeunt.)*

LĀNEIS: Aelia!

AELIA: Adsum, Lāneis.

LĀNEIS: Paene dormiēbam. Calidissimus est diēs. *(Ē templō venit Frontō.)*

FRONTŌ: Aelia! Lāneis! Ōmina optima sunt. Deī nōbīs iter fēlīx dant. Hōc ipsō diē proficīscēmur.

AELIA: Bene, bene est.

FRONTŌ: Et quid agēbat Aelia mea?

AELIA: Duās Furiās vīdī.

FRONTŌ ET LĀNEIS: Quid?

AELIA: Ita. Mē sēcum īre cupiēbant. Cōnābantur mihi nocēre. Malae erant—sed bulla mea mē servāvit.

FRONTŌ *(parvā vōce)*: Quid dīcit, Lāneis?

LĀNEIS *(parvā vōce)*: Nihil est. Calidus diēs est, et puella cōnfecta dormiēbat. Haec in somnō vidēbat; nunc putat omnia vēra esse.

FRONTŌ: Intellegō. Prōcēdāmus, Aelia. Memoriam Furiārum dēpōnāmus, et nōs ad iter parēmus.

AELIA: Ita. Sed bullam meam semper amābō, quod haec mē ā Furiīs dēfendit.

LĀNEIS: Rēctē. *(Frontō et Lāneis rīdent. Exeunt omnēs in dextram partem.)*

Unit III

Livy

UNIT OBJECTIVES
To learn about Livy as a person; To learn some of the stories that are part of the Roman historical tradition, as told by Livy and Eutropius; To learn the dative with compounds; To learn the conjugation of **malō;** To learn the locative case; To review and learn **cum** clauses; To review the gerundive, the gerund, and the dative of agent; To learn the subjunctive with verbs of fearing; To learn Latin sentence structure; To learn additional uses of impersonal verbs; To learn the partitive genitive (genitive of the whole); To review the datives of purpose and reference; To review indirect command; To review the indefinites **quis, aliquis,** and **quīdam**; To learn the relative pronoun as a connector; To learn *place to which* without a preposition; To review the imperative and learn the passive imperative; To learn the use of **quisque** and **quisquam**; To review result clauses; To learn the ablative of separation; To review the genitive and ablative of description and the ablative of degree of difference; To learn relative purpose clauses

In this painting by Jacques-Louis David (1748-1825), we see the contest between the Horatii and the Curiatii that decided the outcome of the war between the Romans and the Albans.

A Great Historian

Livy was one of Rome's most famous historians. Living nearly 2000 years ago in the time of Augustus, the most glorious period in Roman literature, he wrote a history of Rome from its beginnings to his own time. The purpose of the work was to give Roman citizens a better appreciation of the courageous acts and the moral integrity that had brought Rome into world prominence.

The work was divided into 142 books. Of these only 35, including the first ten, still exist. On account of the great importance of the work for the history of Rome, it has always been the dream of historians to find the lost books.

The old Roman tales that Livy weaves into his early history of Rome may be mere legends, but they are, nonetheless, like the story of George Washington and the cherry tree, of great importance and interest and give a good insight into Roman character and ideals. One historian says of them:

If now we take a general view of this wonderful collection of legends, caring little whether the details be wholly or in part imaginary, but regarding the heroes and heroines as at least a gallery of moral types, we may gain a fair notion of the kind of greatness that carried Rome, the city of the Tiber, to the headship of the ancient world. It is simple enough. There is a plain devotion to duty, a disregard of personal inclinations, a pride that disdains submission, a constancy of the finest temper. There is a clear grasp of the object of the hour and a willingness to take the necessary steps . . . We are not dealing with a clever people, like the Greeks. Here there is no constellation of brilliant stars, but a succession of good citizens, able to cooperate and to obey, and preeminent among peoples ancient or modern in steadiness of nerve.

The stories in the following thirteen lessons are adapted chiefly from Livy. However, some parts are based on Eutropius, a writer in the fourth century A.D., who wrote a very brief history of Rome, in the early portion of which he used an abridged edition of Livy.

QUESTIONS

1. Can you name any prominent citizens of the world today with qualities similar to those mentioned in the quotation?
2. What are some of the legends in our history that have become part of our historical tradition?

The Bettmann Archive

Livy, born Titus Livius in 64 B.C., wrote a history of Rome that was immediately recognized as a classic in his own time. He was an eyewitness to civil wars, the fall of the Republic, and the establishment of the Principate by Augustus, although his history only went up to 9 B.C. In all, there were 142 books, of which 35 exist. This rendition of the great historian was done in the 19th century.

LESSON OBJECTIVE
To learn the dative with compounds

STUDY TOPIC
Livy I, 22-26

LESSON XXVII

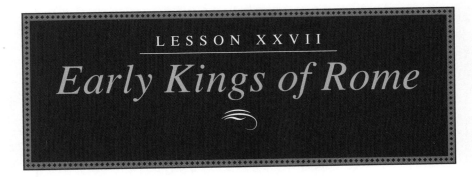

Early Kings of Rome

Rōmānum imperium ā Rōmulō initium habet, quī urbem parvam in Palātīnō cōnstituit. Cīvitāte conditā, quam ex nōmine suō Rōmam vocāvit, haec ēgit: multitūdinem fīnitimōrum in cīvitātem recēpit et centum ex seniōribus dēlēgit, quōs senātōrēs nōmināvit quod senēs erant. Hōrum cōnsiliō omnia ēgit.

Post mortem Rōmulī Numa Pompilius rēx creātus est, quī nūllam partem quidem Rōmae adiēcit, sed nōn minus cīvitātem quam Rōmulus iūvit; nam lēgēs mōrēsque Rōmānīs cōnstituit, quī cōnsuētūdine[1] proeliōrum ā fīnitimīs sēmibarbarī putābantur. Annum dīvīsit in decem mēnsēs et multa sacra ac templa Rōmae[2] cōnstituit.

Huic successit Tullus Hostīlius. Hōc rēge, Rōmānī cum Albānīs bellum gerēbant. Forte in duōbus exercitibus erant trigeminī[3] frātrēs et aetāte et vīribus parēs. Horātiī erant Rōmānī; Cūriātiī, Albānī. Cum hīs agunt[4] rēgēs, ut hī sōlī prō suā patriā exercitūque pugnent.

Tempore cōnstitūtō, arma capiunt. Duo Rōmānī, vulnerātīs tribus Albānīs, interfectī sunt. Forte tertius Rōmānus integer fuit; tribus Cūriātiīs sōlus nōn pār erat, sed contrā singulōs ferōx. Itaque, ut cum singulīs pugnāret, fūgit. Tum respiciēns videt eōs magnīs intervāllīs sequentēs; ūnus nōn multō[5] abest. In eum magnō impetū rediit; et dum Albānus exercitus clāmat Cūriātiīs$_1$ ut opem ferant frātrī, iam Horātius, caesō hoste, secundam pugnam petēbat et alterum Cūriātium interficit. Iamque singulī supererant,$_2$ sed nec spē nec vīribus parēs. Tertiō Cūriātiō quoque interfectō, Rōmānī cum gaudiō Horātium accipiunt.

Horātī soror spōnsa ūnī ex Cūriātiīs erat. Cum Horātius ad urbem accēderet, soror eum vīdit gerentem palūdāmentum[6] Cūriātī quod ipsa cōnfēcerat. Eam flentem[7] frāter interfēcit. "Abī[8] ad spōnsum," inquit, "oblīta[9] frātrum mortuōrum vīvīque,[10] oblīta patriae. Sīc eat quaecumque Rōmāna[11] lūgēbit hostem."

[1] *because of their habit of battles (fighting)*
[2] *at Rome*
[3] *triplet*
[4] *arranged*
[5] *far*
[6] *cloak*
[7] *because she wept*
[8] *Go*
[9] *having forgotten,* with genitive
[10] *your one living brother* refers to himself:
[11] *So may every Roman woman go (to her death) who*

$_1$ indirect object of **clāmat**
$_2$ from **supersum**

PHOTRI/J. A. Cash

The story of the founding of Rome by Romulus was spread throughout the Roman empire. The famous Etruscan statue of the she-wolf is in Spain. Romulus was the first of the seven kings of Rome.

QUESTIONS

1. Who was killed first in the battle of the Horatii?
2. Who was wounded first?
3. Under what king did the Horatii fight?
4. How would you apply the Latin motto "Dīvide et imperā" to the story of the Horatii?

ADDITIONAL QUESTIONS
Who was Romulus? What was the role of the senators? Who were the senators? What was Numa's contribution to Rome? What was odd about the fight between the Horatii and the Curiatii? Why did the surviving Horatius kill his sister?

Grammar

The Dative with Compounds

You have seen that many important verbs are compounded by adding a prefix. Very often, the compounded verb changes its meaning and is followed by the dative. The English equivalent frequently calls for *to* or *for*. The most common prefixes are:

ad	**circum**	**in**	**ob**	**prae**	**sub**
ante	**cum**	**inter**	**post**	**prō**	**super**

If the uncompounded form of the verb is transitive, the compounded form can be followed by both a dative and an accusative.

WORKBOOK
Assign Ex. A to review predicate adjectives.

WORKBOOK
Assign Ex. B to practice the dative with compounds.

Huic successit Tullus Hostīlius.	*Tullus Hostilius succeeded him.*
Nūllam partem Rōmae adiēcit.	*He added no part to Rome.*

ANSWERS
1. Cui Tullius Hostīlius successit? 2. Duōbus Albānīs interfectīs, Horātius ad tertium accessit. 3. Numa nūllam montem Rōmae adiēcit, sed lēgēs Rōmānīs dedit. 4. Numa annum in mēnsēs dīvīsit et multōs mōrēs cōnstituit.

TRANSLATION

1. Whom did Tullus Hostilius succeed?
2. After killing two Albans, Horatius approached the third.
3. Numa added no hill to Rome, but he gave the Romans laws.
4. Numa divided the year into months and established many customs.

Vocabulary

Nouns

cōnsuētūdō, -dinis, *f. custom*	(customary, customize)
fors, fortis, *f. chance*	(fortuity, fortune)
initium, -tī, *n. beginning*	(initial, initiate)
intervāllum, -ī, *n. distance*	(interval)
mōs, mōris, *m. custom; (pl.) character*	(mores)
sponsa, -ae, *f. a betrothed woman*	(sponsor)
sponsus, -i, *m. a betrothed man*	(sponsor)

Adjectives

ferōx, ferōcis (gen.), *bold, fierce*	(ferocious, ferocity)
fīnitimus, -a, -um, *neighboring; (as a noun) neighbor*	
integer, -gra, -grum, *untouched, fresh, unharmed*	(integrate, integrity)
vīvus, -a, -um, *living*	(vivarium)

Verbs

adiciō, -ere, adiēcī, adiectus, *add*	(adjective, adjectival)
iuvō, iuvāre, iūvī, iūtus, *aid*	
sequor, sequī, secūtus, *follow*	(sequel, sequence)
succēdō, -ere, -cessī, -cessūrus, *succeed*	(succedent, success)
vulnerō, 1, *wound*	(vulnerable)

Word Studies

There are many interesting derivatives of **sequor**. From it was derived **secundus**, English "second," whose chief meaning therefore is *following*. Its use as a measure of time arose thus: **hōra** means *hour*; **hōra minūta** means a *diminished hour*, or "minute" (from **minuō**, *make less*, which comes in turn from **minus**); **hōra minūta secunda** means a *second-degree minute*, or smaller division of a minute. The "sequence" of tenses refers to the way one verb *follows* another in the use of a tense. A "suit" of clothes is one which the various pieces *follow* or match one another. A "suite" of rooms consists of several rooms *following* one another, i.e., one after the other. What is a "suitor"? An "executive"? A "prosecutor"?

SUITOR

LESSON OBJECTIVES
To learn the conjugation of **mālō**; To learn the locative case; To review **cum** clauses

LESSON XXVIII

Out Go the Kings

Post Hostīlium Ancus Mārtius suscēpit imperium, tum Prīscus Tarquinius. Circum[1] Rōmae aedificāvit. Lūdōs Rōmānōs īnstituit. Vīcit īdem Sabīnōs. Mūrōs fēcit et cloācās. Capitōlium aedificāvit.

Eō tempore rēs mīra accidit. Servius Tullius puer erat rēgis servus. In capite huius puerī dormientis flamma appāruit multōrum in cōnspectū. Cum quīdam aquam ad exstinguendum ferret, ab rēgīnā retentus est, quae movērī vetuit puerum. Tum cum somnō etiam flamma abiit. Tum rēgīna rēgī sēcrētō "Vidēsne, Tarquinī," inquit, "hunc puerum tam humilem? Hic lūmen rēgnō nostrō erit praesidiumque nōbīs; eī amīcī sīmus et bonīs artibus īnstituāmus."[2] Hōc factō, puer fit vir īnsignis. Cum marītus quaererētur fīliae Tarquinī, nēmō Rōmānus cum Tulliō cōnferrī potuit, rēxque eī sē fīliam suam spondēre mālle dīxit. Post mortem Tarquinī Servius, quī servus fuerat, rēx factus est.

Tullius montēs trēs, Quirīnālem, Vīminālem, Ēsquilīnum, urbī adiūnxit; fossās circum mūrum dūxit. Prīmus[3] omnium cēnsum habuit, quī adhūc per orbem terrārum nōn cognitus erat. Sub eō Rōma, omnibus in cēnsum dēlātīs,[4] habuit LXXXIIII mīlia cīvium.

L. Tarquinius Superbus, fīlius Prīscī Tarquinī, Tullium occīdit et Rōmae rēgnāvit. Cum fīlius eius nōbilissimam mātrōnam Lucrētiam iniūriā affēcisset, eaque dē iniūriā marītō et patrī et amīcīs dīxisset, in omnium cōnspectū Lucrētia sē occīdit. Propter quam causam L. Iūnius Brūtus populum contrā Tarquinium incitāvit. Posteā exercitus quoque eum relīquit. Cum imperāvisset annōs XXV, cum uxōre et līberīs suīs fūgit. Septem rēgēs CCXXXXIIII annōs rēgnāverant. Mors fortis mulieris cīvitātem līberāvit, nam post hoc duo cōnsulēs, quī singulōs annōs imperium habuērunt, ā populō creātī sunt.

[1] noun
[2] *let us train (him) in good arts*
[3] *He was the first of all to*
[4] *enrolled*

STUDY TOPIC
Livy I, 32-60

ADDITIONAL QUESTIONS
What were the contributions of Tarquinius Priscus? Was Servius Tullius of noble birth? What did Tullius do to enlarge Rome? What was the population of Rome at that time?

QUESTIONS

1. Who was the fifth king?
2. How many kings did Rome have?
3. Who was the father of Tarquin the Proud?
4. Who was the son in law of Tarquin the Elder?

Erich Lessing/Art Resource, NY

This painting by Tiziano shows the noble Roman matron Lucretia and Tarquin. Tarquin was the last of the seven kings to rule Rome. He was expelled by the Senate after his son, Sextus, raped the beautiful and virtuous Lucretia. The overthrow of Tarquin led to the establishment of the Republic.

Grammar

The Conjugation of *Mālō*

The irregular verb **mālō**, *prefer*, has the same irregularities are **volō**. The present infinitive is **mālle**.

PRESENT INDICATIVE	PRESENT SUBJUNCTIVE
mālō	mālim
māvīs	mālīs
māvult	mālit
mālumus	mālīmus
māvultis	mālītis
mālunt	mālint

SUGGESTION
Have students work in pairs to review all the irregular verbs by doing synopses. Have one write at the board and the other dictate. You may wish to add compounds of **ferō** and **eō**.

WORKBOOK
Assign Ex. A to practice the forms of **volō, nōlō,** and **mālō**.

SUGGESTION
Remind students that the locative does not use a preposition.

WORKBOOK
Assign Ex. B to practice the locative.

The Locative Case

As you know, to express "place where" in Latin, you use **in** plus the ablative. However, with the names of cities, towns, small islands, **domus** *(home)*, and **rus** *(country)*, "place where" is expressed using the locative case. The endings for the locative are the same as the genitive for first and second declension nouns, and the same as the ablative for the third declension. The locative of **rus** is **rūrī**.

Rōmae domī sunt.	*They are at home in Rome.*
Pūblius Athēnīs erat.	*Publius was in Athens.*
In Ītaliā rūrī mansērunt.	*They stayed in Italy in the country.*

NOTĀ·BENE

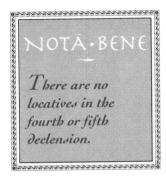

There are no locatives in the fourth or fifth declension.

Review: *Cum* Clauses

Review **cum** clauses in Lesson XVI and find those used in the reading.

TRANSLATION

1. "Dear Servius," the queen said, "we prefer to be your friends."
2. The power of the state was given to the boy when the king died.
3. When the flame appeared on the boy's head, the king adopted him.
4. When he had ruled many years, he lost his power on account of his own son.

NOTE
Starting with this lesson, after new grammatical topics have been introduced, it is suggested that one or more of the more complex constructions should be reviewed. If students are having difficulty, they should go back to the lesson where the material is introduced and redo the translation and workbook assignments.

ANSWERS
1. "Cāre Servī," rēgīna inquit, "amīcī tuī esse mālumus."
2. Potestās cīvitātis puerō datā est cum rēx mortuus esset.
3. Cum flamma in capite puerī appārēret, rēx eum adoptāvit.
4. Cum multōs annos imperāvisset, propter suum fīlium imperium āmīsit.

Scala/Art Resource, NY

Walls and trenches were typically built to help defend a settlement from outsiders. This picture shows part of the reconstructed wall around the Aventine, one of the seven hills of Rome.

Vocabulary

Scala/Art Resource, NY

The Cloaca Maxima was the greatest of the sewers and drains built by the Tarquins in the 6th century B.C. to drain Rome's marshlands. Though rebuilt many times, it remains in use to this day.

Nouns

cloāca, -ae, *f. sewer*
cōnspectus, -ūs, *m. sight*
flamma, -ae, *f. flame* (flammability, flammable)
fossa, -ae, *f. trench* (fossil)
lūmen, lūminis, *n. light, lamp, glory, eye* (luminary, luminous)
marītus, -ī, *m. husband* (marital)
mūrus, -ī, *m. wall* (mural)
orbis, -is, *m. circle, world* (orb, orbicular)

Verbs

adiungō, -ere, adiūnxī, adiūnctus, *join to*
aedificō, 1, *build* (edifice, edify)
conferō, conferre, contulī, collātus, *bring together, compare, give, place* (confer, conference)
dēferō, dēferre, dētulī, dēlātus, *offer, enroll* (defer, deference)
inquit, *he/she says (never first word)*
mālō, mālle, māluī, —, *prefer*
retineō, -ēre, retinuī, retentus, *hold back, restrain, keep* (retain, retention)
vetō, -āre, vetuī, vetitus, *forbid* (veto)

Word Studies

The prefix **sēmi–** means *half* or *partly:* **sēmibarbarus,** *semibarbarous. Semiannual* means *occurring every half year.*

The prefix **bi–** or **bis–** means *twice* or *two:* **biennium,** *a period of two years* (from **annus**). Distinguish carefully *semiannual* and *biennial, semimonthly* and *bimonthly.* **Bi–** is often found in chemical terms: *bicarbonate, bichloride.*

The prefix **ūn–, ūni–** (from **ūnus**) means *one: uniform.*

The prefix **multi–** (from **multus**) means *much, many: multiform, multigraph, multimillionaire.*

Give three other examples of each of these prefixes.

Explain *adjutant, fortuitous, initiate, successor, vulnerable.*

LESSON OBJECTIVE
To review the future passive participle, the gerund, and the dative of agent

LESSON XXIX
How Brutus Got His Name

STUDY TOPIC
Livy I, 56

[1] *slipping*
[2] *to Delphi*
[3] with **ex:** *on purpose*
[4] *wait for, bide*
[5] *laughingstock*
[6] *to chance*
[7] *had another meaning* (*looked in another direction,* literally)

WORKBOOK
Assign Ex. A to review a variety of constructions from the reading.

WORKBOOK
Assign Ex. B to learn and practice a conditional clause of comparison with **velut**.

ADDITIONAL QUESTIONS
What was the omen that Tarquin saw? Was it good or bad? What did Brutus pretend to be? Why? What did they ask the oracle? Who won? Did the prophesy come true?

Altera fābula dē Brūtō nunc nārranda est. Dum Tarquinius, ultimus rēgum Rōmānōrum, Iovis templum Rōmae aedificat, ōmen terribile vīsum est: anguis ex columnā ēlāpsus,[1] rēgis pectus anxiīs cūrīs implēvit. Itaque duōs fīliōs Delphōs[2] ad ōrāculum cōnsulendum mīsit. Comes eīs additus est L. Iūnius. Hic ex industriā[3] imitātus stultitiam, cum sē suaque praedae esse rēgī sineret, Brūtī[1] quoque nōn recūsāvit cognōmen, ab Tarquiniō datum, ut sub eō cognōmine latēns, līberātor ille populī Rōmānī opperīrētur[4] tempora sua. Is tum ab Tarquiniīs, fīliīs rēgis, ductus est Delphōs, lūdibrium[5] vērius quam comes. Quō postquam vēnērunt, perfectīs patris mandātīs, cupīdō incessit animōs iuvenum rogandī ad quem eōrum rēgnum Rōmānum esset ventūrum. Ex īnfimō vōcem redditam audiunt: "Imperium summum Rōmae habēbit quī vestrum prīmus, ō iuvenēs, ōsculum mātrī dederit." Tarquiniī sortī[6] permittunt uter prior, cum ad patriam rediissent, mātri ōsculum daret. Brūtus aliō putāns spectāre[7] vōcem ōrāculī, velut si prōlāpsus cecidisset, terram ōsculō contigit, quod ea commūnis māter omnium mortālium erat. Et sīc ēvēnit: post fugam Tarquinī et fīliōrum suōrum, Brūtus imperium Rōmae obtinuit.

QUESTIONS

1. What is the point of the story?
2. Who went to Delphi and why?
3. How did Junius get the name Brutus?

[1] The name means *stupid.*

Boltin Picture Library

The sons of Tarquin went to consult the oracle at Delphi to learn the significance of the snake omen. The oracle often gave answers that were ambiguous so that no matter what the outcome, the prophesy was accurate. What happened when the Tarquins posed their question?

Grammar

Review: Future Passive Participle and Gerund

Review the future passive participle, the gerund, and the dative of agent in Lessons XXI and XXIII.

Find all the examples of these in the reading.

NOTE
If students have difficulty with these constructions, they should go back to the lessons where the material is introduced and redo the translation and workbook assignments.

TRANSLATION

1. Who did Brutus think was the mother of all men?
2. A temple had to be built at Rome by the citizens.
3. Brutus did not think that he had to fear[2] the king.
4. The two young men went to the oracle for the purpose of asking[3] which would be king.

ANSWERS
1. Quem Brūtus arbitrābātur mātrem omnium (hominum) esse? 2. Templum Rōmae cīvibus aedificandum erat. 3. Brūtus putābat rēgem sibi nōn timendum esse. 4. Duo adulēscentēs ad ōrāculum iērunt ad rogandum uter rēx esset (rogandī causā uter rēx esset).

[2] Use the passive.
[3] Use the gerund with **ad** or **causā.**

Vocabulary

SUGGESTION
Explain to students that Roman citizens had three names: a **praenomen**, a **nomen**, and a **cognomen**.

Nouns

anguis, -is, *m., f. snake, serpent*
cognōmen, -minis, *n. surname*
comes, -itis, *m., f. companion*
iuvenis, -is, *m. young man* (juvenile)
pectus, pectoris, *n. breast, heart* (pectoral)
stultitia, -ae, *f. stupidity* (stultification, stultify)

Adjectives

ānxius, -a, -um, *troubled* (anxiety, anxious)
terribilis, -e, *frightful* (terrible)

Verbs

contingō, -ere, -tigī, -tāctus, *touch* (contact, contagion)
ēveniō, -īre, ēvēnī, ēventūrus, *turn out, happen* (event, eventual)
impleō, -ēre, implēvī, implētus, *fill*
lateō, -ēre, -uī, —, *hide, escape notice* (latent)
sinō, -ere, sīvī, situs, *allow*

Adverb

velut, velutī, *just as, as*

Word Studies

Comes (cum, īre) is one who "goes with" you; a *companion* **(cum, pānis)** is one who shares "bread with" you.

Explain *additive, comity, contingency, elapse, juvenile, latent, narrative, osculatory, pectoral, ultimatum.*

Statue of an Etruscan soldier helping a wounded comrade. The Etruscans flourished in central Italy from the 8th to the 1st centuries B.C. They were well regarded for their seamanship and established a relationship with the Phoenicians in Carthage. Eventually, they were assimilated into the Roman population.

LESSON XXX

How "Lefty" (Scaevola) Got His Name

LESSON OBJECTIVES
To learn the subjunctive with verbs of fearing; To learn Latin sentence structure

STUDY TOPIC
Livy II, 12-13

Tarquinius, ut reciperet rēgnum, bellum Rōmānīs intulit, Porsenā, rēge Etrūscōrum, auxilium ferente. Illō tempore Horātius Coclēs pontem dēfendit et Rōmam servāvit. Urbs tum obsidēbātur ā Porsenā, et frūmentī erat inopia. Sedendō[1] expugnātūrum sē urbem Porsena spērābat. Tum C. Mūcius in hostium castra īre cōnstituit. Nē forte ā mīlitibus Rōmānīs retraherētur, senātum adiit. "Trānsīre Tiberim," inquit, "patrēs,[2] et in castra hostium īre volō. Deīs iuvantibus, magnum in animō factum fīxum habeō." Probant patrēs. Abditō intrā vestem gladiō, proficīscitur. Ubi eō vēnit, in multitūdine hostium ad rēgis tribūnal[3] cōnstitit. Ibi stīpendium mīlitibus forte dabātur, et rēgis scrība,[4] quī rēgī simillimus ōrnātū[5] erat, multa agēbat. Mūcius Porsenam nōn cognōverat, neque rogāre volēbat, nē ipse aperīret quis esset; itaque scrībam, quem rēgem esse crēdidit, prō rēge occīdit. Deinde postquam per hostēs territōs gladiō viam sibi ipse fēcit, rēgis mīlitēs eum prehēnsum retrāxērunt. Ante tribūnal rēgis stāns, tum quoque in tantō perīculō timendus[6] magis quam timēns, "Rōmānus sum," inquit, "cīvis; C. Mūcium mē vocant. Hostem occīdere voluī, sed morī sciō. Nec ego sōlus in tē[7] hōs animōs habeō. Nūllus exercitus timendus tibi, nūllum proelium timendum est; ūnī tibi cum singulīs rēs erit."[8] Tum rēx simul īrā commōtus perīculōque perterritus, ignem circumdarī iussit ut Mūcius īnsidiās statim explicāre cōgerētur. Mūcius autem, "Ēn tibi,"[9] inquit, "ut sentiās quam[10] vīle corpus sit eīs quī magnam glōriam vident," dextramque manum ignī ad sacrificium factō iniēcit. Rēx, tantam virtūtem mīrātus, Mūcium līberum dīmīsit. Huic Mūciō posteā, quod dextram manum āmīserat, nōmen Scaevolae[11] datum est.

1 *by remaining encamped*
2 *senators*
3 *tribunal, platform*
4 *secretary*
5 *dress*
6 *to be feared*
7 *toward you*
8 *the decision will be between you and individual (enemies)*
9 *Look you*
10 *how*
11 *Left-handed ("Lefty")*; pronounced *Sev´ola*

SUGGESTION
Point out the use of the dative (**ignī**) with a compound verb (**iniēcit**).

QUESTIONS

1. Why did Mucius kill Porsena's secretary?
2. How did Mucius get the name Scaevola?
3. Why did Mucius want to cross the Tiber?
4. Why was there a crowd at the king's tribunal?

ADDITIONAL QUESTIONS
Who was Porsena? Why were the Etruscans fighting with the Romans? From whom did Mucius get approval for his plan? How did the king hope to have the plot revealed? Why did Porsena let Mucius go?

Grammar

SUGGESTION
Tell students that when you express a fear, it is usually a fear that something negative might happen. That is why the **nē** is used with the positive construction.

WORKBOOK
Assign Ex. A to practice the subjunctive with verbs of fearing.

The Subjunctive after Verbs of Fearing

After verbs meaning *fear*, such as **timeo** and **vereor**, Latin uses the conjunction **ne** followed by the subjunctive to introduce a positive clause and **ut** to introduce a negative clause. Follow the normal sequence of tenses.

Timēmus ut veniat.	*We fear that he will not come.*
Verēbantur nē ad eōs exercitus noster adducerētur.	*They feared that our army would be led against them.*

SUGGESTION
As students are reading the story in class, have them try a variety of ways of translating the different participial constructions. The goal is to understand the Latin, which can usually best be done by putting it into understandable English.

WORKBOOK
Assign Ex. B to practice various constructions taken from the reading.

Latin Sentence Structure

You may have noticed a striking difference between Latin and English sentence structure. In Latin, it is preferable to vary constructions by using participles, the ablative absolute, and various subordinate clauses. English tends to use coordinate or parallel constructions connected by *and*.

Mīlitēs eum prehēnsum retrāxērunt.	*The soldiers caught him and pulled him back.*

For this reason, it is important to pay attention to the sense of the whole sentence before trying to translate it, word for word, into good English. You may often have to add or delete words to make it flow better.

ANSWERS
1. Mūcius dīxit Rōmam sibi esse servandam. 2. Cum Rōma obsidērētur, Mūcius senātum adiit. 3. Hostibus timendus fuit, nam vēnerat ut Rōmam pugnandō līberāret. 4. Timētis/Verēminī ut servī frūmentō vōs iuvent?

TRANSLATION

1. Mucius said that Rome was to be saved by him.
2. When Rome was being besieged, Mucius approached the senate.
3. He was to be feared by the enemy, for he had come to free Rome by fighting.
4. Do you fear that the slaves will not help you with the grain?

Prenestino Museum, Rome/E.T. Archives, London/SuperStock, Inc.

This detail of what is called the Nile Mosaic was discovered in the sanctuary of a temple dedicated to Fortuna in Praeneste, just east of Rome. It depicts a Roman garrison detachment on the Nile.

Vocabulary

Nouns

inopia, -ae, *f. lack*	
īnsidiae, -ārum, *f. pl. plot, ambush*	(insidious)
pōns, pontis, *m. bridge*	(pontoon)
stīpendium, -dī, *n. pay*	(stipend, stipendiary)

Adjective

vīlis, -e, *cheap, worthless*	(vile, vilipend)

Verbs

abdō, -ere, abdidī, abditus, *put away, hide*	
aperio, -īre, aperuī, apertus, *open, reveal*	(aperture)
circumdō, -dare, -dedī, -datus, *put around*	
fīgō, -ere, fīxī, fīxus, *fix*	(fixate, fixture)
īnferō, īnferre, intulī, illātus, *bring in, to,* or *against; inflict*	(infer, inference)
obsideō, -ēre, obsēdī, obsessus, *beseige*	(obsess, obsession)
retrahō, -ere, retrāxī, retrāctus, *drag back*	(retract, retractor)
vereor, verērī, veritus, *fear, respect*	(rever, reverence)

WORKBOOK
Assign Ex. C to learn about and practice verbs with reduplicative consonants.

Preposition

intrā (+acc.), *within*	(intragalactic, intramural)

Word Studies

We have many silent consonants in English words. They cause trouble in spelling. In some cases the difficulty is cleared up by taking thought of the Latin original, for Latin has no silent letters. Compare the following, often misspelled: *debt* **(dēbitus)**, *honor* **(honor)**, *assign* **(signum)**, *mortgage* **(mortem)**, *receipt* **(receptus)**. Can you find other instances?

LESSON XXXI

The Plebeians Go On Strike

LESSON OBJECTIVE
To learn about impersonal verbs

STUDY TOPICS
Patricians, Plebs; Livy II, 27-33

Paulō post rēgēs exāctōs[1] bellum cīvīle propter aes aliēnum[2] inter senātōrēs et plēbem oritur. Hōrum[3] multī dīxērunt sē in fīnibus hostium prō lībertāte et imperiō pugnantēs ā cīvibus domī oppressōs esse, tūtiōremque in bellō inter hostēs lībertātem plēbis esse quam in pāce inter cīvēs. Quīdam, quī Sabīnō bellō fortis mīles fuerat, "Mē absente," inquit, "ager vāstātus est, vīlla incēnsa, tribūtum imperātum. Aes aliēnum facere[4] mē oportēbat. Posteā agrum āmīsī et ā crēditōribus in vincula coniectus sum." Hōc audītō, multitūdō postulāvit ut senātus vocārētur. Senātū convocātō, nūntiātur Volscōs ad urbem oppugnandam venīre. Omnēs, inimīcitiā dēpositā, pugnant, hostēsque vincuntur. Sed post bellum senātus nihil dē plēbe ēgit. Tum aliud bellum oritur. Cōnsulēs nōmina cīvium legunt.[1] Cum ad nōmen nēmō responderet, omnēs dīcunt lībertātem reddendam esse priusquam arma danda,[5] ut prō patriā cīvibusque, nōn prō dominīs pugnent. Dictātor plēbī meliōrem condiciōnem post bellum pollicitus est. Sed, bellō cōnfectō, nihil āctum est.

Tum plēbs in Sacrum montem sēcessērunt.[2] Hic mōns trāns Aniēnem flūmen est tria ab urbe mīlia passuum. Patribus[6] placuit ad plēbem mittī Menēnium Agrippam. Is hoc nārrāvit:

"Ōlim reliquae partēs corporis hūmānī īrātae erant quod suā cūrā, suō labōre ventrī[7] omnia quaerēbantur, quī ipse nihil agēbat. Coniūrāvērunt nē manūs ad ōs cibum ferrent, nec ōs acciperet, nec dentēs cōnficerent.[8] Dum ventrem hōc modō vincere volunt, ipsa membra paene moriuntur. Inde appāret ventrem nōn magis alī quam alere." Cum Menēnius ostendisset quam[9] corporis discordia similis esset īrae plēbis, pāx facta est hāc condiciōne, ut tribūnī plēbis creārentur neque ūllī patrī[10] licēret eum magistrātum capere. Tribūnī accēpērunt potestātem auxilī dandī[3] contrā cōnsulēs.

[1] *after the expulsion of the kings*
[2] *another's money,* i.e., *debt*
[3] i.e., the plebeians
[4] *go into debt*
[5] *before arms are given* (*to them*)
[6] *senators*
[7] *for the stomach*
[8] *"do up,"* i.e., *chew up*
[9] *how*
[10] *patrician*

SUGGESTION
Explain that in early Rome there were two classes of citizens: the patricians (senators), who had all the power and privileges, and the plebeians, who had none.

NOTE
Point out that this happens also in English. The committee *is* meeting. (an entity) The committee *are* not agreed. (individuals)

NOTE
Point out that we use the Roman tribune's word **veto,** *I forbid,* today in government.

---

[1] They called the roll in the draft.
[2] 494 B.C. As **plēbs** is plural in thought, the plural verb is used.
[3] i.e., to a citizen who appealed to them

The Bettmann Archive

The Sabines were an ancient people who lived in the hills northeast of Rome. Tradition says that the abduction of the Sabine women, supposedly to provide wives for the followers of Romulus, may have developed to explain the Sabine population in Rome.

QUESTIONS

1. How did the civil war start?
2. Where was the Sacred Mount?
3. Who was permitted to be a tribune?
4. What power did the tribunes have?

ADDITIONAL QUESTIONS
What did the common people complain about? What happened to the war hero while he was away? What did the senators learn from the war with the Volscians? Explain the story Menenius Agrippa told.

WORKBOOK
Assign Ex. A to practice impersonal verbs.

Grammar

Impersonal Verbs

Impersonal verbs are always used in the third person singular. They may have no subject or they may have a clause or an infinitive for a subject. Some impersonal verbs take special cases.

licet, *it is permitted*, takes the dative of the person

Mihi hoc facere licet.	*It is permitted to me to do this.* *I may do this.*

placet, *it is decided; it is pleasing*, takes the dative

Mihi discēdere placet.	*It is decided by me to leave.* *I have decided to leave.* *It is pleasing to me to leave.*

oportet, *it is necessary*, takes the accusative

Mē hoc facere oportet.	*It is necessary that I do this.* *I must (ought to) do this.*

NOTĀ · BENE

Remember that necessity may also be expressed in two other ways:
Hoc facere dēbeō.
or **Hoc mihi faciendum est.**

TRANSLATION

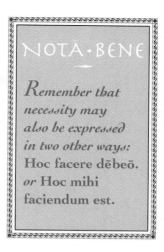

1. No senator will be allowed to oppress the common people.
2. It will not be necessary (for) them to demand better conditions.[4]
3. The citizens ought not to be seized and thrown into chains by creditors.[4]
4. It has been decided by the senate to make peace by promising certain conditions.

[4] Translate in two ways.

WORKBOOK
Assign Ex. B to practice various constructions taken from the reading.

ANSWERS
1. Nūllī senātōrī/patrī plēbem opprimere licēbit. 2. Nōn oportēbit eōs meliōrēs condiciōnēs postulāre./Nōn dēbēbunt meliōrēs condiciōnēs postulāre./Meliōrēs condiciōnēs eīs nōn postulandae erunt. 3. Cīvēs capiendī et in vincula crēditōribus coniciendī nōn sunt./Nōn oportet cīvēs capī et in vincula ā crēditōribus conicī./Crēditōrēs cīvēs capere et in vincula conicere nōn dēbent. 4. Quibusdam condiciōnibus pollicendīs pācem facere senātuī placuit.

Ronald Sheridan/Ancient Art & Architecture Collection

The Roman Senate was the dominant branch of the government. It began with a membership of 300, then grew to 600 under Sulla, increased to 900 under Julius Caesar, and was reduced back to 600 by Augustus. Senators were primarily large landowners who were forbidden to engage in large-scale business.

Vocabulary

Nouns

aes, aeris, *n. bronze, money*
dēns, dentis, *m. tooth* (dental, dentist)
magistrātus, -ūs, *m. magistrate, office* (magistracy)
ōs, ōris, *n. mouth, face, expression* (oral)
plēbs, plēbis, *f. common people* (plebeian, plebiseite)
venter, -tris, *m. belly, stomach* (ventral, ventricle)
vinculum, -ī, *n. bond, chain*

Adjective

tūtus, -a, -um, *safe* (tutelage, tutor)

Verbs

alō, -ere, aluī, alitus, *feed, nourish* (alimony, coalition)
coniūrō, 1, *conspire* (conjure)
licet, -ēre, licuit or **licitum est,** *it is permitted* (illicit, licit)
oportet, -ēre, oportuit, *it is necessary*
oppugnō, 1, *attack* (oppugn)
postulō, 1, *demand* (postulant, postulate)

Adverb

ōlim, *once*

Word Studies

The following words are commonly used in geometry. Define them and find other geometrical or mathematical terms derived from Latin.

acute **(acūtus)**
adjacent **(ad–, iaceō)**
circumscribe **(circum–, scrībō)**
coincide **(co–, incidō)**
complementary **(compleō)**
concurrent **(con–, currō)**
equidistant **(aequus, dis–, stō)**
equilateral **(aequus, latus)**
inscribe **(in–, scrībō)**
locus **(locus)**
median **(medius)**
plane **(plānus)**
quadrilateral **(quattuor, latus)**
Q.E.D. **(quod erat dēmōnstrandum)**
Q.E.F. **(quod erat faciendum)**
subtend **(sub–, tendō)**
tangent **(tangō)**
transversal **(trāns–, vertō)**

LESSON XXXII

Extra! Rome Captured by the Gauls[1]

LESSON OBJECTIVES
To learn the partitive genitive (genitive of the whole); To review and learn more about **cum** clauses

STUDY TOPIC
Livy V, 33-43

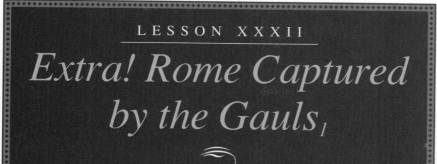

Gallī, Italiae dulcibus frūctibus maximēque vīnō captī, Alpēs trānsiērunt et contrā Rōmānōs prōcessērunt. Sed cum Rōmānī pugnantēs cum fīnitimīs populīs saepe dictātōrem creāvissent, eō tempore nihil extraōrdināriī[2] imperī aut auxilī quaesīvērunt. Plūrimum terrōris ad Rōmānōs celeritās hostium tulit. Ad flūmen Alliam Rōmānī superātī sunt. Maxima pars eōrum ad urbem Veiōs fūgit; nihil praesidī Rōmam[1] mīsērunt. Aliī Rōmam petīvērunt et, nē clausīs quidem portīs urbis, in arcem fūgērunt. Tam facile Rōmānī victī erant ut Gallī mīrantēs prīmum stārent, īnsidiās verentēs. Deinde ad urbem prōgressī sunt. Cum equitēs rettulissent nōn portās urbis clausās, nōn mīlitēs in mūrīs esse, īnsidiās et noctem veritī, inter Rōmam atque flūmen Aniēnem castra posuērunt.

Cum spēs nūlla urbis dēfendendae esset, Rōmānī cōnstituērunt ut iuventūs mīlitāris[2] cum mulieribus ac līberīs in arcem Capitōliumque concēderet. Ibi, frūmentō collātō, deōs hominēsque et Rōmānum nōmen dēfendere parant.

Senēs autem in aedibus[3] suīs adventum hostium obstinātō[4] ad mortem animō exspectāre māluērunt. Eī quī magistrātūs gesserant, augustissimā veste vestītī in mediō aedium in eburneīs sellīs[5] sēdērunt. Posterō diē Gallī urbem ingressī ad praedam properant. Venerābundī[6] spectābant sedentēs virōs, quī ob vestem et maiestātem gravitātemque deīs simillimī vidēbantur. Cum Gallī, ad eōs sedentēs velut ad imāginēs versī, stārent, ūnus ē senibus Gallum barbam suam permulcentem[7] scīpiōne eburneō[3] percussit. Hoc initium caedis fuit. Cēterī in aedibus suīs interfectī sunt. Post prīncipum caedem nēminī parcitur,[8] dīripiuntur aedificia, iniciuntur ignēs. Sed arcem capere Gallī nōndum cōnantur.

[1] *to Rome*
[2] *capable of bearing arms*
[3] *houses*
[4] *resolved*
[5] *ivory*
[6] *full of reverence*
[7] *stroking his* (i.e., the old man's) *beard*
[8] *No one is spared*

---

[1] This was in 390 B.C. Rome was not again captured by a foreign enemy for 800 years.
[2] The genitive of **–ius** adjectives is not contracted like that of nouns.
[3] *ivory staff*—part of the insignia of a triumphing general. He was seated, as we might say, in full uniform, wearing all his medals, awaiting his doom.

The Bettmann Archive

The Gauls were attracted to the Romans initially because of their food and wine. Some Gallic dinners, however, lacked the refinement that one would expect to see in Rome.

QUESTIONS

1. When did the Gauls enter Rome?
2. What did the old Roman men do?
3. Why did the Gauls come into Italy?
4. Why did the Gauls not enter Rome as soon as they arrived there?

Grammar

ADDITIONAL QUESTIONS
To what city did many of the Romans flee? Where did the Gauls pitch their camp? Who went to the citadel? Who was massacred?

SUGGESTION
Do a quick oral drill with a few phrases; since this construction is so much like English, students generally have no difficulty *(a few of the women, some of the horses, many of the slaves)*, etc.

Genitive of the Whole

The genitive of the whole, or partitive genitive, is used to represent the *whole* of which a *part* is mentioned. It is very similar to the English construction.

Hostēs plūrimum terrōris fēcērunt.	*The enemy created a great deal of terror.*
Pars exercitūs in urbe mansit.	*Part of the army remained in the city.*

The partitive genitive is often used after **nihil, satis,** and **quis/quid**.

Plēbēs nihil imperī habuērunt.	*The plebeians had no power.*
Nōn erat satis cibī.	*There was not enough food.*
Quis vestrum ītis?	*Which of you is going?*

NOTĀ·BENE

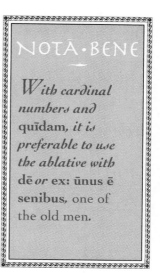

With cardinal numbers and **quīdam,** *it is preferable to use the ablative with* **dē** *or* **ex: ūnus ē senibus,** one of the old men.

More About *Cum* Clauses

You already know that **cum** can be translated *when* in a time clause. In some clauses, **cum** is best translated by *since,* in others by *although.* These are sometimes called *causal* or *concessive* clauses. In such clauses the subjunctive is always used.

Cum tē nōn vidērem, discessī.	*Since I didn't see you, I left.*
Cum vulnerārētur, fortiter pugnāvit.	*Although he was wounded, he fought bravely.*

Find at least one example of each of these uses in the reading.

WORKBOOK
Assign Ex. A to practice the partitive genitive.

SUGGESTION
Before starting the section on **cum** clauses, have students review Lesson XVI.

WORKBOOK
Assign Ex. B to practice and review **cum** clauses.

TRANSLATION

1. Nothing (of) good is inspired by a great deal of terror.
2. Of all the Romans the old men alone determined to die in the city.
3. Although the gates had not been closed, the rest withdrew to the citadel.
4. Since the Romans feared the approach of the enemy's horsemen, they fled and left no (nothing of a) guard.

ANSWERS
1. Nihil bonī plūrimō terrōris inicitur. 2. Omnium Rōmānōrum senēs solī in urbe morī cōnstituērunt. 3. Portīs nōn clausīs, reliquī ad arcem concessērunt. 4. Cum Rōmānī adventum equitum hostium verērentur, fūgērunt et nihil praesidī relīquērunt.

Vocabulary

Nouns

adventus, -ūs, *m. arrival*	(adventure, adventuresome)
arx, arcis, *f. citadel*	
caedēs, -is, *f. slaughter*	
eques, equitis, *m. horseman, knight; (pl.) cavalry*	(equestrian)
fructus, -ūs, *m. fruit*	(fructification, fructify)
sella, -ae, *f. chair, seat, stool*	
terror, -ōris, *m. terror*	(terrorism, terrorize)
vīnum, -ī, *n. wine*	(vine, vinegar)

Adjectives

augustus, -a, -um, *magnificent*
dulcis, -e, *sweet* (dulcet)
mīlitāris, -e, *military*

Verbs

conor, 1, *try, attempt*
dīripiō, -ere, dīripuī, dīreptus, *plunder*
parcō, -ere, pepercī, parsūrus, *spare* (+ dat.) (parsimonious, parsimony)
sedeō, -ēre, sēdī, sessūrus, *sit* (sedate, sedentary)

Adverb

nē... quidem, *not even*

Word Studies

Review the prefix **inter–** in the Appendix. The preposition **intrā** (*within, inside*) is also used as a prefix in English. The two must be carefully distinguished: an *intercollegiate* contest is one *between* two (or more) colleges, as Harvard and Yale; an *intracollegiate* contest is one *within* a single college, as when the freshmen and sophomores of Yale play a game. What is the difference between *interscholastic* and *intrascholastic, interstate* and *intrastate?*

Intrō– (*within*) is also used as a prefix: **intrōdūcō,** *introduce, introspection.*

Extrā– (*outside*) is found in *extraordinary* (from **ōrdō**).

Define *extralegal, intramural, extramural.*

LESSON XXXIII

Rome Sweet Home

LESSON OBJECTIVE
To review the datives of purpose and reference

STUDY TOPIC
Livy V, 44-55

Arx Capitōliumque in magnō perīculō fuērunt. Nam Gallī nocte tantō silentiō in summum ēvāsērunt ut nōn custōdēs sōlum fallerent sed nē canēs quidem excitārent. Ānserēs[1] nōn fefellērunt, quōs sacrōs[2] Iūnōnī in summā inopiā cibī[3] Rōmānī tamen nōn occīderant. Quae rēs Rōmānīs salūtī fuit; nam clangōre[4] eōrum excitātus est M. Mānlius, quī, armīs raptīs, ad arma cēterōs vocāvit. Eī Gallōs facile dēiēcērunt.

Sed posteā nōn sōlum cibus sed etiam spēs dēfēcit. Tum tribūnīs mīlitum negōtium datum ut pācem facerent. Ācta rēs est, et mīlle pondō[1] aurī pretium factum est. Pondera[2] ab Gallīs allāta inīqua et, tribūnō Rōmānō recūsante,[3] additus est ā Gallō ponderī gladius, audītaque vōx Rōmānīs nōn ferenda,[5] "Vae[6] victīs!"

Sed dī[4] et hominēs prohibuērunt esse redēmptōs Rōmānōs. Nam nōndum omnī aurō pēnsō, Camillus, quī absēns iterum dictātor creātus erat, vēnit. Gallōs discēdere iubet et eīs imperat ut sē ad proelium expediant. Suōs ferrō, nōn aurō, recipere patriam iubet. Gallī in Rōmānōs currunt sed vincuntur; castra capiuntur; nē nūntius quidem proelī relīctus.

Sed nunc plēbs voluit ruīnās Rōmae relinquere et in urbem Veiōs migrāre. Camillus ōrātiōnem vehementem habuit et eōs mōvit:

"Nōnne tenet vōs haec terra quam mātrem appellāmus? Mihi quidem, cum patria in mentem venit, haec omnia occurrunt: collēs campīque et Tiberis et hoc caelum sub quō nātus ēducātusque sum. Nōn sine causā dī hominēsque hunc urbī cōnstituendae locum ēlēgērunt, marī propinquum, regiōnum Italiae medium. Argūmentō[7] est ipsa magnitūdō tam novae urbis. Nōn singulae urbēs, nōn coniūnctī cum Aequīs Volscī, nōn tōta Etrūria bellō vōbīs pār est. Hīc Capitōlium est, quod ā deō respōnsum est caput imperī futūrum esse. Hīc Vestae ignēs, hīc ancīlia dē caelō dēmissa, hīc omnēs dī propitiī manentibus vōbīs."

[1] *geese*
[2] *(being) sacred*
[3] *(although) in the greatest need of food*
[4] *cackling*
[5] *intolerable to Romans*
[6] *woe*
[7] *(serves as) proof*

---

[1] Used as an indeclinable noun: *pounds.*
[2] *weights,* for weighing the gold. When the Romans complained that the weights were too heavy, the Gaul insolently threw in a sword as an additional weight.
[3] i.e., the weights
[4] for **deī**

Northwind Picture Archives

The Capitoline Hill, one of the seven hills of Rome, was the center of state religion. The least inhabited of the hills, it was really a fortified citadel and religious sanctuary. According to legend, the sacred geese of Juno alerted the Romans to a sneak attack by the Gauls in 390 B.C.

QUESTIONS

1. How was the Capitol saved?
2. What river flows through Rome?
3. Why did the Romans want to make peace?
4. Why was the gold not given to the Gauls?

ADDITIONAL QUESTIONS
What hill did the Gauls climb? Who (What) awakened Marcus Manlius? What was added to the pile of weights? Why? What happened to the Gauls? Why did some want to move? Did they?

Grammar

Review: Datives of Purpose and Reference

Review the datives of purpose and reference in Lesson XXVI. Find all the examples of these constructions in the reading.

Omission of *Sum*

WORKBOOK
Assign Ex. A to recognize the omission of **sum** as a connector.

A form of **sum** is often omitted either when it might be used as a connector or in compound tenses of the indicative or infinitive of verbs.

Marcus in īnsulā est;	*Marcus is on the island;*
Anna in urbe.	*Anna in the city.*

Can you find five examples in the reading?

TRANSLATION

1. What circumstance was a source of safety to the Romans?
2. "The gods," said he, "have chosen Rome as a home for themselves."
3. The Romans had made peace with the Gauls by paying (*gerundive*) money.
4. When the Gauls were already near the top of the hill, the Romans threw them down.

WORKBOOK
Assign Ex. B to practice various constructions taken from the reading.

ANSWERS
1. Quae rēs Rōmānīs salūtī fuit? 2. "Deī," inquit, "Rōmam sibi domiciliō dēlēgērunt." 3. Rōmānī pecūniā pendendā pācem cum Gallīs fēcerant. 4. Cum Gallī summō collī iam propinquī essent, Rōmānī eōs dēiēcērunt.

Vocabulary

Nouns

ancīle, -is, *n. shield*	
collis, -is, *m. hill*	(collar)
custōs, -ōdis, *m. guard*	(custodian, custody)
mēns, mentis, *f. mind*	(mental, mentality)

Adjectives

inīquus, -a, -um, *uneven, unjust*	(iniquitous, iniquity)
propinquus, -a, -um, *near*	
propitius, -a, -um, *favorable*	(propitiatory, propitious)
vehemēns, vehementis (gen.), *vigorous*	(vehemence, vehement)

C. M. Dixon

The summit of the Capitoline Hill is now occupied by a square designed by Michelangelo. Palaces surround the square on three sides. In the middle of the square is a Roman bronze statue of the the emperor Marcus Aurelius. The statue, erected in the 16th century, was preserved for many centuries because it was believed to be the 4th century Christian emperor, Constantine.

Verbs

dēficiō, -ere, dēfēcī, dēfectus, *fail*	(deficiency, defective)
dēiciō, -ere, dēiēcī, dēiectus, *throw (down), dislodge*	(deject, dejection)
ēvādō, -ere, ēvāsī, ēvāsūrus, *go out, escape*	(evade, evasion)
expediō, -īre, -īvī, -ītus, *set free, prepare*	(expedient, expedite)
fallō, -ere, fefellī, falsus, *deceive*	(fallacy, falsify)
nāscor, nāscī, nātus, *be born*	(nascency, nascent)
occurrō, -ere, occurrī, occursūrus, *meet, occur*	(occurrence, occurrent)
pendō, -ere, pependī, pēnsus, *hang, weigh, pay*	(pendant, pendulous)

Word Studies

Many English words containing *c, g,* or *s* sounds are often misspelled. When these are derived from Latin, it will be helpful to think of the Latin original: *circumstance, voice, concern, suggest, legislation, origin, cordial, graduate, presume, vision, decision.*

Explain *alimentary, custodian, deficient, dementia, expenditure, illicit, impend, iniquitous, nascent, nativity, occurrence, propinquity.* Explain the difference between *liberty* and *license.*

Archivio e Studio Folco Quilici

*Roman armor pieces included body armor (**arma, lorica**), shield (**scutum**), helmet (**galea**), a short stabbing dagger (**sica, pugio**), a sword (**gladius**), and a heavy and a light javelin (**pilum**).*

LESSON XXXIV

Torquatus, or Courage and Discipline[1]

LESSON OBJECTIVES
To review indirect command; To review the indefinites **quis, aliquis**, and **quīdam**

Gallī contrā Rōmānōs pugnābant. Quīdam ex Gallīs quī et vīribus et magnitūdine et virtūte cēterīs praestābat prōcessit et vōce maximā clāmat: "Sī quis mēcum pugnāre vult, prōcēdat." Omnēs recūsant propter magnitūdinem eius atque immānem faciem. Deinde Gallus irrīdēre incipit atque linguam ēicere. Tum T. Mānlius, mīles Rōmānus, prōcessit et contrā Gallum cōnstitit. Gallus, quī duōs magnōs gladiōs habuit, scūtō prōiectō, exspectābat; Mānlius scūtō scūtum percussit[1] atque Gallum dē locō dēiēcit. Eō modō sub Gallī gladium successit atque parvō suō gladiō eum interfēcit. Torquem[2] eius dētrāxit eamque sibi in collum impōnit. Quō ex factō ipse posterīque eius Torquātī sunt nōminātī.

Postquam Torquātus cōnsul factus est, bellum contrā Latīnōs susceptum est.[2] Latīnī Rōmānīs similēs erant linguā, mōribus, armōrum genere, īnstitūtīs mīlitāribus. Itaque Torquātus et alter cōnsul cōnstituērunt cum maximā cūrā pugnāre et imperāvērunt nē quis extrā ōrdinem in hostēs pugnāret.

Forte inter cēterōs quī ad explōrandum et pābulandum dīmissī erant T. Mānlius, cōnsulis fīlius, ad castra hostium ēvāsit. Cum equitem Latīnum vidēret, imperī patris oblītus[3] est et cum hoste pugnāre coepit. Quod ubi audīvit cōnsul, statim mīlitēs convocārī iussit. Tum fīliō, "quoniam tū," inquit, "neque imperium cōnsulis neque maiestātem patris veritus, extrā ōrdinem cum hoste pugnāvistī et disciplīnam mīlitārem, quā stetit ad hanc diem Rōmāna rēs,[4] solvistī, trīste exemplum[3] sed salūbre posterīs nostrīs erō. Mē quidem et amor līberōrum et virtūs tua movet; sed tū quoque, sī quid in tē nostrī sanguinis est, volēs disciplīnam mīlitārem poenā tuā restituere." Hōc dictō, imperāvit ut fīlius statim morte afficerētur.

Post hoc Latīnī magnā pugnā superātī sunt.

STUDY TOPIC
Livy VII, 9-10; VIII, 7

[1] *struck (the Gaul's) shield with his own*
[2] 340 B.C.
[3] *forgot* with the genitive **imperī**
[4] = **rēs pūblica**

---

[1] From Aulus Gellius and Livy. The incident referred to took place in 361 B.C., on the occasion of the second invasion of the Gauls.
[2] *collar of gold,* worn by soldiers as a military decoration, like our medals
[3] Predicate nominative: *I shall be an example.*

ADDITIONAL QUESTIONS
How many people volunteered to fight the Gaul? What did the Gaul carry as weapons? How did Manlius kill the Gaul? How were the Latins like the Romans? What happened to Manlius' son? Why?

NOTE
Remind students that **iubeō** takes an infinitive, not **ut** and the subjunctive.

SUGGESTION
Use the following mnemonic device to help students remember this: "After **sī, nisi, num,** and **nē,** all the **ali**'s drop away."

WORKBOOK
Assign Ex. A to review uses of the ablative.

WORKBOOK
Assign Ex. B to practice various constructions taken from the reading.

ANSWERS
1. Duo cōnsulēs suōs (hominēs/mīlitēs) monuerant ut imperiō/ēdictō pārērent. 2. Cōnsulēs rogāverant nē quis cum hoste/hostibus nisi iussus pugnāret. 3. Cōnsul imperāvit ut suus fīlius interficerētur (iussit suum filium interficī) ut salūbrī exemplō cēterīs esset. 4. Quīdam ē mīlitibus ad explōrandum dīmissī sunt, et cōnsulis fīlius quoque petīverat ut cum eīs īret.

QUESTIONS

1. What happened to Torquatus?
2. How did Manlius get the name Torquatus?
3. Why was Manlius so cautious in his war against the Latins?

Grammar

Indirect Command

Review the indirect command in Lesson XXII. Find examples of such clauses in the reading.

The Indefinites *Quis*, *Aliquis*, and *Quīdam*

After **sī, nisi, num,** and **nē, quis** is used as an indefinite pronoun (*some, any*) in place of **aliquis**. Find at least three examples in the reading. Review the declension of **quis, aliquis,** and **quīdam** in Lessons VI and XX.

ORAL PRACTICE

Tell the form of **quid, cuidam, aliqua, quoddam, quaedam, alicuius, quōrundam, aliquī.**

TRANSLATION

1. The two consuls had warned their (men) to obey the order.
2. The consuls had asked that no one fight with the enemy unless ordered.[4]
3. So as to be a wholesome example to the rest the consul ordered his own son to be killed.
4. Certain of the soldiers were sent out to reconnoiter, and the consul's son too begged to go with them.

Vocabulary

Nouns

faciēs, -ēī, *f. face, appearance* (facial)
sanguis, sanguinis, *m. blood* (sanguinary, sanguine)

Adjectives

immānis, -e, *huge, savage* (immane, immanence)
salūbris, -e, *wholesome, healthy* (salubrious)
trīstis, -e, *sad* (triste)

[4] Use **iubeō.**

Verbs

afficiō, -ere, affēcī, affectus, *affect, afflict, visit* (affection, affective)

coepī, coeptus, *began (perfect tenses only)*

praestō, -āre, -stitī, -stitūrus, *stand before, excel*

prōiciō, -ere, -iēcī, -iectus, *throw, thrust (forward)* (project, projection)

restituō, -ere, restituī, restitūtus, *restore* (restitute, restitution)

suscipiō, -ere, -cēpī, -ceptus, *undertake, incur* (susceptibility, susceptible)

Preposition

extrā (+ acc.), *out of, outside of* (extraordinary)

Conjunctions

forte, *by chance*
quoniam, *since*

Word Studies

The following aviation terms are all derived from Latin.

accelerometer **(ad–, celer)**
aileron **(āla)**
airplane **(āēr, plānus)**
altimeter **(altus)**
aviator **(avis)**
contact **(con–, tangō)**
interceptor **(inter–, capiō)**
jet **(iaciō)**
motor **(moveō)**
propeller **(prō–, pellō)**
retractable **(re–, trahō)**
stabilizer **(stō)**
supersonic **(super–, sonus)**
turbo-prop **(turbō, prō–, pellō)**
visibility **(videō)**

See if you can find other aviation terms.

LESSON OBJECTIVES

To learn the relative pronoun as a connector; To learn *place to which* without a preposition

LESSON XXXV

The Punic Wars[1]

STUDY TOPICS

Livy XXI-XXII; Hannibal; The Battle of Cannae

[1] *was (a battle) fought*
[2] *They made soldiers (of) the slaves*
[3] *(a thing) which*
[4] *pecks of rings*

Prīmō bellō Pūnicō Rōmānī prīmum in marī pugnāvērunt et hostēs vīcērunt. Neque ūlla victōria Rōmānīs grātior fuit, quod, invictī in terrā, iam etiam in marī plūrimum poterant. Postquam Sicilia capta est et Corsica Sardiniaque vāstātae sunt, bellum in Āfricam trānslātum est. Victī Carthāginiēnsēs pācem ā Rōmānīs petīvērunt. Illō tempore Rēgulus, dux Rōmānōrum, senātuī persuāsit nē pācem cum Poenīs faceret. Tandem cōnsul Catulus profectus est cum CCC nāvibus in Siciliam; Poenī contrā ipsum CCCC nāvēs parāvērunt. Numquam in marī tantīs cōpiīs pugnātum est.[1] Carthāginiēnsēs superātī sunt.

Bellum Pūnicum secundum Rōmānīs ab Hannibale illātum est. Cum magnō exercitū Alpēs trānsiit. Post complūrēs parvās victōriās Hannibal Rōmānōs ad lacum Trasumennum gravissimē vīcit.

Rōmae ad prīmum nūntium proelī populus cum magnō terrōre in Forum concurrit. Mulierēs rogāvērunt omnēs quae fortūna exercitūs esset. Tandem praetor, "Pugnā," inquit, "magnā victī sumus." Posterīs diēbus ad portās maior prope multitūdō mulierum quam virōrum stetit, quae aut suōrum aliquem aut nūntiōs dē eīs exspectābat. Ūnam fēminam in ipsā portā incolumī fīliō[2] subitō occurrentem in complexu eius exspīrāvisse dīcunt; alteram, cui mors fīlī falsō nūntiāta erat, sedentem domī ad prīmum cōnspectum redeuntis fīlī gaudiō mortuam esse dīcunt.

Proximō annō Rōmānī ab Hannibale pulsī etiam maius dētrīmentum ad Cannās accēpērunt. Multae Italiae cīvitātēs ad Poenōs dēfēcērunt. Quae tamen rēs Rōmānōs nōn mōvit ut pācis umquam mentiō apud eōs fieret. Servōs mīlitēs[2] fēcērunt, quod[3] numquam ante factum erat. Hannibal trēs modiōs[4] ānulōrum aureōrum Carthāginem mīsit, quōs ex manibus equitum Rōmānōrum mortuōrum dētrāxerat.

Rōmānī tamen post multōs annōs Hannibalem vīcērunt.

---

[1] First Punic War, 264–241 B.C.; Second Punic War, 218–201 B.C. The word "Punic" is derived from **Poenī,** another name for the Carthaginians, who originally came from Phoenicia.

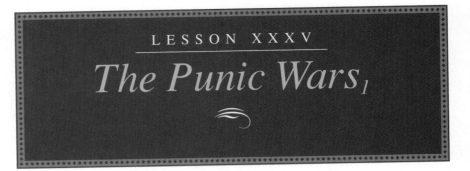

[2] dative, depending on **occurrentem**

Ronald Sheridan/Ancient Art & Architecture Collection

The Roman navy helped ensure Rome's domination of the Mediterranean. With the help of the navy, Rome destroyed Carthage in the Punic Wars. During the Battle of Actium in 31 B.C., the navy under Augustus defeated Mark Antony.

QUESTIONS

1. What was the first war the Romans won on the sea?
2. Why did the victory on the seas please the Romans?
3. What visible evidence did the people of Carthage have of the greatness of Hannibal's victory at Cannae?
4. What other great victory did Hannibal win?

ADDITIONAL QUESTIONS
What three islands were captured by the Romans in battle? Who started the Second Punic War? What was the reaction of some of the women to news about Hannibal's victory? How did the other peoples of Italy react to the Roman losses?

Grammar

The Relative as Connective

In Latin the relative pronoun or adjective is often used to connect a sentence with a preceding sentence. In English a personal or demonstrative pronoun with or without a conjunction (*and, but* etc.) is more common.

WORKBOOK
Assign Ex. A to review the formation of relative and demonstrative pronouns.

Gallus immānis erat. Quae rēs, tamen Manlium nōn terruit.	*The Gaul was savage. This fact, however, did not frighten Manlius.*

Find at least one more example of this construction in the reading.

NOTĀ·BENE

This construction is used under the same conditions as the locative.

WORKBOOK
Assign Ex. B to practice accusative of *place to which* and review the locative.

Place to Which

Ordinarily *place to which* is expressed by the accusative with the preposition **ad** or **in.** The preposition is omitted before names of cities, towns, and a few other words, such as **domus.**

Pūblius Furiānusque Athēnās iērunt.	*Publius and Furianus went to Athens.*
Unō diē, Delphōs īre constituērunt.	*One day, they decided to go to Delphi.*

Find at least one example of this construction in the reading.

TRANSLATION

1. You all know that the Romans received a great loss the next year.
2. Not moved by the words of women and friends, Regulus returned to Carthage.
3. Although terrified by reports of the defeat, nevertheless Rome did not make peace.
4. Regulus, when sent unharmed to Rome, persuaded his country to make war upon the enemy.

The remains of a Roman villa at Carthage, near modern Tunis, date from the 3rd century A.D.

Vanni/Art Resource, NY

Vocabulary

SUGGESTION
Review the locative. If you wish, you may tell students at this point that this same phenomenon happens with ablative of *place from which.*

ANSWERS
1. Omnēs scītis Rōmānōs dētrīmentum magnum proximō annō accēpisse. 2. Verbīs fēminārum/mulierum amīcōrumque nōn mōtus, Rēgulus Carthāginem rediit. 3. Cum nūntiīs calamitātis terrērētur, tamen Rōma pācem nōn fēcit. 4. Rēgulus, incolumis Rōmam missus, patriae suae persuāsit ut hostibus bellum īnferret.

Nouns

calamitās, -tātis, *f. disaster* (calamitous, calamity)
complexus, -ūs, *m. embrace* (complex, complexion)
dētrīmentum, -ī, *n. loss* (detriment, detrimental)
fēmina, -ae, *f. woman* (female, feminine)
lacus, -ūs, *m. lake* (lacustrine)

Adjectives

complūrēs, -a or **-ia,** *several* (falsify, falsity)
falsus, -a, -um, *false*
incolumis, -e, *unharmed*

Verbs

exspīrō, 1, *breathe out, expire* (expiration)
pellō, -ere, pepulī, pulsus, *drive, defeat* (pulse, pulsion)
prōficiō, -ere, -fēcī, -fectus, *accomplish* (proficiency, proficient)
vāstō, 1, *destroy, ruin* (devastate, devastation)

Adverb

prope, *almost*

Conjunction

nisi, *unless, except*

Word Studies

The suffix **–idus** (English *–id*) is added chiefly to verb stems to form adjectives: **timidus,** *timid.* When the noun suffix **–tās** (English *–ty*) is added, **–idus** becomes **–idi–: timiditās,** *timidity.*

The suffix **–īnus** (English *–ine*) is added to noun and adjective stems to form adjectives: **equīnus,** *equine.* When the suffix **–tās** is added, **–īnus** becomes **–īni–: vīcīnitās,** *vicinity.*

Define the following and give the Latin words from which they are derived: *fluid, placid, rapid, valid, vivid, feminine, marine, submarine.* Give additional examples of these suffixes in English words.

LESSON OBJECTIVES
To review the imperative and learn the passive imperative; To learn the use of **quisque** and **quisquam**; To review result clauses

LESSON XXXVI

The Romans Give Liberty to the Greeks

[1] 200–197 B.C.
[2] *as*
[3] *no one could really believe that he had heard correctly*
[4] *one said to another*
[5] *if you agree* (conditional)
[6] Cf. "United we stand, divided we fall."
[7] *flowed for all*

STUDY TOPICS
Livy XXXIII, 31-33; XXXIV, 48-52

Post Pūnicum bellum secūtum est Macedonicum,[1] quod cum Philippō rēge Rōmānī gessērunt ut Graecās cīvitātēs līberārent. T. Quīnctius Flāminīnus contrā Philippum missus rem bene gessit. Corinthum prōcessit ut ibi in lūdīs Isthmiīs[1] condiciōnēs pācis dēferret. Omnēs ad spectāculum cōnsēderant et praecō, ut[2] mōs erat, in medium prōcessit et, tubā silentiō factō, prōnūntiat senātum Rōmānum et Quīnctium imperātōrem iubēre omnēs gentēs Graeciae līberās esse. Audītā vōce praecōnis, vix satis crēdere potest sē quisque bene audīvisse.[3] Tum tantus clāmor est ortus ut facile appārēret nihil omnium bonōrum multitūdinī grātius quam lībertātem esse. Aliī aliīs dīcēbant[4] esse gentem quae suā pecūniā, suō labōre ac perīculō bella gereret[2] prō lībertāte aliōrum.

Duōbus annīs posteā Quīnctius in Italiam profectūrus Graecōs hōc modō monet: "Concordiae cōnsulite. Contrā vōs cōnsentientēs[5] nec rēx quisquam nec tyrannus satis valēbit.[6] Aliēnīs armīs redditam lībertātem vestrā cūrā servāte, ut populus Rōmānus dignīs datam esse lībertātem sciat." Hās velut parentis vōcēs cum audīrent, omnibus mānāvērunt[7] gaudiō lacrimae, ita ut Quīnctium ipsum quoque cōnfunderent dīcentem.

ADDITIONAL QUESTIONS
Against whom did the Romans fight in the Macedonian War? How did the Greeks find out they were free? What was the first reaction of the Greeks?

QUESTIONS

1. Why did Flamininus go to Corinth?
2. What advice did he give the Greeks?
3. How did Flamininus' words affect the Greeks?
4. Why did the Romans start the war against Philip?

[1] *Isthmian;* similar to the Olympic Games. They got their name from being held on the Isthmus of Corinth.
[2] Subordinate clauses in indirect discourse are in the subjunctive.

Erich Lessing/Art Resource, NY

The Temple of Apollo at Corinth still shows its majestic Doric columns.

Grammar

The Imperative

Remember that the present active imperative is formed from the present stem. The plural is formed by adding **–te**.

portā	**portāte**	carry!
docē	**docēte**	teach!
pōne	**pōnite**	place!
capi	**capite**	take!
mūnī	**mūnīte**	build!

There is also a passive imperative, which is formed just like the active imperative, but with passive endings.

portāre	**portāminī**	be carried!
docēre	**docēminī**	be taught!
pōnere	**pōniminī**	be placed!
capere	**capiminī**	be taken!
mūnīre	**mūnīminī**	be built!

SUGGESTION
Ask students what other form of the verb resembles the singular passive imperative.

WORKBOOK
Assign Ex. A to practice the imperative.

SUGGESTION
Do a quick review of the forms of all the indefinites.

WORKBOOK
Assign Ex. B to practice **quisque, quisquam,** and **aliquis**.

Quisque and *Quisquam*

Quisque, *each,* as a pronoun is declined like **quis;** as an adjective, more like **quī. Quisquam** (singular only) is like **quis,** except that **quicquam** is usually used for **quidquam. Quisque** is usually placed after a pronoun or a superlative adjective:

optimus quisque	*all the best men*

Quisquam, *anyone,* is stronger than **aliquis** and is usually found in sentences containing or implying a negative. It is often best translated *any at all:*

Estne quisquam fortior?	*Is anyone braver?*

ORAL PRACTICE

Tell the form of **quōque, quendam, aliquod, quicquam, quaeque, quid, cuiquam, quaedam, quidque, alicuius.**

Result Clauses

Review result clauses in Lesson XIV. Find two examples in the reading.

ANSWERS
1. "Dīc nōbīs quid dīxerit." quisque rogāvit. 2. Omnēs ita superātī sunt ut vix loquī possent. 3. "Cōnsentīte inter vōs nec rēx ūllus erit tam fortis ut vōs oppugnet." 4. Nūntius locūtus erat, neque quisquam eius verbīs crēdere poterat.

TRANSLATION

1. "Tell us what he said," each one asked.
2. All were so overcome that they could hardly speak.
3. "Agree among yourselves and no king will be so brave as to attack you."
4. The messenger had spoken, and not a single one could believe his words.

Vocabulary

Nouns

lacrima, -ae, *f. tear* (lacrimation, lacrimator)
praecō, praecōnis, *m. announcer*
tuba, -ae, *f. trumpet*

Pronouns

quisquam, quicquam, *anyone, anything, any*
quisque, quidque, *each*

Adjectives

equester, -tris, -tre, *(of) cavalry*
necessārius, -a, -um, *necessary*
prīstinus, -a, -um, *former* (pristine)

Verbs

adigō, -ere, adēgī, adāctus, *throw (to)*
confundō, -ere, fūdī, -fūsus, *confuse* (confound)
cōnsīdō, -ere, -sēdī, -sessūrus, *sit down*
subsequor, subsequī, subsecūtus, *follow (closely)* (subsequent)

Adverb

vix, *scarcely*

Word Studies

We have already seen that a few simple principles will enable you to recognize the Latin origin of many Spanish words. On the basis of these principles, explain Spanish *campo, útil, vivo; ocurrir; desierto, puente; vida, virtud; mujer.*

Since *d* is sometimes lost between vowels, what must be the Latin words from which Spanish *caer* and *juicio* are derived?

Since an *e* is added before *sc, sp,* and *st* at the beginning of a word, what must be the Latin words from which the following Spanish words are derived: *esperar, especie, escribir, estar, estudio?*

Since Latin *ex* sometimes becomes *ej* in Spanish, what is the Latin for *ejemplo, ejército?*

QUEM NUMERUM VOCĀS?

LESSON OBJECTIVE
To learn the ablative of separation

LESSON XXXVII
Civil War

M Tulliō Cicerōne ōrātōre et C. Antōnio cōnsulibus,[1] L. Sergius Catilīna, vir nōbilissimī generis, ad dēlendam patriam coniūrāvit cum quibusdam clārīs quidem, sed audācibus virīs. Ā Cicerōne urbe expulsus est. Sociī eius comprehēnsī occīsī sunt. Catilīna ipse victus proeliō est et interfectus.

STUDY TOPIC
Rome, Section IV

Sed Cicerō Rōmānōs timōre bellī cīvīlis nōn līberāvit. C. Iūlius Caesar, quī Catilīnam iūvisse ā quibusdam dīcitur, cōnsul est factus. Dēcrēta est eī Gallia et Īllyricum cum legiōnibus decem. Annīs novem in potestātem populī Rōmānī ferē omnem Galliam redēgit.[2] Britannīs mox bellum intulit, quibus ante eum nē nōmen quidem Rōmānōrum cognitum erat. Eōs victōs, obsidibus acceptīs, stīpendium pendere coēgit. Germānōs trāns Rhēnum aggressus proeliīs vīcit.

Caesar rediēns ex Galliā victor coepit poscere alterum cōnsulātum. Senātū negante, contrā patriam cum exercitū prōcessit.

Deinde in Graeciam trānsiit et contrā Pompeium pugnāvit. Prīmō proeliō victus est, ēvāsit tamen, quod, nocte intercēdente, Pompeius sequī nōluit. Dīxit Caesar Pompeium nōn scīre[1] vincere et illō diē tantum[2] sē potuisse superārī.[3]

[1] *know how*
[2] *only*
[3] *could have been defeated*

Deinde in Thessaliā ad Pharsālum pugnāvērunt. Numquam ante maiōrēs Rōmānae cōpiae in ūnum locum convēnerant neque meliōrēs ducēs habuerant. Tandem Pompeius victus est et Alexandrīam petīvit ut ā rēge Aegyptī auxilia acciperet. Sed rēx occīdit Pompeium et caput eius ad Caesarem mīsit. Caesar lacrimās fūdisse dīcitur, tantī virī vidēns caput et generī[3] quondam suī. Caesar rēgnum Aegyptī Cleopātrae dedit.

---

[1] Ablative absolute expressing time: *in the consulship of* (63 B.C.). The Romans used the names of the consuls to date the year.
[2] 58–50 B.C.
[3] *his former son-in-law* (genitive of **gener**); Pompey had married Caesar's daughter Julia in 60 B.C. After her death in 54 B.C. Caesar and Pompey drifted apart.

THE GRANGER COLLECTION, New York

Marcus Tullius Cicero (106-43 B.C.) was Rome's greatest orator. He was also a political leader and held all the positions in the ***cursus honorum****. He is especially well known for the four orations he delivered against Catiline that exposed a great conspiracy. During the Middle Ages and the Renaissance, Cicero was one of the most popular Roman figures.*

SUGGESTION
Tell students about the Roman system for telling dates with the **Kalends**, the **Nones**, and the **Ides**.

Caesar, bellīs cīvīlibus in tōtō orbe terrārum perfectīs, Rōmam rediit. Agere coepit contrā cōnsuētūdinem Rōmānae lībertātis. Cum honōrēs[4] ex[5] suā voluntāte tribueret quī ā populō anteā dēferēbantur aliaque rēgia[6] faceret, coniūrātum est in eum ā LX vel amplius senātōribus equitibusque Rōmānīs, quōrum prīncipēs fuērunt C. Cassius et duo Brūtī. Itaque Caesar, cum Īdibus Mārtiīs[7] in senātum vēnisset, XXIII vulneribus acceptīs, mortuus est.

[4] *offices*
[5] *in accordance with*
[6] *regal (kinglike) things*
[7] *the Ides of March* (March 15)

QUESTIONS

1. How did Catiline die?
2. Where was Pompey killed?
3. How many years did Caesar fight in Gaul?
4. Why was there a conspiracy against Caesar?
5. Why did Caesar fight against his own country?

ADDITIONAL QUESTIONS
What did Catiline try to do? Who stopped him? How did the Britons hear about Caesar? What did Caesar force the Britons to do? Where else did Caesar fight? How did Caesar feel about the death of Pompey?

Grammar

Ablative of Separation

WORKBOOK
Assign Ex. A to practice the ablative of separation.

Separation is usually expressed by the ablative with **ab**, **dē**, or **ex**. But with some verbs, such as **excēdō** and **līberō**, the preposition is regularly omitted. **Prohibeō** can be used with or without a preposition; **dēfendō** takes the preposition.

NOTĀ·BENE

With līberō, *if the separation is from a person, use the preposition* ā/ab.

Liberī omnī timōre līberātī sunt.	*The children were freed from all fear.*
Prohibēte hostēs arce.	*Keep the enemy from the citadel.*
Manlius nōs Gallō dēfensit.	*Manlius defended us from the Gaul.*
Graecōs ā hostibus līberāvit.	*He freed the Greeks from the enemy.*

Try to find at least two examples of the ablative of separation in the reading.

TRANSLATION

1. Cicero drove Catiline from Rome after seizing his accomplices.
2. You all read that civil war occurred between Caesar and Pompey.
3. Since Caesar had not driven his personal enemies from the city, sixty or more of them later killed him.
4. Having conquered Gaul, Caesar also attacked the Britons, who were much braver than the Gauls.

ANSWERS
1. Cicerō Catilīnam, sociīs eius comprehēnsīs, Rōmā expulit. 2. Vōs omnēs lēgistis bellum cīvīle inter Caesarem et Pompeium intercessisse. 3. Cum inimīcōs suōs Caesar ex urbe nōn expulisset, sexāgintā vel amplius ex hīs (eōrum) posteā eum occīdērunt. 4. Caesar, Galliā victā, etiam Britannōs aggressus est, qui multō fortiōrēs quam Gallī erant.

Vocabulary

Nouns

legiō, -ōnis, *f. legion*	(legionary)
obses, obsidis,[4] *m. hostage*	
ōrātor, -ōris, *m. speaker, orator*	
timor, -ōris, *m. fear*	(timorous)
voluntās, -tātis, *f. wish*	(voluntary)

[4] A hostage is a person of a conquered territory who is held by the conquering nation as a pledge that no unfriendly act will be committed.

Adjectives

adversus, -a, -um, *facing, opposite* (adverse, adversity)
audāx, audācis (gen.), *bold* (audacious, audacity)

Verbs

aggredior, aggredī, aggressus, *attack* (aggression, aggressor)
dēleō, -ēre, ēvī, -ētus, *destroy* (delete, deletion)
fundō, -ere, fūdī, fūsus, *pour, shed* (confound, diffuse)
poscō, -ere, poposcī, —, *demand, call for*

Adverbs

amplius, *more*
anteā, *before*
ferē, *almost, about, generally*

THE GRANGER COLLECTION, New York

Cleopatra, born in 69 B.C., was the seventh and most famous queen of Egypt by that name. She had a forceful personality and was politically skilled. She was well-known for her romantic liaisons with several prominent Romans. She went to Rome with Julius Caesar and stayed there until he was assassinated, after which she returned to Egypt.

Words Easily Confused

Look up and distinguish carefully the following sets of words that are somewhat similar in pronunciation or spelling:

alius, alter, altus	**eques, equus**	**nē, –ne**
audeō, audiō	**gēns, genus**	**post, posteā, postquam**
cadō, caedō, cēdō	**liber, līber, līberī**	**quīdam, quidem**
cīvis, cīvitās	**mora, mors, mōs**	**reddō, redeō**
dīcō, dūcō	**morior, moror**	**Rōma, Rōmānus**

WORKBOOK
Assign Ex. B to practice words that are easily confused.

Word Studies

In English, after the prefix *ex–*, a root word beginning with *s* drops the *s*: **ex–sequor,** *ex–ecute;* **ex–sistō,** *ex–ist;* **ex–spectō,** *ex–pect.*

Explain *aggression, audacity, confusion, delete, indelible, infusion, legionary, projectile, timorous, voluntary.*

LESSON OBJECTIVE
To review the genitive and ablative of description and the ablative of degree of difference

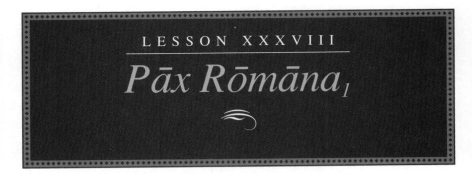

LESSON XXXVIII
Pāx Rōmāna[1]

STUDY TOPIC
Rome, Section V

Octāviānus, nepōs Caesaris,[2] ā Caesare adoptātus, posteā Augustus est dictus. Iuvenis fōrmā praestantī et vultū tranquillō erat. Post mortem Caesaris Octāviānō, adulēscentī XX annōrum, cōnsulātus datur. Nōn multō post cum M. Antōniō contrā Brūtum et Cassium, quī Caesarem interfēcerant, profectus est. Ad Philippōs, Macedoniae urbem, Brūtus et Cassius victī et interfectī sunt.

Antōnius, repudiātā[1] sorōre Caesaris Augustī, Cleopātram, rēgīnam Aegyptī, dūxit[2] uxōrem. Tum magnum bellum cīvīle commōvit, cōgente uxōre Cleopātrā, quae cupīvit in urbe[3] quoque rēgnāre. Victus est ab Augustō nāvālī pugnā clārā apud Actium, quī locus in Ēpīrō est, ex quā fūgit in Aegyptum et, dēspērātīs suīs rēbus, ipse sē occīdit. Cleopātra sibi aspidem admīsit[4] et venēnō eius exstīncta est. Aegyptus ab Augustō imperiō Rōmānō adiecta est.

Pāce Rōmānā cōnstitūtā, Augustus Rōmānōs timōre bellī līberāvit. Ex eō annō rem pūblicam per XLIIII annōs sōlus obtinuit. In campō Mārtiō sepultus est,[5] vir quī meritīs quidem deō similis est putātus. Neque enim quisquam aut in bellīs fēlīcior fuit aut in pāce moderātior. Scythae et Indī, quibus anteā Rōmānōrum nē nōmen quidem cognitum erat, mūnera et lēgātōs ad eum mīsērunt.

Pūblica opera plūrima Rōmae exstrūxit et cēterōs prīncipēs virōs saepe hortātus est ut monumentīs vel novīs vel refectīs urbem adōrnārent. Spatium urbis regiōnēs XIV dīvīsit. Contrā incendia vigiliās īnstituit. Viās et templa refēcit. Annum[3] ā Iūliō Caesare in ōrdinem redāctum, sed posteā neglēctum, rūrsus ad prīstinam ratiōnem redēgit. Sextīlem mēnsem ē suō nōmine Augustum nōmināvit.

[1] *divorced*
[2] *married* (with **uxōrem**)
[3] i.e., Rome
[4] *let an asp* (a poisonous snake) *bite her*
[5] *was buried*

QUESTIONS

1. Where was Cassius killed?
2. Where was Augustus buried?
3. Where and how was Antony killed?

ADDITIONAL QUESTIONS
What was the relationship between Caesar and Augustus? Who accompanied Augustus in his quest for Brutus and Cassius? Who was Cleopatra? Who won the battle of Actium? How did Cleopatra die? What are some of the things that Augustus did for Rome?

---

[1] Under Augustus (31 B.C.–14 A.D.) a long era of peace began.
[2] Actually Octavian was the grandson of Caesar's sister.
[3] i.e., the calendar, which was very inexact before Caesar's time

Scala/Art Resource, NY

The emperor Augustus established his government in 27 B.C., rebuilt Rome, reformed the Senate, made the taxation system more fair, revived the census, and patronized the arts. He ruled the Roman Empire at its height and began the 200 years of peace that came to be called the Pax Romana. He died in A.D. 14 and was buried in this tomb in Rome.

Grammar

Description

Both the genitive and the ablative can be used to describe. Both cases, if modified by an adjective, can be used to describe people or things. Most often, the genitive is used with permanent qualities. The ablative is most often used with temporary qualities.

Māgister magnae sapientiae est.	*He is a teacher of great wisdom.*
Gentēs inimīcō animō Rōmānīs erant.	*They were tribes of an unfriendly spirit toward the Romans.*

SUGGESTION
You might take this opportunity to review several constructions with the ablative, having students find them in the reading.

NOTĀ · BENE

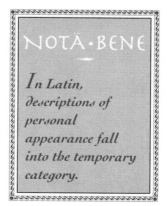

In Latin, descriptions of personal appearance fall into the temporary category.

WORKBOOK
Assign Ex. A and B to practice various constructions taken from the reading.

ANSWERS
1. Cleopātra Antōnium hortāta est ut suās rēs neglegeret. 2. Antōnius fuit vir summā virtūte/summae virtūtis; Augustus fuit adulēscēns XX annōrum. 3. Augustus monumenta templaque maximae magnitūdinis in omnibus partibus imperī Rōmānī exstrūxit. 4. Victōriā dēsperātā, Antonius sē occīdit/interfēcit et nōn multō post cēterī hostēs victī sunt.

Ablative of Degree of Difference

Review the ablative of degree of difference in Lesson XV. Find one example of each of these three constructions in the reading.

TRANSLATION

1. Cleopatra urged Antony to neglect his own interests ("things").
2. Antony was a man of the greatest courage; Augustus was a youth of twenty years.
3. Augustus erected monuments and temples of the greatest size in all parts of the Roman Empire.
4. Despairing of victory, Antony killed himself, and not much later all other enemies were defeated.

Vocabulary

Nouns

incendium, -dī, *n. fire, burning*	(incendiary)
iuvenis, -is, *m. young man*	(juvenile, juvenalia)
nepōs, nepōtis, *m. grandson*	(nepostism)
vigilia, -ae, *f. watchman, watch*	
vultus, -ūs, *m. expression, features*	

Verbs

administrō, 1, *manage, perform*	(administer, administration)
admittō, -ere, admīsī, admissus, *send to, let in, admit*	(admittance)
dēspērō, 1, *despair (of)*	(desperate, desperation)
dīmicō, 1, *fight*	
extruō, -ere, extrūxī, extrūctus, *build*	
neglegō, -ere, -lēxī, -lectus, *neglect*	(negligent)

Adverbs

magis, *more*
rūrsus, *again*

Etiam and *Quoque*; *Quidem*

Distinguish carefully the following words: **etiam** and **quoque** both mean *also,* but **etiam** generally precedes the word it emphasizes, **quoque** always follows. **Quidem** means *certainly, to be sure,* and follows the word it emphasizes. **Nē... quidem** means *not even,* and the emphatic word is placed between **nē** and **quidem. Quidem** alone never means *even,* nor is **nē... etiam** ever used for *not even.*

Word Studies

The suffix **–ārium** (English *–arium, –ary*) is added chiefly to noun stems. The suffix **–ōrium** (English *–orium, –ory, –or*) is added chiefly to participial stems and so is usually preceded by **–t–**. Both suffixes mean a *place where:* granary, a *place where grain* **(grānum)** is kept. The plurals of *–ary* and *–ory* are *–aries* and *–ories.*

Define the following words according to their derivation and give the Latin words from which they come: *aquarium, itinerary, library, laboratory, mirror* **(mīror),** *auditorium, factory, armory.*

NOTĀ · BENE

Other Latin suffixes besides **–ārium** *and* **–ōrium** *sometimes take on the English forms mentioned above; e.g.,* primary *from* **prīmārius,** honor *from* **honor,** cursory *from* **cursōrius.**

SUGGESTION
Point out that in English, *even* generally precedes (like **etiam**) and *too* follows (like **quoque**).

Syria came under Roman domination in the 2nd century B.C. with their victory over Antiochus III at Thermopylae in 190 B.C. as he tried to invade Greece. Evidence of the Roman influence can be seen in these ruins at Palmyra, Syria. Note the 13th century Crusader castle in the background.

N. Thiabaut/Photo Researchers

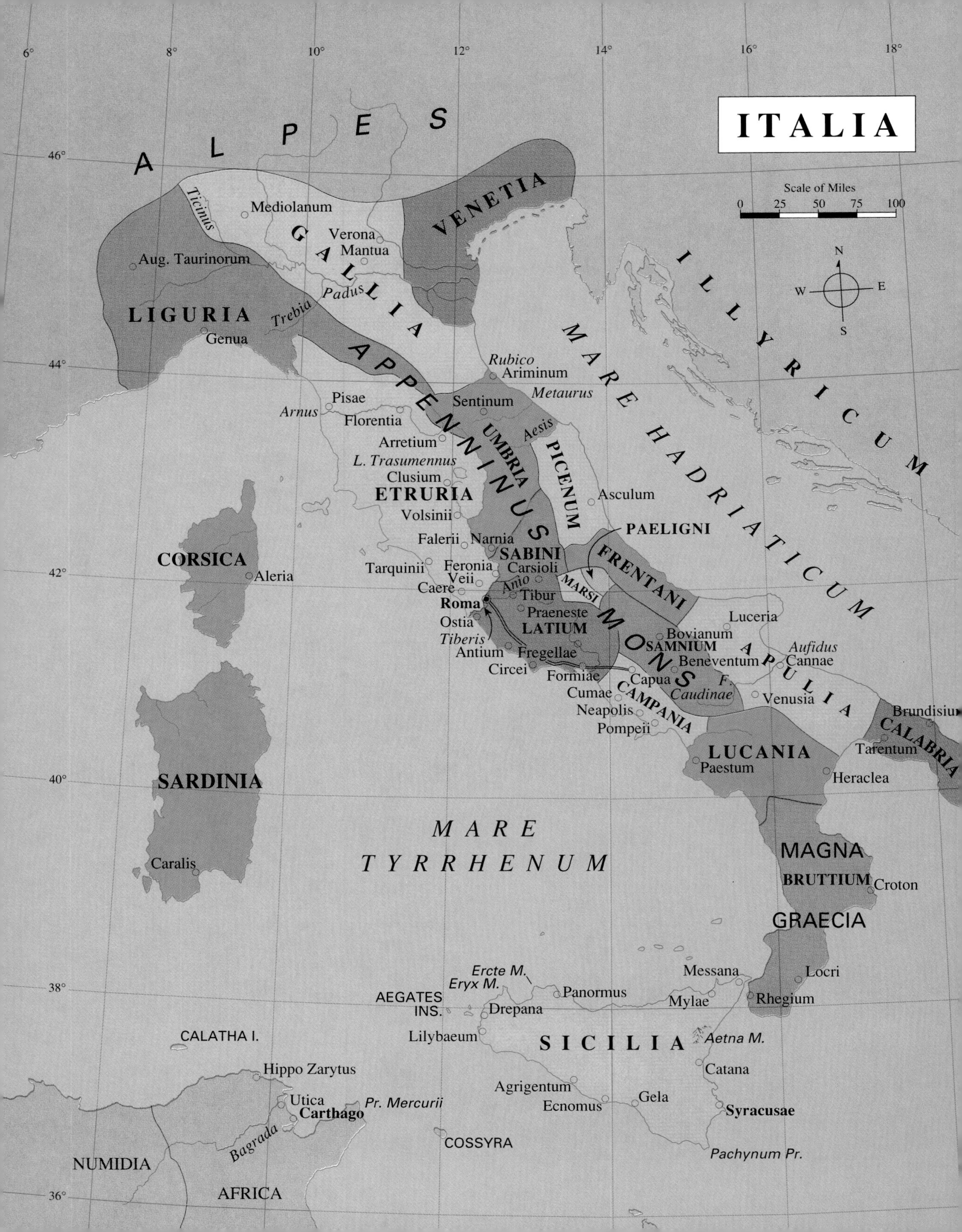
ITALIA
Scale of Miles
0 25 50 75 100
N S E W
ALPES
VENETIA
GALLIA
LIGURIA
APPENNINUS MONS
ILLYRICUM
MARE HADRIATICUM
UMBRIA
PICENUM
ETRURIA
SABINI
PAELIGNI
FRENTANI
MARSI
LATIUM
SAMNIUM
APULIA
CAMPANIA
LUCANIA
CALABRIA
MAGNA GRAECIA
BRUTTIUM
CORSICA
SARDINIA
MARE TYRRHENUM
SICILIA
AEGATES INS.
CALATHA I.
COSSYRA
NUMIDIA
AFRICA
Mediolanum
Verona
Mantua
Aug. Taurinorum
Ticinus
Padus
Trebia
Genua
Rubico
Ariminum
Metaurus
Pisae
Arnus
Florentia
Sentinum
Aesis
Arretium
L. Trasumennus
Clusium
Asculum
Volsinii
Falerii
Narnia
Tarquinii
Feronia
Carsioli
Veii
Caere
Anio
Tibur
Roma
Praeneste
Ostia
Tiberis
Antium
Fregellae
Circei
Formiae
Capua
Cumae
Neapolis
Pompeii
Luceria
Bovianum
Aufidus
Cannae
Beneventum
F. Caudinae
Venusia
Brundisium
Tarentum
Paestum
Heraclea
Aleria
Caralis
Croton
Locri
Messana
Rhegium
Ercte M.
Eryx M.
Panormus
Drepana
Mylae
Lilybaeum
Aetna M.
Catana
Agrigentum
Ecnomus
Gela
Syracusae
Pachynum Pr.
Hippo Zarytus
Utica
Carthago
Pr. Mercurii
Bagrada
6° 8° 10° 12° 14° 16° 18°
46° 44° 42° 40° 38° 36°

LESSON XXXIX

Roman Scandals

LESSON OBJECTIVE
To learn relative purpose clauses

Dē Nerōne[1] multa īnfāmia nārrābantur. Nerō erat prīnceps inūsitātae lūxuriae, adeō ut unguentīs lavāret et rētibus[1] aureīs piscārētur. Nūllam vestem bis gessit. Semper mīlle carrīs vel amplius fēcit iter. Soleae mūlārum eius ex argentō factae sunt. Domum ā Palātiō ad Ēsquiliās exstrūxit, quam auream nōmināvit. In eius vēstibulō locāta est imāgō Nerōnis CXX pedēs alta. Erant lacūs, aedificia, agrī, silvae, cum multitūdine omnis generis animālium. In cēterīs partibus omnia aurō tēcta, ōrnāta gemmīs erant. Cum hanc domum dēdicāret, dīxit: "Tandem quasi homō habitāre coepī."

Etiam saltāvit et cantāvit in scaenā. In Graeciam profectus est ut ibi cantāret. Cantante eō, excēdere theātrō nēminī licitum est. Multī, dēfessī audiendō laudandōque, clausīs oppidōrum portīs, aut fūrtim dēsiluērunt dē mūrō aut, morte simulātā, fūnere ēlātī sunt. In Italiam reversus studium nōn remīsit. Cōnservandae vōcis grātiā neque mīlitēs umquam appellāvit neque quicquam ēgit nisi prope stante phōnascō[2] quī monēret ut parceret sibi ac sūdārium[3] ad ōs applicāret.

Frātrem, uxōrem, sorōrem, mātrem interfēcit. Urbem Rōmam incendit[2] ut spectāculum simile incendiō Troiae antīquae cerneret. Magnam senātūs partem interfēcisse dīcitur.

Tandem ā senātū hostis iūdicātus est. Cum quaererētur ad poenam, fūgit et sē interfēcit. In eō omnis Augustī familia cōnsūmpta est.

[1] *nets*
[2] *singing teacher*
[3] *handkerchief*

STUDY TOPIC
Suetonius' *Life of Nero*

QUESTIONS

1. Who killed Nero?
2. Whom did Nero kill?
3. Where did Nero sing?
4. Where was Nero's statue?

ADDITIONAL QUESTIONS
What were some of the peculiar things Nero did? What were the shoes of his mules' shoes made of? How many wagons did he travel with? Where was his house? How did the audience feel about him?

[1] A.D. 54–68
[2] This was a false charge, as Nero was not in Rome when the fire started, but at Antium. It burned six days and seven nights continuously and then started again.

A. K. G., Berlin/SuperStock, Inc.

The emperor Nero was born in A.D. *37 and ruled Rome from 54-68. He was infamous in his excesses and executed everyone who disagreed with him. He had a passion for art, drama, and music. When several governors rose up against him and the Praetorian Guard deserted him, he committed suicide in 68. In this painting, Nero is giving the death sentence signal to a gladiator.*

SUGGESTION
Have students find an example of the relative purpose clause in the reading.

NOTE
You may want to point out that when the relative pronoun is used, the "purpose" is of the antecedent, not the whole clause.

WORKBOOK
Assign Ex. A to practice relative purpose clauses.

WORKBOOK
Assign Ex. B to review various pronouns.

Grammar

Relative Purpose Clauses

The relative pronoun may be used instead of **ut** to introduce a purpose clause in the subjunctive when there is an antecedent. The pronoun must of course agree with the antecedent in gender and number.

Lēgatōs mīsit quī pacem facerent.	*He sent envoys to make peace.*
Servōs admīsit quī līberōs servārent.	*He let the slaves in to guard the children.*

TRANSLATION

1. Nero built a house covered with gold in which to live.
2. He summoned slaves who were to erect beautiful buildings.
3. He is said to have burned Rome to furnish a spectacle for himself.
4. He led a life of great luxury and cruelty and spent his time in singing.

ANSWERS
1. Nerō domum aurō tectam fēcit/extrūxit in quā habitāret.
2. Servōs convocāvit quī aedificia pulchra exstruerent.
3. Rōmam incendisse dīcitur ut spectāculum sibi praebēret.
4. Vītam magnae lūxuriae crūdēlitātisque ēgit et tempus cantandō cōnsūmpsit.

Vocabulary

Nouns

argentum, -ī, *n. silver* (argent, argentous)
mūla, -ae, *f. mule*
pedes, peditis, *m. foot soldier; (pl.) infantry* (pedestrian)

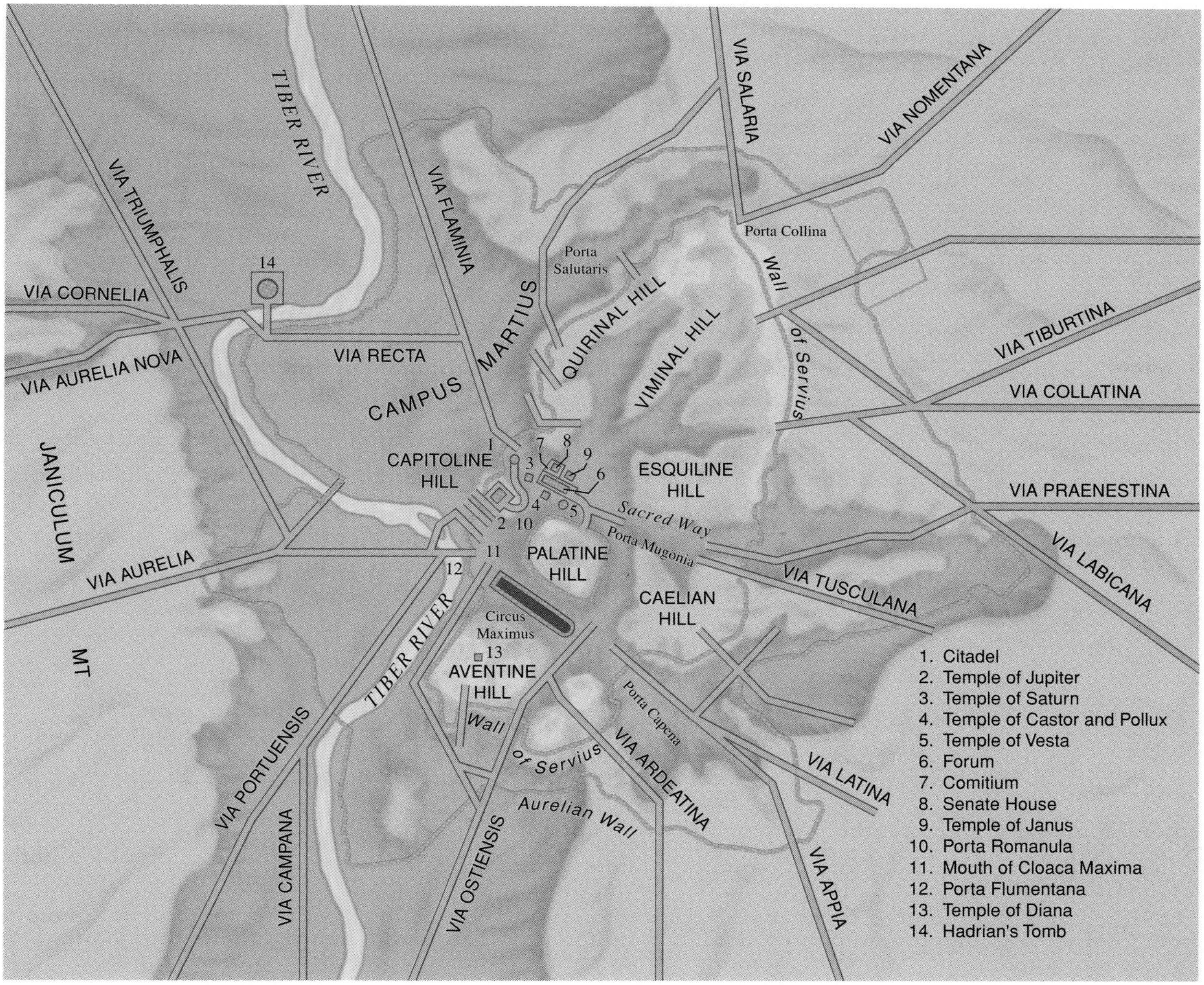

THE CITY OF ROME AS IT WAS IN ANCIENT DAYS

Adjectives

dīversus, -a, -um, *different*	(diverse, diversity)
īnfāmis, -e, *notorious*	(infamous, infamy)
inūsitātus, -a, um, *unusual, strange*	

Verbs

efferō, efferre, extulī, ēlātus, *carry out*	(elate, elation)
locō, 1, *place*	(locate, locative)
piscor, 1, *fish*	
simulō, 1, *pretend*	(dissimulate, simulate)
tegō, -ere, tēxī, tectus, *cover*	(tectum)

Adverbs

adeō, *so, so much*
bis, *twice*
furtim, *secretly*

Word Studies

The prefix **sē–** means *apart from* in Latin and English: **sēparō,** *separate.* Define according to the prefix: *secret* **(cernō),** *secede, seclude, secure* **(cūra).**

The Latin adverb **nōn,** meaning *not,* is freely used as a prefix in English: *nonsense, nonpartisan.* Give three other examples.

The preposition **ultrā** (related to **ultimus**) is used as a prefix in English with the meaning *extremely: ultrafashionable.* Give two other examples.

Explain *admission, collocation, desperation, detective, negligence, simulated (pearls).*

Our Heritage

THE ROMAN EMPIRE

The establishment of the extensive Roman Empire was a remarkable achievement at a time when communications were slow and difficult. A glance at the map (pp. 136–137) shows that, during the second century A.D., the Roman Empire encircled the Mediterranean and covered parts of three continents. Some of these territories have never recovered the prosperity they had in Roman times. Libya in northern Africa, for example, used to be a chief source of wheat for Italy, but today the United States is sending wheat to that country.

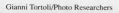

These Roman ruins in Volubilis, Morocco mark one of the most remote Roman bases of the empire. Can you identify the style of the columns?

Gianni Tortoli/Photo Researchers

The Empire brought not only prosperity but also peace and security to Roman citizens. Occasionally foreign wars were fought in remote parts of the Empire, but that meant nothing to most citizens. Sometimes there was a flare-up of civil war, but nothing damaged the stability of the Empire as a whole.

Political liberty was of course diminished during the Empire, compared with the Republic, but for most citizens this meant merely that the emperor and his officials ran things instead of the nobility who composed the senate during the Republic. The government was an efficient bureaucracy, and the emperors were, by and large, very capable administrators. Personal liberty was not affected, nor even the self-rule of the many communities scattered throughout the Empire. In the East the emperors did not force the people to give up their Greek language. In the West the people of their own accord gradually abandoned their native languages in favor of Latin.

The greatest freedom was allowed the individual. The Romans did not look upon themselves as a superior race, although there was of course some race prejudice especially towards the Greeks. There was also occasional persecution of the Christians, but that was not due to a desire to suppress individual religious beliefs but chiefly to the unwillingness of Christians to conform to practices that were considered part of one's duty to the state.

Something is to be said for the claim that the Roman Empire was based on the Stoic doctrine that all men are equal. This was felt by some to be true of slaves too. Roman slavery is not to be confused with some modern forms of slavery, for many Roman slaves won or bought their freedom. Citizenship was granted to men of the most diverse origins. A real world state, a kind of United Nations, was achieved, in which the chief right relinquished by its members was that of making war on their neighbors. The Empire was not an utterly despotic government that aimed at dominating the private lives of its subjects.

Pliny the Elder remarks on the mighty majesty of the Roman peace **(immēnsae Rōmānae pācis maiestāte)**, which made the people and places and products of the whole world known to everyone, and prays that this gift of the gods may last forever, for, he says, the Romans are a gift to humanity comparable only to the sun which shines over all the world. In A.D. 400 the poet Claudian praised Rome for being the only nation that ever welcomed to her arms those she conquered, treating the whole human race as sons, not slaves, giving citizenship to the vanquished and uniting the most remote regions by the bonds of loyalty.

Exaggeration? Without doubt. But the reference to Rome's treatment of human beings as sons, not slaves, is of particular significance in estimating the place of the Roman Empire among the empires of history.

Scala/Art Resource, NY

This 3rd century sarcophagus relief portrays an early Christian agape, or love feast, during which Christians shared food and other goods. Sometimes these functions got out of hand, and the Apostle Paul sent stern words to the Corinthians on this matter (1 Corinthians 11:17-22).

Unit IV

The Argonauts

UNIT OBJECTIVES
To read the story of *Jason and the Argonauts* with understanding and appreciation; To learn new vocabulary in the context of reading; To recognize Latin root words and their derivatives

Scala/Art Resource, NY

***Jason and the Argonauts** is a famous story from Greek mythology. It was one of many Greek tales admired and preserved by the Romans. In this painting by Lorenzo Costa (c. 1460-1535), we see Jason and his friends sailing toward Colchis in search of the Golden Fleece.*

The Story of the Golden Fleece

NOTE
This summary is intended to provide a context for students and to increase their comfort level with more difficult reading selections.

NOTE
The story of the Argonauts as given in Unit IV was published some years ago by Ritchie in *Fabulae Faciles.* It is written in simple Latin and is intended to give intensive drill on the subjunctive and other constructions common in Caesar.

One of the interesting tales told by the Greeks was about the Argonauts, those adventurers who sailed unknown seas in search of the Golden Fleece. A brief summary of the story is as follows:

Aeson (Ēson), king of Thessaly, had a brother Pelias (Pe´lias) and a son Jason. Pelias drove out Aeson, seized the throne, and planned to kill Jason. But Jason escaped with the help of friends, who then told Pelias that his nephew had died.

An oracle told Pelias to beware of a man wearing only one shoe. Some years later Pelias announced a great festival, and crowds came to the city. Among them was Jason, now grown to manhood. On the way he lost one shoe. When Pelias saw him, he recalled the oracle. To get rid of Jason, he gave him the seemingly impossible task of obtaining the Golden Fleece. Jason asked Argus to build him a ship and gathered about him a group of brave friends. After many adventures they finally reached Colchis on the Black Sea.

From this point on the story becomes chiefly that of the enchantress Medea (Medē´a), daughter of Aeetes (Ēē´tēs), king of Colchis. She fell in love with Jason, and with her help he got the Golden Fleece. Jason and the Argonauts returned to Thessaly, taking Medea with them.

Medea now determined to get rid of Pelias so that Jason might be king. Pretending to make Pelias young again, she killed him. But the people were so incensed that they drove out Medea and Jason, who then went to Corinth. Here they quarreled, and Medea killed her own children. She fled to Athens, and Jason was later killed in an accident.

The Argonauts and Latin Grammar

Remember that it is one thing to determine what a Latin sentence means, and another, often much more difficult, to put this meaning into good English. You should *understand* Latin as Latin, but *translate* it as English. Two hints for translation: if you can keep the natural English word order close to the Latin, so much the better; if you cannot, turn the whole Latin sentence upside down, if need be, to produce a smooth English version. Second, wherever you can, avoid the passive voice in English. The passive is very frequent in Latin, but its constant use in English makes the style flat, weak, and stilted.

SUGGESTION
In the lessons in this unit, have students identify every subjunctive, giving its form and construction. Also have students identify all uses of the gerund, gerundive, and the infinitive.

NOTE
Remind students that in their regular writing assignments in any class or subject, it is better style to use the active rather than the passive voice.

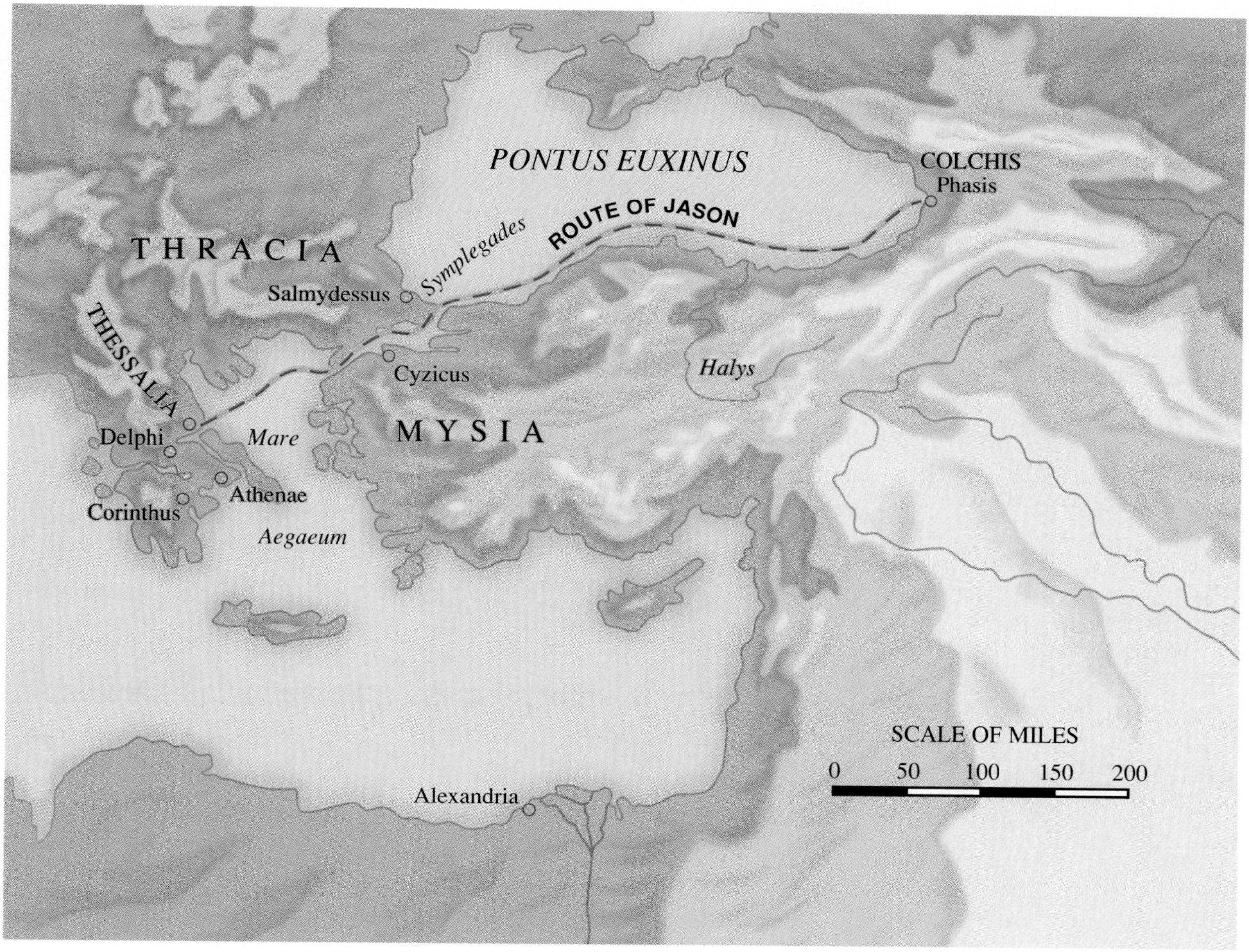

MAP OF THE VOYAGE OF THE ARGONAUTS

LESSON XL

The Wicked Uncle

SUGGESTION
Put the full declension of these proper names on the board for reference: **Iāsōn, Iāsonis; Aesōn, Aesonis; Peliās, Peliae**.

[1] *planned* (with **in animō**)
[2] *fearing*
[3] *that*
[4] *for what reason*
[5] *centaur*
[6] *one*

SUGGESTION
After students finish translating each paragraph line by line, have one student summarize it in good English.

NOTE
Remind students that verbs of fearing take a **nē** for the positive.

NOTE
Explain to students that a *centaur* is a monster that is half man, half horse.

Erant ōlim in Thessaliā duo frātrēs, quōrum alter Aesōn, alter Peliās appellābātur. Aesōn prīmō rēgnum obtinuerat; at post paucōs annōs Peliās rēgnī cupiditāte adductus nōn modo frātrem suum expulit, sed etiam in animō habēbat[1] Iāsonem, Aesonis fīlium, interficere. Quīdam tamen amīcī Aesonis puerum ē tantō perīculō ēripere cōnstituērunt. Noctū igitur Iāsonem ex urbe abstulērunt, et cum posterō diē ad rēgem rediissent, eī renūntiāvērunt puerum mortuum esse. Peliās[1] cum hoc audīvisset, speciem dolōris praebuit et quae causa esset mortis quaesīvit. Illī autem cum bene intellegerent dolōrem eius falsum esse, fābulam dē morte puerī fīnxērunt.

Post breve tempus Peliās, veritus[2] nē[3] rēgnum suum āmitteret, amīcum quendam Delphōs mīsit, quī ōrāculum cōnsuleret. Ille igitur quam celerrimē Delphōs prōcessit et quam ob causam vēnisset dēmōnstrāvit. Ōrāculum monuit Peliam ut, sī quis venīret[4] calceum ūnum gerēns, eum cavēret. Post paucōs annōs accidit ut Peliās magnum sacrificium factūrus esset. Diē cōnstitūtō magnus numerus hominum undique convēnit; inter aliōs vēnit etiam Iāsōn, quī ā pueritiā apud centaurum quendam habitāverat. Dum tamen iter facit,[5] calceum alterum[6] in trānseundō flūmine āmīsit.

Vocabulary

Nouns

calceus, -ī, *m. shoe*
cupiditās, -tātis, *f. desire* (cupidity)
pueritia, -ae, *f. childhood, boyhood*

[1] Subject of **audīvisset** but placed outside the **cum** clause, because it is also the subject of the following verbs. This is common in Latin.

Chiron, the wise and just centaur, on a black-figured Greek vase now in the British Museum. The half-man, half-horse Chiron was the teacher of many Greek heroes, including Jason.

On the other side of the same vase depicting Chiron, we see Achilles' father, King Peleus, handing over his small son for instruction. Chiron's dog greets the visitors.

Adjective

brevis, -e, *short* (abbreviation, brief)

Verbs

caveō, -ēre, cāvī, cautūrus, *beware, take precautions against* (caution, cautious)

morior, morī, mortuus, *die* (mortuary)

renūntiō, 1, *report* (renounce)

Adverbs

noctū, *by night* (nocturne, nocturnal)

undique, *from all sides*

WORKBOOK
Assign Ex. A, B, C, D to review vocabulary used in this lesson.

Word Studies

Review: **etsī, posterus, praebeō, quaerō, quīdam, redeō, tantus, vereor.**

Explain *abbreviate, cupidity, fratricide, inquisition, mortuary, nocturne, posterity, reverend.*

NOTE
Verify that students can supply all the pertinent information for the review vocabulary.

LESSON XLI

The Golden Fleece and the Building of the Argo

Iāsōn igitur, ūnō pede nūdō, in rēgiam pervēnit; quem[1] cum Peliās vīdisset, subitō timōre affectus est; intellēxit enim hunc esse hominem quem ōrāculum dēmōnstrāvisset. Hoc igitur iniit cōnsilium. Rēx erat quīdam nōmine Aeētēs, quī rēgnum Cholchidis illō tempore obtinēbat. Huic commissum erat vellus aureum quod Phrixus ōlim ibi relīquerat. Cōnstituit igitur Peliās Iāsonī negōtium dare, ut hoc vellus obtinēret;[2] cum enim rēs esset magnī perīculī eum in itinere peritūrum esse spērābat. Iāsonem igitur ad sē arcessīvit et quid fierī vellet docuit. Iāsōn autem, etsī intellegēbat rem esse difficillimam, negōtium libenter suscēpit.

Cum Colchis multōrum diērum iter[3] ab eō locō abesset, nōluit Iāsōn sōlus proficīscī. Dīmīsit igitur nūntiōs in omnēs partēs, quī causam itineris docērent et diem certum conveniendī dīcerent. Intereā negōtium dedit Argō[4] ut nāvem aedificāret. In hīs rēbus circiter decem diēs cōnsūmptī sunt; Argus enim tantam dīligentiam praebēbat ut nē noctū quidem labōrem intermitteret. Ad multitūdinem hominum trānsportandam nāvis paulō erat lātior quam quibus[5] ūtī cōnsuēvimus.

NOTE
Have students identify **ūnō pede nūdō** as an ablative absolute.

NOTE
Point out that **dēmōnstrāvisset** is a subjunctive used in a subordinate clause in indirect statement.

SUGGESTION
Put the full declension of these new proper names on the board for reference: **Aeētēs, Aeētae; Colchis, Colchidis**.

SUGGESTION
Either tell students the following story or assign a student to research it. Phrixus and his sister Helle fled from a cruel stepmother on the back of a golden winged ram sent by Jupiter. On the way, Helle fell into the sea, which was then called the Hellespont. Phrixus arrived in Colchis, a country on the Black Sea, and sacrificed the ram to Jupiter. He then gave the fleece to Aeētēs, king of Colchis.

---

1 **quem** is used for **eum** to connect closely with the preceding sentence; translate as if **cum eum**

2 The clause is in apposition with **negōtium**.

3 accusative of extent

4 from **Argus**, a man, not from **Argō**

5 supply **eae**: *those which.*

Ronald Sheridan/Ancient Art & Architecture Collection

This Roman terra-cotta relief shows Athena comfortably seated, helping rig the sails of the Argo. Although the story of the Argonauts is filled with myth and miracle, it probably records some dim memory of the Greeks' first exploration of the Black Sea.

Vocabulary

Noun

vellus, -eris, *n. fleece, wool* (vellum)

Verbs

arcessō, -ere, -īvī, -ītus,
summon
cōnsuēscō, -ere, -suēvī, suētus,
become accustomed; (in perf.) be accustomed
pereō, -īre, -iī (–īvī), -itūrus, (perishable)
perish, pass away, be lost
ūtor, ūtī, ūsus, *use* (+ abl.) (usage, useful)

WORKBOOK
Assign Ex. A, B to review vocabulary used in this lesson.

WORKBOOK
Assign Ex. C to practice various constructions taken from the reading.

Adverbs

intereā, *meanwhile*
libenter, *willingly, gladly*
paulō, *a little*

Word Studies

Review: **circiter, cōnsūmō, enim, ineō, pereō, proficīscor, subitō.**
Explain *consumer, corroborate, public utility, robust, solitary, usage.*

NOTE
Verify that students can supply all the pertinent information for the review vocabulary.

LESSON XLII

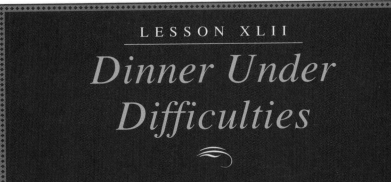

Dinner Under Difficulties

SUGGESTION
Put the full declension of the new proper names on the board for reference: **Herculēs, Herculis; Orpheus, Orpheī; Castor, Castoris, Phīneus, Phīneī; Harpyiae, Harpiarum; Iuppiter, Iovis**.

SUGGESTION
Periodically review these mythological characters as students will encounter them in many stories. Some students may wish to research additional stories.

[1] *about*
[2] *weather*
[3] *set sail*
[4] = **quaesīvissent**
[5] *his*
[6] *as a result*

NOTE
Have students note the interference of the gods (this time, Jupiter) in the lives of mortals. Ask them to recall other stories where this happened.

Intereā is diēs aderat quem Iāsōn per nūntiōs ēdīxerat, et ex omnibus regiōnibus Graeciae multī undique conveniēbant. Trāditum est autem in hōc numerō fuisse Herculem, Orpheum, Castorem, multōsque aliōs quōrum nōmina nōtissima sunt. Ex hīs Iāsōn, quōs[1] arbitrātus est ad omnia subeunda perīcula parātissimōs esse, eōs ad[1] numerum quīnquāgintā dēlēgit; tum paucōs diēs morātus ut ad omnēs cāsūs subsidia comparāret, nāvem dēdūxit, et tempestātem[2] ad nāvigandum idōneam nactus solvit.[3]

Post haec Argonautae ad Thrāciam cursum tenuērunt et ibi in terram ēgressī sunt. Cum ab incolīs quaesīssent[4] quis rēgnum eius regiōnis obtinēret, certiōrēs factī sunt Phīneum quendam tum rēgem esse. Cognōvērunt hunc caecum esse et suppliciō afficī, quod ōlim sē crūdēlissimum in fīliōs suōs praebuisset. Cuius[5] supplicī hoc erat genus. Missa erant ā Iove mōnstra quaedam speciē horribilī, quae capita virginum, corpora volucrum habēbant. Hae volucrēs, quae Harpyiae appellābantur, Phīneō summam molestiam afferēbant; quotiēns enim ille accubuerat, veniēbant et cibum appositum statim auferēbant. Quae cum ita essent,[6] Phīneus fame paene mortuus est.

---

[1] The antecedent is **eōs** (in the next line), which should therefore be translated first.

Luca Tamagnini/Archivio e Studio Folco Quilici

The Mediterranean world, much as Jason would have seen it. The geographical formations are the same today—mountains, forests, islands, and maybe a little mystery.

SUGGESTION
After reading the story, ask students to guess what might happen next. Will the Argonauts help Phineus?

Vocabulary

Nouns

cursus, -ūs, *m. course* (cursive, cursory)
molestia, -ae, *f. annoyance* (molest, molestation)
volucris, -is, *f. bird*

Adjectives

caecus, -a, -um, *blind* (caecilian)
crūdēlis, -e, *cruel* (cruelty)
idōneus, -a, -um, *suitable, fitting*

WORKBOOK
Assign Ex. A, B to practice vocabulary and various constructions taken from the reading.

SUGGESTION
Have students work in pairs and do a quick verb synopsis on the board using regular verbs as well as deponent verbs.

Verbs

accumbō, -ere, accubuī, accubitūrus, *recline (at the table)*

afferō, afferre, attulī, allātus, *bring (to), assign, report*

auferō, auferre, abstulī, ablātus, *take away* (ablative)

comparō, 1, *get ready* (comparative, comparison)

ēgredior, ēgredī, ēgressus, *go out, land* (egress, egression)

nancīscor, nancīscī, nactus, *meet with*

trādō, -ere, -didī, -ditus, *hand over, relate* (tradition, traditional)

Adverb

quotiēns, *as often as, how often* (quotient)

Word Studies

Review: **arbitror, cāsus, famēs, moror, paene.**
Explain *convention, egress, moratorium, subsidy, tradition.*

Caput virginis, corpus volucris habet*. This terra-cotta Harpy once decorated the roof of an Etruscan building in the 5th or 6th century* B.C. *It is called an antefix.*

Alinari/Art Resource

LESSON XLIII

Two Good Turns

Rēs igitur in hōc locō erant cum Argonautae nāvem appulērunt. Phīneus autem, simul atque audīvit eōs in suōs fīnēs ēgressōs esse, magnopere gāvīsus est. Nōn enim dubitābat quīn[1] Argonautae sibi auxilium ferrent. Nūntium igitur ad nāvem mīsit quī Iāsonem sociōsque ad rēgiam vocāret. Eō cum vēnissent, Phīneus prōmīsit sē magna praemia datūrum esse sī illī remedium repperissent. Argonautae negōtium libenter suscēpērunt et cum rēge accubuērunt; at simul ac cēna apposita est, Harpyiae cibum auferre cōnābantur. Argonautae prīmum gladiīs volucrēs petīvērunt; cum tamen vidērent hoc nihil prōdesse, Zētēs et Calais, quī ālīs īnstrūctī sunt, in āera[2] sē sublevāvērunt ut dēsuper impetum facerent. Quod cum sēnsissent Harpyiae, perterritae statim fūgērunt neque posteā umquam rediērunt.

Hōc factō, Phīneus, ut prō tantō beneficiō grātiās referret, Iāsonī dēmōnstrāvit quā ratiōne Symplēgadēs vītāre posset. Symplēgadēs autem duae erant rūpēs ingentī magnitūdine. Hae parvō intervāllō in marī natābant et sī quid in medium spatium vēnerat, incrēdibilī celeritāte concurrēbant. Iāsōn, sublātīs ancorīs, nāvem solvit et mox ad Symplēgadēs appropinquāvit. Tum in prōrā stāns columbam[1] ēmīsit. Illa rēctā viā per medium spatium volāvit et priusquam rūpēs cōnflīxērunt, ēvāsit, caudā tantum āmissā. Tum rūpēs utrimque discessērunt; antequam tamen rūrsus concurrerent, Argonautae summā vī rēmīs contendērunt et nāvem perdūxērunt.

SUGGESTION
You may want to relate the stories of Scylla and Charybdis (or have students research them) as examples of other marine obstacles in the ancient world.

[1] *dove*

NOTE
Point out that **concurrerent** is subjunctive in an anticipatory clause after **antequam**. Refer to the Syntax Appendix under the subjunctive if students require more information.

---

[1] *that,* used after a negative expression of doubting to introduce a clause in the subjunctive **(ferrent)**

[2] accusative singular of **āēr**

Vocabulary

WORKBOOK
Assign Ex. A to practice prepositional phrases.

WORKBOOK
Assign Ex. B, C, D to review vocabulary and verb formation.

WORKBOOK
Assign Ex. E, F to practice various constructions taken from the reading.

Nouns

āēr, āeris, *m. air* (aerial, aeronautics)
impetus, -ūs, *m. attack* (impetuosity, impetus)
ratiō, -ōnis, *f. manner, reason* (ration, rationale)
rēmus, -ī, *m. oar*

Verbs

appropinquō, 1, *come near to, approach*
cōnflīgō, -ere, -flīxī, -flīctus, *dash together* (conflict)
cōnor, 1, *try*
reperiō, -īre, repperī, repertus, *find* (repertory)
sublevō, 1, *raise; (reflex.) rise*
tollō, -ere, sustulī, sublātus, *raise* (sublate)
vītō, 1, *avoid*

Adverbs

magnopere, *greatly*
simul, *at the same time* (simulcast, simultaneous)
simul atque (ac), *as soon as*

Word Studies

Review: **eō** (adv.), **intervāllum, rūrsus, statim.**
Explain *aerial, conflict, impetuous, repertory, simultaneous, volatile.*

LESSON XLIV

A Risky Job

SUGGESTION
Put the full declension of these new proper names on the board for reference: **Phāsis, Phāsidis; Mēdēa, Mēdēae**.

SUGGESTION
Have students keep track of the various obstacles encountered by the Argonauts. Some students may want to read about the 12 labors of Hercules or the problems faced by Ulysses or Aeneas for a later classroom discussion.

Brevī intermissō spatiō, Argonautae ad flūmen Phāsim vēnērunt, quod in fīnibus Colchōrum erat. Eō cum in terram ēgressī essent, statim ad rēgem Aeētem prōcessērunt et ab eō postulāvērunt ut vellus aureum sibi trāderētur. Ille īrā commōtus diū negābat sē vellus trāditūrum esse. Tandem tamen, quod sciēbat Iāsonem nōn sine auxiliō deōrum hoc negōtium suscēpisse, prōmīsit sē vellus trāditūrum esse, sī Iāsōn labōrēs duōs difficillimōs perfēcisset;[1] et cum Iāsōn dīxisset sē ad omnia perīcula subeunda parātum esse, quid fierī vellet ostendit. Prīmum iungendī erant duo taurī speciē horribilī, quī flammās ex ōre ēdēbant; tum, hīs iūnctīs, ager arandus erat, et dentēs dracōnis serendī. Hīs audītīs, Iāsōn, nē hanc occāsiōnem reī bene gerendae[2] āmitteret, negōtium suscēpit.

At Mēdēa, rēgis fīlia, Iāsonem amāvit, et ubi audīvit eum tantum perīculum subitūrum esse, rem aegrē ferēbat. Intellegēbat enim patrem suum hunc labōrem prōposuisse eō ipsō cōnsiliō, ut Iāsōn morerētur. Quae cum ita essent, Mēdēa (quae summam scientiam medicīnae habēbat) hoc cōnsilium iniit. Mediā nocte clam ex urbe ēvāsit et herbās quāsdam carpsit; ex hīs unguentum parāvit quod vī suā corpus aleret[3] nervōsque[4] cōnfirmāret. Hōc factō, Iāsonī unguentum dedit; praecēpit autem ut eō diē quō istī[5] labōrēs cōnficiendī essent corpus suum et arma oblineret. Iāsōn, etsī paene omnibus magnitūdine et vīribus corporis praestābat, tamen hoc cōnsilium nōn neglegendum esse cēnsēbat.

[1] *would perform*
[2] *of accomplishing his mission*
[3] *would nourish*
[4] *muscles*
[5] *the above-mentioned*

NOTE
Point out the phrase beginning with **quod** as a relative purpose clause.

NOTE
Point out that **omnibus** is in the dative after **praestābat** (special verbs/compounds).

Vocabulary

Nouns

dracō, -ōnis, *m. dragon* (Draconian, draconic)
īra, -ae, *f. anger* (ire)
occāsiō, -ōnis, *f. opportunity* (occasion, occasional)
unguentum, -ī, *n. ointment, salve* (unguent)

WORKBOOK
Assign Ex. A, B, C to practice vocabulary and verb forms taken from the reading.

Verbs

arō, 1, *plow* (arable)
carpō, -ere, carpsī, carptus, *pick, take; consume*
cēnseō, -ēre, cēnsuī, cēnsus, *think* (censor, consensus)
ēdō, ēdere, ēdidī, ēditus, *give out, inflict* (edit, editorial)
iungō, -ere, iūnxī, iūnctus, *join, harness* (join, junction)
oblinō, -ere, oblēvī, oblitus, *smear* (obliterate)
serō, -ere, sēvī, satus, *plant, sow*

Adverbs

aegrē, *with difficulty*
clam, *secretly*

Word Studies

Review: **alō, diū, neglegō, postulō, praestō**.
Explain *dental, conjunction, liniment, postulate, Unguentine.*

C. M. Dixon

This portrait of Medea, daughter of King Aeetes, comes from a Roman wall painting in a villa in Herculaneum. It was painted sometime before A.D. *79.*

LESSON XLV

Sowing the Dragon's Teeth

Ubi is diēs vēnit quem rēx ad arandum agrum ēdīxerat, Iāsōn, ortā lūce,[1] cum sociīs ad locum cōnstitūtum prōcessit. Ibi stabulum ingēns repperit in quō taurī erant inclūsī; tum, portīs apertīs, taurōs in lūcem trāxit, et summā cum difficultāte iugum imposuit. Tum Iāsōn, omnibus aspicientibus, agrum arāre coepit; quā in rē tantam dīligentiam praebuit ut ante merīdiem tōtum opus cōnficeret. Hōc factō, ad locum ubi rēx sedēbat adiit et dentēs dracōnis postulāvit; quōs ubi accēpit, in agrum sparsit. Hōrum autem dentium nātūra erat tālis ut in eō locō ubi sparsī essent virī armātī mīrō modō gignerentur.

Postquam igitur omnēs dentēs in agrum sparsit, Iāsōn lassitūdine exanimātus quiētī sē trādidit, dum virī istī gignerentur. Paucās hōrās dormiēbat; sub[2] vesperum tamen ē somnō subitō excitātus rem ita ēvēnisse ut praedictum erat cognōvit; nam in omnibus agrī partibus virī ingentī magnitūdine gladiīs galeīsque armātī mīrō modō ē terrā oriēbantur. Hōc cognitō, Iāsōn cōnsilium quod dedisset Mēdēa nōn omittendum esse putābat. Saxum igitur ingēns in mediōs virōs coniēcit. Illī undique ad locum concurrērunt, et cum sibi quisque id saxum habēre vellet, magna contrōversia orta est. Mox, strictīs gladiīs, inter sē[3] pugnāre coepērunt, et cum hōc modō plūrimī occīsī essent, reliquī vulneribus cōnfectī ā Iāsone nūllō negōtiō[4] interfectī sunt.

1 *at daybreak* (ablative absolute)
2 *toward*
3 *with one another*
4 *without trouble*

SUGGESTION
Have students identify all uses of the ablative in this passage.

Erich Lessing/Art Resource, NY

Jason seizes the horns of a fire-breathing bull. Once he yokes this one with the other, he will plow the field and sow the dragon's teeth.

WORKBOOK
Assign Ex. A, C to practice vocabulary taken from the reading.

WORKBOOK
Assign Ex. B to practice participles taken from the reading.

NOTE
Remind students that **imperō** takes **ut** + subjunctive (indirect command), not an infinitive (like **iubeō**).

Vocabulary

Nouns

contrōversia, -ae, *f. dispute* (controversial, controversy)
galea, -ae, *f. helmet* (galeate, galeiform)
iugum, -ī, *n. yoke* (jugular)
lassitūdō, -dinis, *f. weariness* (lassitude)
merīdiēs, -ēī, *m. midday, noon* (meridian, meridional)

Adjectives

ingēns, ingentis (gen.), *huge*
iste, ista, istud, *that*

Verbs

armō, 1, *arm, equip* (armor, armament)
aspiciō, -ere, aspexī, aspectus, *look on* (aspect)
exanimō, 1, *exhaust, kill* (exanimate)
gignō, -ere, genuī, genitus, *produce; (passive) be born* (genius)
imperō, 1, *command, order* (imperative, imperious)
spargō, -ere, sparsī, sparsus, *scatter, sprinkle* (disperse, sparse)

Word Studies

Review: **aperiō, at, coepī, occīdō, orior, quiēs, saxum, vesper**.
Explain *aspect, disperse* (from **spargō**), *imperative, lassitude, quietus*.

LESSON XLVI

Jason Gets the Fleece

At rēx Aeētēs, ubi cognōvit Iāsonem labōrem prōpositum cōnfēcisse, īrā graviter commōtus est; intellegēbat enim Mēdēam auxilium eī tulisse. Mēdēa autem, cum intellegeret sē in magnō esse perīculō, fugā salūtem petere cōnstituit. Omnibus igitur rēbus ad fugam parātīs, mediā nocte cum frātre Absyrtō ēvāsit et quam celerrimē ad locum ubi Argō[1] subducta erat prōcessit. Eō cum vēnisset, ad pedēs Iāsonis sē prōiēcit et multīs cum lacrimīs eum ōrāvit nē in tantō perīculō sē[2] dēsereret. Ille libenter eam excēpit et hortātus est nē patris īram timēret. Prōmīsit autem sē quam prīmum eam in nāvī suā āvectūrum.[3]

Postrīdiē Iāsōn cum sociīs suīs, ortā lūce, nāvem dēdūxit, et tempestātem idōneam nactī ad eum locum rēmīs contendērunt quō Mēdēa vellus cēlātum esse dēmōnstrāvit. Eō cum vēnissent, Iāsōn in terram ēgressus, ipse cum Mēdēā in silvās contendit. Pauca mīlia passuum per silvam prōgressus vellus quod quaerēbat ex arbore suspēnsum vīdit. Id tamen auferre rēs erat summae difficultātis: nōn modo enim locus ipse ēgregiē et nātūrā et arte mūnītus erat, sed etiam dracō speciē terribilī arborem custōdiēbat. Tum Mēdēa, quae, ut suprā dēmōnstrāvimus, medicīnae summam scientiam habuit, rāmum quem ex arbore proximā arripuerat venēnō īnfēcit. Hōc factō, ad locum appropinquāvit et dracōnem, quī faucibus apertīs eius adventum exspectābat, venēnō sparsit; deinde, dum dracō somnō oppressus dormit, Iāsōn vellus aureum ex arbore arripuit et cum Mēdēā quam celerrimē pedem rettulit.[4]

[1] *Argo* (the ship)
[2] i.e., Medea
[3] *would carry away*
[4] *withdrew* (with **pedem**)

SUGGESTION
Before starting this reading selection, have several students summarize the story thus far.

SUGGESTION
Put the full declension of this new proper name on the board for reference: **Absyrtus, Absyrtī**.

SUGGESTION
Go through the story to find each instance of a subjunctive. Have students identify the reason.

NOTE
Remind students that **quam** + superlative adverb is translated *as . . . as possible.*

Vocabulary

Nouns

difficultās, -tātis, *f. difficulty* (difficult)
rāmus, -ī, *m. branch* (ramification, ramify)
venēnum, -ī, *n. poison* (venom, venomous)

The Metropolitan Museum of Art, Harris Brisbane Dick Fund, 1934. (34.11.7)

On this red-figured vase in New York City, Jason reaches up to steal the Golden Fleece, while Athena (center) looks on. At the right, one of the Argonauts holds the rail of the Argo. We might expect the hero Jason to be a little bigger and less awkward than this.

WORKBOOK
Assign Ex. A to practice infinitives taken from the reading.

WORKBOOK
Assign Ex. B to practice various constructions with **cum** taken from the reading.

WORKBOOK
Assign Ex. C, D to practice dependent clauses with the indicative and subjunctive.

WORKBOOK
Assign Ex. E to practice various uses of the ablative taken from the reading.

Adjective

apertus, -a, -um, *open* (aperture)

Verbs

cēlō, 1, *hide*
contendō, -ere, -tendī, -tentūrus, *struggle, hasten* (contend, contention)

Adverbs

postrīdiē, *on the next day*
quam, *how, as (also conjunction)*
suprā, *above* (supranational, supraorbital)

Word Studies

Review: **arbor, excipiō, hortor, passus.**
Explain *contention, dragon, hortatory, infection, projectile, suspension.*

LESSON XLVII

Escape Through Murder

Postquam Iāsōn et Mēdēa, vellus aureum ferentēs, ad nāvem pervēnissent, omnēs sine morā nāvem rūrsus cōnscendērunt et prīmā vigilia solvērunt. At rēx Aeētēs, ubi cognōvit fīliam suam nōn modo ad Argonautās sē recēpisse sed etiam ad vellus auferendum auxilium tulisse, nāvem longam[1] quam celerrimē dēdūcī iussit et fugientēs[2] īnsecūtus est. Argonautae omnibus vīribus rēmīs contendēbant; cum tamen nāvis quā vehēbantur ingentī esset magnitūdine, nōn eādem celeritāte quā[3] Colchī prōgredī poterant. Quae cum ita essent, ā Colchīs sequentibus paene captī sunt. At Mēdēa, cum vīdīsset quō in locō rēs essent, nefārium cōnsilium cēpit.

Erat in nāvī Argonautārum fīlius rēgis Aeētae, nōmine Absyrtus, quem, ut suprā dēmōnstrāvimus, Mēdēa fugiēns sēcum abdūxerat. Hunc puerum Mēdēa interficere cōnstituit ut, membrīs eius in mare coniectīs, cursum Colchōrum impedīret;[1] sciēbat enim Aeētem, cum membra fīlī vīdisset, nōn longius prōsecūtūrum esse. Neque opīniō eam fefellit.[4] Aeētēs, cum prīmum membra vīdit, ad ea colligenda nāvem dētinērī iussit. Dum tamen ea geruntur, Argonautae mox ex cōnspectū hostium remōtī sunt, neque prius fugere dēstitērunt quam ad flūmen Ēridanum[2] pervēnērunt.

Tandem post multa perīcula Iāsōn in eundem locum pervēnit unde ōlim profectus erat. Tum ē nāvī ēgressus ad rēgem Peliam statim prōcessit et, vellere aureō mōnstrātō, ab eō postulāvit ut rēgnum sibi trāderētur. Peliās prīmum nihil respondit, sed diū in eādem trīstitiā tacitus permānsit; tandem ita locūtus est: "Vidēs mē aetāte iam esse cōnfectum; certē diēs suprēmus mihi adest. Liceat[5] igitur mihi, dum vīvam, hoc rēgnum obtinēre; cum autem tandem dēcesserō, tū in meum locum veniēs." Hāc ōrātiōne adductus Iāsōn respondit sē id factūrum quod ille rogāvisset.

[1] *a warship*
[2] *the fugitives*
[3] *as*
[4] *she was not mistaken*
[5] *let it be permitted*

NOTE
Tell students that a night was divided into four watches.

SUGGESTION
Put the full declension of this new proper name on the board for reference: **Ēridanus, Ēridanī** (now the Po River).

NOTE
Point out that in this sentence, **priusquam** has been separated into two words, **prius** and **quam**.

---

[1] Medea is the subject.
[2] *the Po,* a river of northern Italy

Jason returns to Thessaly and King Pelias, this time with the Golden Fleece.

PHOTRI/AISA

Vocabulary

Nouns

onus, oneris, *n. weight* (onerous, onus)
opīniō, -ōnis, *f. opinion* (opinionated)
tristitia, -ae, *f. sadness* (triste, tristful)

Adjectives

dexter, -tra, -trum, *right (as opposed to left)* (ambidextrous, dexterous)
nefārius, -a, -um, *unspeakable* (nefarious)
tacitus, -a, -um, *silent* (tacit, taciturn)

Verbs

cōnscendō, -ere, -scendī, -scēnsus, *climb (in), embark (in)*
dēsistō, -ere, dēstitī, dēstitūrus, *cease* (desist)
īnsequor, īnsequī, īnsecūtus, *pursue*
tardō, 1, *slow up* (retardant, tardy)

Adverbs

procul, *far off*
unde, *from which (place)*

Conjunctions

cum prīmum, *as soon as*
neve (neu), *and not, nor*
priusquam, *before*

Word Studies

Review: **colligō, cōnficiō, cōnspectus, licet, loquor, mora, ōlim, prōgredior, sequor, vehō.**

Explain *circumlocution, detention, fallacy, illicit, infallible, nefarious, opinionated, survivor, taciturn.*

WORKBOOK
Assign Ex. A to practice participles taken from the reading.

WORKBOOK
Assign Ex. B, C to practice verb formations and uses of the infinitive taken from the reading.

WORKBOOK
Assign Ex. D to practice various constructions taken from the reading.

LESSON XLVIII

Boiled Mutton

NOTE
Ask students to identify the gerund. Ask them how to distinguish a gerund from a participle.

NOTE
Remind students that **num** introduces a question expecting a negative answer.

NOTE
Remind students that **ūtor** is followed by the ablative.

Hīs rēbus cognitīs, Mēdēa rēgnī cupiditāte adducta mortem rēgī per dolum īnferre cōnstituit. Ad fīliās rēgis vēnit atque ita locūta est: "Vidētis patrem vestrum aetāte iam esse cōnfectum neque ad labōrem rēgnandī perferendum satis valēre. Vultisne eum rūrsus iuvenem fierī?" Tum fīliae rēgis ita respondērunt: "Num hoc fierī potest? Quis enim umquam ē sene iuvenis factus est?" At Mēdēa respondit: "Scītis mē medicīnae summam habēre scientiam. Nunc igitur vōbīs dēmōnstrābō quō modō haec rēs fierī possit." Hīs dictīs, cum arietem aetāte iam cōnfectum interfēcisset, membra eius in vāse aēneō posuit et, ignī suppositō,[1] in aquam herbās quāsdam īnfūdit. Tum carmen magicum cantābat. Mox ariēs ē vāse exsiluit et, vīribus refectīs, per agrōs currēbat.

Dum fīliae rēgis hoc mīrāculum stupentēs intuentur, Mēdēa ita locūta est: "Vidētis quantum valeat medicīna. Vōs igitur, sī vultis patrem vestrum in adulēscentiam redūcere, id quod fēcī ipsae faciētis. Vōs patris membra in vās conicite; ego herbās magicās praebēbō." Quod ubi audītum est, fīliae rēgis cōnsilium quod dedisset Mēdēa nōn omittendum putāvērunt. Patrem igitur Peliam necāvērunt et membra eius in vās coniēcērunt. At Mēdēa nōn eāsdem herbās dedit quibus ipsa ūsa erat. Itaque postquam diū frustrā exspectāvērunt, patrem suum rē vērā[2] mortuum esse intellēxērunt. Hīs rēbus gestīs, Mēdēa spērābat sē cum coniuge suō rēgnum acceptūrum esse; sed cīvēs cum intellegerent quō modō Peliās periisset, Iāsone et Mēdēā ē rēgnō expulsīs, Acastum rēgem creāvērunt.

[1] *placed under* (the pot)
[2] *in fact, really* (with **rē**)

White-haired King Pelias watches Medea (center) perform her magic while the ram boils. At the right is one of Pelias' daughters. A slave, or perhaps Jason, tends the fire. Is this vase red-figured or black-figured?

Copyright British Museum

Vocabulary

Nouns

ariēs, -ietis, *m. ram, battering ram*
coniūnx, -iugis, *m., f. husband, wife* (conjugal)
dolus, -ī, *n. treachery, deceit, trickery*
vās, vāsis, *n. kettle, pot, vessel* (vase)

WORKBOOK
Assign Ex. A to practice vocabulary and noun/adjective endings.

Adjective

aēneus, -a, -um, *(of) bronze, copper*

Verbs

coniciō, -ere, -iēcī, -iectus, *throw* (conjecture)
exsiliō, -īre, exsiluī, —, *leap up or out*
īnfundō, -ere, īnfūdī, īnfūsus, *pour in* (infuse, infusion)
necō, 1, *kill*

WORKBOOK
Assign Ex. B to practice verbs, indirect statements taken from the reading.

WORKBOOK
Assign Ex. C to practice various constructions taken from the reading.

Adverbs

frustrā, *in vain* (frustrate, frustration)
satis, *enough* (satiate, satisfy)
umquam, *ever*

Word Studies

Review: **ignis, ita, quantus, spērō.**

Explain *conjugal, dismember, frustrate, imperishable, infusion, internecine, intuition, miraculous, rejuvenate.*

LESSON XLIX

Death and More Death

SUGGESTION
Put the full declension of these proper names on the board for reference: **Corinthus, Corinthī; Creōn, Creontis; Glaucē, Glaucis, Glaucēn** (acc.).

SUGGESTION
Write on the board all the proper names students have encountered in the story of Jason and see how many students can immediately identify them. If you wish, you may make a game out of it. The names include: Jason, Aeson, Pelias, Aeetes, Colchis, Hercules, Orpheus, Castor, Phineus, Harpies, Jupiter, Zetes, Calais, Phasis, Medea, Absyrtus, Acastus, Po, Corinth, Creon, Glauce.

[1] *air* (a Greek form of the accusative)
[2] *falling towards that side (with dēlāpsa)*

Post haec Iāsōn et Mēdēa ad urbem Corinthum vēnērunt, cuius urbis Creōn rēgnum tum obtinēbat. Erat autem Creontī[1] fīlia ūna nōmine Glaucē. Quam cum vīdisset, Iāsōn cōnstituit Mēdēam uxōrem suam repudiāre, ut Glaucēn[2] in mātrimōnium dūceret. At Mēdēa, ubi intellēxit quae ille in animō habēret, īrā graviter commōta iūre iūrandō cōnfirmāvit sē tantam iniūriam ultūram. Hoc igitur cōnsilium cēpit. Vestem parāvit summā arte contextam; hanc īnfēcit venēnō, cuius vīs tālis erat ut, sī quis eam vestem induisset, corpus eius quasi ignī urerētur. Hōc factō, vestem ad Glaucēn mīsit. Illa autem nihil malī suspicāns dōnum libenter accēpit, et vestem novam, mōre fēminārum, sine morā induit.

Statim Glaucē dolōrem gravem per omnia membra sēnsit et post paulum summō cruciātū affecta ē vītā excessit. Tum Mēdēa furōre impulsa fīliōs suōs necāvit et ex eā regiōne fugere cōnstituit. Sōlem ōrāvit ut in tantō perīculō auxilium sibi ferret. Sōl autem hīs precibus commōtus currum mīsit cui dracōnēs ālīs īnstrūctī iūnctī erant. Mēdēa currum cōnscendit, itaque per āera[1] vecta incolumis ad urbem Athēnās pervēnit. Iāsōn autem post breve tempus mīrō modō occīsus est. Ille enim sub umbrā nāvis suae, quae in lītus subducta erat, ōlim dormiēbat. At nāvis in eam partem[2] ubi Iāsōn iacēbat subitō dēlāpsa virum īnfēlīcem oppressit.

Vocabulary

Nouns

cruciātus, -ūs, *m. torture*	(excruciating)
iūs iūrandum, iūris iūrandī, *n. oath*	
prex, precis, *f. prayer*	(deprecate, deprecatory)
turris, -is, *f. tower*	(turret)

[1] dative of possession
[2] accusative (Greek form)

Roman ruins from the city of Corinth, showing a temple and acropolis of Corinth. Here is where the final chapter of the story of Jason took place, with the death of Glauce and the timely disappearance of Medea.

Ronald Sheridan/Ancient Art & Architecture Collection

Adjective

īnfēlix, īnfēlīcis (gen.), *unfortunate, unlucky* (infelicitous, infelicity)

Verbs

induō, -ere, induī, indūtus, *put on, dress, impale*
repudiō, 1, *divorce* (repudiate, repudiation)
suspicor, 1, *suspect* (suspicion, suspicious)
ulcīscor, ulcīscī, ultus, *avenge*
ūrō, -ere, ussī, ustus, *burn*

WORKBOOK
Assign Ex. A, C to practice various constructions taken from the reading.

WORKBOOK
Assign Ex. B to review certain characters in the reading.

WORKBOOK
The Unit IV Review contains a crossword puzzle that includes all the names of the characters mentioned in the Unit IV readings.

Word Studies

Review: **fēmina, incolumis, opprimō, sentiō, sōl, uxor, vestis.**

Explain *context, deprecate, excruciating, investiture, morale, morality, suspicion, tinge, uxoricide.*

5°
0°
BRITANNIA
Cenimagni
Trinovantes
Cassi
Londinium
Tamesis
Ancalites
CANTIUM
Segontiaci
Bibroci
Fretum Gallicum
Morini
Portus Itius
Atrebates
(Arras)
50°
Samara
Ambiani
Samarobriva
BELGI
Bellovaci
Caleti
Veliocasses
Bratuspantium
Sequana
Isera
Noviodunum
Venelli
Lexovii
Essuvii
AREMORICA
Parisii
Matrona
Lutecia
Diablintes
Metiosedum
Osismi
Coriosolites
Aulerci
Redones
Carnutes
Senones
Veneti
Andes
Cenabum
Namnetes
Liger
Ambiliati
Turoni
Bituriges
Avaricum
OCEANUS
ATLANTICUS
CELTI
Pictones
Boii
Lemovices
Santoni
45°
Gergovia
Arverni
Duranius
Garunna
Sotiates
AQUITANIA
M. CEBENN
Tolosates
Tolosa
PROV
Volcae
Garunna
Carcaso
Narbo
HISPANIA
PYRENAEI MONTES
5°
0°

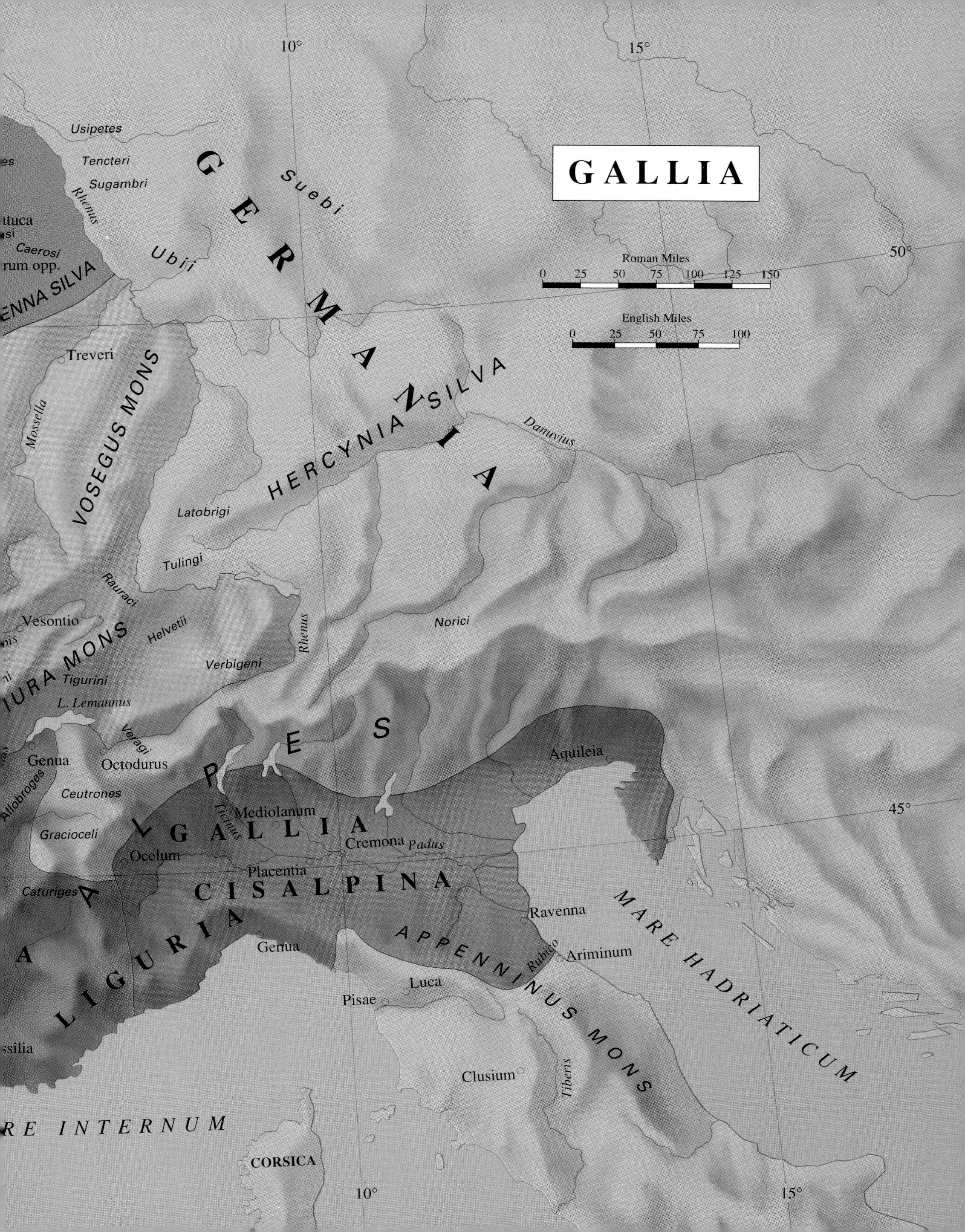

GALLIA
10°
15°
50°
45°
Roman Miles
0 25 50 75 100 125 150
English Miles
0 25 50 75 100
Usipetes
Tencteri
Sugambri
Rhenus
Caerosi
ENNA SILVA
GERMANIA
Suebi
Ubii
Treveri
VOSEGUS MONS
Mossella
HERCYNIA SILVA
Danuvius
Latobrigi
Tulingi
Rauraci
Vesontio
Helvetii
Rhenus
Norici
IURA MONS
Verbigeni
Tigurini
L. Lemannus
Veragi
Genua
Octodurus
Allobroges
Ceutrones
ALPES
Aquileia
Ticinus
Mediolanum
Graciocelli
GALLIA
Ocelum
Cremona
Padus
Placentia
CISALPINA
Caturiges
LIGURIA
Genua
Ravenna
APPENNINUS MONS
Rubico
Ariminum
MARE HADRIATICUM
Luca
Pisae
Clusium
Tiberis
RE INTERNUM
CORSICA

C. M. Dixon

Unit V

Dē Bellō Gallicō I

UNIT OBJECTIVES
To review comparative and superlative adjectives and adverbs; To review the ablative of respect; To review the conjugation of **fīō**; To review the gerundive with **ad**; To review indirect statements and to learn about subordinate clauses in indirect discourse; To review **cum** clauses; To learn the dative of possession; To learn the subjunctive in anticipatory clauses; To learn about causal clauses with **quod** and **quoniam**; To review impersonal verbs; To review the hortatory and jussive subjunctive; To review the **iubeō** construction; To review present and future infinitives in indirect statement; To review the datives of purpose and reference (double dative); To review indirect question

The Senate House in Rome. Originally an advisory group to the early kings, the Senate decreed an end to the kings and thus established the Republic. At this time, they became the dominant governmental group. The ***curia*** *was the meeting place of the Senate. It was the scene of all the major decisions that made Rome a great power. As Julius Caesar came to power and took up the cause of the general populace against the senatorial clique, he had the senate house rebuilt, renamed it the* ***Curia Julia****, and increased the number of senators to 900 to reward his supporters. This number was reduced back to 600 under Augustus. During the Empire, the Senate was returned to its primarily advisory capacity.*

Julius Caesar

SUGGESTION
Have a student research the background behind each of these quotes and others you might add, such as "The die is cast," or "I came, I saw, I conquered."

SUGGESTION
Some students may wish to do additional research by reading (in English) one or more of these works.

NOTE
Remind students that Venus was the mother of Aeneas.

No man is more immediately associated with Rome than is Julius Caesar. To most people the name Caesar symbolizes the dynamism and greatness of the republic that he did so much to turn into an empire. The word Caesar is preserved in the titles Kaiser and Czar, and has come so nearly to be a synonym for royal or dictatorial power that we speak of a minor autocrat as a "little Caesar." Most of us have heard or used many of the phrases that have grown up around him— "crossing the Rubicon," "the Ides of March," "Et tu, Brute," "great Caesar's ghost." No other Roman has been the subject of so much later attention: we have his biography in Latin by Suetonius, one in Greek by Plutarch, plays by Shakespeare and George Bernard Shaw; and several novels and films have celebrated his life and character.

Gaius Julius Caesar was born in 100 B.C. to a patrician family whose members flattered themselves on being so ancient that they could trace their line all the way back to a divine ancestress—Venus. But, in spite of their aristocratic lineage, the Julians became associated with the political program of the common people in the first century B.C. Whether it was from personal conviction or shrewd political insight into the way his ambitions could most easily be realized, Caesar early adopted the popular cause against the senatorial clique, made up of a small number of noble families who had ruled Rome well but autocratically for centuries. Caesar's stand alarmed the conservative dictator Sulla and nearly cost Caesar his life, but, by a combination of a gambler's daring, great acumen in wooing the favor of the people, and an almost irresistible personal magnetism, he steadily made his way up the political ladder.

Somewhat before 60 B.C. Caesar allied himself with Crassus, a wealthy politician (who underwrote the enormous debts Caesar had contracted), and in that year he joined Pompey, the greatest military hero of the time, and Crassus in the coalition called the First Triumvirate ("Three-man Rule"). As a result, in 59 B.C., Caesar was elected to the consulship, the highest office in the Roman government. He so dominated his colleague

Scala/Art Resource, NY

The Temple of Venus and Rome, in the Roman Forum, was restored by the emperor Maxentius in A.D. *307. It was dedicated to Venus, the supposed ancestor of Julius Caesar's family, and to all the local divinities of Rome.*

Bibulus that the year was jestingly called, not "the consulship of Caesar and Bibulus," but "the consulship of Julius and Caesar." Many senators, realizing the danger that Caesar presented to their conservative position, tried to restrict the importance of the command he would hold as an ex-consul, but by political maneuvering Caesar won the proconsulship of Gaul and Illyricum. In all he spent nine years (58–50 B.C.) in subjugating and governing Gaul. In the following pages you will read his own account of that conquest, the *Commentaries* (or *Notes*) *on the Gallic War*.

Caesar is remarkably tight-lipped about his own personal motives. It is apparent, however, that at the start of his command his attitude was a defensive one of simply protecting Italy and the Roman Province in southern France from the barbarian tribes. He then shifted to a more aggressive attitude aimed at reducing all Transalpine Gaul to the status of a Roman province. Possibly he realized that "a good offense is the best defense." He often states that friendly Gallic tribes appealed to him for protection against their more aggressive neighbors. Possibly he was driven farther and farther north by a consuming ambition for military power and glory. It is certain, however, that he used these years to develop his extraordinary military talents and to forge a highly loyal and efficient fighting force. There is also much evidence to show that even while Caesar was away in Gaul he used his prestige and captured gold to build a strong political party at Rome.

Unquestionably he was a great military commander; his absolute physical courage, self-confidence, iron will, fairness, and generosity with praise and rewards made him an unparalleled leader of men. He was a master tactician, relying on great mobility to surprise his enemies, quick to adapt his maneuvers to the terrain and to press every advantage in the field. He showed no less skill in dealing with the people of Gaul, capitalizing on their failure to unite and on their vacillation, trusting those who became his allies, and employing harsh punishments only when the offenders' rebelliousness was incorrigible.

Caesar's successes in Gaul, Britain, and Germany and the growth of his party at Rome led inevitably to conflict with Pompey and the Senate. In 49 B.C., a Civil War began when Caesar crossed the Rubicon, the boundary river between Cisalpine Gaul and Italy proper. The Senatorial army under Pompey's command abandoned Italy and was defeated near Pharsalus (in Greece) in 48 B.C. Within the next three years Caesar had overrun all opposition and become virtually master of the Western world. In the few years before his assassination in 44 B.C., he brought about many reforms in Roman political and economic life, and laid the basis upon which his grandnephew and adopted son Octavian built the Roman Empire.

Caesar was also most expert in "public relations." He wrote his *Commentaries* (or *Notes*) *on the Gallic War* not only to provide a record of the campaigns for future historians, but also to keep himself and his victories before the eyes of the Roman voters. Since he regularly refers to himself in the third person (only occasionally using the modest "we"), the work takes on a deceptively impersonal air, and the reader is inclined to forget that the image of this dynamic and unconquerable, yet understanding and merciful, general is being created by the "hero" himself. The style is likewise deceptively straightforward and clear, and the facts apparently so complete that no ancient historian ever needed or dared to rewrite his story. His three-book account of the Civil War is a valuable document of that bloody period, but it is the earlier work on Gaul that assures Caesar a place among the first rank of military historians.

As a military man, Caesar ranks with such geniuses as Alexander, Hannibal, and Napoleon. Like Pericles, Washington, and Churchill, he was a great statesman, one whose military triumphs and political activities profoundly affected the future of the world. Yet, with all we know about him, there remains some of the mystery and controversy that surround all great

Ronald Sheridan/Ancient Art & Architecture Collection

Pompey (106-48 B.C.) was supported by Julius Caesar for several important military assignments, where he performed well. Pompey, Caesar, and Crassus formed the first triumvirate in 60 B.C. The deaths of Pompey's wife, Julia (Caesar's daughter) in 54 and of Crassus in 53, combined with the huge success of Caesar in Gaul caused a split between Caesar and Pompey, who worked against Caesar for a second consulate.

men. Naturally he had his faults. He was a bit vain about his personal appearance, and particularly sensitive about his baldness. Although not especially superstitious about himself, he capitalized on the people's belief that fortune favored him. Even though "Caesar's wife must be above suspicion," Caesar himself was not. But the gossip that surrounded his personal life served only to spread his reputation and to aid him at the polls. Much more serious is the charge that he was nothing more than a tyrant, bent on destroying the Roman republican form of government to satisfy his own lust for power. This question is still hotly debated, and, as you read his own words in the pages that follow, you will have a chance to decide the answer for yourself.

NOTE
Point out that Caesar was a very versatile man. He was not only a great general, statesman, and writer, but also one of the best orators of his day, known for the vigor of his speeches. He was also something of a poet, and was seriously interested in Latin grammar.

THE GRANGER COLLECTION, New York

The assassination of Julius Caesar took place on March 15, 44 B.C. A brilliant general and formidable politician, it was feared that he wanted to be made king. A conspiracy of senators led by Brutus and Cassius Longinus ended this fear.

Caesar's Army

NOTE
Point out (or elicit) that **exercitus** is literally a body of *trained* men, from **exerceō**.

Caesar's army **(exercitus)** was composed mainly of Roman citizens who served as foot soldiers **(peditēs)**. It also contained a cavalry force **(equitēs)**, which during the Gallic Wars averaged about 4,000 men. The cavalry were foreign mercenaries recruited in Spain, Germany, and Gaul. They were used mainly for scouting and surprise attacks, in preliminary skirmishing to test the enemy's strength, or in pursuit of a retreating foe.

NOTE
Students should not be required to memorize all these terms, but should refer to these pages often to get a clearer picture of Caesar's campaigns.

The Roman army was organized as follows:

I. Groupings

A. Infantry **(peditēs)**

NOTE
A **legiō** is comparable to a *division* in the U.S. Army.

1. **Legiō.** The average size of one of Caesar's legions during the Gallic War was probably about 3,200, though the full strength was supposed to be 6,000.

C. M. Dixon

The Roman cavalry played a crucial role throughout Caesar's campaign in Gaul. This relief shows a Roman ***eques*** *about to kill a barbarian.*

2. **Cohortēs.** Each legion was divided into ten *cohorts* **(cohortēs)**, averaging 360 men each.

3. **Manipulī.** Each cohort was divided into three *maniples* **(manipulī)** of 120 men each.

4. **Ōrdinēs.** Each maniple was divided into two *centuries* **(ōrdinēs**[1]**)**, originally of 100 men each but averaging 60 in Caesar's army.

NOTE
A *cohort* is similar to a *battle group*, which contains a variety of specially trained personnel allowing it to operate independently, at least for limited periods.

NOTE
A *maniple* corresponds to a *company*.

NOTE
A *century* corresponds to a *platoon*.

B. Cavalry **(equitēs)**

1. **Ālae.** The **āla**, or *squadron*, consisted of 300 or 400 men commanded by a **praefectus equitum** (*cavalry prefect*).

2. **Turmae.** Each **āla** was divided into **turmae**, or *troops*, of about 30 men each.

3. **Decuriae.** Each **turma** was divided into **decuriae**, or *squads*, of 10 men each.

C. Auxiliaries **(auxilia)**

1. **Levis armātūrae peditēs.** *Light-armed troops* recruited from allied or dependent states. Their officers were Romans. Caesar did not depend upon his **auxilia** to win battles but used them mostly for raiding and foraging.

2. **Funditōrēs.** *Slingers*, principally from the Balearic Islands (Majorca, etc.), near the east coast of Spain.

3. **Sagittāriī.** *Bowmen*, or *archers*, from Crete in the eastern Mediterranean and Numidia in Africa.

D. Noncombatants

1. **Cālōnēs.** *Camp servants*, including slaves attached to the officers' quarters. Each legion had about 500.

2. **Mūliōnēs.** *Muledrivers* in charge of heavy baggage of the army.

3. **Mercātōrēs.** *Traders* allowed to accompany the army and conduct canteens outside the camp.

II. Personnel

A. Enlisted Men

1. **Mīles legiōnārius.** A *legionary soldier* was usually a citizen volunteer who enlisted for the regular term of twenty years. Roman citizens between the ages of 17 and 46 were subject to military draft (dīlēctus).

2. **Ēvocātus.** A *volunteer* who had served his full time but had reenlisted. Such men were the flower of Caesar's army.

3. **Signifer.** *Standard bearer* of the maniple, resembling the modern color bearer.

4. **Aquilifer.** *Bearer of the eagle*, emblem of the legion.

5. **Centuriō, decuriō.** Each of the 60 centuries of the legion was in charge of a *centurion*, a noncommissioned officer appointed from the ranks

NOTE
The *centurion* corresponds to a *first sergeant* or *top sergeant*.

[1] This term is sometimes used in Caesar in the sense of line, position, or rank.

in recognition of brave and efficient service. The *first centurion* **(prīmipīlus)** was a fearless officer who fought in the ranks, leading his men in person. Much of the success of an army depended on such men. They maintained strict discipline, which they enforced with the **vītis**, similar to a policeman's club. The commander of a squad of cavalry was called a *decurion*.

NOTE
A *military tribune* corresponds to a *second lieutenant*.

B. Commissioned Officers

1. **Tribūnus mīlitum, praefectus equitum.** Each legion had six *military tribunes*, the lowest commissioned officers. They were usually young men, well educated and of good family, but untrained, and were entrusted with duties of minor importance, such as the command of a legion in camp or on the march. These men usually were in the army to get the military experience that was prerequisite to a political career. A *cavalry prefect*, similar in rank to a military tribune, commanded an **āla**.

2. **Quaestor.** Like a *quartermaster*, the **quaestor** supervised the pay of the men and the purchase of supplies; in battle he sometimes commanded a legion.

Ronald Sheridan/Ancient Art & Architecture Collection

The Praetorian Guard was a privileged, politically influential bodyguard established in 27 B.C. to attend and protect the emperor. It consisted of 16,000 men. The Praetorian Guard was disbanded in A.D. 312 by Constantine I.

Ronald Sheridan/Ancient Art & Architecture Collection

Third century depiction of a wounded Gaul.

3. **Lēgātus.** Caesar had a number of *staff officers* (**lēgātī**), who were appointed by the Roman senate with the rank of a modern *lieutenant general* or *major general.* In battle each legion was usually commanded by a **lēgātus**, but the **lēgātī** did not hold permanent command.

4. **Dux, imperātor.** The *general* (**dux**) assumed the title **imperātor** after winning his first important victory. After defeating the Helvetians, Caesar was regularly addressed as **imperātor**, a title which corresponds to that of *commanding general* in a modern army. Any staff officer appointed by the **imperātor** to command a division of troops became temporarily **dux** of that division.

C. Specialists Attached to the General Staff

1. **Fabrī.** *Engineers* specially trained or detailed from the ranks to build ships, bridges, siege engines, and winter quarters. Such work was in charge of the chief of engineers (**praefectus fabrum**).

2. **Speculātōrēs.** *Spies* employed singly by the general to obtain news by going within the enemy's lines, often in disguise.

3. **Explōrātōrēs.** Mounted *scouts*, or *patrols*, who scoured the country for information. They usually went out in small parties.

SUGGESTION
Some students may want to make a poster to illustrate the organization of the Roman army. Others may want to contrast it with the modern U.S. Army.

WORKBOOK
Assign Ex. A-J to learn more about the life and times of Julius Caesar.

LESSON OBJECTIVES

To review comparative and superlative adjectives and adverbs; To review the ablative of respect

LESSON L

A Geography Lesson

I, 1

Gallia est omnis$_{1}$ dīvīsa$_{2}$ in partēs trēs, quārum ūnam$_{3}$ incolunt Belgae, aliam Aquītānī, tertiam eī quī ipsōrum linguā[1] Celtae, nostrā[2] Gallī appellantur. Hī omnēs linguā, īnstitūtīs, lēgibus inter sē[3] differunt. Gallōs$_{4}$ ab Aquītānīs Garunna flūmen, ā Belgīs Matrona[4] et Sēquana dīvidit.

Hōrum omnium fortissimī sunt Belgae, propterea quod ā cultū atque hūmānitāte Prōvinciae longissimē absunt, minimēque saepe mercātōrēs ad eōs veniunt atque ea quae ad effēminandōs animōs pertinent important. Proximī sunt Germānīs quī trāns Rhēnum incolunt, quibuscum semper bellum gerunt. Quā dē causā Helvētiī quoque reliquōs Gallōs virtūte superant, quod ferē cotīdiānīs proeliīs cum Germānīs contendunt, cum[5] aut suīs$_{5}$ fīnibus$_{6}$ eōs prohibent aut ipsī in eōrum[6] fīnibus bellum gerunt.

Eōrum ūna pars, quam Gallī obtinent, initium capit ā flūmine Rhodanō; continētur Garunnā flūmine, Ōceanō, fīnibus Belgārum; attingit etiam ab[7] Sēquanīs et Helvētiīs flūmen[8] Rhēnum; vergit ad septentriōnēs. Belgae ab extrēmīs Galliae fīnibus oriuntur, pertinent ad īnferiōrem partem flūminis Rhēnī, spectant in septentriōnēs et orientem sōlem. Aquītānia ā Garunnā flūmine ad Pyrēnaeōs montēs et eam partem Ōceanī quae est ad$_{7}$ Hispāniam pertinet; spectat inter occāsum sōlis et septentriōnēs.

CASSETTE

This reading is recorded on Cassette 3, Side A.

1 *in their own language*
2 supply **linguā**
3 *from one another*
4 *Garonne, Marne, Seine*
5 conjunction
6 i.e., **Germānōrum**
7 *on the side of;* literally, *from* (*the direction of*)
8 accusative

NOTES:

The **Belgae** are the ancestors of the modern Belgians.

Fairly constant use of a map is critical for students' to best understand the geographical references here and throughout the following lessons. Students should be able to identify all the places named in each lesson.

Southern France is still known as *Provence*.

Some historians think that lines 13-19 were not written by Caesar, but added later.

---

1 *as a whole,* i.e., *Greater Gaul. All Gaul* would be **omnis Gallia**
2 *is divided* (predicate adjective)
3 supply **partem**
4 Caesar here limits the name *Gauls* to the natives of the central part, and this is the sense in which he usually employs the term.
5 Note the emphasis on **suīs** and **eōrum.**
6 ablative of separation
7 *near* what part of the Spanish coast?

QUESTIONS

1. Why were the Helvetians brave?
2. What were three reasons for the bravery of the Belgians?
3. Find the three divisions of Gaul on the map (pp. 228–229) and indicate their boundaries.

ADDITIONAL QUESTIONS
Who are the three major groups that live in Gaul? What geographical features separate one group from the other?

WORKBOOK
Assign Interest Questions 1-5 to review the content of the reading from this lesson.

Consisting of three tiers of arcades, the Pont du Gard in Nîmes, France, is a fine example of a Roman aqueduct. It was built in 19 B.C. over a deep gorge to carry water from a fresh-water source about 15 miles from the city.

Wayne Rowe

NOTE
If students have difficulty recalling the comparatives and superlatives, refer them to Lesson VIII or the Appendix.

Grammar

1. Give the positive of **fortissimus, longissimē**; the comparative of **minimē, saepe**; the superlative of **īnferior, saepe.**
2. Review the ablative of respect in Lesson VII.

ANSWERS
1. Reliquī Gallī ā Belgīs virtūte superātī sunt. 2. Quibus rēbus Gallī inter sē differēbant?

TRANSLATION

1. The rest of the Gauls were surpassed by the Belgians in courage.
2. In what respects (things) did the Gauls differ from one another?

Vocabulary

NOTE
The word for *east* is the present participle from **orior**, *rising*.

NOTE
The word for *north* literally means 7 plow-oxen, from the 7 stars of the constellation Great Bear, or Big Dipper.

Nouns

centuriō, -ōnis, *m. centurion*	
cultus, -ūs, *m. way of living, civilization*	(cult, occult)
īnstitūtum, -ī, *n. custom*	(institute, institution)
oriēns, -entis, *m. east*	(orient, Oriental)
septentriōnēs, -um, *m. pl. north*	(septentrion, septentrional)

Adjective

cotīdiānus, -a, -um, *daily*	(quotidian)

Verbs

effēminō, 1, *weaken*	(effeminacy, effeminate)
incolō, -ere, incoluī, —, *inhabit, live*	
vergo, -ere, —, —, *slope, lie*	(diverge, verge)

Adverbs

ferē, *almost*
propterea, *on this account*

Conjunction

propterea quod, *because*

Review: **differō, initium, mercātor, occāsus, orior, saepe, sōl.**

Foreign Names

Add English endings to Latin proper nouns wherever possible, as in *Belgians, Aquitanians, Celts.* If you keep the Latin form, use the nominative case and pronounce the word as in English but keep the Latin accent. Always give the modern French forms of all Latin names of rivers, mountains, and lakes in Gaul. This will make your translation much smoother.

Word Studies

You may see the extent to which Spanish is like Latin from the following translation of the beginning and end of the first chapter of the *Gallic War:*

La Galia entera está dividida en tres partes, de las cuales los belgas habitan una, otra los aquitanos, y la tercera los que se llaman celtas en su lengua, galos en la nuestra. Todos estos difieren entre sí en cuanto a lengua, instituciones y leyes. . . . Aquitania se extiende desde el río Garona hasta los montes Pirineos y aquella parte del océano que está cerca de España; mira hacia el ocaso y hacia el septentrión.

Explain *culture, differential, effeminate, humanities, mercantile, occident, verge.*

Ronald Sheridan/Ancient Art & Architecture Collection

Maison Carrée. Throughout the Roman provinces smaller temples were found in the cities. This temple is one of the best preserved examples that has come down to us. It is located in Nîmes. An inscription says it was dedicated to Gaius and Lucius Caesar who were adopted sons of Augustus.

LESSON OBJECTIVES
To review the conjugation of **fiō**;
To review the gerundive with **ad**

LESSON LI

An Entire Nation Emigrates

I, 2

Apud Helvētiōs longē nōbilissimus et ditissimus fuit Orgetorīx. Is, M. Messālā M. Pīsōne cōnsulibus,[1] rēgnī cupiditāte inductus coniūrātiōnem nōbilitātis fēcit, et cīvibus persuāsit ut dē fīnibus suīs cum omnibus cōpiīs exīrent.

Id$_1$ facilius eīs persuāsit, quod undique locī nātūrā Helvētiī continentur: ūnā[2] ex parte flūmine Rhēnō lātissimō atque altissimō, quī agrum Helvētium ā Germānīs dīvidit; alterā ex parte monte[3] Iūrā altissimō, quī est inter Sēquanōs et Helvētiōs, tertiā, lacū Lemannō et flūmine Rhodanō, qui prōvinciam nostram ab Helvētiīs dīvidit.

Hīs rēbus fīēbat[4] ut et minus lātē vagārentur et minus facile fīnitimīs bellum īnferre possent; quā dē causā hominēs bellandī$_2$ cupidī magnō dolōre afficiēbantur. Prō[5] multitūdine autem hominum et prō glōriā bellī atque fortitudinis angustōs sē fīnēs habēre arbitrābantur, quī in longitūdinem mīlia passuum CCXL, in lātitūdinem CLXXX patēbant.

3. Hīs rēbus adductī et auctōritāte Orgetorīgis permōtī cōnstituērunt ea quae ad proficīscendum pertinērent comparāre iumentorum et carrōrum quam maximum numerum coemere, sementes quam maximes facere, ut in itinere cōpia frūmentī suppeteret, cum proximīs cīvitātibus pācem et amīcitiam cōnfirmāre. Ad eās rēs cōnficiendās biennium sibi satis esse existīmārērunt; in[6] tertium annum profectiōnem lēge cōnfirmant.

Ad eās rēs cōnficiendās Orgetorīx dēligitur. Is sibi lēgātiōnem ad cīvitātēs suscēpit. In eō itinere persuādet Casticō Sēquanō ut rēgnum in cīvitāte suā occupāret, quod pater ante habuerat; itemque Dumnorīgī Haeduō, frātrī Dīviciācī, quī[7] eō tempore prīncipātum in cīvitāte obtinēbat ac maximē plebī acceptus erat, ut idem cōnārētur persuādet, eīque fīliam suam in mātrimōnium dat. Dīxit sē ipsum suae cīvitātis imperium obtentūrum esse.

[1] 61 B.C.
[2] *on one side*
[3] *mountain range*
[4] *it happened*
[5] *in proportion to*
[6] *for*
[7] Dumnorix

NOTES:
Remind students that **persuādeō** is one of the special verbs that takes the dative; also have students recognize the indirect command construction.

Remind students that when a word is not in its usual position, it is for emphasis, in this case **ūnā** precedes the preposition **ex**.

Point out that **fīnitimīs** is dative after compound verbs (**inferre**).

The verb **pertinērent** is subjunctive by attraction, but should be translated as if indicative.

You may want to review sequence of tenses throughout this paragraph.

$_1$ direct object of **persuāsit**
$_2$ gerund depending on **cupidī**

Erich Lessing/Art Resource, NY

It is said that an "army travels on its stomach." The same can be said for a whole community. The Helvetians sowed grain and then harvested it for two years before beginning their great journey.

QUESTIONS

1. Who was Orgetorix?
2. With whom did Orgetorix conspire?
3. Why did the Helvetians want to migrate?
4. How did the Helvetians prepare for migration?

ADDITIONAL QUESTIONS
What was the geography of Helvetia like? Why were the Helvetians so discontented? How long did they take to prepare to migrate? What happened to the daughter of Orgetorix?

Grammar

1. Review the conjugation of **fīō** in Lesson XXIV.
2. Review the gerundive with **ad** in Lesson XXIII.

WORKBOOK
Assign Interest Questions 6-10 to review the content of the reading from this lesson.

TRANSLATION

1. An embassy was sent to other states for the purpose of encouraging their departure.
2. The Helvetians were always ready to carry on war with those who inhabited that part of Gaul.

ANSWERS
1. Ad profectiōnem cōnfirmandam lēgātiō ad aliās cīvitātēs missa est. 2. Helvētiī ad bellum gerendum cum eīs quī illam partem Galliae incoluērunt semper parātī erant.

S. Fiore/SuperStock, Inc.

In Orange, France, you can still see the well-preserved Roman theater. By 121 B.C., the Romans had established Transalpine Gaul as the first Roman province. Even far from home, the Romans expected to retain their important forms of entertainment, such as drama, dance, and music.

Vocabulary

Nouns

coniūrātiō, -ōnis, *f. conspiracy*

dolor, -ōris, *m. grief, pain, suffering* (dolor, dolorous)

lātitūdō, -dinis, *f. width* (latitude, latitudinarian)

lēgātiō, -ōnis, *f. embassy* (delegation, legation)

nōbilitās, -tātis, *f. nobility* (noble)

prīncipātus, -ūs, *m. first place, leadership* (principate)

profectiō, -ōnis, *f. departure*

Adjective

cupidus, -a, -um, *desirous* (Cupid, cupidity)

Verbs

dīvidō, -ere, dīvīsī, dīvīsus, *divide* (division, divisive)

emō, -ere, ēmī, emptus, *take, buy*

pateō, -ēre, patuī, —, *stand open, extend* (patent)

pertineō, -ēre, -tinuī, -tentūrus, *extend (to), pertain to* (pertinence, pertinent)

vagor, 1, *wander* (vagabond, vague)

Adverb

item, *also* (itemization, itemize)

Idioms: **inter sē, quā dē causā.**

Review: **angustus, arbitror, cōnor, dēligō, persuādeō, proficīscor, undique.**

Word Studies

Item was once used in English as in Latin, to mean "also" in a list: "2 lbs. sugar, item 3 lbs. flour," etc. Then it came to be used wrongly for every article in the list, including the first. *Item* occurs fourteen times in George Washington's will.

Explain *biennial, cupidity, extravagant, itemize, latitude, patent, principate, vagabond, vagary, vagrant.*

LESSON OBJECTIVES
To review indicative clauses with **ubi** and **postquam**; To review subjunctive clauses with **cum**

LESSON LII
A Mysterious Death and a Bonfire

I, 4

[1] *in accordance with*
[2] *in*
[3] *if condemned*
[4] *household* (including all his slaves)
[5] *about*
[6] *nevertheless* (with **nihilō**)
[7] *as allies* (apposition)
[8] *from home*
[9] *where*
[10] *could be drawn*

NOTES:
The ablative of accordance is used with a few words, most commonly *custom*, to express *in accordance with*.

Point out that **ad** is an adverb when used with numerals.

Point out the two meanings of **cogō**: in line 2, it is best translated *compel*, whereas in line 5, *collected* is better.

The name of the Boii is preserved in the word Bohemia.

The Rhone valley for a distance of about 17 miles narrows down to a steep ravine with 1000´ cliffs known as "Mill Race Gorge" (Pas de l'Ecluse). One of the largest dams in Europe has been built there. The railway passes under the mountain through a tunnel over 2 miles long that connects Switzerland and France.

Have students identify **ut... possent** as a result clause.

Ea rēs est Helvētiīs ēnūntiāta. Mōribus[1] suīs Orgetorīgem ex[2] vinculīs causam dīcere coēgērunt. Eum damnātum[3] oportēbat ignī cremārī.

Diē cōnstitūtā Orgetorīx ad iūdicium omnem suam familiam,[4] ad[5] hominum mīlia decem, undique coēgit et omnēs clientēs suōs, quōrum magnum numerum habēbat, eōdem condūxit; per eōs nē causam dīceret sē ēripuit.

Cum cīvitās ob eam rem incitāta armīs iūs suum exsequī cōnārētur, multitūdinemque hominum ex agrīs magistrātūs cōgerent, Orgetorīx mortuus est. Helvētiī autem arbitrantur ipsum sē interfēcisse.

5. Post eius mortem nihilō minus[6] Helvētiī id quod cōnstituerant facere cōnantur, ut$_1$ ē fīnibus suīs exeant. Ubi iam sē ad eam rem parātōs esse arbitrātī sunt, oppida sua omnia, numerō ad duodecim, vīcōs ad quadringentōs, reliqua prīvāta aedificia incendunt. Frūmentum omne, praeter quod sēcum portātūrī erant, combūrunt, ut, domum reditūs spē sublātā, parātiōrēs ad omnia perīcula subeunda essent.

Persuādent Rauracīs et Tulingīs et Latobrīgīs fīnitimīs utī, oppidīs suīs vīcīsque exustīs, ūnā cum eīs proficīscantur. Boiōs, quī trāns Rhēnum incoluerant et in agrum Nōricum trānsierant Nōreiamque oppugnārant, ad sē sociōs[7] recipiunt.

6. Erant omnīnō itinera duo quibus domō[8] exīre possent: ūnum per Sēquanōs, angustum et difficile, inter montem Iūram et flūmen Rhodanum, qua[9] vix singulī carrī dūcerentur;[10] mōns autem altissimus impendēbat, ut facile perparcieōs prohibēre possent; alterum$_2$ per prōvinciam nostram, multō facilius atque expedītius propterea quod inter fīnēs Helvētiōrum et

$_1$ Clause is in apposition with **id**.
$_2$ Supply **iter**.

Alinari/Art Resource, NY

Imagine the difficulty in transporting food, equipment, and other basic necessities through the mountains in all kinds of weather in carts such as these.

Allobrogum quī nuper pacātīerant Rhodanus fluit, isque nōn nūllīs[3] locīs vadō trānsītur. Extrēmum oppidum Allobrogum est,[4] proximumque Helvētiōrum fīnibus, Genua.

Ex eō oppidō pōns ad Helvētiōs pertinet.[5] Allobrogibus sēsē vel persuāsūrōs exīstimābant[11] vel vī coāctūrōs ut per suōs fīnēs eōs īre paterentur. Omnibus rēbus ad profectiōnem comparātīs, diem dīcunt quā diē ad rīpam Rhodanī omnēs conveniant.[6] Is diēs erat a. d. V. Kal. Apr.,[7] L. Pīsōne A. Gabīniō cōnsulibus.[12]

QUESTIONS

1. Why was Orgetorix tried?
2. In what way did he escape?
3. How, apparently, did he die?
4. What was the effect of his death on the Helvetians?
5. What choice did the Helvetians have in leaving their country?

---

3 two negatives made an affirmative: *several,* supply **in**
4 in translating, put **est** after **fīnibus**
5 Parts of this bridge have been found.
6 *on which all are to assemble;* Note the variation in the gender of **diēs.**
7 **Ante diem quīntum Kalendās Aprīlēs,** *the fifth day before the kalends* (*first*) *of April;* i.e., *March 28.*

NOTE
The spelling generally found is **Genava** but all the manuscripts have **Genua**, which is now accepted as the original form.

11 i.e., the Helvetians
12 58 B.C.

SUGGESTION
You might want to review how the Romans set dates with students.

NOTE
Tell students that Piso, a cruel and corrupt politician, was the father of Calpurnia, Caesar's last wife, to whom Caesar had been married for a year before this. Piso had obtained the consulship through Caesar's influence. Gabinius owed his position to Pompey. With the election of these two men, the political activity and maneuvering of the First Triumvirate (formed in 60 B.C.) becomes clearer.

ADDITIONAL QUESTIONS
How would Orgetorix have been punished if found guilty? What did the Helvetians do before leaving their country? Why? What other groups went with them? Which route did they plan to take?

NOTĀ·BENE

Utī is the same as ut.

WORKBOOK

Assign Interest Questions 11-15 to review the content of the reading from this lesson.

ANSWERS

1. Postquam vīdērunt sē ponte trānsīre posse, impulsī sunt ut cum Helvētiīs īrent. 2. Cum hoc nūntiātum esset, Helvētiī suspicātī sunt eum omnēs suōs clientēs conductūrum esse. 3. Ubi ad aedificia incendenda parātī fuērunt, fīnitimīs suīs persuāsērunt ut/utī sēcum proficīscerentur.

Grammar

1. Review indicative clauses with **ubi** and **postquam** in Lesson XVI.
2. Review subjunctive clauses with **cum** in Lesson XVI and XXXII.

TRANSLATION

1. After they saw that they could cross by a bridge, they were impelled to go with the Helvetians.
2. When this had been reported, the Helvetians suspected that he would bring together all his clients.
3. When[8] they were ready to burn their buildings, they persuaded their neighbors to set out with them.

Depiction of a Gallo-Roman officer. After defeat of the Romans, native peoples such as the Gauls and Helvetians gradually adopted many Roman practices, including their use of armor.

Photo Bulloz

8 Use **ubi**.

Vocabulary

Nouns

iūdicium, -cī, *n. trial, investigation*	(judicial, judicious)
vīcus, -ī, *m. village*	(vicinal, vicinity)
vinculum, -ī, *n. bond, chain*	(vinculum)

Adjectives

expedītus, -a, -um, *unencumbered, easy*	(expedition)
prīvātus, -a, -um, *private*	(deprivation)

Verbs

exsequor, exsequi, exsecūtus, *follow up, enforce*	(executor, executrix)
fluō, -ere, flūxī, flūxus, *flow*	(fluid, flux)
recipiō, -ere, recēpī, receptus, *take back, receive*	(receptacle, receptor)
trānseō, -īre, -iī, -itūrus, *cross, pass*	(transition, transitive)

Adverbs

eōdem, *to the same place*
omnīnō, *altogether, in all*
quā, *where*
ūnā, *along*

Preposition

praeter (+acc.), *besides, except*

Review: **aedificium, cliēns, incendō, magistrātus, suspicor, vix.**

Word Studies

Translate the legal phrase **a vinculo matrimonii** which is used in English in divorce cases. Learn the phrase: **sic transit gloria mundi.**

Explain *flux, incendiary, recipient, riparian, transient, transitory.*

LESSON OBJECTIVES

To review indirect statements and to learn about subordinate clauses in indirect discourse

LESSON LIII

Caesar Says: "You Shall Not Pass"

I, 7

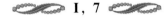

Caesarī cum id nūntiātum esset, eōs per prōvinciam nostram iter facere cōnārī, mātūrat ab urbe[1] proficīscī et quam maximīs potest itineribus[1] in Galliam ulteriōrem[2] contendit et ad[2] Genuam pervenit. Prōvinciae tōtī quam maximum potest mīlitum numerum imperat[3] (erat omnīnō in Galliā ulteriōre legiō ūna[3]), pontem quī erat ad Genuam iubet rescindī.

Ubi dē eius adventū Helvētiī certiōrēs factī sunt,[4] lēgātōs ad eum mittunt nōbilissimōs cīvitātis quī dīcerent, sibī esse in animō sine ullōmaleficiō iter per Prōvinciam facere. Caesar lēgātīs respondit diem[5] sē ad dēlīberandum sūmptūrum.

8. Intereā ab lacū Lemannō, quī in flūmen Rhodanum īnfluit, ad montem Iūram, quī fīnēs Sēquanōrum ab Helvētiīs dīvidit, mīlia passuum XVIII mūrum[6] in altitūdinem pedum XVI fossamque[6] perdūcit. Eō opere perfectō, praesidia dispōnit,[7] castella mūnit, utī eōs trānsīre cōnantēs prohibēre possit.

Ubi ea diēs quam cōnstituerat cum lēgātīs vēnit, et lēgātī ad eum revertērunt, negat sē mōre et exemplō populī Rōmānī posse iter[8] ūllī per Prōvinciam dare; et, sī vim facere[9] cōnentur, sē eōs prohibitūrum ostendit. Eā spē dēiectī,[10] aliī Helvētiōrum nāvibus ratibusque complūribus, aliī vadīs Rhodanī, quā minima altitūdō flūminis erat, nōn numquam interdiū,[11] saepius noctū perrumpere cōnātī sunt. Sed operis mūnītiōne et mīlitum concursū et tēlīs repulsī, hōc cōnātū dēstitērunt.

[1] *by as rapid marches as possible*
[2] *near*
[3] *he levied upon* (with dative and accusative)
[4] *were informed*
[5] *time;* clearly more than a single day
[6] *rampart* (of earth) *and a trench*
[7] *he stations at intervals*
[8] (*right of*) *way*
[9] *use force*
[10] *disappointed in this hope*
[11] *in the daytime*

NOTES:

Plutarch says that Caesar covered the distance in 7 days, an average of 90 miles a day. Of course, he traveled on horseback and had no army with him.

Today the banks of the Rhone are high and steep for the greater part of that distance, so Napoleon III thought that Caesar built the rampart at only a few points; but recent excavations indicate that Caesar strengthened the natural defenses most of the way, especially where the river could be forded.

Point out that **mōre** is another example of the ablative of accordance.

Point out that **eā spē** is an example of the ablative of separation.

---

[1] *The* city is always Rome.
[2] This term would ordinarily mean all of Gaul except the Roman Province. Here it includes the Province.
[3] This one was the famous Tenth, soon to become Caesar's favorite.

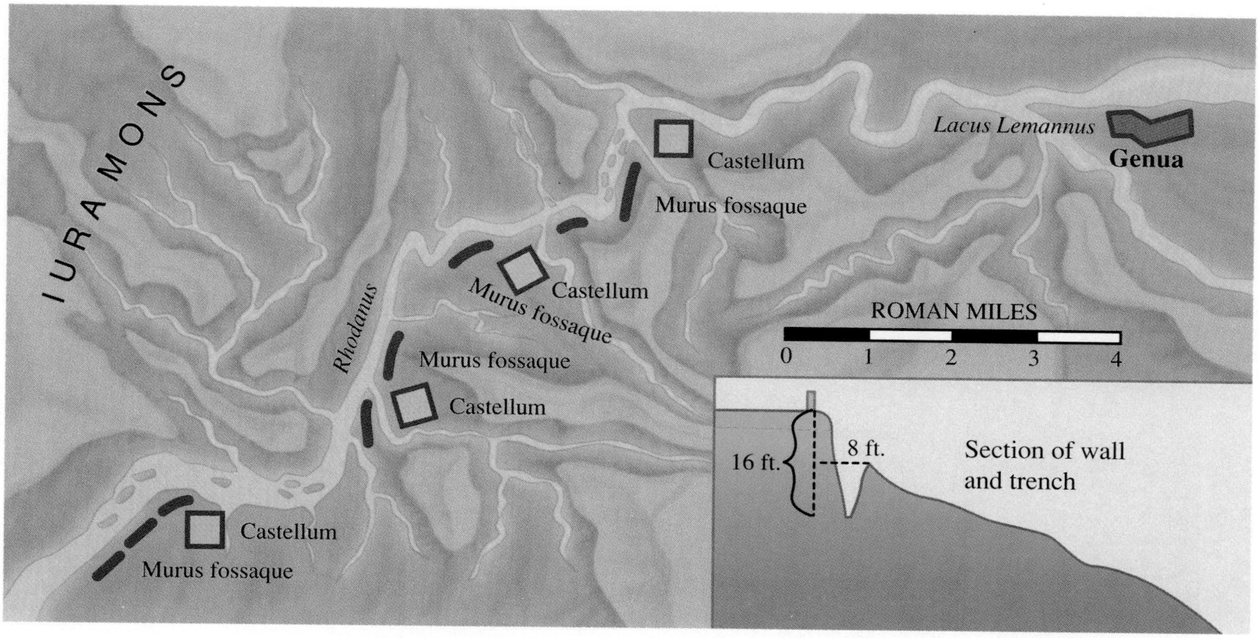

PLAN OF CAESAR'S FORTIFICATIONS ON THE RHONE RIVER

QUESTIONS

1. Where was Caesar when he heard about the Helvetians?
2. What was Caesar's answer and what did he do?
3. What did the Helvetians ask him to let them do?

Grammar

Review indirect statements in Lesson VI. A subordinate clause in indirect discourse is in the subjunctive, following the sequence of tenses.

Dīxit lēgātōs quī ad sē pervēnissent diūtissime exspectavisse.	*He said that the envoys who had come to him had waited for a very long time.*

TRANSLATION

1. Caesar thought that the Helvetians would not cross the river.
2. He said that, if they tried to cross, he would prevent them by defenses.
3. When they were not able to persuade Caesar, they said that they would send envoys to the Haeduans.

ADDITIONAL QUESTIONS
What happened to the bridge near Geneva? Who made the request of Caesar? What was the reaction of the Helvetians? What did some of them try to do?

SUGGESTION
Ask students why they think that Caesar was unwilling to have the Helvetians pass through. The answer is in the next lesson (they were very warlike people and Caesar wanted to protect his part of the empire).

WORKBOOK
Assign Interest Questions 16-20 to review the content of the reading from this lesson.

ANSWERS
1. Caesar arbitrātus est Helvētiōs flūmen nōn trānsitūrōs esse. 2. Dīxit sē, sī trānsīre cōnārentur, eōs mūnītiōnibus prohibitūrum esse. 3. Cum Caesarī persuādēre nōn possent, dīxērunt sē lēgātōs ad Haeduōs missūrōs esse.

SuperStock, Inc.

Modern-day Geneva still carries memories of ancient times, when Caesar aligned his troops and forbade the Helvetians to cross. Founded by the Allobroges, a Celtic tribe, they settled at the tip of Lake Geneva where it was convenient to cross over the Rhone.

Vocabulary

Nouns

altitūdō, -dinis, *f. height, depth*	(altitude, altitudinal)
castellum, -ī, *n. fort*	(castellated, castle)
cornū, -ūs, *n. horn, wing (of an army)*	(cornet, cornucopia)
mūnītiō, -ōnis, *f. fortification*	(ammunition, munition)
tēlum, -ī, *n. weapon*	
vadum, -ī, *n. ford*	

Verbs

dēsum, deesse, dēfuī, dēfutūrus, *be lacking*	
mātūrō, 1, *hasten*	(maturation, maturity)
rescindō, -ere, rescidī, rescissus, *cut down*	(rescind)
sūmō, -ere, sūmpsī, sūmptus, *take, assume*	(resume, sumptuous)

Adverb

nōn numquam, *sometimes*

Idioms: **alter . . . alter, certiōrem faciō, certior fīō, quam** with superlative.

Review: **complūrēs, dēsistō, fossa, intereā, negō, noctū, pōns, spēs.**

Word Studies

From what Latin words are the following derived: **altitūdō, castellum, mūnītiō, noctū, quā?**

Explain *legionary, munitions, renegade.*

LESSON OBJECTIVE
To review **cum** clauses

LESSON LIV

The Harder Way

I, 9

Relinquēbātur ūna per Sēquanōs via, quā, Sēquanīs[1] invītīs, propter angustiās īre nōn poterant. Hīs cum suā sponte persuādēre nōn possent, lēgātōs ad Dumnorīgem Haeduum mittunt, ut hic ā Sēquanīs impetrāret. Dumnorīx grātiā et dōnīs apud Sēquanōs plūrimum poterat et Helvētiīs erat amīcus, quod ex eā cīvitāte Orgetorīgis fīliam in mātrimōnium dūxerat; et cupiditāte rēgnī adductus novīs rēbus[2] studēbat et quam plūrimās cīvitātēs suō beneficiō habēre obstrictās[1] volēbat. Itaque rem suscipit et ā Sēquanīs impetrat ut per fīnēs suōs Helvētiōs īre patiantur, obsidēsque utī inter sē dent perficit:[3] Sēquanī obsidēs dant[4] nē itinere Helvētiōs prohibeant; Helvētiī, ut sine iniūriā trānseant.

10. Caesarī renūntiātur Helvētiīs esse in animō[2] per agrum Sēquanōrum et Haeduōrum iter in Santonōrum fīnēs facere, quī nōn longē ā Tolōsātium fīnibus absunt, quae cīvitās est in Prōvinciā. Caesar intellegēbat magnō cum perīculō Prōvinciae[3] futūrum esse ut hominēs bellicōsī, populī Rōmānī inimīcī, haec loca patentia maximēque frūmentāria occupārent.[4]

Ob eās causās eī mūnītiōnī quam fēcerat T. Labiēnum lēgātum praefēcit. Ipse in Italiam magnīs itineribus contendit duāsque ibi legiōnēs cōnscrībit, et trēs quae circum Aquileiam hiemābant ex hībernīs ēdūcit, et proximō itinere in ulteriōrem Galliam per Alpēs cum hīs quīnque legiōnibus īre contendit.

Summary of the End of Chapter 10. The Ceutrones try to block Caesar's way but are defeated. From Ocelum (near modern Turin) he proceeds to the Province, arriving on the seventh day, then to the Allobroges and Segusiavi.

---

[1] *bound*
[2] *that the Helvetians have in mind*
[3] *to the Province*
[4] *for men . . . to seize*

NOTES:
Elicit that **novīs rēbus** in line 7 is dative after special verbs (**studeō**).

Point out that today's politicians distribute favors in a similar way.

Elicit that **itinere** is ablative of separation.

Point out that **Helvētiīs** is dative of possession. You may want to refer students to the Appendix or simply tell them that the possessor of something may be expressed by the dative with a form of **sum**. This construction will be covered in Lesson LV.

Elicit that **mūnītiōnī** is dative after a compound verb.

Tell students that Titus Labienus was one of the bravest and most trusted of Caesar's staff officers, although later, during the Civil War, he fought against Caesar.

SUGGESTION
Have students summarize, in general terms, what has happened thus far.

[1] Translate with *if*.
[2] In politics "new things" are a revolution.
[3] The English order would be **perficit utī dent obsidēs inter sē.**
[4] i.e., *they guarantee*

G. I. Garvey/Ancient Art & Architecture Collection

The Arch of Tiberius and Germanicus at Saintes. The name of the Santoni, mentioned in the text in this lesson, is preserved in the name of the city (Saintes) where this arch is found.

QUESTIONS

1. Why did Dumnorix help the Helvetians?
2. Why did Caesar object to the Helvetians' plan?
3. Why did he go to Italy at this critical moment?
4. Of what fortifications did Labienus have charge during Caesar's absence?

ADDITIONAL QUESTIONS
What was the problem about going by way of the Sequanians? Was Dumnorix successful in his request? What was exchanged between the Sequanians and the Helvetians? Why?

WORKBOOK
Assign Interest Questions 21-25 to review the content of the reading from this lesson.

Grammar

Review **cum** clauses in Lessons XVI and XXXII.

TRANSLATION

1. What will you do since you cannot influence him by kindness?
2. Although they sent envoys to him, they did not obtain their request.
3. Since the Gauls were eager for a revolution, Caesar placed a general in charge of the legions.

ANSWERS
1. Quid faciētis, cum eum beneficiō addūcere nōn possītis? 2. Cum lēgātōs ad eum mīsissent, nōn impetrāvērunt. 3. Cum Gallī novīs rēbus studērent, Caesar ducem/lēgātum legiōnibus praefēcit.

Developing "Word Sense"

Did you understand the idiom **plurimum poterat** (*"was very powerful"*) in the third sentence of the reading? Here are some more sentences to extend your mastery of this use of the accusative as an adverb with **possum.** Translate:

ANSWERS
In all human affairs, custom is powerful. 2. The fear of death is powerful; more powerful still is the love of glory. 3. Diviciacus was very influential because of his popularity; Dumnorix had very little power because of his youth. 4. How powerful Lady Luck is in the war! 5. The Helvetians were not powerful in cavalry (warfare). 6. Caesar will realize what the undefeated Germans can (do), i.e., how strong they are.

1. In omnibus rēbus hūmānīs cōnsuētūdō multum potest.
2. Multum terror mortis potest, plūs tamen cupiditās glōriae.
3. Dīviciācus grātiā plūrimum poterat, Dumnorīx propter adulēscentiam minimum poterat.
4. Quantum in bellō Fortūna potest!
5. Helvētiī equitātū nihil poterant.
6. Caesar intelleget quid invictī Germānī possint.

Modern lives next to ancient throughout the former Roman empire. These ruins of a Roman arena are in Verona, in northern Italy.

Alan Smith/Tony Stone Images

Vocabulary

Nouns

dōnum, -ī, *n. gift*	(donation, donative)
grātia, -ae, *f. gratitude, grace, favor, influence*	(gratis, ingratiate)
hīberna, -ōrum, *n. pl. winter quarters*	(hibernal, hibernate)

Adjectives

invītus, -a, -um, *unwilling*

Verbs

cōnscrībō, -ere, -scrīpsī, -scrīptus, *write, enlist*	(conscribe, conscription)
hiemō, 1, *spend the winter*	
impetrō, 1, *gain (one's request)*	
patior, patī, passus, *permit*	(passive, patient)
praeficiō, -ere, -fēcī, -fectus, *put in charge of*	(prefect)

Adverbs

plērumque, *usually*	
sponte (with **suā**), *of his/her/their own accord, by his/her/their own influence, voluntarily*	(spontaneity, spontaneous)

Preposition

apud (+acc.), *among, at the house of, near, with*

Idioms: **alicui esse in animō, magnum iter, multum (plūs, plūrimum) posse, novae rēs.**

Word Studies

Things are not always what they seem: *invite* has no connection with **invītus,** nor *Hibernian* with **hīberna.**

From what Latin words are the following derived: **angustiae, cōnscrībō, hīberna, hiemō?**

Explain *conscription, hibernate, impatient, prefect, spontaneous.*

LESSON OBJECTIVES
To learn the dative of possession; To learn the subjunctive in anticipatory clauses

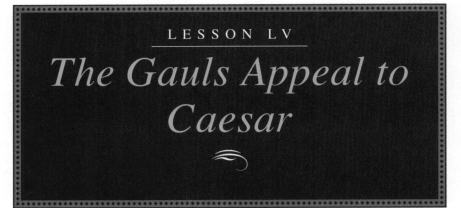

LESSON LV
The Gauls Appeal to Caesar

NOTE
Remind students that the **angustiās** is a reference to the Mill Race Gorge mentioned earlier.

I, 11

Helvētiī iam per angustiās et fīnēs Sēquanōrum suās cōpiās trādūxerant et in Haeduōrum fīnēs pervēnerant eōrumque agrōs populābantur. Haeduī, cum sē suaque[1] ab eīs dēfendere nōn possent, lēgātōs ad Caesarem mīsērunt ut rogārent auxilium. Eōdem tempore Ambarrī, cōnsanguineī Haeduōrum, Caesarem certiōrem faciunt sēsē, vāstātīs agrīs, nōn facile ab oppidīs vim hostium prohibēre posse. Item Allobrogēs, quī trāns Rhodanum vīcōs possessiōnēsque habēbant, fugā sē ad Caesarem recipiunt et dēmōnstrant sibi praeter agrī solum[2] nihil esse reliquī. Quibus rēbus adductus Caesar nōn exspectandum esse sibi statuit dum, omnibus fortūnīs sociōrum cōnsūmptīs, in Santonōs Helvētiī pervenīrent.

12. Flūmen est Arar, quod per fīnēs Haeduōrum et Sēquanōrum in Rhodanum īnfluit incredibilī lenitālē. Id Helvētiī ratibus ac nāvibus iūnctīs trānsībant. Per explōrātōrēs Caesar certior factus est trēs iam partēs cōpiārum Helvētiōs id flūmen trādūxisse, quārtam vērō partem citrā[3] flūmen Ararim[4] reliquam esse. Itaque dē[5] tertiā vigiliā cum legiōnibus tribus ē castrīs profectus, ad eam partem pervēnit quae nōndum flūmen trānsierat.

Eōs impedītōs aggressus[6] magnam partem eōrum concīdit; reliquī sē fugae mandārunt[7] atque in[8] proximās silvās abdidērunt. Is pāgus appellābātur Tigurīnus; nam omnis cīvitās Helvētia in quattuor partēs vel pāgōs dīvīsa est. Hic pāgus ūnus, cum domō[9] exīsset, patrum nostrōrum memoriā[10] L. Cassium cōnsulem interfēcerat et eius exercitum sub iugum mīserat.[11]

Ita sīve cāsū sīve cōnsiliō deōrum immortālium, ea pars cīvitātis Helvētiae quae īnsignem calamitātem populō Rōmānō intulerat, prīnceps[12] poenam dedit. Quā in rē Caesar nōn sōlum pūblicās sed etiam prīvātās iniūriās ultus est; nam Tigurīnī L. Pīsōnem lēgātum, avum Caesaris socerī,[13] eōdem proeliō quō Cassium interfēcerant.

13. Hōc proeliō factō, reliquās cōpiās[1] Helvētiōrum ut cōnsequī posset, pontem in Ararī facit atque ita exercitum trādūcit. Helvētiī repentīnō eius

[1] object of **cōnsequī**

[1] *their possessions*
[2] *soil*
[3] *on this side* i.e., Caesar's side
[4] accusative
[5] *during*
[6] *attacking*
[7] **mandā(vē)runt**
[8] *in*
[9] *from home*
[10] *within the memory of*
[11] *had sent under the yoke,* equivalent to unconditional surrender
[12] *(was the) first (to)*
[13] *father-in-law*

NOTES:
Elicit the genitive of the whole construction with **nihil... reliquī**.

Tell students that Caesar owed much of his success to his efficient intelligence gathering system (**explōrātōrēs**).

Verify that students can identify the **Arar** as the Saône River. Have them locate the areas mentioned on a map.

Remind students that the night was divided into 4 watches, which varied in length with the time of the year.

Have students identify uses of the ablative: **domō**, *place from which*; **memoriā**, *time when.*

SuperStock, Inc.

The Saône River, which in ancient times flowed through the lands of the Haeduans and the Sequanians, today crosses the region where burgundy wine is produced, joining with the Rhone at Lyon.

adventū commōtī, cum id quod ipsī diēbus XX aegerrimē cōnfēcerant, ut[2] flūmen trānsīrent, illum ūnō diē fēcisse intellegerent, lēgātōs ad eum mittunt.

NOTE
The surrender consisted of two spears stuck in the ground and a third tied across the top. The defeated army was forced to march through this arch of spears without arms (cf: sub-jug-ate).

QUESTIONS

1. What reasons does Caesar give for attacking the Helvetians?
2. How long did it take Caesar to cross the Saône?
3. How many cantons of the Helvetians crossed the Saône safely?
4. Which canton did Caesar defeat and why did this particularly please him?

ADDITIONAL QUESTIONS
Which groups (peoples) appealed to Caesar for help? What were the Helvetians doing? How were the Helvetians able to cross the river? What is a canton? How did Caesar and his troops cross the river?

Grammar

The Dative of Possession

The dative, with a form of **sum**, can be used to express possession. The possessor is in the dative.

Trēs līberī mihi sunt.	*I have three children.*
Carrus novus servō est.	*The slave has a new wagon.*

WORKBOOK
Assign Interest Questions 26-30 to review the content of the reading from this lesson.

[2] **ut** clause in apposition with **id**

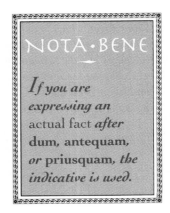

The Subjunctive in Anticipatory Clauses

NOTĀ·BENE

If you are expressing an actual fact *after* **dum, antequam,** *or* **priusquam,** *the indicative is used.*

After **dum** *(until)*, **antequam** *(before)*, and **priusquam** *(before)*, a clause that expresses an anticipated action is in the subjunctive.

Caesar exspectāvit dum murī fossaeque aedificārent.	*Caesar waited until the walls and trenches should be built.*
Priusquam trānsīrent, Caesarem rogāvērunt.	*Before they could pass through, they asked Caesar.*

ANSWERS
1. Hostibus erant multae nāvēs et hominēs. 2. Multī vīcī trāns illud flūmen Haeduīs sunt. 3. Nōlēbant exspectāre dum Caesar pervenīret. 4. Caesar contendit ut pervenīret priusquam trānsīre possent.

TRANSLATION

1. The enemy had many ships and men.
2. The Haeduans have many villages across that river.
3. They were unwilling to wait until Caesar should arrive.
4. Caesar hurried in order to arrive before they could cross.

Brian Brake/Photo Researchers

This aerial view of Timgad, Algeria, shows a typical foundation of a Roman settlement similar to those built in Gaul, Helvetia, and throughout the empire. This colony housed the Third Legion stationed at Lambaesis and contained several baths and a library.

Vocabulary

Nouns

calamitās, -tātis, *f. disaster*	(calamitous, calamity)
cōnsanguineus, -ī, *m. (blood) relative*	(consanguineous, consanguinity)
explōrātor, -ōris, *m. scout*	(exploration, exploratory)
pāgus, -ī, *m. district, canton*	(pagan, paganism)

Adjective

repentīnus, -a, -um, *sudden*

Verbs

populor, 1, *destroy*	(depopulate, population)
statuō, -ere, statuī, statūtus, *decide, determine*	(constitution, statutory)

Conjunctions

sīve (seu), *or if;* **sīve... sīve,** *whether . . . or*

vel, *or;* **vel... vel,** *either . . . or*

Idioms: **dē... vigiliā, fugae mē mandō, mē recipiō.**

Review: **abdō, iugum, nōndum.**

Word Studies

A "pagan" was really a person who lived in a *country district* (**pāgus**). During the time of the Roman Empire new things and ideas, such as Christianity, came to the country districts last of all, and so there was a time when the **pagānī** were pagans after the **urbānī** had become Christians.

From what Latin words are the following derived: **abdō, concīdō, explōrātor, īnferō, nōndum?**

Explain *calamitous, concise, consanguinity, exploratory, inferential, influence, influenza.*

LESSON OBJECTIVE
To review purpose constructions

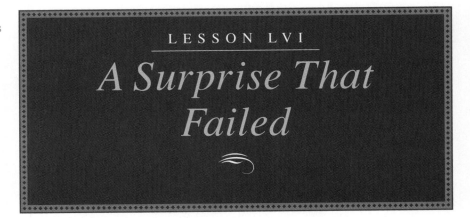

LESSON LVI
A Surprise That Failed

Summary of Chapters 13–20. After crushing the rearguard of the Helvetians at the Saône, Caesar crosses in pursuit of the main body, who now send a deputation to Caesar. The discussion fails, and the Helvetians resume their march. Caesar follows; his cavalry is defeated in a skirmish. Meanwhile his supplies give out because the Haeduans, his Gallic allies, fail to furnish grain any longer. Caesar complains to the Haeduan chiefs who are in his camp and is told secretly that Dumnorix, a rich and powerful noble, is responsible; that he has a Helvetian wife and therefore favors the Helvetians; furthermore, that Dumnorix alone is to blame for the recent defeat of the Roman cavalry, for he led the retreat in person. Caesar decides that Dumnorix must be punished but fears to offend his friend Diviciacus, chief magistrate of the Haeduans and brother of Dumnorix. He therefore urges Diviciacus himsef to punish him. Diviciacus pleads so earnestly for his brother's life that Caesar pardons him.

I, 21

Eōdem diē ab explōrātōribus certior factus hostēs sub monte cōnsēdisse mīlia passuum ab ipsīus castrīs octō, quālis esset nātūra montis et quālis in circuitū[1] ascēnsus, explōrātōrēs quī cognōscerent mīsit. Renūntiātum est ascēnsum facilem esse. Dē tertiā vigiliā T. Labiēnum lēgātum cum duābus legiōnibus et eīs ducibus[2] quī iter cognōverant, summum iugum montis ascendere iubet; suum cōnsilium ostendit. Ipse dē quārtā vigiliā eōdem itinere quō hostēs ierant ad eōs contendit, equitātumque omnem ante sē mittit. P. Cōnsidius, quī reī mīlitāris perītissimus habēbātur[3] et in exercitū L. Sullae et posteā in M. Crassī fuerat, cum explōrātōribus praemittitur.

22. Prīmā lūce, cum summus[4] mōns ā Labiēnō tenērētur et ipse ab hostium castrīs nōn longius MD passibus abesset, neque (ut posteā ex captīvīs comperit) aut ipsīus adventus aut Labiēnī cognitus esset, Cōnsidius,

NOTE
Elicit the indirect question after **quālis** construction.

[1] *on the other side;* literally, *in going around*
[2] appositive to **eīs:** (*as*) *guides*
[3] *was considered*
[4] *top of the mountain*

NOTE
Point out that **reī** is genitive after special adjectives (**peritissimus**).

NOTE
Caesar takes great pains to describe the training and experience of Considius, because his (Considius') conduct later is so bizarre.

Ronald Sheridan/Ancient Art & Architecture Collection

The Romans did battle with many tribes. In this relief, a Roman soldier fights a Celt.

equō admissō,[5] ad eum accurrit. Dīcit montem quem ab Labiēnō occupārī voluerit[1] ab hostibus tenērī; id sē ā Gallicīs armīs atque īnsignibus cognōvisse. Caesar suās cōpiās in proximum collem subdūcit, aciem īnstruit. Labiēnō imperāverat nē proelium committeret, nisi ipsīus cōpiae prope hostium castra vīsae essent, ut undique ūnō tempore in hostēs impetus fieret. Itaque Labiēnus, monte occupātō, nostrōs exspectābat proeliōque abstinēbat. Multō[6] dēnique[7] diē per explōrātōrēs Caesar cognōvit et montem ab suis tenērī et Helvētiōs castra mōvisse et Cōnsidium timōre perterritum quod[2] nōn vīdisset prō[8] vīsō sibi renūntiāvisse. Eō diē, quō intervāllō[3] cōnsuēverat, hostēs sequitur et mīlia passuum tria ab eōrum castrīs castra pōnit.

[5] *with his horse at full speed* (literally, *with horse let go*)
[6] *late in the day*
[7] *finally*
[8] *as seen*

SUGGESTION
Have students summarize, in general terms, what has happened thus far.

QUESTIONS

1. What did Caesar tell Labienus to do?
2. What did Caesar tell Considius to do?
3. What was the mistake that Considius made?
4. What was Caesar's purpose in giving these orders?

ADDITIONAL QUESTIONS
How far apart were the two enemies at the beginning? What did the scouts tell Caesar? At what time of day did Caesar make his move? Was Labienus successful? What did Caesar do after the discovery was made?

[1] The subject is Caesar.
[2] Supply **id** as antecedent.
[3] Translate as **eō intervāllō quō**; the antecedent is sometimes put in the subordinate clause.

WORKBOOK
Assign Interest Questions 31-35 to review the content of the reading from this lesson.

Grammar

Review purpose constructions in Lessons XI, XXIII, and XXVI.

ANSWERS
1. Eīs ut exspectārent dum pervenīret imperāvit. 2. Lēgātōs cōnsilī suī ostendendī causā vocāvit. 3. Rōmānī explōrātōrēs praemittere cōnsuēverant quī ubi hostēs essent cognōscerent.

TRANSLATION

1. He ordered **(imperō)** them to wait until he should arrive.
2. He summoned the generals for the sake of showing his plan.
3. The Romans were accustomed to send ahead scouts who were to learn where the enemy were.

Vocabulary

Nouns

aciēs, aciēī, *f. battle line*
equitātus, -ūs, *m. cavalry* (equitation)
ēruptiō, -iōnis, *f. attack, a bursting forth* (eruption)
īnsigne, -is, *n. ornament* (insignia)

Adjective

quālis, -e, *what kind of, what, such as* (qualify, quality)

Verbs

accurrō, -ere, accurrī, accursūrus, *run*
ascendō, -ere, ascendī, ascēnsus, *climb* (ascend, acension)
comperiō, -īre, -perī, -pertus, *find out*
cōnsīdō, -ere, -sēdī, -sessūrus, *sit down, encamp, settle* (consider, considerable)

Idioms: **castra moveō, castra pōnō, prīmā lūce, rēs mīlitāris, summus mōns.**

Review: **cōnsīdō, cōnsuēscō, perītus.**

ABSTINENCE

Word Studies

From what Latin words are the following derived: **abstineō, equitātus, īnsigne, subdūcō?**

Explain *abstinence, ascension, circuitous, insignia.*

LESSON OBJECTIVE

To learn causal clauses with **quod** and **quoniam**

LESSON LVII

The Fight Is On

I, 23

Postrīdiē eius diēī,[1] quod omnīnō bīduum supererat[2] cum exercituī frūmentum mētīrī oportēret et quod ā Bibracte, oppidō Haeduōrum longē maximō et copiōsissimō, nōn amplius milibus passuum duodeviginti aberat, reī frūmentāriae prōspiciendum[1] exīstimāvit. Itaque iter ab Helvētiīs āvertit ac Bibracte[3] īre contendit. Ea rēs per fugitīvōs L. Aemilī, decuriōnis equitum Gallōrum, hostibus nūntiātur. Helvētiī, seu quod timōre perterritōs Rōmānōs discēdere ā sē exīstimārent,[2] seu quod rē frūmentāriā interclūdī posse[3] cōnfīderent, mūtātō cōnsiliō atque itinere conversō, nostrōs ab novissimō agmine īnsequī ac lacessere coepērunt.

24. Postquam id animadvertit, cōpiās suās Caesar in proximum collem subdūxit equitātumque quī sustinēret hostium impetum mīsit. Ipse interim in colle mediō[4] triplicem aciem īnstrūxit legiōnum quattuor veterānārum. In summō iugō duās legiōnēs quās in Galliā citeriōre proximē cōnscrīpserat et omnia auxilia[4] collocārī ac totum montem hominibus complērī, et intereā sarcinās in ūnum locum cōnferrī, et eum locum ab eīs quī in superiōre aciē cōnstiterant mūnīrī iussit. Helvētiī cum omnibus suīs carrīs secūtī, impedīmenta in ūnum locum contulērunt; ipsī[5] cōnfertissimā aciē, reiectō nostrō equitātū, phalange factā sub prīmam nostram aciem successērunt.

25. Caesar prīmum suō,[5] deinde omnium[6] ex cōnspectū remōtīs equīs ut, aequātō omnium perīculō, spem fugae tolleret. Cohortātus suōs proelium commīsit. Mīlitēs, ē locō superiōre pīlīs missīs, facile hostium phalangem perfregerant. Eā disiectā, et gladiīs in eōs impetum fēcērunt. Gallīs magnō ad pugnam erat impedīmentō quod,[7] plūribus eōrum scūtīs

[1] *next day* (**eius diēī** is superfluous)
[2] *two days were left before* (from **supersum**)
[3] accusative
[4] *halfway up the hill*
[5] i.e., the fighting men

NOTE

Point out that Caesar makes frequent allusions to the problem of feeding his army. He had grain barges on the Saône, but the Helvetians had turned inland, away from the river.

NOTE

Remind students that a *decurion* was a commander of a squad of cavalry.

NOTE

It appears that they built (**mūnīrī**) a trench, remains of which have been discovered in excavations in recent times, to guard the baggage.

---

1 Supply **esse;** impersonal: *he should provide for supplies.*
2 Subjunctive because Caesar assigns these as the reasons of the Helvetians and not as his own.
3 Supply **Rōmānōs** as subject.
4 consisting of friendly Gauls and other foreign troops
5 Supply **equum** from **equōs.**
6 i.e., all the mounted officers, not the cavalry; **omnium** modifies **equōs**
7 The clause is subject of **erat.**

6 *volley*
7 *unprotected* (by a shield)

NOTE
The Gauls overlapped their shields, so two shields were easily pinned together by one spear. Because of the barbed ends and easily bent iron shafts of the spears, it was hard to draw them out. At first, it was probably mere chance that this happened, but the Romans were quick to take advantage of the situation and introduce an element of surprise.

ADDITIONAL QUESTIONS
When they saw Caesar leaving, what did the Helvetians do? What was the cavalry supposed to do? What weapons did they use?

WORKBOOK
Assign Interest Questions 36-40 to review the content of the reading from this lesson.

ūnō ictū[6] pīlōrum trānsfīxīs et colligātīs, cum ferrum sē inflēxisset neque ēvellere neque, sinistrā manū impedītā,[8] satis commodē pugnāre poterant. Multī ut diū iactātō bracchiō praeoptārent scūtum manū emittere et nūdō[7] corpore pugnāre.

QUESTIONS

1. Why did Caesar go to Bibracte?
2. How did Caesar place his troops?
3. What advantages did Caesar have?
4. What disadvantages did the Helvetians have?

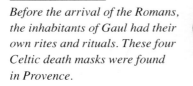

Before the arrival of the Romans, the inhabitants of Gaul had their own rites and rituals. These four Celtic death masks were found in Provence.

Ronald Sheridan/Ancient Art & Architecture Collection

Grammar

Causal Clauses with *Quod* and *Quoniam*

A causal clause, so called because it is translated as *because* or *since*, can be introduced by **quod** or **quoniam** (both of which mean *because, since*). The verb is in the indicative when it expresses the writer's or speaker's reason, and in the subjunctive when it suggests that it is the reason of some other person.

Servus grātiās dominō ēgit quod carrum novum eī dederat.	*The slave thanked the master because he had given him a new wagon.*
Gallī ad Caesarem auxiliō rogāvērunt quoniam Helvētiī fīnēs populārentur.	*The Gauls asked Caesar for help since the Helvetians were destroying their lands.*

8 by the shield, now pinned to that of another soldier

TRANSLATION

1. The enemy advanced crowded together because they did not have their baggage.
2. The Helvetians began to pursue him because (as they thought) he could be cut off.
3. Meanwhile, since Caesar had noticed this, he stationed his cavalry to check[9] them.

ANSWERS
1. Hostēs cōnfertī prōcessērunt/ prōgressī sunt quod impedimenta nōn habuērunt. 2. Helvētiī eum īnsequī coepērunt quod interclūdī posset. 3. Interim Caesar, quoniam/quod id animadverterat, equitātum collocāvit quī/ut eōs sustinēret (ad eōs sustinendōs).

Vocabulary

Nouns

agmen, -inis, *n. line of march*
fugitīvus, -ī, *m. deserter* (fugitive)
pīlum, -ī, *n. spear, javelin*
rēs frūmentāria, reī frūmentāriae, *f. grain supply*

As soldiers travelled, they either lived off the land or used the grain they brought with them. This detail from Trajan's column shows soldiers reaping grain, possibly from the territory of a conquered tribe.

National Historical Museum, Bucharest/E. T. Archives/SuperStock, Inc.

[9] Express in three ways.

Adjectives

cōnfertus, -a, -um, *crowded together*

frūmentārius, -a, -um, *of grain* (frumentaceous)

sinister, -tra, -trum, *left* (sinister, sinistral)

Verbs

NOTE
Point out that **animadvertō** comes from **animum** *(spirit)* + **advertō** *(turn toward).*

aequō, 1, *make equal* (adequate, equate)

animadvertō, -ere, -vertī, -versus, *notice* (animadversion, animadvert)

collocō, 1, *place* (collocate, collocation)

cōnfīdō, -ere, cōnfīsus,[10] *be confident* (confidant, confidential)

lacessō, -ere, -īvī, -ītus, *attack*

mētior, -īrī, mēnsus, *measure (out)*

supersum, -esse, -fuī, -futūrus, *be left (over)*

Adverb

interim, *meanwhile* (interim)

Review: **conferō, facile, mutō, iugum**.

Word Studies

The motto of the state of Maryland is a quotation from the *Book of Psalms:* **scuto bonae voluntatis tuae coronsti nos** (*Thou hast covered us*). The motto of Arkansas is **regnat populus;** of Arizona, **ditat** (*enriches*) **deus.**

From what Latin words are the following derived: **aequō, animadvertō, bīduum, collocō, cōnferō, convertō?**

Explain *collation, collocation, conference, confidence, conversion, equation, prospective, sinister.*

---

[10] Semideponent, i.e., active in the present stem, deponent in the perfect stem.

LESSON OBJECTIVE
To review impersonal verbs

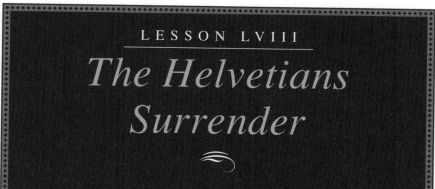

LESSON LVIII
The Helvetians Surrender

I, 26

Ita ancipitī proeliō diū atque ācriter pugnātum est.[1] Diūtius cum sustinēre nostrōrum impetūs nōn possent, alterī sē ut coeperant in montem recēpērunt, alterī ad impedīmenta et carrōs suōs sē contulērunt. Nam hōc tōtō proeliō, cum[2] ab hōrā septimā ad vesperum pugnātum sit, āversum[3] hostem vidēre nēmō potuit. Ad multam noctem[4] etiam ad impedīmenta pugnātum est, propterea quod prō vāllō carrōs obiēcerant et ē locō superiōre in nostrōs venientēs tēla coniciēbant, et nōn nūllī inter carrōs trāgulās subiciēbant nostrōsque vulnerābant. Diū cum esset pugnātum, impedīmentīs[1] castrīsque nostrī potītī sunt. Ibi Orgetorīgis fīlia atque ūnus ē fīliīs captus est. Ex eō proeliō circiter hominum mīlia CXXX superfuērunt, eāque tōtā nocte continenter iērunt. In fīnēs Lingonum diē quārtō pervēnērunt, cum[5] et propter vulnera mīlitum et propter sepultūram occīsōrum nostrī triduum morati eōs sequī nōn potuissent. Caesar ad Lingonas[2] litterās nūntiōsque mīsit nē eōs frūmentō nēve aliā rē iuvārent[3] quī sī iuvissent, sē eōdem locō quō Helvetiōs habitūrum. Ipse, trīduō intermissō, cum omnibus cōpiīs eōs sequī coepit.

27. Helvētiī omnium rērum inopiā adductī lēgātōs dē dēditiōne ad eum mīsērunt. Quī[6] cum eum in itinere convēnissent sēque ad pedēs prōiēcissent flentēsque pācem petīssent,[7] eōs[4] in eō locō quō tum essent suum adventum exspectāre iussit. Eō[8] postquam Caesar pervēnit, obsidēs, arma, servōs quī ad eōs perfūgerant poposcit.

Dum ea[5] conquīruntur et cōnferuntur, nocte intermissā, circiter hominum mīlia VI eius pāgī quī Verbigenus appellātur, sīve timōre perterritī,[6] sīve

[1] *they fought*
[2] *although*
[3] i.e., in retreat
[4] *until late at night*
[5] *since*
[6] i.e., the ambassadors
[7] short for **petīvissent**
[8] *there*
[9] *early in the night*

NOTE
Remind students of who Orgetorix was and what had happened to him.

SUGGESTION
Have students summarize, in general terms, what has happened thus far.

---

1 ablative with **potior**
2 accusative (Greek form)
3 a command in indirect discourse
4 i.e., the Helvetians, not the ambassadors
5 neuter plural, referring to **obsidēs, arma, servōs**
6 The grammatical subject is **mīlia**, but the logical subject is **hominēs**, with which **perterritī** agrees.

spē salūtis inductī, prīmā nocte[9] ē castrīs Helvētiōrum ēgressī ad Rhēnum fīnēsque Germānōrum contendērunt.

QUESTIONS

1. How long did the battle last?
2. What were Caesar's peace terms?
3. Who refused to accept these terms?
4. How many Helvetians escaped to the Lingones?

Grammar

Review impersonal verbs in Lesson XXXI.

TRANSLATION

1. They were not permitted[7] to keep their arms.
2. They fought[7] six hours before they were compelled to flee.
3. After they arrived[7] in the territory of friends, Caesar ordered them to await his arrival.

C. M. Dixon

This detail from a Roman sarcophagus from the 1st or 2nd century A.D. shows Roman soldiers and a captured barbarian. Notice that the barbarian is wearing long pants.

[7] Use an impersonal construction.

NOTE
Verify that students can locate all the territories and geographical features on a map.

ADDITIONAL QUESTIONS
What did the Helvetians use to barricade themselves? Which army was in a higher position? About how many survivors were there? Who were the Lingones and whose side did they support?

WORKBOOK
Assign Interest Questions 41-45 to review the content of the reading from this lesson.

ANSWERS
1. Arma retinēre eīs nōn licuit.
2. Sex hōrās pugnātum est priusquam fugere coāctī sunt.
3. Postquam in fīnēs amīcōrum perventum est Caesar eīs imperāvit ut adventum suum exspectārent.

Vocabulary

Nouns

dēditiō, -ōnis, *f. surrender*
sepultūra, -ae, *f. burial*
trāgula, -ae, *f. javelin*
trīduum, -ī, *n. three days*
vāllum, -ī, *n. rampart, wall, barricade* (interval, wall)

Adjective

nōn nūllī (nōnnūllī), -ae, -a, *some*

Verbs

conquīrō, -ere, -quīsīvī, -quīsītus, *seek for* (conquest, conquistador)
obiciō, -ere, obiēcī, obiectus, *throw against, oppose* (object, objectivity)
potior, potīrī, potītus, *gain possession of* (+ gen. or abl.)

Adverb

circiter, *about*

Word Studies

Some Latin-American countries and cities have names ultimately derived from Latin. Ecuador is the Spanish for our word *equator;* both are derived from **aequō,** because the equator divides the earth into *equal* parts. Argentina was so named because it was mistakenly thought to contain *silver* **(argentum);** its capital, Buenos Aires, is Spanish for *good air* (Latin **bonus āēr**). Montevideo, the capital of Uruguay, has properly a longer name, ending in pure Latin, de Montevideo, **dē monte videō,** or, possibly, it stands for **monte(m) videō.** The capital of Paraguay, Asunción, is named after the Assumption (from **sūmō**), i.e., the taking into Heaven, of the Virgin. The capital of Bolivia, La Paz, has the name of peace **(pāx).** Rio de Janeiro is from Latin (through Portuguese) **rīvus Ianuārī,** *River of (St.) January.* Honduras is from the Spanish *hondo,* Latin **(pro)fundus,** *deep,* perhaps on account of its deep coastal waters. Costa Rica is *rich coast,* and both Spanish *costa* and English *coast* come from Latin **costa,** *rib* or *side.* Puerto Rico is *rich port,* from **portus.** Salvador is from **salvātor,** the Savior.

LESSON OBJECTIVES
To review the hortatory and jussive subjunctive; To review the **iubeō** construction

LESSON LIX

The Price of Peace

I, 28

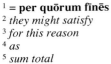

Quod ubi Caesar resciit, hīs quōrum per fīnēs[1] ierant imperāvit utī eōs conquīrerent et redūcerent; eōs reductōs in hostium numerō habuit; reliquōs omnēs, obsidibus, armīs, perfugīs trāditīs, in dēditiōnem accēpit.

Helvētiōs, Tulingōs, Latobrīgōs in fīnēs suōs, unde erant profectī, revertī iussit; et quod, omnibus frūgibus āmissīs, domī nihil erat quō famem sustinērent,[2] Allobrogibus imperāvit ut eīs frūmentī cōpiam facerent; ipsōs oppida vīcōsque, quōs incenderant, restituere iussit. Id eā maximē ratiōne[3] fēcit, quod nōluit eum locum unde Helvētiī discesserant vacāre, nē propter bonitātem agrōrum Germānī, quī trāns Rhēnum incolunt, ē suīs fīnibus in Helvētiōrum fīnēs trānsīrent et fīnitimī Galliae Prōvinciae Allobrogibusque essent. Boiōs,[1] quod ēgregiā virtūte erant, Haeduī in fīnibus suīs collocāre voluērunt; hoc Caesar concessit. Eīs illī agrōs dedērunt, eōsque posteā in parem iūris lībertātisque condiciōnem atque[4] ipsī erant recēpērunt.

29. In castrīs Helvētiōrum tabulae repertae sunt litterīs Graecīs cōnfectae et ad Caesarem relātae, quibus in tabulīs nōminātim ratiō cōnfecta erat, quī numerus domō exīsset[2] eōrum quī arma ferre possent, et item puerī, senēs mulierēsque. Quārum omnium ratiōnum summa[5] erat Helvētiōrum mīlia CCLXIII, Tulingōrum mīlia XXXVI, Latobrīgōrum XIIII, Rauracōrum XXIII, Boiōrum XXXII; ex hīs quī arma ferre possent, ad mīlia XCII.[6] Summa omnium fuērunt[3] ad mīlia CCCLXVIII. Eōrum quī domum rediērunt, cēnsū habitō, ut Caesar imperāverat, repertus est numerus mīlium C et X.

[1] = **per quōrum fīnēs**
[2] *they might satisfy*
[3] *for this reason*
[4] *as*
[5] *sum total*
[6] i.e., 25 percent

NOTES:
Tell students that this is another way of saying that he killed them or sold them into slavery as prisoners of war.

Point out the relative clause of description/characteristic (with **quō**).

NOTES:
They learned the Greek alphabet through contact with the Greek colony Massilia (Marseilles) in southern Gaul (refer to the map).

Point out the relative clause of description/characteristic (with **quī**).

As students translate these numbers, write them on the board. Have a discussion about the logistics of moving, feeding, and leading this quantity of people.

QUESTIONS

1. Why did Caesar want the Helvetians to restore their former homes?
2. What proportion of the Helvetians and their allies returned home?
3. What did Caesar do to the canton which tried to escape after the surrender?

ADDITIONAL QUESTIONS
What were the Allobroges ordered to do? Why? Why was Caesar concerned about the Germans? Why did the Boii settle in with the Haeduans?

---

1 emphatic; direct object of **collocāre**
2 indirect question implied in the noun **ratiō** and introduced by **quī numerus**
3 agrees with the predicate nominative **mīlia**

SuperStock, Inc.

A Gallic town at the foot of the Alps after the Roman conquest. The Roman soldiers, as well as the civilian people that accompanied them, interacted with the Gauls on a regular basis as they went about their daily activities. There were even intermarriages.

WORKBOOK
Assign Interest Questions 46-50 to review the content of the reading from this lesson.

Grammar

Review indirect command in Lesson XXII. Also review the command construction with **iubeō** in the Appendix.

SUGGESTION
Review briefly the infinitive construction with **iubeō**. Remind students that the subject of the infinitive is accusative. Contrast this construction with the indirect command and **imperō**.

TRANSLATION

1. Caesar persuaded the neighbors to give the Helvetians food.
2. He ordered[4] them to throw down their arms and return[5] the slaves.
3. He ordered[4] them to return[5] to their own territory and warned them not to flee.

ANSWERS
1. Caesar fīnitimīs persuāsit ut Helvētiīs cibum darent. 2. Eīs imperāvit ut arma prōicerent et servōs redderent. (Eōs iussit arma prōicere et servōs reddere.) 3. Eīs imperāvit ut in fīnēs suōs redīrent (Eōs iussit in fīnēs suōs redīre) et eōs monuit nē fugerent.

[4] Express in two ways.
[5] Distinguish between transitive *return* in the sense of *give back* and intransitive *return* in the sense of *go back*. Two different verbs are used in Latin.

Vocabulary

Nouns

bonitās, -tātis, *f. goodness, fertility*
famēs, -is (abl. **fame**), *f. hunger* (famine)
frūgēs, -um, *f. pl. crops* (frugal, frugality)
senex, senis, *m. old man* (senile, senescence)
tabula, -ae, *f. writing tablet* (tabulate, tabulation)

Verbs

comperiō, -īre, -perī, -pertus, *find out, learn*
vacō, 1, *be uninhabited, have leisure*

Adverb

nōminātim, *by name*

Review: **ēgregius, iūs.**

Word Studies

The original Roman "senate" consisted of **senēs,** *old men,* i.e., men over forty-five, who were considered too old to fight. A "senior" is *older;* he really ought to be addressed as "sir," for "sir" is derived from **senior.**

Explain *circumvallation, exit, famish, incense, restitution, reversion, tabulate.*

LESSON LX

The German Threat

LESSON OBJECTIVE
To review present and future infinitives in indirect statement

I, 31

Concilium tōtīus Galliae indictum est. Eō conciliō dīmissō, īdem prīncipēs cīvitātum quī ante fueran ad Caesarem revertērunt petiēruntque utī sibi sēcrētō in occultō dē suā omniumque salūte cum eō agere licēret. Locūtus est prō hīs Dīviciācus Haeduus:

"Galliae tōtīus factiōnēs sunt duae; hārum alterius prīncipātum tenent Haeduī, alterius Arvernī. Hī cum dē prīncipātū inter sē multōs annōs contenderent, factum est[1] utī ab Arvernīs Sēquanīsque Germānī mercēde[2] arcesserentur. Hōrum prīmō circiter mīlia XV Rhēnum trānsiērunt; posteāquam agrōs et cultum et cōpiās[3] Gallōrum hominēs ferī ac barbarī amāre coepērunt, trāductī sunt plūrēs; nunc sunt in Galliā ad centum et XX mīlium numerum. Cum hīs Haeduī eōrumque clientēs semel atque iterum[4] armīs contendērunt; magnam calamitātem pulsī accēpērunt, omnem nōbilitātem, omnem senātum, omnem equitātum āmīsērunt.

"Sed peius[5] victōribus Sēquanīs quam Haeduīs victīs accidit, propterea quod Ariovistus, rēx Germānōrum, in eōrum fīnibus cōnsēdit tertiamque partem agrī Sēquanī, quī est optimus tōtīus Galliae, occupāvit, et nunc dē alterā parte tertiā Sēquanōs dēcēdere iubet, propterea quod, paucīs mēnsibus ante, Harūdum mīlia hominum XXIIII ad eum vēnērunt, quibus locus parātur. Paucīs annīs omnēs Gallī ex Galliae fīnibus pellentur atque omnēs Germānī Rhēnum trānsībunt; neque enim cōnferendus est Gallicus ager cum Germānōrum agrō, neque haec cōnsuētūdō vīctūs cum illā.

"Ariovistus autem, ut[6] semel Gallōrum cōpiās proeliō vīcit, superbē et crūdēliter imperat, obsidēs[1] nōbilissimī cuiusque[7] līberōs poscit, et in eōs omnia exempla[8] cruciātūsque ēdit, sī qua rēs nōn ad nūtum aut ad voluntātem eius facta est. Homō est barbarus et īrācundus; nōn possumus eius imperia diūtius sustinēre. Tū vel auctōritāte tuā atque exercitūs recentī victōriā vel nōmine populī Rōmānī dēterrēre[9] potes nē maior multitūdō Germānōrum Rhēnum trādūcātur, Galliamque omnem ab Ariovistī iniūriā potes dēfendere."

NOTE
The fighting between Caesar and Ariovistus took place in Alsace, which has been a trouble spot between the Germans and the French and has changed hands repeatedly. In 1870, it became part of Germany, in 1918 it went back to France, in 1940 back to Germany, and in 1945 returned to France.

1 *it happened*
2 *for pay* ("mercenary" troops)
3 *wealth*
4 *again and again* (literally, *once and again*)
5 *a worse thing*
6 *when*
7 *of all the nobles* (from **quisque**)
8 *all kinds of cruelties* (with **cruciātūsque**)
9 *prevent a larger number . . . from being brought over*

NOTE
These losses, though heavy, are probably an exaggeration.

NOTE
This is an example of the subjunctive with a verb of hindering (**deterrēre**). If you wish to cover it, see the Appendix.

---

1 in apposition with **līberōs**

Although this may appear to be a battle scene, it actually represents a ***decursio****, the military parade that took place when an emperor was deified after his death. In this case, the emperor was Antoninus Pius (A.D. 138-161). On the relief, a troop of cavalry gallop around two groups of infantrymen, each having its own standard-bearer (both at lower left). Note the many details of military dress.*

ADDITIONAL QUESTIONS
Who was the spokesman for the factions? How many Germans were in the first batch of immigrants? What kind of people were they? What was Ariovistus like as a leader?

SUGGESTION
Ask students to predict what they think Caesar's reply will be.

WORKBOOK
Assign Interest Questions 51-55 to review the content of the reading from this lesson.

QUESTIONS

1. Which were the leading tribes in the Gallic factions?
2. What steps did one of them take to gain the supremacy?
3. What was the result and what did the Gauls want Caesar to do about it?

Grammar

Review the use of perfect and future infinitives in indirect discourse in Lesson VI.

NOTE
You may want to do a full review of the sequence of tenses.

TRANSLATION

1. They showed that they themselves would endure tortures and slavery.
2. They said that certain tribes of Gauls had sent for the fierce Germans.
3. They stated that the king of the Germans had seized the best part of all Gaul.

ANSWERS
1. Ostendērunt sē ipsōs cruciātūs et servitūtem lātūrōs esse. 2. Dīxērunt quāsdam gentēs Gallōrum Germānōs ferōs arcessīvisse. 3. Dīxērunt rēgem Germānōrum optimam partem tōtīus Galliae occupāvisse.

George Haling/Photo Researchers

This Roman arena in Arles, France dates from the early years of colonization, about 45 B.C. It measures 446 by 351 feet and seated 21,000. It was restored in 1828.

Vocabulary

Nouns

concilium, -lī, *n. council* (conciliate, conciliatory)
factiō, -ōnis, *f. faction* (faction, factional)
nūtus, -ūs, *m. nod*
victor, -ōris, *m. victor*
vīctus, -ūs, *m. living, food* (victuals, victualler)

Adjectives

ferus, -a, -um, *wild* (feral, ferocious)
īrācundus, -a, -um, *hot-tempered, quick-tempered*
occultus, -a, -um, *secret* (occult, occultism)
recēns, recentis, (gen.) *recent*
victor, -ōris, (gen.) *victorious*

Verbs

arcessō, -ere, -īvī, -ītus, *summon*
indīcō, -ere, indīxī, indictus, *call* (indite)

Adverb

prīmō, *at first*

Review: **cōnsuētūdō, cruciātus, loquor.**

Word Studies

From what Latin words are the following derived: **conquīrō, cōnsuētūdō, dēditiō, ēdō, factiō, prīmō, victor, voluntās?**

Explain *deterrent, factional, ferocity, occult, reiterate.*

Summary of Chapter 32. Caesar notices that during all the time that Diviciacus is speaking, the Sequanians remain silent. He asks the reason and is told that the Sequanians are in such fear of the cruelty of Ariovistus that they do not even dare complain or ask aid because they are so completely at the mercy of the Germans, who had occupied their towns.

LESSON LXI

Caesar Promises to Support the Gauls

LESSON OBJECTIVE
To review the datives of purpose and reference (double dative)

CASSETTE
This reading is recorded on Cassette 3, Side A.

NOTE
Caesar felt this way because, as a consul the year before, he had persuaded the senate to recognize Ariovistus by conferring upon him the honorary title **amīcus populī Rōmānī**.

I, 33

His rēbus cognitīs, Caesar Gallōrum animōs verbīs cōnfirmāvit, pollicitusque est sibi eam rem cūrae futūram: magnam sē habēre spem et beneficio suō et auctōritāte adductum Ariovistum fīnem iniūriīs factūrum. Hāc ōrātiōne habitā, concilium dīmīsit. Et multae rēs eum hortābantur quāre[1] sibi eam rem cōgitandam et suscipiendam putāret: in prīmīs quod Haeduōs, frātrēs[1] cōnsanguineōsque populī Rōmānī saepe ā senātū appellātōs, in servitūte vidēbat Germānōrum tenērī, eōrumque obsidēs esse apud Ariovistum ac Sēquanōs intellegēbat; quod in[2] tantō imperiō populī Rōmānī turpissimum sibi et reī pūblicae esse arbitrābātur. Paulātim autem Germānōs[3] cōnsuēscere Rhēnum trānsīre et in Galliam magnam eōrum multitūdinem venīre, populō Rōmānō perīculōsum vidēbat. Hominēs ferōs ac barbarōs exīstimābat, omnī Galliā occupātā, in Prōvinciam exitūrōs esse atque inde in Italiam contentūrōs, praesertim cum Sēquanōs ā prōvinciā nostrā Rhodanus[4] dīvideret; quibus rēbus[5] quam mātūrrime[6] occurrendum putābat. Ipse autem Ariovistus tantam sibi arrogantiam sūmpserat ut ferendus[7] nōn vidērētur.

34. Quam ob rem placuit eī ut ad Ariovistum lēgātōs mitteret, quī ab eō postulārent utī aliquem locum medium[8] utrīusque colloquiō dīligeret: velle[9] sē dē rē pūblicā et summīs utrīusque rēbus cum eō agere. Eī lēgātiōnī Ariovistus respondit:

"Sī quid mihi ā Caesare opus esset, ego ad eum vēnissem;[10] sī quid ille mē vult, illum ad mē venīre oportet. Praetereā neque sine exercitū in eās partēs Galliae venīre audeō quās Caesar tenet, neque exercitum sine magnō commeātū atque difficultāte in ūnum locum contrahere possum. Mihi autem mīrum vidētur quid in meā Galliā, quam bellō vīcī, aut Caesarī aut omnīnō populō Rōmānō negōtī[11] sit."

[1] = **ut**
[2] *in view of*
[3] *for the Germans*
[4] (*only*) *the Rhone*
[5] *this situation: he ought to meet*
[6] *as promptly as possible*
[7] *unbearable* (with **nōn**)
[8] *midway between them* (literally, *both*)
[9] (*stating*) *that he wished* (indirect statement)
[10] *"If I needed anything from Caesar, I should have come to him"*
[11] with **quid**

NOTES:
Ask students to think of modern day examples of special recognition to foreign dignitaries (e.g., a mayor handing over a key to the city).

Tell students that in this indirect statement, the verb of saying is implied in **postulārent**.

Point out that **Caesarī** is dative of possession with **sit**.

You might tell students that Adolf Hitler had an equally arrogant response in 1938 when he indicated that his demands on the former Czechoslovakia were his business, not England's.

---

[1] An honorary title, like that of **amīcus**, conferred upon foreign leaders for diplomatic reasons.

Wayne Rowe

A triumphal arch in Orange, France. Triumphal arches were freestanding ceremonial gateways erected in honor of a military victory.

ADDITIONAL QUESTIONS
What did Caesar's envoys ask of Ariovistus? Why does Ariovistus say he would not come to Gaul?

WORKBOOK
Assign Interest Questions 56-60 to review the content of the reading from this lesson.

QUESTIONS

1. Why did Caesar think he might influence Ariovistus?
2. What reasons led Caesar to promise the Gauls support?
3. What answer did Ariovistus make to Caesar's request for a conference?

Grammar

Review the datives of purpose and of reference (double dative) in Lesson XXVI.

TRANSLATION

1. He decided to choose a place for a conference.
2. "It will be my concern," he said, "to defend you."
3. He said that the Roman army would be a protection to the Gauls.

ANSWERS
1. Locum colloquiō dēligere cōnstituit. 2. "Mihi cūrae erit," inquit, "vōs dēfendere." 3. Dīxit exercitum Rōmānum Gallīs praesidiō futūrum esse.

Vocabulary

Nouns

colloquium, -quī, *n. conference* (colloquia, colloquial)
commeātus, -ūs, *m. supplies*
servitūs, -tūtis, *f. slavery* (servitude)

Adjectives

perīculōsus, -a, -um, *dangerous* (perilous)
turpis, -e, *disgraceful* (turpitude)

A Germanic war leader, possibly Ariovistus. This bronze head from the 1st century A.D. was found in Switzerland.

PHOTRI/INDEX

Verbs

audeō, -ēre, ausus, *dare (semideponent)*	(audacious)
cōgitō, 1, *think, consider*	(cogitate, cogitation)
cōnsuēscō, -ere, -suēvi, -suētus, *become accustomed; (in perf.) be accustomed*	
contrahō, -ere, -trāxī, -trāctus, *draw* or *bring together; contract*	(contraction, contractual)

Adverbs

paulātim, *little by little*
praesertim, *especially*

Idioms: **opus est, quam ob rem.**
Review: **placeō, praetereā, uterque.**

Word Studies

The original meaning of **commeātus** was *coming and going.* Its use in the sense of *supplies* shows that supply trains for the Roman army must have been on the go all the time and gives an idea of the importance attached to provisioning the soldiers.

From what Latin words are the following derived: **colloquium, praetereā, servitūs?**

Explain *arrogance, cogitate, contract, dividend, turpitude.*

LESSON OBJECTIVES
To review the hortatory and jussive subjunctive; To review indirect question

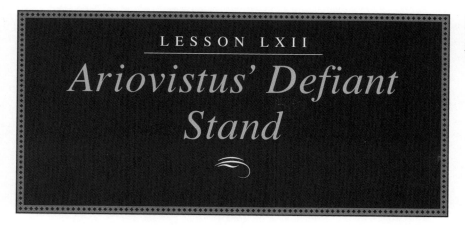

LESSON LXII
Ariovistus' Defiant Stand

Summary of Chapter 35. After receiving Ariovistus' insolent reply, Caesar sends an ultimatum: first, that Ariovistus is not to bring any more Germans into Gaul; second, that he must return the hostages of the Haeduans; third, that he is not to wage war upon the Haeduans and their allies. If Ariovistus will agree to these demands, there will be peace; otherwise Caesar will protect the interest of the Haeduans.

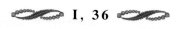

I, 36

Ad haec Ariovistus respondit:

"Iūs est bellī ut victōrēs victīs quem ad modum velint[1] imperent; item populus Rōmānus victīs nōn ad[2] alterius praescrīptum, sed ad[2] suum arbitrium imperāre cōnsuēvit. Sī ego populō Rōmānō nōn praescrībō quem ad modum suō iūre ūtātur, nōn oportet mē ā populō Rōmānō in meō iūre impedīrī. Haeduī mihi,[3] quoniam bellī fortūnam temptāvērunt et armīs congressī ac superātī sunt, stīpendiāriī sunt factī. Magnam Caesar iniūriam facit quī suō adventū vectīgālia[4] mihi dēteriōra facit. Haeduīs obsidēs nōn reddam, neque hīs neque eōrum sociīs iniūriā[5] bellum īnferam, sī in eō manēbunt[6] quod convēnit stīpendiumque quotannīs pendent; sī id nōn fēcerint, longē hīs frāternum[7] nōmen populī Rōmānī aberit.[8] Quod[9] mihi Caesar dēnūntiat sē Haeduōrum iniūriās nōn neglēctūrum, nēmō mēcum sine suā perniciē[10] contendit. Cum volet, congrediātur;[11] intelleget quid invictī Germānī, exercitātissimī in armīs, quī inter annōs XIIII tēctum nōn subiērunt, virtūte possint."[12]

[1] *as they wish*
[2] *according to*
[3] depends on **stīpendiāriī**
[4] *revenues*
[5] *unjustly*
[6] *if they will abide by that* (with **in eō**)
[7] adj., = **frātrum** (a sneer at the honorary title)
[8] i.e., will be of little use to them
[9] *as to the fact that*
[10] *destruction*
[11] *let him come on*
[12] *can* (*do*)

Summary of Chapter 37. On hearing of further German outrages Caesar advances rapidly against Ariovistus.

This marble relief of Caesar from the Louvre shows the great man whose name is synonymous with Rome complete with a laurel leaf crown.

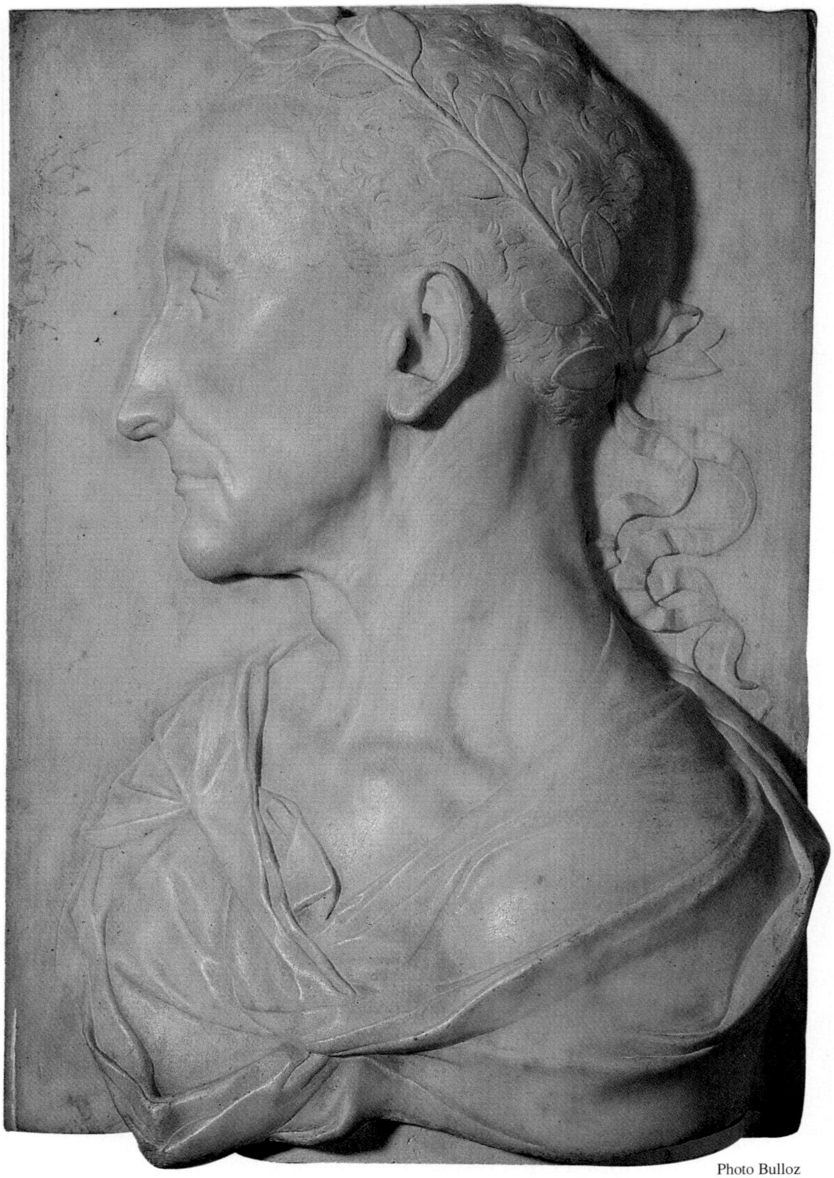

Photo Bulloz

NOTE
Have students locate Besançon on the map.

38. Cum trīduī viam prōcessisset, nūntiātum est eī Ariovistum cum suīs omnibus cōpiīs ad occupandum Vesontiōnem,[1] quod est oppidum maximum Sēquanōrum, contendere trīduīque viam ā suīs fīnibus prōcessisse. Hūc Caesar magnīs nocturnīs diurnīsque itineribus contendit occupātōque oppidō, ibi praesidium collocat.

Summary of Chapters 39–41. Exaggerated reports about the Germans throw Caesar's army into a panic, and throughout the camp soldiers may be seen making their wills. The officers even predict mutiny when Caesar gives the order to advance. He restores confidence by recalling how

[1] Masculine: *Besançon,* one of the strongest natural fortresses in France.

Marius defeated the Germans and by stating that Helvetians, whom they themselves had just defeated, do not fear the Germans, for they have often beaten them in battle. This speech has a bracing effect and his men clamor for an immediate advance. Caesar marches against Ariovistus.

---

42. Cognitō Caesaris adventū, Ariovistus lēgātōs ad eum mittit: quod anteā dē colloquiō postulāvisset, id per sē[13] fierī licēre, quoniam propius accessisset, sēque id sine perīculō facere posse exīstimāret. Nōn respuit condiciōnem Caesar iamque eum ad sānitātem revertī arbitrābātur.

[13] *as far as he was concerned*

QUESTIONS

1. How did Ariovistus defend his actions?
2. Why did he have such confidence in his Germans?
3. How did he explain his willingness to have a conference?
4. What do you think was the real reason for his changing his mind?

ADDITIONAL QUESTIONS
How did Ariovistus feel about the Haeduans? Where did Ariovistus head? What was he thinking of doing? Why did Caesar hurry there?

WORKBOOK
Assign Interest Questions 61-65 to review the content of the reading from this lesson.

Grammar

Review the hortatory and jussive subjunctives in Lesson X.
Review the subjunctive in indirect questions in Lesson XIX.

TRANSLATION

1. Let us not tempt fortune too often.
2. Let Caesar meet (in battle) with us and learn how Germans conquer.
3. The Germans did not know whether **(utrum)** to kill the prisoner or **(an)** reserve him for **(in)** another time.

ANSWERS
1. Nē saepius fortūnam temptēmus. 2. Caesar nōbīscum congrediātur et cognōscat quō modō Germānī vincant. 3. Germānī nōn scīvērunt utrum captīvum occīderent an eum in aliud tempus reservārent.

Vocabulary

Noun

tēctum, -ī, *n. roof, house*

Adjective

stīpendiārius, -a, -um, *tributary* (stipend)

Verbs

congredior, congredī, congressus, *meet* (congress, congressional)

praescrībō, -ere, -scrīpsī, -scrīptus, *direct* (prescribe, prescription)

respuō, -ere, respui, —, *reject*

temptō, 1, *try, test* (tempt, temptation)

Adverb

hūc, *to this side, here*

Idiom: **quem ad modum**.
Review: **pendō, stīpendium, ūtor**.

Word Studies

Explain *convention, covenant, denunciation, deteriorate, journal, journey, pernicious, prescription, sanitation.*

A Gallic warrior fallen in battle. Many tribes of Gauls and Germans wore pants to protect them from the elements.

Ronald Sheridan/Ancient Art & Architecture Collection

Ronald Sheridan/Ancient Art & Architecture Collection

Reading Caesar's ***Gallic War*** *sometimes gives the impression that every eligible Gallic male fought against the Romans. Men were still needed for building and agricultural occupations. This 3rd century bronze shows a farmer. The odd way in which he is holding his hands shows us that a wheelbarrow or plow is missing from this piece.*

Summary of Chapters 42–54. Caesar grants the request but guards against treachery. In his speech Caesar pleads for peace but insists upon his former demands. Ariovistus is as arrogant as before and demands that Caesar withdraw from *his* Gaul before he drives him out of it. Caesar rejects appeasement and replies that he will not forsake his allies. The conference is brought to a sudden end when the German cavalry attack Caesar's escort. Ariovistus later arrests two Roman envoys as spies whom Caesar sent in response to his request for another conference. Ariovistus then begins actual hostilities by cutting off Caesar's line of communication, but Caesar later reestablishes it by a skillful maneuver. Learning that the superstitious Germans are waiting for a full moon in order to attack, Caesar, like the good general that he was, takes the initiative and attacks at once. The fighting on both sides is desperate. At the critical moment Crassus sends up the reserves and the Romans win a decisive victory. Ariovistus escapes across the Rhine in a small boat. After establishing his legions in winter quarters at Vesontio, Caesar returns to Cisalpine Gaul.

Our Heritage

THE GALLIC CONQUEST AND ITS EFFECT ON THE WORLD

The immediate result of Caesar's conquest of Gaul was to free Italy for centuries from the fear of another invasion like that of the Gauls who had swept down from the north and sacked Rome in 390 B.C. "Let the Alps sink," Cicero exclaimed; "the gods raised them to shelter Italy from the barbarians; they are now no longer needed."

The Roman conquest of Gaul likewise relieved Italy from the German menace. Two German tribes, the Teutons and the Cimbri, had annihilated two Roman armies before Marius and his legions succeeded in stopping their advance in the Alpine passes. Caesar not only drove the Germans out of Gaul but bridged the Rhine and pushed the German tribes back into their own forests. It was Caesar who fixed the frontier of Gaul at the Rhine. Had it not been for Caesar's conquest of Gaul, the country extending from the Rhine to the Pyrenees and from the Alps to the ocean might have become an extension of Germany, embracing the Iberian peninsula as well.

This subjugation of Gaul by the Romans gave the Greco-Italic culture time to become thoroughly rooted, not only in Gaul, but also in Spain, before the breakup of the Roman Empire. Belgium, France, Portugal, and Spain became *Latin* instead of *Teutonic*. The language, customs, and arts of Rome were gradually introduced and the "vulgar," or spoken, Latin of Gaul became early French. Thus the whole history of western Europe was profoundly affected by the Roman conquest of Gaul. We should not forget, moreover, that through the Norman-French language our own English speech became predominantly Latin, though Caesar in his two invasions of the island of Britain (England) had merely, according to Tacitus, "revealed Britain to the Romans." The distinguished historian, T. Rice Holmes, has written that the French nation is the monument of Caesar's conquest of Gaul.

QUESTIONS

1. Is our English speech the richer because of its Latin elements?
2. What would have been the probable effect upon the history of Europe if the Germans had conquered Gaul?
3. Was Rome, as the possessor of a superior culture, justified in imposing her civilization upon the Gauls?

SEF/Art Resource, NY

Everywhere the Romans governed, they established theaters for public entertainment. From the Greeks, the Romans borrowed the dramatic styles of comedy and tragedy. Masks were used so that the audience could identify various characters at a glance. This Roman theater was constructed by Agrippa in A.D. *18 in Mérida, Spain. In no province did Roman ways take firmer root outside of Italy than in Spain.*

Scala/Art Resource, NY

Unit VI

Dē Bellō Gallicō II-V

UNIT OBJECTIVES
To review purpose and result clauses; To review the conjugation of **ferō**; To review the genitive of the whole; To review indirect command; To review the datives of purpose and reference (double dative); To review the ablative of separation; To review the gerundive and gerund

*The Forum of Julius Caesar is located a short distance from the Roman Forum. It was begun in 54 B.C., during the period of Caesar's military campaign. The Forum contains the Temple of Venus Genetrix, from whom Caesar claimed descent. In this photo, you can see the **tabernae** (shops) behind the columns of the double colonnade.*

Summary of Book II – Caesar's **Gallic War**

Book II is the story of the campaign against the Belgians. Several Belgian groups, primarily descendants of German tribes, decided to join together to claim their independence. Since there were many disparate groups, Caesar tried to move quickly to prevent them from coming together in a large army, but he was too late. Taking a strong position in the territory of his allies the Remi, on the banks of the Aisne River, Caesar tested the strength of both armies with his cavalry. The Belgians tried to surround Caesar's camp by crossing the river, but Caesar got to the bridge first, crossed it, and engaged the Belgians in a fierce battle. The Belgians were running low on grain and heard that help was on the way for Caesar. As a result, they decided to withdraw in the middle of the night. Caesar's legions pursued them at dawn and killed many of those at the rear of the withdrawing Belgian Army.

Caesar then moved quickly by forced marches to the territories of the Suessiones and the Bellovaci. The speed of the Romans and the size of their fortifications so alarmed the two groups that they decided to surrender. Hostages and information about other tribes were exchanged and Caesar moved on. He soon arrived at the territory of the Nervii, whom it is said, were very fierce and courageous, and would never consider any terms of surrender or peace.

The battle with the Nervii was the most exciting of Caesar's battles in Gaul. Upon learning that Caesar's army was on the move but still widely separated, the Nervii made the first attack. The first attack came so fast that Caesar did not have time to give orders. But his men were so experienced by this time that they knew what had to be done. The heavily wooded terrain made the fighting difficult. As additional troops arrived on the scene, they were largely unable to see where their services were needed, nor how best to prepare themselves. The enemy pushed their way into the main camp as fierce fighting continued on the flanks. The Treveri arrived as reinforcements for Caesar, but when they saw that all was turmoil and the enemy were in the camp, they left and went home and reported that the Romans had been beaten.

Caesar saw that his lines were being broken and that his legions were too tightly crowded together to fight efficiently. Spirits were sagging. He suddenly snatched a shield from a soldier and advanced to the front line, shouting the names of specific centurions and rousing the men with his own courage. The men, wanting to show the general their best efforts, were spurred on by him, and the rush of the enemy was slowed. Then Caesar directed the military tribunes to advance on another side to push the enemy back. Finally, the reinforcements from the rear, commanded by Labienus, were able to see from their higher position where they were most needed, and came on the scene as fast as they could. When the enemy saw them, they were greatly discouraged, although they continued to fight with the last of their strength.

Meanwhile, the Atuatuci were coming as reinforcements for the Nervii. When they arrived at the battle site, however, and saw what looked like a lost cause, they decided to turn back and fortify their own town.

When the Romans approached the town of the Atuatuci, they constructed a tower far off from the fortified wall. At first, the Atuatuci laughed and jeered. Then, when they saw the tower moving toward them, they immediately decided to sue for peace. They asked that they be allowed to retain their weapons, since they were surrounded by hostile tribes. Caesar said that he would only accept their surrender if it were done before the battering ram reached their fortified wall, and required that all arms be given up,

Ronald Sheridan/Ancient Art & Architecture Collection

Julius Caesar spent the years from 58-50 B.C. in his military campaigns in the Gallic provinces. This frieze from a sarcophagus shows the Roman soldiers fighting the Gauls in battle.

since Caesar would command all the neighboring tribes to leave untouched the prisoners of the Romans. The Atuatuci agreed and began to throw out their weapons. However, they kept almost a third of them hidden in the town. That night, they launched a final sortie against the Romans. The Atuatuci fought very bravely, but were beaten back by the Romans, the town was destroyed, and all survivors were sold off as slaves.

NOTE
The selections in Lessons LXIII and LXIV are from Book III of Caesar's *Gallic War,* which deals with the campaign against the Veneti. The events described took place in 56 B.C.

SUGGESTION
Verify that students can locate the Great St. Bernard Pass on a map. As students read through this section, indicate each position and leader on a larger map. Discuss with students the incredible communication system of the Roman army under Caesar.

NOTE
Remind students that Caesar's legion consisted of approximately 3,200 men.

Summary of Chapters 1–13. After subduing the Belgians, Caesar decides to make access to their northern country easy and safe for Roman traders by opening a road through the Alps to Italy by way of what we now call the Great St. Bernard Pass. He accordingly sends Servius Galba with a small force to guard this pass and hold the Alpine tribes in check. Galba takes up winter quarters in Octodurus (see map, pp. 228–229). This proves to be a death trap, for the mountaineers, who had pretended to submit, suddenly gather in large numbers on the heights above and attack the Romans before they have completed their fortifications. Galba beats them off, but finding it impossible to get supplies, he burns the village, destroys his camp, and withdraws to the Province.

Caesar had sent Publius Crassus with a legion to establish winter quarters among the coast tribes of what is now Brittany and Normandy. Foremost of these tribes were the Vĕn´etī. They, too, had pretended to submit and had even sent hostages to Crassus. Later, in order to force him to restore their hostages, they seize some of the officers sent by him to arrange for supplies. All the northwestern seacoast tribes combine to resist the Romans and send an embassy to Crassus, demanding the hostages. Caesar at once orders ships to be built at the mouth of the Liger (Loire) and oarsmen to be procured from the Province. He hastens north in the early spring. He sends Labienus to the Treveri, near the Rhine, to keep the Belgians under control and to prevent the Germans, whom the Belgians had asked for aid, from crossing the Rhine. Crassus is sent to Aquitania to prevent help from being sent from there into Gaul. Brutus is sent to prevent the coast tribes of the north from aiding the Veneti. Decimus Brutus is put in charge of the fleet that is being obtained from the pacified districts.

The towns of the Veneti are almost inaccessible from the land side because high tide cuts them off, and from the sea because low tide causes ships to be stranded in the shallows. In case of extreme danger the Veneti move from town to town by ship, taking all with them. They have a powerful fleet of seagoing vessels that have every advantage over the Roman galleys, because they have high prows and flat keels and are fitted with sails, being well adapted to fighting in shallow water or to riding out storms at sea.

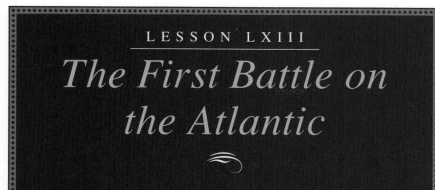

LESSON LXIII
The First Battle on the Atlantic

LESSON OBJECTIVE
To review purpose and result clauses

III, 14

Complūribus expugnātīs oppidīs, Caesar, ubi intellēxit frūstrā tantum labōrem sūmī, neque hostium fugam, captīs oppidīs, reprimī neque eīs nocērī[1] posse, statuit exspectandam classem.[2] Quae ubi convēnit ac prīmum ab hostibus vīsa est, circiter CCXX nāvēs eōrum parātissimae atque omnī genere armōrum ōrnātissimae ex portū profectae nostrīs adversae cōnstitērunt; neque satis Brūtō,[3] quī classī praeerat, vel tribūnīs mīlitum centuriōnibusque, quibus singulae nāvēs erant attribūtae, cōnstābat quid agerent[4] aut quam ratiōnem pugnae īnsisterent. Rōstrō enim nocērī nōn posse cognōverant; turribus autem excitātīs, tamen hās altitūdō puppium ex[5] barbarīs nāvibus superābat ut neque ex īnferiōre locō satis commodē tēla adigī possent et missa[6] ā Gallīs gravius acciderent. Ūna erat magnō ūsuī rēs praeparāta ab nostrīs—falcēs praeacūtae īnsertae affīxaeque longuriīs[7] nōn absimilī[8] fōrmā mūrālium falcium. Hīs[1] cum[9] fūnēs quī antemnās ad mālōs dēstinābant[10] comprehēnsī adductīque erant, nāvigiō[11] rēmīs incitātō, praerumpēbantur. Quibus abscīsīs, antemnae necessāriō concidēbant; ut, cum omnis Gallicīs nāvibus[12] spēs in vēlīs armāmentīsque cōnsisteret, hīs ēreptīs, omnis ūsus nāvium ūnō tempore ēriperētur.[2] Reliquum erat certāmen positum in virtūte, quā nostrī mīlitēs facile superābant atque eō magis, quod in cōnspectū Caesaris atque omnis exercitūs rēs gerēbātur, ut nūllum paulō fortius[13] factum latēre posset; omnēs enim collēs ac loca superiōra, unde erat propinquus dēspectus in mare, ab exercitū tenēbantur.

[1] *that they could not be injured*
[2] i.e., his own
[3] with **cōnstābat**
[4] *what they should do*
[5] *on*
[6] *those thrown*
[7] *long poles*
[8] *not unlike that of*
[9] *whenever*
[10] *bound to the masts*
[11] i.e., the attacking Roman ship
[12] *in the case of the Gallic ships* (dative of reference)
[13] *a little braver (than usual)*

NOTE
Point out that **nocērī** is one of the special verbs that takes the dative.

NOTE
Elicit that **classī** is dative after a compound verb.

NOTE
Tell students that ramming a ship (with the bow, **rostrum**) was a common battle technique, but the ships of the Veneti were made of oak.

NOTE
Point out that **formā** is an ablative of description.

NOTE
Have students describe the battle in their own words after reading about it to verify comprehension. There are several technical naval terms in this reading.

[1] ablative of means, with **comprehēnsī**
[2] The Gallic ships, unlike those of the Romans, had no oars.

Scala/Art Resource, NY

A large Roman vessel, used for carrying men and goods, usually had two banks of oars. The master at the front of the ship set the cadence, or tempo, for the rowers to follow. This was sometimes done with a drum, his voice, or with his own oar. This detail is from the Column of Trajan.

ADDITIONAL QUESTIONS
What made Caesar decide to await the fleet? How many enemy ships were there? Why did Brutus and the other ship commanders not know what to do? How much experience do you think the Romans had in naval warfare?

WORKBOOK
Assign Interest Questions 66-70 to review the content of the reading from this lesson.

ANSWERS
1. Nāvēs hostium tam altae erant ut Rōmānī pīla nōn iacere possent. 2. Mīlitēs magnā virtūte pugnāvērunt nē in conspectū Caesaris superārentur.

QUESTIONS

1. Who commanded the Roman fleet?
2. Why were the Romans particularly brave?
3. In what three ways did the Roman and Venetan ships differ?

Grammar

Review purpose and result clauses in Lessons XI, XII, and XIV.

TRANSLATION

1. The ships of the enemy were so high that the Romans could not throw their spears.
2. The soldiers fought with great courage in order not to be beaten in the sight of Caesar.

Vocabulary

Nouns

antemna, -ae, *f. yardarm (of a ship; the spar to which sails are fastened)*
classis, -is, *f. fleet* (class, classic)
falx, falcis, *f. hook* (falcate, falchion)
fūnis, -is, *m. rope*
nāvigium, -gī, *n. boat*
puppis, -is, *f. stern*
rostrum, -ī, *n. prow (of a ship); beak* (rostral, rostrum)
ūsus, -ūs, *m. use, practice, experience*
vēlum, -ī, *n. sail*

Adjective

praeacūtus, -a, -um, *pointed*

Verbs

attribuō, -ere, attribuī, attribūtus, *assign* (attribute, attribution)
cōnstat, *it is evident, it is clear, it is certain*
cōnsto, -āre, -stitī, -stātūrus, *stand together* (constancy, constant)
īnsistō, -ere, īnstitī, —, *adopt, stand (on)* (insist, insistence)

The rocky coast of Brittany, France. Caesar's fleet, with ships powered by oars, defeated the Gallic fleet in this region by pulling down their sails and rigging, rendering them immobile.

Joe Cornish/Tony Stone Images

Word Studies

Classis originally meant a calling out of citizens for military service, or draft. Then it came to mean any group, or *class*. One specialized meaning was that of the naval *class*, or *fleet*.

From what Latin words are the following derived: **abscīdō, absimilis, affīgō, attribuō, concidō, praerumpō, reprimō?**

Explain *affix, attribution, insertion, latent, repression.*

LESSON OBJECTIVES
To review the conjugation of **ferō**; To review the genitive of the whole

LESSON LXIV

A Decisive Victory

III, 15

Dēiectīs (ut dīximus) antemnīs, cum[1] singulās[2] bīnae ac ternae nāvēs circumsteterant, mīlitēs summā vī trānscendere in hostium nāvēs contendēbant. Quod postquam barbarī fierī animadvertērunt, expugnātīs complūribus nāvibus, cum eī reī nūllum reperīrētur auxilium, fugā salūtem petere contendērunt. Ac iam conversīs in eam partem nāvibus quō[3] ventus ferēbat,[4] tanta subitō tranquillitās exstitit ut sē ex locō movēre nōn possent. Quae quidem rēs ad negōtium cōnficiendum maximē fuit opportūna; nam singulās nostrī cōnsecūtī expugnāvērunt, ut perpaucae ex omnī numerō noctis interventū ad terram pervenīrent, cum$_1$ ab hōrā ferē quārtā usque ad sōlis occāsum pugnārētur.

16. Quō proeliō bellum Venetōrum tōtīusque ōrae maritimae cōnfectum est. Nam cum[5] omnis iuventūs, omnēs etiam graviōris[6] aetātis, in quibus aliquid cōnsilī aut dignitātis fuit, eō convēnerant, tum nāvium$_2$ quod ubīque fuerat$_2$ in ūnum locum coēgerant; quibus āmissīs reliquī neque quō[7] sē reciperent neque quem ad modum oppida dēfenderent habēbant. Itaque sē suaque omnia Caesarī dēdidērunt. In quōs eō[8] gravius Caesar vindicandum[9] statuit, quō dīligentius in reliquum tempus ā barbarīs iūs lēgātōrum cōnservārētur. Itaque omnī senātū necātō, reliquōs sub corōnā[10] vēndidit.

1 *whenever*
2 *each (Gallic vessel)*
3 *where* adverb
4 *was blowing*
5 with **tum:** *not only . . . but also*
6 *more advanced*
7 *(a place) where they might take refuge or means whereby*
8 *all the more severely* (looking forward to **quō**)
9 *that punishment ought to be inflicted.*
10 "under the crown," i.e., *as slaves*

NOTE
Tell students that the Roman hour was one-twelfth of daylight and therefore varied from 45 to 74 minutes according to the time of year. Roughly, the fourth hour would be 10:00 A.M.

NOTE
Point out that **quō** here is introducing a purpose clause.

Summary of Chapters 17–19. Caesar sends Sabinus to subdue the northern allies of the Veneti near Avranches in Normandy. Knowing that he must employ strategy to deal with their overwhelming numbers, Sabinus bribes a Gaul to play the role of a deserter and tell the Gauls that Sabinus is going to Caesar's aid. The ruse works, for the Gauls immediately attack Sabinus in his camp, whereupon, having the advantage of position, he orders his trained soldiers to charge them from the right and left gates and sends them flying. The enemy at once surrenders.

NOTE
Tell students that prisoners of war were crowned with wreaths when offered for sale.

$_1$ loosely attached to the preceding: *the fighting going on,* etc.
$_2$ Depends on **quod:** *all the ships there were anywhere*

Erich Lessing/Art Resource, NY

Fortasse trans aquam in Britanniam procedemus. *This wall painting from Pompeii shows Roman warships in battle. The soldiers are visible but the rowers are protected below deck.*

19. Sīc ūnō tempore et dē nāvālī pugnā Sabīnus et dē Sabīnī victōriā Caesar est certior factus, cīvitātēsque omnēs sē statim Titūriō dēdidērunt. Nam ut ad bella suscipienda Gallōrum alacer ac prōmptus est animus, sīc mollis ac minimē resistēns ad calamitātēs ferendās mēns eōrum est.

QUESTIONS

1. What won the sea battle for the Romans?
2. Why did Caesar punish the Veneti more severely than he had punished others?
3. From Caesar's description of the spirit of the Gauls, what do you infer was his idea of Roman spirit?

ADDITIONAL QUESTIONS
What were the weather conditions that helped the Romans? About how long did the battle last? What did the Roman victory mean for supremacy on the seas? Why? What did Caesar do to the Senate?

WORKBOOK
Assign Interest Questions 71-75 to review the content of the reading from this lesson.

Grammar

1. Review the conjugation of **ferō** in Lesson XIII.
2. Review the genitive of the whole in Lesson XXXII.

TRANSLATION

1. Two of Caesar's ships surrounded one of the enemy's ships.
2. When Caesar had brought together enough ships, he attacked the enemy.

ANSWERS
1. Duae ē nāvibus Caesaris ūnam ē hostium nāvibus circumstetērunt. 2. Cum Caesar satis nāvium condūxisset, hostēs aggressus est.

Vocabulary

Nouns

ōra maritima, ōrae maritimae, *f. seacoast*
ventus, -ī, *m. wind* (vent, ventilate)

Adjectives

bīnī, -ae, -a, *two at a time*	(binary, binational)
maritimus, -a, -um, *of the sea*	(maritime)
mollis, -e, *tender*	(mollification, mollify)
opportūnus, -a, -um, *opportune, advantageous*	(opportune, opportunity)
perpaucī, -ae, -a, *very few*	

Verbs

circumsistō, -ere, -stetī, —, *surround*	
exsistō, -ere, exstitī, —, *stand out, arise*	(exist, existential)
trānscendō, -ere, -cendī, —, *board, climb over*	(transcend, transcendental)

Adverb

usque, *up to*

Review: **alacer, expugnō, necō, statim.**

Word Studies

From what Latin words are the following derived: **dēiciō, dignitās, interventus, maritimus, nāvālis, perpaucī?**

Explain *alacrity, binary, combine, coronation, dejection, dignitary, intervention, maritime, mollify, ventilate.*

Summary of Chapters 20–29. Crassus, who had been sent by Caesar to subdue Aquitania, is attacked by the Sotiates. He defeats them and captures their city. Advancing farther, Crassus faces a formidable Aquitanian army, which fights according to Roman tactics. Since the enemy's forces are being strengthened daily, Crassus decides to attack their camp at once. Finding that the rear gate is not well guarded, he makes a surprise attack and routs the enemy. The various tribes of Aquitania now surrender and send hostages. In the north, Caesar defeats the Morini and Menapii, who, avoiding a pitched battle, seek refuge in their forests. The Romans pursue and attempt to cut their way after them, but storms prevent this. After ravaging the enemy's country, Caesar returns to winter in recently conquered territory.

A Gallic warrior is taken prisoner by the Romans. Compare his weapons and armor to that of the Romans. What differences do you see?

Ronald Sheridan/Ancient Art & Architecture Collection

LESSON LXV

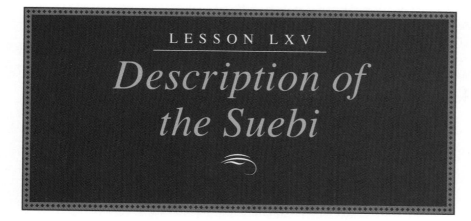

Description of the Suebi

LESSON OBJECTIVE
There is no specific grammar review for this lesson. You may, however, want to review the uses of the ablative that appear in this reading.

In Book IV of the *Gallic War,* represented by Lessons LXV to LXXII, Caesar describes his war with the Suebi, a German tribe, and his first expedition to Britain, made in 55 B.C.

NOTE
Ask students to describe what they remember of Ariovistus, then tell them that Ariovistus was a Sueban.

IV, 1

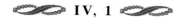

Eā quae secūta est hieme, quī[1] fuit annus Cn. Pompeiō M. Crassō cōnsulibus, Usipetēs Germānī[1] et item Tencterī magnā cum multitūdine hominum flūmen Rhēnum trānsiērunt, nōn longē ā marī quō[2] Rhēnus īnfluit. Causa trānseundī fuit quod ab Suēbīs complūrēs annōs exagitātī bellō premēbantur et agrī cultūrā prohibēbantur.

Suēbōrum gēns est longē maxima et bellicōsissima Germānōrum omnium. Hī centum pāgōs habēre dīcuntur, ex quibus quotannīs singula[3] mīlia armātōrum bellandī causā suīs ex fīnibus ēdūcunt. Reliquī, quī domī mānsērunt, sē atque illōs alunt. Hī rūrsus in vicem annō post in armīs sunt, illī domī remanent. Sīc neque agrī cultūra nec ratiō atque ūsus bellī intermittitur. Sed prīvātī agrī apud eōs nihil est, neque longius annō[4] remanēre ūnō in locō colendī causā licet. Neque multum frūmentō, sed maximam partem[5] lacte atque pecore vīvunt, multumque[6] sunt in vēnātiōnibus; quae rēs[7] et cibī genere et cotīdiānā exercitātiōne et lībertāte vītae, quod ā puerīs[8] nūllō officiō aut disciplīnā assuēfactī[9] nihil omnīnō contrā voluntātem faciunt, et vīrēs alit et immānī corporum magnitūdine hominēs efficit. Atque in eam sē cōnsuētūdinem addūxērunt ut locīs[10] frīgidissimīs neque[11] vestītūs praeter pellēs habeant quicquam, quārum propter exiguitātem magna est corporis pars aperta, et laventur in flūminibus.

[1] *the German Usipetes*
[2] adverb
[3] *a thousand each*
[4] *than a year*
[5] *for the most part*
[6] *they are much given to*
[7] *this manner of life* (subject of **alit** and **efficit**)
[8] *from boyhood*
[9] *accustomed to*
[10] ablative of place
[11] with **et:** *not only not . . . but even*

NOTE
Pompey and Crassus had been elected to the consulship for 55 B.C., with Caesar's political support. The understanding was that they would gain for him a 5-year extension of his term as proconsular governor of Gaul, giving him the opportunity to complete his conquest.

NOTE
Ask students what this adds up to as total military strength (100,000).

NOTE
Remind students that after a comparative, the ablative is used if **quam** is omitted (**annō**).

[1] refers to **hieme** (*fem.*) but agrees with **annus** (*masc.*)

A Roman general in full armor but wearing a laurel crown stands next to a German warrior, possibly one of the Suebi, who holds his tribe's standard.

North Wind Picture Archives

ADDITIONAL QUESTIONS
What was happening to the Usipetes and Tencteri? What did they do as a result? How were the German men physically built? How did they get this way? What was the nature of their clothing?

WORKBOOK
Assign Interest Questions 76-80 to review the content of the reading from this lesson.

QUESTIONS

1. What were the chief foods of the Suebi?
2. What do you infer was the Romans' chief food?
3. What was the nature of the military system of the Suebi?
4. What modern system of land ownership resembles theirs?
5. Why did the Germans cross the Rhine into Gaul? Where?

Summary of Chapters 2–12. The Suebi tolerate the presence of traders solely that they may sell what they take in war. They are teetotalers. They ride bareback, often fighting on foot, making a speedy getaway on horseback if the fighting goes against them. They live in isolation, allowing no one to settle near their borders. They drive out the German Usipetes and Tencteri, who go to the Rhine, where they are held in check by the Menapii, a Gallic tribe, who have settlements on both sides of the river. The Germans, however, make a surprise attack and cross into Gaul. Caesar, knowing the fickle character of the Gauls, fears that they may unite with the Germans against him. He therefore decides to drive out the Germans. When their envoys come to him asking for lands in Gaul, he orders them to leave the country. They plead for delay and gain a truce, but later make a treacherous attack upon the Roman cavalry.

Vocabulary

Nouns

cultūra, -ae, *f. cultivation* (culture, cultural)
exiguitās, -tātis, *f. scantiness, shortness, smallness* (exiguity)
lac, lactis, *n. milk* (lactic acid)
pecus, pecoris, *n. cattle*
pellis, -is, *f. skin* (pellicule)
vēnātiō, -ōnis, *f. hunting, hunt*
vestītus, -ūs, *m. clothing* (vest)
vicis, -is, *f. change;* (vicissitude)
  in vicem, *in turn*

Adjectives

bellicōsus, -a, -um, *warlike* (bellicose)
frīgidus, -a, -um, *cold* (frigid)

Verbs

alō, -ere, aluī, alitus, *support, feed, nourish, raise*
exagitō, 1, *harass, drive about*

Adverbs

longē, *by far*
quotannīs, *every year*

Word Studies

From what Latin words are the following derived: **bellicōsus, exercitātiō, omnīnō, vestītus, voluntās?**

Explain *lactic acid, lave, pellagra, pelt.*

LESSON OBJECTIVE
There is no specific grammar review for this lesson. You may, however, want to review the ablative absolutes that appear in this reading.

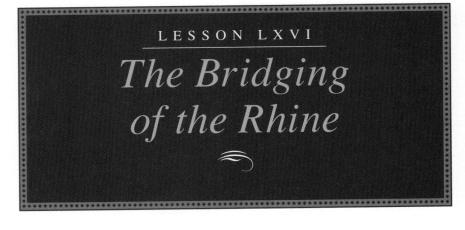

LESSON LXVI
The Bridging of the Rhine

NOTE
You may want to point out that **genere** is an ablative of origin. Have students refer to the Appendix if they require further information.

NOTE
Tell students that Caesar wanted to give the Germans a taste of their own medicine. Up until now, they had done their fighting in Gallic territory.

NOTE
You may want to tell students that **dignitātis** is a predicate genitive of possession.

NOTE
The building of the bridge was a phase of psychological warfare intended to impress and scare the Germans, since the Rhine had never before been bridged.

IV, 12

In eō proeliō ex equitibus nostrīs interficiuntur IIII et LXX; in hīs vir fortissimus, Pīsō Aquītānus, amplissimō genere nātus, cuius avus in cīvitāte suā rēgnum obtinuerat, amīcus ā senātū nostrō appellātus. Hic cum frātrī interclūsō ab hostibus auxilium ferret, illum ex perīculō ēripuit, ipse equō vulnerātō dēiectus quoad potuit fortissimē restitit; cum circumventus, multīs vulneribus acceptīs, cecidisset, atque id frāter, quī iam proeliō excesserat, procul animadvertisset, incitātō equō, sē hostibus obtulit atque interfectus est.

Summary of Chapters 13–15. After this attack, the Germans send some of their chiefs to ask for a truce. Caesar seizes them and then, advancing upon the leaderless force of Germans, annihilates it.

---

16. Germānicō bellō cōnfectō, multīs dē causīs Caesar statuit sibi Rhēnum esse trānseundum. Quārum illa fuit iūstissima, quod, cum vidēret Germānōs tam facile impellī ut in Galliam venīrent, suīs quoque rēbus[1] eōs timēre voluit, cum intellegerent et posse et audēre populī Rōmānī exercitum[1] Rhēnum trānsīre.

17. Caesar hīs dē causīs quās commemorāvimus Rhēnum trānsīre dēcrēverat; sed nāvibus trānsīre neque satis tūtum esse arbitrābātur neque suae neque populī Rōmānī dignitātis[2] esse statuēbat. Itaque, etsī summa difficultās faciendī pontis prōpōnēbātur propter lātitūdinem, rapiditātem, altitūdinemque flūminis, tamen id sibi contendendum[3] aut aliter nōn trādūcendum exercitum exīstimābat.

1 *for their own possessions* (**suīs** is emphatic)
2 *not in accord with the dignity*
3 *he must make the effort*

NOTE
Tell students that during World War II, American troops crossed the Rhine by capturing a bridge at Remagen, about 15 miles north of where Caesar built his bridge. Near Remagen, a Roman milestone marked (A.D.) 162 was found, giving the distance to Cologne as **m(ilia) p(assuum) XX**.

---

1 subject of **posse** and **audēre**

PHOTRI/AISA

In order to cross rivers efficiently with thousands of ***copiae, impedimenta****, and* ***equi****, the Romans built bridges. This model shows Caesar's bridge over the Rhine according to the description in Book IV of* ***Dē Bellō Gallicō****.*

QUESTIONS

1. What single reason does Caesar give for crossing the Rhine?
2. What other reasons can you give?
3. What method of crossing did he use?
4. What were his reasons for using this method?

Summary of Chapters 18–19. Caesar invades Germany and terrifies the Germans. After eighteen days he returns to Gaul and destroys the bridge.

ADDITIONAL QUESTIONS
How many men were killed in the battle? Were they foot soldiers? Who had been called a friend of the senate? From what region of Gaul was Piso descended? Which other relative of his was killed?

WORKBOOK
Assign Interest Questions 81-85 to review the content of the reading from this lesson.

Vocabulary

Noun

avus, -ī, *m. grandfather*

Adjective

iūstus, -a, -um, *just, proper, regular* (just, justice)

Verbs

commemorō, 1, *mention* (commemorate, commemoration)

dēcernō, -ere, dēcrēvī, dēcrētus, *decide*

impellō, -ere, impulī, impulsus, *drive on, influence, incite* (impel, impulse)

incitō, 1, *urge on, arouse* (incite, incitement)

interclūdō, -ere, -clūsī, -clūsus, *shut off, cut off*

offerō, offerre, obtulī, oblātus, *offer*; **mē offerō,** *rush against* (offer, proffer)

Adverb

aliter, *otherwise*

Conjunction

quoad, *as long as*

Review: **amplus, eques, nāscor, tūtus.**

Word Studies

From what Latin words are the following derived: **dēiciō, ēripiō, interclūdō, trānseō?**

Explain *amplitude, commemorate, proposition, renaissance.*

LESSON LXVII

Scarcity of Information about Britain

LESSON OBJECTIVE
To review indirect command

NOTE
Point out that Caesar feels the need to justify the invasion of Britain at this time by blaming the enemy.

NOTE
Point out that **subministräta** would normally have been followed by **sunt** but that it was omitted; you may want to review this in Lesson XXXIII.

IV, 20

Exiguā parte aestātis reliquā,[1] Caesar, etsī in hīs locīs (quod omnis Gallia ad septentriōnēs vergit) mātūrae sunt hiemēs, tamen in Britanniam proficīscī contendit, quod omnibus ferē Gallicīs bellīs[2] hostibus nostrīs inde[3] subministräta[4] auxilia intellegēbat; et, sī tempus ad bellum gerendum dēficeret, tamen magnō sibi ūsuī fore[5] arbitrābātur, sī modo īnsulam adīsset,[6] genus hominum perspexisset, loca, portūs, aditūs cognōvisset, quae omnia ferē Gallīs erant incognita. Neque enim temere[7] praeter mercātōrēs illō[8] adit quisquam, neque eīs ipsīs quicquam praeter ōram maritimam atque eās regiōnēs quae sunt contrā Galliam nōtum est. Itaque ēvocātīs[9] ad sē undique mercātōribus, neque quanta esset īnsulae magnitūdō, neque quae aut quantae nātiōnēs incolerent, neque quem ūsum bellī habērent aut quibus īnstitūtīs ūterentur, neque quī essent ad maiōrem nāvium multitūdinem idōneī portūs reperīre poterat.

21. Ad haec cognōscenda priusquam perīculum[10] faceret, idōneum esse arbitrātus C. Volusēnum[1] cum nāvī longā praemittit. Huic mandat ut, explōrātīs omnibus rēbus, ad sē quam prīmum revertātur. Ipse cum omnibus cōpiīs in Morinōs proficīscitur, quod inde erat brevissimus in Britanniam trāiectus.[11] Hūc[12] nāvēs undique ex fīnitimīs regiōnibus et quam[2] superiōre aestāte ad Veneticum bellum fēcerat classem iubet convenīre. Interim, cōnsiliō eius cognitō et per mercātōrēs perlātō ad Britannōs, ā complūribus eius īnsulae cīvitātibus ad eum lēgātī veniunt, quī polliceantur obsidēs dare atque imperiō populī Rōmānī obtemperāre. Quibus audītīs, līberāliter pollicitus hortātusque ut in eā sententiā permanērent, eōs domum remittit et cum eīs ūnā Commium, quem ipse, Atrebātibus superātīs, rēgem ibi

[1] (being) *left*
[2] ablative of time
[3] i.e., **ē Britanniā**
[4] Supply **esse.**
[5] = **futūrum esse**
[6] = **adiisset**
[7] **neque temere,** *scarcely*
[8] adverb
[9] *although he called*
[10] *the attempt*
[11] *passage*
[12] *to this point*

NOTE
This entire last sentence contains a whole series of indirect questions introduced by **reperīre.**

NOTE
Point out that **hūc** here refers to the shortest crossing point, the modern Boulogne. Be sure students can locate it on a map.

NOTE
Remind students that **Veneticus** is *Venetan,* not *Venetian.*

NOTE
You might tell students that a couple of years later, in 52 B.C., Commius deserted Caesar.

[1] subject of **esse** and object of **praemittit**
[2] The antecedent is **classem.**

[13] *was considered great*
[14] i.e., Caesar
[15] *as far as opportunity* (with **quantum**)

NOTE
Elicit that **ut** introduces a series of indirect commands.

NOTE
Point out that **quī** introduces a relative clause of description (characteristic).

cōnstituerat, cuius et virtūtem et cōnsilium probābat, et quem sibi fidēlem esse arbitrābātur, cuiusque auctōritās in hīs regiōnibus magnī habēbātur,[13] mittit. Huic imperat quās[3] possit adeat[4] cīvitātēs, hortēturque ut populī Rōmānī fidem sequantur, sēque[14] celeriter eō ventūrum nūntiet. Volusēnus, perspectīs regiōnibus quantum eī facultātis[15] darī potuit quī[5] ex nāvī ēgredī ac sē barbarīs committere nōn audēret, quīntō diē ad Caesarem revertitur quaeque ibi perspexisset renūntiat.

QUESTIONS

1. At what time of year did Caesar go to Britain?
2. What were his reasons for crossing into Britain?
3. How did he try to get information about the island?
4. Why did Caesar and his forces set out for the land of the Morini?

ADDITIONAL QUESTIONS
Who were the only people who went to Britain at all regularly? Who was Gaius Volusenus? What was his mission? How long was he gone? How did the Britons find out Caesar's plan? What was their response?

Summary of Chapter 22. The Morini submit as Caesar prepares to cross the Channel. He gathers together eighty transports for two legions and eighteen for the cavalry, besides several warships for the officers.

WORKBOOK
Assign Interest Questions 86-90 to review the content of the reading from this lesson.

Grammar

Review indirect command in Lesson XXII.

TRANSLATION

1. "Persuade the Britons to send hostages and to refrain from war."
2. He urged his friend to investigate everything and to report as soon as possible.

ANSWERS
1. "Persuādē Britannīs ut obsidēs mittant et bellō abstineant." 2. Amīcum hortātus est ut omnia explōrāret et quam prīmum nūntiāret.

[3] The antecedent is **cīvitātēs.**
[4] Supply **ut** before **adeat, hortētur**, and **nūntiet.**
[5] The antecedent is **eī:** *to one who.*

Vocabulary

Nouns

aestās, -tātis, *f. summer* (estival, estivation)
nātiō, -ōnis, *f. nation, tribe* (nationalization, nationalize)

Adjectives

exiguus, -a, -um, *small* (exiguous)
mātūrus, -a, -um, *early, ripe, mature* (maturation, maturity)

Verbs

obtemperō, 1, *submit to*
subministrō, 1, *furnish*

Adverbs

inde, *then, from there, thereafter, therefore*
līberāliter, *liberally, courteously*
temere, *rashly, without reason*

Review: **brevis, modo, perspiciō.**

Word Studies

Motto of the United States Marine Corps: **semper fidelis.**

From what Latin words are the following derived: **ēvocō, fidēlis, incognitus, līberāliter, trāiectus?**

Explain *converge, divergent, fidelity, incognito.*

LESSON OBJECTIVE
To review the datives of purpose and reference (double dative)

LESSON LXVIII
Midnight Sailing

CASSETTE
This reading is recorded on Cassette 3, Side A.

NOTE
Tell students that Caesar probably landed near the steep chalk cliffs of Dover; have them locate the site on a map.

[1] *while they had carried out his order a little too slowly*
[2] *chariot fighters*
[3] *in deep water*
[4] *while they,* i.e., the Britons
[5] *trained*
[6] i.e., *on land*
[7] *artillery*

NOTE
After you have finished the first paragraph, have one student summarize it in good English. Since this passage is somewhat longer than the others, it will help reinforce the content.

NOTE
Elicit that **cōpiīs** is ablative of accompaniment; remind students that **cum** is often omitted in military phrases if modified by an adjective.

NOTE
Point out that **generis** is genitive after certain adjectives, in this case **imperītī**.

NOTE
Have a student summarize the second paragraph.

IV, 23

His cōnstitūtīs rēbus, nactus idōneam ad nāvigandum tempestātem tertiā ferē vigiliā nāvēs solvit, equitēsque in ulteriōrem portum prōgredī et nāvēs cōnscendere et sē sequī iussit. Ā quibus cum[1] paulō tardius esset administrātum, ipse hōrā diēī circiter quārtā cum prīmīs nāvibus Britanniam attigit atque ibi in omnibus collibus expositās hostium cōpiās armātās cōnspexit. Hunc ad ēgrediendum nēquāquam idōneum locum arbitrātus, dum reliquae nāvēs eō convenīrent ad hōram nōnam in ancorīs exspectāvit. Interim lēgātīs tribūnīsque mīlitum convocātīs, et quae ex Volusēnō cognōvisset et quae fierī vellet ostendit. Hīs dīmissīs et ventum et aestum ūnō tempore nactus secundum, datō signō et sublātīs ancorīs, circiter mīlia passuum VII ab eō locō prōgressus, apertō ac plānō lītore nāvēs cōnstituit.

24. At barbarī, cōnsiliō Rōmānōrum cognitō, praemissō equitātū et essedāriīs,[2] reliquīs cōpiīs subsecūtī nostrōs nāvibus ēgredī prohibēbant. Erat ob hās causās summa difficultās quod nāvēs propter magnitūdinem nisi in altō[3] cōnstituī nōn poterant; mīlitibus$_1$ autem, ignōtīs locīs, impedītīs manibus, magnō et gravī onere armōrum pressīs, simul et dē nāvibus dēsiliendum et in flūctibus cōnsistendum et cum hostibus erat pugnandum; cum illī[4] aut ex āridō aut paulum in aquam prōgressī, omnibus membrīs expedītīs, nōtissimīs locīs, audācter tēla conicerent et equōs īnsuēfactōs[5] incitārent. Quibus rēbus nostrī perterritī atque huius omnīnō generis pugnae imperītī nōn eādem alacritāte ac studiō quō in pedestribus[6] ūtī proeliīs cōnsuēverant ūtēbantur.

25. Quod ubi Caesar animadvertit, nāvēs$_2$ longās, quārum speciēs erat barbarīs inūsitātior, paulum removērī ab onerāriīs nāvibus et rēmīs incitārī et ad latus apertum hostium cōnstituī, atque inde fundīs, sagittīs, tormentīs[7] hostēs prōpellī ac submovērī iussit. Quae rēs magnō ūsuī nostrīs fuit. Nam

$_1$ Dative of agent with **dēsiliendum, cōnsistendum, pugnandum;** make it the subject in English.
$_2$ Subject of **removērī, incitārī, cōnstituī;** note change of subject in **hostēs... submovērī.**

North Wind Picture Archives

Caesar was finally able to land in Britain after redeploying his warships. Notice that the standardbearer, holding his eagle aloft, urges on the spirit of the other soldiers.

et nāvium figūrā et rēmōrum mōtū et inūsitātō genere tormentōrum permōtī barbarī cōnstitērunt ac paulum pedem rettulērunt. At nostrīs mīlitibus cūnctantibus, maximē propter altitūdinem maris, quī[3] decimae legiōnis aquilam ferēbat obtestātus deōs ut ea rēs legiōnī fēlīciter ēvenīret, "Dēsilīte," inquit, "commīlitōnēs, nisi vultis aquilam hostibus prōdere; ego certē meum reī pūblicae atque imperātōrī officium praestiterō." Hoc cum magnā vōce dīxisset, sē ex nāvī prōiēcit atque in hostēs aquilam ferre coepit. Tum nostrī cohortātī inter sē[8] nē tantum dēdecus admitterētur, ūniversī ex nāvī dēsiluērunt. Hōs item ex proximīs nāvibus[4] cum cōnspexissent, subsecūtī hostibus appropinquāvērunt.

[8] *one another*

NOTE
Tell students that the Roman eagle, or ensign, like our flag, was regarded with patriotism and respect; its loss was considered a great disgrace.

NOTE
Have another student summarize the third paragraph.

QUESTIONS

1. Why did Caesar not land immediately?
2. What were the difficulties faced by the Romans?
3. With what types of troops did the Britons keep the Romans from landing?
4. What was Caesar's motive in telling the story of the standard-bearer?

ADDITIONAL QUESTIONS
How long did it take Caesar to sail to Britain? Were the rest of the troops there at the same time? When did they arrive? What bearing did unfamiliar weapons and tactics have on each side? How did Caesar change his strategy to help the Romans?

WORKBOOK
Assign Interest Questions 91-95 to review the content of the reading from this lesson.

[3] Supply the antecedent: *the one who.*
[4] Supply **eī:** *the men on the nearest ships* (used as subject of **cōnspexissent** and **appropinquāvērunt**).

Grammar

Review the datives of purpose and reference (double dative) in Lesson XXVI.

ANSWERS
1. Putātisne nāvēs nōbīs praesidiō futūrās esse?
2. Scūta mīlitibus in aquā labōrantibus auxiliō nōn erant.

TRANSLATION

1. Do you think that the ships will be any protection to us?
2. The shields were of no help to the soldiers struggling in the water.

Vocabulary

Nouns

aestus, -ūs, *m. tide*	(estuarine, estuary)
ancora, -ae, *f. anchor*	(anchorage)
aquila, -ae, *f. eagle*	(aquiline)
funda, -ae, *f. sling, slingshot*	
mōtus, -ūs, *m. motion*	(motif, motive)
sagitta, -ae, *f. arrow*	(Sagittarius, sagitate)

Adjectives

aridus, -a, -um, *dry*	(arid)
imperītus, -a, -um, *inexperienced, ignorant*	
ūniversus, -a, -um, *all (together)*	(universal, universe)

Verbs

cūnctor, 1, *hesitate*	(cunctation)
dēsiliō, -īre, dēsiluī, dēsultūrus, *jump down*	(desultory, expository)
expōnō, -ere, -posuī, -positus, *put out, draw up*	(exponent, exponential)
obtestor, 1, *entreat, pray*	
prōdō, -ere, -didī, -ditus, *give (forth), betray*	

Idioms: **nāvis longa, nāvis onerāria.**

Word Studies

From what Latin words are the following derived: **alacritās, commīlitō, flūctus, ignōtus, inūsitātus, mōtus, onerārius, praefectus, prōdō?**

Explain *aquiline, arid, dismember, estuary, expository, fluctuate.*

LESSON LXIX
Difficult Fighting

LESSON OBJECTIVE
There is no specific grammar review for this lesson. You may, however, want to review deponent and semi-deponent verbs.

IV, 26

Pugnātum est ab utrīsque ācriter. Nostrī tamen, quod neque ōrdinēs servāre neque firmiter īnsistere neque signa subsequī poterant, atque alius[1] aliā ex nāvī quibuscumque signīs occurrerat sē aggregābat, magnopere perturbābantur; hostēs vērō, nōtīs omnibus vadīs, ubi ex lītore aliquōs singulārēs ex nāvī ēgredientēs cōnspexerant, incitātīs equīs, impedītōs adoriēbantur, plūrēs[2] paucōs circumsistēbant, aliī ab latere apertō in ūniversōs tēla coniciēbant. Quod cum animadvertisset Caesar, scaphās[3] longārum nāvium, item speculātōria nāvigia[4] mīlitibus complērī iussit, et quōs labōrantēs cōnspexerat hīs[1] subsidia submittēbat. Nostrī simul[5] in āridō cōnstitērunt, suīs omnibus cōnsecūtīs,[6] in hostēs impetum fēcērunt atque eōs in fugam dedērunt; neque longius prōsequī potuērunt, quod equitēs cursum tenēre atque īnsulam capere[7] nōn potuerant. Hoc ūnum ad prīstinam fortūnam Caesarī dēfuit.

27. Hostēs proeliō superātī, simul atque sē ex fugā recēpērunt, statim ad Caesarem lēgātōs dē pāce mīsērunt. Ūnā cum hīs lēgātīs Commius Atrebās vēnit, quem suprā dēmōnstrāverāmus ā Caesare in Britanniam praemissum. Hunc illī ē nāvī ēgressum, cum[8] ad eōs ōrātōris modō[9] Caesaris mandāta dēferret, comprehenderant atque in vincula coniēcerant. Tum, proeliō factō, remīsērunt[2] et in petendā pāce eius reī culpam in multitūdinem contulērunt, et propter imprūdentiam ut ignōscerētur[10] petīvērunt. Caesar questus quod,[3] cum ultrō, in continentem lēgātīs missīs, pācem ab sē petīssent, bellum sine causā intulissent, ignōscere[4] imprūdentiae dīxit obsidēsque imperāvit. Quōrum illī partem statim dedērunt, partem ex longinquiōribus locīs arcessītam paucīs diēbus sēsē datūrōs dīxērunt. Intereā suōs in agrōs remigrāre iussērunt, prīncipēsque undique convenīre et sē cīvitātēsque suās Caesarī commendāre coepērunt.

CASSETTE
This reading is recorded on Cassette 3, Side A.

[1] *one from one vessel, another from another would join whatever standard he met*
[2] *several*
[3] *boats*
[4] *scout boats,* i.e., *patrol craft*
[5] *as soon as* (**atque** or **ac** is understood)
[6] *and their fellow soldiers caught up with them* (ablative absolute)
[7] *reach*
[8] *although*
[9] *as an envoy*
[10] impersonal

NOTE
Remind students that the Roman cavalry was still in the **ulterior portus** as described in Chapter 23.

NOTE
The reference here to **fortūna** shows how much importance the Romans placed on luck as a factor to a general's success.

NOTE
Tell students that **imprudentiae** is dative after special verbs (**ignōscō**).

---

[1] antecedent of **quōs**
[2] Supply **eum.**
[3] Introduces **intulissent; cum** goes with **petīssent.**
[4] Supply **sē** as subject.

Robert Estall/Tony Stone Images

The remains of a Roman amphitheater in St. Albans, England. Since the Romans knew that the people who were garrisoned so far away would miss the comforts of home, they felt it was important to ensure that sports and dramatic entertainment was available. Thus they built their monuments to last.

ADDITIONAL QUESTIONS
What tactic did the Britons use to cause initial problems for the Romans? Who won this battle? What happened to Commius? What did Caesar demand of the Britons? Did he get it?

WORKBOOK
Assign Interest Questions 96-100 to review the content of the reading from this lesson.

QUESTIONS

1. What advantage did the Britons have?
2. What caused confusion among the Romans?
3. Why did Caesar have no cavalry to pursue the enemy?
4. How did Caesar come to the aid of those in difficulty?
5. What two things did Caesar complain about to the Britons?

Vocabulary

Nouns

imprūdentia, -ae, *f. poor sense* (imprudence, imprudent)
latus, lateris, *n. side, flank* (lateral, unilateral)
subsidium, -dī, *n. aid, reserve* (subsidiary, subsidy)

Pronoun

quīcumque, quaecumque, quodcumque, *whoever, whatever*

Adjective

longinquus, -a, -um, *distant*

Verbs

ignōscō, -ere, ignōvī, ignōtus, *pardon* (ignoble)

queror, querī, questus, *complain* (quarrel, querulous)

remigrō, 1, *go back*

Adverbs

firmiter, *firmly*

ultrō, *voluntarily*

Word Studies

Distinguish carefully the forms and derivatives of **quaerō** and **queror.** Derivatives of **quaerō** include *conquest, query, quest, question;* of **queror,** *quarrel, querulous.*

From what Latin words are the following derived: **commendō, comprehendō, continēns, imprūdentia, longinquus, mandātum, remigrō, speculātōrius?**

Explain *aggregation, comprehension, mandate, recommendation.*

LESSON OBJECTIVE
To review the ablative of separation

LESSON LXX
Storm and Tide Cause Trouble

IV, 28

Hīs rēbus pāce cōnfirmātā, diē quārtō postquam est in Britanniam ventum,[1] nāvēs XVIII dē quibus suprā dēmōnstrātum est, quae equitēs sustulerant, ex superiōre portū lēnī ventō solvērunt. Quae cum appropinquārent Britanniae et ex castrīs vidērentur, tanta tempestās subitō coorta est ut nūlla eārum cursum tenēre posset sed aliae eōdem unde erant profectae referrentur,$_{1}$ aliae ad īnferiōrem partem īnsulae, quae est propius sōlis occāsum, magnō suō[2] cum perīculō dēicerentur. Quae[3] tamen, ancorīs iactīs, cum fluctibus complērentur, necessāriō adversā nocte[4] in altum prōvectae continentem petīvērunt.

29. Eādem nocte accidit ut esset lūna plēna, quī diēs[4] maritimōs aestūs maximōs in Ōceanō efficere cōnsuēvit, nostrīsque id erat incognitum. Ita ūnō tempore et longās nāvēs, quibus Caesar exercitum$_{2}$ trānsportandum cūrāverat quāsque in āridum subdūxerat, aestus complēbat, et onerāriās, quae ad ancorās erant dēligātae, tempestās afflīctābat, neque ūlla nostrīs facultās aut administrandī aut auxiliandī dabātur. Complūribus nāvibus frāctīs, reliquae cum essent ad nāvigandum inūtilēs, magna tōtīus exercitūs perturbātiō facta est. Neque enim nāvēs erant aliae quibus reportārī possent, et omnia deerant quae ad reficiendās nāvēs erant ūsuī; et, quod omnibus cōnstābat hiemārī in Galliā oportēre, frūmentum in hīs locīs[5] in hiemem prōvīsum nōn erat.

[1] *they came,* literally, *it was come*
[2] *to themselves*
[3] *Nevertheless, when after anchoring they were filling with water, in the face of the night*
[4] *time*
[5] i.e., in Britain

NOTE
This statement about the full moon has enabled astronomers to compute the exact date: August 30, 55 B.C.

NOTE
Point out that **possent** is subjunctive because it is in a relative clause of description (characteristic).

$_{1}$ still part of the **ut** clause
$_{2}$ Only part of the army had been transported in the warships.

C. M. Dixon

These roof tiles are from a 1st century Roman villa in Fishbourne, England. The Romans constructed many buildings in the English countryside, expecting their occupation to be permanent. Parts of homes, municipal buildings, walls, and fortifications are not only visible but in use today.

SUGGESTION
Have a few students summarize each paragraph of this reading. Then have a few others summarize the "British invasion" thus far.

30. Quibus rēbus cognitīs, prīncipēs Britanniae, quī post proelium ad ea quae iusserat Caesar facienda convēnerant, inter sē collocūtī, cum et equitēs et nāvēs et frūmentum Rōmānīs deesse intellegerent, et paucitātem mīlitum ex castrōrum exiguitāte cognōscerent—quae hōc[6] erant etiam angustiōra quod sine impedīmentīs Caesar legiōnēs trānsportāverat—optimum esse dūxērunt,[7] rebelliōne factā, frūmentō commeātūque nostrōs prohibēre et rem in hiemem prōdūcere; quod, hīs[8] superātīs aut reditū interclūsīs, nēminem posteā bellī īnferendī causā in Britanniam trānsitūrum cōnfīdēbant. Itaque rūrsus coniūrātiōne factā, paulātim ex castrīs discēdere et suōs clam ex agrīs dēdūcere[9] coepērunt.

[6] *on this account*
[7] *thought*
[8] i.e., Caesar's army
[9] i.e., to mobilize an army

ADDITIONAL QUESTIONS
How long after the battle did it take for the other ships to arrive? Who started the conspiracy? What did they begin to do?

QUESTIONS

1. What became of the cavalry?
2. What happened to the main fleet?
3. What three things did the Romans lack?

WORKBOOK
Assign Interest Questions 101-105 to review the content of the reading from this lesson.

Grammar

Review the ablative of separation in Lesson XXXVII.

TRANSLATION

1. Caesar was unwilling to depart from Britain until he received hostages.
2. The Britons thought that they could keep the Romans from their supplies.
3. "Let us cut these Romans off from (the possibility of) return; no one will cross the sea again to attack us."

ANSWERS
1. Caesar ē Britanniā excēdere nōlēbat dum obsidēs acciperet. 2. Britannī putāvērunt sē commeātibus Rōmānōs prohibēre posse. 3. "Interclūdāmus reditū hōs Rōmānōs; nēmō mare iterum ad nōs oppugnandōs trānsībit."

Vocabulary

Nouns

continēns, -entis, *f. mainland* (continent, continental)
reditus, -ūs, *m. return*

Adjective

lēnis, -e, *gentle* (leniency, lenient)

Verbs

colloquor, colloquī, collocūtus, *talk with, confer* (colloquium, colloquy)
coorior, coorīrī, coortus, *arise*
cūrō, 1, *care (for), cause (to be done)* (curative, curator)
frangō, -ere, frēgī, frāctus, *break, wreck* (fraction, fracture)
prōvehō, -ere, -vexī, -vectus, *carry forward*

Review: **clam, commeātus, compleō, prope, subitō.**

Word Studies

The moon was thought to have an effect not merely on the tide, as Caesar discovered, but also on the human mind: "lunatic" means *moon-struck*.

From what Latin words are the following derived: **auxilior, colloquor, cūrō, exiguitās, inūtilis, perturbātiō, prōvehō, rebelliō, reditus, reportō?**

Explain *colloquy, curative, lunacy, lunar, plenipotentiary.*

LESSON LXXI

New Difficulties

LESSON OBJECTIVE
To review the gerundive and gerund

IV, 31

At Caesar, etsī nōndum eōrum cōnsilia cognōverat, tamen et ex ēventū[1] nāvium suārum et ex eō[2] quod obsidēs dare intermīserant, fore$_1$ id quod accidit suspicābātur. Itaque ad omnēs cāsūs subsidia comparābat. Nam et frūmentum ex agrīs cotīdiē in castra cōnferēbat et quae$_2$ gravissimē afflīctae erant nāvēs, eārum māteriā atque aere ad reliquās reficiendās ūtēbātur, et quae[3] ad eās rēs erant ūsuī ex continentī comportārī iubēbat. Itaque cum summō studiō ā mīlitibus administrārētur,[4] XII nāvibus āmissīs, reliquīs ut nāvigārī satis commodē posset effēcit.[5]

[1] *accident to his ships*
[2] *from the fact that*
[3] Supply **ea.**
[4] impersonal
[5] *he made it possible to sail well enough in the others* (**nāvigarī** is used impersonally)
[6] *in a favorable position*
[7] i.e., Britons, to join the revolt
[8] *of freeing themselves forever*
[9] *if they should drive*
[10] *by this means*

Summary of Chapters 32–33. The Britons attack the seventh legion while it is collecting grain. They use chariots, which give them the mobility of cavalry. Caesar comes to the rescue.

---

34. Quibus rēbus perturbātīs nostrīs$_3$ tempore opportūnissimō Caesar auxilium tulit. Namque eius adventū hostēs cōnstitērunt, nostrī sē ex timōre recēpērunt. Quō factō, ad lacessendum hostem et committendum proelium aliēnum esse tempus arbitrātus, suō sē locō[6] continuit et, brevī tempore intermissō, in castra legiōnēs redūxit. Dum haec geruntur, nostrīs omnibus occupātīs, quī erant in agrīs reliquī discessērunt.[7] Secūtae sunt continuōs complūrēs diēs tempestātēs quae et nostros in castrīs continērent et hostem ā pugnā prohibērent. Interim barbarī nūntiōs in omnēs partēs dīmīsērunt paucitātemque nostrōrum mīlitum suīs praedicāvērunt, et quanta praedae faciendae atque in perpetuum suī līberandī[8] facultās darētur, sī Rōmānōs castrīs expulissent,[9] dēmōnstrāvērunt. Hīs rēbus[10] celeriter magnā multitūdine peditātūs equitātūsque coāctā, ad castra vēnērunt.

NOTE
Point out that **continērent** is subjunctive because it is in a relative clause of description (characteristic).

$_1$ = **futūrum esse.** Its subject is **id.**
$_2$ Translate as if **eārum nāvium quae.**
$_3$ dative with **auxilium tulit**

PHOTRI/INDEX

This detail from the Arch of Titus depicts the celebration of the sack of Jerusalem. You can see soldiers carrying off sacred vessels and a seven-pronged menorah.

36. Lēgātī ab hostibus missī ad Caesarem dē pāce vēnērunt. Hīs[11] Caesar numerum obsidum quem ante imperāverat duplicāvit, eōsque in continentem addūcī iussit. Ipse idōneam tempestātem nactus paulō post mediam noctem nāvēs solvit; quae omnēs incolumēs ad continentem pervēnērunt; sed ex eīs onerāriae duae eōsdem portūs quōs[12] reliquae capere[13] nōn potuērunt et paulō īnfrā[14] dēlātae sunt.

[11] *for them*
[12] *as*
[13] *reach*
[14] i.e., down the coast

QUESTIONS

1. What led Caesar to expect trouble?
2. What preparations did Caesar make?
3. How did he use the ships that could not be repaired?
4. What postponed the final battle?

ADDITIONAL QUESTIONS
How many ships were actually lost from the fleet? How was the weather during this period? Did it favor one side or the other? How did the Britons use their time? Where did Caesar go with his troops? Did they arrive safely?

Summary of Chapters 37–38. Three hundred soldiers from the two transports are attacked by the Morini. The Romans fight bravely and are rescued by reinforcements. Caesar then sends Labienus to pacify the Morini. Winter quarters are established among the Belgians. The Roman senate decrees a thanksgiving of twenty days for Caesar's victories.

WORKBOOK
Assign Interest Questions 106-110 to review the content of the reading from this lesson.

Grammar

Review the gerundive and gerund in Lessons XXI and XXIII.

TRANSLATION

1. The men were sent to fight.
2. There was no chance of attacking.
3. Caesar was occupied in repairing the ships.
4. They went out for the purpose of collecting grain.

ANSWERS
1. Virī ad pugnandum missī sunt. 2. Nūlla cōpia oppugnandī erat. 3. Caesar in nāvibus reficiendīs occupātus est. 4. Frūmentī cōnferendī causā exiērunt.

Vocabulary

Nouns

equitātus, -ūs, *m. cavalry* (equitation)
ēventus, -ūs, *m. outcome, result* (event, eventuality)
peditātus, -ūs, *m. infantry*

Adjective

continuus, -a, -um, *successive* (continual, continuous)

Verbs

duplicō, 1, *double* (duplicate, duplicity)
intermittō, -ere, -mīsī, -missus, *let go, stop, interrupt, intervene* (intermission, intermittent)
praedicō, 1, *announce* (predicament, predicate)

Adverbs

commodē, *well, suitably, effectively*
īnfrā, *below, farther on* (infrared)

Word Studies

From what Latin words are the following derived: **adventus, complūrēs, cōnferō, ēventus, paucitās?**

Explain *affliction, continuity, perpetuity, propinquity.*

Our Heritage

CAESAR'S INVASIONS OF BRITAIN

The recorded history and culture of Britain, now called England, probably began with Caesar's two invasions of 55 and 54 B.C., although centuries before that traders had gone there for tin. On August 25, 1946, in recognition of the significance of Caesar's invasion, a tablet "to commemorate the two thousandth anniversary of the landing" was unveiled at Deal (north of Dover), where historians think Caesar first set foot on British soil. It is hard for us to imagine what an adventure it was for the Romans to set sail over strange seas from a port in a country that they were just conquering, to an entirely unknown land.

The Bettmann Archive

Tiberius Claudius Drusus Nero Germanicus, or just Claudius, reigned from A.D. 41-54. Since he suffered from a kind of paralysis, he was thought dim-witted and unfit for public office. When Caligula was assassinated in 41, the Praetorian Guard made Claudius emperor, thinking he could be easily controlled. Claudius, however, was a shrewd administrator who added Britain, Mauritania, and Thrace to the Roman Empire.

Caesar made no attempt at a permanent conquest, perhaps because he saw that it would take too long and he was afraid that the hostile Gallic tribes at his back might cause trouble. He was, of course, a long way from home. As the historian Tacitus said a century and a half later, Caesar did not hand Britain over to future generations of Romans but merely revealed it to them. But that in itself was a very important contribution.

Almost exactly a century after Caesar, when all of Gaul, thanks to his efforts, had not only been pacified but Romanized, the Romans began the serious task of conquering Britain. This was under the emperor Claudius in A.D. 43. By the end of the century most of the island had been thoroughly Romanized.

The historian R. G. Collingwood, quoting Sir Mortimer Wheeler, writes of the civilizing influence of the Romans on London (Londinium): "Londinium was a civilized city, a comfortable one, with an efficient drainage system and an adequate water supply. There were probably more buildings of stone and brick than at any subsequent period until after the Great Fire of 1666. There were more adequate and attractive facilities for bathing than ever until the latter part of Queen Victoria's reign."[1]

[1] R.G. Collingwood, *Roman Britain* (London, 1953), p. 58.

LESSON LXXII

Britain and Its People

LESSON OBJECTIVE
There is no specific grammar review for this lesson. You may, however, want to review the adjectives and adverbs that are irregularly compared.

Book V of the *Gallic War,* from which Lessons LXXII to LXXIV are taken, gives an account of Caesar's second invasion of Britain (54 B.C.) and of the Gallic uprisings he faced upon his return.

Summary of Chapters 1–11. The winter following the first expedition to Britain is spent in preparation for a second invasion. After issuing orders for a large fleet to be ready early the next spring, Caesar sets out for Illyricum because he hears that the Pirustae are raiding the country adjoining his province. After subduing them, he sets out for Gaul, where he finds the ships ready. First, however, he decides to subdue the Treveri, among whom an anti-Roman spirit has developed. Caesar's appearance with an army is sufficient to quell the revolt. He then gives orders for his fleet to assemble at Portus Itius. He decides to take Dumnorix, the crafty and ambitious Haeduan, to Britain, for he fears that in his absence Dumnorix will cause trouble. While the troops are embarking and there is confusion in the Roman camp, Dumnorix escapes. He is soon captured and is killed resisting arrest.

SUGGESTION
Ask students to do research on naval battles in U.S. history, either during the Revolutionary War or the Civil War. Compare the number of ships in use during these wars with the 800 that the Romans produced over the winter.

Caesar, leaving Labienus in charge in Gaul with three legions, takes five legions and 2,000 cavalry with him in more than 800 ships. After some difficulty with the tide, he lands in Britain without opposition. He afterwards learns that the Britons, frightened by the number of ships, had taken to the hills. Leaving a force under Quintus Atrius sufficient to guard the ships, Caesar advances inland against the Britons and captures one of their forest strongholds. On the following day, while preparing to pursue them, he learns that a great storm has destroyed about forty of his ships and damaged many others. These are beached and repaired. The Britons put Cassivellaunus in charge of their army.

NOTE
Tell students that today, white lead is a different substance. The mines of Cornwall, since early times, have supplied a large supply of tin, which was carried to all parts of the world.

1 *originated*
2 *as those from which they originated and from which they migrated to this place*
3 *bars*
4 *instead of*
5 *tin* (literally, *white lead*)
6 *bronze*
7 *beech and fir*
8 *hare*
9 *chicken*
10 *goose;* The origin of these taboos is uncertain.
11 *for pastime and pleasure* (as pets)
12 *three-cornered*
13 *as it is from*
14 *in mid-channel*
15 Supply **esse:** *are thought to lie off the coast.*
16 *winter solstice;* Caesar's source was incorrect on this point.
17 *with a water* (*glass*), resembling in principle the sand or hour glass
18 *as their opinion goes*
19 supply **latus**
20 *woad* (a plant)

NOTE
Bronze is an alloy of copper and tin. Its widespread use during one period of history accounts for the name Bronze Age (which preceded the Iron Age). Earliest humans lived in the Stone Age, when tools were made of stone.

NOTE
Point out that Chapter 13, though not geographically accurate, is interesting in that it describes Britain as the Romans imagined it to be. Until this time, no Roman had ever sailed around the island or explored its interior.

SUGGESTION
You might want to review compass directions with students: **septentriones, oriens solis, occidens solis, regio meridiana**.

V, 12

Britanniae pars interior ab eīs incolitur quōs nātōs[1] in īnsulā ipsī dīcunt; maritima pars ab eīs quī praedae ac bellī īnferendī causā ex Belgiō trānsiērunt (quī omnēs ferē eīs nōminibus cīvitātum appellantur quibus[2] ortī ex cīvitātibus eō pervēnērunt) et, bellō illātō, ibi remānsērunt atque agrōs colere coepērunt. Hominum est īnfīnīta multitūdō crēberrimaque aedificia ferē Gallicīs cōnsimilia, pecoris magnus numerus. Ūtuntur aut aere aut nummō aureō aut tāleīs[3] ferreīs ad certum pondus exāminātīs prō[4] nummō. Nāscitur ibi plumbum[5] album in mediterrāneīs regiōnibus, in maritimīs ferrum, sed eius exigua est cōpia; aere[6] ūtuntur importātō. Māteria cuiusque generis ut in Galliā est praeter fāgum atque abietem.[7] Leporem[8] et gallīnam[9] et ānserem [10] gustāre fās nōn putant; haec tamen alunt animī voluptātisque causā. [11] Loca sunt temperātiōra quam in Galliā, remissiōribus frīgoribus.

13. Īnsula nātūrā triquetra,[12] cuius ūnum latus est contrā Galliam. Huius lateris alter angulus, quī est ad Cantium, quō ferē omnēs ex Galliā nāvēs appelluntur, ad orientem sōlem, īnferior ad merīdiem spectat. Hoc latus pertinet circiter mīlia passuum D. Alterum vergit ad Hispāniam atque occidentem sōlem; quā ex parte est Hibernia, īnsula dīmidiō minor (ut exīstimātur) quam Britannia, sed parī spatiō atque[13] ex Galliā est in Britanniam. In hōc mediō cursū[14] est īnsula quae appellātur Mona; complūrēs praetereā minōrēs obiectae[15] īnsulae exīstimantur; dē quibus īnsulīs nōn nūllī scrīpsērunt diēs continuōs XXX sub brūmam[16] esse noctem. Nōs nihil dē eō reperiēbāmus, nisi certīs ex aqua[17] mēnsūrīs breviōrēs esse quam in continentī noctēs vidēbāmus. Huius[1] est longitūdō lateris, ut[18] fert illōrum opīniō, DCC mīlium. Tertium est contrā septentriōnēs, cui partī nūlla est obiecta terra; sed eius angulus lateris maximē ad Germāniam spectat. Hoc[19] mīlia passuum DCCC in longitūdinem esse exīstimātur. Ita omnis īnsula est in circuitū vīciēs centum mīlium passuum.

14. Ex hīs omnibus longē sunt hūmānissimī quī Cantium incolunt (quae regiō est maritima omnis), neque multum ā Gallicā differunt cōnsuētūdine. Interiōrēs plērīque frūmenta nōn serunt, sed lacte et carne vīvunt pellibusque sunt vestītī. Omnēs vērō sē Britannī vitro[20] īnficiunt, quod caeruleum efficit colōrem, atque hōc horridiōrēs sunt in pugnā aspectū; capillōque sunt prōmissō.

---

1 the side of Britain facing Ireland

S. Vidler/SuperStock, Inc.

Stonehenge is the famous prehistoric megalith complex that dates from 2800 B.C. It was a ceremonial and religious center made of precisely positioned stones. It may have functioned as an astronomical observatory. At one time, it was thought that the Druids caused it to be built.

NOTE
Actually, the circumference is more than twice as great, although the measurement of coastlines is difficult. We do not know how Caesar arrived at his estimate.

NOTE
Have students identify the three different ablatives used in this sentence.

QUESTIONS

1. What was the origin of the Britons?
2. What did the natives do with chickens?
3. What metals were once found in Britain?
4. Describe the inhabitants of Britain.

ADDITIONAL QUESTIONS
What were the houses of the Britons like? What do they use for money? What animals are found in abundance in Britain? Why do the Britons appear particularly terrible in battle?

Vocabulary

Nouns

capillus, -ī, *m. hair* (capillary)
fas, *n. (indeclinable) right*
ferrum, -ī, *n. iron* (ferroconcrete, ferrous)
nummus, -i, *m. coin, money* (numismatics, nummular)
voluptās, -tātis, *f. pleasure* (voluptuary, voluptuous)

WORKBOOK
Assign Interest Questions 111-115 to review the content of the reading from this lesson.

Adjectives

albus, -a, -um, *white* (albino, albumen)
caeruleus, -a, -um, *blue* (cerulean)
cōnsimilis, -e, *very similar*
crēber, -bra, -brum, *frequent, numerous* (crebation)
īnfīnītus, -a, -um, *endless, countless* (infinitive, infinity)
interior, -ius, *interior*

Verb

appellō, -ere, appulī, appulsus, *land, drive to, bring up*

Adverb

vīciēs, *twenty times*

The Roman lighthouse at Dover, England, 380 feet high, as it appears today. The solidity of its construction (during the 1st century A.D.) is an indication of the Romans' interest in a permanent conquest and colonization of Britain.

Robert Estall/Tony Stone Images

Summary of Chapters 15–43. The Romans on their march are attacked by British charioteers and cavalry, but beat them off. The Britons, by retreating, induce the Roman cavalry to pursue. Then, leaping down from their chariots, they fight on foot, relieving one another at intervals. Later, when Caesar sends out a detachment to forage, the Britons attack his scattered troops and drive them to seek the protection of the legions who are standing guard. The latter charge and drive the Britons off. Caesar leads his army to the Tamesis (Thames) River, which he fords, and again routs the enemy. Cassivellaunus, the British leader, avoiding a general engagement, confines himself to guerrilla tactics. Meanwhile the Trinovantes, the strongest British tribe of that region, surrender and send hostages to Caesar. Other tribes do the same. After an unsuccessful attack on the Roman camp, Cassivellaunus surrenders. Caesar returns to Gaul with his army and prisoners. During the two invasions of Britain not a single ship carrying troops was lost.

Caesar finds it necessary, on account of the scarcity of provisions, to distribute his legions in six divisions among various Gallic tribes. The Gauls seize this opportunity to revolt. The Carnutes kill Tasgetius, whom Caesar had made king over them. Ambiorix, leader of the Eburones, attacks the camp of Sabinus and Cotta. In a conference, Ambiorix, assuming the role of friend, urges Sabinus to leave his camp and join either Cicero or Labienus. Sabinus and Cotta call a council of war. Sabinus favors acting upon the advice given by Ambiorix, but Cotta opposes. In the end Cotta yields. The army then leaves camp, loaded down with baggage, and is ambushed in a valley. Though the Romans fight bravely, they are gradually worn down. After Cotta is wounded, Sabinus has a conference with Ambiorix, at which he is treacherously murdered. The Romans then fight on till they are killed or commit suicide. Only a few escape; not one surrenders. Ambiorix then stirs up the Atuatuci and the Nervii. All proceed to attack Quintus Cicero, brother of the famous orator, in his winter quarters. All the Romans, including the sick and wounded, work day and night on the fortifications. At a conference with Cicero, the Nervii promise to let him and his army withdraw unharmed if Caesar will refrain from quartering his troops in their territory. Cicero is not deceived and refers them to Caesar. The Gauls then begin a siege. They set fire to the Roman camps with fire bombs and burning arrows.

Word Studies

Believe it or not, *goose* and **ānser** are derived from the same word. Latin, English, and most European languages are descended from a language called Indo-European, which we know only from the common elements in its descendants. The masculine of goose is *gander,* which looks a bit more like **ānser.**

Brūma is from **brevima (diēs),** the *shortest day* of the year; **brevima** is a variant of **brevissima.**

From what Latin words are the following derived: **cōnsimilis, importō, īnfīnītus, mediterrāneus?**

Explain *album, albumen, angular, commensurate, disgust, gustatory, gusto, oriole, plumber, ponderous, voluptuous.*

LESSON LXXIII

Two Rival Heroes

LESSON OBJECTIVE

There is no specific grammar review for this lesson. You may, however, want to review various participles, since several appear in this reading.

V, 44

CASSETTE

This reading is recorded on Cassette 3, Side A.

Erant in eā legiōne fortissimī virī, centuriōnēs, quī iam prīmīs ōrdinibus appropinquārent, T. Pullō et L. Vorēnus. Hī perpetuās inter sē contrōversiās habēbant uter alterī anteferrētur, omnibusque annīs[1] dē locō contendēbant. Ex hīs Pullō, cum ācerrimē ad mūnītiōnēs pugnārētur, "Quid dubitās," inquit, "Vorēne, aut quem locum probandae virtūtis tuae exspectās? Hic diēs dē nostrīs contrōversiīs iūdicābit."

Haec cum dīxisset, prōcēdit extrā mūnītiōnēs quaeque pars hostium cōnfertissima est vīsa in eam irrumpit. Nē Vorēnus quidem sēsē tum vāllō continet, sed omnium veritus opiniōnem subsequitur. Mediocrī spatiō relīctō, Pullō pīlum in hostēs immittit atque ūnum ex multitūdine prōcurrentem trāicit; quo[1] percussō exanimātōque, hunc scūtīs dēfendunt hostēs, in illum ūniversī tēla coniciunt neque dant prōgrediendī facultātem. Trānsfīgitur scūtum Pullōnī et iaculum in balteō dēfīgitur. Āvertit hic cāsus vāgīnam[2] et gladium ēdūcere cōnantī[3] dextram morātur manum, impedītumque hostēs circumsistunt. Succurrit inimīcus illī Vorēnus et labōrantī subvenit. Ad hunc sē cōnfestim ā Pullōne omnis multitūdō convertit. Vorēnus gladiō rem gerit atque, ūnō interfectō, reliquōs paulum prōpellit; dum cupidius īnstat, in locum dēiectus īnferiōrem concidit. Huic rūrsus circumventō subsidium fert Pullō, atque ambō incolumēs, complūribus interfectīs, summā cum laude intrā mūnītiōnēs sē recipiunt. Sīc fortūna in certāmine utrumque versāvit[4] ut alter alterī inimīcus auxiliō salūtīque esset, neque dīiūdicārī posset uter[5] virtūte anteferendus vidērētur.

[1] *every year* (they were rivals for promotion, **locō**)
[2] *scabbard* (It was pushed to one side and hard to get at.)
[3] Supply **eī:** *when he tried.*
[4] *dealt with*
[5] *which seemed superior*

NOTE

Tell students that **Pullo** is nominative (**Pullo, Pullonis**).

NOTE

Remind students that according to the rule, an ablative absolute must not be grammatically connected to the rest of the sentence; **hunc** breaks this rule.

[1] the wounded Gaul (ablative absolute). Contrary to the rule, **hunc** refers to the same person.

C. M. Dixon

Marcus Favonius Facilis was a centurion with the 20th legion of the Pollian tribe. He fought with Caesar in Britain. Notice that he carries a ***gladius****, a* ***pugio****, and a* ***vitis*** *as a symbol of his rank.*

45. Erat ūnus in castrīs Nervius nōmine Verticō, locō nātus honestō, quī ad Cicerōnem perfūgerat suamque eī fidem praestiterat. Hic servō spē lībertātis magnīsque persuādet praemiīs ut litterās ad Caesarem dēferat. Hās ille in iaculō illigātās[2] effert, et Gallus inter Gallōs sine ūllā suspīciōne versātus ad Caesarem pervenit. Ab eō dē perīculīs Cicerōnis legiōnisque cognōscitur.

NOTE
Tell students that **loco** here is ablative of origin.

QUESTIONS

1. Who quarreled and why?
2. Which attacked the enemy first?
3. What difficulty did he run into?
4. Which of the two soldiers was the braver?
5. How did Caesar get word of Cicero's situation?

ADDITIONAL QUESTIONS
Of what rank were Pullo and Vorenus? Were either Pullo or Verenis wounded? What difficulty happened to Vorenus? Who was Vertico?

WORKBOOK
Assign Interest Questions 116-120 to review the content of the reading from this lesson.

Summary of Chapters 46–47. Caesar immediately advances with two legions to relieve Cicero. The Treveri, elated by their recent victory over Sabinus, now menace Labienus, preventing him from joining Caesar.

[2] Perhaps concealed in the shaft, which may have been wrapped as if mended.

Vocabulary

Nouns

balteus, -ī, *m. belt*
certāmen, -minis, *n. contest, struggle*
iaculum, -ī, *n. dart, javelin*

Adjectives

mediocris, -e, *short, moderate* (mediocre, mediocrity)
perpetuus, -a, -um, *constant, lasting* (perpetual, perpetuate)

Verbs

anteferō, -ferre, -tulī, -lātus, *prefer*
dēfīgō, -ere, dēfīxī, dēfīxus, *drive in*
dubitō, 1, *hesitate* (dubitable, dubitation)
iūdicō, 1, *judge, decide* (prejudice, judicature)

Adverb

cōnfestim, *immediately, at once*

Word Studies

From what Latin words are the following derived: **anteferō, dēfīgō, dīiūdicō, honestus, illigō, immittō, irrumpō, succurrō, trāiciō, trānsfīgō?**

Explain *irruption, laudatory, percussion, succor.*

LESSON LXXIV

A Coded Message and a Clever Trick

LESSON OBJECTIVE
There is no specific grammar review for this lesson. You may, however, want to review any constructions with which your students seem to be having difficulty. This is the last lesson in Unit VI.

V, 48

Caesar vēnit magnīs itineribus in Nerviōrum fīnēs. Ibi ex captīvīs cognōscit quae apud Cicerōnem gerantur quantōque in perīculō rēs sit. Tum cuidam ex equitibus Gallīs magnīs praemiīs persuādet utī ad Cicerōnem epistulam dēferat. Hanc Graecīs[1] cōnscrīptam litterīs mittit, nē, interceptā epistulā, nostra ab hostibus cōnsilia cognōscantur. Sī adīre nōn possit, monet ut trāgulam cum epistulā dēligātā intrā mūnītiōnēs castrōrum abiciat. In litterīs scrībit sē cum legiōnibus profectum celeriter adfore;[1] hortātur ut prīstinam virtūtem retineat. Gallus perīculum veritus, ut erat praeceptum, trāgulam mittit. Haec cāsū ad turrim adhaesit, neque ā nostrīs bīduō animadversa, tertiō diē ā quōdam mīlite cōnspicitur; ad Cicerōnem dēfertur. Ille perlēctam[2] in conventū mīlitum recitat maximāque omnēs laetitiā afficit. Tum fūmī incendiōrum[2] procul vidēbantur, quae rēs omnem dubitātiōnem adventūs legiōnum expulit.

NOTE
Tell students that this message was written in code.

[1] = **adfutūrum esse**
[2] *read through* (*silently*); supply **epistulam.**
[3] *not one soldier in ten*

Summary of Chapters 49–51. The Gauls rush to meet Caesar, who is warned by a message from Cicero. By pretending fear, Caesar induces the enemy to attack him on his own ground and defeats them with great loss.

NOTE
Ask students to recall some of the other tricks and tactics that have been used by Caesar and his men.

---

52. Longius prōsequī veritus, quod silvae palūdēsque intercēdēbant, omnibus suīs incolumibus, eōdem diē ad Cicerōnem pervēnit. Īnstitūtās turrēs, testūdinēs mūnītiōnēsque hostium admīrātur; prōductā legiōne, cognōscit nōn decimum quemque[3] esse reliquum mīlitem sine vulnere. Ex hīs omnibus iūdicat rēbus quantō cum perīculō et quantā virtūte rēs sint administrātae. Cicerōnem prō eius meritō legiōnemque collaudat; centuriōnēs singillātim tribūnōsque mīlitum appellat, quōrum ēgregiam fuisse virtūtem testimōniō Cicerōnis cognōverat.

SUGGESTION
Use a large map to show the range of territory Caesar and his troops covered over a relatively short time.

---

[1] probably Latin written in Greek letters
[2] not of camp fires but of flaming villages fired by the Romans as they advanced

The Romans were not the only army with a cavalry. These two horsemen are Gauls. Do you notice anything different about them, compared with the Romans?

North Wind Picture Archives

ADDITIONAL QUESTIONS
Into what territory did Caesar march? Who delivered the message? Did Cicero receive the message immediately? What was the reaction of Cicero's troops when he read the message?

WORKBOOK
Assign Interest Questions 121-125 to review the content of the reading from this lesson.

QUESTIONS

1. How did Cicero get the message from Caesar?
2. What confirmation of the message did he get?
3. What percentage of Cicero's men were wounded?

Summary of Chapters 53–58. Despite this victory, the spirit of revolt spreads fast among the Gauls, and Caesar decides to spend the winter with his army. The leader of the Treveri prepares to attack the camp of Labienus, but the latter, feigning fear, lures the enemy to the very walls of his camp; then, by a surprise attack, he routs the Gauls, and the leader is killed. After that Caesar states that he "found Gaul a little more peaceful."

Vocabulary

Nouns

dubitātiō, -iōnis, *f. doubt* (dubitation)
epistula, -ae, *f. letter* (epistle, epistolary)
fūmus, -ī, *m. smoke* (fume, fumigate)
meritum, -ī, *n. merit, service* (meritorious)
testūdō, -dinis, *f. shed, turtle*

Adverb

singillātim, *one by one, individually*

Word Studies

From what Latin words are the following derived: **admīror, conventus, dubitātiō, intercēdō, praecipiō, singillātim?**

Explain *adhesive, cohesive, conspicuous, epistolary, indubitable.*

ADHESIVE TAPE

ANNO DNI
SARTIVS PINGEBAT

Scala/Art Resource, NY

Unit VII

Dē Bellō Gallicō VI-VII

UNIT OBJECTIVES
No specific grammar topics are taught in this unit. You may want to review structures as needed, depending on the abilities of your students. These are the last of the Caesar selections. If you wish, you may assign projects to be presented at the end of this unit. A Latin play, "Caesar the Dictator," ends the unit.

After spending nine years (58-50 B.C.) conquering and governing Gaul, Julius Caesar crossed the Rubicon River into Italy proper in 49 B.C., precipitating Civil War. Within three years, he had overpowered his opposition and had become ruler of the Western world. In the next few years, he brought about many reforms in Roman political and economic life. Caesar has been painted, sculpted, and drawn throughout the ages. In this painting by del Sarto (c. 1487-1530), various conquered tribes bring tribute to their conqueror, Julius Caesar. Notice the variety of animals in this scene.

LESSON LXXV

Gallic Leaders

The readings in Lessons LXXV to LXXXI, selected from Book VI of the *Gallic War,* are devoted to Caesar's comparison of the way of life of the Gauls with that of the Germans.

Summary of Chapters 1–10. Caesar, expecting a more serious revolt in Gaul, increases his force by three legions, one of which is supplied by Pompey. Ambiorix and the Treveri are plotting against him. The Nervii, Atuatuci, Menapii, and all the Germans on the Gallic side of the Rhine are in arms against the Romans, and the Senones are conspiring with the Carnutes and other states. Accordingly, before the winter is over, Caesar leads a strong force against the Nervii and compels them to surrender. He next marches against the Senones, and they, as well as the Carnutes, surrender. Caesar, now free to attack Ambiorix, proceeds to cut him off from allied aid. He first crushes the Menapii. Meanwhile, with reinforcements received from Caesar, Labienus defeats the Treveri. Caesar again builds a bridge and crosses the Rhine, partly to prevent the Germans from sending aid to the Treveri, partly to prevent Ambiorix from finding refuge in Germany. He learns that the Suebi have sent aid to the Treveri and are now mobilizing in a large forest.

Photo Bulloz

Coinage was used throughout the empire. This Gallic coin was from the Parisii tribe, who settled in the area of modern day Paris around 250-200 B.C. Though they were primarily fishermen, horses obviously played an important part in their lives.

VI, 11

Quoniam ad hunc locum[1] perventum est, nōn aliēnum esse vidētur dē Galliae Germāniaeque mōribus et quō[2] differant hae nātiōnēs inter sē prōpōnere. In Galliā nōn sōlum in omnibus cīvitātibus atque in omnibus pāgīs partibusque, sed paene etiam in singulīs domibus factiōnēs sunt, eārumque factiōnum sunt prīncipēs quī summam auctōritātem eōrum[3] iūdiciō habēre exīstimantur, quōrum[1] ad arbitrium iūdiciumque summa omnium rērum cōnsiliōrumque redeat.[4]

12. Cum Caesar in Galliam vēnit, alterius factiōnis prīncipēs erant Haeduī, alterius Sēquanī. Hī cum per sē minus valērent, quod summa auctōritās antīquitus erat in Haeduīs magnaeque eōrum erant clientēlae, Germānōs atque Ariovistum sibi adiūnxerant eōsque ad sē magnīs iactūrīs pollicitātiōnibusque perdūxerant. Proeliīs vērō complūribus factīs secundīs atque omnī nōbilitāte Haeduōrum interfectā, tantum potentiā antecesserant ut magnam partem clientium ab Haeduīs ad sē trādūcerent obsidēsque[5] ab eīs prīncipum fīliōs acciperent, et pūblicē iūrāre cōgerent nihil sē contrā Sēquanōs cōnsilī[6] initūrōs,[7] et partem fīnitimī agrī per vim occupātam possidērent[8] Galliaeque tōtīus prīncipātum obtinērent. Quā necessitāte adductus Dīviciācus auxilī petendī causā Rōmam ad senātum profectus, īnfectā rē, redierat. Adventū Caesaris factā commūtātiōne rērum, obsidibus Haeduīs redditīs, veteribus clientēlīs restitūtīs, novīs per Caesarem comparātīs, quod eī quī sē ad eōrum amīcitiam aggregāverant meliōre condiciōne atque aequiōre imperiō sē ūtī[9] vidēbant, reliquīs rēbus[10] eōrum grātiā dignitāteque amplificātā, Sēquanī prīncipātum dīmīserant. In eōrum locum Rēmī successerant; quōs quod adaequāre apud Caesarem grātiā intellegēbātur,[2] eī[11] quī propter veterēs inimīcitiās nūllō modō cum Haeduīs coniungī poterant, sē Rēmīs in clientēlam dicābant.[12] Hōs illī dīligenter tuēbantur; ita et novam et repente collēctam auctōritātem tenēbant. Eō tum statū[13] rēs erat ut longē prīncipēs habērentur Haeduī, secundum locum dignitātis Rēmī obtinērent.

[1] i.e., in the story
[2] *in what respect*
[3] i.e., the Gauls
[4] *is referred*
[5] *(as) hostages*
[6] object of **nihil**
[7] Supply **esse.**
[8] *kept* (coordinate with **trādūcerent, acciperent, cōgerent**)
[9] *that they were enjoying*
[10] *in all other respects*
[11] *those (other tribes)*
[12] with **in clientēlam:** *they attached themselves*
[13] *situation*

QUESTIONS

1. How were the Gallic leaders chosen?
2. Which tribe had the most power before Caesar came?
3. Which tribe was first after Caesar's arrival? Which was second?

1 *so that to their decision* (the antecedent is **prīncipēs**, not **eōrum**)
2 Used impersonally: *because it was understood that these* **(quōs)** *equaled* (*the Haeduans*).

NOTE
You might tell students (or elicit) that **redeat** is subjunctive because it is in a relative clause of description (characteristic).

NOTE
Discuss with students the widespread use of hostages in ancient times.

NOTE
Point out that **initūrōs (esse)** is an indirect statement after **iūrāre**.

NOTE
If students are having any difficulty with this section, you might want to review ablative absolutes.

SUGGESTION
Many tribes/groups are mentioned in this reading. Have students sort them out one by one to determine who gained status, who lost it, and how alliances were put together.

ADDITIONAL QUESTIONS
Who was Ariovistus? Which tribe had he influenced? Who was Diviciacus? Which tribe did he represent? Did Caesar support the Roman Senate's decision?

WORKBOOK
Assign Interest Questions 126-130 to review the content of the reading from this lesson.

Vocabulary

SUGGESTION
As a quick drill, have students decline aloud using nouns and adjectives from this lesson.

Nouns

arbitrium, -trī, *n. decision, judgment*	(arbiter, arbitrary)
clientēla, -ae, *f. clientship*	(clientele)
iactūra, -ae, *f. loss, expense, sacrifice*	
pollicitātiō, -ōnis, *f. promise*	

Adjectives

aequus, -a, -um, *equal, fair, calm*	(equal, inequity)
infectus, -a, -um, *not done*	(infect, infectious)
vetus, veteris (gen.), *old*	(inveterate, veteran)

Verbs

adaequō, 1, *equal*	(adequacy, adequate)
aggregō, 1, *attach*	(aggregate, aggregation)
iūrō, 1, *swear*	(adjure, adjuration)
tueor, tuērī, tūtus, *guard*	(tutor, tutorial)

Adverbs

publicē, *publicly*
repente, *suddenly*

Review: **colligō, nōn sōlum... sed etiam, redeō.**

Word Studies

From what Latin words are the following derived: **adaequō, antīquitus, arbitrium, clientēla, commūtātiō, iactūra, īnfectus, iūdicium, necessitās, pollicitātiō, potentia, status?**

Explain *adjunct, dedicate, inveterate, status, tutor, veteran.*

LESSON LXXVI

The Druids

SUGGESTION
You might want to review the various uses of the ablative that appear in this reading.

VI, 13

In omnī Galliā eōrum hominum quī aliquō sunt numerō[1] atque honōre genera sunt duo. Nam plēbēs[2] paene servōrum habētur locō, quae nihil audet per sē, nūllī adhibētur cōnsiliō. Plērīque, cum aut aere aliēnō aut magnitūdine tribūtōrum aut iniūriā potentiōrum premuntur, sēsē in servitūtem dant nōbilibus; quibus in hōs[3] eadem omnia sunt iūra quae[4] dominīs in servōs. Sed dē hīs duōbus generibus alterum est druidum, alterum equitum. Illī rēbus dīvīnīs intersunt, sacrificia pūblica ac prīvāta prōcūrant, religiōnēs[5] interpretantur. Ad hōs magnus adulēscentium numerus disciplīnae causā concurrit, magnōque hī[6] sunt apud eōs[7] honōre. Nam ferē dē omnibus contrōversiīs pūblicīs prīvātīsque cōnstituunt; et, sī quod est facinus admissum, sī caedēs facta, sī dē hērēditāte, dē fīnibus contrōversia est, īdem[8] dēcernunt; praemia poenāsque cōnstituunt; sī quī aut prīvātus aut populus eōrum dēcrētō nōn stetit,[9] sacrificiīs prohibent. Haec poena apud eōs est gravissima. Quibus$_1$ ita est prohibitum, hī numerō impiōrum ac sceleratorum habentur, hīs[10] omnēs dēcēdunt, aditum eōrum sermōnemque dēfugiunt, nē quid ex contāgiōne incommodī[11] accipiant, neque hīs petentibus iūs redditur neque honōs$_2$ ūlius commūnicātur. Hīs autem omnibus druidibus praeest ūnus, quī summam inter eōs habet auctōritātem. Hōc mortuō, aut, sī quī$_3$ ex reliquīs praestat dignitāte, succēdit, aut, sī sunt parēs plūrēs, suffrāgiō druidum dēligitur; nōn numquam etiam armīs dē prīncipātū contendunt. Hī certō annī tempore in fīnibus Carnutum, quae regiō tōtīus Galliae media habētur, cōnsīdunt in locō cōnsecrātō; hūc omnēs undique quī contrōversiās habent conveniunt eōrumque dēcrētīs iūdiciīsque pārent. Disciplīna$_4$ in Britanniā reperta atque inde in Galliam trānslāta esse exīstimātur; et nunc quī dīligentius eam rem cognōscere volunt plērumque illō[12] discendī causā proficīscuntur.

[1] of *some account* (with **aliquō**)
[2] = **plēbs**
[3] *over them* (the enslaved plebeians)
[4] *as*
[5] *religious questions*
[6] i.e., the druids
[7] i.e., all the Gauls
[8] *likewise*
[9] *did not abide by;* **dēcrētō** is ablative
[10] *from these*
[11] genitive
[12] adverb

NOTES:
Point out that **hīs** is dative of separation (or reference).

The name of the Carnutes is preserved in Chartres. It is possible that the annual Council on the Isle of Man is a survival of such meetings.

The druids met in groves of oak trees, which were sacred, as was the mistletoe that grew on them. Our use of mistletoe at Christmas is inherited from the druids.

Some students may want to do additional research on the druids, Stonehenge, and the dolmens and menhirs in northwestern France.

$_1$ dative; the antecedent is **hī.**
$_2$ old form of **honor**
$_3$ for the more usual **quis**
$_4$ *system* of druidism

Ancient Art & Architecture Collection

Among the ancients Celts, the Druids were priests and learned individuals. They were held in high esteem and enjoyed enormous prestige in the community. Druid cults were found in Gaul, Britain, and Ireland. Much of what we know about the Druids comes from Roman texts, since the Druids themselves preferred to pass on their knowledge in the oral tradition rather that writing it down.

ADDITIONAL QUESTIONS
What was the status of the common people in Gaul? What is the most severe punishment that the druids inflict? What happens when the head druid dies? Why do they meet in the land of the Carnutes?

WORKBOOK
Assign Interest Questions 131-135 to review the content of the reading from this lesson.

QUESTIONS

1. What three classes were there among the Gauls?
2. What were the functions and powers of the druids?
3. What business did the druids transact at their annual meetings?

Vocabulary

Nouns

facinus, facinoris, *n. crime*	
hērēditās, -tātis, *f. inheritance*	(heredity)
honor, -ōris, *m. honor, office*	(honorable, honorary)
incommodum, -ī, *n. harm*	(incommode, incommodious)
religiō, -ōnis, *f. religion, superstition*	(religious)
sermō, -ōnis, *m. conversation, talk*	(sermon, sermonize)
suffrāgium, -gī, *n. vote*	(suffrage, suffragette)

Adjective

impius, -a, -um, *impious*	(impish)

Verbs

adhibeō, -ēre, adhibuī, adhibitus, *hold toward, admit to*	
commūnicō, 1, *share*	(commune, communicate)
intersum, -esse, -fuī, -futūrus, *be between, take part (in)*	(interest)
pāreō, -ēre, pāruī, pāritūrus, *obey* (+ dat.)	
praesum, -esse, -fuī, -futūrus, *be in charge of*	
prōcūrō, 1, *take care of*	(procuration, procure)

Review: **admittō, adulēscēns, caedēs, hūc, morior.**

Word Studies

Proxy is shortened from *procuracy* and therefore means *taking care* of something *for* someone.

From what Latin words are the following derived; **adhibeō, commūnicō, cōnsecrātus, dēfugiō, sacrificium, tribūtum?**

Explain *consecration, heredity, interpretation, suffrage.*

LESSON LXXVII

Druids and Knights

NOTE
Point out that this practice is comparable to the Egyptian priests and their hieroglyphs (sacred writing).

NOTE
Elicit that they believed in reincarnation.

VI, 14

Druidēs ā bellō abesse[1] cōnsuērunt neque tribūta ūnā cum reliquīs pendunt. Tantīs excitātī praemiīs et suā sponte multī in disciplīnam conveniunt et ā parentibus propinquīsque mittuntur. Magnum ibi numerum versuum ēdiscere dīcuntur. Itaque annōs nōn nūllī vīcēnōs in disciplīnā permanent. Neque fās esse exīstimant ea[2] litterīs mandāre, cum[3] in reliquīs ferē rēbus, pūblicīs prīvātīsque ratiōnibus, Graecīs ūtantur litterīs. Id mihi duābus dē causīs īnstituisse videntur; quod neque in vulgus disciplīnam efferrī velint neque eōs quī discunt litterīs cōnfīsōs minus memoriae studēre[4] —quod ferē plērīsque accidit ut praesidiō litterārum dīligentiam in perdiscendō ac memoriam remittant. In prīmīs hoc volunt persuādēre,[5] nōn interīre animās,[6] sed ab aliīs post mortem trānsīre ad aliōs; atque hōc maximē ad virtūtem excitārī[1] putant, metū mortis neglēctō. Multa praetereā dē sīderibus atque eōrum mōtū, dē mundī ac terrārum magnitūdine, dē rērum nātūrā, dē deōrum immortālium vī ac potestāte disputant et iuventūtī trādunt.

15. Alterum genus est equitum. Hī cum[7] est ūsus[8] atque aliquod bellum incidit (quod[9] ante Caesaris adventum ferē quotannīs accidere solēbat, utī aut ipsī iniūriās īnferrent aut illātās prōpulsārent[10]), omnēs in bellō versantur, atque eōrum ut[11] quisque est genere cōpiīsque amplissimus, ita plūrimōs circum sē ambactōs[12] clientēsque habet. Hanc ūnam grātiam potentiamque nōvērunt.

1 *to be exempt from*
2 *these principles*
3 *although*
4 *pay less attention to the memory*
5 *prove*
6 *souls*
7 *whenever*
8 *need*
9 *and this*
10 *warded off injuries inflicted (by others)*
11 *(in proportion) as*
12 *retainers* (a Gallic word)

SUGGESTION
You might have an interesting class discussion about the notion that writing things down impairs the memory. The Greeks also used a primarily oral form of teaching. Today, however, we seem to feel that books and computers hold the answers to everything, and rarely are facts committed to memory.

ADDITIONAL QUESTIONS
Why did parents and relatives send young men for druid training? How long do some men spend in their studies? Name some of the things the druids taught about. What was the principal role of the knights? How often did wars break out prior to Caesar's arrival? What determines a knight's influence?

QUESTIONS

1. What exemptions did the druids have?
2. What were the teaching methods of the druids?
3. What was their belief about the souls of the dead?
4. Why did the druids not put their teachings in writing?

WORKBOOK
Assign Interest Questions 136-140 to review the content of the reading from this lesson.

[1] Supply **hominēs** as subject.

Ancient Art & Architecture Collection

Druids were in charge of educating the sons of chiefs and guarding the sacred traditions. Oak trees and mistletoe figured heavily in their rituals, as did human sacrifice. They resisted the Latin culture and were eventually suppressed by the Romans.

Vocabulary

Nouns

anima, -ae, *f. soul* (animal, animate)
iuventūs, -tūtis, *f. youth, young people*
metus, -ūs, *m. fear*
sīdus, sīderis, *n. star* (sidereal)
versus, -ūs, *m. line, verse*
vulgus, -ī, *n. common people* (vulgar, Vulgate)

NOTE
Point out that **vulgus** is neuter, even though it would seem to follow the "masculine" pattern.

Verbs

ēdiscō, -ere, ēdidicī, —, *learn by heart* (edit, editor)
intereō, -īre, -iī, -itūrus, *perish*
soleō, -ēre, solitus, *be used to, be accustomed (semideponent)*

Review: **efferō, neglegō, suā sponte.**

Word Studies

The suffix **–tō (–sō, –itō)** is added to the stems of past participles to form verbs expressing the idea of *keeping on* ("frequentative" verbs): **prōpulsō** (from **prōpulsus**), *keep on warding off.*

From what Latin words are the following derived: **disputō, immortālis?**

Explain *disciple, disputant, divulge, immortality, mundane, sidereal, spontaneity, vulgar, Vulgate.*

The great Gallic Hammer-God. The hammer associates him with both the heavens and the underworld, and the rustic panpipe with the woodlands. The Romans appear to have identified him with their own Jupiter, Dispater, and Silvanus. By the Gauls he was variously called Sucellus or Taranis. About 200 of his images have been found.

C. M. Dixon

LESSON LXXVIII

Religion

VI, 16

Nātiō est omnis Gallōrum admodum dēdita religiōnibus; atque ob eam causam quī sunt affectī graviōribus morbīs, quīque in proeliīs perīculīsque versantur, aut prō victimīs hominēs immolant aut sē immolātūrōs vovent, administrīsque [1] ad ea sacrificia druidibus ūtuntur, quod, prō vītā hominis nisi hominis vīta reddātur, nōn posse deōs immortālēs plācārī arbitrantur; pūblicēque eiusdem generis habent īnstitūta sacrificia. Aliī immānī magnitūdine simulācra [2] habent, quōrum contexta vīminibus [3] membra vīvīs hominibus complent; quibus incēnsīs, circumventī flammā exanimantur hominēs. Supplicia eōrum quī in fūrtō aut latrōciniō aut aliquā noxiā sint comprehēnsī grātiōra dīs [4] immortālibus esse arbitrantur; sed, cum eius generis cōpia dēficit, etiam ad innocentium supplicia dēscendunt.

17. Deōrum maximē Mercurium colunt. Huius sunt plūrima simulācra; hunc omnium inventōrem artium ferunt,[5] hunc viārum atque itinerum ducem, hunc ad quaestūs pecūniae mercātūrāsque habēre vim maximam arbitrantur; post hunc[6] Apollinem et Mārtem et Iovem et Minervam. Dē hīs eandem ferē quam[7] reliquae gentēs habent opīniōnem: Apollinem morbōs dēpellere, Minervam operum atque artificiōrum[8] initia trādere, Iovem imperium deōrum tenēre, Mārtem bella regere. Huic, cum proelio climicare cōnstituērunt, ea quae bellō cēperint plērumque dēvovent;[9] cum superāvērunt, animālia capta immolant, reliquās rēs in ūnum locum cōnferunt. Multīs in cīvitātibus hārum rērum exstrūctōs tumulōs locīs cōnsecrātīs cōnspicārī licet. Neque saepe accidit ut neglectā quispian religione aut capta apud sē occultāre aut posita tollere audēret; gravissimumque eī reī supplicium cum cruciatū cōnstitūtum est.

18. Gallī sē omnēs ab Dīte patre prōgnātōs praedicant idque ab druidibus prōditum dīcunt. Ob eam causam spatia omnis temporis nōn numerō diērum sed noctium fīniunt; diēs nātālēs et mēnsium et annōrum initia sīc observant ut noctem diēs subsequātur.

NOTE
Have students recognize that Caesar assigns the Roman names to the Gallic deities based on the supposed resemblances as Romans did with the Greek deities also.

[1] *(as) ministers*
[2] *figures (of men)*
[3] *twigs*
[4] = **deīs**
[5] *they say*
[6] Supply **colunt.**
[7] *as*
[8] *crafts*
[9] *they vow*

SUGGESTION
Ask students to provide the names of the corresponding Greek gods (Hermes, Apollo, Ares, Zeus, Athena).

NOTE
Tell students that this was because Dis (Pluto) was the god of Hades, i.e., of Darkness. A similar custom that reckons time by nights has survived from Anglo-Saxon days in the expression "fortnight" (fourteen nights).

NOTE
For holidays beginning in the evening we may compare Christmas Eve. All Jewish holidays begin and end at sunset. The phases of the moon probably had a great deal to do with this, since it is relatively easy to mark time by full moons.

ADDITIONAL QUESTIONS
What kinds of people were generally chosen to be sacrificed? How were these sacrifices sometimes carried out? What are some of the reasons for their worship of Mercury? Over what domains do the major gods and goddesses have influences? Did they differ much from the Roman's beliefs? From what god do the Gauls believe they are descended?

WORKBOOK
Assign Interest Questions 141-145 to review the content of the reading from this lesson.

QUESTIONS

1. Who was chief god of the Gauls?
2. Why did the Gauls sacrifice human beings?
3. Which god did they consider their ancestor?

Vocabulary

Nouns

ars, artis, *f. skill, art*	(artisan)
cumulus, -ī, *m. heap, pile*	(accumulate, cumulative)
furtum, -ī, *n. theft*	(furtive)
initium, -tī, *n. beginning, element*	(initial, initiate)
latrōcinium, -nī, *n. robbery*	
mercātūra, -ae, *f. trade*	(mercantile)
morbus, -ī, *m. disease*	(morbid, morbidity)
noxia, -ae, *f. crime*	(noxious)
quaestus, -ūs, *m. gain*	(quest, question)
simulācrum, -ī, *n. figure, image*	

Adjective

prōgnātus, -a, -um, *descended*	(prognathus)

Verbs

dēpellō, -ere, dēpulī, dēpulsus, *drive away*	
immolō, 1, *sacrifice*	(immolate, immolation)
voveō, -ēre, vōvī, vōtus, *vow, promise*	

Adverb

admodum, *very (much)*

Word Studies

From what Latin words are the following derived: **artificium, inventor, noxa, prōgnātus?**

Explain *accumulate, artificial, cumulative, furtive, immolate, implacable, mercantile, morbid, noxious, victimize, votive.*

LESSON LXXIX

Marriages and Funerals; Censorship

VI, 19

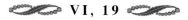

Virī, quantās pecūniās[1] ab uxōribus dōtis nōmine accēpērunt, tantās ex suīs bonīs, aestimātiōne factā, cum dōtibus commūnicant.[2] Huius omnis pecūniae coniūnctim ratiō habētur frūctūsque[3] servantur; uter eōrum vītā superāvit,[4] ad eum pars utrīusque cum frūctibus superiōrum temporum pervenit. Virī in[5] uxōrēs sīcutī in līberōs vītae necisque habent potestātem; et cum pater familiae illūstriōre locō nātus dēcessit, eius propinquī conveniunt et dē morte, sī rēs in suspīciōnem vēnit, dē uxōribus in servīlem modum[6] quaestiōnem habent, et sī[7] compertum est, ignī atque omnibus tormentīs excruciātās interficiunt. Fūnera sunt prō cultū Gallōrum magnifica; omniaque quae vīvīs cāra fuisse arbitrantur in ignem īnferunt, etiam animālia; ac paulō suprā hanc memoriam[8] servī et clientēs quōs ab eīs dilectūs esse cōnstābat, iūstīs fūneribus cōnfectīs, ūnā cremābantur.

20. Quae cīvitātēs[9] commodius suam rem pūblicam administrāre exīstimantur habent lēgibus sānctum,[10] sī quis quid[11] dē rē pūblicā ā fīnitimīs rūmōre ac fāmā accēperit, utī ad magistrātum dēferat nēve cum quō[12] aliō commūnicet, quod saepe hominēs temerāriōs[13] atque imperītōs falsīs rūmōribus terrērī et ad facinus impellī et dē summīs rēbus cōnsilium capere cognitum est. Magistrātūs quae vīsa sunt[14] occultant, quaeque esse ex ūsū[15] iūdicāvērunt multitūdinī prōdunt. Dē rē pūblicā nisi per concilium loquī nōn concēditur.

1 *property*
2 *they combine with*
3 *profits, income*
4 *survives* (with **vītā**)
5 *over*
6 *as is done in the case of slaves,* i.e., by torture
7 *if (their guilt)*, etc.
8 *before our time*
9 *those states which*
10 *have it ordained by law* (explained by the **utī** clauses)
11 *if anyone has heard anything*
12 *anyone*
13 *rash*
14 *whatever seems best*
15 *of advantage*

QUESTIONS

1. What rights did the Gallic women have?
2. What power did the husband have over his wife?
3. What was an individual required to do if he got information about public matters?

NOTE
You might point out that **locō** is ablative of origin.

NOTE
Elicit that **uxōribus** is plural. Ask students what this means.

NOTE
Have students summarize what this is saying and compare it to some societies today (particularly the totalitarian countries).

ADDITIONAL QUESTIONS
What happens if relatives feel that a death is suspicious? Is the position of women in Gaul different from what you know about the position of Roman women? What is a Gallic funeral like? What is the role of magistrates?

WORKBOOK
Assign Interest Questions 146-150 to review the content of the reading from this lesson.

Vocabulary

Nouns

aestimātiō, -ōnis, *f. estimate*
dōs, dōtis, *f. dowry*
fūnus, -eris, *n. funeral* (funereal)
nex, necis, *f. death*
quaestiō, -ōnis, *f. investigation* (inquest, question)

Adjectives

illūstris, -e, *noble* (illustrious)
servīlis, -e, *of a slave* (servile)

Verb

cremō, 1, *burn* (cremate, crematorium)

Adverbs

coniūnctim, *jointly*
sīcutī (sīcut), *just as, as if*

Conjunction

nēve (neu), *and not, nor*

Word Studies

From what Latin words are the following derived: **coniūnctim, cultus, dēcēdō, falsus, magnificus, quaestiō, servīlis, temerārius?**

Explain *cremate, crematory, decease, excruciating, funereal, inquest.*

Photo Bulloz

A bronze statue of a Gallic divinity. This is possibly Cernunnos, a Celtic god whose significance is unknown but whose cult was widespread from northern Italy, throughout Romano-Celtic Gaul, and into Britain.

LESSON LXXX

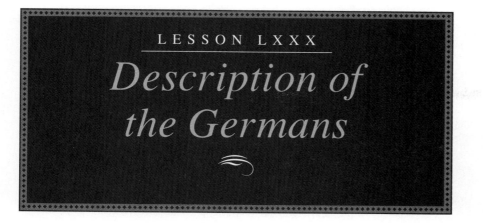

Description of the Germans

VI, 21

Germānī multum ab hāc cōnsuētūdine differunt. Nam neque druidēs habent quī rēbus dīvīnīs praesint neque sacrificiīs student. Deōrum numerō eōs sōlōs dūcunt quōs cernunt et quōrum apertē opibus iuvantur, Sōlem et Vulcānum et Lūnam; reliquōs nē fāmā quidem accēpērunt. Vīta omnis in vēnātiōnibus atque in studiīs reī mīlitāris cōnsistit; ā parvīs[1] labōrī ac dūritiae student.

SUGGESTION
Have students compare this description with that of the Suebi in Lesson LXV.

22. Agrī cultūrae nōn student, maiorque pars eōrum vīctūs in lacte, cāseō, carne cōnsistit. Neque quisquam agrī modum certum aut fīnēs habet propriōs; sed magistrātūs ac prīncipēs in annōs singulōs[2] gentibus cognātiōnibusque hominum quantum et quō locō vīsum est agrī[3] attribuunt, atque annō post aliō[4] trānsīre cōgunt. Eius reī multās afferunt causās: nē assiduā cōnsuētūdine captī[5] studium bellī gerendī agrī cultūrā[6] commūtent; nē lātōs fīnēs parāre studeant potentiōrēsque humiliōrēs[7] possessiōnibus expellant; nē accūrātius ad frīgora atque aestūs vītandōs aedificent; nē qua oriātur pecūniae cupiditās, quā ex rē factiōnēs dissēnsiōnēsque nāscuntur; ut animī aequitāte[8] plēbem contineant, cum suās quisque opēs cum potentissimīs aequārī videat.

23. Cīvitātibus maxima laus est quam lātissimē circum sē, vāstātīs fīnibus, sōlitūdinēs habēre. Hoc proprium[9] virtūtis exīstimant, expulsōs agrīs fīnitimōs[10] cēdere neque quemquam prope sē audēre cōnsistere. Simul hōc sē fore tūtiōrēs arbitrantur, repentīnae incursiōnis timōre sublātō. Cum bellum cīvitās aut illātum dēfendit aut īnfert,[11] magistrātūs quī eī bellō praesint et vītae necisque habeant potestātem dēliguntur. In pāce nūllus est commūnis magistrātus, sed prīncipēs regiōnum atque pāgōrum inter suōs iūs dīcunt[12] contrōversiāsque minuunt. Latrōcinia nūllam habent īnfāmiam quae extrā fīnēs cuiusque cīvitātis fīunt, atque ea iuventūtis exercendae ac dēsidiae[13] minuendae causā fierī praedicant. Hospitem violāre fās nōn putant; quī quācumque dē causā ad eōs vēnērunt ab iniūriā prohibent sānctōsque habent hīsque omnium domūs patent vīctusque commūnicātur.

[1] *from childhood*
[2] *for a single year*
[3] with **quantum**
[4] *elsewhere*
[5] *captivated by fixed habits (of life)*
[6] *for agriculture*
[7] object of **expellant**
[8] *contentment*
[9] *a sign of*
[10] subject of **cēdere**
[11] *fights either a defensive or an offensive war*
[12] *pronounce judgment*
[13] *laziness*

NOTE
Remind students that **fas** is indeclinable and represents a very important concept to the Romans.

Ronald Sheridan/Ancient Art & Architecture Collection

The baths from the 4th century A.D. at Trier, Germany are just some of the remains from the Roman occupation. Trier, founded by Augustus in 15 B.C. as Augusta Treverorum, was named after the Treveri, an eastern Gallic people who had inhabited the area.

ADDITIONAL QUESTIONS
Did the Germans believe in sacrifices? Who were the most important gods and goddesses to the Germans? What were the two main points of emphasis in their lives? How do you think the Germans' lack of housing stability influenced their attitude toward others? How did the Germans treat guests?

WORKBOOK
Assign Interest Questions 151 155 to review the content of the reading from this lesson.

QUESTIONS

1. What were the chief German foods?
2. How did the Gauls and Germans differ?
3. What was the German attitude toward robbery?
4. How did the government differ in war and peace?
5. What advantages were claimed for the German system of public ownership of land?

Summary of Chapter 24. The Gauls had once been powerful enough to invade and seize the most fertile districts of Germany; but now, as a result of their contact with civilization, they have deteriorated to such an extent that they have grown accustomed to defeat at the hands of the Germans.

Vocabulary

Nouns

carō, carnis, *f. meat* (carnival, carnivorous)
cāseus, -ī, *m. cheese* (caseate, casein)
cognātiō, -ōnis, *f. related group*
dūritia, -ae, *f. hardship*
frīgus, frīgoris, *n. cold* (frigorific)
incursiō, -ōnis, *f. raid* (incursion)
laus, laudis, *f. praise* (laud, laudable)

Adjective

proprius, -a, -um, *(one's) own, characteristic of* (proper, property)

Verbs

cernō, -ere, crēvī, crētus, *separate, see* (concern, discern)
minuō, -ere, minuī, minūtus, *lessen, settle* (diminutive, minute)

Word Studies

Cognātiō is from **co–** and **gnātus,** whose later form was **nātus.** Cf. English *cognate. Cheese* comes from **cāseus,** through the French. When you are "assiduous" you *sit by* **(ad–sedeō)** a job.

ASSIDUOUS

From what Latin words are the following derived: **accūrātus, aequitās, dissēnsiō, dūritia, īnfāmia, possessiō, sōlitūdō, vīctus?**

Explain *casein, diminutive, hospital, hospitality, infamy, inviolate, victuals, volcano, vulcanize.*

LESSON LXXXI

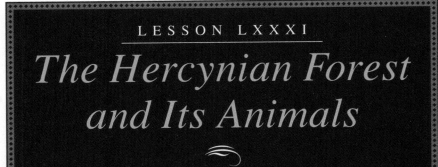

The Hercynian Forest and Its Animals

NOTE
Explain that since reindeer have two horns that are shed every year, it is probable here that Caesar (or his informant) saw one that had just shed one horn.

NOTE
Elicit that **hīs** is an ablative of comparison.

[1] *for one unencumbered* (with baggage)
[2] i.e., by miles.
[3] *than those horns*
[4] *spotted appearance*
[5] *joints*
[6] *beds*
[7] *whenever*
[8] *hunters*
[9] modifies **arborēs**
[10] i.e., the trees.
[11] *against these*
[12] *buffaloes*
[13] *pits*
[14] *to serve as proof*
[15] = **parvī ūrī**
[16] Supply **cornua.**
[17] *at the edges*
[18] *feasts*
[19] *cups*

NOTE
Ask students if they think Caesar believed this tale or if he was merely passing on a good story.

NOTE
Tell students that some believe that Caesar is describing the almost extinct aurochs (the European cousin of the American buffalo), now found only in a primeval forest in Poland; others hold that he means the broad-horned "wild ox" (the ancestor of our domesticated cattle), which became extinct in Europe in 1627.

VI, 25

Hercyniae silvae lātitūdō VIIII diērum iter expedītō[1] patet; nōn enim aliter fīnīrī potest, neque mēnsūrās[2] itinerum nōvērunt. Multa in eā genera ferārum nāscī cōnstat quae reliquīs in locīs vīsa nōn sint; ex quibus quae maximē differant ā cēterīs et memoriae prōdenda videantur haec sunt.

26. Est bōs cervī figūrā, cuius ā mediā fronte inter aurēs ūnum cornū exsistit excelsius magisque dērēctum hīs[3] quae nōbīs nōta sunt cornibus. Ab eius summō sīcut palmae rāmīque lātē diffunduntur. Eadem est fēminae marisque nātūra, eadem fōrma magnitūdōque cornuum.

27. Sunt item quae appellantur alcēs. Hārum est cōnsimilis caprīs figūra et varietās[4] pellium; sed magnitūdine paulō antecēdunt mutilaeque sunt cornibus et crūra sine articulīs[5] habent; neque quiētis causā prōcumbunt neque, sī quō afflīctae cāsū concidērunt, ērigere sēsē possunt. Hīs sunt arborēs prō cubīlibus;[6] ad eās sē applicant atque ita paulum modo reclīnātae quiētem capiunt. Quārum ex vēstigiīs cum[7] est animadversum ā vēnātōribus[8] quō sē recipere cōnsuērint, omnēs[9] eō locō aut ab rādīcibus subruunt aut accīdunt arborēs, tantum ut speciēs eārum[10] stantium relinquātur. Hūc[11] cum sē cōnsuētūdine reclīnāvērunt, īnfirmās arborēs pondere afflīgunt atque ūnā ipsae concidunt.

28. Tertium est genus eōrum quī ūrī[12] appellantur. Hī sunt magnitūdine paulō īnfrā elephantōs; speciē et colōre et figūrā taurī. Magna vīs eōrum est et magna vēlōcitās; neque hominī neque ferae quam cōnspexērunt parcunt. (Hōs foveīs[13] captōs interficiunt. Hōc sē labōre dūrant adulēscentēs atque hōc genere vēnātiōnis exercent; et quī plūrimōs ex hīs interfēcērunt, relātīs in pūblicum cornibus quae[14] sint testimōniō, magnam ferunt laudem.) Sed assuēscere ad hominēs nē parvulī[15] quidem exceptī possunt. Amplitūdō cornuum et figūra et speciēs multum ā nostrōrum boum cornibus differt. Haec[16] conquīsīta ab labrīs[17] argentō circumclūdunt atque in amplissimīs epulīs[18] prō pōculīs[19] ūtuntur.

Giraudon/Art Resource, NY

Animals always played a significant role for the Romans. This mosaic shows Orpheus, the Thracian musician who could charm not only animals, but also trees, rivers, and stones, with his lyre. How many of these animals can you identify?

QUESTIONS

1. How was the "urus" trapped?
2. What were its chief characteristics?
3. What was peculiar about the elk described by Caesar?

Summary of Chapters 29–44. Caesar, finding it impossible to pursue the Suebi in their forests, decides to return to Gaul. As a constant threat to the Germans, he leaves a large part of the bridge standing, protected by a garrison. Ambiorix is still at large, and Caesar devotes all his energy toward his capture. He divides his army into four divisions to prevent the escape of Ambiorix, but that wily chieftain always eludes capture. At last Caesar gives up the pursuit and, after placing his legions in winter quarters, returns to Italy.

ADDITIONAL QUESTIONS
How big is the Hercynian forest? What are some of the unusual animals that live there? How were the elk hunted? Were the buffaloes able to be domesticated?

WORKBOOK
Assign Interest Questions 156-160 to review the content of the reading from this lesson.

Vocabulary

Nouns

alcēs, -is, *f. elk*	
auris, -is, *f. ear*	(aural, auricular)
bōs, bovis (gen. pl., **boum**), *m. ox, bull*	(bovine)
caper, -rī, *m. goat*	(Capricorn, caprine)
cervus, -ī, *m. deer, stag*	(cervine)
crūs, crūris, *n. leg*	(crural)
mās, maris, *m. male*	(masculine)
mēnsūra, -ae, *f. measurement*	(commensurate, mensural)
palma, -ae, *f. hand*	(palm, palmistry)
rādix, -dīcis, *f. root*	(radiate, radish)

Adjectives

dērēctus, -a, -um, *straight*	
excelsus, -a, -um, *high*	(excelsior)

Verbs

assuēscō, -ere, assuēvī, assuētus, *become accustomed*	
dērigō (dīrigō), -ere, dērēxī, dērēctus, *direct*	(directive, directory)
fīniō, -īre, -īvī, -ītus, *limit, determine*	(finite, infinity)
pateō, -ēre, patuī, —, *stand open, extend*	(patent, patentee)
subruō, -ere, -ruī, -rutus, *undermine*	

Review: **cōnstat, cornū, parcō, quiēs.**

Word Studies

The motto of the state of Maine is **Dirigo.**

To "caper" is to act like a *goat* **(capra).** The old-fashioned "cab" bounced around like a *goat;* some taxicabs still do.

From what Latin words are the following derived: **accīdō, amplitūdō, arbor, cōnsimilis, dērigō, diffundō, varietās?**

Explain *aural, bovine, Capricorn, eradicate, excelsior, finite, inarticulate, mutilate, radical, ramification, toreador, vestige.*

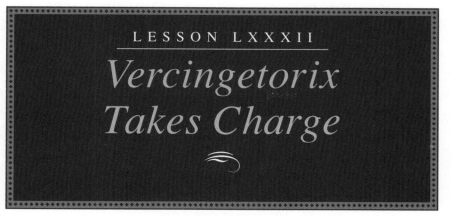

LESSON LXXXII

Vercingetorix Takes Charge

NOTE
Make sure students can locate the areas mentioned on a map.

Vercingetorix, the Gallic leader who heads the final desperate revolt against the Romans in 52 B.C., is the dominant figure of Book VII (Lessons LXXXII to LXXXVII) of the *Gallic War*.

Ronald Sheridan/Ancient Art & Architecture Collection

The Romans were not the only ones who honored their leaders on their coinage. Here is Vercingetorix, the first hero of Gaul on a coin that dates from the 1st century B.C.

Summary of Chapters 1–3. The Gauls, learning of political unrest at Rome, feel that the hour for freedom has come. This is the third and greatest of the Gallic revolts (the first was that of the Veneti and their allies; the second, that of Ambiorix). At a secret council a general uprising is planned. The Carnutes strike the first blow by massacring the Romans in Cenabum (Orleans).

VII, 4

Similī ratiōne ibi Vercingetorīx, Celtillī fīlius, Arvernus, summae potentiae adulēscēns, cuius pater prīncipātum tōtīus Galliae obtinuerat et ob eam causam, quod rēgnum appetēbat, ā cīvitāte erat interfectus, convocātīs suīs clientibus, facile incendit.[1] Cognitō eius cōnsiliō, ad arma concurritur. Prohibētur ā patruō[2] suō reliquīsque prīncipibus, quī hanc temptandam fortūnam nōn exīstimābant; expellitur ex oppidō Gergoviā. Nōn dēsistit tamen atque in agrīs habet dīlēctum[3] egentium ac perditōrum.[4] Hāc coāctā manū, quōscumque adit ex cīvitāte, ad suam sententiam perdūcit; hortātur ut commūnis lībertātis causā arma capiant, magnīsque coāctīs cōpiīs, adversāriōs suōs, ā quibus paulō ante erat ēiectus, expellit ex cīvitāte. Rēx ab suīs appellātur. Dīmittit quōqueversus[5] lēgātiōnēs; obtestātur ut in fidē maneant. Celeriter sibi omnēs quī Ōceanum attingunt adiungit; omnium cōnsēnsū ad eum dēfertur imperium. Quā oblātā potestāte, omnibus hīs cīvitātibus obsidēs imperat, certum numerum mīlitum ad sē celeriter addūcī iubet, armōrum quantum quaeque cīvitās domī quodque ante tempus efficiat[6] cōnstituit; in prīmīs equitātuī studet. Summae dīligentiae summam imperī

[1] i.e., the clients
[2] *uncle*
[3] *levy*
[4] *of the needy and desperate*
[5] *in every direction*
[6] *how many arms each state should produce and by what time*

NOTE
You might want students to do research on Vercingetorix, since he is an important figure in French history.

sevēritātem addit; magnitūdine supplicī dubitantēs cōgit. Nam maiōre commissō dēlīctō, ignī atque omnibus tormentīs necat, leviōre dē causā, auribus dēsectīs aut singulīs effossīs oculīs, domum remittit, ut sint reliquīs documentō et magnitūdine poenae perterreant aliōs.

Summary of Chapters 5–7. The Bituriges join the revolt. Caesar hastens from Italy to Gaul on receipt of the news. He reinforces his troops at Narbo (Narbonne) in the Province, which is threatened with invasion. Caesar's problem is to reach his scattered legions through possibly hostile tribes. As usual, he depends on speed.

NOTE
Tell students that Cebenna is modern day Cévennes.

8. Etsī mōns Cebenna, quī Arvernōs ab Helviīs disclūdit, dūrissimō tempore annī altissimā nive iter impediēbat, tamen, discussā nive sex in altitūdinem pedum atque ita viīs patefactīs, summō mīlitum labōre ad fīnēs Arvernōrum pervēnit. Quibus oppressīs inopīnantibus, quod sē Cebennā ut mūrō mūnītōs exīstimābant, ac nē singulārī[7] quidem umquam hominī eō tempore annī sēmitae patuerant, equitibus imperat ut quam lātissimē possint vagentur, ut quam maximum hostibus terrōrem īnferant.

[7] *all alone*

NOTE
Point out that one man had a better chance of getting across than an army. "It can't be done," they said; so Caesar did it.

Hubertus Kanus/Photo Researchers

In the Haute Alpes region of Provence, France, the mountains are covered with snow all year, even in the summer. Crossing this region was therefore treacherous at any time.

QUESTIONS

1. How did Vercingetorix raise an army?
2. How did he become leader of all the Gauls?
3. How did he keep the various tribes faithful?
4. Why did Caesar catch the Arvernians unprepared?

ADDITIONAL QUESTIONS
What happened to the father of Vercingetorix? Why was he killed? Did his relatives support Vercingetorix? Was he particularly interested in infantry or cavalry? Was he a gentle leader? How did he deal with the snow?

Summary of Chapters 9–16. Caesar gathers together his scattered troops before the Gauls are aware of what is going on. In rapid succession he captures several towns and then advances against Avaricum (Bourges). This place the Gauls had considered impregnable and had therefore spared, while following a "scorched earth" policy in the rest of the country in their effort to check Caesar's advance by cutting off his supplies. Though harassed in the rear by Vercingetorix, who concentrates on attacking the Romans' foraging parties, Caesar begins the siege of Avaricum.

WORKBOOK
Assign Interest Questions 161-165 to review the content of the reading from this lesson.

Vocabulary

Nouns

nix, nivis, *f. snow* (nival)
patrūus, -ī, *m. uncle*
sēmita, -ae, *f. path, footpath*

Adjectives

commūnis, -e, *common* (commonality, communicate)
inopīnāns, inopīnantis (gen.), *unsuspecting*

Verbs

appetō, -ere, appetīvī, appetītus, *seek, approach* (appetite, appetizer)
effodiō, -ere, effōdī, effossus, *dig up*

Word Studies

From what Latin words are the following derived: **adversārius, appetō, cōnsēnsus, disclūdō, documentum?**

Explain *corpus delicti, dissect, document, perdition.*

LESSON LXXXIII

Roman Spirit

NOTE
Remind students that part of the supplies problem is due to the season of the year and part to the "scorched earth" policy of the Gauls.

[1] *so much so that*
[2] *suffer too severely (from)* (with **ferrent**)
[3] *that they would regard as*

NOTE
Tell students that **frumento** is an ablative of separation.

NOTE
Tell students that the adjectives **dignus** (*worthy*) and **indignus** (*unworthy*) are followed by the ablative, which explains **maiestāte** and **victoriīs**. See the Appendix if further explanation is required.

VII, 17

Summā difficultāte reī frūmentāriae affectō exercitū, usque eō ut[1] complūrēs diēs frūmentō mīlitēs caruerint, et, pecore ex longinquiōribus vīcīs adāctō, extrēmam famem sustinuerint, nūlla tamen vōx est ab eīs audīta populī Rōmānī maiestāte et superiōribus victōriīs indigna. Quīn etiam Caesar cum in opere singulās legiōnēs appellāret, et, sī[1] acerbius[2] inopiam ferrent, sē dīmissūrum oppugnātiōnem dīceret, ūniversī ab eō nē id faceret petēbant sīc sē complūrēs annōs, illō imperante, meruisse[2] ut nūllam ignōminiam acciperent, numquam, īnfectā rē, discēderent; hoc sē ignōminiae locō lātūrōs,[3] sī inceptam oppugnātiōnem relīquissent; praestāre omnēs perferre acerbitātēs quam nōn cīvēs Rōmānōs quī perfidiā Gallōrum interīssent ulcīscī.

Summary of Chapters 18–56. Vercingetorix tempts Caesar to attack him, but Caesar, finding him too well entrenched, resumes the siege of Avaricum. The Gauls then accuse Vercingetorix of treason because he did not attack the Romans when he was in a position to do so. He successfully defends himself against this charge. The Gauls with renewed determination resolve to hold Avaricum at any cost. Vercingetorix sends a strong reinforcement. The besieged manage to set fire to the Roman siege works and display marked heroism. At length, however, Avaricum falls, and most of the inhabitants are killed. Vercingetorix consoles his troops for the loss of the town by stating that he had from the beginning opposed the defense of the place as untenable. He raises fresh troops. Caesar now marches along the Elaver (Allier) River, passing, no doubt, the site of Vichy (the hot springs of Vichy were known in antiquity). Vercingetorix anticipates Caesar in seizing the hillside near Gergovia, and Caesar can only follow.

[1] the clause depends upon **dīmissūrum**
[2] depends (with **sē** as subject) on the idea of saying in **petēbant**

MOPY/Photo Researchers

Paris has come a long way in the past 2,000 years, since the Île de la Cité, a tiny island of land in the middle of the Seine River, was first inhabited by the Parisii tribe. You can see the even smaller Ile St. Louis just behind the Île de la Cité and the cathedral of Notre Dame de Paris, begun in the 12th century, on the right.

At this point the Haeduans, who were on their way to join Caesar, mutiny at the instigation of their leader, who had been bribed, but Caesar, making a forced march, meets them and wins them back to his cause. He returns to Gergovia just in time to save his camp from capture by Vercingetorix. Later the Romans attack the town but are badly defeated. In spite of the critical situation, Caesar does not, as his enemies might expect, retreat to the Province, but goes north to protect his supplies at his headquarters on the Loire River.

57. Dum haec apud Caesarem geruntur, Labiēnus cum quattuor legiōnibus Luteciam proficīscitur. Id est oppidum Parīsiōrum positum in īnsulā flūminis Sēquanae. Cuius adventū ab hostibus cognitō, magnae ex fīnitimīs cīvitātibus cōpiae convēnērunt. Summa imperī trāditur Camulogenō Aulercō. Is cum animadvertisset perpetuam esse palūdem quae īnflueret in Sēquanam atque illum omnem locum magnopere impedīret, hīc cōnsēdit.

NOTE
Tell students that this is the capital of the **Parisii** (the original "Parisians"), on the site of modern-day Paris. The spelling of **Lutecia** instead of the more usual **Lutetia** is that of most of the best manuscripts.

ADDITIONAL QUESTIONS
What did the Romans do for food? What was the reaction of the Roman soldiers when Caesar offerred to abandon the seige? Who was Camulogenus? Why did he choose to encamp where he did?

QUESTIONS

1. Whom did Caesar send to Paris?
2. Where was ancient Paris situated?
3. What was the greatest hardship for the Romans?

WORKBOOK
Assign Interest Questions 166-170 to review the content of the reading from this lesson.

Summary of Chapters 58–68. Labienus retires to Metiosedum (Melun), which he captures. He then again marches toward Lutecia, which he finds in flames. He then learns of Caesar's defeat at Gergovia and receives alarming reports of a general Gallic uprising. Labienus decides to join Caesar and reaches him on the third day. The Haeduans now openly revolt and demand the supreme command, but at a council of the Gauls the command is given to Vercingetorix, who orders the Gauls to furnish hostages and troops, especially cavalry. Caesar sends to Germany for cavalry. The Gallic cavalry attack but are defeated. Vercingetorix heads for Alesia and occupies it. Caesar follows and plans to shut up the Gauls in that town by a series of trenches around it.

Vocabulary

Nouns

acerbitās, -tātis, *f. suffering, bitterness*

ignōminia, -ae, *f. disgrace* (ignominious, ignominy)

maiestās, -tātis, *f. dignity, honor* (majestic, majesty)

perfidia, -ae, *f. faithlessness, treachery* (perfidious, perfidy)

Adjective

ūniversus, -a, -um, *all (together)* (universal, universe)

Verb

careō, -ēre, caruī, caritūrus, *be without* (+ abl.) (caret)

Conjunctions

quīn, *that*

quīn etiam, *moreover*

Word Studies

A "caret" mark (^) indicates that something is *lacking* **(caret).** Explain *acerbity, ignominious, influx, perfidious.*

LESSON LXXXIV

The Siege of Alesia

VII, 69

Ipsum erat oppidum in colle summō admodum ēditō locō, ut nisi obsidiōne expugnārī nōn posse vidērētur. Ante oppidum plānitiēs circiter mīlia passuum tria in longitūdinem patēbat; reliquīs ex omnibus partibus collēs, mediocrī interiectō spatiō, oppidum cingēbant. Sub mūrō, quae pars collis ad orientem sōlem spectābat, hunc omnem locum[1] cōpiae Gallōrum complēverant fossamque et māceriam sex in altitūdinem pedum praedūxerant. Eius mūnītiōnis quae ab Rōmānīs īnstituēbātur circuitus X mīlia passuum tenēbat.[2] Castra opportūnīs locīs erant posita ibique castella XXIII facta, quibus in castellīs interdiū[3] statiōnēs pōnēbantur, nē qua subitō ēruptiō fieret; haec eadem noctū firmīs praesidiīs tenēbantur.

NOTE
Tell students that 8 of these forts have been found. Alesia is now Mont Auxois, near Dijon. During a recent drought, crops were found growing in certain places. It was concluded that they were drawing moisture from the walls of the ancient town, which lay underneath.

[1] **hunc omnem locum,** i.e., **eam partem (quae ... spectābat)**
[2] *extended*
[3] *in the daytime*
[4] i.e., the Atrebatians
[5] *free from tribute*
[6] *agreement to claim*
[7] Supply **Gallī,** including Commius.
[8] *lent their efforts*

Summary of Chapters 70–75. The Gauls attempt to interfere with Caesar's operations but are repulsed in a great slaughter. Vercingetorix sends his cavalry to get reinforcements. Food runs short and is rationed. Caesar constructs an inner and an outer line of siege works, the former to hem Vercingetorix in Alesia, the latter to defend his own army from attack from without, for Caesar had already learned that the Gauls were raising a great army for the relief of Alesia.

76. Operā Commī fidēlī atque ūtilī superiōribus annīs erat ūsus in Britanniā Caesar; prō quibus meritīs cīvitātem[4] eius immūnem[5] esse iusserat, iūra lēgēsque reddiderat atque ipsī[1] Morinōs attribuerat. Tanta tamen ūniversae Galliae cōnsēnsiō fuit lībertātis vindicandae[6] et prīstinae bellī laudis recuperandae ut neque beneficiīs neque amīcitiae memoriā movērentur,[7] omnēsque et animō et opibus in id bellum incumberent.[8] Coāctīs equitum mīlibus VIII et peditum circiter CCL, haec in Haeduōrum fīnibus recēnsēbantur, et praefectī cōnstituēbantur. Omnēs alacrēs et fīdūciae plēnī ad Alesiam proficīscuntur; neque erat omnium quisquam quī aspectum

NOTE
In 50 B.C., Commius, who had once been a prisoner in Britain (refer back to Lessons LXVII and LXIX), escaped to that island and there became a powerful king.

NOTE
The representatives of the various states formed a war council, which produced a further division of authority, rather than one commander-in-chief with supreme power.

[1] Commius, as ruler

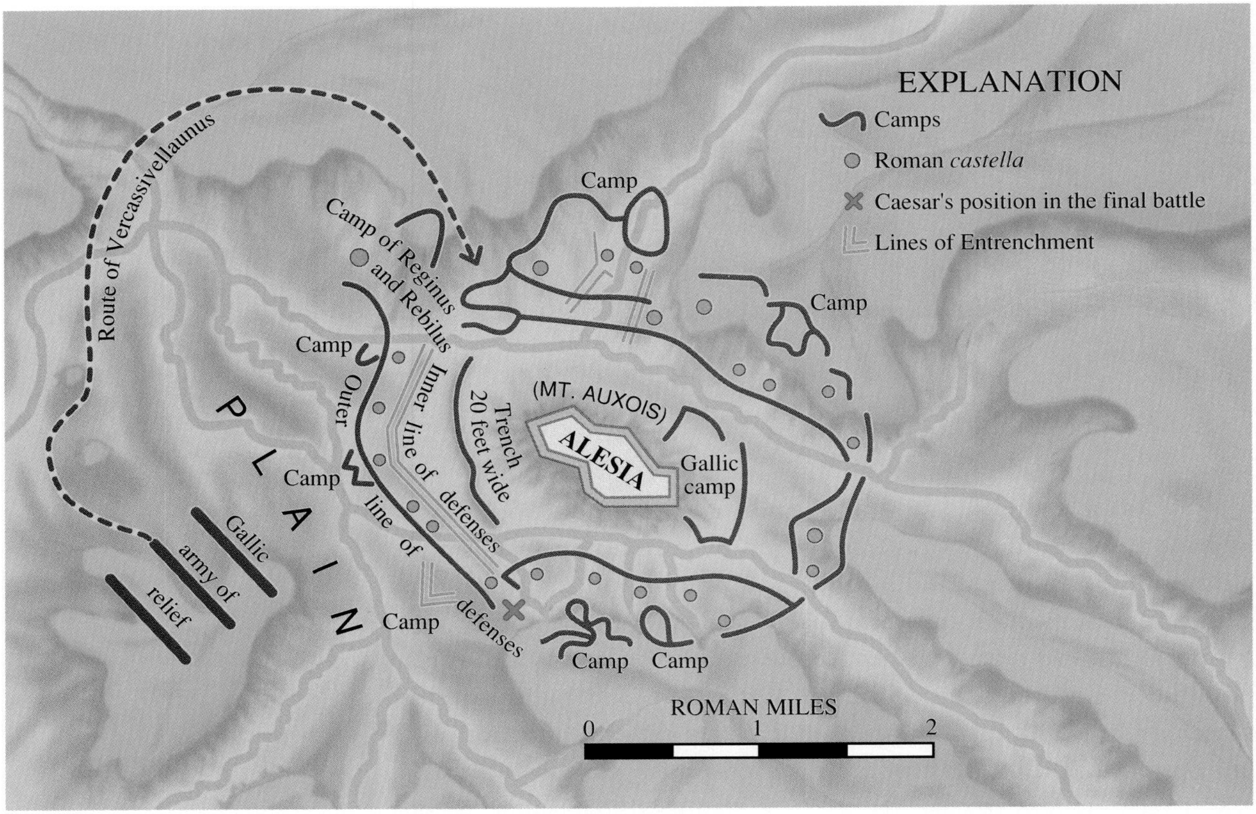

PLAN OF THE SIEGE OF ALESIA

[9] *on two fronts*
[10] *outside*

modo tantae multitūdinis sustinērī posse arbitrārētur, praesertim ancipitī[9] proeliō, cum ex oppidō ēruptiōne pugnārētur, forīs[10] tantae cōpiae equitātūs peditātūsque cernerentur.

ADDITIONAL QUESTIONS
What did the Gauls build to help defend themselves? How many forts and camps were assembled? What had Commius negotiated for in the past? Were the Gauls unified in their thinking? What effect did the Gauls think the sight of their army would have on the Romans?

WORKBOOK
Assign Interest Questions 171-175 to review the content of the reading from this lesson.

QUESTIONS

1. Describe the location of Alesia.
2. What two things led the Gauls to forget Caesar's previous kindnesses?
3. How many Gallic soldiers came to the rescue of Alesia?

Vocabulary

Nouns

castellum, -ī, *n. fort*	(castle, castellated)
circuitus, -ūs, *m. distance around*	(circuit, circuitous)
fīdūcia, -ae, *f. confidence*	(fiduciary)
māceria, -ae, *f. wall*	
obsidiō, -ōnis, *f. siege*	
plānitiēs, -ēī, *f. plain*	

Adjectives

mediocris, -e, *moderate* (mediocre, mediocrity)
opportūnus, -a, -um, *convenient, advantageous* (opportune, opportunist)

Verbs

cingō, -ere, cīnxī, cīnctus, *surround* (cinch, cinture)
incumbō, -ere, incubuī, incubitūrus, *lean over* (incumbency, incumbent)
recēnseō, -ēre, recēnsuī, recēnsus, *count again, review* (recension)
recuperō, 1, *get back, recover* (recuperate, recuperation)
vindicō, 1, *claim, appropriate* (vindicate, vindication)

Review: **ēditus, opportūnus, praesertim, prīstinus.**

Word Studies

From what Latin words are the following derived: **ēruptiō, fidēlis, interdiū, intericiō, mediocris, plānitiēs?**

Explain *fidelity, fiduciary, immunity, incumbent, infidel, recuperate, replenish, vindication.*

Wayne Rowe

A Roman army camp included towers, walls, and trenches to help protect it against invaders, especially in a potentially hostile territory. Any invading force would be slowed down by the outerworks, giving those in the towers the opportunity to pick them off.

LESSON LXXXV

A Horrible Suggestion

VII, 77

At eī quī Alesiae obsidēbantur, praeteritā diē quā auxilia suōrum exspectāverant, cōnsūmptō omnī frūmentō, ignōrantēs quid in Haeduīs gererētur, conciliō coāctō, dē exitū suārum fortūnārum cōnsultābant. Apud quōs variīs dictīs sententiīs, quārum pars dēditiōnem, pars, dum vīrēs essent, ēruptiōnem cēnsēbat,[1] nōn praetereunda[2] vidētur ōrātiō Critognātī propter eius singulārem ac nefāriam crūdēlitātem.

Hic summō in Arvernīs ortus locō et magnae habitus auctōritātis, "Nihil," inquit, "dē eōrum sententiā dictūrus sum quī turpissimam servitūtem dēditiōnis nōmine appellant, neque hōs habendōs cīvium locō neque adhibendōs ad concilium cēnseō. Cum hīs mihi rēs sit[3] quī ēruptiōnem probant; quōrum in cōnsiliō omnium vestrum cōnsēnsū prīstinae residēre virtūtis memoria vidētur. Animī est ista$_1$ mollitia, nōn virtūs, paulisper inopiam ferre nōn posse. Quī[4] sē ultrō mortī offerant facilius reperiuntur quam quī dolōrem patienter ferant. Atque ego hanc sententiam probārem[5] (tantum apud mē dignitās potest[6]), sī nūllam praeterquam vītae nostrae iactūram fierī vidērem; sed in cōnsiliō capiendō omnem Galliam respiciāmus, quam ad nostrum auxilium concitāvimus. Quid, hominum mīlibus LXXX ūnō locō interfectīs, propinquīs cōnsanguineīsque nostrīs animī$_2$ fore exīstimātis, sī paene in ipsīs cadāveribus proeliō dēcertāre cōgentur? Nōlīte[7] hōs vestrō auxiliō spoliāre quī vestrae salūtis causā suum perīculum neglēxērunt; nec stultitiā ac temeritāte vestrā aut animī imbēcillitāte omnem Galliam prōsternere et perpetuae servitūtī subicere.

"Quid[8] ergō meī cōnsilī est? Facere quod nostrī maiōrēs nēquāquam parī bellō Cimbrōrum Teutonumque fēcērunt; quī in oppida compulsī ac similī inopiā subāctī, eōrum corporibus quī aetāte ad bellum inūtilēs vidēbantur

1 *voted for*
2 *should not, it seems (to me), be passed over*
3 *Let my speech deal with those.*
4 *(men) who*
5 *I might approve, if I saw*
6 *the standing (of its backers) has so much weight with me*
7 *do not*
8 *What is my plan?*

NOTE
Remind students that **nōlō** is acting as a negative imperative here, which explains the three infinitives.

$_1$ For **istud;** it is the subject and is explained by **posse.**
$_2$ depends on **Quid**

vītam sustinuērunt, neque sē hostibus trādidērunt. Cuius reī sī exemplum nōn habērēmus, tamen lībertātis causā īnstituī et posterīs prōdī pulcherrimum iūdicārem.[9] Nam quid illī simile bellō fuit? Vāstātā Galliā, Cimbrī, magnāque illātā calamitāte, fīnibus quidem nostrīs aliquandō[10] excessērunt atque aliās terrās petīvērunt; iūra, lēgēs, agrōs, lībertātem nōbīs relīquērunt. Rōmānī vērō quid petunt aliud aut quid volunt, nisi invidiā adductī, quōs[3] fāmā nōbilēs potentēsque bellō cognōvērunt, hōrum in agrīs cīvitātibusque cōnsīdere atque hīs aeternam iniungere servitūtem? Neque enim umquam aliā condiciōne bella gessērunt. Quod sī ea quae in longinquīs nātiōnibus geruntur ignōrātis, respicite fīnitimam Galliam, quae in prōvinciam redācta, iūre et lēgibus commūtātīs, secūribus[11] subiecta perpetuā premitur servitūte!"

[9] *I should consider*
[10] *at last*
[11] *authority*

QUESTIONS

1. What three suggestions were made in the council of the Gauls?
2. What was the objection of Critognatus to fighting their way out?
3. In what way, according to Critognatus, were the Romans worse than the Cimbri?

Ronald Sheridan/Ancient Art & Architecture Collection

The inland waterways connecting many of the long rivers in France provided transportation for the various Gallic tribes. Trade goods could be moved much more economically from one region to another in barges, such as the one in this relief. It looks as if even the dog will be going along for the ride.

NOTE
Tell students that the lictors who accompanied a consul carried bundles of rods (**fasces**) enclosing an ax (**securis**). The former represented the consul's power to flog a criminal; the latter his right to put him to death.

SUGGESTION
Before reading the next selection, ask students to predict what will happen. Will the council accept his suggestion?

ADDITIONAL QUESTIONS
Why did the leaders come together to form a council? Who was Critognatus? Was there a precedent for his recommendation?

WORKBOOK
Assign Interest Questions 176-180 to review the content of the reading from this lesson.

[3] Supply **esse;** the antecedent is **hōrum.**

Vocabulary

Nouns

cadāver, -eris, *n. corpse* (cadaver, cadaverous)
dēditiō, -ōnis, *f. surrender*
exitus, -ūs, *m. outlet, outcome, departure, death* (exit)
imbecillitās, -tātis, *f. weakness* (imbecile, imbecility)
invidia, -ae, *f. envy* (envious, envy)
mollitia, -ae, *f. weakness*

Verbs

cēnseō, -ēre, cēnsuī, cēnsus, *think* (censor, consensus)
concitō, 1, *rouse*
obsideō, -ēre, obsēdī, obsessus, *besiege, blockade* (obsess, obsession)
praetereō, -īre, -iī, -itus, *go by, pass* (preterite)
resideō, -ēre, resēdī, —, *remain* (reside, residence)
spoliō, 1, *rob* (despoil, spoil)

Adverbs

nēquāquam, *by no means*
patienter, *patiently*
praeterquam, *other than*

Word Studies

From what Latin words are the following derived: **cōnsultō, ignōrō, patienter, praetereō, resideō, subiciō, subigō, temeritās?**

Explain *consultative pact, eternity, ignoramus, imbecile, nefarious, prostrate, residence.*

Yet another dog is immortalized. This Roman pot with a hunting dog was found in Alesia.

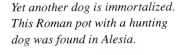

Ronald Sheridan/Ancient Art & Architecture Collection

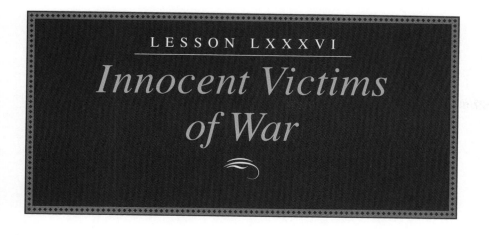

LESSON LXXXVI

Innocent Victims of War

VII, 78

Sententiīs dictīs, cōnstituunt ut eī quī valētūdine aut aetāte inūtilēs sint bellō oppidō excēdant, atque omnia prius experiantur quam[1] ad Critognātī sententiam dēscendant; illō tamen potius ūtendum[2] cōnsiliō, sī rēs cōgat atque auxilia morentur, quam aut dēditiōnis aut pācis subeundam condiciōnem. Mandubiī, quī eōs oppidō recēperant, cum līberīs atque uxōribus exīre cōguntur. Hī cum ad mūnītiōnēs Rōmānōrum accessissent, flentēs omnibus precibus ōrābant ut sē in servitūtem receptōs cibō iuvārent. At Caesar, dispositīs in vāllō custōdiīs, recipī[3] prohibēbat.

79. Intereā Commius reliquīque ducēs, quibus summa imperī permissa erat, cum omnibus cōpiīs ad Alesiam perveniunt, et, colle exteriōre occupātō, nōn longius mīlle passibus ā nostrīs mūnītiōnibus cōnsīdunt. Posterō diē, equitātū ex castrīs ēductō, omnem eam plānitiem quae in longitūdinem mīlia passuum III patēbat, complent; pedestrēsque cōpiās paulum ab eō locō abductās in locīs superiōribus cōnstituunt. Erat ex oppidō Alesiā dēspectus in[4] campum. Concurrunt, hīs auxiliīs vīsīs; fit grātulātiō inter eōs atque omnium animī ad laetitiam excitantur. Itaque, prōductīs cōpiīs, ante oppidum cōnsīdunt, sēque ad ēruptiōnem atque omnēs cāsūs comparant.

[1] *before* (with **prius**)
[2] *but that plan was to be used*
[3] Supply **eōs.**
[4] *over*
[5] *spurs* (pointed iron stakes)
[6] *wolf-holes*

NOTE
These innocent townspeople perished of starvation between the lines.

NOTE
Ask students if any behavior of this nature has happened in recent times. (There are many parallels in countries that are going through or who have undergone a civil or religious war.)

NOTE
Napoleon III erected a statue honoring Vercingetorix near the spot from which the relief army was seen.

Summary of Chapters 80–81. Caesar sends his cavalry out of camp to engage that of the enemy; after a long struggle the enemy is finally defeated. The Gallic relief army, under cover of night, makes a second attack upon the outer works, while Vercingetorix leads an attack upon the inner lines.

---

82. Dum longius ā mūnītiōne aberant Gallī, plūs multitūdine tēlōrum prōficiēbant; posteāquam propius successērunt, aut sē ipsī stimulīs[5] inopīnantēs induēbant aut in scrobēs[6] dēlātī trānsfodiēbantur aut ex vāllō ac turribus

A detail from the painting "Thusnelda in the Triumphal Procession of Germanicus" by Karl Theodor von Piloty (1826-1886). Germanicus Caesar was an immensely popular commander in Germany and Gaul. He was able to suppress a mutiny of the legions after the death of Augustus. He crossed the Rhine to fight the Germans several times, and returned to a triumph in A.D. *17 in Rome. Were it not for his early death in* A.D. *19, he would have been emperor. He was the brother of Claudius and the father of Caligula.*

Blauel/Gnamm-ARTOTHEK

[7] *heavy wall javelins*
[8] *before* (with **prius**)

trāiectī pīlīs mūrālibus[7] interībant. Multīs undique vulneribus acceptīs, nūllā mūnītiōne perruptā, cum lūx appeteret, veritī nē ab latere apertō ex superiōribus castrīs ēruptiōne circumvenīrentur, sē ad suōs recēpērunt. At interiōrēs,[1] dum ea quae ā Vercingetorīge ad ēruptiōnem praeparāta erant prōferunt, priōrēs fossās explent: diūtius in hīs rēbus administrandīs morātī prius suōs discessisse cognōvērunt quam[8] mūnītiōnibus appropinquārent. Ita, rē īnfectā, in oppidum revertērunt.

QUESTIONS

1. What plan did the Gauls adopt?
2. What happened to the Mandubii?
3. Why did the night attack of the Gauls fail?

ADDITIONAL QUESTIONS
How did the Romans react to the Mandubii? Why do you think they reacted this way? Which side was Commius on? Where did he position his infantry and cavalry? What kinds of weapons and tactics were used in the battle?

WORKBOOK
Assign Interest Questions 181-185 to review the content of the reading from this lesson.

[1] i.e., the army within Alesia

Summary of Chapters 83–87. The Gauls send out scouts and find that the Roman camp on the north is in a weak position. So Vercassivellaunus makes a surprise march by night and attacks the camp the next noon. Vercingetorix attacks from Alesia, and the Romans are forced to fight on all sides. Caesar, perceiving that his men are weakening under the attack of Vercassivellaunus, sends Labienus with six cohorts to reinforce them. He then addresses his troops, reminding them that the reward of all their struggles depends upon that day and hour. Vercingetorix attempts a diversion from Alesia. Caesar sends reinforcements and finally goes to the rescue himself.

Vocabulary

Nouns

grātulātiō, -ōnis, *f. congratulation*	
prex, precis, *f. prayer, entreaty*	(precarious, imprecate)
valētūdō, -dinis, *f. health, illness*	(valetudinarian)

Adjective

prior, prius, *former, first*	(prior, prioritize)

Verbs

experior, experīrī, expertus, *try*	(experience, expert)
expleō, -ēre, explēvī, explētus, *fill up*	
moror, 1, *delay*	(moratorium)
prōficiō, -ere, -fēcī, -fectus, *accomplish*	(proficiency, proficient)
trānsfodiō, -ere, -fōdī, -fossus, *pierce through*	

Review: **cibus, fleō, posteāquam, posterus, prex, turris.**

Word Studies

From what Latin words are the following derived: **appetō, custōdia, dēspectus, dispōnō, grātulātiō, mūrālis, perrumpō?**

Explain *appetite, priority, stimulation, trajectory, translucent.*

LESSON LXXXVII

Near Disaster Followed by Victory

VII, 88

NOTE
Caesar wore a scarlet uniform.

[1] *answers*
[2] *and*
[3] *might have been*
[4] *they must yield to*
[5] *for either*
[6] *one to each (soldier)*

Eius adventū ex colōre vestītūs cognitō, quō īnsignī in proeliīs ūtī cōnsuēverat, turmīsque equitum et cohortibus vīsīs quās sē sequī iusserat, ut dē locīs superiōribus haec dēclīvia cernēbantur, hostēs proelium committunt. Utrimque, clāmōre sublātō, excipit[1] rūrsus ex vāllō atque omnibus mūnītiōnibus clāmor. Nostrī, omissīs pīlīs, gladiīs rem gerunt. Repente post tergum[1] equitātus cernitur; cohortēs aliae appropinquant. Hostēs terga vertunt; fugientibus equitēs occurrunt; fit magna caedēs. Signa mīlitāria LXXIII ad Caesarem referuntur; paucī ex tantō numerō incolumēs sē in castra recipiunt. Cōnspicātī ex oppidō caedem et fugam suōrum, dēspērātā salūte, cōpiās ā mūnītiōnibus redūcunt. Fit prōtinus, hāc rē audītā, ex castrīs Gallōrum fuga. Quod[2] nisi crēbrīs subsidiīs ac tōtīus diēī labōre mīlitēs essent dēfessī, omnēs hostium cōpiae dēlērī potuissent.[3] Dē mediā nocte missus equitātus novissimum agmen cōnsequitur; magnus numerus capitur atque interficitur; reliquī ex fugā in cīvitātēs discēdunt.

89. Posterō diē Vercingetorīx, conciliō convocātō, id bellum sē suscēpisse nōn suārum necessitātum sed commūnis lībertātis causā dēmōnstrat; et quoniam sit fortūnae cēdendum,[4] ad utramque[5] rem sē illīs offerre,[2] seu morte suā Rōmānīs satisfacere seu vīvum trādere velint. Mittuntur dē hīs rēbus ad Caesarem lēgātī. Iubet arma trādī, prīncipēs prōdūcī. Ipse in mūnītiōne prō castrīs cōnsīdit; eō ducēs prōdūcuntur. Vercingetorīx dēditur; arma prōiciuntur. Reservātīs Haeduīs atque Arvernīs, sī per eōs cīvitātēs recuperāre posset, ex reliquīs captīvīs tōtī exercituī capita singula[6] praedae nōmine distribuit.

90. Huius annī rēbus ex Caesaris litterīs cognitīs Rōmae diērum vīgintī supplicātiō redditur.

---

[1] of the enemy; the cavalry is Roman.
[2] depends upon **dēmōnstrat**

The Bettmann Archive

The Gauls, under many leaders but especially Vercingetorix, shown here surrendering to Caesar, fought long and hard for their homeland, but finally succumbed to the more powerful Roman troops.

QUESTIONS

1. What led the enemy to begin the attack?
2. What changed the situation and made the enemy flee?
3. What offer did the defeated Vercingetorix make to his soldiers?

ADDITIONAL QUESTIONS
How could Caesar be identified on the battlefield? How did the cavalry impact the battle? How many standards were handed over to Caesar? What happened to Vercingetorix?

Vocabulary

Nouns

color, -ōris, *m. color* (colorize, discolor)
dēclīvia, -um, *n. pl. slopes* (declivity)
tergum, -ī, *n. back* (tergal)
turma, -ae, *f. troop (of cavalry)*

Adjective

dēclīvis, -e, *sloping downward*

Verbs

deleō, -ēre, -ēvī, -ētus, *destroy, wipe out* (delete, deletion)
omittō, -ere, omīsī, omissus, *let go, drop, disregard* (omit, omission)

Adverbs

prōtinus, *immediately*
utrimque, *on both sides*

Word Studies

Tollō is a good word to know well, both for its irregular principal parts and for its basic meaning, *raise up or away from a lower position.* Thus, in the proper contexts, **tollō** can mean: *weigh anchor, cheer up a friend, praise someone highly,* or, on the other hand, *plunder booty, get rid of something,* or *"do away" with a man,* i.e., *murder him.*

After the death of the dictator Caesar, his nineteen-year-old adopted son and heir, Octavian (later the Emperor Augustus), began to seize power for himself. The orator Cicero, fearful of what might happen to the Roman Senate, suggested that: **laudandum (esse) adulēscentem, ornandum, tollendum.** Octavian, who had a good sense of humor, was not exactly pleased by the pun.

SUGGESTION
Have students try several possible translations. One is "The young man ought to be praised, given all sorts of honors, and promoted out of sight."

WORKBOOK
The Unit VII Review contains four crossword puzzles that review Caesar's army, the tribes in Gaul, and special terms that Caesar used.

Our Heritage

VERCINGETORIX AND ALESIA

In strategic skill, organizing ability, and leadership, Vercingetorix was by far the ablest foreign opponent that Caesar faced, but he was unable in a short time to give the Gauls the discipline and military knowledge that the Romans had acquired through centuries of experience. He did succeed for a time in producing Gallic unity, and for that he has been considered the first national hero of France.

After his surrender, Vercingetorix was sent to Rome and remained in prison there for six years. In 46 B.C. he was led through the streets before Caesar's chariot in a triumphal procession and then executed as part of the ceremony.

Historians agree that the fall of Alesia constitutes a turning point in the history of northern Europe, for it settled the question of Roman supremacy in Gaul. The striking contrast between Roman efficiency and Gallic inefficiency is here seen most clearly. With all their courage and physical strength, the Gauls were defeated in their own territory by an army scarcely one seventh the size of their own.

The military operations of the two years (51–50 B.C.) following the capture of Alesia were not included by Caesar in his *Commentaries,* but we are indebted to one of his generals, Aulus Hirtius, for a full account, which he added as an eighth book. The military strength of the Gauls had been broken forever, and there remained only the task of subduing certain states that had not yet been fully reduced and of garrisoning the country. Caesar's term as proconsular governor expired in 49 B.C. Thus the conquest of Gaul, with its momentous results, occupied nine years in all.

Vercingetorix is a national hero in the history of France. In 52 B.C. he led a coalition of tribes against the encroaching Romans. Caesar besieged Vercingetorix at Alesia and finally won as famine overcame them. Vercingetorix was taken to Rome and executed in 46 B.C.

Ronald Sheridan/Ancient Art & Architecture Collection

A Latin Play

Caesar Dictātor

Persōnae

C. Iūlius Caesar	**Senātōrēs I** *et* **II**
Babidus, *scrība senex*	**Aedīlis**
Frontō, *scrība adulēscēns*	**Būbulō,** *frāter pistōris*[1] *Caesaris*
M. Terentius Varrō	**Syphāx,** *margarītārius*
Sōsigenēs, *astronomus*	**Calpurnia,** *uxor Caesaris*
M. Flāvius, *amīcus Sōsigenis*	**Rhoda,** *serva*

[1] *baker*
[2] *Sometimes he even faints*
[3] *Nonsense!*

[The scene is a room in Caesar's house. The time is somewhere between 49 and 44 B.C. The Civil War with Pompey and his followers has ended victoriously for Caesar. Established in Rome as dictator, Caesar is putting into effect his plans for the reorganization of the war-torn state.]

(*Intrant Babidus et Frontō. Tabulās, libellōs, stilōs ferunt.*)

BABIDUS: Dēpōne libellōs, Frontō.

FRONTŌ: Aderuntne hodiē multī salūtātōrēs?

BABIDUS: Multī. Caesarī dictātōrī omnis rēs pūblica cūrae est.

FRONTŌ: Labōrat magis quam servus.

BABIDUS: Prō eō saepe timeō. Semper labōrat; cibum nōn capit. Valētūdine minus commodā iam ūtitur. Aliquandō animō quidem linquitur.[2]

FRONTŌ: Rūmōrem in urbe audīvī—Caesarem cupere rēgem esse.

BABIDUS: Nūgās![3] Caesar pācem, concordiam, tranquillitātem in urbe et orbe terrārum cōnfirmāre vult.

FRONTŌ: Candidātōs magistrātuum certē ipse nōminat.

BABIDUS: Aliōs nōminat Caesar, aliōs populus. Rēs pūblica antīqua autem mortua est.

FRONTŌ: Suntne libellī bene parāti? Memoriā teneō Caesarem quondam interfēcisse scrībam suum Philēmonem.

BABIDUS: Philēmon erat nefārius. Servus Caesaris inimīcīs Caesaris prōmīserat sē dominum per venēnum necātūrum esse. Tū es neque nefārius neque servus. Nōlī timēre.

FRONTŌ: Audī! Appropinquat Caesar. (*Intrat C. Iūlius Caesar.*)

CAESAR: Salvēte.

BABIDUS et FRONTŌ: Salvē, imperātor.

CAESAR: Prīmum, acta diurna senātūs populīque. Suntne parāta?

FRONTŌ: Ecce, imperātor. (*Caesarī dat libellum, quem Caesar legit.*)

CAESAR: Bene! Bene scrīpta! Nunc ad commentāriōs meōs Dē Bellō Cīvīlī animadvertāmus.

BABIDUS: Ecce, Caesar. (*Caesarī libellum dat.*)

CAESAR: Pauca verba addere volō.

BABIDUS: Parātus sum. (*Cōnsīdit Babidus; notās*[4] *scrībere parat. Frontō exit.*)

CAESAR: (*dictat*): "Caesar, omnibus rēbus relīctīs, persequendum sibi Pompeium exīstimāvit, quāscumque in partēs sē ex fugā recēpisset, nē rūrsus cōpiās comparāre aliās et bellum renovāre posset."

BABIDUS: Scrīptum est.

CAESAR: Estne scrīpta epistula mea ad Mārcum Cicerōnem, quam herī dictāvī? (*Intrat Frontō.*)

BABIDUS: Ecce, Caesar. (*Caesarī epistulam dat.*)

CAESAR: Mūtā litterās. Scrībe D prō A, et deinceps.[5]

BABIDUS: Intellegō.

FRONTŌ: Adsunt salūtātōrēs, imperātor.

CAESAR: Intret Varrō. (*Exit Frontō, tum intrat cum Varrōne.*) Salvē, Varrō.

VARRŌ: Salvē, imperātor.

CAESAR: Varrō, tū es vir doctus. Mihi in animō est maximam bibliothēcam, Graecam Latīnamque, aedificāre. Pūblica erit bibliothēca. Tē bibliothēcae praefectum facere volō.

VARRŌ: Mē?

CAESAR: Tē certē.

VARRŌ: Ego autem Pompeiī, inimīcī tuī, eram lēgātus.

CAESAR: Nōlī timēre, Varrō. Dictātor sum—nōn autem tālis dictātor quālis erat Sulla. Prōscrīptiōnēs neque dē capite neque dē bonīs Caesarī placent.

VARRŌ: Imperātor, quō modō tibi grātiam referre possum?

CAESAR: Dē grātiā loquī necesse nōn est. Optimus eris bibliothēcae praefectus. Valē, Varrō.

VARRŌ: Dī bene vertant! Valē. (*Exit.*)

CAESAR: Intrent astronomī. (*Exit Frontō. Intrat cum Sōsigene et Flāviō.*) Salvēte, Sōsigenēs et Flāvī.

SŌSIGENĒS et FLĀVIUS: Salvē, imperātor.

CAESAR: Quid effēcistis?

SŌSIGENĒS: Nostrā sententiā, annus ad cursum sōlis accommodandus est. Necesse est annum trecentōrum sexāgintā quīnque diērum esse; necesse est quoque ūnum diem quārtō quōque[6] annō intercalārī.[1]

CAESAR: Rēctam viam capitis, meā quidem sententiā.

FLĀVIUS: Sī Caesarī placet, mēnsis nātālis Caesaris, nunc Quīnctīlis, nōminētur Iūlius.

[4] *shorthand notes*

[5] *and so on* (Caesar used a simple cipher in writing important letters.)

[6] *every*

---

[1] *insert* (Caesar had the calendar revised to approximately its present form. The insertion of the leap-year day was a feature of his revision.)

CAESAR: Dē hāc rē posteā loquāmur. Intereā, prōcēdite ut incēpistis. Valēte.

SŌSIGENĒS et FLĀVIUS: Valē, imperātor. (*Exeunt.*)

CAESAR: Intrent nunc senātōrēs. (*Exit Frontō. Intrat cum senātōribus.*) Salvēte.

SENĀTŌRĒS: Salvē, Caesar.

CAESAR: Quid est in animō?

SENĀTOR I: Nōbīs sunt magnae cūrae, Caesar. Audīvimus tē sine auctōritāte senātūs mīlitēs Rōmānōs ad rēgēs per orbem terrārum submittere ut eīs auxiliō sint; tē pecūniā pūblicā urbēs Asiae, Graeciae, Hispāniae, Galliae operibus ōrnāre.

SENĀTOR II: Tū cīvitātem Rōmānam medicīs et grammaticīs et aliīs dōnāvistī. In senātum Gallōs sēmibarbarōs cōnscrīpsistī. Mīlitēs tuī domōs cīvium ingressī sunt et cibum abstulērunt.[2] Ipse dirēmistī[7] nūptiās cīvium Rōmānōrum.

[7] *annual*

SENĀTOR I: Rūmōrēs malī per urbem eunt. Quid agis, Caesar?

CAESAR: Dictātor sum. Rem pūblicam, bellō dēiectam, restituō.

SENĀTOR II: Rem pūblicam dēlēs, Caesar.

CAESAR: Omnia bene erunt. Nōlīte īram meam concitāre. Valēte, amīcī.

SENĀTŌRĒS: Valē, Caesar. (*Exeunt.*)

CAESAR: Ad rēs fēlīciōrēs animum advertāmus. Intret aedīlis. (*Exit Frontō. Intrat cum aedīle.*) Salvē.

AEDĪLIS: Salvē, imperātor. Omnia parāta sunt, ut imperāvistī—mūnus gladiātōrum, vēnātiō, naumachia, lūdī scaenicī, lūdī circēnsēs.

CAESAR: Bene.

AEDĪLIS: Spectācula erunt omnium maxima.

CAESAR: Optimē factum. Tibi grātiās agō.

AEDĪLIS: Mihi est honōrī Caesarem iuvāre. Valē.

CAESAR: Valē. (*Exit Aedīlis. Intrat Rhoda. Cibum et epistulās fert. Epistulās Babidō dat.*)

RHODA: Domina ōrat ut dominus cibum recipiat.

CAESAR: Abī, abī! (*Rhoda, cibum ferēns, exit.*) Quae sunt illae epistulae?

BABIDUS: Architectus scrīpsit dē Forō Iūliō, dē templō novō, dē statuā equī tuī.[3]

CAESAR: Ita, ita.

BABIDUS: Alius scrīpsit dē viā novā mūniendā, dē Isthmō perfodiendō,[4] dē palūdibus Pomptīnīs siccandīs.

---

[2] In an attempt to reduce inflation, Caesar forbade the sale of certain luxurious foods. He sent soldiers to markets and even to private houses to seize such luxuries.

[3] Caesar had a horse of which he was very fond; to it he set up a statue in his own Forum.

[4] *digging* (*a canal through*) *the Isthmus* (*of Corinth*) (This project was not completed until 1893 and the next one has only recently been finished.)

CAESAR: Dā mihi hanc epistulam.

BABIDUS: Veterānus tibi grātiās ēgit prō praedā, servīs, agrīs quōs eī dedistī. Pauper vir Rōmānus tibi grātiās ēgit, aurō et frūmentō receptō.

CAESAR: Illās epistulās iam legam. Quis in vēstibulō manet?

FRONTŌ: Vir magnus—Būbulō. Et margarītārius.

CAESAR: Būbulōne?

FRONTŌ: Frāter est pistōris tuī.

CAESAR: Quid petit? Intret. (*Exit Frontō. Intrat cum Būbulōne.*)

BŪBULŌ: Caesar imperātor, tē ōrō, tē ōrō!

CAESAR: Quid petis?

BŪBULŌ: Līberā frātrem meum, pistōrem tuum, in vincula coniectum.

CAESAR: Alium pānem mihi, alium amīcīs meīs in trīclīniō meō dedit.[5]

BŪBULŌ: Tū autem es Caesar.

CAESAR: Īdem cibus erit mihi et amīcīs meīs. Frāter tuus autem poenās iam solvit. Eum līberābō. (*In tabulā scrībit; tabulam Būbulōnī dat.*)

BŪBULŌ: Ōh, dī tē ament, Caesar! (*Exit. Caesar rīdet.*)

CAESAR: Intret Syphāx margarītārius. (*Exit Frontō. Intrat cum Syphāce.*)

SYPHĀX: Avē, imperātor. Margarītam habeō—maximam. (*Margarītam Caesarī mōnstrat.*)

CAESAR: Quid dīcis? Haec margarīta nōn est magna. (*Intrat Calpurnia.*) Haec margarīta est parva. Volō rēgīnam margarītārum—prō uxōre meā.

CALPURNIA: Quid audiō?

CAESAR: Calpurnia!

CALPURNIA: Mihi margarītam mōnstrā.—Est pulcherrima.

CAESAR: Placetne tibi? Maiōrem tibi dare voluī.

CALPURNIA: Certē placet. Pulchra est—et satis magna.

CAESAR: Tua erit. (*Scrībīs dīcit.*) Cūrāte omnia.

SYPHĀX: Tibi grātiās agō, imperātor. (*Exit cum scrībīs.*)

CALPURNIA: Utinam tē aequē ac mē cūrārēs!

CAESAR: Ego valeō.

CALPURNIA: Cibum reicis; nōn satis quiētem capis; etiam per somnum terrērī solēs.

CAESAR: Nihil est.

CALPURNIA: Vītam prō rē pūblicā dēdis. Ōmina quoque mala sunt.

CAESAR: Ōmina nōn mē terrent. (*Intrat Babidus. Margarītam Caesarī dat.*) Ecce! Pulcherrimae uxōrī pulcherrimam gemmam dō. Nunc ad prandium eāmus.

(*Exeunt Caesar et Calpurnia, tum Babidus.*)

---

[5] Some rich Romans had special foods served to themselves and less fine foods to their guests. Of this practice Caesar violently disapproved.

C. M. Dixon

Unit VIII

The Letters of Pliny

UNIT OBJECTIVES
To read selections of Pliny's letters with understanding and appreciation; To learn about Pliny the Younger, and his times

Ancient Pompeii was a thriving metropolis when it was snuffed out in A.D. *79. Though it had suffered heavy damage from an earthquake in* A.D. *62, some of the buildings had been rebuilt and there were plans to redo many others. This view of a main street shows how the practical Romans constructed their roads. The stepping stones allowed pedestrians to cross without getting their feet wet, while chariots and wagons could still pass their wheels between the stones without being hindered.*

SUGGESTION
In many of the following letters, the ideas that are presented have strong parallels to today's world. You may want to discuss many of them, using the adage "The more things change, the more they stay the same."

The workbook offers several essay assignments at the end of the unit.

An Ancient Letter Writer

Pliny the Younger, whose name distinguishes him from his uncle and adoptive father, Pliny the Elder, was born at Comum (Como) in northern Italy in A.D. 62 during the reign of Nero. His famous teacher Quintilian filled him with admiration of Cicero, whom he tried to imitate in many ways. Like Cicero he became consul and governor of a province. His highest ambition was to rival Cicero as an orator, but only one of his many speeches has survived—and no one reads that.

The fact that many of Cicero's letters were collected and published by his secretary and others gave Pliny the idea of selecting for publication some of his own more polished and less personal letters. These have survived and make fascinating reading for the light they throw on Pliny himself and on life in his day.

An excavated street in ancient Herculaneum. Located on the Bay of Naples, Herculaneum was known as a resort town. It was much smaller than Pompeii, but was destroyed by the same eruption of Vesuvius in A.D. *79. Herculaneum was covered by a layer of hot mud from 50-65 feet thick that filled the buildings and eventually carbonized, preserving much of the contents. Most of the inhabitants escaped.*

Scala/Art Resource, NY

Pliny was a man of fine character, a good representative of the honest and efficient officials who developed and governed the Roman Empire. He was generous and kind and for these reasons we can forgive him his conceit and overseriousness.

Among Pliny's most interesting letters are two that give a vivid account of the famous eruption of Mt. Vesuvius near Naples in A.D. 79. The author was seventeen years old at the time and was living with his mother and uncle near Naples, at Misenum, where the elder Pliny was stationed as admiral of the fleet. Many years later Pliny wrote the letters describing the eruption.

This great disaster has been a blessing for us, since it preserved as if in a huge plaster cast, the towns of Pompeii and Herculaneum. The excavation of these two towns during the last two centuries has made it possible for us to walk into the houses and shops of the people who once lived there and has given us an intimate view of their daily life.

The Eruption of Vesuvius

CASSETTE
This reading is recorded on Cassette 3, Side A.

This letter is a reply to a request by Pliny's great friend, the historian Tacitus, who was gathering eyewitness material for his *Histories*. Although part of *Histories* has survived, the section dealing with the eruption has unfortunately been lost, and we are unable to tell how Tacitus used the information furnished by Pliny.

NOTE
There is a short selection from Tactitus' *Agricola* in the next unit.

Petis ut tibi dē avunculī meī morte scrībam ut hoc trādere posterīs possīs. Grātiās agō; nam videō mortī eius immortālem glōriam esse prōpositam. Quamquam ipse opera plūrima et mānsūra scrīpsit, multum tamen eius librōrum aeternitātī[1] tuōrum aeternitās addet. Beātōs eōs putō quibus deōrum mūnere datum est aut facere scrībenda[1] aut scrībere legenda,[1] beātissimōs vērō eōs quibus utrumque.[2] Hōrum in numerō avunculus meus et suīs librīs[3] et tuīs erit.

Erat Mīsēnī.[4] Hōrā ferē septimā māter mea ostendit eī nūbem inūsitātā magnitūdine et speciē. Ille ascendit locum ex quō optimē mīrāculum illud cōnspicī poterat. Nūbēs ex monte Vesuviō oriēbātur. Fōrmam pīnūs[5] habēbat.

NOTE
This comment would seem to say that since Pliny knew that his contributions were going to be published, he was perhaps more conscious of what and how he wrote.

[1] *(things) to be* (i.e., *worthy of being*), etc.
[2] Supply **datum est.**
[3] *because of*
[4] *at Misenum*
[5] *pine* (tree)

NOTE
Tell students that **librīs** is ablative of cause. If they would like further explanation, they may consult the Appendix.

---

[1] dative with **addet;** supply **librōrum** with **tuōrum**

6 i.e., with him
7 *pumice stones*
8 *cushions* (used by his slaves as a protection against falling stones)
9 *lying down*
10 (*this has*) *nothing* (*to do*) *with*

NOTES:
Tell students that Misenum was near Naples. Have them locate Naples, Pompeii, and Herculaneum on a map.

Tell students that **septimā hōrā** would have been shortly after noon.

Have students identify **eundī** as the gerund of **eō**.

Tell students that **Fortēs fortūna iuvat** was a common Roman proverb. Perhaps they can think of something comparable in English.

Tell students his death was more likely due to a cause such as heart disease rather than to the eruption.

WORKBOOK
Assign Ex. A-D to practice various constructions taken from the reading.

Iubet nāvēs parārī; mihi cōpiam eundī[6] facit. Respondī studēre mē mālle. Tum accipit litterās cuiusdam mulieris perīculō territae. Nāvem ascendit ut nōn illī mulierī modo sed multīs auxilium ferret. Properat illūc unde aliī fugiunt rēctumque cursum in perīculum tenet, tam solūtus timōre ut omnia vīsa ēnotāret.

Iam nāvibus cinis dēnsior incidēbat, iam pūmicēs[7] etiam nigrīque lapidēs. Cum gubernātor monēret ut retrō flecteret, "Fortēs," inquit, "fortūna iuvat." Ubi ad lītus vēnit, amīcum vīdit. Eum territum hortatur. Tum in balneum it et postea ad cenam, aut hilaris aut similis hilarī.

Interim ē Vesuviō monte lātissimās flammās vīdērunt. Ille, nē cēterī timērent, dīcēbat ignēs ab agricolīs relīctōs esse. Tum sē quiētī dedit. Sed nōn multō post servī eum excitāvērunt nē exitus ob cinerem negārētur. Domus crēbrīs tremōribus nunc hūc nunc illūc movērī vidēbātur. Itaque placuit ēgredī in lītus. Cervīcālia[8] capitibus impōnunt. Sed ille recubāns[9] aquam poposcit et hausit. Tum surrēxit et statim concidit. Cēterī fugiunt. Posterō diē corpus inventum est integrum. Similior erat dormientī quam mortuō.

Interim Mīsēnī ego et māter—sed nihil ad[10] historiam, nec tū aliud quam de exitū eius scīre voluistī. Fīnem ergō faciam.

Flight from Disaster

CASSETTE
This reading is recorded on Cassette 3, Side A.

NOTE
You might tell students that this line is in quotation marks because Pliny is quoting Vergil.

1 from **proficīscor**
2 from **crēscō**
3 *to be turning upside down*
4 *whether,* introducing **dēbeam**
5 *at length*

WORKBOOK
Assign Ex. A to answer questions about the content of the reading.

Taking the hint given in the last sentence in the preceding selection, Tacitus asked about Pliny the Younger's own adventures during the eruption. Pliny replied as follows.

Dīcis tē adductum litterīs quās tibi dē morte avunculī meī scrīpsī cupere cognōscere quōs timōrēs et cāsūs ego pertulerim. "Quamquam animus meminisse horret, incipiam."

Profecto[1] avunculō, ipse reliquum tempus studiīs dedī. Tum balneum, cēna, somnus brevis. Praecesserat per multōs diēs tremor terrae. Illā vērō nocte ita crēvit[2] ut nōn movērī omnia sed vertī[3] vidērentur. Māter et ego in āream domūs iimus et cōnsēdimus. Dubitō utrum[4] cōnstantiam vocāre an imprūdentiam dēbeam (nātus enim eram XVII annōs), sed poscō librum T. Līvī et legō.

Iam hōra diēī prīma erat. Magnus et certus erat ruīnae timor. Tum dēmum[5] excēdere oppidō placuit. Multī nōs sequuntur. Ēgressī cōnsistimus. Multa ibi mīranda, multōs timōrēs patimur. Nam carrī quōs prōdūcī

This ***cubiculum*** *(bedroom) from a home in ancient Pompeii shows the elaborate wall paintings and floor mosaics that mark it as an upper class home during the 1st century* B.C.

iusserāmus, quamquam in plānissimō campō, in contrāriās partēs agēbantur. Ab alterō latere nūbēs ātra et horrenda appārēbat. Paulō post, illa nūbēs dēscendit in terrās. Tum māter ōrat, hortātur, iubet mē fugere. "Tū potes," inquit; "ego et annīs et corpore gravis bene moriar sī tibi causa mortis nōn erō." Ego vērō dīcō mē nōn incolumem nisi cum eā futūrum esse. Deinde eam prōcēdere cōgō. Pāret aegrē. Iam cinis cadit. Tum nox, nōn quālis sine lūnā est, sed quālis in locīs clausīs, lūmine exstīnctō. Audiuntur ululātūs[6] fēminārum, īnfantium quirītātūs,[7] clāmōrēs virōrum. Aliī parentēs, aliī līberōs, aliī coniugēs vōcibus quaerēbant, vōcibus nōscēbant. Quīdam timōre mortis mortem ōrābant. Multī ad deōs manūs tollēbant, plūrēs nōn iam deōs ūllōs esse aeternamque illam et ultimam noctem dīcēbant. Cinis multus et gravis. Hunc identidem surgentēs excutiēbāmus[8] nē pondus nōbīs nocēret. Possum dīcere mē nōn gemitum in tantīs perīculīs ēdidisse. Tandem nūbēs discessit. Tum diēs vērus. Omnia mūtāta erant altōque cinere tamquam nive tēcta.

[6] *shrieks*
[7] *wails*
[8] *shook off*

WORKBOOK
Assign Ex. B, C to practice various constructions taken from the reading.

The Secret of Success

SUGGESTION
A student may want to research Pliny the Elder.

This letter and the next are interesting revelations of the Romans' genius for organization, even of their personal lives.

Mīrāris quō modō tot librōs avunculus meus, homō occupātus, scrībere potuerit. Magis mīrāberis sī scīveris illum causās ēgisse, vīxisse LV annōs, medium[1] tempus impedītum esse officiīs maximīs et amīcitiā prīncipum. Sed erat ācre ingenium, incrēdibile studium. Studēre incipiēbat hieme ab hōrā septimā noctis. Erat somnī[2] parātissimī, nōn numquam[3] etiam inter ipsa studia īnstantis[4] et dēserentis.[4] Ante lūcem ībat ad Vespasiānum imperātōrem (nam ille quoque noctibus ūtēbātur), inde ad officium datum. Reversus domum, reliquum tempus studiīs reddēbat. Post levem cibum saepe aestāte iacēbat in sōle; liber legēbātur,[5] ille ēnotābat. Dīcere solēbat nūllum esse librum tam malum ut nōn aliquā parte ūtilis esset. Post sōlem plērumque frīgidā aquā lavābātur[6]; deinde dormiēbat minimum. Tum quasi aliō diē studēbat in cēnae tempus.

Meminī quendam ex amīcīs, cum lēctor quaedam verba male prōnūntiāvisset, eum revocāvisse et iterum prōnūntiāre coēgisse. Huic avunculus meus dīxit, "Nōnne intellēxerās?" Cum ille nōn negāret, "Cūr revocābās? Decem versūs hōc modō perdidimus."

Etiam dum lavātur audiēbat servum legentem. In itinere, quasi solūtus cēterīs cūrīs, huic ūnī reī vacābat; ad latus servus erat cum librō et tabulīs, cuius manūs hieme manicīs[7] mūniēbantur, nē ūllum tempus studī āmitterētur. Perīre omne tempus nōn studiīs datum arbitrābātur.

[1] *time in between*
[2] *(a man) of*
[3] *not never,* i.e., *sometimes*
[4] *which came and went* (modifies **somnī**)
[5] i.e., to him by a slave.
[6] *bathed (himself)* (the passive is used reflexively)
[7] *gloves*

NOTES:
Tell students that other famous people, including Napoleon, were accustomed to taking naps at any time or place.

Remind students that **ūtor** takes the ablative (**noctibus**).

The reference here to the sun (**post sōlem**) means after his bath.

Remind students that **Nōnne** introduces a question that expects *yes* as a reply.

WORKBOOK
Assign Ex. A to practice various constructions taken from the reading.

WORKBOOK
Assign Ex. B to answer questions about the content of the reading.

How to Keep Young

NOTE
It is said that Winston Churchill did much of his thinking and writing on his feet, and even had special desks constructed so that he could stand and write as he passed by. That way, no time was lost.

Spūrinna senex omnia ōrdine agit. Hōrā secundā calceōs poscit, ambulat mīlia passuum tria nec minus animum quam corpus exercet. Sī adsunt amīcī, sermōnēs explicantur;[1] sī nōn, liber legitur dum ambulat. Deinde cōnsīdit et liber rūrsus aut sermō. Tum vehiculum ascendit cum uxōre vel aliquō amīcō. Cōnfectīs septem mīlibus passuum iterum ambulat mīlle, iterum cōnsīdit. Ubi hōra balneī nūntiāta est (est autem hieme nōna, aestāte octāva), in sōle ambulat. Deinde pilā[2] lūdit vehementer et diū; nam hōc quoque exercitātiōnis genere pugnat cum senectūte. LXXVII annōs ēgit sed aurium et oculōrum et corporis vigor adhūc est integer.

[1] *take place*
[2] *ball*

NOTE
Have students think of people today who are well into their "golden years" but continue to play competitive sports and whose minds and ideas are still strong and well respected. Clearly, the idea of keeping fit is not a new one.

WORKBOOK
Assign Ex. A, C to practice various constructions taken from the reading.

WORKBOOK
Assign Ex. B to answer questions about the content of the reading.

The Good Die Young

In addition to being a touching expression of grief, this letter gives us an idea of the qualities the Romans appreciated most in women.

CASSETTE
This reading is recorded on Cassette 3, Side A.

Trīstissimus haec tibi scrībō, Fundānī nostrī fīliā minōre mortuā. Nihil umquam fēstīvius[1] aut amābilius quam illam puellam vīdī. Nōndum annōs XIII complēverat, et iam illī anūs[2] prūdentia, mātrōnae gravitās erat et tamen suāvitās puellae.[1] Ut[3] illa patris cervīcibus[4] haerēbat! Ut nōs, amīcōs patris, et amanter et modestē complectēbātur![5] Ut magistrōs amābat! Quam studiōsē, quam intellegenter legēbat! Ut parcē lūdēbat! Quā patientiā, quā etiam cōnstantiā ultimam valētūdinem tulit! Medicīs pārēbat, sorōrem, patrem adhortābātur, ipsamque sē vīribus animī sustinēbat. Hae vīrēs nec spatiō valētūdinis nec timōre mortis frāctae sunt. Itaque plūrēs graviōrēsque causās dolōris nōbīs relīquit. Iam spōnsa erat ēgregiō iuvenī, iam ēlēctus nūptiārum diēs, iam nōs vocātī.

[1] *more charming*
[2] *of an old woman*
[3] *how*
[4] *neck*
[5] *embraced*

NOTE
Elicit that **illī** is a dative of possession with **erat**.

NOTE
Tell students that the parts in parentheses in footnote 1 complete the abbreviations in the inscription. The first two words mean *to the deified shades (of)*.

---

[1] The urn containing the girl's ashes was actually found in 1881 in the family tomb three miles north of Rome. The inscription on it reads: **d(īs) m(ānibus) Miniciae Mārcellae Fundānī f(īliae). V(īxit) a(nnīs) xii, m(ēnsibus) xi, d(iēbus) vii.**

This wall painting from the 1st century A.D. shows a young girl wearing a laurel wreath. Perhaps the artist was inspired by someone like the daughter of Fundanus.

Erich Lessing/Art Resource, NY

SUGGESTION
A student may want to research funeral rites or the catacombs in ancient Rome.

Nōn possum exprimere verbīs quantum animō vulnus accēperim, cum audīvī Fundānum ipsum imperantem ut illa pecūnia quam in vestēs et gemmās impēnsūrus esset in unguenta et odōrēs impenderētur.[6] Āmīsit fīliam quae nōn minus mōrēs eius quam vultum referēbat.

[6] *giving orders that the money which . . . be spent on perfumes* (for the funeral)

WORKBOOK
Assign Ex. A to answer questions about the content of the reading.

WORKBOOK
Assign Ex. B to practice various constructions taken from the reading.

A Ghost Story

Erat Athēnīs magna domus sed īnfāmis.[1] Per silentium noctis sonus vinculōrum, longius prīmō, deinde ē proximō audiēbātur. Tum appārēbat lārva, senex horrentī capillō. Vincula gerēbat. Deinde malae noctēs erant eīs quī ibi habitābant; mors sequēbātur. Domus dēserta est et illī lārvae relīcta. Prōscrībēbātur[2] tamen, sed nēmō vel emere vel condūcere voluit.

Vēnit Athēnās philosophus Athēnodōrus, lēgit titulum, audītōque pretiō, quaesīvit cūr tam vīlis esset. Omnia cognōscit sed tamen condūcit. Ubi nox vēnit, poposcit tabulās, stilum, lūmen; servōs suōs omnēs dīmīsit, ipse ad scrībendum animum, oculōs, manum intendit nē mēns timōrēs fingeret. Prīmō silentium, deinde vincula audiuntur. Ille nōn tollit oculōs. Tum sonus vinculōrum crēscit, propius venit. Iam in līmine,[3] iam intrā līmen audītur. Ille respicit, videt lārvam. Stābat innuēbatque[4] digitō similis vocantī. Sed philosophus rūrsus studiīs sē dat. Iterum sonus vinculōrum audītur. Ille rūrsus respicit lārvam innuentem. Nōn morātus tollit lūmen et sequitur. Postquam lārva dēflexit in āream domūs, eum dēserit; is signum in locō pōnit. Posterō diē philosophus adit magistrātūs et monet ut illum locum effodī iubeant. Inveniuntur ossa et vincula. Haec collēcta sepeliuntur.[5] In eō aedificiō numquam posteā lārva vīsa est.

[1] *with a bad reputation*
[2] *advertised*
[3] *threshold*
[4] *beckoned*
[5] *are buried*

SUGGESTION
Ask students what **prōscrībēbātur** means literally.

NOTE
Ask students if they are familiar with this kind of ghost story—the parallels should be evident. Literature in all cultures contains stories of "unfinished" burials and the consequences.

WORKBOOK
Assign Ex. A-C to practice various constructions taken from the reading.

Don't Be a Harsh Father

NOTE
This short reading says so much about relationships in so little space. Elicit parallels to "The Golden Rule" or simply ask students how they might feel as both parent and child.

Castīgābat quīdam fīlium suum quod paulō sūmptuōsius equōs et canēs emeret. Huic ego: "Heus[1] tū, numquamne fēcistī quod ā patre tuō culpārī posset? Nōn etiam nunc facis quod fīlius tuus, sī pater tuus esset, parī gravitāte culpet?"

Haec tibi admonitus magnae sevēritātis exemplō scrīpsī nē tū quoque fīlium acerbius dūriusque tractārēs.[2] Cōgitā et illum puerum esse et tē fuisse atque hominem esse tē et hominis patrem.

[1] *Say!*
[2] *handle*

WORKBOOK
Assign Ex. A to practice various constructions taken from the reading.

Graded Friendship Is Degraded Friendship

Longum est altius repetere[1] quō modō acciderit ut cēnārem apud quendam, ut sibi vidēbātur, lautum et dīligentem, ut mihi, sordidum simul et sūmptuōsum. Nam sibi et paucīs opīma[2] quaedam, cēterīs vīlia pōnēbat. Vīnum etiam parvulīs lagunculīs[3] in tria genera dīvīserat, nōn ut potestās ēligendī, sed nē iūs esset recūsandī, aliud sibi et nōbīs, aliud minōribus amīcīs (nam gradātim[4] amīcōs habet), aliud suīs nostrīsque lībertīs. Animadvertit[5] quī mihi proximus accumbēbat et an probārem interrogāvit. Negāvī. "Tū ergō," inquit, "quam cōnsuētūdinem sequeris?" "Eadem omnibus pōnō; ad cēnam enim, nōn ad contumēliam invītō omnibusque rēbus aequō quōs mēnsā aequāvī." "Etiamne lībertōs?" "Etiam: amīcōs enim tum, nōn lībertōs putō." Et ille, "Magnō[6] tibi cōnstat?" "Minimē." "Quō modō fierī potest?" "Quia lībertī meī nōn idem quod ego bibunt, sed idem ego quod lībertī."

[1] *go into too deeply*
[2] *rich (foods)*
[3] *bottles*
[4] *of different degrees*
[5] Supply **is.**
[6] *It costs a great deal?*

NOTE
Remind students that Caesar criticized the same practice.

WORKBOOK
Assign Ex. A to practice various constructions taken from the reading.

Wanted, a Teacher

NOTE
Perhaps students can make parallels to choosing the colleges they might want to attend (and asking others for advice) or electing certain classes for the following year (based on who is teaching the course).

WORKBOOK
Assign Ex. A to practice various constructions taken from the reading.

WORKBOOK
Assign Ex. B to answer questions about the content of the reading.

Note the exquisite courtesy that turns a chore into a pleasure.

Quid ā mē grātius potuistī petere quam ut magistrum frātris tuī līberīs quaererem? Nam beneficiō tuō in scholam redeō et illam dulcissimam aetātem quasi resūmam. Sedeō inter iuvenēs, ut solēbam, atque etiam experior quantum apud illōs auctōritātis ex studiīs meīs habeam. Nam proximē inter sē iocābantur: intrāvī, silentium factum est. Hoc ad illōrum laudem magis quam ad meam pertinet.

Cum omnēs professōrēs audīverō, quid dē quōque sentiam scrībam. Dēbeō enim tibi, dēbeō memoriae frātris tuī hanc fidem, hoc studium, praesertim in tantā rē.

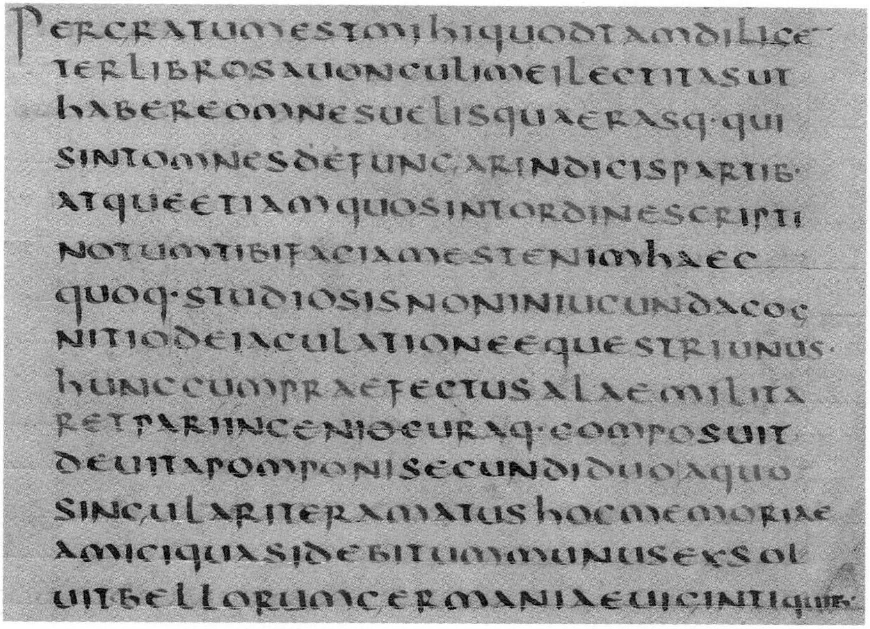

The Pierpont Morgan Library/Art Resource, NY. M. (462,F.6V)

The oldest manuscript of Pliny's letters in existence. It dates from about A.D. *500 and is in the Pierpont Morgan Library, New York City. What words can you identify?*

A Courageous Wife

Aeger erat Paetus, marītus Arriae, aeger etiam fīlius. Fīlius dēcessit. Huic illa ita fūnus parāvit ut ignōrāret marītus. Cum[1] cubiculum eius intrāret, vīvere fīlium atque etiam commodiōrem esse dīcēbat, ac saepe marītō interrogantī quid ageret puer respondēbat, "Bene quiētem cēpit et cibum sūmpsit." Deinde, cum lacrimae vincerent, ēgrediēbātur. Tum sē dolōrī dabat. Compositō vultū redībat.

Paetus cum Scrībōniānō arma in Īllyricō contrā Claudium mōverat. Occīsō Scrībōniānō, Rōmam Paetus trahēbātur.[2] Erat ascēnsūrus nāvem; Arria mīlitēs ōrābat ut simul impōnerētur. "Datūrī estis," inquit, "marītō meō, cōnsulārī virō, servōs aliquōs quōrum ē manū cibum capiat[3] et vestem et calceōs. Omnia haec ego sōla faciam." Hōc negātō, illa condūxit parvum nāvigium et magnam nāvem secūta est.

Postquam Rōmam pervēnērunt, illa gladium strīnxit, in corde suō dēfīxit, extrāxit, marītō dedit, addidit vōcem immortālem ac paene dīvīnam: "Paete, nōn dolet."[4]

NOTE
Pliny gives three examples of Arria's devotion. Have students identify them.

NOTE
Ask students how they feel about these actions of Arria in today's world? Would they be interpreted the same way?

[1] *whenever*
[2] i.e., as a prisoner
[3] *he may take*
[4] *it doesn't hurt*

NOTE
Ask students why she handed the sword to Paetus? Although the letter does not say, ask students what they think Paetus' reaction would be.

WORKBOOK
Assign Ex. A, B to practice various constructions and content from the reading.

Two Love Letters

Written by Pliny to his third wife, who was much younger than he.

[1] *complain* (from **queror**)
[2] *two*

Numquam magis dē occupātiōnibus meīs sum questus,[1] quae mē nōn sunt passae sequī tē proficīscentem in Campāniam valētūdinis causā. Nunc enim maximē tēcum esse cupiō ut oculīs meīs videam quid vīrium cōnsecūta sīs. Et absentia et īnfirmitās tua mē terrent. Vereor omnia, fingō omnia, ea maximē quae maximē timeō. Itaque rogō ut cotīdiē singulās vel etiam bīnās[2] epistulās scrībās. Sine cūrā erō dum legō statimque timēbō cum lēgerō. Valē.

WORKBOOK
Assign Ex. A, C to practice various constructions taken from the reading.

Scrībis tē absentiā meā magnopere afficī ūnumque habēre sōlācium, quod prō mē librōs meōs teneās. Grātum est quod mē requīris. Ego epistulās tuās legō atque identidem in manūs quasi novās sūmō. Tū quam frequentissimē scrībe. Valē.

WORKBOOK
Assign Ex. B to answer questions about the content of the reading.

A Fish Story

[1] *people of all ages*
[2] depends on **studiō**
[3] i.e., than the rest
[4] *made for*
[5] *comes up from under,* i.e., takes the boy on its back
[6] *leaps up and dives*
[7] *is carried (out) and back*

Est in Āfricā colōnia marī proxima. Hīc omnis aetās[1] piscandī,[2] nāvigandī, atque etiam natandī studiō tenētur, maximē puerī, quī ōtium habent et lūdere cupiunt. Hīs glōria et virtūs est longissimē natāre; victor ille est quī longissimē lītus et aliōs natantēs relīquit. Puer quīdam audācior[3] in ulteriōra tendēbat.[4] Delphīnus occurrit et nunc praecēdit puerum, nunc sequitur, tum subit,[5] dēpōnit, iterum subit territumque puerum perfert prīmum in altum, deinde flectit ad lītus redditque terrae.

Concurrunt omnēs, ipsum puerum tamquam mīrāculum spectant, rogant, audiunt. Posterō diē rūrsus natant puerī, rūrsus delphīnus ad puerum venit. Fugit ille cum cēterīs. Delphīnus, quasi revocāns, exsilit et mergitur.[6] Hoc plūribus diēbus facit. Tandem puerī accēdunt, appellant, tangunt etiam. Crēscit audācia. Maximē puer quī prīmus expertus est natat ad eum, īnsilit tergō, fertur referturque.[7] Amārī sē putat, amat ipse. Neuter timet, neuter timētur.

Boltin Picture Library

Ancient coin of a dolphin and rider. The Greeks and Romans were just as fascinated with dolphins, as we are today.

NOTE
Explain that the town had to pay for the entertainment of the visiting officials.

Veniēbant omnēs magistrātūs ad spectāculum, quōrum adventū et morā parva rēs pūblica novīs sūmptibus[8] cōnficitur. Posteā locus ipse quiētem suam āmittēbat. Placuit delphīnum interficī ad quem videndum omnēs veniēbant.

[8] *expenses*

WORKBOOK
Assign Ex. A to practice various constructions taken from the reading.

WORKBOOK
Assign Ex. B to answer questions about the content of the reading.

Advice to a Provincial Governor

NOTE
This letter indicates Pliny's respect for Greek culture as well as his belief that, although man is born free, he must preserve this right to freedom by the way he lives.

Cōgitā tē missum in prōvinciam Achaiam, illam vēram Graeciam, in quā prīmum hūmānitās, litterae, etiam frūgēs inventae esse crēduntur; missum ad hominēs vērē hominēs, ad līberōs[1] vērē līberōs, quī iūs ā nātūrā datum virtūte et meritīs tenuērunt. Reverēre glōriam veterem. Sint antīquitās et magna facta in magnō honōre apud tē. Habē ante oculōs hanc esse terram quae nōbīs mīserit iūra, quae lēgēs nōn victīs sed petentibus dederit, Athēnās esse quās adeās, Lacedaemonem esse quam regās. Plūs potest amor ad obtinendum quod[1] velīs quam timor.

WORKBOOK
Assign Ex. A to practice various constructions taken from the reading.

WORKBOOK
Assign Ex. B to answer questions about the content of the reading.

[1] Supply **id** as antecedent.

[1] from **līber,** not **līberī**; he means that true manhood and true freedom had their beginnings in Greece.

A Humane Master

Cōnfēcērunt mē īnfirmitātēs servōrum meōrum, mortēs etiam. Sōlācia duo sunt, nōn paria tantō dolōrī: ūnum, cōpia manūmittendī (videor enim nōn omnīnō perdidisse quōs iam līberōs[1] perdidī); alterum, quod permittō servīs quoque quasi[2] testāmenta facere. Mandant rogantque in hīs id quod volunt; pāreō ut[3] iussus. Dīvidunt, dōnant, relinquunt, dumtaxat[4] intrā domum; nam servīs rēs pūblica quaedam et quasi cīvitās domus est.

Nōn ignōrō aliōs[5] eius modī cāsūs nihil amplius vocāre quam damnum.[6] Fortasse[7] sunt magnī sapientēsque, ut sibi videntur; hominēs nōn sunt. Homō enim dēbet afficī dolōre.

Dīxī dē hīs plūra fortasse quam dēbuī, sed pauciōra quam voluī. Est enim quaedam etiam dolendī voluptās.

[1] from **līber**
[2] *as it were*
[3] *as*
[4] *only, however*
[5] *other men*
[6] *loss* (of property)
[7] *perhaps*

WORKBOOK
Assign Ex. A to answer questions about the content of the reading.

WORKBOOK
Assign Ex. B to practice various constructions taken from the reading.

Household slaves pouring and serving wine. As Roman slaves were by law merely so much property, they could not legally own money or make wills. In actual practice, however, most Roman slaves had these and other privileges.

Ronald Sheridan/Ancient Art & Architecture Collection

Jack Novak/SuperStock, Inc.

Chariot races were major entertainment for the Romans—so much so that they built a ***circus*** *to hold the shows in many major provincial cities.*

A Busy Holiday

Omne hoc tempus inter tabulās ac librōs grātissimā quiēte ēgī. "Quō modō," inquis, "in urbe potuistī?" Circēnsēs lūdī erant, quō genere spectāculī minimē teneor. Nihil novum, nihil varium, nihil quod nōn semel spectāvisse sufficiat. Mīror tot mīlia virōrum tam puerīliter cupere identidem vidēre currentēs equōs, īnsistentēs curribus[1] hominēs. Nōn vēlōcitāte equōrum aut hominum arte trahuntur.[2] Favent pannō,[3] pannum amant. Sī in ipsō cursū hic color illūc, ille hūc trānsferātur,[4] studium favorque trānsferētur,[1] et statim aurīgās illōs, equōs illōs quōs procul nōscunt, quōrum clāmant nōmina, relinquent. Tanta grātia, tanta auctōritās in ūnā vīlissimā tunicā, nōn modo apud vulgus sed apud quōsdam gravēs hominēs. Capiō aliquam voluptātem quod hāc voluptāte nōn capior. Et ōtium meum in litterīs per hōs diēs collocō, quōs aliī perdunt. Valē.

[1] Singular because the two subjects represent one idea.

NOTE
Have students compare the colors of high school, college, or professional athletic teams. The point is that the spectators are not interested in the skill of the drivers, but in the side they represent.

[1] *standing in chariots*
[2] *they are attracted*
[3] *the cloth*
[4] *should be transferred*

WORKBOOK
Assign Ex. A, B to answer questions about the content of the reading.

WORKBOOK
Assign Ex. C to practice various constructions taken from the reading.

Unit IX

Latin Literature

UNIT OBJECTIVES
To learn biographical information about numerous Latin authors; To read, with understanding and appreciation, selections from Latin literature from the third century B.C. to the sixteenth century A.D.

PHOTRI/INDEX

This wall painting from a home in Rome depicts Rome's greatest orator, Marcus Tullius Cicero addressing the senate, denouncing Catiline, and exposing the conspiracy. In all, Cicero delivered four orations against Catiline. The eloquence of these orations set the standard of excellence for all who followed.

SUGGESTION
You may want to assign students to do some brief biographical research on the authors presented in this unit. If you assign all of them early on, as you arrive at each one, the student responsible for that author can provide the class with background information.

SUGGESTION
As another project, you may want to assign other literary pieces by these or other authors to be read in translation.

WORKBOOK
There is an acrostic that includes most of the authors' names who appear in this unit at the end of the Workbook unit.

Latin literature, as it exists, extends from the third century B.C. to the present time. It contains material of almost every description: fine poetry, absorbing history and biography, amusing stories, moral essays, pithy sayings, passionate oratory, comic and tragic drama, scientific treatises, and much that is pertinent to life today. In this unit you will find a wide variety of samples that cover over two thousand years.

Ennius

NOTE
In the translation by E. H. Warmington, the alliteration comes through beautifully: "Thyself to thyself, Titus Tatius the tyrant, thou tookest terrible troubles."

Ennius (239–169 B.C.) has been called the father of Latin poetry. His *Annals*, an epic poem dealing with the history of Rome down to his own time, remained the chief epic of Rome until it was supplanted by Vergil's *Aeneid*. Only fragments of the *Annals* and his plays have survived, preserved in quotations by later authors. Ennius was a bold experimenter with verse. One of his experiments in alliteration might remind you of "Peter Piper picked a peck of pickled peppers." It is addressed to Titus Tatius, the Sabine king, by the man who killed him.

Ō, Tite, tūte,[1] Tatī, tibi tanta,$_1$ tyranne, tulistī.

Like many Roman writers, Ennius stressed patriotic and moral qualities:

Mōribus[2] antīquīs stat rēs[3] Rōmāna virīsque.[2]

[1] = **tū**
[2] *because of*
[3] = **rēs pūblica**

WORKBOOK
Assign Ex. A to practice additional alliterative epigrams.

$_1$ neuter plural accusative; i.e., misfortunes

Plautus and Terence

CASSETTE
This reading is recorded on Cassette 3, Side B.

CASSETTE
A reading from the **Menaechmi** is recorded on Cassette 3, Side B. The actual piece can be found in *Latin for Americans, Third Book.*

SUGGESTION
You may want to assign the entire **Miles Gloriosus** to be read in translation, as well as a play by Terence for comparison. If students are very interested in comedy, they may want to read the plays of Aristophanes.

As early as the third century B.C. the Romans had begun to borrow and adapt from the Greeks a type of comedy based on the manners (or bad manners) of middle-class citizens. Its themes were general: thwarted but eventually successful love, paternal strictness versus the frivolity of an ungovernable teen-aged son, the cleverness of a slave who outwits his master to make everything come out right at the end. The plots are complicated, with all sorts of mistaken identities and surprise twists. Much of the humor consists in clever puns, in constant involvement of the characters in embarassing and humiliating situations, and in the wildest sort of slapstick.

Rome's two masters of comedy were Plautus (ca. 254–184 B.C.), twenty of whose plays survive, and Terence (ca. 190–159 B.C.), who has left us six plays. Terence is much the milder, and, if we consider that originally he was a slave of African birth, the purity of his Latin is remarkable. The following selection is taken from the more boisterous Plautus.

C. M. Dixon

Plautus and Terence were Rome's most famous dramatic comedians. This mosaic from Pompeii shows masked actors in a comedy playing a magician and clients.

The Boastful Soldier

The title of the play, *Miles Gloriosus (The Boastful Soldier)*, describes the subject of the play. The soldier, Pyrgopolinices (whose name means "tower-city-conqueror" in Greek) has a good imagination in recounting his deeds, but his sponging friend Artotrogus ("bread-eater") has an even better one, inventing fantastic tales about his companion.

NOTE
Cilicia and Cappadocia are in Asia Minor; the Sardinians are west of Italy; the Macedonians north of Greece.

AR. Meminī centum in Ciliciā
et quīnquāgintā, centum in Scytholatrōniā,[1]
trīgintā Sardōs, sexāgintā Macedonēs—
sunt hominēs quōs tū—occīdistī ūnō diē.
PY. Quanta istaec[1] hominum summa est? AR. Septem mīlia.
PY. Tantum esse oportet. Rēctē ratiōnem tenēs.
AR. Quid in Cappadociā, ubi tū quīngentōs simul,
nī hebes machaera foret,[2] ūnō ictū[3] occīderās?
Quid tibi ego dīcam, quod omnēs mortālēs sciunt,
Pyrgopolinīcem tē ūnum in terrā vīvere
virtūtē et fōrmā et factīs invictissimīs?
Amant tē omnēs mulierēs neque iniūriā,[4]
quī sīs tam pulcher; vel[5] illae quae herī palliō
mē reprehendērunt.[6] PY. Quid eae dīxērunt tibi?
AR. Rogitābant: "Hicine[7] Achillēs est?"
"Immo[8] eius frāter," inquam, "est."

[1] = **ista**
[2] *if your sword had not been dull*
[3] *blow*
[4] *and not without reason*
[5] *for example*
[6] *caught me by the coat.*
[7] = **hicne**
[8] *No, but*

NOTE
Ask students if they can think of other literary "heroes" who are given to boastfulness and exaggeration.

WORKBOOK
Assign Ex. A to work with the content of this reading.

---

[1] a nonexistent place: "Scythia-robber-land"

Lucretius

CASSETTE
This reading is recorded on Cassette 3, Side B.

NOTE
If students wish to read more Lucretius, the section on how ears hear is very interesting.

NOTE
Although no one knows the exact dates of Lucretius, we do know he was contemporary with Cicero, and some plausible dates are 99-55 B.C.

NOTE
Students interested in philosophy may want to read the works of Epicurus.

Almost nothing certain is known about the life of this great poet, who lived during the first half of the first century B.C. His one poem, the *De Rerum Natura (On the Nature of Things)*, is a poetic exposition of the theories of the Greek philosopher Epicurus. It is important because it is an attempt to explain the universe in the scientific terms of an atomic theory often surprisingly similar to our own, and to dispel our superstitious fears about death and terrifying natural phenomena, such as thunder, lightning, and earthquakes, which were commonly attributed to the actions of the gods. It also anticipates modern notions of biological and social evolution.

Knowledge Produces a Tranquil Mind

Suāve,[1] marī$_1$ magnō turbantibus aequora[2] ventīs,
ē terrā magnum alterius spectāre labōrem,
nōn quia vexārī quemquam est iūcunda voluptās,
sed quibus ipse malīs careās[3] quia cernere$_2$ suāve est.
Sed nīl dulcius est, bene quam mūnīta tenēre
ēdita doctrīnā sapientum templa[4] serēnā,
dēspicere unde queās[5] aliōs passimque[6] vidēre
errāre atque viam pālantēs[7] quaerere vītae,
certāre ingeniō, contendere nōbilitāte,
noctēs atque diēs nītī[8] praestante labōre
ad summās ēmergere opēs rērumque potīrī.
Ō miserās hominum mentēs,$_3$ ō pectora caeca![9]

[1] Supply **est.**
[2] *waters*
[3] *you are free from* (with ablative)
[4] *regions*
[5] *you can*
[6] *everywhere*
[7] *wandering*
[8] *to strive* (deponent infinitive)
[9] *blind*
[10] i.e., of matter
[11] *in turn*
[12] *of living beings*
[13] = **vītae**

Two features of Lucretius' scientific explanation of the universe are that nothing is produced from nothing and that the universe consists only of matter and empty space:

Nīl posse creārī dē nīlō.$_4$
Corpora[10] sunt et ināne.

Men are like relay racers; they pass on the torch of life to the next generation:

Sīc rērum summa novātur
semper, et inter sē mortālēs mūtua[11] vīvunt.
Augēscunt aliae gentēs, aliae minuuntur,
inque brevī spatiō mūtantur saecla animantum[12]
et quasi cursōrēs vītāī[13] lampada trādunt.

$_1$ ablative of place without a preposition
$_2$ The antecedent of **quibus** (**ea** understood) is the object of **cernere.**
$_3$ accusative of exclamation
$_4$ from **nīl** (ablative)

Ronald Sheridan/Ancient Art & Architecture Collection

The Greek philosopher Epicurus (341-270 B.C.) founded his own school in Athens. Called the Garden, it was one of the few that accepted women and slaves. The followers of Epicurus focused heavily on sense perceptions and enjoyed much pleasure; many thought the Epicureans were hedonistic.

WORKBOOK
Assign Ex. A to practice various constructions taken from the reading.

WORKBOOK
Assign Ex. B to learn about poetic forms.

WORKBOOK
Assign Ex. C, D to work with the content of this reading.

Cornelius Nepos

Nepos wrote biographies of famous Greeks and Romans. He, too, lived in the first century B.C. and he outlived Lucretius. In this selection he tells about an honest politician who could not be bought.

NOTE
Students might be interested in discussing this politician's view with what they know of politicians and lobbyists today.

Phōcion Athēniēnsis saepe exercitibus praefuit summōsque magistrātūs cēpit, sed tamen multō nōtior est ob prīvātam vītam quam ob glōriam reī mīlitāris. Fuit enim semper pauper, quamquam dītissimus esse poterat propter honōrēs dēlātōs potestātēsque summās quae eī ā populō dabantur. Cum magna mūnera pecūniae ā lēgātīs rēgis Philippī dēlāta reiceret, lēgātī dīxērunt: "Sī ipse haec nōn vīs,[1] līberīs tamen tuīs prōspicere tē oportet, quibus difficile erit in summā inopiā tantam patris glōriam servāre." Hīs ille, "Sī meī[2] similēs erunt," inquit, "īdem hic parvus ager illōs alet quī mē ad hanc dignitātem perdūxit; sī dissimilēs sunt futūrī, nōlō meā pecūniā illōrum lūxuriam alī augērīque."

[1] from **volō**
[2] *like me* (genitive of **ego,** with **similis**)

WORKBOOK
Assign Ex. A to practice various constructions taken from the reading.

WORKBOOK
Assign Ex. B to work with the content of this reading.

Catullus

CASSETTE
These two poems are recorded on Cassette 3, Side B.

NOTE
Catullus didn't live to be very old; he was born in 87 B.C. and died around 54 B.C.

Catullus, a younger contemporary of Caesar, Cicero, and Nepos, was Rome's most inspired lyric poet. Many of his poems are addressed to his sweetheart Lesbia. His love affair had its ups and downs, but it did not end happily. Other short poems of his are written to friends and enemies, including Caesar, who at different times was a friend and foe. He also wrote marriage songs, a short epic, and a lament for his dead brother.

"Poor Little Sparrow"

In the poem on the next page, Catullus mourns the death of the pet sparrow (**passer**) of his sweetheart Lesbia.

Lūgēte, ō Venerēs Cupīdinēsque$_{1}$
et quantum est hominum venustiōrum![1]
Passer mortuus est meae puellae,
passer, dēliciae[2] meae puellae,
quem plūs illa oculīs suīs amābat;
nam mellītus[3] erat, suamque nōrat$_{2}$
ipsam tam bene quam puella mātrem,
nec sēsē ā gremiō[4] illius movēbat,
sed circumsiliēns modo[5] hūc modo illūc
ad sōlam dominam usque pīpiābat.[6]
Quī nunc it per iter tenebricōsum[7]
illūc unde negant redīre quemquam.
At vōbīs male sit, malae tenebrae
Orcī, quae omnia bella$_{3}$ dēvorātis;
tam bellum mihi passerem abstulistis.
Ō factum male! Iō miselle$_{4}$ passer!
Tuā nunc operā meae puellae
flendō turgidulī rubent ocellī.$_{5}$

[1] *all of the handsome men there are*
[2] *pet* (nominative)
[3] *sweet as honey*
[4] *lap*
[5] *now. . . now*
[6] *chirped*
[7] *shadowy* (to Hades); see also **tenebrae,** *darkness* (line 13)

NOTE
Point out that **oculīs** is ablative of comparison.

NOTE
Point out the onomatopoeia in **pipiābat** (it sounds like a chirp).

NOTE
Ask students what a comparable diminutive ending is in English *(-ette).*

WORKBOOK
Assign Ex. A to work with the content of this reading; Ex. B to practice various constructions taken from the reading.

$_{1}$ i.e., all the gods of love and beauty
$_{2}$ = **nōverat;** with **suam** supply **dominam** (Lesbia); **ipsam** modifies **mātrem:** *as the girl (knew) her own mother*
$_{3}$ adjective, from **bellus,** *beautiful*
$_{4}$ diminutive of **miser:** *poor little.*
$_{5}$ The diminutives (**ocellus** from **oculus, turgidulus** from **turgidus,** *swollen*) are used, like **miselle** above, for pathetic effect, as they heighten the tenderness and affection of the expression; **rubent** means *are red.*

Passer, deliciae meae puellae. *This detail from a wall painting in a Roman villa shows the Romans' fondness for birds.*

Scala/Art Resource, NY

NOTE
You may want to do a little work with students on meter so they can read the poems better. Unit X begins with a section on meter.

[1] *at one penny*
[2] i.e., life
[3] = **mihi**
[4] *kisses* (from **bāsium**)

WORKBOOK
Assign Ex. A, C to work with the content of this reading.

WORKBOOK
Assign Ex. B to practice various constructions taken from the reading.

Counting Kisses

Vīvāmus, mea Lesbia, atque amēmus,
rūmōrēsque senum sevēriōrum
omnēs ūnius aestimēmus assis.[1]
Sōlēs occidere et redīre possunt;
nōbīs cum semel occidit brevis lūx,[2]
nox est perpetua ūna dormienda.
Dā mī[3] bāsia[4] mīlle, deinde centum,
dein mīlle altera, dein secunda centum,
deinde usque altera mīlle, deinde centum.
Dein, cum mīlia multa fēcerīmus,
Conturbābimus illa, nē sciāmus
aut nē quis malus invidēre[1] possit,
cum tantum sciat esse bāsiōrum.

[1] i.e., cast the evil eye

Cicero

You have already become slightly acquainted with M. Tullius Cicero, now you will get to know him a little better. If you continue Latin next year, you will become intimately acquainted with him.

Cicero (106–43 B.C.) was Rome's greatest prose writer. He was the leading public speaker at a time when the ability to make an effective speech was even more important than it is today. Many of his orations still exist, including those against Catiline and Mark Antony, and the one for Archias the poet, in which he shows his appreciation of poetry. He wrote fine essays on moral and philosophical subjects: on friendship, on old age, on one's duties, etc. He also wrote on the history and technique of oratory. A large number of his letters, which he himself had no intention of publishing, have been preserved. Many are addressed to his intimate friend Atticus. They cover all sorts of subjects, from bathtubs to politics, from the birth of a son to the divorce and death of his daughter. He died while vainly attempting to defend constitutional government against Mark Antony.

The Regulation of War

Adapted from Cicero's treatise *De Officiis*, which was written for his son.

In rē pūblicā maximē cōnservanda sunt iūra bellī. Nam sunt duo genera dēcertandī, ūnum per disputātiōnem, alterum per vim. Illud proprium est hominis, hoc animālium. Itaque nōn fugiendum est[1] ad vim et bellum nisi ūtī nōn licet disputātiōne. Suscipienda quidem bella sunt ut sine iniūriā in pāce vīvāmus; post autem victōriam cōnservandī sunt eī quī nōn crūdēlēs in bellō fuērunt, ut maiōrēs nostrī Tusculānōs, Volscōs, Sabīnōs in cīvitātem etiam accēpērunt. At Carthāginem omnīnō sustulērunt; etiam Corinthum (et hoc vix probō), sed crēdō eōs hoc fēcisse nē locus[2] ipse ad bellum faciendum hortārī[1] posset. Nam pāx quae nihil habitūra sit īnsidiārum semper est petenda. Sed eī quī, armīs positīs, ad imperātōrum fidem fugiunt recipiendī sunt. In quō magnopere apud nostrōs iūstitia culta est. Nūllum bellum est iūstum nisi quod[3] aut, rēbus repetītīs, gerātur aut dēnūntiātum ante sit. Bellum autem ita suscipiātur ut nihil nisi pāx quaerī videātur.

NOTE
Remind students that **ūtor** takes the ablative (**disputatiōne**).

[1] impersonal; translate *as we must not resort to*
[2] *site*
[3] *except (one) which*

WORKBOOK
Assign Ex. A, B to work with the content of this reading.

---

[1] Supply as object "the inhabitants of Corinth."

A 15th century manuscript page from Cicero's treatise ***De Officiis****. Cicero's essays deal with a wide range of subjects, from oratorical training, to Greek philosophy, to practical behavior.*

PHOTRI

Good Citizenship

NOTE
Elicit the ablative of comparison (**patriā**).

[1] *associations*
[2] *which each one of us has with* (from **quisque**)
[3] *would hesitate*
[4] *therefore*
[5] *ferocity*
[6] *it is the special duty*
[7] *represents*
[8] *administer justice*
[9] *a private citizen*

NOTE
Point out that **nostrum** is from **ego**, not **noster**.

NOTE
Point out that **se gerere persōnam** means literally to *wear the mask of, play the part of.*

NOTE
Point out the contrast between **privātum** and **magistrātus**.

WORKBOOK
Assign Ex. C to work with the content of this reading.

WORKBOOK
Assign Ex. D to practice various constructions taken from the reading.

Adapted from various works of Cicero, primarily the *De Officiis.*

Nec locus tibi ūllus dulcior esse dēbet patriā.

Omnium societātum[1] nūlla est gravior, nūlla cārior quam ea quae cum rē pūblicā est ūnī cuique[2] nostrum. Cārī sunt parentēs, cārī līberī, propinquī, familiārēs, sed omnēs omnium cāritātēs patria ūna continet, prō quā nēmō bonus dubitet[3] mortem petere. Quō[4] est dētestābilior istōrum immānitās[5] quī lacerāvērunt omnī scelere patriam et in eā dēlendā occupātī et sunt et fuērunt.

Est proprium mūnus[6] magistrātūs intellegere sē gerere persōnam[7] cīvitātis dēbēreque eius dignitātem sustinēre, servāre lēgēs, iūra dīscrībere,[8] ea[1] fideī suae commissa meminisse. Prīvātum[9] autem oportet aequō et parī iūre cum cīvibus vīvere, atque in rē pūblicā ea velle quae tranquilla et honesta sint: tālem enim solēmus et sentīre bonum cīvem et dīcere.

Sī pecūniam aequam omnibus esse nōn placet, sī ingenia omnium paria esse nōn possunt, iūra certē paria dēbent esse eōrum quī sunt cīvēs in eādem rē pūblicā.

Mēns et animus et cōnsilium et sententia cīvitātis posita est in lēgibus. Ut corpora nostra sine mente, sīc cīvitās sine lēge suīs partibus ūtī nōn potest.

Fundāmentum iūstitiae est fidēs.

---

[1] neuter plural, object of **meminisse**; modified by **commissa**

Quotations from Cicero

NOTE
Ask students what the modern version of proverb 6 is.

[1] *gather*

1. Aliae nātiōnēs servitūtem patī possunt; populī Rōmānī rēs est propria lībertās.
2. Cavēte, patrēs cōnscrīptī, nē spē praesentis pācis perpetuam pācem āmittātis.
3. Cēdant arma togae.[1]
4. Cōnsuētūdinis magna vīs est.
5. Ō tempora, ō mōrēs!
6. Parēs cum paribus facillimē congregantur.[1]
7. Salūs populī suprēma lēx estō.[2]

WORKBOOK
Assign Ex. E to work with additional famous sayings.

---

[1] The toga represents *civil life,* as contrasted with *military.* Motto of the state of Wyoming.
[2] *let. . . be.* Motto of the state of Missouri.

Sallust

Sallust (86–34 B.C.) was a politician and officer who held important commands under Caesar during the Civil War. With the fortune he amassed, supposedly from plundering the province of Numidia, he bought a palatial estate in Rome, with magnificent gardens that are still famous. Two of his surviving works are the *Catiline* and the *Jugurtha*, the former dealing with the conspiracy of Catiline, the latter with a war against an African king. Sallust claimed impartiality, but he is bitterly critical of the old Roman aristocracy and the decadence for which he thinks they are responsible.

NOTE
There is a reading about this conspiracy in Lesson XXXVII.

The Good Old Days of Early Rome

Igitur domī mīlitiaeque[1] bonī mōrēs colēbantur; concordia maxima, minima avāritia erat; iūs bonumque apud eōs nōn lēgibus magis quam nātūrā valēbat. Iūrgia,[2] discordiās, simultātēs[3] cum hostibus exercēbant, cīvēs cum cīvibus dē virtūte certābant. In suppliciīs deōrum magnificī, domī parcī, in amīcōs fidēlēs erant. Duābus hīs artibus, audāciā in bellō, ubi pāx ēvēnerat aequitāte, sēque remque pūblicam cūrābant. Quārum rērum ego maxima documenta haec habeō, quod in bellō saepius vindicātum est[4] in eōs quī contrā imperium in hostem pugnāverant quīque tardius[5] revocātī proeliō excesserant, quam$_1$ quī signa relinquere aut pulsī locō cēdere ausī erant; in pāce vērō quod beneficiīs magis quam metū imperium agitābant et, acceptā iniūriā, ignōscere quam persequī mālēbant.

[1] *abroad*
[2] *quarrels*
[3] *hatreds*
[4] *punishment was inflicted* (*on*)
[5] *too slowly* (with **excesserant**)

NOTE
See if students can identify **domī** and **mīlitiae** as locatives.

NOTE
You may want to refer students back to the reading about Manlius in Lesson XXXIV.

NOTE
Elicit the ablative of separation (**proeliō**).

WORKBOOK
Assign Ex. A to practice various constructions taken from the reading.

WORKBOOK
Assign Ex. B to work with the content of this reading.

$_1$ take with **saepius;** supply **in eōs**

Publilius Syrus

Publilius Syrus was a writer of a type of comedy that was very popular when he wrote, which was in the time of Caesar. One reason why he won so much favor was his use of many proverbial expressions. Although the plays themselves have disappeared, someone made a collection of the proverbs in them, and these have been preserved. Many are as fresh and applicable today as they were two thousand years ago.

NOTE
Wherever possible, have students come up with modern equivalents of these sayings.

[1] Supply **id** as antecedent.
[2] *free*
[3] *eloquent, interesting*
[4] Supply **is** as antecedent.
[5] *very little things*

NOTE
Point out the use of the subjunctive used in a command.

SUGGESTION
These sayings lend themselves well to a short writing assignment.

WORKBOOK
Assign Ex. A to work with the content of the proverbs.

1. Ab aliīs exspectēs alterī quod[1] fēcerīs.
2. Aliēna[1] nōbīs, nostra plūs aliīs placent.
3. Aliēnum aes hominī ingenuō[2] acerba est servitūs.
4. Aut amat aut ōdit mulier; nihil est tertium.
5. Avārus ipse miseriae causa est suae.
6. Avārus, nisi cum moritur, nihil rēctē facit.
7. Bis vincit quī sē vincit in victōriā.
8. Comes fācundus[3] in viā prō vehiculō est.
9. Cui[4] plūs licet quam pār est plūs vult quam licet.
10. Discordiā fit cārior concordia.
11. Effugere cupiditātem rēgnum est vincere.
12. Etiam capillus ūnus habet umbram suam.
13. Inopī bis dat quī cito dat.
14. Male imperandō summum imperium āmittitur.
15. Necesse est minima[5] maximōrum esse initia.
16. Paucōrum improbitās est multōrum calamitās.
17. Perīcula timidus etiam quae nōn sunt videt.
18. Quicquid fit cum virtūte fit cum glōriā.
19. Spīna etiam grāta est ex quā spectātur rosa.
20. Stultī timent fortūnam, sapientēs ferunt.
21. Stultum facit fortūna quem vult perdere.
22. Taciturnitās stultō hominī prō sapientiā est.

---

[1] **Aliēna** and **nostra** are both used as subjects of **placent**.

Livy

NOTE
For background information on Livy, refer students back to the Unit III introduction.

NOTE
This reading should elicit considerable class discussion.

Cato and the Women

Inter bellōrum magnōrum cūrās intercessit rēs parva sed quae[1] in magnum certāmen excesserit.[1] In mediō Pūnicī bellī lēx lāta erat nē qua mulier plūs quam sēmunciam[2] aurī habēret nec veste versicolōrī ūterētur nec vehiculō in urbe veherētur. Post bellum mulierēs voluērunt hanc lēgem abrogārī. Nec auctōritāte nec imperiō virōrum continērī poterant; omnēs viās urbis obsidēbant; etiam audēbant adīre cōnsulēs. Sed cōnsul, M. Porcius Catō, haec verba fēcit: "Sī in[3] suā quisque uxōre, cīvēs, iūs virī

[1] (*one*) *which*
[2] *half an ounce*
[3] *in* (*the case of*); **quisque** is the subject

[1] Translate as if indicative: *developed into.*

The Bettmann Archive

Often when the men were away fighting battles, the women stayed home. They would frequently offer sacrifices to help ensure that their loved ones would return safely.

[4] *had begun to hold on to the rights of the husband*
[5] *we should have*
[6] *only* (adverb)
[7] *is beneficial* (from **prōsum**)

WORKBOOK
Assign Ex. A, C to work with the content of this reading.

WORKBOOK
Assign Ex. B to practice various constructions taken from the reading.

retinēre īnstituisset,[4] minus negōtī cum omnibus fēminīs habērēmus.[5] Quia singulās nōn continuimus, omnēs timēmus. Maiōrēs nostrī voluērunt fēminās agere nūllam rem, nē prīvātam quidem, sine parentibus vel frātribus vel virīs; nōs, sī deīs placet, iam etiam rem pūblicam capere eās patimur. Hāc rē expugnātā, quid nōn temptābunt? Sī eās aequās virīs esse patiēminī, tolerābilēs vōbīs eās futūrās esse crēditis? Simul ac parēs esse coeperint, superiōrēs erunt. Nūlla lēx satis commoda omnibus est; id modo[6] quaeritur, sī maiōrī partī prōsit."[7] Tum ūnus ex tribūnīs contrā lēgem locūtus est, et lēx abrogāta est. Mulierēs vīcerant.

Horace

NOTE
Remind students that these quotations are from various poems, and poetry generally uses a freer word order than prose.

Horace (65–8 B.C.) was one of the greatest of Roman poets. He was a friend of Augustus and Vergil. His *Odes*, *Satires*, and *Epistles* are delightful reading. Because his poems are not always easy to read, only quotations are given here. They often tell much in very brief but exquisitely phrased language.

NOTE
This phrase was made popular in the film, "Dead Poets Society."

[1] *nothing hard* (with **nīl**)
[2] = **vīxērunt**

NOTE
Tell students that **Agamemnona** is accusative. Remind them that it was Agamemnon who led the Greeks in the Trojan War.

1. Aequam mementō[1] rēbus in arduīs servāre mentem.
2. Aurea mediocritās.
3. Carpe diem.
4. Crēscentem sequitur cūra pecūniam.
5. Est modus[2] in rēbus.
6. Levius fit patientiā quicquid[3] corrigere est nefās.
7. Magnās inter opēs inops.
8. Nīl mortālibus arduī[1] est.
9. Nīl sine magnō vīta labōre dedit mortālibus.
10. Permitte dīvīs cētera.
11. Rāra avis.
12. Rīdentem dīcere vērum.
13. Vīxēre[2] fortēs ante Agamemnona.

[1] *remember* (imperative); **aequam** modifies **mentem.**
[2] in the same sense as **mediocritās** in No. 2
[3] *whatever;* the clause is the subject of **fit.**

WORKBOOK
Assign Ex. A, B to work with the content of the quotations.

Sulpicia

Sulpicia is the only known Latin woman poet. She was of aristocratic birth and was the niece of Messalla, a prominent citizen and supporter of the arts. She was welcome in Tibullus' literary circle, and probably wrote around 30 B.C. Her contributions indicate the more prominent role women were beginning to play in fashionable society. Only six of her love-poems, written to Cerinthus, have survived.

Scala/Art Resource, NY

Sometimes mothers taught their daughters to read so that they could enjoy poetry and literature as well as letters from family that may be far away. Sulpicia was welcomed into Tibullus' literary circle—perhaps the girl in this wall painting hopes to be a poet also when she grows up.

NOTE
Elicit the ablative of comparison (**urbe**).

[1] *hateful*
[2] *to be spent*
[3] *river* (with **frigidus**)
[4] *at the right time, convenient* (with **nōn**)
[5] *does not allow*

NOTE
Point out that **quiescas** is a command in the subjunctive.

NOTE
Tell students that **meōs** is plural to agree with both **animum** and **sensus**.

WORKBOOK
Assign Ex. A to practice various constructions taken from the readings.

[1] *unexpected*

Here, Sulpicia laments having to spend her birthday away from Rome and Cerinthus.

Invisus nātālis adest, quī rūre molestō[1]
 et sine Cerinthō tristis agendus erit.[2]
Dulcius urbe quid est? An villa sit apta puellae
 atque Arretinō frīgidus amnis[3] agrō?
Iam, nimium Messalla meī studiōse, quiescas:
 nōn tempestīvae[4] saepe, propinque, viae.
Hic animum sensusque meōs abducta relinquō,
 arbitriō quam vis nōn sinit[5] esse meō.

In this poem, it appears that the trip was, at last, called off.

Scīs iter ex animō sublātum triste puellae?
 nātālī Rōmae iam licet esse meō.
Omnibus ille diēs nōbīs nātālis agatur,
 quī nec opināta[1] nunc tibi sorte vēnit.

Ovid and Roman Elegy

NOTE
Chronologically, Vergil would be covered here, but a selection of excerpts from the *Aeneid* is covered in Unit X.

NOTE
Explain that the Roman underworld was divided into sections, and the Elysian Fields corresponded to heaven.

NOTE
Remind students that bodies were cremated, not buried, in Rome.

[1] i.e., poets
[2] *come to meet him;* **obvius** is an adjective
[3] *your temples crowned with ivy*
[4] *I pray*

WORKBOOK
Assign Ex. A to practice various constructions taken from the reading; Ex. B to work with the content of this reading.

The Greeks used the elegiac meter for drinking and military songs, for historical and political subjects, for inscriptions on tombstones and laments for the dead, and even for love poetry. It was this last category that the three most famous Roman elegists, Tibullus, Propertius, and Ovid, developed into an extremely personal and sensitive form. Each immortalized the sweetheart to whom he addressed his verse, Tibullus' Delia, Propertius' Cynthia, and Ovid's Corinna. The following selection from Ovid exemplifies elegy's traditional role of mourning for the dead. Ovid here laments the loss of Tibullus, who had joined the earlier elegists in the Elysian Fields.

Sī tamen ē nōbīs[1] aliquid nisi nōmen et umbra
restat, in Ēlysiā valle Tibullus erit.
Obvius huic veniās[2] hederā iuvenālia cīnctus
tempora[3] cum Calvō, docte Catulle, tuō.
Hīs comes umbra tua est. Sī qua est modo corporis umbra,
auxistī numerōs, culte Tibulle, piōs.
Ossa quiēta, precor,[4] tūtā requiēscite in urnā,
et sit humus cinerī nōn onerōsa tuō.[1]

[1] a variant of the phrase found on hundreds of Roman tombstones: **sit tibi terra levis**

Phaedrus

The fable is an ancient form of literature, in which animals generally speak and act like human beings. Usually a moral is attached. The most famous of all fabulists was the Greek writer Aesop, and his stories are still much read in many languages. In Rome during the age of Augustus, Phaedrus put these fables into simple Latin verse. Here are three of them, rewritten in prose.

NOTE
Ask students if they can think of any modern parallels to these stories.

The Wolf and the Lamb

Ad rīvum eundem lupus et agnus vēnerant; superior stābat lupus, longēque īnferior agnus. Tum lupus famē incitātus contrōversiae causam intulit. "Cūr," inquit, "turbulentam fēcistī mihi aquam bibentī?" Agnus timēns respondit: "Quō modō possum hoc facere, lupe? Ā tē dēcurrit aqua ad mē." Repulsus ille vēritātis vīribus: "Ante sex mēnsēs," ait, "male dīxistī[1] mihi." Respondit agnus: "Equidem nātus nōn eram." "Pater certē tuus," ille inquit, "male dīxit mihi." Atque ita raptum lacerat iniūstā nece.

Haec propter illōs scrīpta est hominēs fābula quī fictīs causīs innocentēs opprimant.

[1] *swore at* (with **male**)

WORKBOOK
Assign Ex. A to work with the content of this reading.

WORKBOOK
Assign Ex. B to practice various constructions taken from the reading.

The Greedy Dog

Āmittit meritō[1] suum quī aliēnum appetit. Canis dum per flūmen carnem ferret natāns, in aquā vīdit simulācrum suum, aliamque praedam ab aliō cane ferrī putāns ēripere voluit; sed dēceptus avidus, quem tenēbat ōre dīmīsit cibum nec quem petēbat potuit attingere.

[1] *deservedly*

WORKBOOK
Assign Ex. C, E to work with the content of this reading.

WORKBOOK
Assign Ex. D to practice various constructions taken from the reading.

The ancient Romans loved their dogs just as much as we do. Perhaps a particularly big one lived in the house in Pompeii where this mosaic was found.

Ronald Sheridan/Ancient Art & Architecture Collection

Sour Grapes

Famē coācta vulpes[1] in altā vīneā ūvam[2] petēbat, summīs vīribus saliēns. Quam ubi tangere nōn potuit, discēdēns, "Nōndum mātūra est," inquit; "nōlō acerbam sūmere."

Eī quī verbīs ēlevant[3] quae nōn facere possunt hoc exemplum sibi ascrībere dēbent.

[1] *fox*
[2] *grapes, bunch of grapes*
[3] *make light of*

WORKBOOK
Assign Ex. F to work with the content of this reading.

WORKBOOK
Assign Ex. G to practice various constructions taken from the reading.

Valerius Maximus

In the first century A.D. Valerius Maximus compiled a book of well-known stories from history, both Roman and foreign, to illustrate various human qualities and conditions such as courage, superstition, cruelty. The purpose of the book was to provide material for a public speaker who wanted to illustrate his points by means of examples from history, just as today many speakers make use of jokebooks.

NOTE
Very little is known about Valerius Maximus, except that he seemed to have lived during the time of Tiberius.

NOTE
Ask students how they feel about the depth of trust and loyalty shown in this story. Is it common today?

Damon and Pythias

Cum Dionȳsius, rēx Syrācūsārum, Pythiam philosophum interficere vellet, hic ā Dionȳsiō petīvit ut sibi licēret domum proficīscī rērum suārum dispōnendārum causā. Amīcus eius Dāmōn erat. Tanta erat amīcitia inter Dāmōnem et Pythiam ut Dāmōn sē vadem[1] prō reditū alterius rēgī dare nōn dubitāret. Appropinquante cōnstitūtō diē nec illō redeunte, ūnus quisque stultitiam Dāmōnis damnāvit. At is nihil sē dē amīcī fidē timēre dīcēbat. Hōrā cōnstitūtā Pythiās vēnit. Admīrātus utrīusque animum Dionȳsius supplicium remīsit et eōs rogāvit ut sē[2] socium amīcitiae reciperent.

WORKBOOK
Assign Ex. A, C to work with the content of this reading.

[1] *(as) bail*
[2] i.e., Dionysius

WORKBOOK
Assign Ex. B to practice various constructions taken from the reading.

A Costly Joke

P. Scīpiō Nāsīca, cum aedīlitātem[1] adulēscēns peteret, mōre candidātōrum manum cuiusdam agricolae rūsticō opere dūrātam prehendit. Iocī causā rogāvit agricolam num manibus solitus esset ambulāre. Quod[2] dictum ā circumstantibus audītum ad populum allātum est causaque fuit repulsae[3] Scīpiōnis. Nam omnēs agricolae paupertātem suam ab eō rīdērī iūdicantēs īram suam contrā eius iocum ostendērunt.

[1] *aedileship* (a public office)
[2] = **hoc**
[3] *defeat*

NOTE
Tell students that an *aedileship* (part of the **cursus honōrum**) was a public office that, among other things, supervised public games and festivals.

WORKBOOK
Assign Ex. D to work with the content of this reading.

WORKBOOK
Assign Ex. E to practice various constructions taken from the reading.

Seneca

Seneca, who wrote many books on philosophy, was the tutor and later the adviser of the emperor Nero (A.D. 54–68), who eventually forced him to commit suicide. His books preach Stoic philosophy.

1. Magna rēs est vōcis et silentī tempora nōsse.[1]
2. Maximum remedium īrae mora est.
3. Nōn est in rēbus vitium, sed in ipsō animō.
4. Nōn sum ūnī angulō nātus; patria mea tōtus hic mundus est.
5. Omnis ars imitātiō est nātūrae.
6. Optimum est patī quod ēmendāre nōn possīs.[1]
7. Ōtium sine litterīs mors est.
8. Quī beneficium dedit taceat: nārret quī accēpit.
9. Sī vīs amārī, amā.
10. Ubicumque homō est, ibi beneficī locus est.

[1] = **nōvisse**

NOTE
Have students compare the quotations from Cicero, Syrus, Horace, and Seneca. Which do they find most appealing? Why?

WORKBOOK
Assign Ex. A to work with the content of this reading.

[1] Translate as if indicative.

Petronius

CASSETTE
This reading is recorded on Cassette 3, Side B.

Nothing in Latin literature is quite so zany and ludicrous as the *Satiricon* of Petronius. It is a kind of novel, containing a wild medley of prose and poetry, dealing mostly with the escapades of three lower-class rogues who must live by their wits and who are constantly in trouble with the authorities. Best known of their adventures is the account of a fantastic dinner party at the house of an ex-slave named Trimalchio, who was so illiterate that he thought Hannibal took part in the Trojan War and so enormously wealthy that he bought the whole west coast of Italy so that, when he sailed to Sicily, he would not have to sail past anyone else's coastline! The selection below should give you still more indications of the size of Trimalchio's fortune.

THE GRANGER COLLECTION, New York

Quite a feast was set on this reconstructed ***triclinium*** *(dining room) table from the House of the Moralist in Pompeii. Notice the couches for reclining while one ate.*

NOTE
Remind students that this was only one of his properties!

Petronius is thought to have lived in the first century A.D. and has been identified as the Petronius who was called the *elegantiae arbiter* of Nero's court because of his exquisite refinement.

In this selection, Trimalchio has his own newspaper read aloud to the guests at his dinner party.

Āctuārius[1] tamquam urbis ācta[2] recitāvit: "Hōc diē in praediō Cūmānō[3] quod est Trimalchiōnis, nātī sunt puerī XXX, puellae XL; sublāta in horreum[4] trīticī mīlia modium quīngenta;[5] bovēs domitī[6] quīngentī. Eōdem diē: in arcam[7] relātum est quod collocārī nōn potuit sēstertium centiēs.[8] Eōdem diē: incendium factum est in hortīs Pompeiānīs." "Quid," inquit Trimalchiō, "quandō mihi Pompeiānī hortī ēmptī sunt?" "Annō priōre," inquit āctuārius, "et ideō[9] in ratiōnem nōndum vēnērunt." Trimalchiō, "Quīcumque," inquit, "mihi fundī[10] ēmptī fuerint, nisi intrā sextum mēnsem scierō,[11] in ratiōnēs meās īnferrī vetō."

[1] *newsman, secretary*
[2] *doings, news*
[3] *the estate at Cumae*
[4] *barn*
[5] *500,000 pecks of wheat*
[6] *tamed, broken in*
[7] *vault*
[8] *10,000,000 sesterces* (about $500,000)
[9] *therefore*
[10] *estates*
[11] = **scīverō**

NOTE
Tell students that 500,000 pecks of wheat would be enough to feed 10,000 people for a year.

WORKBOOK
Assign Ex. A to try writing in the style of a satyrist.

Quintilian

Possibly the most famous schoolteacher of all time is Quintilian (ca. A.D. 35–96), who was appointed the first state-paid professor of rhetoric (oratory) by the emperor Vespasian. After a lifetime of teaching and practice at the bar, at the request of his devoted pupils he put his theories of education into twelve books called the *Institutio Oratoria (Introduction to Public Speaking)*, which carry the training of the orator from the cradle to the grave, for he believed in beginning education when the child was born and continuing it all one's life. So the nursery school and the kindergarten are not new, nor is adult education. Quintilian's favorite orator was Cicero, although he does not hesitate to criticize even him. The basic principle of his teaching was that a man could not be a great orator, whatever his skill, unless he were first of all a good man.

NOTE
Vespasian was emperor from 69-79. He brought prosperity to the empire, was a patron of the arts, and began the building of the Colosseum.

Ante omnia nē sit vitiōsus sermō nūtrīcibus,[1] quās, sī fierī posset, sapientēs Chrysippus[1] optāvit, certē quantum rēs paterētur, optimās ēligī voluit. Et mōrum quidem in hīs haud dubiē[2] prior ratiō est; rēctē tamen etiam loquantur. Hās prīmum audiet puer, hārum verba effingere[3] imitandō cōnābitur. Et nātūrā tenācissimī sumus eōrum quae rudibus animīs percēpimus. Et haec ipsa magis pertināciter haerent quō[4] dēteriōra sunt. Nam bona facile mūtantur in peius; num quandō[5] in bonum verteris vitia? Nōn adsuēscat[6] ergō, nē dum īnfans quidem[7] est, sermōnī quī dēdiscendus sit.[8]

In parentibus vērō quam plūrimum esse ērudītiōnis optāverim,[9] nec dē patribus tantum loquor, nam Gracchōrum ēloquentiae multum contulisse accēpimus Cornēliam mātrem, cuius doctissimus sermō in posterōs quoque est epistulīs trāditus; et Laelia C.[10] fīlia reddidisse in loquendō paternam ēlegantiam dīcitur; et Hortēnsiae Q. fīliae ōrātiō legitur. Nec tamen iī quibus discere[11] ipsīs nōn contigit minōrem cūram docendī līberōs habeant, sed sint propter hoc ipsum ad cētera magis dīligentēs.

[1] *nurses*
[2] *undoubtedly* (with **haud**)
[3] *form*
[4] *according as*
[5] *at any time*
[6] *he should not accustom himself*
[7] *not even* (with **nē**)
[8] *must be unlearned*
[9] *I could wish*
[10] **Gāī**
[11] i.e., to get an education

WORKBOOK
Assign Ex. A to practice various constructions taken from the reading.

WORKBOOK
Assign Ex. B, C to work with the content of this reading. Ex. C is a writing exercise.

[1] a Greek philosopher and teacher

Martial

Like Seneca and Quintilian, Martial was born in Spain but moved to Rome. He is the writer who gave the word epigram its present meaning. It is generally a short poem that makes fun of someone. Its clever and often unexpected point is at the end, at times in the last word.

CASSETTE
These six epigrams are recorded on Cassette 3, Side B.

An Unfair Exchange

1. Cūr nōn mitto meōs tibi, Pontiliāne, libellōs?
   Nē mihi tū mittās, Pontiliāne, tuōs.

A Friend and His Faults

2. Difficilis, facilis, iūcundus, acerbus es īdem.
   Nec tēcum possum vīvere nec sine tē.

NOTE
Tell students that **nubere** is used for a woman; **ducere** for a man.

"Fifty-Fifty"

3. Nūbere[1] vīs Prīscō: nōn mīror, Paula; sapīstī.[2]
   Dūcere[1] tē nōn vult Prīscus: et[3] ille sapit.

Rich Wives

4. Uxōrem quārē locuplētem[4] dūcere nōlim
   quaeritis? Uxōrī nūbere[1] nōlo meae.
   Īnferior mātrōna suō sit, Prīsce, marītō;
   nōn aliter fīunt fēmina virque parēs.

The Plagiarist

5. Quem recitās meus est, ō Fīdentīne, libellus,
   sed, male cum recitās, incipit esse tuus.

A Good Match

6. Cum sītis similēs parēsque vītā,
   uxor pessima, pessimus marītus,
   mīror nōn bene convenīre[5] vōbīs.

[1] *marry*
[2] *you are wise* (= **sapīvistī**)
[3] *also*
[4] *rich*
[5] *that you are not well suited* (impersonal)

WORKBOOK
Assign Ex. A to work with the content of the reading.

---

[1] A man who marries a rich wife becomes the "lady" of the house.

Tacitus

Last of the great Roman historians was Cornelius Tacitus (ca. A.D. 55–120). His two most extensive works are the *Annals* and the *Histories*, which between them originally covered the period of Roman history from the death of Augustus through the reign of Domitian, i.e., from A.D. 14 to A.D. 96. He also wrote monographs on oratory, on Germany, and on the deeds of his father-in-law, Agricola. He was a distinguished orator and public figure, rising to the consulship in 97. His cynical tone, his austerity, and his intense brevity have made him a favorite of students of Latin style, while his bitter senatorial prejudice against the imperial regime has been chiefly responsible for our present impression, largely incorrect, of the corruption and cruelty of Roman emperors. The *Agricola*, from which the following selection is taken, deals largely with Britain, because Tacitus' father-in-law was a successful general there.

Agricola brings Roman culture to Britain.

Iam vērō prīncipum fīliōs līberālibus artibus ērudīre,[1] et ingenia Britannōrum studiīs Gallōrum anteferre,[1] ut quī modo[2] linguam Rōmānam abnuēbant,[3] ēloquentiam concupīscerent.[4] Inde etiam habitūs[5] nostrī honor et frequēns toga. Paulātimque dēscēnsum ad dēlēnīmenta[6] vitiōrum, porticūs et balineās[7] et convīviōrum[8] ēlegantiam. Idque apud imperītōs hūmānitās vocābātur, cum pars servitūtis esset.

[1] The infinitives are used instead of a past tense of the indicative.

NOTE
The Roman baths in Bath, England are still a tourist attraction.

[1] *put ahead of* (with dative)
[2] *recently*
[3] *were rejecting*
[4] *were eager for*
[5] *clothing*
[6] *enticements*
[7] = **balnea**
[8] *banquets*

WORKBOOK
Assign Ex. A, B to work with the content of the reading.

Juvenal

NOTE
Have students compare these sayings to the others in this unit.

Juvenal was a satirist who lived at the beginning of the second century A.D. He was a contemporary of Pliny the Younger. The vices of his times are the themes of his poems.

1. Probitās laudātur et alget.[1]
2. Pānem et circēnsēs.[2]
3. Nēmō malus fēlīx.
4. Quis custōdiet ipsōs custōdēs?
5. Mēns sāna in corpore sānō.

WORKBOOK
Assign Ex. A to work with the content of the reading.

---

[1] *shivers,* i.e., the honest man is usually too poor to buy warm clothing.
[2] *bread and circus games,* i.e., all that the degenerate Romans of his day are interested in, according to Juvenal.

Aulus Gellius

NOTE
Chronologically, Suetonius, Rome's most important writer of biography should appear here. You may want to refer students to Lesson XXXIX and the story of Nero for an example.

NOTE
Fabricius was the hero of the war with Pyrrhus, who admired him so much that he offered him part of his kingdom.

NOTE
The *censor* had the right to expel senators who committed offenses or whose manner of living was not in accord with the best Roman tradition.

The two stories that follow are adapted from Aulus Gellius, a writer of the second century A.D., who tells many curious and interesting anecdotes. His *Noctes Atticae*, or *Attic Nights*, is a sort of literary scrapbook, written during winter evenings in Attica, Greece, to amuse and instruct his children.

A Lesson in Voting

Fabricius magnā glōriā vir magnīsque rēbus gestīs fuit. P. Cornēlius Rūfīnus imperātor bonus et fortis et mīlitāris disciplīnae perītus[1] fuit, sed avārus erat. Hunc Fabricius nōn probābat et eī inimīcus ob mōrēs fuit. Sed cum tempore difficillimō reī pūblicae cōnsulēs creandi essent et Rūfīnus peteret cōnsulātum competītōrēsque eius nōn essent bellī perītī, summā ope[2] Fabricius labōrāvit ut Rūfīnō cōnsulātus dēferrētur. Eam rem quibusdam mīrantibus, "Mālō," inquit, "ā cīve spoliārī quam ab hoste vēnīre."[3] M. Cicerō refert hoc esse dictum, nōn aliīs, sed ipsī Rūfīnō, cum hic Fabriciō ob opem[4] grātiās ageret.

Hunc Rūfīnum, postquam bis cōnsul et dictātor fuit, cēnsor Fabricius ob lūxuriam ē senātū ēiēcit.

[1] with the genitive
[2] *effort*
[3] *to be sold* (from **vēneō**)
[4] *help*

WORKBOOK
Assign Ex. A to work with the content of the reading.

WORKBOOK
Assign Ex. B to practice various constructions taken from the reading.

Androclus and the Lion

In Circō Maximō vēnātiō[1] populō dabātur. Multae ibi ferae erant, sed praeter aliās omnēs ūnus leō magnitūdine corporis animōs oculōsque omnium in sē converterat.

Inductus erat servus inter complūrēs aliōs ad pugnam ferārum. Eī servō Androclus nōmen fuit. Hunc ille leō ubi vīdit procul, statim quasi admīrāns stetit ac deinde lēniter, quasi cognōscēns ad hominem accēdit. Tum caudam mōre canis movet hominisque manūs linguā lēniter dēmulcet. Androclus, prīmum territus, nunc leōnem spectat. Tum quasi leōne cognitō, homō gaudēre vīsus est.

Eā rē tam mīrā maximī clāmōrēs populī excitātī sunt. Caesar[2] Androclum vocāvit et quaesīvit causam cūr illī ūnī ferōcissimus leō pepercisset. Tum Androclus rem mīrandam nārrat.

[1] *hunt,* i.e., a fight between men and wild beasts
[2] probably Tiberius

NOTE
Androclus is generally known as *Androcles.*

NOTE
Elicit that **servō** is dative of possession (with **fuit**).

Venatio *(the hunt). In addition to the occasional hunts staged in the Colosseum, Roman nobles sometimes went hunting wild boar or deer for food as well as sport.*

Erich Lessing/Art Resource, NY

[3] *cave*
[4] *pus*
[5] *strap*

"Cum prōvinciae," inquit, "Āfricae dominus meus imperāret, ego iniūstē verberātus fugere coāctus sum. Specum[3] quendam remōtum inveniō et eum ingredior. Neque multō post ad eundem specum venit hic leō, vulnerātō ūnō pede, gemitūs ob dolōrem ēdēns. Prīmō quidem cōnspectū leōnis territus sum. Sed postquam leō ingressus mē vīdit, lēniter accessit et pedem ostendere mihi quasi opis petendae grātiā vīsus est. Ibi ego spīnam magnam, pedī eius haerentem, ēripuī et saniem[4] expressī. Ille tum, pede in manibus meīs positō, quiētem cēpit. Ex eō diē trēs annōs ego et leō in eōdem specū vīximus. Membra ferārum leō mihi ferēbat, quae ego, ignis cōpiam nōn habēns, sōle torrēbam. Sed tandem specum relīquī et ā mīlitibus prehēnsus ad dominum ex Āfricā Rōmam dēductus sum. Is mē statim ad ferās mīsit. Intellegō autem hunc quoque leōnem, posteā captum, grātiam mihi referre."

Haec dīxit Androclus. Omnibus petentibus, dīmissus est et leō eī dōnātus. Posteā Androclus et leō, lōrō[5] ligātus, circum tabernās ībant. Androclus pecūniam accipiēbat, leō flōrēs. Omnēs dīcēbant: "Hic est leō hospes hominis; hic est homō medicus leōnis."

WORKBOOK
Assign Ex. C to work with the content of the reading.

Miscellaneous Quotations

NOTE
Varro was a contemporary of Cicero.

[1] Supply **pūblicae.**
[2] *fall*
[3] *even*
[4] Supply **itinere.**
[5] *of a foreigner*
[6] Supply *is taken for,* i.e., *is regarded as.*

1. Dīvīna nātūra dedit agrōs, ars hūmāna aedificāvit urbēs. (Varro)
2. Concordiā parvae rēs[1] crēscunt, discordiā maximae dīlābuntur.[2] (Sallust)
3. Est deus in nōbīs. (Ovid)
4. Fās est et[3] ab hoste docērī. (Ovid)
5. Mediō[4] tūtissimus ībis. (Ovid)
6. Externus[5] timor maximum concordiae vinculum. (Livy)
7. In cīvitāte līberā linguam mentemque līberās esse (dīcēbat). (Tiberius)
8. Damnant quod nōn intellegunt. (Quintilian)
9. Omne ignōtum prō magnificō.[6] (Tacitus)
10. Ipsa quidem virtūs pretium sibi. (Claudian)
11. Omnia mors aequat. (Claudian)
12. Facis dē necessitāte virtūtem. (St. Jerome)

NOTE
Claudian was a poet around A.D. 400.

NOTE
The *Vulgate* is Jerome's translation of the Bible.

13. Magna est vēritās et praevalet. (the *Vulgate*)
14. Quī dēsīderat pācem praeparet bellum. (author unknown)
15. Cōgitātiōnis poenam nēmō patitur. *(Corpus Iuris Civilis)*
16. Iūris praecepta sunt haec: honestē vīvere, alterum nōn laedere, suum cuique tribuere. *(Corpus Iuris Civilis)*
17. Glōriōsa est scientia litterārum, quia, quod prīmum est, in homine mōrēs pūrgat; quod secundum, verbōrum grātiam subministrat. (Cassiodorus)
18. Necessitās nōn habet lēgem. (author unknown)
19. Dē duōbus malīs, minus est semper ēligendum. (Thomas à Kempis)
20. Ō quam cito trānsit glōria mundī! (Thomas à Kempis)
21. Ipsa scientia potestās est. (Francis Bacon)
22. Ego cōgitō, ergō sum. (René Descartes)
23. Ēripuit[1] caelō fulmen,[7] mox scēptra tyrannīs. (author unknown)
24. Crocodīlī lacrimae. (proverb)
25. Vestis virum facit. (proverb)
26. Festīnā lentē.[8] (proverb)
27. Nōlī dīcere[9] omnia quae scīs; nōlī crēdere omnia quae audīs; nōlī scrībere omnia quae facis; nōlī facere omnia quae potes. (author unknown)

[1] The subject is Benjamin Franklin.

NOTES:
The *Corpus Iuris Civilis* is the great law code compiled in the sixth century, the basis of modern law in many countries.

Cassiodorus lived in the sixth century.

Thomas à Kempis was a well-known writer in the Middle Ages.

Francis Bacon (1561-1626) was an English philosopher, essayist, jurist, and statesman.

[7] *lightning*
[8] *Make haste slowly.*
[9] *Do not tell*

NOTE
René Descartes (1596-1650) was a French mathematician and philosopher.

NOTE
Quote 27 was found in a medieval manuscript.

WORKBOOK
Assign Ex. A to work with the content of this reading.

Augustine

NOTE
Saint Augustine (354-430) was an early Christian church father and philosopher who served as the bishop of Hippo (in present-day Algeria).

Teaching School

Here Augustine tells us why he preferred to teach in a boys' school in Rome rather than in Carthage.

Ēgistī[1] ergō mēcum ut mihi persuādērētur Rōmam pergere[2] et potius ibi docēre quod docēbam Carthāginī. Nōn ideo[3] Rōmam pergere[2] voluī, quod maiōrēs quaestūs maiorque mihi dignitās ab amīcīs quī hoc suādēbant prōmittēbātur (quamquam et ista dūcēbant animum tunc meum), sed illa erat causa maxima et paene sōla, quod audiēbam quiētius ibi studēre adulēscentēs et disciplīnā sēdārī, nē in scholam protervē[4] irrumpent. Contrā apud Carthāginem intemperāns est licentia scholasticōrum: irrumpunt impudenter et perturbant ōrdinem.

NOTE
Elicit that **Carthāginī** is locative.

WORKBOOK
Assign Ex. A to work with the content of this reading.

[1] addressed to God
[2] *go*
[3] *on this account* (explained by the **quod** clause)
[4] *boldly*

WORKBOOK
Assign Ex. B to practice various constructions taken from the reading.

*Roman boys attended school taught by a **magister** or **grammaticus**. Teachers were often strict and students could be beaten if they did not learn their lessons.*

Photo Bulloz

Liutprand

NOTE
Liutprand was a 10th century Lombard who was sent to Constantinople as ambassador.

A Palace Full of Tricks

Est Cōnstantīnopolī domus palātiō proxima, mīrae magnitūdinis et pulchritūdinis. Aerea[1] sed aurō tēcta arbor ante imperātōris solium[2] stābat, cuius rāmōs aereae et aurō tēctae avēs explēbant, quae dīversārum avium vōcēs ēmittēbant. Imperātōris vērō solium huius modī erat arte compositum ut nunc humile, tum excelsius, posteā excelsissimum vidērētur. Leōnēs (incertum est utrum ex aere an lignō[3] factī) aurō tēctī solium custōdiēbant, quī caudā terram percutientēs, apertō ōre, rugītum[4] ēmittēbant.

[1] *made of bronze*
[2] *throne*
[3] *wood*
[4] *roar*

NOTE
In other words, the tree, birds, and lions were all artificial.

Ante imperātōris praesentiam sum dēductus. Cum in adventū meō rugītum leōnēs ēmitterent et avēs cantārent, nūllō sum terrōre commōtus, quoniam omnia eī quī bene nōverant mē docuerant. Prōnus imperātōrem adōrāns, caput sustulī, et quem prius moderātā mēnsūrā ā terrā ēlevātum sedēre vīdī, mox aliīs indūtum vestibus ad domūs laquear[5] sedēre prōspexī; quod quō modō fieret cōgitāre nōn potuī, nisi forte sit māchinā hydraulicā sublevātus.

[5] *ceiling*

WORKBOOK
Assign Ex. A to work with the content of this reading.

Adam of Bremen

The Norse Discovery of America

NOTE
Ask students which parts of this story are possible fact and which are obviously fiction. Can any inferences be made about its accuracy based on the age of the manuscript (11th century) and the story of Leif Ericson (ca. 1000)?

Adam of Bremen (eleventh century) tells of the supposed discovery of America (Vinland or Winland) by Leif Ericson and his Norsemen. Cape Cod is one of the latest suggestions for the site where they landed. The story is full of possible fact and obvious fiction.

Rēx Dāniae[1] īnsulam recitāvit in eō repertam ōceanō[2] quae dīcitur Wīnland quod ibi vītēs[3] sponte nāscantur vīnum optimum ferentēs. Item nōbīs rettulit beātae memoriae pontifex Adalbertus quōsdam nōbilēs virōs in septentriōnēs nāvigāvisse ad ōceanum explōrandum. Relinquentēs Britanniam et glaciālem Īsland[4] subitō in cālīginem[5] cecidērunt quae vix oculīs penetrārī posset. Et iam perīculum cālīginis ēvadentēs appulērunt ad quandam īnsulam altissimīs saxīs mūnītam. Hūc videndōrum grātiā locōrum ēgressī, repperērunt hominēs in antrīs[6] subterrāneīs merīdiē latentēs; prō quōrum iānuis īnfīnīta iacēbat cōpia vāsōrum aureōrum. Itaque sūmptā parte quam sublevāre poterant, laetī ad nāvēs rēmigant, cum subitō venientēs vīdērunt hominēs mīrae altitūdinis. Ā quibus raptus est ūnus dē sociīs; reliquī vērē ēvāsērunt perīculum.

[1] *Denmark*
[2] i.e., the Atlantic
[3] *grapevines*
[4] *icy Iceland*
[5] *fog*
[6] *caves*

WORKBOOK
Assign Ex. A to work with the content of this reading.

WORKBOOK
Assign Ex. B to practice various constructions taken from the reading.

Hildegard von Bingen

Hildegard von Bingen (1098-1179) was a poet, mystic, composer, scholar, and herbalist. She was also the abbess of a Benedictine convent in Germany. She wrote at least two treatises, numerous songs, and at least one play embracing good virtues and showing the constant battle between good and evil. The following are excerpts from her play, *The Virtues*.

PATRIĀRCHE ET PROPHETE: Nōs sumus rādicēs[1] et vōs rāmī,[2]
fructūs viventis oculī,
et nōs umbrā in illō fuimus.[3]

HUMILITĀS: Ego, Humilitās, rēgina Virtūtum, dīcō:
venīte ad mē, Virtūtēs, et enūtriam[4] vōs
ad requīrendam[5] perditam dragmam[6]
et ad coronandum in persevērantiā fēlicem.

DISCRETIŌ: Ego Discretīō sum lux et dispensatrix[7]
omnium creāturārum
indifferentia[8] deī, quam Adam ā sē
fugāvit per lasciviam morum.[9]

MISERICORDIA: Ō quam amara[10] est illa duricia[11]
que nōn cēdit in mentibus
misericorditer[12] dolōrī succurrēns![13]
Ego autem omnibus dolentibus
manum porrigere[14] volō.

[1] *roots*
[2] *branches*
[3] *we grew up*
[4] *give*
[5] *seek*
[6] *drachma*
[7] *moderator*
[8] *impartiality*
[9] *wanton behavior*
[10] *bitter*
[11] *harshness*
[12] *mercifully*
[13] *ease*
[14] *to reach out*

WORKBOOK
Assign Ex. A to practice various constructions taken from the readings.

THE GRANGER COLLECTION, New York

An illumination of the self-portrait of Hildegard von Bingen (1098-1179). Here, she receives the divine light from heaven.

From the *Carmina Burana*

NOTE
The goliards were wandering students in medieval Europe disposed to conviviality, license, and the making of ribald and satirical Latin songs.

The following three pieces are from the *Carmina Burana*, songs of poor wandering students, or goliards. They date from the twelfth and thirteenth centuries.

This Crazy World

WORKBOOK
Assign Ex. A, B to work with the content of this reading.

Iste mundus
furibundus
falsa praestat gaudia,
quae dēfluunt
et dēcurrunt
ceu[1] campī līlia.

Rēs mundāna,
vīta vāna
vēra tollit praemia:
nam impellit
et submergit
animās in Tartara.

[1] *like*

Spring Song

WORKBOOK
Assign Ex. C to work with the content of this reading.

CASSETTE
This reading is recorded on Cassette 3, Side B.

Ecce grātum
et optātum
vēr[1] redūcit gaudia.
Purpurātum
flōret prātum,[2]

sōl serēnat omnia.
Iam iam cēdant trīstia.
Aestās redit,
nunc recēdit
hiemis saevitia.

[1] *spring*
[2] *meadow*

In the Tavern

WORKBOOK
Assign Ex. D to practice various constructions taken from the reading.

1. In tabernā quandō sumus,
nōn cūrāmus quid sit humus,
sed ad lūdum[1] properāmus,
cui semper īnsūdāmus.[2]
Quid agātur in tabernā,
ubi nummus est pincerna,[3]
hoc est opus[4] ut quaerātur,
sīc quid loquar audiātur.

2. Quīdam lūdunt, quīdam bibunt,
quīdam indiscrētē vīvunt.
Sed in lūdō quī morantur
ex hīs quīdam dēnūdantur;
quīdam ibi vestiuntur,
quīdam saccīs[1] induuntur.
Ibi nūllus timet mortem,
sed prō Bacchō[5] mittunt sortem.[6]

[1] *game*, i.e., of dice
[2] *perspire, work hard*
[3] *waiter,* i.e., money brings service
[4] *there is need that*
[5] *wine*
[6] *cast lots,* i.e., in throwing dice

[1] *sacks* (put on by those who lose their shirts in gambling, contrasted with the winners of the preceding line)

WORKBOOK
Assign Ex. E to work with the content of this reading.

Iacopone of Todi

A hymn about the Virgin Mary who is mourning Jesus.

NOTE
This hymn dates from the thirteenth century.

Stābat Māter

1. Stābat māter dolōrōsa
iūxtā crucem lacrimōsa
dum pendēbat fīlius;
cuius animam gementem,
contrīstantem et dolentem
pertrānsīvit gladius.

3. Quis est homō quī nōn flēret,
mātrem Christī sī vidēret
in tantō suppliciō?
Quis nōn posset contrīstārī
piam mātrem contemplārī
dolentem cum fīliō?

5. Pia māter, fōns amōris,
mē sentīre vim dolōris
fac ut tēcum lūgeam,
fac ut ārdeat cor meum
in amandō Christum Deum,
ut sibi complaceam.

10. Fac mē cruce custōdīrī,
morte Christī praemūnīrī,
cōnfovērī grātiā;
quandō corpus moriētur,
fac ut animae donētur
Paradīsī glōria.

WORKBOOK
Assign Ex. A to practice various constructions taken from the reading.

WORKBOOK
Assign Ex. B to work with the content of this reading.

Thomas of Celano

CASSETTE
This reading is recorded on Cassette 3, Side B.

Another famous hymn, this one about the Judgment Day.

NOTE
Thomas of Celano wrote this famous hymn in the thirteenth century.

Diēs Īrae

1. Diēs īrae, diēs illa
solvet saeclum in favillā,[1]
teste Dāvīd cum Sibyllā.[2]

2. Quantus tremor est futūrus
quandō iūdex est ventūrus,
cūncta strictē[3] discussūrus!

3. Tuba mīrum spargēns sonum
per sepulchra regiōnumr
cōget omnēs ante thronum.

4. Mors stupēbit et nātūra
cum resurget creātūra[4]
iūdicantī respōnsūra.

[1] *ashes*
[2] i.e., in both Biblical and Roman prophecy
[3] *completely*
[4] *(every) creature*

WORKBOOK
Assign Ex. A to practice various constructions taken from the reading.

5. Liber scrīptus prōferētur,
in quō tōtum continētur
unde mundus iūdicētur.

11. Iūstae iūdex ultiōnis,[5]
dōnum fac remissiōnis
ante diem ratiōnis.

18. Lacrimōsa diēs illa,
quā resurget ex favillā

19. iūdicandus homō reus,
huic ergō parce, Deus.

20. Pie Iēsū Domine,
dōnā eīs requiem.

[5] *vengeance*

The theme of the crucifixion and the Judgment Day, shown in this painting and the poem by Thomas of Celano, are typical of many that inspired medieval writers, painters, and poets.

Arena Chapel, Cappella Degli Scrovegni, Padua/M. Magliani/SuperStock, Inc.

From *Gesta Romanorum*

The *Gesta Romanorum* is a collection of curious stories, some gathered from ancient sources. The collection was probably made about the fourteenth century in England. Most of these stories have fanciful "morals" attached to them. Shakespeare and other modern writers made use of this collection. This story is also told by Cicero.

The "Hanging Tree"

Homō quīdam flēns dīxit omnibus vīcīnīs suīs: "Heu, heu![1] Habeō in horto[2] meō arborem īnfēlīcem, in quā uxor mea prīma sē suspendit, posteā secunda, nunc tertia, et dolōre afficior." Ūnus ex vīcīnīs, "Mīror," inquit, "tē in tantīs successibus lacrimās ēmīsisse. Dā mihi, rogō tē, trēs surculōs[3] illīus arboris, quod volō hōs inter vīcīnōs dīvidere ut habeāmus arborēs ad uxōrēs nostrās suspendendās."

[1] *alas!*
[2] *garden*
[3] *sprouts*

WORKBOOK
Assign Ex. A to work with the content of this reading.

Petrarch

Petrarch (1304–1374) has been called the first modern man. He was largely responsible for initiating the movement known as the *Renaissance*. He had an intense interest in the ancient classics, especially in Cicero. This letter tells of his attempts to secure Cicero's works. If it had not been for the activity of Petrarch and some of his followers, many ancient works would have been lost forever.

Ab ipsā pueritiā, ubi cēterī Aesōpō sē dant, ego librōs Cicerōnis lēgī. Et illā quidem aetāte nihil intellegere poteram, sōla dulcia quaedam verba mē dētinēbant.

NOTE
Tell students that Liège is in Belgium.

NOTE
Only Book VI has survived complete.

Posteā variās amīcitiās contrāxī, quod concursus ex omnī regiōne factus est in locō in quō eram. Amīcīs abeuntibus et petentibus quid vellem ē patriā suā mittī, respondēbam nihil praeter librōs Cicerōnis. Et saepe litterās, saepe pecūniam mīsī, nōn per Italiam modo, ubi eram nōtior, sed per Galliam atque Germāniam et usque ad Hispāniam atque Britanniam. Etiam in Graeciam mīsī, et ē locō ē quō Cicerōnem exspectābam habuī Homērum. "Labor omnia vincit," inquit Vergilius. Multō studiō multāque cūrā multōs librōs collēgī. Sōlus Cicerō mihi[1] sapiēns erat. Dē quō Quīntiliānus dīxit: "Bene dē sē spēret[2] cui Cicerō placēbit."

Posteā, cum Leodium[3] pervēnissem, invēnī duās ōrātiōnēs Cicerōnis; ūnam meā manū scrīpsī, alteram amīcus scrīpsit. Et, ut rīdeās, in tam bonā urbe aliquid ātrāmentī[4] (et id crocō[5] simillimum) reperīre difficillimum erat.

Et dē librīs quidem *Reī Pūblicae* iam dēspērāns, librum *Dē Cōnsōlātiōne* quaesīvī, nec invēnī. Magnum librum epistulārum manū propriā scrīpsī, adversā tum valētūdine; sed valētūdinem magnus amor operis et gaudium et habendī cupiditās vincēbant. Hunc librum, ut mihi semper ad manum esset, ad iānuam pōnere solēbam.

[1] *in my eyes*
[2] *let him hope*; the subject is the antecedent of **cui.**
[3] *Liège*
[4] *ink*
[5] *saffron, yellow*

NOTE
The reference here is to Cicero's letters to his friend, Atticus.

WORKBOOK
Assign Ex. A to work with the content of this reading.

SEF/Art Resource

Petrarch (1304-1374) was an Italian Renaissance poet, scholar, and humanist. Born in Arezzo, he moved to Avignon, France, when he was 8 and grew up there. After studies at the University in Montpellier, he entered the Church and did much writing, especially love poems to a woman he called Laura. In 1341, he was named poet laureate in Rome.

Poggio

From the *Facetiae* (joke book) of Poggio, a secretary of the Pope (fifteenth century). When he and his colleagues had nothing to do they got together and told stories in what he called a "Lie Factory."

The Shrewd Priest

Erat quīdam sacerdōs rūsticus admodum dīves. Hic canem sibi cārum, cum mortuus esset, sepelīvit in coemētēriō. Sēnsit hoc episcopus et in eius pecūniam animum intendēns,[1] sacerdōtem pūniendum ad sē vocat. Sacerdōs, quī animum episcopī satis nōverat, quīnquāgintā aureōs[2] sēcum dēferēns ad episcopum dēvēnit. Quī sepultūram canis graviter accūsāns iussit ad carcerēs[3] sacerdōtem dūcī. Hic vir callidus: "Ō pater," inquit, "sī nōscerēs quā prūdentiā canis fuit, nōn mīrārēris[4] sī sepultūram inter hominēs meruit. Fuit enim plūs quam hūmānus, et in vītā et maximē in morte." "Quidnam hoc est?" ait episcopus. "Testāmentum," inquit sacerdōs, "in fīne vītae condēns sciēnsque paupertātem tuam tibi quīnquāgintā aureōs ex testāmentō relīquit, quōs mēcum tulī." Tum episcopus et testāmentum et sepultūram probāns, acceptā pecūniā, sacerdōtem solvit.

[1] *casting his thoughts towards*
[2] *gold pieces*
[3] *prison*
[4] *if you knew . . . you would not wonder*

WORKBOOK
Assign Ex. A, B to practice various constructions taken from the reading.

WORKBOOK
Assign Ex. C to work with the content of this reading.

Pietro Bembo

Pietro Bembo, an Italian man of letters (1470–1547), wrote this letter to his young son.

An Alarm Clock

Hōrologiō[1] ē meā bibliothēcā tibi allātō, ā quō expergēfierī,[2] quā hōrā volēs, possīs, tē libenter ūtī nōn molestē[3] ferō. Modo tē id nōn intemperātē[4] ā somnō āvocet. Valētūdinis enim tuae cūram tē habēre in prīmīs volō. Dē tuōrum studiōrum ratiōne nihil tibi mandō nunc quidem nisi ūnum: fac ut in tuīs quās ad mē dās litterīs Cicerōnem accūrātius exprimās mōremque illīus scrībendī, verba, numerōs,[5] gravitātem, dīligentius imitēre. Hoc sī fēceris, omnia tē cōnsecūtum putābō. Magistrō tuō multam salūtem. Valē. MDXLIIII. Rōmā.

[1] *clock*
[2] *be awakened*
[3] *I don't mind* (with **ferō**)
[4] *too early*
[5] *rhythm*

WORKBOOK
Assign Ex. A to work with the content of this reading.

Unit X

Ovid and Vergil

UNIT OBJECTIVES
To read selections from the Roman poets Ovid and Vergil with understanding and appreciation; To learn the scanion of the dactylic hexameter; To develop an understanding and appreciation of poetic word order in Latin verse

In Greek mythology, Medusa was a Gorgon and the daughter of the sea god Phorcys. She had been beautiful in her youth, but when she bragged of her beauty, the goddess Athena became so jealous that she transformed Medusa into an ugly woman with protruding eyes and snakes for hair. Medusa was so ugly that anyone who looked at her was immediately turned into stone. She was eventually killed by Perseus.

Scala/Art Resource, NY

Reading Latin Verse

NOTE
Remind students that the diphthongs in Latin are: **ae, au, oe, ei, eu,** and **ui** (in **huic** and **cui** only).

NOTE
Students may need to be reminded regularly at the beginning that a vowel's length is often affected by the word that follows it.

The word order of Latin poetry is freer than that of prose. Adjectives often are widely separated from their nouns. Words are often taken out of subordinate clauses and precede the introductory words (**quī, ut,** etc.). Subjects often come at or near the end of sentences.

The rhythm of Latin verse does not depend on a words accent as in English, but rather on the length of syllables. The rules for determining the length of syllables are:

1. A syllable is long *by nature* if it contains a long vowel or a diphthong.

auferrō	**ī**nsul**ae**

2. A syllable is long *by position* if it contains a short vowel followed by two or more consonants or the consonant **x** (= **cs**).

am**an**t	n**ox**

A mute consonant (**p, b, t, d, c, g**) followed by a liquid consonant (**l, r**) does not make a syllable long. There are occasional exceptions.

ŭt legam	ăd regiònem

The letter **h** is disregarded entirely. The combinations **qu** and **gu** (before a vowel) constitute one consonant; the **u** is disregarded.

In poetry, a long syllable is twice the length of a short syllable. Since a line of poetry is considered one long word, in a case like **in mē** the first word is treated as a long syllable because the (short) vowel is followed by two consonants (**n, m**).

Several syllables are combined to form a foot. The *dactyl* is a foot consisting of a long syllable followed by two short syllables, written —˘˘.[1] The *spondee* consists of two long syllables, — —. When a line contains six feet, it is called a hexameter. The *Metamorphoses* and *Aeneid*, from

[1] Do not confuse this marking of syllables with the identical signs used in marking vowels.

which you will read excerpts, are written in the dactylic hexameter. A spondee may be substituted for a dactyl in every foot except the fifth. The sixth foot is always a spondee.[2] The beat is on the first syllable of each foot.

If a word ends in a vowel or a vowel plus **m** and the next word begins with a vowel (or **h**), the first vowel disappears entirely. This is called "elision"; the vowel is said to be "elided."

mar(e) et	pronounced **maret**
iacer(e) (h)ōs	pronounced **iacerōs**
cūnctant(em) et	pronounced **cūnctantet**

NOTE
Encourage to mark long and short syllables at the beginning, until they become used to the rhythm.

WORKBOOK
Assign Ex. A-G to practice determining long and short vowels (A-C); to practice elision (D); to recognize dactyls and spondees (E-F); and to put it all together (G).

[2] The last syllable is often short, but the "rest" at the end of the line fills out the foot.

Ronald Sheridan/Ancient Art & Architecture Collection

Orpheus and Eurydice, in a painting by French artist Nicolas Poussin (1594-1665).

Ovid's *Metamorphoses*

NOTE
Remind students that they have already read a little about Ovid's life in Lessons IV and XV.

Ovid (Publius Ovidius Naso) was born in 43 B.C. Trained for the law and public life, he abandoned his career to devote himself to his great passion, the writing of poetry. In A.D. 8 he incurred the displeasure of the Emperor Augustus and was banished to a little town, Tomi (present-day Constanza, Romania), on the Black Sea. Here he died in A.D. 17.

NOTE
Tell students that the title *Metamorphoses* comes from the Greek meaning *transformations*.

Ovid was a very facile poet and left us many poems. The greatest of these is the *Metamorphoses*. This consists of a series of mythical tales dealing with the transformation of humans, animals, and things into different forms. The tales are loosely joined together with considerable cleverness and reveal Ovid's great ability as a storyteller. They cover so much of Greek and Roman mythology that they are now our chief source of information about it. The work, from which several selections are given below, has always been a favorite and has left a strong influence on literature and art throughout the ages.

CASSETTE
This entire reading is recorded on Cassette 4, Side A.

The Flood: Deucalion and Pyrrha

NOTE
You might point out (or elicit) that Deucalion is the Greek Noah and Mt. Parnassus corresponds to Mt. Ararat.

Because of the wickedness of human beings, Jupiter sends a flood to destroy the earth. Only Deucālion and his wife Pyrrha survive, landing from their boat on Mt. Parnassus. The first four lines are "scanned" (marked) to show the meter.

Stones thrown by Deucalion and Pyrrha "grow" into people; from a 1589 edition of Ovid.

The Flood at Its Height—a Topsy-Turvy World

Iamque ma r(e) et tel lūs nūl lum dis crīmen ha bēbant.
Ōmnia pontus e rant; dee rant quoque lītora pontō.
Occupat hic[1] col lem, cum bā sedet alter ad uncā[2]
et dū cit[3] rē mōs il līc ubi nūper a rārat,

ille[1] su prā sege tēs[4] aut mersae culmina[5] villae
nāvigat, hic summā piscem dēprēndit in ulmō.[6]
Fīgitur in viridī,[7] sī fors tulit, ancora prātō
aut subiecta terunt[8] curvae vīnēta carīnae;[9]
et, modo quā[10] gracilēs grāmen carpsēre[11] capellae,[12]
nunc ibi dēfōrmēs pōnunt sua corpora phōcae.[13]
Mīrantur sub aquā lūcōs[14] urbēsque domōsque
Nēreidēs, silvāsque tenent delphīnes[15] et altīs incursant rāmīs
agitātaque rōbora[16] pulsant.
Nat[17] lupus inter ovēs,[18] fulvōs[19] vehit unda leōnēs,
unda vehit tigrēs.

NOTE
Have students listen to the recording and repeat several lines aloud to become accustomed to the meter.

1 *one man*
2 *in a curved boat (*with **cumbā**)
3 *plies*
4 *crops*
5 *top* (poetic plural for singular)
6 *on top of an elm* (with **summā**)
7 *green meadow (*with **prātō**)
8 *scrape*
9 *keels,* i.e., *ships (*subject)
10 = **quā modo**
11 = **carpsērunt**
12 *goats*
13 *seals*
14 *groves*
15 = **delphīnī** (Greek form)
16 *oaks*
17 *swims*
18 *sheep*
19 *tawny*

When the waters recede, Deucalion seeks dry land. He laments the fact that Pyrrha and he are the only two people left in the world: **Nōs duo turba sumus,** *We two are a crowd,* he says, for two are a crowd in a world which consists of only two persons. He finds the temple of Themis, goddess of prophecy, and prays for aid and advice.

Deucalion Interprets a Strange Oracle

Mōta dea est sortemque dedit: "Discēdite templō
et vēlāte caput cīnctāsque[20] revolvite vestēs
ossaque post tergum magnae iactāte parentis." [21]
Obstupuēre[22] diū, rumpitque silentia vōce
Pyrrha prior iussīsque deae parēre recūsat,
detque[23] sibī veniam pavidō rogat ōre pavetque
laedere iactātīs māternās ossibus umbrās.[24]
Inde Promēthīdēs[25] placidīs Epimēthida[26] dictīs
mulcet[27] et "aut fallāx," ait, "est sollertia[28] nōbīs[29]
aut pia sunt nūllumque nefās ōrācula suādent.
Magna parēns terra est, lapidēs in corpore terrae
ossa reor[30] dīcī: iacere hōs post terga iubēmur."

The Stones Come to Life

Coniugis auguriō[31] quamquam Tītānia[32] mōta est,
spēs tamen in dubiō est; adeō caelestibus ambō
diffīdunt monitīs.[33] Sed quid temptāre nocēbit?
Discēdunt vēlantque caput tunicāsque recingunt
et iussōs lapidēs sua post vēstīgia mittunt.
Saxa (quis hoc crēdat,[34] nisi sit prō teste vetustās?)[35]
pōnere[36] dūritiem coepēre[37] suumque rigōrem
mollīrīque morā[38] mollītaque dūcere[39] fōrmam.
Inque brevī spatiō superōrum nūmine saxa
missa virī manibus faciem trāxēre virōrum,
et dē fēmineō reparāta est fēmina iactū.
Inde genus dūrum sumus experiēnsque[40] labōrum
et documenta damus quā sīmus orīgine nātī.
(Met. I. 291–415)

NOTE
You may want to have students write additional lines on the board to practice the meter, or you can write lines on a transparency for practice.

NOTE
Tell students that in religious services, the head was covered and the tunic was allowed to hang down, unbelted.

[20] *girt up*
[21] Modifies **ossa.**
[22] *they were astounded*
[23] Supply **ut:** *asks that (Themis) grant her pardon.*
[24] *to offend her mother's ghost by throwing her bones*
[25] *son of Promētheus,* i.e., Deucalion
[26] acc. s.: *daughter of Epimētheus,* i.e., Pyrrha
[27] *calms*
[28] *skill*
[29] for **mihi; = mea.**
[30] *I think that the bones are meant to be*

[31] *interpretation*
[32] *the Titan's daughter,* i.e., Pyrrha
[33] *advice*
[34] *would believe*
[35] *if antiquity were not a witness*
[36] = **dēpōnere**
[37] = **coepērunt**
[38] *gradually*
[39] *take on*
[40] *used to* (with genitive)

NOTE
Point out that **monitīs** is dative after special verbs (**diffidunt**).

NOTE
Crēdat (line 400) is an example of a future less vivid condition, which takes present subjunctive in both clauses.

NOTE
Ask students what they think of the argument that the age of a story proves it to be true.

WORKBOOK
Assign Ex. A to practice scansion; Ex. B-D to practice various constructions taken from the reading.

Echo and Narcissus

Juno punishes the nymph Echo for her talkativeness by curtailing her power of speech. Thereafter Echo can merely echo what others say. She falls in love with the handsome but cold youth Narcissus.

CASSETTE
This entire reading is recorded on Cassette 4, Side A.

Echo Falls in Love with Narcissus

NOTE
She was still a living being.

Corpus adhūc Ēchō, nōn vōx erat et tamen ūsum
360 garrula nōn alium quam nunc habet ōris[1] habēbat,
361 reddere dē multīs ut verba novissima[2] posset.
370 Ergō ubi Narcissum per dēvia rūra[3] vagantem
vīdit et incaluit,[4] sequitur vēstīgia fūrtim,
372 quōque magis[5] sequitur, flammā propiōre calēscit.
375 Ō quotiēns voluit blandīs accēdere dictīs
et mollēs adhibēre precēs! Nātūra repugnat
nec sinit[6] incipiat; sed, quod[7] sinit, illa parāta est
exspectāre sonōs ad quōs sua verba remittat.

[1] *no other use of speech* (with **ūsum alium**)
[2] *(only) the last of many*
[3] *trackless countryside*
[4] *fell in love*
[5] *the more . . . the hotter* (literally, *the nearer*) *the flame* (*with which*) *she is inflamed*
[6] *permits*; supply **ut** with **incipiat**
[7] *a thing which*

NOTE
Remind students that the genitive of the whole becomes the ablative with **dē** or **ex** with numerals, **multī**, **paucī**, etc.

NOTE
The main clause is the antecedent, which explains the use of **quod**.

Narcissus Calls to His Companions and Echo Answers

Forte puer comitum sēductus ab agmine fīdō
380 dīxerat "ecquis[8] adest?" et "adest" responderat Ēchō.
Hic stupet, utque aciem[9] partēs dīmittit in omnēs,
vōce "venī!" magnā clāmat; vocat illa vocantem.
Respicit et rūrsus, nūllō veniente, "quid," inquit,
"mē fugis?" et totidem quot dīxit verba recēpit.
385 Perstat et alternae[10] dēceptus imāgine vōcis
"hūc coeāmus," ait, nūllīque[11] libentius umquam
respōnsūra sonō "coeāmus" rettulit Ēchō,
et verbīs favet[1] ipsa suīs ēgressaque silvā
ībat ut iniceret spērātō bracchia collō.
390 Ille fugit fugiēnsque "manūs complexibus[12] aufer.
Ante," ait, "ēmoriar[13] quam[14] sit tibi cōpia nostrī."[15]
Rettulit illa nihil nisi "sit tibi cōpia nostrī."

[8] *is there anyone?*
[9] *glance*
[10] *answering*
[11] Modifies **sonō.**
[12] *from embraces*
[13] *may I die*
[14] *before* (with **ante**)
[15] = **meī:** *a chance at me*

---

[1] i.e., she suits the action to the words

Giraudon/Art Resource, NY

Mythological scenes were a favorite of Nicolas Poussin (1594-1665). Here he has painted his interpretation of Echo and Narcissus. The poet Milton called Echo a "nymph that liv'st unseen."

Echo Wastes Away to a Mere Voice

Sprēta[16] latet silvīs pudibundaque[17] frondibus ōra
prōtegit et sōlīs ex illō[18] vīvit in antrīs.
Sed tamen haeret amor crēscitque dolōre repulsae,[19]
et tenuant vigilēs corpus miserābile cūrae,
addūcitque cutem[20] maciēs et in āera[21] sūcus[22]
corporis omnis abit. Vōx tantum atque ossa supersunt—
vōx manet; ossa ferunt[23] lapidis trāxisse figūram.
Inde latet silvīs nūllōque in monte vidētur,
omnibus[24] audītur; sonus est quī vīvit in illā.
(Met. III. 359–401)

[16] *spurned*
[17] *ashamed*
[18] Supply **tempore.**
[19] *refusal*
[20] *skin*
[21] *air* (accusative singular)
[22] *life, strength*
[23] *they say*
[24] *by all*

WORKBOOK
Assign Ex. A to work with the content of the reading.

WORKBOOK
Assign Ex. B to practice oral work with a classmate that could be presented in class.

Perseus and Atlas

Medusa was a maiden with snaky locks — one look at her turned a person into stone. Perseus, son of Jupiter, is commissioned to bring back her head. With the help of the gods he does this without injury to himself. On his way back he stops at the home of the giant Atlas, in northwest Africa. Atlas is the owner of the famous golden apples. When Atlas refuses hospitality to Perseus, the latter turns Atlas into a mountain of stone by means of Medusa's head.

Themis Predicts the Loss of the Golden Apples

Mīlle gregēs[1] illī[2] totidemque armenta[3] per herbās
errābant, et humum vīcīnia[4] nūlla premēbant.
Arboreae frondēs aurō radiante nitentēs[5]
ex aurō rāmōs, ex aurō pōma[6] tegēbant.
"Hospes," ait Perseus illī, "seu glōria tangit
tē generis[7] magnī, generis mihi Iuppiter auctor;
sīve es mīrātor rērum,[8] mīrābere nostrās.
Hospitium requiemque petō." Memor ille[9] vetustae
sortis erat (Themis hanc dederat Parnassia[10] sortem):
"Tempus, Atlās, veniet tua quō spoliābitur aurō
arbor, et hunc praedae titulum[11] Iove nātus[12] habēbit."
Id metuēns solidīs pōmāria clauserat Atlās
montibus et vāstō dederat servanda dracōnī
arcēbatque[13] suīs externōs fīnibus omnēs.
Huic[14] quoque "vade procul, nē longē glōria rērum
quam mentīris,"[15] ait, "longē tibi Iuppiter absit."[16]
Vimque minīs[17] addit manibusque expellere temptat
cūnctantem et placidīs miscentem fortia dictīs.
Vīribus īnferior (quis enim pār esset[18] Atlantis
vīribus?) "at quoniam parvī[19] tibi grātia nostra est,
accipe mūnus," ait, laevāque ā parte[20] Medūsae,
ipse retrō versus,[21] squālentia prōtulit ōra.
Quantus[22] erat, mōns factus Atlās; nam barba comaeque[23]
in silvās abeunt, iuga sunt umerīque[24] manūsque,
quod caput ante fuit summō est in monte cacūmen.
Ossa lapis fīunt; tum partēs altus in omnēs
crēvit in immēnsum[25] (sīc, dī,[26] statuistis), et omne
cum tot sīderibus caelum requiēvit in illō.
(Met. IV. 636–662)

CASSETTE
This reading is recorded on Cassette 4, Side A.

NOTES:
This is a reference to the famous golden apples of the Hesperides. It is thought that the mythical apples were actually oranges, which were unknown in Europe in antiquity.

Hercules was meant here, but when Atlas hears that Perseus is the son of Jupiter, he thinks that he is the one mentioned in the oracle and refuses to admit him.

You might point out that Perseus was rather cocky.

Tell students that **illī** is a dative of reference.

1 *flocks*
2 i.e., Atlas
3 *herds*
4 *no neighbors hemmed in his land,* i.e., he had vast tracts of land
5 *gleaming* (modifies **frondēs**)
6 *apples of gold* (**ex aurō** modifies **pōma**)
7 i.e., of Perseus
8 *deeds,* referring to his defeat of Medusa
9 i.e., Atlas
10 with Themis
11 *the glory for this loot*
12 *a son of Jupiter*
13 *shut out* (with ablative)
14 i.e., Perseus
15 *which you falsely claim*
16 *be far from you,* i.e., *be of no help to you*
17 *threats*
18 *could be*
19 *of little value*
20 *on his left side*
21 i.e., turning his face away, so as not to look at Medusa's head
22 *as huge as he had been* (in life)
23 *beard and hair*
24 *his shoulders become* (**sunt**)
25 *to an immense size*
26 = **deī**

WORKBOOK
Assign Ex. A to practice scansion.

WORKBOOK
Assign Ex. B, C to work on poetic techniques and devices.

Orpheus and Eurydice

CASSETTE
This reading is recorded on Cassette 4, Side A.

NOTE
Tell students that the German composer Christoph Gluck (1714-1787) wrote an opera on the theme of this story in 1762.

Orpheus was such a fine musician that he could make even the trees and stones listen to and follow him. When his wife Eurydice (Urid´i-sē) died, he followed her to Hades and by his wonderful singing persuaded the king of Hades to let her go back to the land of the living. But there was one condition, that Orpheus should not look back until he had come out of Hades. At the last moment Orpheus looked back to see whether Eurydice was following, and she disappeared forever.

"Omnia dēbēmus vōbīs,[1] paulumque morātī
sērius aut citius sēdem properāmus ad ūnam.
Tendimus hūc omnēs, haec est domus ultima, vōsque
hūmānī generis[1] longissima rēgna tenētis.
Haec[2] quoque, cum iūstōs mātūra perēgerit annōs,
iūris erit vestrī; prō mūnere poscimus ūsum.[2]
Quod sī fāta negant veniam[3] prō coniuge, certum est
nōlle[4] redīre mihī; lētō[5] gaudēte duōrum."
Tālia dīcentem[3] nervōsque[6] ad verba moventem
exsanguēs flēbant animae.[4]
Hanc simul et lēgem[7] Rhodopēius[8] accipit Orpheus,
nē flectat retrō sua lūmina, dōnec[9] Avernās[10]
exierit vallēs; aut irrita[11] dōna futūra.
Carpitur acclīvis per mūta silentia trāmes,[12]
arduus, obscūrus, cālīgine[13] dēnsus opācā.
Nec procul āfuerunt tellūris margine summae.
Hic nē dēficeret[14] metuēns avidusque videndī,
flexit amāns oculōs; et prōtinus illa relāpsa est,
bracchiaque intendēns prēndīque et prēndere captāns
nīl nisi cēdentēs īnfēlīx arripit aurās.[15]
(Met. X, 32–59)

[1] *over the human race*
[2] Eurydice
[3] *boon* (of longer life)
[4] Supply the subject from **mihī:** *I have resolved that I.*
[5] *death*
[6] *strings* (of the lyre).
[7] *condition* (the **nē** clause is in apposition with **lēgem**)
[8] *Thracian*
[9] *until*
[10] adjective modifying **vallēs:** *of Avernus,* the entrance of Hades
[11] *void*
[12] *ascending path* (to the upper world) (with **acclīvis**)
[13] *mist*
[14] The subject is Eurydice.
[15] *breezes*

NOTE
Point out that **lētō** is an ablative of cause.

WORKBOOK
Assign Ex. A to work with the content of the reading.

WORKBOOK
Assign Ex. B to practice various constructions taken from the reading.

---

[1] Orpheus is speaking to Pluto and Proserpina, king and queen of Hades.
[2] i.e., not for a permanent gift but as a temporary loan
[3] Modifies **eum** understood, object of **flēbant.**
[4] Pluto and Proserpina are so moved that they allow Eurydice to return.

Erich Lessing/Art Resource, NY

This marble relief from the Louvre shows Orpheus and Eurydice with the messenger god, Hermes.

Pygmalion

CASSETTE

This reading is recorded on Cassette 4, Side A.

NOTE

George Bernard Shaw borrowed the name and idea for his play, in which he has a professor educate a poor girl into a fine lady. Later, Lerner and Loewe's musical comedy *My Fair Lady* was based on this play.

The sculptor Pygmalion of Cyprus carved an ivory statue of a woman so beautiful that he fell in love with it. Venus gave it life, and Pygmalion married the girl.

Intereā niveum mīrā fēlīciter arte
sculpsit ebur[1] fōrmamque dedit quā[2] fēmina nāscī
nūlla potest; operisque suī concēpit amōrem.
Virginis est vērae faciēs, quam vīvere crēdās[3]
et, sī nōn obstet reverentia, velle movērī;
ars adeō latet arte suā. Mīrātur et haurit
pectore Pygmaliōn simulātī corporis ignēs.[4]

[1] *ivory*
[2] *in which*
[3] *you could believe*
[4] *the fires (of love)*

5 *he admits*
6 *kisses*
7 *sink in, dent*
8 *bruise*
9 *now*
10 *shells and smooth pebbles*
11 *colored*
12 *tears of the Heliades, fallen from*
13 *necklaces*
14 *in Cyprus* (feminine)
15 *incense*
16 *having performed* (with ablative)
17 = **deī**
18 *of ivory*
19 i.e., home from the altar
20 *couch*
21 *thumb* (he felt her pulse)

Saepe manūs operī temptantēs admovet an sit
corpus an illud ebur; nec adhūc ebur esse fatētur.[5]
Ōscula[6] dat reddīque putat; loquiturque tenetque
et crēdit tactīs digitōs īnsīdere[7] membrīs;
et metuit, pressōs veniat nē līvor[8] in artūs.
Et modo[9] blanditiās adhibet, modo[9] grāta puellīs
mūnera fert illī, conchās teretēsque lapillōs,[10]
et parvās volucrēs et flōrēs mīlle colōrum,
līliaque pictāsque[11] pilās et ab arbore lāpsās
Hēliadum lacrimās.[12] Ōrnat quoque vestibus artūs.
Dat digitīs gemmās, dat longa monīlia[13] collō.
Fēsta diēs Veneris tōtā celeberrima Cyprō[14] vēnerat,
tūraque[15] fūmābant, cum mūnere fūnctus[16] ad ārās
cōnstitit et timidē "sī, dī,[17] dare cūncta potestis,
sit coniūnx, optō," nōn ausus, "eburnea[18] virgō,"
dīcere Pygmaliōn, "similis mea," dīxit, "eburnae."
Ut rediit,[19] simulācra suae petit ille puellae,
incumbēnsque torō[20] dedit ōscula. Vīsa tepēre est.
Corpus erat; saliunt temptātae pollice[21] vēnae,
dataque ōscula virgō
sēnsit et ērubuit.
(Met. X. 247–293)

WORKBOOK
Assign Ex. A, B to work with the content of the reading.

Vergil's *Aeneid*

NOTE
Students have come across references to Vergil in Lessons IV and XXIII.

Vergil (Publius Vergilius Maro) was born in 70 B.C. Two thousand years later, in 1930, the entire western world celebrated his birthday, for he is one of the world's greatest and best-loved poets. His earlier works were the *Bucolics* (or *Eclogues*) about shepherds, and the *Georgics,* dealing with farming. His chief work, the *Aeneid,* is an epic poem in twelve books that tells of the wanderings of the Trojan Aeneas in his attempt to find a new home after the capture of Troy by the Greeks in the twelfth century B.C., according to tradition. The *Aeneid* also tells of Aeneas' arrival in Italy, where he established his kingdom and where his descendants founded Rome. Thus Vergil gave a background for Roman history. It is no wonder that the Roman people greeted the *Aeneid* as a national poem glorifying Rome and the Roman Empire.

The Bettmann Archive

A page from a 4th century manuscript of Vergil's ***Aeneid****. Notice that no spaces are left between individual words.*

Vergil was planning to spend three years putting the finishing touches on the *Aeneid* when he died in 19 B.C. He left word to have the poem burned but Augustus insisted that it be published—and the world has been grateful to him ever since.

So popular was Vergil in the Middle Ages that he was called a magician, and all sorts of tales were told about his deeds.

CASSETTE
All excerpts from Books I, IV, and VI are recorded on Cassette 4, Side A.

NOTE
Have students continue to scan and read aloud the verses; remind them that this was an epic poem.

NOTE
Terrīs and **altis** (line 3) are examples of ablative of *place where*, without the preposition.

[1] *a fugitive by fate*
[2] = **superōrum**
[3] *also*
[4] *until he could found*
[5] *his gods,* statues of which he had brought along
[6] = **in Latium,** *to Lā´shium*

NOTE
Latiō (line 6) is a poetic use of the dative.

Book I

Juno's anger causes the Trojans to be shipwrecked off the coast of Africa. They make their way to the place where Queen Dido, a refugee from Tyre in Phoenicia, is building the new city of Carthage. They are cordially welcomed. The poem opens with the poet's statement of his theme.

Arma virumque canō, Troiae quī prīmus ab ōrīs
Ītaliam[1] fātō profugus[1] Lāvīniaque[2] vēnit
lītora,[1] multum ille et terrīs iactātus et altō[3]
vī superum,[2] saevae memorem Iūnōnis ob īram,
multa quoque et[3] bellō passus, dum conderet[4] urbem
īnferretque deōs[5] Latiō,[6] genus unde Latīnum
Albānīque patrēs atque altae moenia Rōmae.

[1] Poetic usage of accusative of *place to which* without **ad**
[2] *of Lavinium,* a town near Rome
[3] **Altō** is used as a noun for **marī.**

A painting by the English artist William Turner (1775-1851) shows Dido building Carthage after fleeing Tyre with many followers and much treasure.

Bridgeman/Art Resource, NY

Venus goes to Jupiter to complain that the great destiny of her son Aeneas is not being fulfilled. Jupiter's predictions reassure her.

"Bellum ingēns geret Ītalia populōsque ferōcēs 263
contundet[7] mōrēsque virīs et moenia pōnet.
At puer Ascanius,[4] cui nunc cognōmen Iūlō[5] 267
additur,
longam multā vī mūniet Albam.[8]
Rōmulus excipiet gentem et Māvortia[9] condet 276
moenia Rōmānōsque suō dē nōmine dīcet.
Hīs ego nec mētās[10] rērum nec tempora pōnō;
imperium sine fīne dedī. Quīn[11] aspera Iūnō,
quae mare nunc terrāsque metū[12] caelumque fatīgat, 280
cōnsilia in melius referet[13] mēcumque fovēbit
Rōmānōs rērum dominōs gentemque togātam.[14]
Nāscētur pulchrā Troiānus orīgine Caesar,[15] 286
imperium Ōceanō, fāmam quī terminet[16] astrīs
Iūlius,[15] ā magnō dēmissum nōmen Iūlō.
Aspera tum positīs[17] mītēscent saecula[18] bellīs; 291
cāna[19] Fidēs et Vesta, Remō cum frātre Quirīnus[20]
iūra dabunt; dīrae ferrō et compāgibus artīs[21]
claudentur bellī portae; Furor impius intus[22]
saeva sedēns super arma et centum vīnctus aēnīs[23] 295
post tergum nōdīs fremet[24] horridus ōre cruentō."

[7] *he* (Aeneas) *will crush*
[8] *Alba Longa,* a town southeast of Rome
[9] *of Mars*
[10] *bounds for their state* (**rērum**)
[11] = **quīn etiam**
[12] *with her fears*
[13] *will change for the better*
[14] *toga-clad*
[15] Augustus
[16] *to bound*
[17] = **dēpositīs**
[18] *the ages will become gentle*
[19] *white-haired, venerable*
[20] = **Rōmulus**
[21] *tight joints*
[22] *within* (the temple)
[23] *by bronze* (i.e., *hard*) *knots* (with **nōdīs**)
[24] *will rage*

[4] Aeneas' son, whose other name (**cognōmen**) was Iulus
[5] attracted into the case of **cui**

NOTES:
Remind students that Mars was the father of Romulus.

Tell students that the toga was the garment of peace.

Vergil emphasizes Augustus' relationship to Julius Caesar and through him to Iulus, Aeneas' son.

The doors of the Temple of Janus were closed in peace by Augustus for the first time in 200 years.

WORKBOOK
Assign Ex. A to practice scansion.

WORKBOOK
Assign Ex. B, D to practice various constructions taken from the reading.

WORKBOOK
Assign Ex. C to work with the content of the reading.

WORKBOOK
Assign Ex. E to do oral work with meter.

Book IV

NOTE
If students want to read more works of Vergil, there are several excerpts in *Latin for Americans, First Book.*

Books II and III tell of a banquet Dido gives for Aeneas, at which he relates his adventures, beginning with the fall of Troy. The Trojan War was caused by the abduction of Helen, the wife of the Greek Menelaus, by the Trojan Paris. As Book IV opens, Dido discovers that she is falling in love with Aeneas.

At rēgīna gravī iam dūdum[1] saucia[2] cūrā
vulnus alit vēnīs et caecō[3] carpitur ignī.
Multa virī virtūs animō multusque recursat
gentis honōs;[4] haerent īnfīxī pectore vultūs[5]
verbaque, nec placidam membrīs dat cūra quiētem.
Postera Phoebēā[6] lūstrābat[7] lampade terrās
ūmentemque[8] Aurōra polō[9] dīmōverat umbram,
cum sīc ūnanimam alloquitur male[10] sāna sorōrem:
"Anna soror, quae mē suspēnsam īnsomnia[11] terrent!
Quis novus hic nostrīs successit sēdibus hospes,[12]
quem sēsē ōre ferēns,[13] quam fortī pectore et armīs!
Crēdō equidem, nec vāna fidēs, genus esse deōrum.
Dēgenerēs animōs timor arguit.[14] Heu, quibus ille
iactātus fātīs! Quae bella exhausta canēbat!"

[1] *for a long time*
[2] *wounded, stricken*
[3] *blind, unseen*
[4] = **honor** (nominative)
[5] i.e., of Aeneas.
[6] *with Apollo's lamp,* i.e., the sun
[7] *lighted;* the subject is **Aurōra** (*Dawn*)
[8] *damp*
[9] *from the heavens*
[10] with **sāna** = *insane*
[11] *dreams*
[12] *who (is) this strange guest (who)*
[13] *What a man he shows himself in his looks*
[14] *Fear reveals ignoble souls.*

NOTE
Point out the ablative of description (**pectore**).

Dido and Aeneas fall in love, but Jupiter (representing Aeneas' conscience) sends Mercury to remind Aeneas of his duty to establish the Trojans in a new country of their own. Aeneas' reaction is immediate.

NOTE
Tell students that the odd thing here is that Aeneas shows no signs of fear.

At vērō Aenēās aspectū obmūtuit āmēns,[15]
arrēctaeque horrōre comae,[16] et vōx faucibus haesit.
Ārdet abīre fugā dulcīsque relinquere terrās,
attonitus[17] tantō monitū imperiōque deōrum.
Heu quid agat?[18] Quō nunc rēgīnam ambīre[19] furentem
audeat affātū? Quae prīma exōrdia[20] sūmat?

[15] *confused, he becomes silent*
[16] *hair (stood) on end* (with **arrēctae**)
[17] *astounded*
[18] *What should he do?*
[19] *get around, approach*
[20] *beginnings*

Aeneas orders his men to prepare the ships secretly, hoping to sail away without Dido's knowledge.

At rēgīna dolōs (quis fallere possit[21] amantem?)
praesēnsit mōtūsque excēpit prīma futūrōs,
omnia tūta[22] timēns; eadem impia Fāma furentī[23]
dētulit armārī classem cursumque parārī.
Tandem hīs Aenēān compellat[24] vōcibus ultrō:
"Dissimulāre etiam spērāstī, perfide, tantum
posse nefās tacitusque meā dēcēdere terrā?
Nec tē noster amor nec tē data dextera[25] quondam
nec moritūra tenet crūdēlī fūnere Dīdō?"
At pius Aenēās, quamquam lēnīre dolentem
sōlandō[26] cupit et dictīs āvertere cūrās,
multa[27] gemēns magnōque animum labefactus[28] amōre,
iussa tamen dīvum exsequitur classemque revīsit.
Tum vērō Teucrī[29] incumbunt[30] et lītore celsās
dēdūcunt tōtō nāvīs.

[21] *would be able*
[22] *(even if) safe*
[23] i.e., Dido.
[24] *addresses*
[25] = **dextra,** i.e., *pledge*
[26] *by consoling (her)*
[27] *much, a great deal*
[28] *his heart overcome*
[29] *Trojans*
[30] *get to work* (literally, *bend to*)

NOTE
For the contracted form, refer students to the Appendix.

WORKBOOK
Assign Ex. A, B to practice various constructions taken from the reading; Ex. C, E to work with the content of the reading; Ex. D to practice uses of the ablative that appear in the reading.

Book VI

NOTE
Inspired by this book of Vergil's, the Italian poet Dante (1265-1321) wrote *The Divine Comedy*.

After consulting the Sibyl at Cumae (near Naples), Aeneas descends to Hades, where he sees the shades of his father, Dido, and many other famous persons and learns about the great future of the new country he is about to establish.

NOTE
Lake Avernus was considered the entrance to Hades.

Tālibus ōrābat dictīs ārāsque[1] tenēbat,
cum sīc ōrsa[2] loquī vātēs:[3] "Sate[4] sanguine dīvum,
Trōs Anchīsiadē,[5] facilis dēscēnsus Avernō[6]
(noctēs atque diēs patet ātrī iānua Dītis);
sed revocāre gradum superāsque ēvādere ad aurās,[7]
hoc opus, hic labor est. Paucī, quōs aequus amāvit
Iuppiter aut ārdēns ēvexit ad aethera[8] virtūs,
dīs genitī[9] potuēre."[10]

[1] *altar*
[2] Supply **est:** *began.*
[3] *prophetess*
[4] *sprung from* (vocative)
[5] *Trojan son of Anchises* (vocative)
[6] *to Hades*
[7] *air*
[8] accusative singular: *sky*
[9] *descended from the gods* (from **gignō**)
[10] i.e., to do so

Aeneas and the Sibyl come to the entrance of Hades.

Ībant obscūrī[11] sōlā sub nocte per umbram
perque domōs Dītis vacuās[1] et inānia rēgna
quāle[12] per incertam lūnam sub lūce malignā[13]
est iter in silvīs, ubi caelum condidit umbrā
Iuppiter et rēbus[14] nox abstulit ātra colōrem.
Vēstibulum ante ipsum prīmīsque in faucibus Orcī
Lūctus[15] et ultrīcēs posuēre cubīlia[16] Cūrae
pallentēsque[17] habitant Morbī trīstisque Senectūs
et Metus et malesuāda[18] Famēs ac turpis Egestās,[19]
terribilēs vīsū[20] fōrmae, Lētumque[21] Labōsque,[22]
tum cōnsanguineus Lētī Sopor et mala[23] mentis
Gaudia mortiferumque adversō in līmine Bellum
ferreīque Eumenidum thalamī[24] et Discordia dēmēns.

[11] *in the dark*
[12] *just as one goes*
[13] *stingy*
[14] dative
[15] *Grief*
[16] *couches*
[17] *pale*
[18] *urging to do wrong*
[19] *Need*
[20] *to look at*
[21] *Death*
[22] = **Labor**
[23] *wicked*
[24] *chambers of the Furies*

NOTE
Point out **rēbus** as a dative of separation.

NOTE
The reference to couches means that the worries of conscience are there to stay.

Aeneas meets the shade of his father, who points out to him the souls of various notables.

"Huc geminās[25] nunc flecte aciēs, hanc aspice gentem
Rōmānōsque tuōs; hīc Caesar et omnis Iūlī
prōgeniēs magnum caelī ventūra sub axem.[26]
Hic vir, hic est tibi quem prōmittī saepius audīs,
Augustus Caesar, Dīvī[2] genus, aurea condet
saecula quī rūrsus Latiō[27] rēgnāta per arva[28]
Sāturnō[29] quondam; super et Garamantas[30] et Indōs
prōferet imperium (iacet extrā sīdera tellūs,
extrā annī sōlisque viās,[3] ubi caelifer Atlās[31]
axem umerō torquet stēllīs ārdentibus aptum[32])."

[25] *both eyes* (with **aciēs**)
[26] *up to the vault of heaven* (with **sub**)
[27] *in Latium*
[28] *lands*
[29] *by Saturn* (dative of agent)
[30] *the Garamantēs,* an African tribe
[31] *heaven-carrying Atlas*
[32] *the sky studded with* (with **axem**)

NOTE
Remind students that Saturn was a god in the mythical "Golden Age" when life was peaceful.

Anchises tells Aeneas that the great contribution of the Romans will be good government and peace.

"Excūdent[33] aliī spīrantia[34] mollius[35] aera
(crēdō equidem), vīvōs dūcent dē marmore vultūs;
ōrābunt causās melius caelīque meātūs[36]
dēscrībent radiō[37] et surgentia sīdera dīcent.
Tū regere imperiō populōs, Rōmāne, mementō[38]
(hae tibi erunt artēs) pācīque impōnere mōrem,[39]
parcere subjectīs et dēbellāre superbōs."

[33] *will mold*; the Greeks are meant
[34] *breathing, lifelike*
[35] *more delicately*
[36] *movements* (of the stars)
[37] *with the rod*—with which the movements of the stars were traced in sand
[38] *remember* (imperative)
[39] i.e., to make peace customary

[1] Because only ghosts lived there.
[2] Julius Caesar, deified after his death
[3] i.e., beyond the constellations of the zodiac through which the sun seems to travel in the course of a year

Aeneas returns to the upper world through the gate of false dreams.

Sunt geminae somnī portae; quārum altera fertur
cornea,[40] quā vērīs facilis datur exitus umbrīs,[41]
altera candentī[42] perfecta nitēns[43] elephantō,
sed falsa ad caelum mittunt īnsomnia[41] Mānēs.[44]
Hīs[4] ibi tum nātum Anchīsēs ūnāque Sibyllam
prōsequitur dictīs portāque ēmittit eburnā.[45]
Ille viam secat[46] ad nāvīs sociōsque revīsit;
tum sē ad Caiētae[5] rēctō[47] fert lītore portum.
Ancora dē prōrā iacitur; stant lītore puppēs.

[40] *(to be) of horn*
[41] *dreams*
[42] *white* (ablative)
[43] *gleaming*
[44] *the spirits*
[45] *of ivory*
[46] *makes* (literally, *cuts*)
[47] *straight along the shore*

NOTE
Ask students how they would feel if they were given the opportunity to know their future. How would they live their lives differently?

WORKBOOK
Assign Ex. A, B to practice various constructions taken from the reading; Ex. C to work with the content of the reading.

[4] with **dictīs,** referring to Anchises' speech
[5] *Caiēta,* a town on the coast near Formiae

Quotations from Vergil

Some of Vergil's famous lines are given in the preceding selections. Here are a few more.

NOTE
Quotation 3 plays a part in a famous story of two rival English shoemakers whose shops adjoined each other. One of them put out a sign with the Vergilian quotation on it. Not to be outdone, his rival, who did not know Latin, promptly hung out a sign that read, "Mens and Womens Conscia Recti."

1. Forsan[1] et[1] haec ōlim meminisse iuvābit.
2. Hīc domus, haec patria est.
3. Mēns cōnscia rēctī.[2]
4. Nōn omnia possumus omnēs.
5. Pedibus timor addidit ālās.
6. Quōrum[2] pars magna fuī.
7. Ūna salūs victīs, nūllam spērāre salūtem.
8. Varium et mūtābile[3] semper fēmina.

[1] *perhaps*
[2] *right,* with **cōnscia**

WORKBOOK
Assign Ex. A to work with additional quotations.

[1] *even.* **Haec** refers to the misfortunes of Aeneas.
[2] Neuter, referring to the destruction of Troy, as seen by Aeneas.
[3] Supply **est**; used as nouns in the predicate nominative.

Appendix

Important Dates and Events

B.C.	
753	(Traditional date) Rome founded
753–509	Legendary kings
509	Republic established
496	Battle of Lake Regillus
494	Secession of the plebs
451–450	Laws of the Twelve Tables
390	Gauls capture Rome
343–290	Samnite Wars
280–275	War with Pyrrhus
264–241	First Punic War
218–201	Second Punic War
200–197	War with Philip
171–168	War with Perseus
157?–86	Marius, general
149–146	Third Punic War
146	Capture of Corinth
111–106	War with Jugurtha
106–48	Pompey, general
106–43	Cicero, orator, statesman
102	Marius defeats Cimbri and Teutons
100–44	Caesar, general, statesman
88–63	Mithridatic Wars
86	Sulla captures Athens
80–78	Caesar in Asia
63	Cicero consul; conspiracy of Catiline
63–A.D. 14	Augustus
62	Caesar praetor (propraetor in Spain in **61**)
60	First triumvirate (Caesar, Crassus, Pompey)
59	Caesar consul (proconsul in Gaul and Illyricum, **58–50**)
55 and 54	Caesar invades Britain
55 and 53	Caesar invades Germany
52	Fall of Alesia
49	Caesar crosses the Rubicon, thus precipitating civil war
48	Caesar consul; Battle of Pharsalus—Pompey defeated
48–46	Caesar dictator
46	Caesar consul and dictator, reforms calendar
45	Caesar sole consul
44	Caesar assassinated, March 15
42	Battle of Philippi
31	Battle of Actium
31–A.D. 14	Reign of Augustus
A.D.	
9	Defeat of Varus
14–37	Reign of Tiberius
37–41	Reign of Caligula
41–54	Reign of Claudius
54–68	Reign of Nero
68–69	Reigns of Galba, Otho, Vitellius
69–79	Reign of Vespasian
79	Eruption of Mt. Vesuvius
79–81	Reign of Titus
81–96	Reign of Domitian
96–98	Reign of Nerva
98–117	Reign of Trajan
117–138	Reign of Hadrian
138–161	Reign of Antoninus Pius
161–180	Reign of Marcus Aurelius

Life Spans of Major Latin Authors

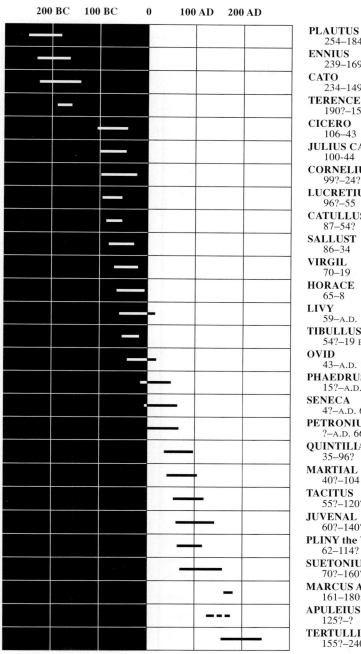

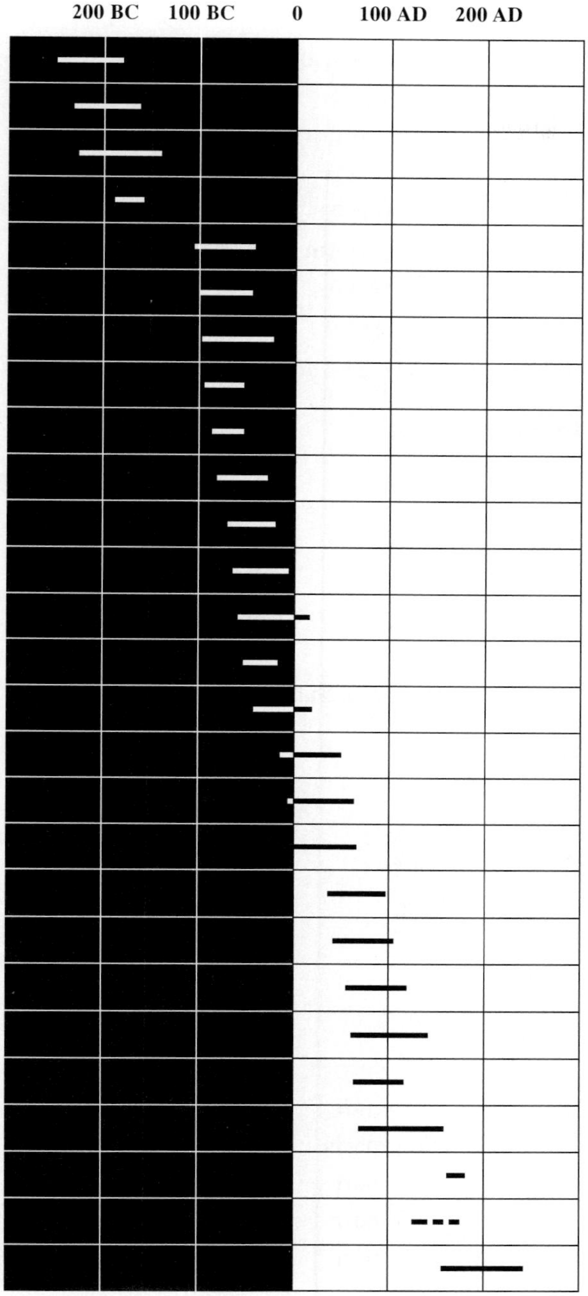

PLAUTUS
254–184
ENNIUS
239–169
CATO
234–149
TERENCE
190?–159
CICERO
106–43
JULIUS CAESAR
100-44
CORNELIUS NEPOS
99?–24?
LUCRETIUS
96?–55
CATULLUS
87–54?
SALLUST
86–34
VIRGIL
70–19
HORACE
65–8
LIVY
59–A.D. 17
TIBULLUS
54?–19 B.C.
OVID
43–A.D. 18?
PHAEDRUS
15?–A.D. 50?
SENECA
4?–A.D. 65
PETRONIUS
?–A.D. 66?
QUINTILIAN
35–96?
MARTIAL
40?–104
TACITUS
55?–120?
JUVENAL
60?–140?
PLINY the Younger
62–114?
SUETONIUS
70?–160?
MARCUS AURELIUS
161–180: reign
APULEIUS
125?–?
TERTULLIAN
155?–240?

Basic Forms

Nouns

First Declension / **Second Declension**

	SINGULAR	PLURAL	SINGULAR	PLURAL
NOM.	vi**a**	vi**ae**	serv**us**	serv**ī**
GEN.	vi**ae**	vi**ārum**	serv**ī**	serv**ōrum**
DAT.	vi**ae**	vi**īs**	serv**ō**	serv**īs**
ACC.	vi**am**	vi**ās**	serv**um**	serv**ōs**
ABL.	vi**ā**	vi**īs**	serv**ō**	serv**īs**
(VOC.)			(serv**e**)	

Nouns in **–ius** have –ī in the genitive and vocative singular: **fīlī, Cornēlī.** The accent does not change.

Second Declension

	SING.	PLUR.	SING.	PLUR.	SING.	PLUR.
NOM.	ager	agr**ī**	puer	puer**ī**	sign**um**	sign**a**
GEN.	agr**ī**	agr**ōrum**	puer**ī**	puer**ōrum**	sign**ī**	sign**ōrum**
DAT.	agr**ō**	agr**īs**	puer**ō**	puer**īs**	sign**ō**	sign**īs**
ACC.	agr**um**	agr**ōs**	puer**um**	puer**ōs**	sign**um**	sign**a**
ABL.	agr**ō**	agr**īs**	puer**ō**	puer**īs**	sign**ō**	sign**īs**

Nouns in **–ium** have **–ī** in the genitive singular: **cōnsilī.** The accent does not change.

Third Declension

	SING.	PLUR.	SING.	PLUR.	SING.	PLUR.
NOM.	mīles	mīlit**ēs**	lēx	lēg**ēs**	corpus	corpor**a**
GEN.	mīlit**is**	mīlit**um**	lēg**is**	lēg**um**	corpor**is**	corpor**um**
DAT.	mīlit**ī**	mīlit**ibus**	lēg**ī**	lēg**ibus**	corpor**ī**	corpor**ibus**
ACC.	mīlit**em**	mīlit**ēs**	lēg**em**	lēg**ēs**	corpus	corpor**a**
ABL.	mīlit**e**	mīlit**ibus**	lēg**e**	lēg**ibus**	corpor**e**	corpor**ibus**

Third Declension I–Stems

	SINGULAR	PLURAL	SINGULAR	PLURAL
NOM.	cīv**is**	cīv**ēs**	mar**e**	mar**ia**
GEN.	cīv**is**	cīv**ium**	mar**is**	mar**ium**
DAT.	cīv**ī**	cīv**ibus**	mar**ī**	mar**ibus**
ACC.	cīv**em**	cīv**ēs (–īs)**	mar**e**	mar**ia**
ABL.	cīv**e**	cīv**ibus**	mar**ī**	mar**ibus**

Turris and a few proper nouns have **–im** in the accusative singular. **Turris, ignis, nāvis,** and a few proper nouns sometimes have **–ī** in the ablative singular.

(a) The classes of masculine and feminine **i**-stem nouns are:

1. Nouns ending in **–is** and **–ēs** having no more syllables in the genitive than in the nominative: **cīvis, nūbēs.**
2. Nouns of one syllable whose base ends in two consonants: **pars** (gen. **part–is**), **nox** (gen. **noct–is**).
3. Nouns whose base ends in **–nt** or **–rt: cliēns** (gen. **client–is**).

(b) Neuter **i**-stem nouns ending in **–e, –al, –ar: mare, animal, calcar.**

Fourth Declension

	SINGULAR	PLURAL	SINGULAR	PLURAL
NOM.	cās**us**	cās**ūs**	corn**ū**	corn**ua**
GEN.	cās**ūs**	cās**uum**	corn**ūs**	corn**uum**
DAT.	cās**uī**	cās**ibus**	corn**ū**	corn**ibus**
ACC.	cās**um**	cās**ūs**	corn**ū**	corn**ua**
ABL.	cās**ū**	cās**ibus**	corn**ū**	corn**ibus**

Fifth Declension

	SINGULAR	PLURAL	SINGULAR	PLURAL
NOM.	di**ēs**	di**ēs**	**rēs**	**rēs**
GEN.	di**ēī**	di**ērum**	**reī**	**rērum**
DAT.	di**ēī**	di**ēbus**	**reī**	**rēbus**
ACC.	di**em**	di**ēs**	**rem**	**rēs**
ABL.	di**ē**	di**ēbus**	**rē**	**rēbus**

Irregular Nouns

	SING.	PLUR.	SING.	SING.	PLUR.
NOM.	**vīs**	vīr**ēs**	nēm**ō**	dom**us**	dom**ūs**
GEN.	———	vīr**ium**	(nūll**īus**)	dom**ūs** (**–ī**)	dom**uum** (**–ōrum**)
DAT.	———	vīr**ibus**	nēmin**ī**	dom**uī** (**–ō**)	dom**ibus**
ACC.	v**im**	vīr**ēs** (**–īs**)	nēmin**em**	dom**um**	dom**ōs** (**–ūs**)
ABL.	v**ī**	vīr**ibus**	(nūll**ō**)	dom**ō** (**–ū**)	dom**ibus**
(LOC.)				(dom**ī**)	

Adjectives and Adverbs

First and Second Declensions

	SINGULAR			PLURAL		
	M	F	N	M	F	N
NOM.	magn**us**	magn**a**	magn**um**	magn**ī**	magn**ae**	magn**a**
GEN.	magn**ī**	magn**ae**	magn**ī**	magn**ōrum**	magn**ārum**	magn**ōrum**
DAT.	magn**ō**	magn**ae**	magn**ō**	magn**īs**	magn**īs**	magn**īs**
ACC.	magn**um**	magn**am**	magn**um**	magn**ōs**	magn**ās**	magn**a**
ABL.	magn**ō**	magn**ā**	magn**ō**	magn**īs**	magn**īs**	magn**īs**
(VOC.)	(magn**e**)					

	SINGULAR			SINGULAR		
NOM.	līber	līber**a**	līber**um**	noster	nostr**a**	nostr**um**
GEN.	līber**ī**	līber**ae**	līber**ī**	nostr**ī**	nostr**ae**	nostr**ī**
DAT.	līber**ō**	līber**ae**	līber**ō**	nostr**ō**	nostr**ae**	nostr**ō**
ACC.	līber**um**	līber**am**	līber**um**	nostr**um**	nostr**am**	nostr**um**
ABL.	līber**ō**	līber**ā**	līber**ō**	nostr**ō**	nostr**ā**	nostr**ō**

Plural, **līberī, līberae, lībera,** etc. Plural, **nostrī, –ae, –a,** etc.

Third Declension

(a) THREE ENDINGS

	SINGULAR			PLURAL		
	M	F	N	M	F	N
NOM.	ācer	ācr**is**	ācr**e**	ācr**ēs**	ācr**ēs**	ācr**ia**
GEN.	ācr**is**	ācr**is**	ācr**is**	ācr**ium**	ācr**ium**	ācr**ium**
DAT.	ācr**ī**	ācr**ī**	ācr**ī**	ācr**ibus**	ācr**ibus**	ācr**ibus**
ACC.	ācr**em**	ācr**em**	ācr**e**	ācr**ēs (–īs)**	ācr**ēs (–īs)**	ācr**ia**
ABL.	ācr**ī**	ācr**ī**	ācr**ī**	ācr**ibus**	ācr**ibus**	ācr**ibus**

(b) TWO ENDINGS — *(c)* ONE ENDING[1]

	(b) SINGULAR		(b) PLURAL		(c) SINGULAR		(c) PLURAL	
	M F	N	M F	N	M F	N	M F	N
NOM.	fort**is**	fort**e**	fort**ēs**	fort**ia**	pār	pār	par**ēs**	par**ia**
GEN.	fort**is**	fort**is**	fort**ium**	fort**ium**	par**is**	par**is**	par**ium**	par**ium**
DAT.	fort**ī**	fort**ī**	fort**ibus**	fort**ibus**	par**ī**	par**ī**	par**ibus**	par**ibus**
ACC.	fort**em**	fort**e**	fort**ēs (–īs)**	fort**ia**	par**em**	pār	par**ēs (–īs)**	par**ia**
ABL.	fort**ī**	fort**ī**	fort**ibus**	fort**ibus**	par**ī**	par**ī**	par**ibus**	par**ibus**

PRESENT PARTICIPLE

	SINGULAR		PLURAL	
	M F	N	M F	N
NOM.	portāns	portāns	portant**ēs**	portant**ia**
GEN.	portant**is**	portant**is**	portant**ium**	portan**ium**
DAT.	portant**ī**	portant**ī**	portant**ibus**	portant**ibus**
ACC.	portant**em**	portāns	portant**ēs (–īs)**	portant**ia**
ABL.	portant**e (–ī)**	portant**e (–ī)**	portant**ibus**	portant**ibus**

The ablative singular regularly ends in **–e**, but **–ī** is used wherever the participle is used simply as an adjective.

IRREGULAR ADJECTIVES AND NUMERALS

	M	F	N	M F	N
NOM.	ūn**us**	ūn**a**	ūn**um**	tr**ēs**	tr**ia**
GEN.	ūn**īus**	ūn**īus**	ūn**īus**	tr**ium**	tr**ium**
DAT.	ūn**ī**	ūn**ī**	ūn**ī**	tr**ibus**	tr**ibus**
ACC.	ūn**um**	ūn**am**	ūn**um**	tr**ēs**	tr**ia**
ABL.	ūn**ō**	ūn**ā**	ūn**ō**	tr**ibus**	tr**ibus**

	M	F	N	M F N *(adj.)*	N *(noun)*
NOM.	du**o**	du**ae**	du**o**	mīlle	mīl**ia**
GEN.	du**ōrum**	du**ārum**	du**ōrum**	mīlle	mīl**ium**
DAT.	du**ōbus**	du**ābus**	du**ōbus**	mīlle	mīl**ibus**
ACC.	du**ōs**	du**ās**	du**o**	mīlle	mīl**ia**
ABL.	du**ōbus**	du**ābus**	du**ōbus**	mīlle	mīl**ibus**

[1] **Vetus** has **vetere** in the ablative singular and **veterum** in the genitive plural.

Like **ūnus** are **alius, alter, ūllus, nūllus, sōlus, tōtus, uter, neuter, uterque;** plural regular. The nom. and acc. sing. neuter of **alius** is **aliud;** for the genitive sing., **alterius** is generally used. **Ambō** is declined like **duo.**

Comparison of Regular Adjectives and Adverbs

POSITIVE		COMPARATIVE		SUPERLATIVE	
ADJ.	ADV.	ADJ.	ADV.	ADJ.	ADV.
alt**us**	alt**ē**	alt**ior**	alt**ius**	alt**issimus**	alt**issimē**
fort**is**	fort**iter**	fort**ior**	fort**ius**	fort**issimus**	fort**issimē**
līber	līber**ē**	līber**ior**	līber**ius**	līber**rimus**	līber**rimē**
ācer	ācr**iter**	ācr**ior**	ācr**ius**	ācer**rimus**	ācer**rimē**
facil**is**	facil**e**	facil**ior**	facil**ius**	facil**limus**	facil**limē**

Like **facilis** are **difficilis, similis, dissmilis, gracilis, humilis,** but their adverbs (not used in this book) vary in the positive degree. Adjectives in **–er** are like **līber** or **ācer.**

Comparison of Irregular Adjectives

POSITIVE	COMPARATIVE	SUPERLATIVE
bon**us**	mel**ior**	opt**imus**
mal**us**	pe**ior**	pess**imus**
magn**us**	ma**ior**	max**imus**
parv**us**	min**or**	min**imus**
mult**us**	——, plūs	plūr**imus**
īnfer**us**	īnfer**ior**	īnf**imus** *or* **īmus**
super**us**	super**ior**	supr**ēmus** *or* summ**us**
——	pr**ior**	pr**īmus**
——	prop**ior**	prox**imus**
——	ulter**ior**	ult**imus**

Comparison of Irregular Adverbs

ben**e**	mel**ius**	opt**imē**
mal**e**	pe**ius**	pess**imē**
(magnopere)	mag**is**	max**imē**
——	min**us**	min**imē**
mult**um**	plūs	plūr**imum**
diū	diūt**ius**	diūt**issimē**
prop**e**	prop**ius**	prox**imē**

Declension of Comparatives

	SINGULAR		PLURAL		SINGULAR	PLURAL	
	M F	N	M F	N	N	M F	N
NOM.	altior	altius	altiō**res**	altiō**ra**	plūs[1]	plūr**ēs**	plūr**a**
GEN.	altiō**ris**	altiō**ris**	altiō**rum**	altiō**rum**	plūr**is**	plūr**ium**	plūr**ium**
DAT.	altiō**rī**	altiō**rī**	altiō**ribus**	altiō**ribus**	——	plūr**ibus**	plūr**ibus**
ACC.	altiō**rem**	altius	altiō**rēs**	altiō**ra**	plūs	plūr**ēs**	plūr**a**
ABL.	altiō**re**	altiō**re**	altiō**ribus**	altiō**ribus**	plūr**e**	plūr**ibus**	plūr**ibus**

[1] Masculine and feminine lacking in the singular.

Numerals

	ROMAN	CARDINALS	ORDINALS
1.	**I.**	**ūnus, –a, –um**	**prīmus, –a, –um**
2.	**II.**	**duo, duae, duo**	**secundus (alter)**
3.	**III.**	**trēs, tria**	**tertius**
4.	**IIII** *or* **IV.**	**quattuor**	**quārtus**
5.	**V.**	**quīnque**	**quīntus**
6.	**VI.**	**sex**	**sextus**
7.	**VII.**	**septem**	**septimus**
8.	**VIII.**	**octō**	**octāvus**
9.	**VIIII** *or* **IX.**	**novem**	**nōnus**
10.	**X.**	**decem**	**decimus**
11.	**XI.**	**ūndecim**	**ūndecimus**
12.	**XII.**	**duodecim**	**duodecimus**
13.	**XIII.**	**tredecim**	**tertius decimus**
14.	**XIIII** *or* **XIV.**	**quattuordecim**	**quārtus decimus**
15.	**XV.**	**quīndecim**	**quīntus decimus**
16.	**XVI.**	**sēdecim**	**sextus decimus**
17.	**XVII.**	**septendecim**	**septimus decimus**
18.	**XVIII.**	**duodēvīgintī**	**duodēvīcēsimus**[1]
19.	**XVIIII** *or* **XIX.**	**ūndēvīgintī**	**ūndēvīcēsimus**
20.	**XX.**	**vīgintī**	**vīcēsimus**
21.	**XXI.**	**vīgintī ūnus** *or* **ūnus et vīgintī**	**vīcēsimus prīmus** *or* **ūnus et vīcēsimus**
30.	**XXX.**	**trīgintā**	**trīcēsimus**
40.	**XXXX** *or* **XL.**	**quadrāgintā**	**quadrāgēsimus**
50.	**L.**	**quīnquāgintā**	**quīnquāgēsimus**
60.	**LX.**	**sexāgintā**	**sexāgēsimus**
70.	**LXX.**	**septuāgintā**	**septuāgēsimus**
80.	**LXXX.**	**octōgintā**	**octōgēsimus**
90.	**LXXXX** *or* **XC.**	**nōnāgintā**	**nōnāgēsimus**
100.	**C.**	**centum**	**centēsimus**
101.	**CI.**	**centum (et) ūnus**	**centēsimus (et) prīmus**
200.	**CC.**	**ducentī, –ae, –a**	**ducentēsimus**
300.	**CCC.**	**trecentī, –ae, –a**	**trecentēsimus**
400.	**CCCC.**	**quadringentī, –ae, –a**	**quadringentēsimus**
500.	**D.**	**quīngentī, –ae, –a**	**quīngentēsimus**
600.	**DC.**	**sescentī, –ae, –a**	**sescentēsimus**
700.	**DCC.**	**septingentī, –ae, –a**	**septingentēsimus**
800.	**DCCC.**	**octingentī, –ae, –a**	**octingentēsimus**
900.	**DCCCC.**	**nōngentī, –ae, –a**	**nōngentēsimus**
1000.	**M.**	**mīlle**	**mīllēsimus**
2000.	**MM.**	**duo mīlia**	**bis mīllēsimus**

[1] The forms in **–ēsimus** are sometimes spelled **–ēnsimus.**

Pronouns

Personal

	SING.	PLUR.	SING.	PLUR.	M	F	N
NOM.	**ego**	**nōs**	**tū**	**vōs**	**is**	**ea**	**id**
GEN.	**meī**	**nostrum (nostrī)**	**tuī**	**vestrum (–trī)**	(for declension see demonstrative **is** chart)		
DAT.	**mihi**	**nōbīs**	**tibi**	**vōbīs**			
ACC.	**mē**	**nōs**	**tē**	**vōs**			
ABL.	**mē**	**nōbīs**	**tē**	**vōbīs**			

Reflexive

	FIRST PERSON		SECOND PERSON		THIRD PERSON	
	SINGULAR	PLURAL	SINGULAR	PLURAL	SINGULAR	PLURAL
GEN.	**meī**	**nostrī**	**tuī**	**vestrī**	**suī**	**suī**
DAT.	**mihi**	**nōbīs**	**tibi**	**vōbīs**	**sibī**	**sibi**
ACC.	**mē**	**nōs**	**tē**	**vōs**	**sē (sēsē)**	**sē (sēsē)**
ABL.	**mē**	**nōbīs**	**tē**	**vōbīs**	**sē (sēsē)**	**sē (sēsē)**

Not being used in the nominative, reflexives have no nominative form.

Demonstrative

	SINGULAR			PLURAL		
	M	F	N	M	F	N
NOM.	**hic**	**haec**	**hoc**	**hī**	**hae**	**haec**
GEN.	**huius**	**huius**	**huius**	**hōrum**	**hārum**	**hōrum**
DAT.	**huic**	**huic**	**huic**	**hīs**	**hīs**	**hīs**
ACC.	**hunc**	**hanc**	**hoc**	**hōs**	**hās**	**haec**
ABL.	**hōc**	**hāc**	**hōc**	**hīs**	**hīs**	**hīs**
NOM.	**is**	**ea**	**id**	**eī (iī)**	**eae**	**ea**
GEN.	**eius**	**eius**	**eius**	**eōrum**	**eārum**	**eōrum**
DAT.	**eī**	**eī**	**eī**	**eīs (iīs)**	**eīs (iīs)**	**eīs (iīs)**
ACC.	**eum**	**eam**	**id**	**eōs**	**eās**	**ea**
ABL.	**eō**	**eā**	**eō**	**eīs (iīs)**	**eīs (iīs)**	**eīs (iīs)**

	SINGULAR			PLURAL		
	M	F	N	M	F	N
NOM.	**īdem**	**eadem**	**idem**	**eīdem (īdem)**	**eaedem**	**eadem**
GEN.	**eiusdem**	**eiusdem**	**eiusdem**	**eōrundem**	**eārundem**	**eōrundem**
DAT.	**eīdem**	**eīdem**	**eīdem**	**eīsdem (īsdem)**	**eīsdem (īsdem)**	**eīsdem (īsdem)**
ACC.	**eundem**	**eandem**	**idem**	**eōsdem**	**eāsdem**	**eadem**
ABL.	**eōdem**	**eādem**	**eōdem**	**eīsdem (īsdem)**	**eīsdem (īsdem)**	**eīsdem (īsdem)**

	SINGULAR		
	M	F	N
NOM.	**ille**	**illa**	**illud**
GEN.	**illīus**	**illīus**	**illīus**
DAT.	**illī**	**illī**	**illī**
ACC.	**illum**	**illam**	**illud**
ABL.	**illō**	**illā**	**illō**

(Plural regular like **magnus**)

	SINGULAR		
	M	F	N
NOM.	**ipse**	**ipsa**	**ipsum**
GEN.	**ipsīus**	**ipsīus**	**ipsīus**
DAT.	**ipsī**	**ipsī**	**ipsī**
ACC.	**ipsum**	**ipsam**	**ipsum**
ABL.	**ipsō**	**ipsā**	**ipsō**

(Plural regular)

Iste is declined like **ille.**

Relative / Interrogative

	Relative						Interrogative	
	SINGULAR			PLURAL			SINGULAR	
	M	F	N	M	F	N	M F	N
NOM.	**quī**	**quae**	**quod**	**quī**	**quae**	**quae**	**quis**	**quid**
GEN.	**cuius**	**cuius**	**cuius**	**quōrum**	**quārum**	**quōrum**	**cuius**	**cuius**
DAT.	**cui**	**cui**	**cui**	**quibus**	**quibus**	**quibus**	**cui**	**cui**
ACC.	**quem**	**quam**	**quod**	**quōs**	**quās**	**quae**	**quem**	**quid**
ABL.	**quō**	**quā**	**quō**	**quibus**	**quibus**	**quibus**	**quō**	**quō**

Plural of **quis** like **quī.** Interrogative adjective **quī** like relative **quī.**

Indefinite

	SINGULAR		PLURAL		
	M F	N	M	F	N
NOM.	**aliquis**	**aliquid**	**aliquī**	**aliquae**	**aliqua**
GEN.	**alicuius**	**alicuius**	**aliquōrum**	**aliquārum**	**aliquōrum**
DAT.	**alicui**	**alicui**	**aliquibus**	**aliquibus**	**aliquibus**
ACC.	**aliquem**	**aliquid**	**aliquōs**	**aliquās**	**aliqua**
ABL.	**aliquō**	**aliquō**	**aliquibus**	**aliquibus**	**aliquibus**

The adjective form is **aliquī, –qua, –quod,** etc.

	M	F	N
	SINGULAR		
NOM.	**quīdam**	**quaedam**	**quiddam**
GEN.	**cuiusdam**	**cuiusdam**	**cuiusdam**
DAT.	**uidam**	**cuidam**	**cuidam**
ACC.	**quendam**	**quandam**	**quiddam**
ABL.	**quōdam**	**quādam**	**quōdam**
	PLURAL		
NOM.	**quīdam**	**quaedam**	**quaedam**
GEN.	**quōrundam**	**quārundam**	**quōrundam**
DAT.	**quibusdam**	**quibusdam**	**quibusdam**
ACC.	**quōsdam**	**quāsdam**	**quaedam**
ABL.	**quibusdam**	**quibusdam**	**quibusdam**

The adjective has **quoddam** for **quiddam.**

	SINGULAR		SINGULAR	
	M F	N	M F	N
NOM.	**quisquam**	**quicquam (quidquam)**	**quisque**	**quidque**
GEN.	**cuiusquam**	**cuiusquam**	**cuiusque**	**cuiusque**
DAT.	**cuiquam**	**cuiquam**	**cuique**	**cuique**
ACC.	**quemquam**	**quicquam (quidquam)**	**quemque**	**quidque**
ABL.	**quōquam**	**quōquam**	**quōque**	**quōque**
	(Plural lacking)		(Plural rare)	

The adjective form of **quisque** is **quisque, quaeque, quodque,** etc.

The indefinite pronoun **quis** (declined like the interrogative) and adjective **quī** (declined like the relative, but in the nom. fem. sing. and the nom. and acc. neut. plur. **qua** may be used for **quae**) are used chiefly after **sī, nisi,** and **nē.**

Verbs

First Conjugation

PRINCIPAL PARTS: **portō, portāre, portāvī, portātus**

	ACTIVE		PASSIVE	
		INDICATIVE		
PRESENT	*I carry,* etc.		*I am carried,* etc.	
	port**ō**	portā**mus**	port**or**	portā**mur**
	portā**s**	portā**tis**	portā**ris (–re)**	portā**minī**
	porta**t**	porta**nt**	portā**tur**	porta**ntur**
IMPERFECT	*I was carrying,* etc.		*I was (being) carried,* etc.	
	portā**bam**	portā**bāmus**	portā**bar**	portā**bāmur**
	portā**bās**	portā**bātis**	portā**bāris (–re)**	portā**bāminī**
	portā**bat**	portā**bant**	portā**bātur**	portā**bantur**
FUTURE	*I shall carry,* etc.		*I shall be carried,* etc.	
	portā**bō**	portā**bimus**	portā**bor**	portā**bimur**
	portā**bis**	portā**bitis**	portā**beris (–re)**	portā**biminī**
	portā**bit**	portā**bunt**	portā**bitur**	porta**buntur**
PERFECT	*I carried, have carried,* etc.		*I was carried, have been carried,* etc.	
	portāv**ī**	portāv**imus**	portā**tus** (–a, –um) { **sum**	portā**tī** (–ae, –a) { **sumus**
	portāv**istī**	portāv**istis**	**es**	**estis**
	portāv**it**	portāv**ērunt**	**est**	**sunt**
PLUPERFECT	*I had carried,* etc.		*I had been carried,* etc.	
	portāv**eram**	portāv**erāmus**	portā**tus** (–a, –um) { **eram**	portā**tī** (–ae, –a) { **erāmus**
	portāv**erās**	portāv**erātis**	**erās**	**erātis**
	portāv**erat**	portāv**erant**	**erat**	**erant**

	ACTIVE		PASSIVE	
FUTURE PERFECT	*I shall have carried,* etc.		*I shall have been carried,* etc.	
	portāv**erō**	portāv**erimus**	portāt**us** (–a, –um) **erō**	portāt**ī** (–ae, –a) **erimus**
	portāv**eris**	portāv**eritis**	**eris**	**eritis**
	portāv**erit**	portāv**erint**	**erit**	**erunt**

SUBJUNCTIVE

PRESENT	port**em**	port**ēmus**	port**er**	port**ēmur**
	port**ēs**	port**ētis**	port**ēris (–re)**	port**ēminī**
	port**et**	port**ent**	port**ētur**	port**entur**
IMPERFECT	portā**rem**	portā**rēmus**	portā**rer**	portā**rēmur**
	portā**rēs**	portā**rētis**	portā**rēris** (**–re**)	portā**rēminī**
	portā**ret**	portā**rent**	portā**rētur**	portā**rentur**
PERFECT	portāv**erim**	portāv**erīmus**	portāt**us** (–a, –um) **sim**	portāt**ī** (–ae, –a) **sīmus**
	portāv**erīs**	portāv**erītis**	**sīs**	**sītis**
	portāv**erit**	portāv**erint**	**sit**	**sint**
PAST PERFECT	portāv**issem**	portāv**issēmus**	portāt**us** (–a, –um) **essem**	portāt**ī** (–ae, –a) **essēmus**
	portāv**issēs**	portāv**issētis**	**essēs**	**essētis**
	portāv**isset**	portāv**issent**	**esset**	**essent**

PRESENT IMPERATIVE

2ND SING.	port**ā**, *carry*	port**āre**, *be carried*
2ND PLUR.	port**āte**, *carry*	port**āminī**, *be carried*

INFINITIVE

PRESENT	port**āre**, *to carry*	port**ārī**, *to be carried*
PERFECT	portāv**isse**, *to have carried*	portāt**us esse**, *to have been carried*
FUTURE	portāt**ūrus esse**, *to be going to carry*	

PARTICIPLE

PRESENT	port**āns**, *carrying*	
PERFECT		portāt**us** (*having been*) *carried*
FUTURE	portāt**ūrus**, *going to carry*	port**andus**, (*necessary*) *to be carried*

GERUND

GEN. port**andī** DAT. port**andō** ACC. port**andum** ABL. port**andō**, *of carrying*, etc.

Second, Third, and Fourth Conjugations

2d Conj.	*3d Conj.*	*4th Conj.*	*3d Conj.* (*–iō*)
PRINCIPAL PARTS			
doceō	**pōnō**	**mūniō**	**capiō**
docēre	**pōnere**	**mūnīre**	**capere**
docuī	**posuī**	**mūnīvī**	**cēpī**
doctus	**positus**	**mūnītus**	**captus**

	2d Conj.	*3d Conj.*	*4th Conj.*	*3d Conj.* **(–*iō*)**
		INDICATIVE ACTIVE		
PRESENT	doce**ō**	pōn**ō**	mūni**ō**	capi**ō**
	docē**s**	pōni**s**	mūnī**s**	capi**s**
	doce**t**	pōni**t**	mūni**t**	capi**t**
	docē**mus**	pōni**mus**	mūnī**mus**	capi**mus**
	docē**tis**	pōni**tis**	mūnī**tis**	capi**tis**
	doce**nt**	pon**unt**	mūni**unt**	capi**unt**
IMPERFECT	docē**bam**	pōnē**bam**	mūni**ēbam**	capi**ēbam**
	docē**bās**	pōnē**bās**	mūni**ēbās**	capi**ēbās**
	docē**bat**	pōnē**bat**	mūni**ēbat**	capi**ēbat**
	docē**bāmus**	pōnē**bāmus**	mūni**ēbāmus**	capi**ēbāmus**
	docē**bātis**	pōnē**bātis**	mūni**ēbātis**	capi**ēbātis**
	docē**bant**	pōnē**bant**	mūni**ēbant**	capi**ēbant**
FUTURE	docē**bō**	pōn**am**	mūni**am**	capi**am**
	docē**bis**	pōn**ēs**	mūni**ēs**	capi**ēs**
	docē**bit**	pōn**et**	mūni**et**	capi**et**
	docē**bimus**	pōn**ēmus**	mūni**ēmus**	capi**ēmus**
	docē**bitis**	pōn**ētis**	mūni**ētis**	capi**ētis**
	docē**bunt**	pōn**ent**	mūni**ent**	capi**ent**
PERFECT	docu**ī**	posu**ī**	mūnīv**ī**	cēp**ī**
	docu**istī**	posu**istī**	mūnīv**istī**	cēp**istī**
	docu**it**	posu**it**	mūnīv**it**	cēp**it**
	docu**imus**	posu**imus**	mūnīv**imus**	cēp**imus**
	docu**istis**	posu**istis**	mūnīv**istis**	cēp**istis**
	docu**ērunt**	posu**ērunt**	mūnīv**ērunt**	cēp**ērunt**
	(–ēre)	**(–ēre)**	**(–ēre)**	**(–ēre)**
PAST PERFECT	docu**eram**	posu**eram**	mūnīv**eram**	cēp**eram**
	docu**erās**	posu**erās**	mūnīv**erās**	cēp**erās**
	docu**erat**	posu**erat**	mūnīv**erat**	cēp**erat**
	docu**erāmus**	posu**erāmus**	mūnīv**erāmus**	cēp**erāmus**
	docu**erātis**	posu**erātis**	mūnīv**erātis**	cēp**erātis**
	docu**erant**	posu**erant**	mūnīv**erant**	cēp**erant**
FUTURE PERFECT	docu**erō**	posu**erō**	mūnīv**erō**	cēp**erō**
	docu**eris**	posu**eris**	mūnīv**eris**	cēp**eris**
	docu**erit**	posu**erit**	mūnīv**erit**	cēp**erit**
	docu**erimus**	posu**erimus**	mūnīv**erimus**	cēp**erimus**
	docu**eritis**	posu**eritis**	mūnīv**eritis**	cēp**eritis**
	docu**erint**	posu**erint**	mūnīv**erint**	cēp**erint**

	2d Conj.	*3d Conj.*	*4th Conj.*	*3d Conj.* **(–*iō*)**
		SUBJUNCTIVE ACTIVE		
PRESENT	doce**am**	pōn**am**	mūni**am**	capi**am**
	doce**ās**	pōn**ās**	mūni**ās**	capi**ās**
	doce**at**	pōn**at**	mūni**at**	capi**at**
	doce**āmus**	pōn**āmus**	mūni**āmus**	capi**āmus**
	doce**ātis**	pōn**ātis**	mūni**ātis**	capi**ātis**
	doce**ant**	pōn**ant**	mūni**ant**	capi**ant**
IMPERFECT	docē**rem**	pōne**rem**	mūnī**rem**	cape**rem**
	docē**rēs**	pōne**rēs**	mūnī**rēs**	cape**rēs**
	docē**ret**	pōne**ret**	mūnī**ret**	cape**ret**
	docē**rēmus**	pōne**rēmus**	mūnī**rēmus**	cape**rēmus**
	docē**rētis**	pōne**rētis**	mūnī**rētis**	cape**rētis**
	docē**rent**	pōne**rent**	mūnī**rent**	cape**rent**
PERFECT	docu**erim**	posu**erim**	mūnīv**erim**	cēp**erim**
	docu**erīs**	posu**erīs**	mūnīv**erīs**	cēp**erīs**
	docu**erit**	posu**erit**	mūnīv**erit**	cēp**erit**
	docu**erīmus**	posu**erīmus**	mūnīv**erīmus**	cēp**erīmus**
	docu**erītis**	posu**erītis**	mūnīv**erītis**	cēp**erītis**
	docu**erint**	posu**erint**	mūnīv**erint**	cēp**erint**
PAST PERFECT	docu**issem**	posu**issem**	mūnīv**issem**	cēp**issem**
	docu**issēs**	posu**issēs**	mūnīv**issēs**	cēp**issēs**
	docu**isset**	posu**isset**	mūnīv**isset**	cēp**isset**
	docu**issēmus**	posu**issēmus**	mūnīv**issēmus**	cēp**issēmus**
	docu**issētis**	posu**issētis**	mūnīv**issētis**	cēp**issētis**
	docu**issent**	posu**issent**	mūnīv**issent**	cēp**issent**
		PRESENT IMPERATIVE ACTIVE		
2D SING.	docē	pōne[1]	mūnī	cape[1]
2D PLUR.	docē**te**	pōni**te**	mūnī**te**	capi**te**
		INFINITIVE ACTIVE		
PRESENT	docē**re**	pōne**re**	mūnī**re**	cape**re**
PERFECT	docu**isse**	posu**isse**	mūnīv**isse**	cēp**isse**
FUTURE	doct**ūrus esse**	posit**ūrus esse**	mūnīt**ūrus esse**	capt**ūrus esse**
		PARTICIPLE ACTIVE		
PRESENT	docē**ns**	pōnē**ns**	mūniē**ns**	capiē**ns**
FUTURE	doct**ūrus**	posit**ūrus**	mūnīt**ūrus**	capt**ūrus**

[1] **Dīcō, dūcō,** and **faciō** have **dīc, dūc, fac** in the imperative singular.

	2d Conj.	*3d Conj.*	*4th Conj.*	*3d Conj.* **(–*iō*)**
		GERUND		
GEN.	doce**ndī**	pōne**ndī**	mūnie**ndī**	capie**ndī**
DAT.	doce**ndō**	pōne**ndō**	mūnie**ndō**	capie**ndō**
ACC.	doce**ndum**	pōne**ndum**	mūnie**ndum**	capie**ndum**
ABL.	doce**ndō**	pōne**ndō**	mūnie**ndō**	capie**ndō**
		INDICATIVE PASSIVE		
PRESENT	doce**or**	pōn**or**	mūni**or**	capi**or**
	docē**ris (–re)**	pōne**ris (–re)**	mūnī**ris (–re)**	cape**ris (–re)**
	docē**tur**	pōni**tur**	mūnī**tur**	capi**tur**
	docē**mur**	pōni**mur**	mūnī**mur**	capi**mur**
	docē**minī**	pōni**minī**	mūnī**minī**	capi**minī**
	doce**ntur**	pōnu**ntur**	mūni**untur**	capi**untur**
IMPERFECT	docē**bar**	pōnē**bar**	mūniē**bar**	capiē**bar**
	docē**bāris (–re)**	pōnē**bāris (–re)**	mūniē**bāris (–re)**	capiē**bāris (–re)**
	docē**bātur**	pōnē**bātur**	mūniē**bātur**	capiē**bātur**
	docē**bāmur**	pōnē**bāmur**	mūniē**bāmur**	capiē**bāmur**
	docē**bāminī**	pōnē**bāminī**	mūniē**bāminī**	capiē**bāminī**
	docē**bantur**	pōnē**bantur**	mūniē**bantur**	capiē**bantur**
FUTURE	docē**bor**	pōn**ar**	mūni**ar**	capi**ar**
	docē**beris (–re)**	pōn**ēris (–re)**	mūni**ēris (–re)**	capi**ēris (–re)**
	docē**bitur**	pōn**ētur**	mūni**ētur**	capi**ētur**
	docē**bimur**	pōn**ēmur**	mūni**ēmur**	capi**ēmur**
	docē**biminī**	pōn**ēminī**	mūni**ēminī**	capi**ēminī**
	docē**buntur**	pōn**entur**	mūni**entur**	capi**entur**
PERFECT	doct**us sum**	posit**us sum**	mūnīt**us sum**	capt**us sum**
	doct**us es**	posit**us es**	mūnīt**us es**	capt**us es**
	doct**us est**	posit**us est**	mūnīt**us est**	capt**us est**
	doctī **sumus**	positī **sumus**	mūnītī **sumus**	captī **sumus**
	doctī **estis**	positī **estis**	mūnītī **estis**	captī **estis**
	doctī **sunt**	positī **sunt**	mūnītī **sunt**	captī **sunt**
PAST PERFECT	doct**us eram**	posit**us eram**	mūnīt**us eram**	capt**us eram**
	doct**us erās**	posit**us erās**	mūnīt**us erās**	capt**us erās**
	doct**us erat**	posit**us erat**	mūnīt**us erat**	capt**us erat**
	doctī **erāmus**	positī **erāmus**	mūnītī **erāmus**	captī **erāmus**
	doctī **erātis**	positī **erātis**	mūnitī **erātis**	captī **erātis**
	doctī **erant**	positī **erant**	mūnītī **erant**	captī **erant**

	2d Conj.	*3d Conj.*	*4th Conj.*	*3d Conj.* (*–iō*)
FUTURE PERFECT	doct**us erō**	posit**us erō**	mūnīt**us erō**	capt**us erō**
	doct**us eris**	posit**us eris**	mūnīt**us eris**	capt**us eris**
	doct**us erit**	posit**us erit**	mūnīt**us erit**	capt**us erit**
	doct**ī erimus**	posit**ī erimus**	mūnīt**ī erimus**	capt**ī erimus**
	doct**ī eritis**	posit**ī eritis**	mūnīt**ī eritis**	capt**ī eritis**
	doct**ī erunt**	posit**ī erunt**	mūnīt**ī erunt**	capt**ī erunt**

SUBJUNCTIVE PASSIVE

PRESENT	doce**ar**	pōn**ar**	mūni**ar**	capi**ar**
	doce**āris (–re)**	pōn**āris (–re)**	mūni**āris (–re)**	capi**āris (–re)**
	doce**ātur**	pōn**ātur**	mūni**ātur**	capi**ātur**
	doce**āmur**	pōn**āmur**	mūni**āmur**	capi**āmur**
	doce**āminī**	pōn**āminī**	mūni**āminī**	capi**āminī**
	doce**antur**	pōn**antur**	mūni**antur**	capi**antur**
IMPERFECT	docē**rer**	pōne**rer**	mūnī**rer**	cape**rer**
	docē**rēris (–re)**	pōne**rēris (–re)**	mūnī**rēris (–re)**	cape**rēris (–re)**
	docē**rētur**	pōne**rētur**	mūnī**rētur**	cape**rētur**
	docē**rēmur**	pōne**rēmur**	mūnī**rēmur**	cape**rēmur**
	docē**rēminī**	pōne**rēminī**	mūnī**rēminī**	cape**rēminī**
	docē**rentur**	pōne**rentur**	mūnī**rentur**	cape**rentur**
PERFECT	doct**us sim**	posit**us sim**	mūnīt**us sim**	capt**us sim**
	doct**us sīs**	posit**us sīs**	mūnīt**us sīs**	capt**us sīs**
	doct**us sit**	posit**us sit**	mūnīt**us sit**	capt**us sit**
	doct**ī sīmus**	posit**ī sīmus**	mūnīt**ī sīmus**	capt**ī sīmus**
	doct**ī sītis**	posit**ī sītis**	mūnīt**ī sītis**	capt**ī sītis**
	doct**ī sint**	posit**ī sint**	mūnīt**ī sint**	capt**ī sint**
PAST PERFECT	doct**us essem**	posit**us essem**	mūnīt**us essem**	capt**us essem**
	doct**us essēs**	posit**us essēs**	mūnīt**us essēs**	capt**us essēs**
	doct**us esset**	posit**us esset**	mūnīt**us esset**	capt**us esset**
	doct**ī essēmus**	posit**ī essēmus**	mūnīt**ī essēmus**	capt**ī essēmus**
	doct**ī essētis**	posit**ī essētis**	mūnīt**ī essētis**	capt**ī essētis**
	doct**ī essent**	posit**ī essent**	mūnīt**ī essent**	capt**ī essent**

PRESENT IMPERATIVE PASSIVE

2D SING.	docē**re**	pōne**re**	mūnī**re**	cape**re**
2D PLUR.	docē**minī**	pōni**minī**	mūnī**minī**	capi**minī**

INFINITIVE PASSIVE

PRESENT	docē**rī**	pōn**ī**	mūnī**rī**	cap**ī**
PERFECT	doct**us esse**	posit**us esse**	mūnīt**us esse**	capt**us esse**

	2d Conj.	*3d Conj.*	*4th Conj.*	*3d Conj.* (**–iō**)
		PARTICIPLE PASSIVE		
PERFECT	doct**us**	posit**us**	mūnīt**us**	capt**us**
FUTURE	doc**endus**	pōn**endus**	mūni**endus**	capi**endus**

Deponent Verbs[1]

	1st Conj.	*2d Conj.*	*3d Conj.*	*4th Conj.*	*3d Conj.* (**–iō**)
			PRINCIPAL PARTS		
	arbitror **arbitrārī** **arbitrātus**	**vereor** **verērī** **veritus**	**loquor** **loquī** **locūtus**	**orior** **orīrī** **ortus**	**gradior** **gradī** **gressus**
			INDICATIVE		
PRESENT	arbitr**or,** *I think*	vere**or,** *I fear*	loqu**or,** *I talk*	ori**or,** *I rise*	gradi**or,** *I walk*
IMPERFECT	arbitrā**bar**	verē**bar**	loquē**bar**	oriē**bar**	gradiē**bar**
FUTURE	arbitrā**bor**	verē**bor**	loqu**ar**	ori**ar**	gradi**ar**
PERFECT	arbitrāt**us** **sum**	verit**us** **sum**	locūt**us** **sum**	ort**us** **sum**	gress**us** **sum**
PAST PERFECT	arbitrāt**us** **eram**	verit**us** **eram**	locūt**us** **eram**	ort**us** **eram**	gress**us** **eram**
FUTURE PERFECT	arbitrāt**us** **erō**	verit**us** **erō**	locūt**us** **erō**	ort**us** **erō**	gress**us** **erō**
			SUBJUNCTIVE		
PRESENT	arbitr**er**	vere**ar**	loqu**ar**	ori**ar**	gradi**ar**
IMPERFECT	arbitrā**rer**	verē**rer**	loque**rer**	orī**rer**	grade**rer**
PERFECT	arbitrāt**us** **sim**	verit**us** **sim**	locūt**us** **sim**	ort**us** **sim**	gress**us** **sim**
PAST PERFECT	arbitrāt**us** **essem**	verit**us** **essem**	locūt**us** **essem**	ort**us** **essem**	gress**us** **essem**
			PRESENT IMPERATIVE		
2D SING.	arbitrā**re**	verē**re**	loque**re**	orī**re**	grade**re**
2D PLUR.	arbitrā**minī**	verē**minī**	loqui**minī**	orī**minī**	gradi**minī**
			INFINITIVE		
PRESENT	arbitrā**rī**	verē**rī**	loqu**ī**	orī**rī**	grad**ī**
PERFECT	arbitrāt**us** **esse**	verit**us** **esse**	locūt**us** **esse**	ort**us** **esse**	gress**us** **esse**
FUTURE	arbitrāt**ūrus** **esse**	verit**ūrus** **esse**	locūt**ūrus** **esse**	ort**ūrus** **esse**	gress**ūrus** **esse**

1 See p. 98.

	1st Conj.	*2d Conj.*	*3d Conj.*	*4th Conj.*	*3d Conj.* **(–*iō*)**
			PARTICIPLE		
PRESENT	arbitrā**ns**	verē**ns**	loquē**ns**	ori**ēns**	gradi**ēns**
PERFECT	arbitrāt**us**	verit**us**	locūt**us**	ort**us**	gress**us**
FUTURE ACTIVE	arbitrāt**ūrus**	verit**ūrus**	locūt**ūrus**	ort**ūrus**	gress**ūrus**
FUTURE PASSIVE	arbitra**ndus**	vere**ndus**	loque**ndus**	ori**endus**	gradi**endus**
			GERUND		
GEN.	arbitra**ndī,** etc.	vere**ndī,** etc.	loque**ndī,** etc.	ori**endī,** etc.	gradi**endī,** etc.

A few verbs (called "semideponent") are active in the present system and deponent in the perfect system, as **audeō, audēre, ausus.**

Irregular Verbs

PRINCIPAL PARTS: **sum, esse, fuī, futūrus**

	INDICATIVE			SUBJUNCTIVE	
PRESENT	s**um,** *I am*	s**umus,** *we are*	PRESENT	s**im**	s**īmus**
	es, *you are*	es**tis,** *you are*		s**īs**	s**ītis**
	es**t,** *he is*	s**unt,** *they are*		s**it**	s**int**
IMPERFECT	*I was,* etc.				
	er**am**	er**āmus**	IMPERFECT	ess**em**	ess**ēmus**
	er**ās**	er**ātis**		ess**ēs**	ess**ētis**
	er**at**	er**ant**		ess**et**	ess**ent**
FUTURE	*I shall be,* etc.				
	er**ō**	er**imus**			
	er**is**	er**itis**			
	er**it**	er**unt**			
PERFECT	*I was,* etc.				
	fu**ī**	fu**imus**	PERFECT	fu**erim**	fu**erīmus**
	fu**istī**	fu**istis**		fu**erīs**	fu**erītis**
	fu**it**	fu**ērunt (–ēre)**		fu**issem**	fu**issēmus**
PAST PERFECT	*I had been,* etc.				
	fu**eram**	fu**erāmus**	PAST PERFECT	fu**issem**	fu**issēmus**
	fu**erās**	fu**erātis**		fu**issēs**	fu**issētis**
	fu**erat**	fu**erant**		fu**isset**	fu**issent**
FUTURE PERFECT	*I shall have been,* etc.				
	fu**erō**	fu**erimus**			
	fu**eris**	fu**eritis**			
	fu**erit**	fu**erint**			

INFINITIVE			IMPERATIVE	
PRESENT	**esse,** *to be*	2D SING. es, *be*	2D PLUR. es**te**, *be*	
PERFECT	fu**isse,** *to have been*			
		PARTICIPLE		
FUTURE	fut**ūrus esse,** *to be going to be*	FUTURE	fut**ūrus,** *going to be*	

PRINCIPAL PARTS: **possum, posse, potuī, ——**

	INDICATIVE			SUBJUNCTIVE	
PRESENT	*I am able, I can* etc.				
	pos**sum**	pos**sumus**	PRESENT	pos**sim**	pos**sīmus**
	pot**es**	pot**estis**		pos**sīs**	pos**sītis**
	pot**est**	pos**sunt**		pos**sit**	pos**sint**
IMPERFECT	*I was able, I could* etc.				
	pot**eram,** etc.		IMPERFECT	pos**sem,** etc.	
FUTURE	*I shall be able,* etc.				
	pot**erō,** etc.				
PERFECT	*I was able, I could,* etc.				
	potu**ī,** etc.		PERFECT	pot**erim,** etc.	
PAST PERFECT	*I had been able,* etc.				
	potu**eram,** etc.		PAST PERFECT	potu**issem,** etc.	
FUTURE PERFECT	*I shall have been able,* etc.				
	potu**erō,** etc.				

	INFINITIVE		PARTICIPLE
PRESENT	pos**se,** *to be able*	PRESENT	pot**ēns** (*adj.*), *powerful*
PERFECT	potu**isse,** *to have been able*		

PRINCIPAL PARTS: **ferō, ferre, tulī, lātus**

	ACTIVE		PASSIVE	
	INDICATIVE			
PRESENT	**ferō**	**ferimus**	**feror**	**ferimur**
	fers	**fertis**	**ferris (–re)**	**feriminī**
	fert	**ferunt**	**fertur**	**feruntur**
IMPERFECT	**ferēbam,** etc.		**ferēbar,** etc.	
FUTURE	**feram, ferēs,** etc.		**ferar, ferēris,** etc.	
PERFECT	**tulī,** etc.		**lātus sum,** etc.	
PAST PERFECT	**tuleram,** etc.		**lātus eram,** etc.	
FUTURE PERFECT	**tulerō,** etc.		**lātus erō,** etc.	

	ACTIVE		PASSIVE	
		SUBJUNCTIVE		
PRESENT	**feram, ferās**, etc.		**ferar, ferāris**, etc.	
IMPERFECT	**ferrem**, etc.		**ferrer**, etc.	
PERFECT	**tulerim**, etc.		**lātus sim**, etc.	
PAST PERFECT	**tulissem**, etc.		**lātus essem**, etc.	
		PRESENT IMPERATIVE		
2D PERS.	**fer**	**ferte**	**ferre**	**feriminī**
		INFINITIVE		
PRESENT	**ferre**		**ferrī**	
PERFECT	**tulisse**		**lātus esse**	
FUTURE	**lātūrus esse**			
		PARTICIPLE		
PRESENT	**ferēns**			
PERFECT	**lātus**			
FUTURE	**lātūrus**		**ferendus**	

GERUND

GEN. **ferendī**	DAT. **ferendō**	ACC. **ferendum**	ABL. **ferendō**

PRINCIPAL PARTS: **eō, īre, iī, itūrus**

	INDICATIVE		SUBJUNCTIVE	INFINITIVE
PRESENT	**eō**	**īmus**	**eam**, etc.	**īre**
	īs	**ītis**		
	it	**eunt**		
IMPERFECT	**ībam**, etc.		**īrem**, etc.	
FUTURE	**ībō**	**ībimus**		**itūrus esse**
	ībis	**ībitis**		
	ībit	**ībunt**		
PERFECT	**iī**	**iimus**	**ierim**, etc.	**īsse**
	īstī	**īstis**		
	iit	**iērunt (–ēre)**		
PAST PERFECT	**ieram**, etc.		**īssem**, etc.	
FUTURE PERFECT	**ierō**, etc.			

	PARTICIPLE	IMPERATIVE		GERUND	
PRESENT	**iēns**, GEN. **euntis**	**ī**	**īte**	GEN.	**eundī**
				DAT.	**eundō**
FUTURE	**itūrus** (PASSIVE **eundus**)			ACC.	**eundum**
				ABL.	**eundum**

	PRINCIPAL PARTS					
	volō		**nōlō**		**mālō**	
	velle		**nōlle**		**mālle**	
	voluī		**nōluī**		**māluī**	
	INDICATIVE					
PRESENT	**volō**	**volumus**	**nōlō**	**nōlumus**	**mālō**	**mālumus**
	vīs	**vultis**	**nōn vīs**	**nōn vultis**	**māvīs**	**māvultis**
	vult	**volunt**	**nōn vult**	**nōlunt**	**māvult**	**mālunt**
IMPERFECT	**volēbam**, etc.		**nōlēbam**, etc.		**mālēbam**, etc.	
FUTURE	**volam, volēs**, etc.		**nōlam, nōlēs**, etc.		**mālam, mālēs**, etc.	
PERFECT	**voluī**, etc.		**nōluī**, etc.		**māluī**, etc.	
PAST PERFECT	**volueram**, etc.		**nōlueram**, etc.		**mālueram**, etc.	
FUTURE PERFECT	**voluerō**, etc.		**nōluerō**, etc.		**mālerō**, etc.	
	SUBJUNCTIVE					
PRESENT	**velim**	**velīmus**	**nōlim**	**nōlīmus**	**mālim**	**mālīmus**
	velīs	**velītis**	**nōlīs**	**nōlītis**	**mālīs**	**mālītis**
	velit	**velint**	**nōlit**	**nōlint**	**mālit**	**mālint**
IMPERFECT	**vellem**, etc.		**nōllem**, etc.		**māllem**, etc.	
PERFECT	**voluerim**, etc.		**nōluerim**, etc.		**māluerim**, etc.	
PAST PERFECT	**voluissem**, etc.		**nōluissem**, etc.		**māluissem**, etc.	
	PRESENT IMPERATIVE					
2D PERS.	——	——	**nōlī**	**nōlīte**	——	——
	INFINITIVE					
PRESENT	**velle**		**nōlle**		**mālle**	
PERFECT	**voluisse**		**nōluisse**		**māluisse**	
	PARTICIPLE					
PRESENT	**volēns**		**nōlēns**		——	——

PRINCIPAL PARTS: **fīō, fierī, (factus)**

	INDICATIVE		SUBJUNCTIVE	IMPERATIVE		INFINITIVE
PRESENT	**fīō**	——	**fīam**, etc.			**fierī**
	——	——		**fī**	**fīte**	
	fit	**fīunt**				
IMPERFECT	**fīēbam**, etc.		**fierem**, etc.			
FUTURE	**fīam, fīēs,** etc.					

Defective Verbs

Coepī is used only in the perfect system. For the present system **incipiō** is used. With a passive infinitive the passive of **coepī** is used: **Lapidēs iacī coeptī sunt,** *Stones began to be thrown.* **Meminī** and **ōdī** likewise are used only in the perfect system, but with present meaning. The former has an imperative **mementō, mementōte.**

Contracted Forms

Verbs having perfect stems ending in **–āv–** or **–ēv–** are sometimes contracted by dropping **–ve–** before **–r–** and **–vi–** before **–s–: amārunt, cōnsuēsse.** Verbs having perfect stems ending in **–īv–** drop **–vi–** before **–s–** but only **–v–** before **–r–: audīsset, audierat.**

Syntax[1]

Agreement

1. *Adjectives.* Adjectives and participles agree in number, gender, and case with the nouns which they modify.
2. *Adjectives as Nouns.* Sometimes adjectives are used as nouns: **nostrī,** *our* (*men*); **malum,** *evil.*
3. *Verbs.* Verbs agree in person and number with their subjects. When two subjects are connected by **aut, aut... aut, neque... neque,** the verb agrees with the nearer subject.
4. *Relative Pronoun.* The relative pronoun agrees in gender and number with its antecedent but its case depends upon its use in its own clause.
5. *Appositives.* Appositives agree in case.

Noun Syntax

Nominative

1. *Subject.* The subject of a finite verb is in the nominative case.
2. *Predicate. a.* A noun or adjective used in the predicate with a linking verb (*is, are, seem,* etc.) is in the nominative.

Īnsula est magna.	*The island is large.*
Sicilia est īnsula.	*Sicily is an island.*

b. Predicate nouns and adjectives are used not only with **sum** but also with **fīō** and the passive voice of verbs meaning *call, choose, appoint, elect,* and the like.

Caesar dux factus est.	*Caesar was made leader.*
Cicerō Pater Patriae appellātus est.	*Cicero was called the Father of his Country.*

Genitive

1. *Possession.* Possession is expressed by the genitive.

viae īnsulae	*the roads of the island*

2. *Description.* The genitive, if modified by an adjective, may be used to describe a person or thing.

virī magnae virtūtis	*men of great courage*

3. *Of the Whole.* The genitive of the whole (also called partitive genitive) represents the whole to which the part belongs.

hōrum omnium fortissmī	*the bravest of all these*
nihil praesidī	*no guard*

4. *With Adjectives.* The genitive is used with certain adjectives. In many cases the English idiom is the same; in others, it is not.

bellandī cupidus	*desirous of waging war*
reī mīlitāris perītus	*skilled in warfare*

NOTĀ · BENE

A plural verb may be used with a singular subject which is plural in thought.

a. The antecedent of the relative pronoun is often omitted.
b. Sometimes the antecedent is represented by an entire clause, in which case the pronoun is best translated *a thing which.*
c. In Latin a relative pronoun is often used at the beginning of a sentence to refer to the thought of the preceding sentence. The English idiom calls for a demonstrative or personal pronoun.

quā dē cuasā
for this reason

It is often best to supply *as* in translating the appositive.

eōdem homine magistrō ūtī
to use the same man as teacher

[1] In this summary only those constructions are included which are relatively more important and which recur repeatedly in the text, or are referred to in the book.

Dative

1. *Indirect Object.* The indirect object of a verb is in the dative. It is used with verbs of *giving, reporting, telling,* etc.

Nautae pecūniam dōnō.	*I give money to the sailor.*

2. *Purpose.* The dative is sometimes used to express purpose.

Locum castrīs dēlēgit.	*He chose a place for a camp.*

3. *Reference.* The dative of reference shows the person concerned or referred to.

sī mihi dignī esse vultis	*if you wish to be worthy in my sight* (lit., *for me*)

4. *Separation.* The dative of separation (really reference) is usually confined to persons and occurs chiefly with verbs compounded with **ab, dē**, and **ex.**

scūtō ūnī mīlitī dētrācto	*having seized a shield from a soldier*

5. *With Adjectives.* The dative is used with certain adjectives, as **amīcus, idōneus, pār, proximus, similis, ūtilis,** and their opposites. In many cases the English idiom is the same.

Hic liber est similis illī.	*This book is similar to that.*

6. *With Special Verbs.* The dative is used with a few intransitive verbs, such as **cōnfīdō, crēdō, dēsum, faveō, ignōscō, imperō, invideō, noceō, parcō, pārēō, persuādeō, placeō, praestō, resistō,** and **studeō.**

Tibi pāret sed mihi resistit.	*He obeys you but resists me.*

a. Some of these verbs become impersonal in the passive and the dative is retained. The perfect passive participle of such verbs is used only in the neuter.

Eī persusāsum est.	*He was persuaded.*

b. A neuter pronoun or adjective or an **ut** clause may be used as a direct object with **imperō** and **persuādeō.**

Hoc mihi persuāsit.	*He persuaded me of this.*

7. *With Compounds.* The dative is often used with certain compound verbs, especially when the noun goes closely with the prefix of the verb. No general rule can be given. Sometimes both an accusative and a dative are used when the main part of the verb is transitive.

Gallīs bellum intulit.	*He made war against the Gauls.*

8. *Possession.* The possessor may be expressed by the dative with **sum.**

Liber mihi est.	*I have a book.*

NOTĀ·BENE

With the active voice of the verbs discussed in the Nominative section, two accusatives are used.

The descriptive genitive (p. 475) is largely confined to permanent qualities such as measure and number.

spatium decem pedum
a space of ten feet

a. The genitive of the whole (p. 475) is similar to the English idiom except when the genitive is used with such words as **nihil, satis, quid.**

b. Instead of the genitive of the whole, the ablative with **ex** or **dē** is regularly used with cardinal numerals (except **mīlia**) and **quīdam,** often also with other words, such as **paucī** and **complūrēs.**

quīnque ex nostrīs
five of our men

quīdam ex mīlitibus
certain of the soldiers.

9. *Agent.* The dative of agent is used with the future passive participle to indicate the person upon whom the obligation rests.

Hoc opus vōbīs faciendum est.	*This work is to be done by you.* i.e., *This work must be done by you.*

Accusative

1. *Direct Object.* The direct object of a transitive verb is in the accusative.

Viam parāmus.	*We are preparing a way.*

2. *Extent.* Extent of time or space is expressed by the accusative.

Duōs annōs remānsit.	*He remained two years.*
Flūmen decem pedēs altum est.	*The river is ten feet deep.*

3. *Place to Which.* The accusative with **ad** (*to*) or **in** (*into*) expresses *place to which.* These prepositions, however, are omitted before **domum** and names of towns and cities.

Lēgātōs ad eum mittunt.	*They send envoys to him.*
Rōmam eunt.	*They go to Rome.*

4. *Subject of Infinitive.* The subject of an infinitive is in the accusative.

Puerōs esse bonōs volumus.	*We want the boys to be good.*

5. *Two Accusatives.* With **trādūcō** and **trānsportō** two accusatives are used. In the passive the word closely connected with the prefix remains in the accusative.

Cōpiās *Rhēnum* trādūcit.	*He leads his forces across the Rhine.*
Cōpiae *Rhēnum* trādūcuntur.	*The forces are led across the Rhine.*

6. *With Prepositions.* The accusative is used with prepositions (except those listed on p. 479, 19). When **in** and **sub** show the direction toward which a thing moves, the accusative is used.

Ablative

Summary. The uses of the ablative may be grouped under three heads:

I. The *true* or *"from" ablative* (**ab,** *from,* and **lātus,** *carried*), used with the prepositions **ab, dē,** and **ex**—if any preposition is used.

II. The *associative* or *"with" ablative,* used with the preposition **cum**—if any preposition is used.

III. The *place* or *"in" ablative,* used with the prepositions **in** and **sub**—if any preposition is used.

1. *Separation.* Separation may be expressed by the ablative without a preposition, always so with **careō** and **līberō,** often also with **abstineō, dēsistō, excēdō,** and other verbs.

NOTĀ·BENE

The dative of reference (p. 476) is often used with the dative of purpose to show the person or thing affected ("double" dative).

Haec castra erunt praesidiō oppidō.
This camp will be (for) a protection to the town.

When the preposition **ad** is used with names of towns, it means *to the vicinity of.*

a. Caesar uses **prohibeō,** *keep from,* usually without a preposition, but occasionally with it.

Suīs fīnibus eōs prohibent.
They keep them from their own territory.

b. Other verbs expressing separation regularly require the prepositions **ab, dē,** or **ex.**

> **NOTĀ·BENE**
>
> The preposition is regularly omitted before **domō** as well as before names of towns and cities. When it is used with such names, it means *from the vicinity of.*

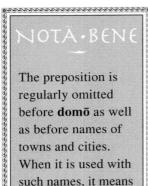

2. *Place from Which.* The ablative with **ab, dē,** or **ex** expresses *place from which.*

ex agrīs	*out of the fields*

3. *Origin.* The ablative without or with a preposition **(ab, dē ex)** expresses origin.

amplissimō genere nātus	*born of most illustrious family*

4. *Agent.* The ablative with **ā** or **ab** is used with a passive verb to show the person (or animal) by whom something is done.

Amāmur ab amīcīs.	*We are loved by our friends.*

5. *Comparison.* After a comparative the ablative is used when **quam** (*than*) is omitted.

amplius pedibus decem	*more than ten feet*
Nec locus tibi ūllus dulcior esse dēbet patriā.	*No spot ought to be dearer to you than your native land.*

6. *Accompaniment.* The ablative with **cum** expresses accompaniment.

Cum servō venit.	*He is coming with the slave.*

   a. When **cum** is used with a personal, relexive, or relative pronoun, it is attached to it as an enclitic: **vōbīscum,** *with you;* **sēcum,** *with himself;* **quibuscum,** *with whom.*

   b. **Cum** may be omitted in military phrases indicating accompaniment, if modified by an adjective other than a numeral.

omnibus suīs cōpiīs	*with all his forces*
cum tribus legiōnibus	*with three legions*

7. *Manner.* The ablative of manner with **cum** describes how something is done. **Cum** is sometimes omitted if an adjective modifies the noun.

(Cum) magnō studiō labōrat.	*He labors with great eagerness (very eagerly).*

8. *Absolute.* A noun in the ablative used with a participle, adjective, or other noun and having no grammatical connection with any other word in its clause is called an ablative absolute.

   In translating, an ablative absolute should, as a rule, be changed to a clause expressing *time, cause, condition, means,* or *concession,* according to the context. At times it may best be rendered by a coodinate clause.

Servō accūsātō, dominus discessit.	*After accusing the slave* (lit., *the slave having been accused*), *the master departed.*
Oppidīs nostrīs captīs, bellum gerēmus.	*If our towns are captured* (lit., *ourtowns captured*), *we shall wage war.*

9. *Means.* The means by which a thing is done is expressed by the ablative without a preposition.

Ratibus trānsībant.	*They were trying to cross by means of rafts.*

10. *With Special Verbs.* The ablative is used with a few verbs, notably **potior** and **ūtor,** whose English equivalents govern a direct object.

Castrīs potītī sunt.	*They got possession of the camp.*

11. *Cause.* The ablative of cause is used chiefly with verbs and adjectives expressing feeling.

labōrāre iniūriā	*to suffer because of the wrong*
vīribus cōnfīsī	*relying on their strength*

12. *Measure of Difference.* The ablative without a preposition expresses the measure of difference.

tribus annīs ante	*three years ago* (lit., *before by three years*)
multō maior	*much larger* (lit., *larger by much*)

13. *Description.* The ablative, like the genitive, is used with an adjective to describe a noun. It is regularly used of temporary qualities, such as personal appearance.

hominēs inimīcā faciē	*men with an unfriendly appearance*

14. *Place Where.* The ablative with **in** or **sub** expresses *place where.* The preposition may be omitted, however, with certain words like **locō, locīs,** and **parte,** also in certain fixed expressions like **tōtō orbe terrārum,** *in the whole world.* In poetry the omission of the preposition is more frequent. See also Locative.

15. *Time When. Time when* or *within which* is expressed by the ablative without a preposition.

aestāte	*in summer*
paucīs diēbus	*within a few days*

16. *Respect.* The ablative tells in what respect the statement applies.

Nōs superant numerō.	*They surpass us in number.*

17. *Accordance.* The ablative is used with a few words to express the idea *in accordance with.*

mōre suō	*in accordance with his custom*

18. *With Dignus.* The ablative is used with **dignus** and **indignus.**

dignus patre	*worthy of his father*

19. *With Prepositions.* The ablative is used with the prepositions **ab, cum, dē, ex, prae, prō, sine;** sometimes with **in** and **sub** (see 14).

Locative

Domus and the names of towns and cities require a separate case, called the locative, to express *place where*. The locative has the same ending as the genitive in the singular of nouns of the first and second declensions; it has the same ending as the ablative in the plural of these declensions and in the third declension, singular and plural.

domī	*at home*
Rōmae	*at Rome*
Athēnīs	*at Athens*

Vocative

The vocative is used in addressing a person. Unless emphatic it never stands first.

Quid facis, amīce?	*What are you doing, my friend?*

Verb Syntax

Tenses

The tenses of the indicative in Latin are in general used like those in English, but the following points are to be noted.

1. *Present.* The Latin present has the force of the English simple present and of the progressive present.

Vocat.	*He calls.* or *He is calling.*

2. *Historical Present.* The historical present is used for vivid effect instead of a past tense in Latin as in English.

Rōmam proficīscuntur.	*They depart(ed) for Rome.*

a. In clauses introduced by **dum** meaning *while,* the historical present is always used. In translating use the English past.

dum haec geruntur	*while these things were going on*

3. *Imperfect.* The Latin imperfect expresses repeated, customary, or continous action in the past and is usually best translated by the English progressive past, sometimes by the auxiliary *would*, or by a phrase, such as *used to* or *kept on.*

Pugnābant.	*They were fighting.*

4. *Perfect.* The Latin perfect is generally equivalent to the English past, occasionally to the present perfect.

Vīcī.	*I conquered.* or *I have conquered.*

5. *Sequence of Tenses.* The subjunctive mood is used chiefly in subordinate clauses, in which its tenses are determined by the principle of "sequence of tenses," as shown in the following summary and examples:

a. PRIMARY TENSES (referring to the present or future)
Indicative: present, future, future perfect.
Subjunctive: present, perfect.

1. **Venit ut mē videat.** *He is coming to see me* (*that he may see me*).
2. **Veniet ut mē videat.** *He will come to see me* (*that he may see me*).
3. **Excesserō priusquam veniat.** *I shall have departed before he comes.*
4. **Rogō quid crās faciās** (or **factūrus sīs**). *I ask what you will do tomorrow.*
5. **Rogō quid herī fēcerīs.** *I ask what you did yesterday.*

b. SECONDARY TENSES (referring to the past)
Indicative: imperfect, perfect, past perfect.
Subjunctive: imperfect, past perfect.

1. **Vēnit ut mē vidēret.** *He came to see me* (*that he might see me*).
2. **Rogābam quid facerēs.** *I kept asking what you were doing.*
3. **Rogābam quid anteā fēcissēs.** *I kept asking what you had done before.*
4. **Excesseram priusquam venīret.** *I had departed before he came.*

Primary indicative tenses are followed by primary subjunctive tenses, secondary by secondary.

NOTĀ·BENE

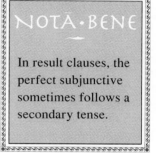

In result clauses, the perfect subjunctive sometimes follows a secondary tense.

Indicative Mood

The indicative mood is generally used in Latin as in English. The following points are to be noted.

1. *Relative Clauses.* Most relative clauses are in the indicative, as in English.
2. *Adverbial Clauses.* Clauses introduced by **postquam, posteāquam** (*after*), **ubi, ut** (*when*), **cum prīmum, simul ac** (*as soon as*), **dum** (*while, as long as*), **quamquam, etsī** (*although*) are in the indicative.

   Postquam id cōnspexit, signum dedit. *After he noticed this, he gave the signal.*

3. *Noun Clauses.* A clause introduced by **quod** (*the fact that, that*) is in the indicative and may be used as subject or object of the main verb or in apposition with a demonstative.

   Grātum est quod mē requīris. *It is gratifying that you miss me.*

Subjunctive Mood

1. *Volitive.* The volitive (**volō**) subjunctive represents an act as *willed* and is translated by *let.* The negative is **nē.**

Patriam dēfendāmus.	*Let us defend our country.*
Nē id videat.	*Let him not see it.*

2. *Purpose Clauses.* The subjunctive is used in a subordinate clause with **ut** or **utī** (negative **nē**) to express the purpose of the act expressed by the principal clause.

Venīmus ut videāmus.	*We come that we may see.* or *We come to see.*
Fugit nē videātur.	*He flees that he may not be seen.*

3. *Relative Purpose Clauses.* If the principal clause contains (or implies) a definite antecedent, the purpose clause may be introduced by the relative pronoun **quī** (= **ut is** or **ut eī**) instead of **ut.**

Mīlitēs mīsit quī hostem impedīrent.	*He sent soldiers to hinder the enemy.*

4. *Quō Purpose Clauses.* If the purpose clause contains an adjective or adverb in the comparative degree, **quō** is generally used instead of **ut.**

Accēdit quō facilius audiat.	*He approaches in order that he may hear more easily.*

(For other ways to express purpose see Dative, Future Passive Participle, Gerund.)

5. *Volitive Noun Clauses.* Clauses in the subjunctive with **ut** (negative **nē**) are used as the objects of such verbs as **moneō, rogō, petō, hortor, persuādeō,** and **imperō.**

Mīlitēs hortātus est ut fortēs essent.	*He urged the soldiers to be brave.*
Helvētiīs persuāsit ut exīrent.	*He persuaded the Helvetians to leave.*

6. *Clauses with Verbs of Hindering.* With verbs of hindering and preventing, as **impediō** and **dēterreō,** the subjunctive introduced by **nē** or **quō minus** is used if the main clause is affirmative, by **quīn** if negative.

Tū dēterrēre potes nē maior multitūdō trādūcātur.	*You can prevent a greater number from being brought over.*

7. *Clauses of Fear.* With verbs of fearing, clauses in the subjunctive introduced by **nē** (*that*) and **ut** (*that not*) are used.

Verēbātur nē tū aeger essēs.	*He feared that you were sick.*
Timuī ut venīrent.	*I was afraid that they would not come.*

NOTĀ·BENE

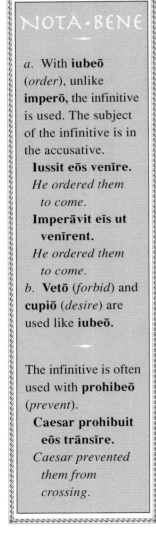

a. With **iubeō** (*order*), unlike **imperō,** the infinitive is used. The subject of the infinitive is in the accusative.

Iussit eōs venīre.
He ordered them to come.

Imperāvit eīs ut venīrent.
He ordered them to come.

b. **Vetō** (*forbid*) and **cupiō** (*desire*) are used like **iubeō.**

The infinitive is often used with **prohibeō** (*prevent*).

Caesar prohibuit eōs trānsīre.
Caesar prevented them from crossing.

8. *Result Clauses.* The result of the action or state of the principal verb is expressed by a subordinate clause with **ut (utī)**, negative **ut nōn (utī nōn)**, and the subjunctive.

Tantum est perīculum ut paucī veniant.	*So great is the danger that few are coming.*
Ita bene erant castra mūnīta ut nōn capī possent.	*So well had the camp been fortified that it could not be taken.*

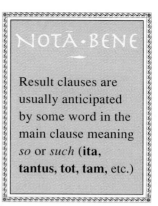

9. *Noun Clauses of Result.* Verbs meaning *to happen* **(accidō)** or *to cause* or *effect* **(efficiō)** require clauses of result in the subjunctive with **ut (utī)** or **ut (utī nōn,** used as subject or object of the main verb:

Accidit ut mē nōn vidēret.	*It happened that he did not see me.*
Efficiam ut veniat.	*I shall cause him to come.*

10. *Descriptive Relative Clauses.* A relative clause with the subjunctive may be used to describe an indefinite antecedent. Such clauses are called relative clauses of description (characteristic) and are especially common after such expressions as **ūnus** and **sōlus, sunt quī** (*there are those who*), and **nēmō est quī** (*there is no one who*).

11. ***Cum*** *Clauses.* In secondary sequence **cum** (*when*) is used with the imperfect of the past perfect subjunctive to describe the circumstances under which the action of the main verb occurred.

Cum mīlitēs redīssent, Caesar ōrātionem habuit.	*When the soldiers returned, Caesar made a speech.*

a. In some clauses **cum** with the subjunctive is best translated *since.*

Quae cum ita sint, nōn ībō.	*Since this is so, I shall not go* (literally, *When this is so*).

b. In some clauses **cum** with the subjunctive is best translated *although.*

Cum ea ita sint, tamen nōn ībō.	*Although this is so, yet I shall not go* (literally, *When,* etc.).

When **ut** means *although, granted that,* its clause is in the subjunctive.

12. *Anticipatory Clauses.* **Dum** (*until*), **antequam,** and **priusquam** (*before*) introduce clauses (*a*) in the indicative to indicate *an actual fact,* (*b*) in the subjunctive to indicate an act *as anticipated.*

Silentium fuit dum tū vēnistī.	*There was silence until you came.*
Caesar exspectāvit dum nāvēs convenīrent.	*Caesar waited until the ships should assemble.*
Priusquam tēlum adigī posset, omnēs fūgērunt.	*Before a weapon could be thrown, all fled.*

NOTĀ·BENE

Result clauses are usually anticipated by some word in the main clause meaning *so* or *such* (**ita, tantus, tot, tam,** etc.)

NOTĀ·BENE

Sometimes a descriptive clause expresses cause.

> **NOTĀ·BENE**
>
> The first member of a double indirect question is introduced by **utrum** or **–ne,** the second by **an.**
>
> **Quaerō utrum vērum an falsum sit.**
> *I ask whether it is true or false.*

13. *Indirect Questions.* In a question indirectly quoted or expressed after some introductory verb such as *ask, doubt, learn, know, tell, hear,* etc., the verb is in the subjunctive.

Rogant quis sit.	*They ask who he is.*

14. *Subordinate Clauses in Indirect Discourse.* An indicative in a subordinate clause becomes subjunctive in indirect discourse. If the clause is not regarded as an essential part of the quotation but is merely explanatory or parenthetical, its verb may be in the indicative.

Dīxit sē pecūniam invēnisse quam āmīsisset.	*He said that he found the money which he had lost.*

15. *Attraction.* A verb in a clause dependent upon a subjunctive or an infinitive, is frequently "attracted" to the subjunctive, especially if its clause is an essential part of the statement.

Dat negōtium hīs utī ea quae apud Belgās gerantur cognōscant.	*He directs them to learn what is going on among the Belgians.*

16. ***Quod*** *Causal Clauses.* Causal clauses introduced by **quod** (or **propterea quod**) and **quoniam** (*since, because*) are in the indicative when they give the writer's or speaker's reason, the subjunctive when the reason is presented as that of another person.

Amīcō grātiās ēgī quod mihi pecūniam dederat.	*I thanked my friend because he had given me money.*
Rōmānīs bellum intulit quod agrōs suōs vāstāvissent.	*He made war against the Romans because (as he alleged) they had laid waste his lands.*

Outline of Conditions

a. Subordinate clause ("condition") introduced by **sī, nisi,** or **sī nōn.**
b. Principal clause ("conclusion").

1. *Simple* (nothing implied as to truth). Any possible combination of tenses of the indicative, as in English.

Sī mē laudat, laetus sum.	*If he praises me, I am glad.*

2. *Contrary to Fact.*

a. Present: imperfect subjunctive in both clauses.

Sī mē laudāret, laetus essem.	*If he were praising me* (but he isn't), *I should be glad* (now).

b. Past: past perfect subjunctive in both clauses.

Sī nē laudāvisset, laetus fuissem.	*If he had praised me* (but he didn't), *I should have been glad* (then).

*c. Mixed:*past condition and present conclusion.

Sī mē laudāvisset, laetus essem.	*If he had praised me* (but he didn't), *I should be glad* (now).

3. *Future Less Vivid* ("should," "would"). Present subjunctive in both clauses.

Sī mē laudet, laetus sim.	*If he should praise me, I should be glad.*

Imperative Mood

Affimative commands are expressed by the imperative; negative commands by the present imperative of **nōlō (nōlī, nōlīte)** and the infinitive. The imperative with **nē** is used in poetry.

Amā inimīcōs tuōs.	*Love your enemies.*
Nōlīte īre.	*Do not go* (lit., *Be unwilling to go*).

Reflexive Use of the Passive

Occasionally the passive form of a verb or participle is used in a reflexive sense: **armārī,** *to arm themselves.*

Participle

1. The tenses of the participle (present, perfect, future) indicate time *present, past,* or *future* from the standpoint of the main verb.
2. *a.* Perfect participles are often used simply as adjectives: **nōtus,** *known.*
   b. Participles, like adjectives, may be used as nouns: **factum,** "having been done," *deed.*
3. The Latin participle is often a *one-word substitute* for a subordinate clause in English introduced by *who* or *which, when* or *after, since* or *because, although,* and *if.*

Future Passive Participle

The future passive participle (gerundive) is a verbal adjective, having thirty forms. It has two distinct uses:

1. As a predicate adjective with forms of **sum**[1] when it naturally indicates, as in English, *what must be done.* The person upon whom the obligation rests is in the dative.

Caesarī omnia erant agenda.	*Caesar had to do all things* (lit., *all things were to be done by Caesar*).

2. As modifier of a noun or pronoun in various constructions, with no idea of obligation:

dē Rōmā cōnstituendā	*about founding Rome* (lit. *about Rome to be founded*)

[1] The so-called passive periphrastic, a term not used in this book. The term should be avoided because it is not only useless but troublesome.

NOTĀ·BENE

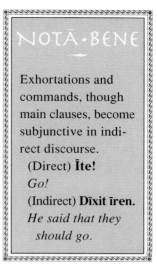

Exhortations and commands, though main clauses, become subjunctive in indirect discourse.
(Direct) **Īte!**
Go!
(Indirect) **Dīxit īren.**
He said that they should go.

NOTĀ·BENE

With phrases introduced by **ad** and the accusative or by **causā** (or **grātiā**) and the genitive it expresses purpose. **Causā** and **grātiā** are always placed after the participle.
Ad eās rēs cōnficiendās Mārcus dēligitur.
Marcus is chosen to accomplish these things (lit., *for these things to be accomplished*).
Caesaris videndī causā (or **grātiā**) **vēnit.**
He came for the sake of seeing Caesar (lit., *for the sake of Caesar to be seen*).

> **NOTĀ·BENE**
>
> The gerund usually does not have an object. Instead, the future passive participle is used, modifying the noun.

Gerund

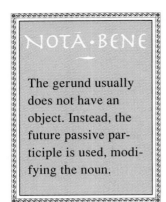

The gerund is a verbal noun of the second declension with only four forms—genitive, dative, accusative, and ablative singular.

The uses of the gerund are similar to some of those of the future passive participle:

cupidus bellandī	*desirous of waging war*
Ad discendum vēnī.	*I came for learning* (i.e., *to learn*).
Discendī causā (or **grātiā**) **vēnī.**	*I came for the sake of learning.*

Infinitive

1. The infinitive is an indeclinable neuter verbal noun, and as such it may be used as the subject of a verb.

Errāre hūmānum est.	*To err is human.*
Vidēre est crēdere.	*To see is to believe.*

2. With many verbs the infinitive, like other nouns, may be used as a direct object. (Sometimes called the complementary infinitive.)

Cōpiās movēre parat.	*He prepares to move the troops.*

3. The infinitive object of some verbs, such as **iubeō, volō, nōlō,** and **doceō,** often has a noun or pronoun subject in the accusative.

4. Statements that give indirectly the thoughts or words of another, used as the objects of verbs of *saying, thinking, knowing, hearing, perceiving,* etc., have verbs in the infinitive with their subjects in the accusative.

(Direct) **Dīcit, "Puerī veniunt."**	*He says, "The boys are coming."*
(Indirect) **Dīcit puerōs venīre.**	*He says that the boys are coming.*

> **NOTĀ·BENE**
>
> With the passive third singular (impersonal) of these verbs the infinitive is the subject.
>
> **Caesarī nūntiātur eōs trānsīre.**
>
> *It is reported to Caesar that they are crossing.*

5. *a.* The present infinitive represents time or actions as *going on,* from the standpoint of the introductory verb:

Dīcit / **Dīxit** } **eōs pugnāre.** He { *says* / *said* } (*that*) *they* { *are* / *were* } *fighting.*

b. The future infinitive represents time or actions as *subsequent to* that of the introductory verb:

Dīcit / **Dīxit** } **eōs pugnātūrōs esse.** He { *says* / *said* } (*that*) *they* { *will* / *would* } *fight.*

c. The perfect infinitive represents time or action as *completed before* that of the introductory verb:

Dīcit / **Dīxit** } **eōs pugnāvisse.** He { *says* / *said* } (*that*) *they* { *have* / *had* } *fought.*

Summary of Prefixes and Suffixes

Prefixes

Many Latin words are formed by joining prefixes (**prae,** *in front;* **fīxus,** *attached*) to *root* words. These same prefixes, most of which are prepositions, are also those used most often in English.

Some prefixes change their final consonants to make them like the initial consonants of the words to which they are attached. This change is called assimilation (**ad,** *to;* **similis,** *like*).

Many prefixes in Latin and English may have intensive force, especially **con–, ex–, ob–, per–.** They are then best translated either by an English intensive, such as *up* or *out,* or by an adverb, such as *completely, thoroughly, deeply.* Thus **commoveō** means *move greatly,* **permagnus,** *very great,* **obtineō,** *hold on to,* **concitō,** *rouse up,* **excipiō,** *catch, receive.*

1. **ab (abs, ā),** *from:* **abs-tineō;** *ab-undance, abs-tain, a-vocation.*
2. **ad,** *to, toward:* **ad-iciō;** *ac-curate, an-nounce, ap-paratus, ad-vocate.*
3. **ante,** *before:* **ante-cēdō;** *ante-cedent.*
4. **bene,** *well:* **bene-dīcō;** *bene-factor.*
5. **bi–, bis–,** *twice, two:* **bi-ennium;** *bi-ennial.*
6. **circum,** *around:* **circum-eō;** *circum-ference.*
7. **con–,** *with, together:* **con-vocō;** *con-voke, col-lect, com-motion, cor-rect.*
8. **contrā,** *against: contra-dict.*
9. **dē,** *from, down from, not:* **dē-ferō;** *de-ter.*
10. **dis–,** *apart, not:* **dis-cēdō;** *dis-locate, dif-fuse, di-vert.*
11. **ex (ē),** *out of, from:* **ex-eō;** *ex-port, e-dit, ef-fect.*
12. **extrā,** *outside: extra-legal.*
13. **in,** *in, into, against:* **in-dūcō;** *in-habit, im-migrant, il-lusion, en-chant.*
14. **in–,** *not, un–:* **im-mēnsus;** *il-legal, im-moral, ir-regular.*
15. **inter,** *between, among:* **inter-clūdō;** *inter-class.*
16. **intrā,** *within, inside: intra-collegiate.*
17. **intrō–,** *within: intro-duce.*
18. **male,** *ill: male-factor, mal-formation.*
19. **multi–,** *much, many: multi-graph.*
20. **nōn,** *not: non-sense.*
21. **ob,** *against, toward:* **ob-tineō;** *oc-cur, of-fer, o-mit, op-pose, ob-tain.*
22. **per,** *through, thoroughly:* **per-moveō;** *per-fect.*
23. **post,** *after: post-pone.*
24. **prae,** *before, in front of:* **prae-ficiō;** *pre-cede.*
25. **prō,** *for, forward:* **prō-dūcō;** *pro-mote.*
26. **re– (red–),** *back, again:* **re-dūcō, red-igō;** *re-fer.*
27. **sē–,** *apart from:* **sē-cēdō;** *se-parate.*
28. **sēmi–,** *half, partly:* **sēmi-barbarus;** *semi-annual.*
29. **sub,** *under, up from under:* **suc-cēdō;** *suf-fer, sug-gest, sup-port, sub-let.*
30. **super (sur–),** *over, above:* **super-sum;** *super-fluous, sur-mount.*
31. **trāns (trā–),** *through, across:* **trā-dūcō;** *trans-fer.*
32. **ultrā,** *extremely: ultra-fashionable.*
33. **ūn– (ūni–),** *one: uni-form.*

Suffixes

Particles that are attached to the ends of words are called suffixes (**sub,** *under, after;* **fīxus,** *attached*). Like the Latin prefixes, the Latin suffixes play a very important part in the formation of English words.

The meaning of suffixes is often far less definite than that of prefixes. In many cases they merely indicate the part of speech.

Suffixes are often added to words that already have suffixes. Thus, *functionalistically* has six suffixes, all of Latin or Greco-Latin origin except the last. A suffix often combines with a preceding letter or letters to form a new suffix. This is especially true of suffixes added to perfect participles whose base ends in **–s–** or **–t–**. In the following list no account is taken of such English suffixes as *–ant,* derived from the ending of the Latin present participle.

1. **–ālis** (*–al*), *pertaining to:* **līber-ālis;** *annu-al.*
2. **–ānus** (*–an, –ane, –ain*), *pertaining to:* **Rōm-ānus;** *capt-ain, hum-ane.*
3. **–āris** (*–ar*), *pertaining to:* **famili-āris;** *singul-ar.*
4. **–ārium** (*–arium, –ary*), *place where: aqu-arium, gran-ary.*
5. **–ārius** (*–ary*), *pertaining to:* **frūment-ārius;** *ordin-ary.*
6. **–āticum** (*–age*): *bagg-age.*
7. **–āx** (*–ac–ious*), *tending to:* **aud-āx;** *rap-acious.*
8. **–faciō, –ficō** (*–fy*), *make:* **cōn-ficiō;** *satis-fy.*
9. **–ia** (*–y*), **–cia, –tia** (*–ce*), **–antia** (*–ance, –ancy*), **–entia** (*–ence, –ency*), *condition of:* **memor-ia, grā-tia, cōnst-antia, sent-entia;** *memor-y, provin-ce, gra-ce, const-ancy, sent-ence.*
10. **–icus** (*–ic*), *pertaining to:* **pūbl-icus;** *civ-ic.*
11. **–idus** (*–id*), *having the quality of:* **rap-idus;** *flu-id.*
12. **–ilis** (*–ile, –il*), **–bilis** (*–ble, –able, –ible*), *able to be:* **fac-ilis, laudā-bilis;** *fert-ile, no-ble, compar-able, terr-ible.*
13. **–īlis** (*–ile, –il*), *pertaining to:* **cīv-īlis;** *serv-ile.*
14. **–īnus** (*–ine*), *pertaining to:* **mar-īnus;** *div-ine.*
15. **–iō** (*–ion*), **–siō** (*–sion*), **–tiō** (*–tion*), *act* or *state of:* **reg-iō, mān-siō, ōrā-tiō;** *commun-ion, ten-sion, rela-tion.*
16. **–ium** (*–y*), **–cium, –tium** (*–ce*): **remed-ium, sōlā-cium, pre-tium;** *stud-y, edifi-ce.*
17. **–īvus** (*–ive*), *pertaining to:* **capt-īvus;** *nat-ive.*
18. **–lus, ellus, –ulus** (*–lus, –le*) *little* ("diminutive"): **parvu-lus, castel-lum;** *gladio-lus, parti-cle.*
19. **–men** (*–men, –min, –me*): **lū-men;** *cri-min-al, cri-me.*
20. **–mentum** (*–ment*), *means of:* **im-pedī-mentum;** *comple-ment.*
21. **–or** (*–or*), *state of:* **tim-or;** *terr-or.*
22. **–or, –sor, –tor** (*–sor, –tor*), *one who:* **scrīp-tor;** *inven-tor.*
23. **–ōrium** (*–orium, –ory, –or*) *place where: audit-orium, fact-ory, mirr-or.*
24. **–ōsus** (*–ous, –ose*), *full of:* **ōti-ōsus;** *copi-ous.*
25. **–tās** (*–ty*), *state of:* **līber-tās;** *integri-ty.*
26. **–tō, –sō, –itō,** *keep on* ("frequentative"): **dic-tō, prēn-sō, vent-itō.**
27. **–tūdō** (*–tude*), *state of:* **magni-tūdō;** *multi-tude.*
28. **–tūs** (*–tue*), *state of:* **vir-tūs;** *vir-tue.*
29. **–ūra, –sūra, –tūra** (*–ure, –sure, –ture*): **fig-ūra, mēn-sūra, agricul-tūra;** *proced-ure, pres-sure, na-ture.*

Vocabulary

Latin–English

Verbs of the first conjugation whose parts are regular (i.e., like **portō**, p. 463) are indicated by the figure 1. Proper names are not included unless they are spelled differently in English or are difficult to pronounce in English. Their English pronunciation is indicated by a simple system. The vowels are as follows: ā as in *hate,* ă as in *hat,* ē as in *feed,* ĕ as in *fed,* ī as in *bite,* ĭ as in *bit,* ō as in *hope,* ŏ as in *hop,* ū as in *cute,* ŭ as in *cut.* In the ending *ēs* the *s* is soft as in *rose.* When the accented syllable ends in a consonant, the vowel is short; otherwise it is long.

A

A., *abbreviation for* **Aulus, –ī,** *m.,* Aulus
ā, ab, abs, *prep. w. abl.,* from, by
abdō, –ere, abdidī, abditus, put away, hide
abdūcō, –ere, abdūxī, abductus, lead *or* take away
abeō, abīre, abiī, abitūrus, go away, depart; change (into)
abiciō, –ere, abiēcī, abiectus, throw away
abrogō, 1, repeal
abscīdō, –ere, –cīdī, –cīsus, cut away
absēns, *gen.* **absentis,** absent
absentia, –ae, *f.,* absence
abstineō, –ēre, –tinuī, –tentus, hold away; refrain
abstulī, *see* **auferō**
absum, –esse, āfuī, āfutūrus, be away, be absent
abundō, 1, be well supplied
ac, *see* **atque**
accēdō, –ere, accessī, accessūrus, come to, approach, be added
accidō, –ere, accidī, —, fall, happen
accīdō, –ere, accīdī, accīsus, cut into
accipiō, –ere, accēpī, acceptus, receive, accept, be told
accommodō, 1, fit (on)
accumbō, –ere, accubuī, accubitūrus, recline (at the table)
accūrātē, *adv.,* carefully
accurrō, –ere, accurrī, accursūrus, run
accūsō, 1, blame, criticize
ācer, ācris, ācre, sharp, keen, fierce
acerbē, *adv.,* severely
acerbitās, –tātis, *f.,* bitterness; suffering
acerbus, –a, –um, sour, bitter
Achaia, –ae, *f.,* Achaia (Akā´ya), Greece
aciēs, aciēī, *f.,* battle line
ācriter, *adv.,* fiercely; *comp.* **ācrius;** *superl.* **ācerrimē**
Actium, –tī, *n.,* Actium (Ak´shĭum), *a promontory in Epirus*
acūtus, –a, –um, sharp
ad, *prep. w. acc.,* to, toward, for, near, at, until; *adv., w. numbers,* about
adāctus, *part of* **adigō**
adaequō, 1, equal
addō, –ere, addidī, additus, add
addūcō, –ere, addūxī, adductus, lead (to), pull in, bring, influence; contract
adeō, adīre, adiī, aditūrus, go to, approach
adeō, *adv.,* so, so much
adfore, *fut. inf. of* **adsum**
adhaereō, –ēre, adhaesī, adhaesus, stick (to)
adhibeō, –ēre, adhibuī, adhibitus, hold toward; admit to, use
adhūc, *adv.,* up to this time, still
adiciō, –ere, adiēcī, adiectus, add
adigō, –ere, adēgī, adāctus, bring (to), bring near, throw (to)
aditus, –ūs, *m.,* approach, access
adiungō, –ere, adiūnxī, adiūnctus, join to
administrō, 1, manage, perform
admīrātiō, –ōnis, *f.,* admiration
admīror, 1, wonder (at), admire
admittō, –ere, admīsī, admissus, send to, let in, commit, admit
admodum, *adv.,* very (much)
admoneō, –ēre, admonuī, admonitus, remind, advise
admoveō, –ēre, admōvī, admōtus, move (to)
adoptiō, –ōnis, *f.,* adoption
adoptō, 1, adopt
adorior, adorīrī, adortus, rise up to, attack
adōrnātus, –a, –um, decorated
adōrō, 1, worship
adsum, adesse, adfuī, adfutūrus, be near, be present, come
adulēscēns, –entis, *m.,* young man, youth

adulēscentia, –ae, *f.,* youth
adveniō, –īre, advēnī, adventūrus, approach
adventus, –ūs, *m.,* arrival, approach
adversārius, –rī, *m.,* opponent
adversus, –a, –um, facing, opposite, unfavorable
aedificium, –cī, *n.,* building
aedificō, 1, build
aedīlis, –is, *m.,* aedile (*an official*)
aeger, aegra, aegrum, sick
aegrē, *adv.,* with difficulty, reluctantly; *w.* **ferre,** be indignant (at)
Aegyptus, –ī, *f.,* Egypt
aēneus, –a, –um, (of) bronze, copper
Aequī, –ōrum, *m.,* the Aequians (Ē´quians), *a people of Italy*
aequitās, –tātis, *f.,* fairness
aequō, 1, make equal
aequus, –a, –um, equal, fair, calm
āēr, āeris, *m.,* air
aes, aeris, *n.,* bronze, money, bronze statue; **aes aliēnum,** (another's money), debt
Aesculāpius, –pī, *m.,* Aesculapius (Esculā´pius), *god of healing*
Aesōpus, –ī, *m.,* Aesop (Ē´sop), *writer of fables*
aestās, –tātis, *f.,* summer
aestimātiō, –ōnis, *f.,* estimate
aestimō, 1, estimate
aestus, –ūs, *m.,* heat; tide
aetās, –tātis, *f.,* age, time of life
aeternitās, –tātis, *f.,* immortality
aeternus, –a, –um, eternal
Aethiopēs, –um, *m. pl.,* the Ethiopians, *a people of Africa*
affātus, –ūs, *m.,* speech
afferō, afferre, attulī, allātus, bring (to), assign, report
afficiō, –ere, affēcī, affectus, affect, afflict, visit, fill (with joy, *etc.*), move
affīgō, –ere, affīxī, affīxus, fasten to
afflīctō, 1, wreck
afflīgō, –ere, afflīxī, afflīctus, throw down, afflict, damage
Āfrī, –ōrum, *m. pl,* the Africans, Carthaginians; **Āfricānus, –a, –um,** African; *as noun, m.,* an African; Africā´nus, *an honorary name of Scipio*
ager, agrī, *m.,* field, land, farm, country
agger, aggeris, *m.,* mound, rampart
aggredior, aggredī, aggressus, attack
aggregō, 1, attach
agitō, 1, carry on; shake
agmen, –minis, *n.,* line of march, column; **novissimum agmen,** rear; **prīmum agmen,** front
agnōscō, –ere, agnōvī, agnitus, recognize
agnus, –ī, *m.,* lamb
agō, –ere, ēgī, āctus, drive, move forward; live *or* spend (*of time*), live (a life); do, perform; discuss, plead; carry on; **grātiās agō,** thank; **quid agit,** how is; **vītam agō,** lead a life
agricola, –ae, *m.,* farmer
ait, (he) says
ala, –ae, *f.,* wing
alacer, –cris, –cre, eager
alacritās, –tātis, *f.,* eagerness
Albānus, –a, –um, Alban; *as noun, m.,* an Alban
albus, –a, –um, white
alces, –is, *f.,* elk
Alesia, –ae, *f.,* Alē´sia, now Alise-Sainte-Reine
Alexander, –drī, *m.,* Alexander
Alexandrīa, –ae, *f.,* Alexandria, *a city in Eqypt*
aliēnus, –a, –um, another's, unfavorable, out of place
aliquī, aliqua, aliquod, *adj.,* some(one), any
aliquis, aliquid, someone, some, any, something, anything
aliter, *adv.,* otherwise
alius, alia, aliud, other, another; **alius... alius,** one . . . another; **aliī... aliī,** some . . . others; **quid aliud,** what else.
allātus, *part. of* **afferō**
Allobrogēs, –um, *m. pl.,* the Allobroges (Allŏb´rojēs)
alloquor, alloquī, allocūtus, address
alō, –ere, aluī, alitus, support, feed, nourish, raise
Alpēs, –ium, *f. pl.,* the Alps
altē, *adv.,* high, deeply
alter, altera, alterum, the other (*of two*), another, the second; **alter... alter,** the one . . . the other
altitūdō, –dinis, *f.,* height, depth
altus, –a, –um, high, deep, tall
amābilis, –e, lovely
amanter, *adv.,* lovingly
ambō, –ae, –ō, both
ambulō, 1, walk
amīcitia, –ae, *f.,* friendship
amīcus, –a, –um, friendly; **amīcus, –ī,** *m.,* friend; **amīca, ae,** *f.,* (girl) friend
āmittō, –ere, āmīsī, āmissus, let go, lose
amō, 1, love, like
amor, –ōris, *m.,* love, affection
amphitheātrum, –ī, *n.,* amphitheater
amplē, *adv.,* fully; *comp.* **amplius,** more
amplificō, 1, increase
amplitūdō, –dinis, *f.,* size
amplius, *see* **amplē**
amplus, –a, –um, great; distinguished, magnificent
an, *conj.,* or, *introducing the second part of a double question*
ancīle, –is, *n.,* shield
ancora, –ae, *f.,* anchor
anguis, –is, *m. and f.,* snake, serpent
angulus, –ī, *m.,* corner, little place
angustiae, –ārum, *f. pl.,* narrowness, narrow pass
angustus, –a, –um, narrow, small
anima, –ae, *f.,* soul, spirit
animadvertō, –ere, –vertī, –versus, turn attention, notice
animal, –ālis, *n.,* animal

animus, –ī, *m.,* mind, spirit, courage, feeling; **in animō est,** intend; **in animō habeō,** plan
Aniō, Aniēnis, *m.,* the Ăn´io river
annus, –ī, *m.,* year
ante, *adv. and prep. w. acc.,* before (*of time and space*); *see* **antequam**
anteā, *adv.,* before
antecēdō, –ere, –cessī, –cessūrus, go before; surpass
anteferō, –ferre, –tulī, –lātus, prefer
antemna, ae, *f.,* yardarm (*of a ship; the spar to which sails are fastened*)
antequam (ante... quam), *conj.,* before
antīquitās, –tātis, *f.,* antiquity
antīquitus, *adv.,* long ago
antīquus, –a, –um, ancient
Antōnius, –nī, *m.,* Antony
antrum, –ī, *n.,* cave
ānxius, –a, –um, troubled
aperio, –īre, aperuī, apertus, open, reveal; **apertus,** open, exposed
apertē, *adv.,* openly, manifestly
apertus, –a, –um, open
Apollō, –inis, *m.,* Apŏl´lo, *god of music, prophecy, and medicine*
appāreō, –ēre, appāruī, appāritūrus, appear
appellō, 1, call, call upon, speak to
appellō, –ere, appulī, appulsus, land, drive to, bring up
appetō, –ere, appetīvī, appetītus, seek; approach
Appius, –a, –um, of Ăp´pius, Ăp´pian; *as noun, m.,* Ăp´pius
applicō, 1, apply (to); lean against
appōnō, –ere, apposuī, appositus, set before, serve
appropinquō, 1, come near to, approach *(w. dat.)*
aptus, –a, –um, suited; **aptē,** *adv.,* suitably

apud, *prep. w. acc.,* among, at the house of, near, with
aqua, –ae, *f.,* water
aquaeductus, –ūs, *m.,* aqueduct
aquila, –ae, *f.,* Aquilē´ia, *a town of Cisalpine Gaul;* eagle
Aquītānia, –ae, *f.,* Aquitā´nia; **Aquītānus, –a, –um,** Aquitā´nian
āra, –ae, *f.,* altar
Arar, –aris, *acc.* **–im,** *abl.* **–ī,** *m.,* Arar river, *now* Saône
arbitrium, –trī, *n.,* decision, judgment
arbitror, 1, think
arbor, –oris, *f.,* tree
arboreus, –a, –um, of a tree
arcessō, –ere, –īvī, –ītus, summon, send for
architectus, –ī, *m.,* architect
ārdeō, –ēre, ārsī, ārsūrus, burn, be eager
arduus, –a, –um, steep, hard
ārea, –ae, *f.,* courtyard
arēna, –ae, *f.,* sand, arena
argentum, –ī, *n.,* silver
āridum, –ī, *n.,* dry land
aridus, –a, –um, dry
ariēs, –ietis, *m.,* ram, battering-ram
Aristotelēs, –is, *m.,* Ăr´istŏtle, *a Greek philosopher*
arma, –ōrum, *m. pl.,* arms, armor
armāmenta, –ōrum, *n. pl.,* equipment
armātūra, –ae, *f.,* armor; **levis armātūrae,** light-armed
armō, 1, arm, equip
arō, 1, plow
arripiō, –ere, arripuī, arreptus, seize
arrogantia, –ae, *f.,* insolence
ars, artis, *f.,* skill, art
artus, –ūs, *m.,* limb
Arvernus, –ī, *m.,* an Arver´nian
arx, arcis, *f.,* citadel
ascendō, –ere, ascendī, ascēnsus, climb (up); embark
ascēnsus, –ūs, *m.,* ascent
ascrībō, –ere, ascrīpsī, ascrīptus, add to (*in writing*), apply

aspectus, –ūs, *m.,* appearance, sight
asper, –era, –erum, harsh
aspiciō, –ere, aspexī, aspectus, look on *or* at
assistō, –ere, astitī, —, stand
assuēscō, –ere, assuēvī, assuētus, become accustomed
astronomus, –ī, *m.,* astronomer
astrum, –ī, *n.,* star
at, *conj.,* but
āter, ātra, ātrum, black, gloomy
Athēna, –ae, *f.,* Athena, *Greek goddess of wisdom, the Roman Minerva*
Athēnae, –ārum, *f. pl.,* Athens
Athēniēnsis, –is, *adj. and n.,* Athenian
atomus, –ī, *f.,* atom
atque (ac), *conj.,* and, as than
Atrebās, –ātis, *m.,* an Atrebatian (Atrebā´shian)
ātrium, ātrī, *n.,* atrium, hall
attingō, –ere, attigī, attāctus, touch, reach, border
attribuō, –ere, attribuī, attribūtus, assign
auctor, –ōris, *m.,* author, founder
auctōritās, –tātis, *f.,* authority, influence
audācia, –ae, *f.,* daring, boldness
audācter, *adv.,* boldly
audāx, *gen.* **audācis,** daring, bold
audeō, –ēre, ausus, *semideponent,* dare
audiō, –īre, –īvī, –ītus, hear, hear of
auferō, auferre, abstulī, ablātus, take away
augeō, –ēre, auxī, auctus, increase, enlarge, make grow
augēscō, –ere, —, —, increase
augustus, –a, –um, magnificent; (*cap.*), of Augustus; August; *as noun, m.,* Augus´tus, *the emperor*
Aulercus, –ī, *m.,* an Auler´can
aureus, –a, –um, of gold, golden

aurīga, –ae, *m.,* charioteer
auris, –is, *f.,* ear
aurum, –ī, *n.,* gold
auspicium, –cī, *n.,* auspices
aut, or; **aut... aut,** either . . . or
autem, *conj.* (*never first word*), however, but, moreover
auxilior, 1, help
auxilium, –lī, *n.,* help, aid; *pl.,* auxiliary troops, reserves
avāritia, –ae, *f.,* greed
avārus, –a, –um, avaricious
Aventīnus (mōns), –ī, *m.,* the Av´entīne Hill
āvertō, –ere, āvertī, āversus, turn away, turn aside
avidus, –a, –um, desirous, greedy
avis, –is, *f.,* bird
āvocō, 1, call away
avunculus, ī, *m.,* uncle
avus, –ī, *m.,* grandfather
Axona, –ae, *m.,* Axona river, *now* Aisne

B

balneum, –ī, *n.,* bath
balteus, –ī, *m.,* belt
barbarus, –a, –um, foreign, barbarous; *as noun, m.,* barbarian
beātus, –a, –um, happy
Belgae, –ārum, *m. pl,* the Belgians
bellicōsus, –a, –um, warlike
bellicus, –a, –um, of war
bellō, 1, carry on war
bellum, –ī, *n.,* war; **bellum gerō,** carry on war; *(with dat.)* **bellum īnferō,** make war upon
bene, *adv.,* well, good; *comp.* **melius,** better; *superl.* **optimē,** best
beneficium, –cī, *n.,* kindness
benignus, –a, –um, kindly
bibliothēca, –ae, *f.,* library
bibō, –ere, bibī, —, drink
Bibracte, –actis, *n.,* Bibrăc´te, *now* Mont Beauvray *near Autun*
bīduum, –ī, *n.,* two days
biennium, –nī, *n.,* two years
bīnī, –ae, –a, two at a time
bis, *adv.,* twice
blanditia, –ae, *f.,* caress
blandus, –a, –um, caressing
bonitās, –tātis, *f.,* goodness, fertility
bonus, –a, –um, good; *comp.* **melior, melius,** better; *superl.* **optimus, –a, –um,** best; **bona, –ōrum,** *n.,* possessions
bōs, bovis (*gen. pl.,* **boum**), *m.,* ox, bull
bracchium, bracchī, *n.,* arm
brevis, –e, short
brevitās, –tātis, *f.,* shortness
Britannia, –ae, *f.,* Britain
Britannus, –ī, *m.,* a Briton
Brundisium, –sī, *n.,* Brundisium (Brundizh´ium), *a town in Italy, now* Brindisi
bulla, –ae, *f.,* fulla, *an ornament worn on the neck by children*

C

C., *abbreviation for* **Gāius**
cacūmen, –minis, *n.,* peak
cadāver, –eris, *n.,* corpse
cadō, –ere, cecidī, cāsūrus, fall
Caecilius, –a, –um, Caecilian (Sēsil´ian); **Caedilius, –lī,** *m.,* Caecilius; **Caecilia, –ae,** *f.,* Caecilia
caecus, –a, –um, blind
caedēs, –is, *f.,* slaughter, murder
caedō, –ere, cecīdī, caesus, cut (down), beat, kill
caelestis, –e, heavenly
Caelius (mōns), –ī, *m.,* the Caelian (Sē´lian) Hill
caelum, –ī, *n.,* sky
caeruleus, –a, –um, blue
Caesar, –aris, *m.,* Caesar
calamitās, –tātis, *f.,* disaster, defeat
calceus, –ī, *m.,* shoe
calidus, –a, –um, hot
callidus, –a, –um, clever
cālō, –ōnis, *m.,* camp servant
campus, –ī, *m.,* plain, field; **campus Mārtius, campī Mārtiī,** *m.,* Campus Martius (Mar´shius), *a park in Rome*
candidātus, –ī, *m.,* candidate
canis, –is, *m.,* dog
Cannae, –ārum, *f. pl.,* Cannae (Can´ē), *a town in Italy*
canō, –ere, cecinī, cantus, sing, tell (about)
Cantium, –tī, *n.,* Kent, *a district in Britain*
cantō, 1, sing
Capēna (porta), porta Capena (Capē´na), *a gate in the wall of Rome*
caper, –rī, *m.,* goat
capillus, –ī, *m.,* hair
capiō, –ere, cēpī, captus, take, seize, capture, hold, receive; captivate; adopt
Capitōlium, –lī, *n.,* the Capitol, *temple of Jupiter at Rome;* the Capitoline Hill
captīva, –ae, *f.,* (female) prisoner; **captīvus, –ī,** *m.,* prisoner
captō, 1, strive
caput, capitis, *n.,* head, person
careō, –ere, caruī, caritūrus, be without *(+ abl.)*
cāritās, –tātis, *f.,* affection
carmen, –minis, *n.,* song, poem
Carneadēs, –is, *m.,* Carnē´adēs, *a Greek philosopher*
carō, carnis, *f.,* meat
carpō, –ere, carpsī, carptus, pick; take; consume
carrus, –ī, *m.,* cart, wagon
Carthāginiēnsēs, –ium, *m. pl.,* the Carthaginians (Carthajin´ians)
Carthāgō, –ginis, *f.,* Carthage, *a city in northern Africa*
cārus, –a, –um, dear, expensive, esteemed
cāseus, –ī, *m.,* cheese
Castalius, –a, –um, Castā´lian
castellum, –ī, *n.,* fort
castīgō, 1, punish
castra, –ōrum, *n. pl.,* camp
cāsus, –ūs, *m.,* chance, accident, misfortune, fate, emergency
Catilīna, –ae, *m.,* Căt´ilīne
cauda, –ae, *f.,* tail
causa, –ae, *f.,* cause, reason; case; **causā,** for the sake of (*w. gen. preceding*)

caveō, –ēre, cāvī, cautūrus, beware (of), take precautions against
cecīdī, *see* **caedō**
cēdō, –ere, cessī, cessūrus, move, retreat, yield
celeber, –bris, –bre, celebrated
celer, celeris, celere, swift
celeritās, –tātis, *f.,* swiftness, speed
celeriter, swiftly, quickly
cēlō, 1, hide, conceal
celsus, –a, –um, high
cēna, –ae, *f.,* dinner
cēnō, 1, dine
cēnseō, –ēre, cēnsuī, cēnsus, think
cēnsus, –ūs, *m.,* census
centum, *indeclinable adj.,* hundred
centuriō, –ōnis, *m.,* centurion
Cerēs, Cereris, *f.,* Ceres (Sē´rēs), *goddess of agriculture*
cernō, –ere, crēvī, crētus, separate, see
certāmen, –minis, *n.,* contest, struggle
certē, *adv.,* certainly, at least
certō, 1, strive
certus, –a, –um, fixed, certain, sure; **certiōrem eum faciō dē,** inform him about; **certior fīō,** be informed
cervus, –ī, *m.,* deer, stag
cēterī, –ae, –a, the other(s), the rest (of), all other
Christus, –ī, *m.,* Christ
cibus, –ī, *m.,* food
cingō, –ere, cīnxī, cīnctus, surround
cinis, cineris, *m.,* ashes
circēnsis, –e, of the circus
circiter, *adv.,* about
circuitus, –ūs, *m.,* distance around
circulus, –ī, *m.,* circle
circum, *prep. w. acc.,* around
circumclūdō, –ere, –clūsī, –clūsus, surround
circumcursō, 1, run around
circumdō, –dare, –dedī, –datus, put around, surround
circumiciō, –ere, –iēcī, –iectus, throw around
circumsiliō, –īre, –siluī, —, hop around
circumsistō, –ere, –stetī, —, surround
circumstō, –āre, –stetī, —, stand around
circumveniō, –īre, –vēnī, –ventus, surround; cheat
circus, –ī, *m.,* circle; circus; **Circus Maximus,** the Circus Maximus, *at Rome*
citerior, –ius, nearer
cito, *adv.,* quickly; *comp.* **citius,** sooner
citrā, *prep. w. acc.,* on this side of
cīvīlis, –e, civil
cīvis, –is, *m.,* citizen
cīvitās, –tātis, *f.,* citizenship, state
clam, *adv.,* secretly
clāmō, 1, cry (out), shout, declare, exclaim
clāmor, –ōris, *m.,* shout
clārus, –a, –um, clear, loud; famous
classis, –is, *f.,* fleet
claudō, –ere, clausī, clausus, close
clēmentia, –ae, *f.,* clemency, mercy
cliēns, –entis, *m.,* client
clientēla, –ae, *f.,* clientship
cloāca, –ae, *f.,* sewer
Cn., *abbreviation for* **Gnaeus, –ī,** *m.,* Gnaeus (Nē´us)
Cnidiī, –ōrum, *m. pl.,* the Cnidians (Nĭd´ians)
coacervō, 1, pile up
coctus, –a, –um, cooked
coemētērium, –rī, *n.,* cemetery
coeō, coīre, coiī, coitūrus, meet
coepī, coeptus (*perf. tenses only*), began, have begun
cōgitātiō, –ōnis, *f.,* thought
cōgitō, 1, think, consider
cognātiō, –ōnis, *f.,* related group
cognōmen, –minis, *n.,* cognomen, surname
cognōscō, –ere, –nōvī, –nitus, become acquainted with, learn, recognize; *perf.,* have learned, know
cōgō, –ere, coēgī, coāctus, drive together, collect, compel
cohors, cohortis, *f.,* cohort
cohortātiō, –ōnis, *f.,* encouragement
cohortor, 1, encourage
Colchī, –ōrum, *m. pl.,* the Colchians (Kol´kians)
colligō, 1, fasten together
colligō, –ere, –lēgī, –lēctus, collect, acquire
collis, –is, *m.,* hill
collocō, 1, place, invest, station
colloquium, –quī, *n.,* conference
colloquor, colloquī, collocūtus, talk with, confer
collum, –ī, *n.,* neck
colō, –ere, coluī, cultus, cultivate, inhabit, worship
colōnia, –ae, *f.,* colony
color, –ōris, *m.,* color
columna, –ae, *f.,* column
combūrō, –ere, –ussī, –ustus, burn up
comes, –itis, *m. and f.,* companion
Comitium, –tī, *n.,* Comitium (Comish´ium), *the assembly place of the Romans;* **comitia, –ōrum,** *n. pl.,* assemblies, election
commeātus, –ūs, *m.,* (going to and fro), supplies
commemorō, 1, mention
commendō, 1, entrust
commentārius, –rī, *m.,* commentary, notes
commīlitō, –ōnis, *m.,* fellow soldier
committō, –ere, –mīsī, –missus, commit, do, entrust; **proelium committō,** begin battle
commodē, *adv.,* well, suitably, effectively
commodus, –a, –um, suitable, convenient, well

commoveō, –ēre, –mōvī, –mōtus, move (away), disturb, stir up; influence
commūnicō, 1, share
commūniō, –īre, –īvī, –ītus, fortify on all sides
commūnis, –e, common
commūtātiō, –ōnis, *f.,* change
commūtō, 1, change wholly, exchange
comparō, 1, prepare, get ready; procure
compellō, –ere, –pulī, –pulsus, drive (together), collect
comperiō, –īre, –perī, –pertus, find out
competītor, –ōris, *m.,* competitor
complaceō = placeō
compleō, –ēre, –ēvī, –ētus, fill, cover, complete
complexus, –ūs, *m.,* embrace
complūrēs, –a *or* **–ia,** several, many
compōnō, –ere, –posuī, –positus, put together, compose
comportō, 1, collect
comprehendō, –ere, –hendī, –hēnsus, seize, grasp, catch, understand
cōnātus, –ūs, *m.,* attempt
concēdō, –ere, –cessī, –cessūrus, yield, withdraw, grant, permit
concidō, –ere, –cidī, —, fall down, collapse
concīdō, –ere, –cīdī, –cīsus, cut up, kill
concilium, –lī, *n.,* meeting, council
concipiō, –ere, –cēpī, –ceptus, conceive
concitō, 1, rouse
concordia, –ae, *f.,* harmony
concurrō, –ere, –currī, –cursūrus, run *or* dash together, rush, flock
concursus, –ūs, *m.,* running together, gathering, onset
condēnsātus, –a, –um, condensed
condiciō, –ōnis, *f.,* condition, terms
condīmentum, –ī, *n.,* seasoning
condō, –ere, –didī, –ditus, found, establish, make; conceal
condūcō, –ere, –dūxī, –ductus, bring together; hire, rent
conferō, conferre, contulī, collātus, bring together, collect, compare; give, place; **mē conferō,** proceed
cōnfertus, –a, –um, crowded together, dense
cōnfestim, *adv.,* immediately, at once
cōnficiō, –ere, –fēcī, –fectus, complete; do up, exhaust; make, furnish, accomplish
cōnfīdō, –ere, cōnfīsus, *semideponent,* have confidence (in), rely on, be confident
cōnfirmō, 1, encourage, strengthen, establish, assert
cōnfīsus, *part of* **cōnfīdō**
cōnflīgō, –ere, –flīxī, –flīctus, dash together
cōnfoveō = foveō
cōnfundō, –ere, –fūdī, –fūsus, confuse
congredior, congredī, congressus, meet (in battle)
coniciō, –ere, –iēcī, –iectus, throw, conjecture
coniūnctim, *adv.,* jointly
coniungō, –ere, –iūnxī, –iūnctus, join (with), unite
coniūnx, –iugis, *m. and f.,* husband, wife
coniūrātiō, –ōnis, *f.,* conspiracy
coniūrō, 1, swear together, conspire
cōnor, 1, try, attempt
conquīrō, –ere, –quīsīvī, –quīsītus, seek for
cōnsanguineus, –ī, *m.,* (blood) relative
cōnscendō, –ere, –scendī, –scēnsus, climb (in); embark (in)
cōnscius, –a, –um, conscious
cōnscrībō, –ere, –scrīpsī, –scrīptus, write, enlist; **patrēs cōnscrīptī,** senators
cōnsecrātus, –a, –um, sacred
cōnsecūtus, *part. of* **cōnsequor**
cōnsēnsiō, –ōnis, *f.,* agreement
cōnsēnsus, –ūs, *m.,* agreement
cōnsentiō, –īre, –sēnsī, –sēnsus, agree, conspire
cōnsequor, cōnsequī, cōnsecūtus, follow, reach, attain
cōnservō 1, save, preserve, spare
cōnsīdō, –ere, –sēdī, –sessūrus, sit down, encamp, settle
consilium, –lī, *n.,* plan, policy; prudence; advice, counsel; council
cōnsimilis, –e, very similar
cōnsistō, –ere, –stitī, –stitūrus, stand still, stand, stop, take one's place, settle; consist in; depend on
cōnsōlātiō, –ōnis, *f.,* consolation
cōnspectus, –ūs, *m.,* sight
cōnspiciō, –ere, –spexī, –spectus, catch sight of, see
cōnspicor, 1, catch sight of, see
cōnstantia, –ae, *f.,* steadfastness
cōnstitī, *see* **cōnsistō**
cōnstituō, –ere, –stituī, –stitūtus, set up, establish, found; appoint, determine, decide; station
cōnsto, –āre, –stitī, –stātūrus, stand together; **cōnstat,** it is evident, it is clear, it is certain
cōnsuēscō, –ere, –suēvī, –suētus, become accustomed; *in perf.,* be accustomed
cōnsuētūdō, –dinis, *f.,* custom, habit
cōnsul, –ulis, *m.,* consul
cōnsulāris, –e, of consular rank
cōnsulātus, –ūs, *m.,* consulship
cōnsulō, –ere, –suluī, –sultus, consult (for)
cōnsultō, 1, consult
cōnsūmō, –ere, –sūmpsī, –sūmptus, use up, spend, waste
contāgiō, –ōnis, *f.,* contact

contemnō, –ere, –tempsī, –temptus, despise
contemplor, 1, look at
contemptus, –ūs, *m.,* contempt
contendō, –ere, –tendī, –tentūrus, struggle, hasten, contend, strive
contentus, –a, –um, contented
contexō, –ere, –texuī, –textus, weave (together)
continēns, –entis, *f.,* mainland
contineō, –ēre, –tinuī, –tentus, contain, keep; hem in, bound; restrain
contingō, –ere, –tigī, –tāctus, touch; happen
continuus, –a, –um, successive, continuous
contrā, *prep. w. acc.,* against, contrary to, opposite; *adv.,* on the other hand
contrahō, –ere, –trāxī, –trāctus, draw *or* bring together, contract
contrārius, –a, –um, opposite
contrīstō, 1, sadden
contrōversia, –ae, *f.,* dispute
contumēlia, –ae, *f.,* insult
conturbō, 1, confuse, mix up
conveniō, –īre, –vēnī, –ventūrus, come together, assemble, meet; **convenit,** it is agreed upon
conventus, –ūs, *m.,* meeting
convertō, –ere, –vertī, –versus, turn
convocō, 1, call together, summon
coorior, coorīrī, coortus, arise
cōpia, –ae, *f.,* supply, abundance, opportunity, chance; *pl.* forces, troops; resources
cor, cordis, *n.,* heart
Corinthus, –ī, *f.,* Corinth, *a Greek city*
cornū, –ūs, *n.,* horn; wing (*of an army*)
corōna, –ae, *f.,* crown, wreath
corpus, corporis, *n.,* body
corrigō, –ere, –rēxī, –rēctus, correct
cotīdiānus, –a, –um, daily
cotīdiē, *adv.,* daily
crās, *adv.,* tomorrow
crēber, –bra, –brum, frequent, numerous
crēditor, –ōris, *m.,* creditor
crēdō, –ere, crēdidī, crēditus, believe
cremō, 1, burn
creō, 1, elect, appoint
crēscō, –ere, crēvī, crētus, grow, increase
crocodīlus, –ī, *m.,* crocodile
cruciātus, –ūs, *m.,* torture
crūdēlis, –e, cruel
crūdēlitās, –tātis, *f.,* cruelty
crūdēliter, *adv.,* cruelly
cruentus, –a, –um, bloody
crūs, crūris, *n.,* leg
crux, crucis, *f.,* cross
cubiculum, –ī, *n.,* bedroom
culmen, –minis, *n.,* top, roof
culpa, –ae, *f.,* blame, fault
culpō, 1, blame
cultūra, –ae, *f.,* cultivation
cultus, –a, –um, cultured
cultus, –ūs, *m.,* way of living, civilization
cum, *prep. w. abl.,* with; although
cum, *conj.,* when, whenever, since, although; **cum prīmum,** as soon as; **cum... tum,** not only . . . but also
cumulus, –ī, *m.,* heap, pile
cūnctor, 1, hesitate
cūnctus, –a, –um, all
cupidē, *adv.,* eagerly
cupiditās, –tātis, *f.,* desire
cupīdō, –dinis, *m.,* desire; Cupid, *god of love*
cupidus, –a, –um, eager, desirous
cupiō, –ere, –īvī, –ītus, desire, wish
cūr, *adv.,* why
cūra, –ae, *f.,* care, anxiety, love, concern
cūria, –ae, *f.,* senate house; **Cūria Iūlia,** *a senate house named for Julius Caesar*
cūriōsitās, –tātis, *f.,* curiosity
cūrō, 1, care (for), cause (to be done)
currō, –ere, cucurrī, cursūrus, run
currus, –ūs, *m.,* chariot
cursor, –ōris, *m.,* runner
cursus, –ūs, *m.,* running, speed, race, course; **cursus honōrum,** course of offices, career
curvus, –a, –um, curved
custōdia, –ae, *f.,* guard
custōdiō, –īre, –īvī, –ītus, guard
custōs, –ōdis, *m.,* guard

D

damnō, 1, condemn
dē, *prep. w. abl.,* from, down from, concerning, about, during
dea, –ae, *f.,* goddess
dēbellō, 1, crush (*in war*)
dēbeō, –ēre, dēbuī, dēbitus, owe, ought
dēbitum, –ī, *n.,* debt
dēcēdō, –ere, dēcessī, dēcessūrus, depart, go away, die
decem, ten
decemvirī, –ōrum, *m. pl.,* decemvirs (*a board of ten men*)
dēcernō, –ere, dēcrēvī, dēcrētus, decide, vote
dēcertō, 1, fight (it out), contend
decimus, –a, –um, tenth
dēcipiō, –ere, dēcēpī, dēceptus, deceive
dēclīvia, –um, *n. pl.,* slopes
dēclīvis, –e, sloping (downward)
dēcrētum, –ī, *n.,* decree, decision
dēcrētus, *part. of* **dēcernō**
dēcurrō, –ere, dēcucurrī, dēcursūrus, run down *or* off
dēdecus, –coris, *n.,* disgrace
dēdicō, 1, dedicate
dēditīcius, –cī, *m.,* prisoner
dēditiō, –ōnis, *f.,* surrender
dēdō, dēdere, dēdidī, dēditus, surrender, devote

dēdūcō, –ere, dēdūxī, dēductus, lead, withdraw, bring, launch
dēfendō, –ere, dēfendī, dēfēnsus, defend, repel
dēfēnsor, –ōris, *m.,* defender
dēferō, dēferre, dētulī, dēlātus, carry, bestow, offer, enroll, report; *passive,* fall
dēfessus, –a, –um, tired
dēficiō, –ere, dēfēcī, dēfectus, fail, revolt
dēfīgō, –ere, dēfīxī, dēfīxus, drive in
dēflectō, –ere, dēflexī, dēflexus, turn aside
dēfluō, –ere, dēflūxī, dēflūxus, flow away
dēfōrmis, –e, unshapely
dēfugiō, –ere, dēfūgī, dēfugitūrus, avoid
dēiciō, –ere, dēiēcī, dēiectus, throw (down), dislodge, drive
dein, deinde, *adv.,* then
dēlātus, *part. of* **dēferō**
dēlēctus, *part. of* **dēligō**
dēleō, –ēre, –ēvī, –ētus, destroy, wipe out
dēlīberō, 1, consider
dēlīctum, –ī, *n.,* crime
dēligō, 1, fasten, select
dēligō, –ere, dēlēgī, dēlēctus, select
Delphī, –ōrum, *m. pl.,* Delphi
delphīnus, –ī, *m.,* dolphin, porpoise
dēmēns, *gen.* **dēmentis**, mad
dēmittō, –ere, dēmīsī, dēmissus, let *or* drop down, send down, derive
dēmocraticus, –a, –um, democratic
dēmōnstrō, 1, point out, show, mention
Dēmosthenēs, –is, *m.,* Dēmŏs´thenēs, *a Greek orator*
dēmulceō, –ēre, dēmulsī, dēmulctus, lick
dēns, dentis, *m.,* tooth
dēnsus, –a, –um, thick
dēnūdō, 1, strip
dēnūntiō, 1, declare
dēpellō, –ere, dēpulī, dēpulsus, drive away
dēpōnō, –ere, dēposuī, dēpositus, put *or* lay aside, put down, leave with
dēprēndō, –ere, dēprēndī, dēprēnsus, catch
dērigō (dīrigō), –ere, dērēxī, dērēctus, direct; **dērēctus**, straight
dēscendō, –ere, dēscendī, dēscēnsus, descend, resort
dēscēnsus, –ūs, *m.,* descent
dēscrībō, –ere, dēscrīpsī, dēscrīptus, write down, copy, describe
dēsecō, –āre, dēsecuī, dēsectus, cut off
dēserō, –ere, dēseruī, dēsertus, desert
dēsertor, –ōris, *m.,* deserter
dēsīdero, 1, long for
dēsiliō, –īre, dēsiluī, dēsultūrus, jump down
dēsistō, –ere, dēstitī, dēstitūrus, (stand away), cease
dēspectus, –ūs, *m.,* view
dēspērō, 1, despair (of)
dēspiciō, –ere, dēspexī, dēspectus, look down
dēstitī, *see* **dēsistō**
dēsum, deesse, dēfuī, dēfutūrus, be lacking
dēsuper, *adv.,* from above
dēterior, –ius, poorer, less, worse
dētestābilis, –e, detestable
dētineō, –ēre, dētinuī, dētentus, detain
dētrahō, –ere, dētrāxī, dētrāctus, draw off, take (off)
dētrīmentum, –ī, *n.,* loss
deus, –ī, *m.,* god
dēveniō, –īre, dēvenī, dēventūrus, come
dēvorō, 1, devour
dexter, –tra, –trum, right (hand), right *(as opposed to left)*
dī = deī
dīcō, –ere, dīxī, dictus, say, tell, speak, state, name; **salūtem dīcō**, pay respects; **causam dīcō**, plead a case
dictātor, –ōris, *m.,* dictator
dictō, 1, dictate
dictum, –ī, *n.,* word, remark
didicī, *see* **discō**
diēs, diēī, *m. and f.,* day
differō, differre, distulī, dīlātus, spread; differ
difficilis, –e, difficult
difficultās, –tātis, *f.,* difficulty
diffīdō, –ere, diffīsus, *semi-deponent,* distrust
diffundō, –ere, –fūdī, –fūsus, spread out
digitus, –ī, *m.,* finger
dignitās, –tātis, *f.,* worth, rank, position
dignus, –a, –um, worthy
dīiūdicō, 1, determine
dīligēns, *gen.* **–entis**, careful, diligent
dīligenter, *adv.,* carefully
dīligentia, –ae, *f.,* care, diligence
dīmicō, 1, fight
dīmidium, –dī, *n.,* half
dīmittō, –ere, dīmīsī, dīmissus, let go, lose, abandon, send (away), dismiss, send out
dīmoveō, –ēre, dīmōvī, dīmōtus, move away
dīrigō, *see* **dērigō**
dīripiō, –ere, dīripuī, dīreptus, plunder
dīrus, –a, –um, horrible
Dīs, Dītis, *m.,* Pluto, *god of Hades*
discēdō, –ere, –cessī, –cessūrus, go away, depart, draw back
disciplīna, –ae, *f.,* discipline, training, instruction, system
discipulus, –ī, *m.,* pupil
disclūdō, –ere, –clūsī, –clūsus, separate
discō, –ere, didicī, —, learn
discordia, –ae, *f.,* discord
discrīmen, –minis, *n.,* difference

discutiō, –ere, –cussī, –cussus, push aside, destroy
disiciō, –ere, –iēcī, –iectus, scatter
dispergō, –ere, dispersī, dispersus, scatter
dispōnō, –ere, –posuī, –positus, put here and there, arrange
disputātiō, –ōnis, *f.*, discussion
disputō, 1, discuss
dissēnsiō, –ōnis, *f.*, dissension
dissimilis, –e, unlike
dissimulō, 1, conceal
dissipō, 1, scatter
distineō, –ēre, –tinuī, –tentus, keep apart
distribuō, –ere, –tribuī, –tribūtus, distribute, divide, assign
dītissimus, *see* **dīves**
diū, *adv.*, (for) a long time, long; *comp.* **diūtius;** *superl.* **diūtissimē**
diurnus, –a, –um, (by) day; **acta diurna,** journal, newspaper
dīversus, –a, –um, different
dīves, *gen.* **dīvitis,** rich; *comp.* **dītior;** *superl.* **dītissimus**
Dīviciācus, –ī, *m.*, Diviciacus (Divishiā´cus)
dīvidō, –ere, dīvīsī, dīvīsus, divide, separate
dīvīnus, –a, –um, divine
dīvitiae, –ārum, *f. pl.*, riches
dīvus, –ī (*gen. pl.* **dīvum**), *m.*, god
dō, dare, dedī, datus, give; **poenam dō,** pay the penalty; **in fugam dō,** put to flight
doceō, –ēre, docuī, doctus, teach, explain; **doctus,** skilled
doctrīna, –ae, *f.*, teaching
documentum, –ī, *n.*, proof, warning
doleō, –ēre, doluī, dolitūrus, grieve, be sorry
dolor, –ōris, *m.*, grief, pain, suffering
dolōrōsus, –a, –um, grieving
dolus, –ī, *m.*, treachery, deceit, trick(ery)
domesticus, –a, –um, one's own
domicilium, –lī, *n.*, home
domina, –ae, *f.*, mistress
dominor, 1, be master
dominus, –ī, *m.*, master
domus, –ūs, *f.*, home, house
dōnō, 1, give
dōnum, –ī, *n.*, gift
dormiō, –īre, –īvī, –ītus, sleep
dōs, dōtis, *f.*, dowry
dracō, –ōnis, *m.*, dragon
druidēs, –um, *m. pl.*, druids
dubitātiō, –iōnis, *f.*, doubt
dubitō, 1, hesitate, doubt
dubium, –bī, *n.*, doubt
dūcō, –ere, dūxī, ductus, lead, draw, construct, consider, influence
dulcis, –e, sweet, agreeable; *as noun, n. pl.*, cakes
dum, *conj.*, while, until, as long as
duo, –ae, –o, two
duodecim, twelve; **duodecimus, –a, –um,** twelfth
duplex, *gen.* **duplicis,** double
duplicō, 1, double
dūrē, *adv.*, harshly
dūritia, –ae, *f.*, hardship
dūritiēs, –ēī, *f.*, hardness
dūrō, 1, harden
dūrus, –a, –um, hard, harsh, cruel
dux, ducis, *m.*, leader, guide, general; **dux,** under the direction of
Dyrrachium, –chī, *n.*, Dyrrachium, *now* Durazzo, *a city on the east coast of the Adriatic*

E

ē, *see* **ex**
ea, she
ecce! *interj.*, look!
ēdīcō, –ere, ēdīxī, ēdictus, appoint
ēdiscō, –ere, ēdidicī, —, learn by heart
ēditus, –a, –um, elevated
ēdō, ēdere, ēdidī, ēditus, give out, publish, inflict, utter
ēducō, 1, bring up
ēdūcō, –ere, ēdūxī, ēductus, lead out; draw
effēminō, 1, weaken
efferō, efferre, extulī, ēlātus, carry out, make known
efficiō, –ere, effēcī, effectus, make, bring about, accomplish, complete, produce, achieve, cause
effodiō, –ere, effōdī, effossus, dig up
effugiō, –ere, effūgī, effugitūrus, escape
ego, meī, I
ēgredior, ēgredī, ēgressus, go *or* march out, leave, land
ēgregiē, *adv.*, excellently
ēgregius, –a, –um, distinguished, excellent, outstanding
ēheu! *interj.*, alas!
eī, eae, ea, they
ēiciō, –ere, ēiēcī, ēiectus, throw (out), stick out, expel
eius, his, her
ēlegantia, –ae, *f.*, elegance, style
elephantus, –ī, *m.*, elephant, ivory
Eleusis, –is, *f.*, Eleu´sis, *a Greek city*
ēlevō, 1, raise
ēligō, –ere, –ēlēgī, ēlēctus, pick out
ēloquentia, –ae, *f.*, eloquence, rhetoric
ēmendō, 1, correct
ēmergō, –ere, ēmersī, ēmersus, emerge
ēmittō, –ere, ēmīsī, ēmissus, let drop, let *or* send out, shed
emō, –ere, ēmī, emptus, take, buy
enim, *conj.* (*never first word*), for
ēnotō, 1, take notes (on)
ēnūntiō, 1, announce, report
eō, īre, iī, itūrus, go
eō, *adv.*, there
eōdem, *adv.*, to the same place
eōrum, eārum, eōrum, their
Ēpīrus, –ī, *f.*, Ēpī´rus, *a province in northern Greece*

episcopus, –ī, *m.,* bishop
epistula, –ae, *f.,* letter
eques, equitis, *m.,* horseman, knight; *pl.,* cavalry
equester, –tris, –tre, (of) cavalry
equidem, *adv.,* to be sure
equitātus, –ūs, *m.,* cavalry
equus, –ī, *m.,* horse
ergō, *adv.,* therefore
ērigō, –ere, ērēxī, ērēctus, raise up
ēripiō, –ere, ēripuī, ēreptus, snatch away, remove, save
errō, 1, wander; be mistaken
ērubēscō, –ere, ērubuī,—, blush
ērudiō, –īre, –īvī, –ītus, instruct
ērudītiō, –ōnis, *f.,* learning
ēruptiō, –ōnis, *f.,* sally, attack, a bursting forth
Ēsquiliae, –ārum, *f. pl.,* **Ēsquilīnus (mōns),** the Es´quilīne Hill
et, *conj.,* and, even; **et... et,** both . . . and
etiam, *adv.,* also, even
Etrūscī, –ōrum, *m. pl.,* the Etruscans, the people of Etruria
etsī, *conj.,* although
ēvādō, –ere, ēvāsī, ēvāsūrus, go out, escape
ēvehō, –ere, ēvexī, ēvectus, carry up
ēvellō, –ere, ēvellī, ēvulsus, pull out
ēveniō, –īre, ēvēnī, ēventūrus, turn out, happen
ēventus, –ūs, *m.,* outcome, result
ēvertō, –ere, ēvertī, ēversus, overturn
ēvocō, 1, call out, summon
ex (ē), *prep. w. abl.,* from, out of, of, as a result of, in accordance with
exāctus, *part. of* **exigō**
exagitō, 1, weigh, harass, drive about
exanimō, 1, exhaust, kill
excēdō, –ere, excessī, excessūrus, go away, depart, withdraw
excelsus, –a, –um, high
excipiō, –ere, excēpī, exceptus, receive, capture, sense
excitō, 1, arouse, erect
exclāmō, 1, exclaim
excruciō, 1, torture
exemplum, –ī, *n.,* example, sample, precedent
exeō, exīre, exiī, exitūrus, go out (from), go forth
exerceō, –ēre, exercuī, exercitus, train, exercise, make use of
exercitātiō, –ōnis, *f.,* exercise
exercitātus, –a, –um, trained
exercitus, –ūs, *m.,* (trained) army
exhauriō, –īre, exhausī, exhaustus, draw out, endure
exigō, –ere, exēgī, exāctus, drive out, demand
exiguē, *adv.,* scarcely
exiguitās, –tātis, *f.,* scantiness, shortness, smallness
exiguus, –a, –um, small
existimō, 1, think
exitus, –ūs, *m.,* outlet, outcome, departure, death
expediō, –īre, –īvī, –ītus, set free, prepare; **expedītus,** unencumbered; free, easy
expedītus, –a, –um, unencumbered, easy
expellō, –ere, expulī, expulsus, drive out, banish
experior, experīrī, expertus, try; **expertus,** experienced
expleō, –ēre, explēvī, explētus, fill up
explicō, 1, unroll, develop, explain
explōrātor, –ōris, *m.,* scout
explōrō, 1, investigate, explore, reconnoiter; **explōrātus,** assured
expōnō, –ere, –posuī, expositus, put out, draw up, expose
exprimō, –ere, expressī, expressus, press out, express, portray, imitate
expugnō, 1, capture, gain
exsanguis, –e, bloodless
exsequor, exsequi, exsecūtus, follow up, enforce
exsiliō, –īre, exsiluī, —, leap up *or* out
exsilium, –lī, *n.,* exile
exsistō, –ere, exstitī, —, stand out, arise
exspectō, 1, expect, wait, await
exspīrō, 1, breathe out, expire
exstinguō, –ere, exstīnxī, exstīnctus, put out, kill
exstruō, –ere, exstrūxī, exstrūctus, pile up, build, erect
exterior, –ius, outer
externus, –ī, *m.,* stranger
extrā, *prep. w. acc.,* out of, outside of, beyond
extrahō, –ere, extrāxī, extrāctus, draw out
extraōrdinārius, –a, –um, (out of order), extraordinary
extrēmus, –a, –um, farthest, last, extreme, end of
extruō, –ere, extrūxī, extrūctus, build

F

fābula, –ae, *f.,* story, play
faciēs, –ēi, *f.,* face, appearance
facile, *adv.,* easily
facilis, –e, easy
facinus, facinoris, *n.,* crime
faciō, –ere, fēcī, factus, do, make, act; **verba faciō,** speak, make a speech; **certiōrem eum faciō dē,** inform him about; **iter faciō,** march, travel
factiō, –ōnis, *f.,* faction
factum, –ī, *n.,* deed, act
facultās, –tātis, *f.,* faculty, opportunity; *pl.,* means
fallāx, *gen.* **–ācis,** false
fallō, –ere, fefellī, falsus, deceive
falsus, –a, –um, false; **falsō,** *adv.,* falsely

falx, falcis, *f.*, hook
fāma, –ae, *f.*, report, fame
famēs, –is, *abl.* **fame,** *f.*, hunger
familia, –ae, *f.*, household, family
familiāris, –e, (of the family), friendly; *as noun, m.*, friend
fas, *indeclinable, n.*, right
fatīgō, 1, weary, wear out
fātum, –ī, *n.*, fate
faucēs, –ium, *f. pl.*, throat, jaws
faveō, –ēre, fāvī, fautūrus, be favorable to, favor
favor, –ōris, *m.*, favor
fefellī, *see* **fallō**
fēlīcitās, –tātis, *f.*, happiness
fēlīciter, *adv.*, fortunately, successfully; good luck!
fēlīx, *gen.* **fēlīcis,** happy, fortunate, successful, lucky
fēmina, –ae, *f.*, woman, female
fēmineus, –a, –um, of a woman
fera, –ae, *f.*, wild beast
ferē, *adv.*, almost, about, generally
fēriae, –ārum, *f. pl.*, holidays; **fēriae Latīnae,** *festival of the allied Latins.*
ferō, ferre, tulī, lātus, bear, endure, carry, bring, receive, report, propose (*of a law*)
ferōx, *gen.* **ferōcis,** bold, fierce
ferreus, –a, –um, iron
ferrum, –ī, *n.*, iron
fertilis, –e, fertile
fertilitās, –tātis, *f.*, fertility
ferus, –a, –um, wild, fierce
fēstus, –a, –um, festal
fidēlis, –e, faithful
fidēs, –eī, *f.*, trust, protection; word, loyalty
fīdūcia, –ae, *f.*, confidence
fīdus, –a, –um, faithful
fīgō, –ere, fīxī, fīxus, fix
figūra, –ae, *f.*, figure, shape
fīlia, –ae, *f.*, daughter
fīlius, –lī, *m.*, son
fingō, –ere, fīnxī, fictus, form, invent, imagine
fīniō, –īre, –īvī, –ītus, limit, determine
fīnis, fīnis, *m. or f.*, end; *pl.*, borders, territory
fīnitimus, –a, –um, neighboring; *as noun,* neighbor
fīō, fierī, —, (factus), be made, become, be done, happen; **certior fīō,** be informed
firmiter, *adv.*, firmly
firmus, –a, –um, strong, firm
fissus, –a, –um, split
flagellum, –i, *n.*, whip
flamma, –ae, *f.*, flame
flectō, –ere, flexī, flexus, bend, turn
fleō, flēre, flēvī, flētus, weep (for)
flōreō, –ēre, flōruī, —, bloom
flōs, flōris, *m.*, flower
flūctus, –ūs, *m.*, wave
flūmen, flūminis, *n.*, river
fluō, –ere, flūxī, flūxus, flow
fōns, fontis, *m.*, spring
fore = futūrum esse, *from* **sum**
fōrma, –ae, *f.*, shape, form, beauty
fors, fortis, *f.*, chance
fortasse, *adv.*, perhaps
forte, by chance
fortis, –e, brave
fortiter, *adv.*, bravely
fortūna, –ae, *f.*, fortune, fate; *pl.*, property
forum, –ī, *n.*, marketplace; Forum (*at Rome*)
fossa, –ae, *f.*, trench
foveō, –ēre, fōvī, fōtus, cherish
frangō, –ere, frēgī, frāctus, break, wreck
frāter, frātris, *m.*, brother
fraus, fraudis, *f.*, fraud, wrong
frequēns, *gen.* **frequentis,** frequent, numerous
frequenter, *adv.*, often
frīgidus, –a, –um, cold
frīgus, frīgoris, *n.*, cold
frōns, frondis, *f.*, leaf
frōns, frontis, *f.*, forehead, front
fructus, –ūs, *m.*, fruit
frūgēs, –um, *f. pl.*, crops
frūmentārius, –a, –um, of grain; fertile; **rēs frūmentāria,** grain supply
frūmentum, –ī, *n.*, grain; *pl.*, ears of grain, crops
frūstrā, *adv.*, in vain
fuga, –ae, *f.*, flight
fugiō, –ere, fūgī, fugitūrus, flee, avoid, escape
fugitīvus, –ī, *m.*, deserter
fūmō, 1, smoke
fūmus, –ī, *m.*, smoke
funda, –ae, *f.*, sling, slingshot
fundāmentum, –ī, *n.*, foundation
funditor, –ōris, *m.*, slinger
fundō, –ere, fūdī, fūsus, pour, shed
fūnis, –is, *m.*, rope
fūnus, –eris, *n.*, funeral
Furiae, –ārum, *f. pl.*, the Furies, *avenging and tormenting spirits*
furibundus, –a, –um, mad
furō, –ere, —, —, rage
furor, –ōris, *m.*, madness
fūrtim, *adv.*, secretly
furtum, –ī, *n.*, theft
futūrus, *fut. part. of* **sum**

G

galea, –ae, *f.*, helmet
Gallia, –ae, *f.*, Gaul, *ancient France*
Gallicus, –a, –um, Gallic
Gallus, –a, –um, Gallic; *as noun, m.*, a Gaul
garrulus, –a, –um, talkative
gaudeō, –ēre, gāvīsus, *semideponent,* rejoice, be glad
gaudium, –dī, *n.*, joy
gāvīsus, *part. of* **gaudeō**
geminus, –a, –um, twin
gemitus, –ūs, *m.*, groan
gemma, –ae, *f.*, precious stone
gemō, –ere, gemuī, —, groan
Genava, *see* **Genua**
gēns, gentis, *f.*, family, people, nation, tribe
Genua, –ae, *f.*, Geneva
genus, generis, *n.*, birth, family, race; kind, class
Germānia, –ae, *f.*, Germany
Germānicus, –a, –um, German
Germānus, –a, –um, German; *as noun, m.*, a German

gerō, –ere, gessī, gestus, carry on, manage, do, hold; wear; *passive,* go on; **mē gerō,** act; **rēs gestae,** deeds
gignō, –ere, genuī, genitus, produce; *passive,* be born
gladiātor, –ōris, *m.,* gladiator
gladiātōrius, –a, –um, gladiatorial
gladius, –dī, *m.,* sword
glōria, –ae, *f.,* glory
glōriōsus, –a, –um, glorious
gracilis, –e, slender
gradior, gradī, gressus, walk
gradus, –ūs, *m.,* step
Graecia, –ae, *f.,* Greece
Graecus, –a, –um, Greek; *as noun, m.,* a Greek
grāmen, grāminis, *n.,* grass
grammaticus, –ī, *m.,* grammarian, teacher of literature
grātia, –ae, *f.,* gratitude, grace, favor, influence; **grātiās agō,** thank; **grātiā,** for the sake of (*w. gen. preceding*)
grātulātiō, –ōnis, *f.,* congratulation
grātus, –a, –um, pleasing, grateful
gravis, –e, heavy, serious, severe, important
gravitās, –tātis, *f.,* weight, dignity, seriousness
graviter, *adv.,* heavily, seriously, severely, decisively
gubernātor, –ōris, *m.,* pilot
gustō, 1, taste
gustus, –ūs, *m.,* taste

H

ha! *interj.,* ha!
habeō, –ēre, habuī, habitus, have, hold, consider; **ōrātiōnem habeō,** deliver a speech
habitō, 1, live
Haeduus, –a, –um, Haeduan (Hĕd´uan); *as noun, m.,* a Haeduan
haereō, –ēre, haesī, haesus, stick, cling
Hamburgiēnsis, –e, of Hamburg
Harpyiae, –ārum, *f. pl.,* the Harpies
haud, *adv.,* by no means
hauriō, –īre, hausī, haustus, drain, drink
Helvētius, –a, –um, Helvetian (Helvē´shian); *as noun, m. pl.,* the Helvetians
herba, –ae, *f.,* grass, plant, herb
Herculēs, –is, *m.,* Her´culēs
hērēditās, –tātis, *f.,* inheritance
herī, *adv.,* yesterday
heu! *interj.,* alas!
hīberna, –ōrum (*i.e.,* **castra**), *n. pl.,* winter quarters
Hibernia, –ae, *f.,* Ireland
hic, haec, hoc, this, the latter; *as pron.,* he, she, it
hīc, *adv.,* here
hiemō, 1, spend the winter
hiems, hiemis, *f.,* winter
hilaris, –e, gay, cheerful
Hispānia, –ae, *f.,* Spain
Hispānus, –a, –um, Spanish
historia, –ae, *f.,* history
hodiē, *adv.,* today
hodiernus, –a, –um, of today
Homērus, –ī, *m.,* Homer, *a Greek poet*
homō, hominis, *m.,* man, human being; *pl.,* people
honestē, *adv.,* honorably
honestus, –a, –um, honorable
honor, –ōris, *m.,* honor, office
hōra, –ae, *f.,* hour
Horātius, –tī, *m.,* Horace, *a Roman poet;* Horatius (Horā´shius) Cocles
horrēns, *gen.* **horrentis,** shaggy
horreō, –ēre, horruī, —, shudder, dread
horribilis, –e, horrible
horridus, –a, –um, frightful
horror, –ōris, *m.,* horror
hortor, 1, urge, encourage
hortus, –ī, *m.,* garden, park
hospes, hospitis, *m.,* guest, guest-friend, host
hospitium, –tī, *n.,* hospitality
hostis, –is, *m.,* (national) enemy (*usually pl.*)
hūc, *adv.,* to this side, here
hūmānitās, –tātis, *f.,* culture
hūmānus, –a, –um, human, civilized
humilis, –e, low, humble
humus, –ī, *f.,* ground, earth
hydraulicus, –a, –um, hydraulic

I

iaceō, –ēre, iacuī, —, lie
iaciō, –ere, iēcī, iactus, throw, build
iactō, 1, throw, toss
iactūra, –ae, *f.,* (throwing), loss, expense, sacrifice
iactus, –ūs, *m.,* throw
iaculum, –ī, *n.,* dart, javelin
iam, *adv.,* already, by this time, at last, (*w. fut.*) soon; **nōn iam,** no longer
iānua, –ae, *f.,* door
ibi, *adv.,* there
īdem, eadem, idem, same, likewise
identidem, *adv.,* again and again
idōneus, –a, –um, suitable, fitting
igitur, *adv.,* therefore
ignis, –is, *m.,* fire
ignōminia, –ae, *f.,* disgrace
ignōrō, 1, not know
ignōscō, –ere, ignōvī, ignōtus, pardon
ignōtus, –a, –um, unknown, strange
illātus, *part. of* **īnferō**
ille, illa, illud, that, the former; *as pron.,* he, she it; **ille... hic,** the former . . . the latter
illī, illae, illa, they
illigō, 1, tie to
illō, *adv.,* there, to that place
illūc, *adv.,* to that place *or* side
illūstris, –e, noble
Illyricum, –ī, *n.,* Illy̆r´icum, *a region along the east coast of the Adriatic*
imāgō, imāginis, *f.,* statue, likeness, echo
imbecillitās, –tātis, *f.,* weakness
imitātiō, –ōnis, *f.,* imitation
imitor, 1, imitate
immānis, –e, huge, savage

immittō, –ere, immīsī, immissus, let go, throw
immolō, 1, sacrifice
immortālis, –e, undying, immortal
impār, *gen.* **imparis,** unequal
impedīmenta, –orum, *n. pl.,* baggage
impedīmentum, –ī, *n.,* hindrance
impediō, –īre, –īvī, –ītus, hinder, obstruct; **impedītus,** burdened
impellō, –ere, impulī, impulsus, drive on, influence, incite, impel, urge
impendeō, –ēre, —, —, hang over
impendō, –ere, impendī, impēnsus, spend
imperātor, –ōris, *m.,* commander, general, emperor
imperātum, –ī, *n.,* order
imperītus, –a, –um, inexperienced, ignorant
imperium, –rī, *n.,* command, control, military power, order; empire, government; **nova imperia,** revolution
imperō, 1, command, order, rule, demand
impetrō, 1, gain *or* obtain (one's request)
impetus, –ūs, *m.,* attack, fury
impius, –a, –um, impious
impleō, –ēre, implēvī, implētus, fill
impōnō, –ere, imposuī, impositus, put on, impose
importō, 1, bring in, import
improbitās, –tātis, *f.,* dishonesty
imprōvīsus, –a, –um, unforeseen; **dē imprōvīsō,** suddenly
imprūdentia, –ae, *f.,* poor sense
impudenter, *adv.,* impudently
impulsus, *part. of* **impellō**
īmus, *see* **īnferior**
in, *prep. w. acc.,* into, to, towards, against, on; *w. abl.,* in, on, among, at
inānis, –e, empty
incēdō, –ere, incessī, incessus, enter
incendium, –dī, *n.,* fire, burning
incendō, –ere, incendī, incensus, set on fire, burn; rouse
incertus, –a, –um, uncertain
incidō, –ere, incidī, —, fall (into *or* upon), happen
incipiō, –ere, incēpī, inceptus, take to, begin
incitō, 1, urge on, arouse
inclūdō, –ere, inclūsī, inclūsus, shut up
incognitus, –a, –um, unknown
incolō, –ere, incoluī, — inhabit, live
incolumis, –e, unharmed, safe
incommodum, –ī, *n.,* harm
incrēdibilis, –e, unbelievable
incumbō, –ere, incubuī, incubitūrus, lean over
incursiō, –ōnis, *f.,* raid
incursō, 1, run against
inde, *adv.,* then, from there, thereafter, therefore
Indī, –ōrum, *m. pl.,* the Indians, inhabitants of India
indīcō, –ere, indīxī, indictus, call
indignitās, –tātis, *f.,* outrage
indīligenter, *adv.,* carelessly
indiscrētē, *adv.,* indiscreetly
indoctus, –a, –um, untrained
indūcō, –ere, indūxī, inductus, lead in, bring in; influence
induō, –ere, induī, indūtus, put on, dress, impale
ineō, inīre, iniī, initūrus, enter upon; **cōnsilium ineō,** form a plan
inermis, –e, unarmed
īnfāmia, –ae, *f.,* dishonor
īnfāmis, –e, notorious
īnfāns, –fantis, *m.,* infant
īnfectus, –a, –um, not done
īnfēlīx, *gen.* **īnfēlīcis,** unfortunate,unlucky, unhappy
īnferior, –ius, lower, inferior; *superl.* **īmus, īnfimus,** lowest
īnferō, īnferre, intulī, illātus, bring in, to, *or* against; place upon, inflict, enter; **signa īnferō,** charge
īnficiō, –ere, īnfēcī, īnfectus, stain, infect
īnfimus, *see* **īnferior**
īnfīnītus, –a, –um, endless, countless
īnfirmitās, –tātis, *f.,* illness
īnfirmus, –a, –um, fixed
īnfluō, –ere, īnfūxī, īnfūxus, flow (in)
īnfrā, *adv.,* below, farther on; *prep. w. acc.,* below
īnfundō, –ere, īnfūdī, īnfūsus, pour in
ingenium, –nī, *n.,* ability
ingēns, *gen.* **ingentis,** huge
ingredior, ingredī, ingressus, step into, enter
iniciō, –ere, iniēcī, iniectus, throw *or* thrust into, inspire
inimīcitia, –ae, *f.,* enmity, feud
inimīcus, –a, –um, unfriendly, hostile; *as noun, m.,* (personal) enemy
inīquitās, –tātis, *f.,* unfavorableness
inīquus, –a, –um, uneven, unfavorable, unjust
initium, –tī, *n.,* beginning, element
iniungō, –ere, iniūnxī, iniūnctus, join to, impose on
iniūria, –ae, *f.,* wrong, injustice, injury
iniūstē, *adv.,* unjustly
iniūstus, –a, –um, unjust
innocēns, *gen.* **innocentis,** innocent
inopia, –ae, *f.,* lack, scarcity, poverty
inopīnāns, *gen.* **inopīnantis,** unsuspecting
inops, *gen.* **inopis,** poor, helpless
inquit, says, says he (*after one or more words of a direct quotation*); **inquis,** you say
īnsānia, –ae, *f.,* madness
īnsānus, –a, –um, mad
īnsciēns, *gen.* **īnscientis,** not knowing

īnscrībō, –ere, īnscrīpsī, īnscrīptus, inscribe
īnsequor, īnsequī, īnsecūtus, follow up, pursue
īnserō, –ere, īnseruī, īnsertus, insert
īnsidiae, –ārum, *f. pl.*, plot, ambush, treachery
īnsignis, –e, remarkable, noted, conspicuous; *as noun*, **īnsigne, –is**, *n.*, ornament, signal
īnsiliō, –īre, īnsiluī, —, leap upon
īnsistō, –ere, īnstitī, —, adopt, stand (on)
instituō, –ere, instituī, institūtus, establish, decide upon; begin, train; build, provide
īnstitūtum, –ī, *n.*, custom
īnstō, –āre, īnstitī, —, press on
īnstrūmentum, –ī, *n.*, instrument
īnstruō, –ere, –īnstrūxī, īnstrūctus, draw up, provide
īnsula, –ae, *f.*, island
integer, –gra, –grum, untouched, fresh, unharmed
intellegenter, *adv.*, intelligently
intellegō, –ere, –lēxī, –lēctus, realize, understand
intemperāns, *gen.* **–antis**, intemperate
intendō, –ere, intendī, intentus, stretch out, direct
inter, *prep. w. acc.*, between, for, among; **inter sē**, with each other from one another
intercēdō, –ere, –cessī, –cessūrus, go between, intervene
intercipiō, –ere, –cēpī, –ceptus, intercept
interclūdō, –ere, –clūsī, –clūsus, shut off, cut off
intereā, *adv.*, meanwhile
intereō, –īre, –iī, –itūrus, perish
interest, *see* **intersum**
interficiō, –ere, –fēcī, –fectus, kill
intericiō, –ere, –iēcī, –iectus, throw between, intervene
interim, *adv.*, meanwhile
interior, –ius, interior; **interiōrēs**, those in the interior
intermittō, –ere, –mīsī, –missus, let go, stop, interrupt, intervene
interpōnō, –ere, –posuī, –positus, present
interpretor, 1, explain
interrogō, 1, ask, question
intersum, –esse, –fuī, –futūrus, be between, take part (in); **interest**, it makes a difference
intervāllum, –ī, *n.*, interval, distance
interventus, –ūs, *m.*, coming on
intrā, *prep. w. acc.*, within
intrō, 1, enter
intrōmittō, –ere, –mīsī, –missus, let in
intueor, intuērī, intuitus, look at
inūsitātus, –a, –um, unusual, strange
inūtilis, –e, useless
inveniō, –īre, invēnī, inventus, come upon, find
inventor, –ōris, *m.*, discoverer
invictus, –a, –um, unconquered
invideō, –ēre, invīdī, invīsus, envy
invidia, –ae, *f.*, envy
invītō, 1, invite
invītus, –a, –um, unwilling
iō! *interj.*, oh! ah! hurrah!
iocor, 1, joke
iocus, –ī, *m.*, joke
Iovis, *see* **Iuppiter**
ipse, ipsa, ipsum, -self, very
īra, –ae, *f.*, anger, wrath
īrācundus, –a, –um, hot-tempered, quick-tempered
īrātus, –a, –um, angry
irrīdeō, –ēre, irrīsī, irrīsus, laugh at, jeer
irrumpō, –ere, irrūpī, irruptus, break in, rush in
is, ea, id, this, that; *as pron.*, he, she, it
iste, ista, istud, that
ita, *adv.*, so, in such a way, thus, yes; **ita ut(ī)**, just as
Italia, –ae, *f.*, Italy
itaque, *adv.*, and so, therefore
item, *adv.*, also, likewise
iter, itineris, *n.*, journey, road, march, way; **iter faciō**, march, travel
iterum, *adv.*, again
iubeō, –ēre, iussī, iussus, order
iūcundus, –a, –um, pleasant
iūdex, iūdicis, *m.*, judge
iūdicium, –cī, *n.*, trial, investigation, judgment
iūdicō, 1, judge, decide
iugum, –ī, *n.*, yoke, ridge
Iūlius, –a, –um, of Julius; *as noun, f., m.*, Julia, Julius; July
iungō, –ere, iūnxī, iūnctus, join, harness
iūnior, –ius (*comp. of* **iuvenis**), younger
Iūnō, –ōnis, *f.*, Juno, *a goddess, wife of Jupiter*
Iuppiter, Iovis, *m.*, Jupiter, *king of the gods*
Iūra, –ae, *m.*, Jura, *a mountain range*
iūrō, 1, swear
iūs, iūris, *n.*, right, justice, law; **iūs iūrandum, iūris iūrandī**, *n.*, oath
iussum, –ī, *n.*, order
iūstitia, –ae, *f.*, justice
iūstus, –a, –um, just, proper, regular
iuvenālis, –e, youthful
iuvenis, –is, *m.*, young man
iuventūs, –tūtis, *f.*, youth, young people
iuvō, –āre, iūvī, iūtus, help, aid, please
iūxtā, *adv.*, close by

L

L., *abbreviation for* **Lūcius, Lūcī**, *m.*, Lucius (Lū´shius)
labor, –ōris, *m.*, work, task, trouble, hardship
labōrō, 1, work, be hard pressed, struggle
lac, lactis, *n.*, milk

Lacedaemon, –onis, *f.,* Sparta, *a region in Greece*
lacerō, 1, tear to pieces
lacessō, –ere, –īvī, –ītus, attack
lacrima, –ae, *f.,* tear
lacrimōsus, –a, –um, tearful
lacus, –ūs, *m.,* lake
laetitia, –ae, *f.,* joy
laetus, –a, –um, joyful
lampas, –adis, *f.,* lamp, torch
lanterna, –ae, *f.,* lantern
lapis, lapidis, *m.,* stone
Lār, Laris, *m.,* Lar (*pl.* Lā´rēs), *a household god*
lārva, –ae, *f.,* ghost
lassitūdō, –dinis, *f.,* weariness
lātē, *adv.,* widely
lateō, –ēre, –uī, —, hide, escape notice
later, lateris, *m.,* brick, tile
Latīnus, –a, –um, Latin; *as noun, m.,* a Latin
lātitūdō, –dinis, *f.,* width
latrō, –ōnis, *m.,* robber, bandit
latrōcinium, –nī, *n.,* robbery
latus, lateris, *n.,* side, flank
lātus, –a, –um, wide, broad
lātus, *see* **ferō**
laudō, 1, praise
laus, laudis, *f.,* praise
lautus, –a, –um, magnificent
lavō, –āre, lāvī, lautus, wash, bathe
laxō, 1, open out
lēctor, –ōris, *m.,* reader
lēgātiō, –ōnis, *f.,* embassy
lēgātus, –ī, *m.,* envoy; general, staff officer; governor
legiō, –ōnis, *f.,* legion
legiōnārius, –a, –um, legionary
legō, –ere, lēgī, lēctus choose, read, select
Lemannus, –ī, *m., w.* **lacus,** Lake Geneva
lēniō, –īre, –īvī, –ītus, soothe
lēnis, –e, gentle
lēniter, *adv.,* gently
leō, –ōnis, *m.,* lion
Leōnidās, –ae, *m.,* Leŏn´idas
levis, –e, light
levitās, –tātis, *f.,* lightness, inconstancy
lēx, lēgis, *f.,* law
libellus, –ī, *m.,* little book
libenter, *adv.,* willingly, gladly
liber, librī, *m.,* book
līber, –era, –erum, free
līberālis, –e, liberal
līberāliter, *adv.,* liberally, courteously
līberātor, –ōris, *m.,* liberator
līberī, –ōrum, *m. pl.,* children
līberō, 1, free, set free
lībertās, –tātis, *f.,* freedom, liberty
lībertus, –ī, *m.,* freedman
librārius, –rī, *m.,* bookseller
licentia, –ae, *f.,* license
licet, –ēre, licuit *or* **licitum est,** it is permitted, one may, allow
ligō, 1, tie, bind
līlium, līlī, *n.,* lily
līmen, līminis, *n.,* threshold
lingua, –ae, *f.,* tongue, language
liquidus, –a, –um, liquid
littera, –ae, *f.,* letter (*of the alphabet*); *pl.,* letter (*epistle*), letters (*if modified by an adjective such as* **multae**), literature
lītus, lītoris, *n.,* shore
Līvius, –vī, *m.,* Livy, *a Roman historian*
locō, 1, place
locus, –ī, *m.* (*pl.* **loca, locōrum,** *n.*), place, country; rank, situation; opportunity
longē, *adv.,* far away, far, by far; **longē lātēque,** far and wide
longinquus, –a, –um, distant
longitūdō, –dinis, *f.,* length
longus, –a, –um, long
loquor, loquī, locūtus, talk, speak
lūdificō, 1, make sport of
lūdō, –ere, lūsī, lūsus, play
lūdus, –ī, *m.,* game, play, school
lūgeō, –ēre, lūxī, lūctus, mourn for
lūmen, lūminis, *n.,* light, lamp; glory; eye
lūna, –ae, *f.,* moon
lupus, –ī, *m.,* wolf
lūx, lūcis, *f.,* light; **prīmā** *or* **ortā lūce,** at dawn
lūxuria, –ae, *f.,* luxury
Lycurgus, –ī, *m.,* Lȳcur´gus

M

M., *abbreviation for* **Mārcus**
Macedonia, –ae, *f.,* Macedonia, *a country northeast of Greece;* **Macedonicus, –a, –um,** Macedonian
māceria, –ae, *f.,* wall
māchina, –ae, *f.,* machine
māchinātiō, –ōnis, *f.,* engine
maciēs, –ēī, *f.,* thinness
magicus, –a, –um, magic
magis, *adv.,* more, rather; *superl.* **maximē,** most, very, very greatly, especially, very hard
magister, –trī, *m.,* teacher
magistrātus, –ūs, *m.,* magistrate, official, office
magnificus, –a, –um, magnificent, generous
magnitūdō, –dinis, *f.,* greatness, size
magnopere, *adv.,* greatly
magnus, –a, –um, large, great, much, loud; *w.* **iter,** forced; *comp.* **maior, maius,** larger, greater; **maiōrēs, –um,** older men, ancestors; *superl.* **maximus, –a, –um,** greatest, very great
maiestās, –tātis, *f.,* dignity, honor
maior, *see* **magnus**
male, *adv.,* badly
mālō, mālle, māluī, —, prefer
malus, –a, –um, bad; *comp.* **peior, peius,** worse; *superl.* **pessimus, –a, –um,** very bad, worst; **malum, –ī,** *n.,* trouble
mandātum, –ī, *n.,* order
mandō, 1, commit, entrust, give, command; **fugae mē mandō,** take to flight
maneō, –ēre, mānsī, mānsūrus, remain, endure
manifēstus, –a, –um, obvious
manipulus, –ī, *m.,* maniple
manūmittō, –ere, –mīsī, –missus, make free
manus, –ūs, *f.,* hand, force
mare, maris, *n.,* sea
margarīta, –ae, *f.,* pearl

margarītārius, –rī, *m.,* pearl dealer
margō, marginis, *m.,* edge
maris, *see* **mare** *and* **mās**
maritimus, –a, –um, of the sea, near the sea; **ōra maritima, ōrae maritimae,** *f.,* seacoast
marītus, –ī, *m.,* husband
marmor, –oris, *n.,* marble
marmoreus, –a, –um, of marble
Mārs, Mārtis, *m.,* Mars, *god of war*
Mārtius, –a, –um, of Mars; of March; *as noun, m.,* Martius (Mar´shius)
mās, maris, *m.,* male
māter, mātris, *f.,* mother
māteria, –ae, *f.,* timber, wood
mātrimōnium, –nī, *n.,* marriage; **in mātrimōnium dō,** give in marriage; **in mātrimōnium dūcō,** marry
mātrōna, –ae, *f.,* wife, married woman
mātūrē, *adv.,* soon, quickly
mātūrō, 1, hasten
mātūrus, –a, –um, ripe, early, mature
maximē, *see* **magis; maximus,** *see* **magnus**
mēcum = cum mē
medicīna, –ae, *f.,* medicine
medicus, –ī, *m.,* doctor
mediocris, –e, short, moderate
mediocritās, –tātis, *f.,* mean
mediterrāneus, –a, –um, inland
medius, –a, –um, middle (of), midst of
mel, mellis, *n.,* honey
melior, *see* **bonus; melius,** *see* **bene**
membrum, –ī, *n.,* member, part of the body, limb
meminī (*perf. translated as pres.*), remember
memor, *gen.* **memoris,** mindful, unforgetting
memoria, –ae, *f.,* memory; **memoriā teneō,** remember
mēns, mentis, *f.,* mind
mēnsa, –ae, *f.,* table
mēnsis, –is, *m.,* month
mēnsūra, –ae, *f.,* measurement
mentiō, –ōnis, *f.,* mention
mercātor, –ōris, *m.,* trader, merchant
mercātūra, –ae, *f.,* trade
Mercurius, –rī, *m.,* Mercury, *god of trade and gain and messenger of the gods*
mereō, –ēre, meruī, meritus, deserve, earn, win
merīdiēs, –ēī, *m.,* midday, noon; south
meritum, –ī, *n.,* merit, service
mersus, –a, –um, submerged
mētior, –īrī, mēnsus, measure (out)
metuō, –ere, –uī, —, fear
metus, –ūs, *m.,* fear
meus, –a, –um, my mine
migrō, 1, move, depart
mīles, mīlitis, *m.,* soldier
mīlitāris, –e, military
mīlitia, –ae, *f.,* military service
mīlle, *pl.* **mīlia,** thousand
mīlle passūs, mile
Minerva, –ae, *f.,* Minerva, *goddess of wisdom*
minimē, *see* **minus**
minimus, *see* **parvus**
minor, *see* **parvus**
minuō, –ere, minuī, minūtus, lessen, settle
minus, *adv.,* less; *superl.* **minimē,** least, by no means
mīrābilis, –e, wonderful
mīrāculum, –ī, *n.,* wonderful thing
mīrātor, –ōris, *m.,* admirer
mīror, 1, wonder, wonder at, admire
mīrus, –a, –um, wonderful, strange
misceō, –ēre, –uī, mixtus, mix
miser, –era, –erum, unhappy, poor
miserābilis, –e, wretched
miseria, –ae, *f.,* wretchedness
mittō, –ere, mīsī, missus, let go, send, throw
mixta, *see* **misceō**
mōbilis, –e, moving
mōbilitās, –tātis, *f.,* changeableness
moderātus, –a, –um, moderate
modernus, –a, –um, modern
modestē, *adv.,* modestly
modo, *adv.,* only, merely, even; **nōn modo . . . sed etiam,** not only . . . but also
modus, –ī, *m.,* measure, manner, kind, plan, way; **quem ad modum,** how
moenia, –ium, *m. pl.,* (city) walls
molestia, –ae, *f.,* annoyance
molliō, –īre, –īvī, –ītus, soften
mollis, –e, tender
mollitia, –ae, *f.,* weakness
Mona, –ae, *f.,* the Isle of Man, *between England and Ireland*
moneō, –ēre, monuī, monitus, remind, advise, warn
monitus, –ūs, *m.,* warning
mōns, montis, *m.,* mountain, hill, mount
mōnstrō, 1, point out, show
mōnstrum, –ī, *n.,* monster
monumentum, –ī, *n.,* monument
mora, –ae, *f.,* delay, stay
morbus, –ī, *m.,* disease
morior, morī, mortuus, die; **mortuus, –a, –um,** dead, having died; **moritūrus,** about to die
moror, 1, delay, stay
mors, mortis, *f.,* death
mortālis, –e, mortal
mortifer, –fera, –ferum, deadly
mortuus, *see* **morior**
mōs, mōris, *m.,* custom; *pl.,* character
mōtus, –ūs, *m.,* motion, movement
moveō, –ēre, mōvī, mōtus, move, stir (up)
mox, *adv.,* soon
mūla, –ae, *f.,* mule
mulier, mulieris, *f.,* woman
multitūdō, –dinis, *f.,* multitude, (great) number
multō, *adv.,* much
multum, *adv.,* much, great; *comp.* **plūs,** more; *superl.* **plūrimum,** most, very much, great deal

multus, –a, –um, much; *pl.*, many; *comp.* **plūrēs, plūra**, more, several; *superl.* **plūrimus, –a, –um**, most, very many
mundānus, –a, –um, of the world
mundus, –ī, *m.*, world, universe
mūniō, –īre, –īvī, –ītus, fortify, protect; **viam mūniō**, build a road
mūnītiō, –ōnis, *f.*, fortification, defenses
mūnus, –eris, *n.*, duty, gift; *pl.*, shows (of gladiators), games
mūrālis, –e, wall
mūrus, –ī, *m.*, wall
Mūsae, –ārum, *f. pl.*, the Muses
mūtābilis, –e, changeable, fickle
mutilus, –a, –um, broken
mūtō, 1, change
mūtus, –a, –um, mute

N

nactus, *part of* **nancīscor**
nam, namque, *conj.*, for
nancīscor, nancīscī, nactus, gain, obtain, find, meet with
narrō, 1, tell, relate
nāscor, nāscī, nātus, be born, be found; **duōs annōs nātus**, two years old; **nātus, –ī**, *m.*, son
nātālis, –e, of birth; **diēs nātālis**, birthday
nātiō, –ōnis, *f.*, nation, tribe
natō, 1, swim, float
nātūra, –ae, *f.*, nature
nātus, *part. of* **nāscor**
naumachia, –ae, *f.*, sea fight
nauta, –ae, *m.*, sailor
nāvālis, –e, naval
nāvigium, –gī, *n.*, boat
nāvigō, 1, sail
nāvis, nāvis, *f.*, ship; **nāvis longa**, warship; **nāvis onerāria**, transport
–ne, *introduces questions; indirect questions*, whether
–nē, *conj.*, not, (so) that . . . not, in order that . . . not, that; *adv.*, not; **ne... quidem** (*emphatic word between*), not even

nec, *see* **neque**
necessāriō, *adv.*, necessarily
necessārius, –a, –um, necessary
necesse, *indeclinable adj.*, necessary
necessitās, –tātis, *f.*, necessity
necō, 1, kill
nefārius, –a, –um, unspeakable
nefās, *n.*, *indeclinable*, sin, wrong
neglegō, –ere, –lēxī, –lectus, disregard, neglect
negō, 1, say no, deny, say . . . not
negōtium, –tī, *n.*, business, trouble, task, job
nēmō, *dat.* **nēminī**, *acc.* **nēminem** (*no other forms*), no one
nepōs, nepōtis, *m.*, grandson
nēquāquam, *adv.*, by no means
neque (*or* **nec**), and not, not; **neque... neque**, neither . . . nor; **neque quisquam**, not a single one
nesciō, nescīre, nescīvī, —, not know
neu, *see* **nēve**
neuter, –tra, –trum, neither (*of two*)
nēve (neu), *conj.*, and not, nor
nex, necis, *f.*, death
niger, –gra, –grum, black
nihil, nīl, nothing, not
nimis, too much
nisi, *conj.*, unless, except
niveus, –a, –um, snow-white
nix, nivis, *f.*, snow
nōbilis, –e, distinguished, noble
nōbilitās, –tātis, *f.*, nobility
nōbīscum = cum nōbīs
noceō, –ēre, nocuī, nocitūrus, do harm to, injure (*w. dat.*)
noctū, *adv.*, by night
nocturnus, –a, –um, of night, night
nōlō, nōlle, nōluī, —, not want, not wish, be unwilling
nōmen, nōminis, *n.*, name
nōminātim, *adv.*, by name
nōminō, 1, name

nōn, *adv.*, not; **nōn iam**, no longer; **nōn nūllī (nōnnūllī), –ae, –a**, some; **nōn numquam**, sometimes
nōndum, *adv.*, not yet
nōnus, –a, –um, ninth
Nōreia, –ae, *f.*, Norē´ia, *a city of the Norici*
Nōricus, –a, –um, Norican, of the Norici
nōs, we, *pl. of* **ego**
nōscō, –ere, nōvī, nōtus, learn, recognize; *perf.*, have learned, know
noster, –tra, –trum, our, ours
nōtus, –a, –um, known, familiar, well-known, noted
novem, nine
novō, 1, renew
novus, –a, –um, new, strange; **novis-simum agmem** *or* **novissimī**, the rear; *w.* **rēs** *or* **imperia**, revolution
nox, noctis, *f.*, night
noxia, –ae, *f.*, crime
nūbēs, –is, *f.*, cloud
nūdō, 1, strip, expose
nūgae, –ārum, *f.*, nonsense
nūllus, –a, –um, no, none; *as noun, m.*, no one; **nōn nūllī**, some
num, *adv.*, *introduces questions expecting negative answer; conj.*, whether
nūmen, nūminis, *n.*, divinity, will
numerus, –ī, *m.*, number
Numidae, –ārum, *m. pl.*, the Numidians
nummus, –i, *m.*, coin, money
numquam, *adv.*, never
nunc, *adv.*, now
nūntiō, 1, report, announce
nūntius, –tī, *m.*, messenger; message, news, report
nūper, *adv.*, recently
nūptiae, –ārum, *f. pl.*, wedding
nūtriō, –īre, –īvī, –ītus, nourish, foster
nūtus, –ūs, *m.*, nod
nux, nucis, *f.*, nut
nympha, –ae, *f.*, nymph

O

ō! *interj.*, O!
ob, *prep. w. acc.*, because of, on account of, for
obiciō, –ere, obiēcī, obiectus, throw to *or* against, put in the way, oppose
oblinō, –ere, oblēvī, oblitus, smear
obscūrus, –a, –um, dark
observō, 1, observe, watch
obses, obsidis, *m.*, hostage
obsideō, –ēre, obsēdī, obsessus, besiege, blockade
obsidiō, –ōnis, *f.*, siege
obstō, –āre, obstitī, obstātūrus, 1prevent
obtemperō, 1, submit to
obtestor, 1, entreat, pray
obtineō, –ēre, obtinuī, obtentus, hold, obtain
occāsiō, –ōnis, *f.*, opportunity
occāsus, –ūs, *m.*, setting; **occāsus sōlis**, sunset, west
occidō, –ere, occidī, occāsūrus, set
occīdo, –ere, occīdi, occīsus, kill
occultō, 1, conceal
occultus, –a, –um, secret
occupātiō, –ōnis, *f.*, business
occupō, 1, seize, occupy; **occupātus**, busy
occurrō, –ere, occurrī, occursūrus, run against, meet, occur
Ōceanus, –ī, *m.*, ocean (*esp. the Atlantic Ocean*)
Octāviānus, –ī, *m.*, Octā´vian, *the emperor Augustus*
octāvus, –a, –um, eighth
octō, eight
oculus, –ī, *m.*, eye
ōdī, ōsūrus (*perf. translated as pres.*), hate
offerō, offerre, obtulī, oblātus, offer; **mē offerō,** rush against
officium, –cī, *n.*, duty
ōh! *interj.*, oh!
ōlim, *adv.*, once, formerly, sometime
Olympia, –ae, *f.*, Olympia, *a Greek city;* **Olympicus, –a, –um,** Olympic
Olympiēum, –ī, *n.*, Olympiē´um, *temple of the Olympian Jupiter*
ōmen, ōminis, *n.*, omen, sign
omittō, –ere, omīsī, omissus, let go, drop, disregard
omnīnō, *adv.*, altogether, in all
omnis, omne, all, every, whole
onerārius, –a, –um, for freight; **nāvis onerāria**, transport
onerōsus, –a, –um, heavy
onus, oneris, *n.*, weight
opācus, –a, –um, gloomy
opera, –ae, *f.*, work, effort
opēs, –um, *f. pl.*, resources
opīniō, –ōnis, *f.*, opinion, expectation; reputation
oportet, –ēre, oportuit, it is necessary, ought
oppidum, –ī, *n.*, town
opportūnus, –a, –um, opportune, convenient, advantageous
opprimō, –ere, oppressī, oppressus; overcome, surprise, crush, oppress
oppugnātiō, –ōnis, *f.*, siege, method of attack
oppugnō, 1, attack, besiege
ops, opis, *f.*, aid; *pl.*, wealth, resources
optimē, *see* **bene**
optimus, *see* **bonus**
optō, 1, desire
opus, operis, *n.*, work
opus, *n.*, *indeclinable,* need; necessary
ōra, –ae, *f.*, coast, edge
ōrāculum, –ī, *n.*, oracle, prophesy
ōrātiō, –ōnis, *f.*, speech
ōrātor, –ōris, *m.*, speaker, orator
orbis, –is, *m.*, circle; *esp. w.* **terrārum**, the world (*i.e., the circle of lands around the Mediterranean*)
Orcus, –ī, *m.*, Orcus, *god of Hades;* Hades
ōrdō, ōrdinis, *m.*, order, rank
oriēns, –entis, m., east
orīgo, originis, *f.*, origin
orior, orīrī, ortus, rise, arise, begin, be descended from
ōrnō, 1, adorn; **ōrnātus**, fitted out
ōrō, 1, beg, ask, pray (for), plead
Orpheus, –ī, *m.*, Orpheus (Or´fūs), *a famous musician*
ōs, ōris, *n.*, mouth, face, expression
os, ossis, *n.*, bone
ōsculum, –ī, *n.*, kiss
ostendō, –ere, ostendī, ostentus, (stretch out), show, display
ōtium, ōtī, *n.*, leisure, quiet
Ovidius, –dī, *m.*, Ovid
ōvum, –ī, *n.*, egg

P

P., *abbreviation for* **Pūblius**
pābulos, 1, forage
pābulum, –ī, *n.*, food (for cattle), fodder
pācō, 1, pacify, subdue
paene, *adv.*, almost
Paestum, –ī, *n.*, Paestum (Pĕs´tum), *a town in southern Italy*
pāgus, –ī, *m.*, district, canton
Palātīnus (mōns), –ī, *m.*, **Palātium, –tī,** *n.*, the Palatine Hill; palace
palma, –ae, *f.*, hand
palūs, palūdis, *f.*, marsh, swamp
pānis, –is, *m.*, bread
pār, *gen.* **paris**, equal, fair; *as noun, n.*, pair
parcē, *adv.*, sparingly
parcō, –ere, pepercī, parsūrus, spare, save
parcus, –a, –um, sparing, economical
parēns, –entis, *m. and f.*, parent
pāreō, –ēre, pāruī, pāritūrus, (appear), obey
pariō, –ere, peperī, partus, gain
Parnassius, –a, –um, Parnassian
parō, 1, get, get ready (for), prepare; **parātus, –a, um,** prepared, ready

pars, partis, *f.,* part, side, direction
parvulus, –a, –um, very small, little
parvus, –a, –um, small, low; *comp.* **minor, minus,** smaller, less, lesser, younger; *superl.* **minimus, –a, –um,** smallest, least, very little, youngest
passus, –ūs, *m.,* step, pace (*about five feet*); **mīlle passūs,** mile
passus, *part. of* **patior**
pāstor, –ōris, *m.,* shepherd
patefaciō, –ere, –fēcī, –factus, open
patēns, *gen.* **patentis,** open
pateō, –ēre, patuī, —, stand open, extend
pater, patris, *m.,* father, senator; **patrēs cōnscrīptī,** senators
paternus, –a, –um, of the father
patienter, *adv.,* patiently
patientia, –ae, *f.,* patience
patior, patī, passus, suffer, permit
patria, –ae, *f.,* fatherland, country
patrius, –a, –um, of a father, ancestral
patrūus, –ī, *m.,* uncle
paucī, –ae, –a, few, only a few
paucitās, –tātis, *f.,* small number
paulātim, *adv.,* little by little; a few at a time
paulisper, *adv.,* for a little while
paulō *and* **paulum,** *adv.,* shortly, a little
pauper, *gen.* **pauperis,** poor
paupertās, –tātis, *f.,* poverty
paveō, –ēre, pāvī, —, fear
pavidus, –a, –um, trembling
pāx, pācis, *f.,* peace
pectus, pectoris, *n.,* breast, heart
pecūnia, –ae, *f.,* money
pecus, pecoris, *n.,* cattle
pedes, peditis, *m.,* foot soldier; *pl.,* infantry
pedester, –tris, –tre, (of) infantry; on foot
peditātus, –ūs, *m.,* infantry
perior, *see* **malus**
pellis, –is, *f.,* skin
pellō, –ere, pepulī, pulsus, drive, defeat
pendeō, –ēre, pependī, —, hang
pendō, –ere, pependī, pēnsus, hang, weigh, pay
penetrō, 1, penetrate
per, *prep. w. acc.,* through, by, during, along
peragō, –ere, –ēgī, –āctus, complete
percipiō, –ere, –cēpī, –ceptus, feel, learn
percutiō, –ere, –cussī, –cussus, strike
perdiscō, –ere, –didicī, —, learn thoroughly
perdō, –ere, –didī, –ditus, lose, destroy, waste
perdūcō, –ere, –dūxī, –ductus, lead *or* bring through, extend, win over
pereō, –īre, –iī (–īvī), –itūrus, perish, pass away, be lost
perfero, –ferre, –tulī, –lātus, carry (through), report, endure
perficiō, –ere, –fēcī, –fectus, make of, bring about, finish
perfidia, –ae, *f.,* faithlessness, treachery
perfidus, –a, –um, treacherous
perfuga, –ae, *m.,* deserter
perfugiō, –ere, –fūgī, —, flee
perīculōsus, –a, –um, dangerous
perīculum, –ī, *n.,* trial, danger
perītus, –a, –um, skilled, experienced
perlegō, –ere, –lēgī, –lēctus, read through
permaneō, –ēre, –mānsī, –mānsūrus, remain
permittō, –ere, –mīsī, –missus, let go through, leave, allow, grant, entrust, permit
permoveō, –ēre, –mōvī, –mōtus, move deeply, induce, alarm
perpaucī, –ae, –a, very few
perpetuus, –a, –um, constant, lasting
perrumpō, –ere, –rūpī, –ruptus, break through
Persae, –ārum, *m. pl.,* the Persians
persequor, –sequī, –secūtus, pursue, punish
perspiciō, –ere, –spexī, –spectus, see (clearly), examine
perstō, –āre, –stitī, –stātūrus, persist
persuādeo, –ēre, –suāsī, –suāsūrus, persuade
perterreō, –ēre, –terruī, –territus, scare thoroughly, alarm
pertināciter, *adv.,* persistently
pertineō, –ēre, –tinuī, –tentūrus, extend (to), pertain to
pertrānseō, –īre, –īvī, –itūrus, pass through
perturbātiō, –ōnis, *f.,* confusion
perturbō, 1, disturb, throw into confusion
perveniō, –īre, –vēnī, –ventūrus, come (through), arrive (at)
pēs, pedis, *m.,* foot; **pedibus,** on foot
pessimus, *see* **malus**
petō, –ere, petīvī, petītus, seek, ask, beg; attack
Pharsālus, –ī, *f.,* Pharsā´lus, *a town in Thessaly*
Philippī, –ōrum, *m. pl.,* Philippi (Filĭp´ī), *a city in Macedonia*
Philippus, –ī, *m.,* Philip
philosophus, –ī, *m.,* philosopher
pictūra, –ae, *f.,* picture
pila, –ae, *f.,* ball
pilula, –ae, *f.,* pill
pīlum, –ī, *n.,* spear (*for throwing*), javelin
piscis, –is, *m.,* fish
piscor, 1, fish
pius, –a, –um, dutiful, righteous, pious

placeō, –ēre, placuī, placitūrus, be pleasing to, please; **placet,** it pleases (him), *i.e.,* (he) decides, be decided
placidus, –a, –um, gentle
plācō, 1, appease
plānitiēs, –ēī, *f.,* plain
plānus, –a, –um, level
Platō, –ōnis, *m.,* Plā´tō, *a Greek philosopher*
plēbs, plēbis, *f.,* common people
plēnus, –a, –um, full
plērīque, –aeque, –aque, most
plērumque, *adv.,* usually
plūrēs, *see* **multus**
plūrimum, *see* **multum**
plūrimus, *see* **multus**
plūs, *see* **multum, multus**
poena, –ae, *f.,* penalty, punishment; **poenam dō,** pay the penalty
Poenī, –ōrum, *m. pl.,* the Carthaginians
poēta, –ae, *m.,* poet
polliceor, pollicērī, pollicitus, promise
pollicitātiō, –ōnis, *f.,* promise
pōmārium, –rī, *n.,* orchard
pompa, –ae, *f.,* parade, procession
Pompeiānus, –a, –um, at Pompeii
Pompeius, –peī, *m.,* Pompey
Pomptīnae palūdēs, Pŏn´tīne Marshes, *south of Rome*
pondus, ponderis, *n.,* weight
pōnō, –ere, posuī, positus, put, place, serve, lay down; *passive,* be situated, depend upon; *w.* **castra,** pitch
pōns, pontis, *m.,* bridge
pontifex, pontificis, *m.,* priest
pontus, –ī, *m.,* sea
poposci, *see* **poscō**
populor, 1, destroy
populus, –ī, *m.,* people; *pl.,* peoples
porta, –ae, *f.,* gate, door
porticus, –ūs, *f.,* colonnade
portō, 1, carry
portus, –ūs, *m.,* harbor, port
poscō, –ere, poposcī, —, demand, call for
possessiō, –ōnis, *f.,* possession
possum, posse, potuī, —, can, can do, be able; **multum (plūs, plūrimum) possum,** be very powerful
post, *adv. and prep. w. acc.,* behind; after, later; **paulō post,** a little later
posteā, *adv.,* afterwards, later; **posteāquam,** *conj.,* after
posterus, –a, –um, following, next; *as noun, m. pl.,* posterity, descendants
postquam, *conj.,* after
postrēmō, *adv.,* finally
postrīdiē, *adv.,* on the next day
postulō, 1, demand
potēns, *gen.* **potentis,** powerful
potentia, –ae, *f.,* power
potestās, –tātis, *f.,* power
potior, potīrī, potītus, gain possession of (*w. gen. or abl.*)
potius, *adv.,* rather
prae, *prep. w. abl.,* before; in comparison with
praeacūtus, –a, –um, pointed
praebeō, –ēre, –uī, –itus, hold forth, furnish, present, show
praecēdō, –ere, –cessī, –cessūrus, go before, precede
praeceps, *gen.* **praecipitis,** headlong
praeceptum, –ī, *n.,* rule, instruction
praecipiō, –ere, –cēpī, –ceptus, instruct
praecō, parecōnis, *m.,* announcer
praeda, –ae, *f.,* loot
praedicō, 1, announce, declare
praedīcō, –ere, –dīxī, –dictus, predict
praedor, 1, loot
praedūcō, –ere, –dūxī, –ductus, extend
praefectus, –ī, *m.,* commander, prefect
praeficiō, –ere, –fēcī, –fectus, put *or* place in charge of
praemittō, –ere, –mīsī, –missus, send ahead
praemium, –mī, *n.,* reward
praemūniō = mūniō
praenōscō, –ere, –nōvī, –nōtus, learn beforehand
praeparō, 1, prepare
praerumpō, –ere, –rūpī, –ruptus, break off
praescrībō, –ere, –scrīpsī, –scrīptus, direct
praescrīptum, –ī, *n.,* order
praesēns, *gen.* **praesentis,** present
praesentiō, –īre, –sēnsī, –sēnsus, foresee
praesertim, *adv.,* especially
praesidium, –dī, *n.,* garrison, guard, protection, aid
praestāns, *gen.* **praestantis,** outstanding
praestō, –āre, –stitī, –stitūrus, stand before, excel; offer, perform, show; **praestat,** it is better
praesum, –esse, –fuī, –futūrus, be in charge of, be in command of
praeter, *prep. w. acc.,* besides, except, beyond
praetereā, *adv.,* besides
praetereō, –īre, –iī, –itus, go by, pass
praeterquam, *adv.,* other than
praetor, –ōris, *m.,* praetor (*an official*), judge
praevaleō, –ēre, –valuī, –valitūrus, prevail
prandium, –dī, *n.,* lunch
prātum, –ī, *n.,* meadow
prehendō, –ere, –hendī, –hensus, grasp, seize, catch
premō, –ere, pressī, pressus, press, press hard, oppress, crowd
prēndō = prehendō
pretium, –tī, *n.,* price; reward
prex, precis, *f.,* prayer, entreaty
prīdiē, *adv.,* on the day before
prīmō, *adv.,* at first
prīmum, *adv.,* first, at first, for the first time; **quam prīmum,** as soon as possible
prīmus, –a, –um, first; **in prīmīs,** especially

prīnceps, prīncipis, *adj. and noun, m.,* chief, first (man), leader, emperor; **prīnceps,** under the direction of
prīncipātus, –ūs, *m.,* first place, leadership
prior, prius, former, first
prīstinus, –a, –um, former
prius, *adv.,* before, first; **priusquam (prius... quam),** *conj.,* before
prīvātus, –a, –um, private; *as noun, m.,* private citizen
prō, *prep. w. abl.,* in front of, before, for, instead of, as, in accordance with, in proportion to
probitās, –tātis, *f.,* honesty
probō, 1, prove, approve
prōcēdō, –ere, –cessī, –cessūrus, go forward, advance, proceed
procul, *adv.,* at a distance, far off
prōcumbō, –ere, –cubuī, –cubitūrus, lie down, sink down
prōcūrō, 1, take care of
prōcurrō, –ere, –currī, –cursūrus, run forward
prōdō, –ere, –didī, –ditus, give (forth), hand down, betray
prōdūcō, –ere, –dūxī, –ductus, lead *or* bring out, prolong
proelium, –lī, *n.,* battle
profectiō, –ōnis, *f.,* departure
prōferō, prōferre, prōtulī, prōlātus, bring out, extend
professor, –ōris, *m.,* professor
prōficiō, –ere, –fēcī, –fectus, accomplish
proficīscor, proficīscī, profectus, set out, start
profugiō, –ere, –fūgī, –fugitūrus, flee
prōgeniēs, –iēī, *f.,* descendants
prōgnātus, –a, –um, descended
prōgredior, prōgredī, prōgressus, step forward, advance
prohibeō, –ēre, –hibuī, –hibitus, prevent, keep from, cut off
prōiciō, –ere, –iēcī, –iectus, throw, thrust (forward), abandon
prōlabor, –ī, prōlāpsus, slip
prōmittō, –ere, –mīsī, –missus, let go; promise; **prōmissus,** long
prōmoveō, –ēre, –mōvī, –mōtus, move forward
prōmptus, –a, –um, ready
prōnūntiō, 1, announce, recite
prōnus, –a, –um, flat
prope, *adv.,* almost; *prep. w. acc.,* near
prōpellō, –ere, –pulī, –pulsus, drive away, dislodge
properō, 1, hasten, hurry (on)
propinquitās, –tātis, *f.,* nearness
propinquus, –a, –um, near; *as noun, m.,* relative
propitius, –a, –um, favorable
prōpōnō, –ere, –posuī, –positus, explain, present, offer, raise, propose
proprius, –a, –um, (one's) own, characteristic of
propter, *prep. w. acc.,* because of, on account of
propterea, *adv.,* on this account; **propterea quod,** because
prōpugnō, 1, fight on the offensive
prōra, –ae, *f.,* prow
prōscrīptiō, –ōnis, *f.,* proscription, list of condemned
prōsequor, prōsequī, prōsecūtus, pursue, address
prōspectus, –ūs, *m.,* view
prōspiciō, –ere, –spexī, –spectus, look out for, see
prōsternō, –ere, –strāvī, –strātus, overthrow
prōsum, prōdesse, prōfuī, —, benefit, help
prōtegō, –ere, –tēxī, –tēctus, cover
prōtinus, *adv.,* immediately
prōvehō, –ere, –vexī, –vectus, carry forward
prōvideō, –ēre, –vīdī, –vīsus, provide, look out for
prōvincia, –ae, *f.,* province
proximē, *adv.,* recently
proximus, –a, –um, nearest, last, next, very near
prūdēns, *gen.* **prūdentis,** sensible
prūdentia, –ae, *f.,* foresight, good sense
publicē, *adv.,* publicly
pūblicus, –a, –um, public
Pūblius, Pūblī, *m.,* Pub´lius
puella, –ae, *f.,* girl
puer, puerī, *m.,* boy, child
puerīlis, –e, boyish, childish
puerīliter, *adv.,* childishly
pueritia, –ae, *f.,* childhood, boyhood
pugna, –ae, *f.,* fight, battle
pugnō, 1, fight
pulcher, –chra, –chrum, beautiful
pulchritūdō, –dinis, *f.,* beauty
pulsō, 1, dash against
pulsus, *part. of* **pellō**
Pūnicus, –a, –um, Punic, Carthaginian
pūniō, –īre, –īvī, –ītus, punish
puppis, –is, *f.,* stern
pūrgō, 1, cleanse
purpurātus, –a, –um, purple
putō, 1, think, consider
Pȳrēnaeī montēs, Pyrenees Mountains

Q

Q., *abbreviation for* **Quīntus**
quā, *adv.,* where
quadringentī, –ae, –a, four hundred
quaerō, –ere, quaesīvī, quaesītus, seek, inquire
quaestiō, –ōnis, *f.,* investigation
quaestor, –ōris, *m.,* quaestor (*a Roman official*), treasury official
quaestus, –ūs, *m.,* gain
quālis, –e, what kind of, what, such as
quam, *adv. and conj.,* how, as; *w. comp.,* than; *w. superl.,* as . . . as possible; **quam prīmum,** as soon as possible
quamquam, *conj.,* although

quandō, *conj.*, when
quantus, –a, –um, how great, how much, what, as (great *or* much as)
quārē, why
quartus, –a, –um, fourth; **quārtus decimus,** fourteenth
quasi, *adv. and conj.*, as if, like, as it were
quattuor, four
–que, *conj.* (*added to second word*), and
queror, querī, questus, complain
quī, quae, quod, *rel. pron.*, who, which, what, that; *interrog. adj.*, what; **quī, qua, quod,** *indef. adj.*, any
quia, *conj.*, because
quīcumque, quaecumque, quodcumque, whoever, whatever
quid, *adv.*, why
quīdam, quaedam, quiddam *and* (*adj.*) **quoddam,** a certain one *or* thing; *adj.*, certain, some, a, one
quidem, *adv.* (*follows emphasized word*), at least, to be sure; **nē . . . quidem**, not even
quidnam, what in the world
quiēs, quiētis, *f.*, rest, sleep, quiet
quiētus, –a, –um, quiet; **quiētē**, *adv.*, quietly
quīn, *conj.*, that; **quīn etiam**, moreover
Quīnctīlis, –e, (of) July
quīngentī, –ae, –a, five hundred
quīnquāgintā, fifty
quīnque, five
Quīntiliānus, –ī, *m.*, Quintil´ian
quīntus, –a, –um, fifth
Quirīnālis (mōns), –is, *m.*, Quĭr´inal Hill
quis, quid, *interrog, pron.*, who, what; *indef. pron.*, anyone, anything
quisquam, quicquam, anyone, anything, any; **neque quisquam,** not a single one
quisque, quidque, each one, each thing, each
quō, *adv.*, where, to which; **quō modō**, how
quō, *conj.*, in order that; **quō minus (quōminus),** that not
quoad, *conj.*, as long as
quod, *conj.*, because, that, since; **quod sī**, but if
quondam, *adv.*, once (upon a time)
quoniam, *conj.*, since, because
quoque, *adv.*, too (*follows the word it emphasizes)*
quot, *indeclinable adj.*, how many; as (many as)
quotannīs, *adv.*, every year
quotiēns, *adv.*, as often as, how often

R

radiō, 1, shine
rādīx, –dīcis, *f.*, root
raeda, –ae, *f.*, carriage, bus
rāmulus, –ī, *m.*, branch
rāmus, –ī, *m.*, branch
rana, –ae, *f.*, frog
rapiditās, –tātis, *f.*, swiftness
rapiō, –ere, rapuī, raptus, seize, carry off
rārus, –a, –um, rare
ratiō, –ōnis, *f.*, account, plan, manner, reason, consideration, method, theory, system, judgment
ratis, –is, *f.*, raft
rebelliō, –ōnis, *f.*, rebellion
recēdō, –ere, recessī, recessūrus, withdraw
recēns, *gen.* **recentis,** new, recent
recēnseō, –ēre, recēnsuī, recēnsus, count again, review
recingō, –ere, recīnxī, recīnctus, loosen
recipiō, –ere, recēpī, receptus, take (back), receive, recover; **mē recipiō**, withdraw, recover, retire
recitō, 1, recite, read aloud
reclīnō, 1, bend back; *passive*, lean
rectē, *adv.*, rightly
rēctus, *see* **regō**
recuperō, 1, get back, recover
recursō, 1, run back and forth
recūsō, 1, refuse
reddō, –ere, reddidī, redditus, give (back), render, return, restore, reflect
redeō, –īre, rediī, reditūrus, go back, return
redigō, –ere, redēgī, redāctus, bring (back), drive back, reduce
redimō, –ere, redēmī, redēmptus, buy back, ransom
redintegrō, 1, renew
reditus, –ūs, *m.*, return
redūcō, –ere, redūxī, reductus, lead back, bring back
referō, referre, rettulī, relātus, bring *or* carry (back), report, reproduce; **pedem referō**, withdraw; **grātiam referō**, show gratitude
reficiō, –ere, refēcī, refectus, repair, refresh, restore
rēgia, –ae, *f.*, palace
rēgīna, –ae, *f.*, queen
regiō, –ōnis, *f.*, district, region
rēgnō, 1, reign, rule
rēgnum, –ī, *n.*, royal power, kingdom, rule
regō, –ere, rēxī, rēctus, rule, direct; **rēctus**, straight
reiciō, –ere, reiēcī, reiectus, drive back, reject
relābor, relābī, relāpsus, slip back
relanguēscō, –ere, –languī, —, become weak
religiō, –ōnis, *f.*, religion, superstition
relinquō, –ere, relīquī, relictus, leave (behind), abandon
reliquus, –a, –um, remaining, rest (of), left; *w.* **tempus,** the future
remaneō, –ēre, remānsī, remānsūrus, remain
remedium, –dī, *n.*, remedy

rēmigō, –āre, —, —, row
remigrō, 1, go back
remissiō, –ōnis, *f.,* forgiveness
remittō, –ere, remīsī, remissus, send *or* throw back, remit, relax; **remissus,** mild
removeō, –ēre, remōvī, remōtus, move back, remove; **remōtus,** remote
rēmus, –ī, *m.,* oar
Rēmus, –ī, *m.,* a Rē´man
renūntiō, 1, report
reparō, 1, restore
repellō, –ere, reppulī, repulsus, drive back, repulse
repente, *adv.,* suddenly
repentīnus, –a, –um, sudden
reperiō, –īre, repperī, repertus, find
repetō, –ere, –īvī, –ītus, seek back
reportō, 1, carry *or* bring back
reprimō, –ere, repressī, repressus, stop
repudiō, 1, divorce
repugnō, 1, oppose
requiēs, –ētis, *f.,* rest
requiēscō, –ere, –ēvī, –ētus, rest
requīrō, –ere, requīsīvī, requīsītus, miss
rēs, reī, *f.,* thing, matter, affair, circumstance; **novae rēs, novārum rerum,** *f. pl.,* revolution; **rēs frūmentāria, reī frūmentāriae,** *f.,* grain supply; **rēs mīlitāris,** military affairs, art of war; **rēs pūblica,** public affairs, government, state; **rēs gestae,** deeds
rescindō, –ere, rescidī, rescissus, cut down
reservō, 1, reserve
resideō, –ēre, resēdī, —, remain
resistō, –ere, restitī, —, stand against; resist
resolvō, –ere, resolvī, resolūtus, loosen
respiciō, –ere, respexī, respectus, look back, consider
respondeō, –ēre, respondī, respōnsus, reply, answer; **respōnsum, –ī,** *n.,* answer
respuō, –ere, respui, —, reject
restituō, –ere, restituī, restitūtus, restore
restō, –āre, restitī, —, remain
resūmō, –ere, resūmpsī, resūmptus, take up again, resume
resurgō = surgō
retineō, –ēre, retinuī, retentus, hold back, restrain, keep
retrahō, –ere, retrāxī, retrāctus, drag back
retrō, *adv.,* back
rettulī, *see* **referō**
reus, –ī, *m.,* defendant
revereor, reverērī, reveritus, respect
revertō, –ere, revertī, reversus, (*sometimes deponent*), turn back, return
revīsō, –ere, —, —, revisit
revocō, 1, recall, call back
rēx, rēgis, *m.,* king
Rhēnus, –ī, *m.,* Rhine river
rhētor, –ōris, *m.,* rhetorician
Rhodanus, –ī, *m.,* Rhone river
rīdeō, –ēre, rīsī, rīsus, laugh (at)
rigor, –ōris, *m.,* stiffness
rīpa, –ae, *f.,* bank (*of a river*)
rōborō, 1, strengthen
rogitō, 1, keep on asking
rogō, 1, ask
Rōma, –ae, *f.,* Rome
Rōmānus, –a, –um, Roman; *as noun,* a Roman
rosa, –ae, *f.,* rose
rostrum, –ī, *n.,* prow (of a ship); beak
rotundus, –a, –um, round
rudis, –e, untrained, ignorant
ruīna, –ae, *f.,* ruin, destruction
rūmor, –ōris, *m.,* rumor
rumpō, –ere, rūpī, ruptus, break
rūpēs, –is, *f.,* cliff, rock
rūrsus, *adv.,* again
rūsticus, –a, –um, rustic

S

Sabīnus, –a, –um, Sā´bīne: *as noun, f.,* a Sabine woman; *pl.,* the Sā´bīnes, *a people of Italy*
sacer, sacra, sacrum, sacred
sacerdōs, –dōtis, *m.,* priest
sacrificium, –cī, *n.,* sacrifice
sacrificō, 1, sacrifice
saeculum (saeclum), –ī, *n.,* age
saepe, *adv.,* often
saevitia, –ae, *f.,* fierceness
saevus, –a, –um, cruel
sagitta, –ae, *f.,* arrow
sagittārius, –rī, *m.,* bowman
Saliī, –ōrum, *m. pl.,* the Sā´liī *or* "Jumpers" (*priests of Mars*)
saliō, –īre, saluī, saltūrus, jump, beat
saltō, 1, dance
salūbris, –e, wholesome, healthy
salūs, –ūtis, *f.,* health, safety, greeting
salūtātor, –ōris, *m.,* greeter, visitor
salvē, salvēte, be well, greetings, hail
sānctus, –a, –um, sacred
sanguis, sanguinis, *m.,* blood
sānitās, –tātis, *f.,* sanity
sānus, –a, –um, sound
sapiēns, *gen.* **sapientis,** wise
sapienter, wisely
sapientia, –ae, *f.,* wisdom
satis, *adv. and indeclinable adj.,* enough, rather
satisfaciō, –ere, –fēcī, –factus, satisfy
saxum, –ī, *n.,* rock, stone
scaena, –ae, *f.,* stage
scaenicus, –a, –um, of the theater; *w.* **lūdī,** stage plays
scelus, sceleris, *n.,* crime
scēptrum, –ī, *n.,* scepter
schola, –ae, *f.,* school
scholasticus, –a, –um, scholastic; *as noun, m.,* student
scientia, –ae, *f.,* knowledge
sciō, scīre, scīvī, scītus, know, know how
scrība, –ae, *m.,* secretary

scrībō, –ere, scrīpsī, scrīptus, write
sculpō, –ere, sculpsī, sculptus, carve
scūtum, –ī, *n.,* shield
Scythae, –ārum, *m. pl.,* the Scythians (Sĭth´ians), *people beyond the Black Sea*
sē, *acc. and abl. of* **suī**
sēcēdō, –ere, sēcessī, sēcessūrus, secede, withdraw
sēcrētō, *adv.,* in private, secretly
sēcum = cum sē
secundus, –a, –um, second, favorable
sed, *conj.,* but
sedeō, –ēre, sēdī, sessūrus, sit
sēdēs, –is, *f.,* abode
sēdō, 1, quiet
sēductus, –a, –um, separated
sella, –ae, *f.,* chair, seat, stool
semel, *adv.,* once
sēmibarbarus, –a, –um, half-barbarian
semita, –ae, *f.,* path, footpath
semper, *adv.,* always
senātor, –ōris, *m.,* senator
senātus, –ūs, *m.,* senate
senectūs, –tūtis, *f.,* old age
senex, senis, *m.,* old man; *adj.,* old; *comp.* **senior**
sententia, –ae, *f.,* feeling, opinion
sentiō, –īre, sēnsī, sēnsus, feel, think, realize, vote
sepeliō, –īre, –īvī, sepultus, bury
septem, seven
septentriōnēs, –um, *m. pl.,* seven plow-oxen (*the seven stars of the constellation Great Bear or Big Dipper*), north
septimus, –a, –um, seventh
sepulchrum, –ī, *n.,* tomb
sepultūra, –ae, *f.,* burial
Sēquana, –ae, *m.,* the Seine river
Sēquanus, –a, –um, Sequā´nian; *as noun, m. pl.,* the Sequanians
sequor, sequī, secūtus, follow, pursue, seek
serēnō, 1, clear up
serēnus, –a, –um, quiet
sērius, *comp. adv.,* later
sermō, –ōnis, *m.,* conversation, talk
serō, –ere, sēvī, satus, plant, sow
serpēns, –entis, *f.,* snake
serva, –ae, *f.,* slave
servīlis, –e, of a slave
servitūs, –tūtis, *f.,* slavery
servō, 1, save, preserve, guard
servus, –ī, *m.,* slave
sēsē, *acc. and abl. of* **suī**
seu, *see* **sīve**
sevērē, *adv.,* severely
sevēritās, –tātis, *f.,* severity
sevērus, –a, –um, stern
sex, six; **sexāgintā,** sixty
Sextīlis, –e, August
sextus, –a, –um, sixth
sī, *conj.,* if
Sibylla, –ae, *f.,* the Sibyl, *a prophetess*
sīc, *adv.,* so, thus
siccō, 1, dry up
Sicilia, –ae, *f.,* Sicily (Sis´ily)
sīcutī (sīcut), *adv.,* just as, as if
sīdus, sīderis, *n.,* star
signifer, –ferī, *m.,* standard bearer
significātiō, –ōnis, *f.,* signal
significō, 1, indicate, mean
signum, –ī, *n.,* sign, signal, standard
silentium, –tī, *n.,* silence
silva, –ae, *f.,* forest, woods
similis, –e, like, similar
simul, *adv.,* at the same time; **simul atque (ac),** as soon as
simulācrum, –ī, *n.,* figure, image
simulō, 1, pretend
sine, *prep. w. abl.,* without
singillātim, *adv.,* one by one, individually
singulāris, –e, one by one, remarkable
singulī, –ae, –a, *pl. only,* one at a time; one each, single
sinister, –tra, –trum, left
sinō, –ere, sīvī, situs, allow
sīve (seu), *conj.,* or if; **sīve (seu)... sīve (seu),** whether . . . or, either . . . or
socius, –cī, *m.,* comrade, ally, accomplice
sōl, sōlis, *m.,* sun
sōlācium, –cī, *n.,* comfort
solea, –ae, *f.,* sandal, shoe
soleō, –ēre, solitus, *semideponent,* be used to, be accustomed
solidus, –a, –um, solid
sōlitūdō, –dinis, *f.,* wilderness
sollicitō, 1, stir up
sōlum *adv.,* only
sōlus, –a, –um, alone, only, lonely
solvō, –ere, solvī, solūtus, loosen, break, free; set sail; *w.* **poenam,** pay
somnus, –ī, *m.,* sleep
sonus, –ī, *m.,* sound
sopor, –ōris, *m.,* sleep
sordidus, –a, –um, dirty, mean
soror, –ōris, *f.,* sister
sors, sortis, *f.,* lot, prophecy
spargō, –ere, sparsī, sparsus, scatter, sprinkle
Sparta, –ae, *f.,* Sparta, *a Greek city*
Spartacus, –ī, *m.,* Spartacus, *leader in a revolt of gladiators*
Spartānus, –ī, *m.,* a Spartan
spatium, –tī, *n.,* space, distance; time, period
speciēs, speciēī, *f.,* appearance, sight
spectāculum, –ī, *n.,* spectacle, show
spectō, 1, look at *or* on, face
speculātor, –ōris, *m.,* spy
spērō, 1, hope (for)
spēs, speī, *f.,* hope
spīna, –ae, *f.,* thorn
spoliō, 1, rob
spondeo, –ēre, spopondi, sponsus, promise, engage
sponsa, –ae, *f.,* a betrothed woman
sponsus, –i, *m.,* a betrothed man

sponte, *w.* **suā**, of his/her/their own accord, by his/her/their own influence, voluntarily
squālēns, *gen.* **squālentis**, foul
st! *interj.*, hush!
stabulum, –ī, *n.*, stable
statim, *adv.*, at once, immediately
statiō, –ōnis, *f.*, outpost, guard, picket
statua, –ae, *f.*, statue
statuō, –ere, statuī, statūtus, decide, determine
statūra, –ae, *f.*, stature
stēlla, –ae, *f.*, star
stetī, *see* **stō**
stilus, –ī, *m.*, stylus (*instrument used in writing on wax tablets*)
stīpendiārius, –a, –um, tributary
stīpendium, –dī, *n.*, pay, tribute
stō, stāre, stetī, stātūrus, stand, stop
stringō, –ere, strīnxī, strictus, draw
studeō, –ēre, studuī, —, be eager (for), study
studiōsē, *adv.*, eagerly
studium, –dī, *n.*, eagerness, interest, enthusiasm; study, pursuit
stultitia, –ae, *f.*, stupidity, folly
stultus, –a, –um, foolish
stupeō, –ēre, –uī, —, be amazed
suādeō, –ēre, suāsī, suāsūrus, urge
suāvis, –e, sweet
suāvitās, –tātis, *f.*, sweetness
sub, *prep.*, under, close to, at the foot of, just before (*w. acc. after verbs of motion; w. abl. after verbs of rest or position*)
subdūcō, –ere, –dūxī, –ductus, lead up; draw up
subeō, –īre, –iī, –itūrus, go under, enter, come up, undergo
subiciō, –ere, –iēcī, –iectus, throw from below, subject, conquer; **subiectus**, lying beneath
subigō, –ere, –ēgī, –āctus, force, subdue
subitō, *adv.*, suddenly
sublātus, *part. of* **tollō**
sublevō, 1, lighten, raise; *w. reflex.*, rise
submergō, –ere, –mersī, –mersus, plunge
subministrō, 1, furnish
submittō, –ere, –mīsī, –missus, send
submoveō, –ēre, –mōvī, –mōtus, drive back
subruō, –ere, –ruī, –rutus, undermine
subsequor, subsequī, subsecūtus, follow (closely)
subsidium, –dī, *n.*, aid, reserve
subterrāneus, –a, –um, subterranean
subveniō, –īre, –vēnī, –ventūrus, come to help
succēdō, –ere, –cessī, –cessūrus, come up, succeed (*w. dat.*)
successus, –ūs, *m.*, success
succurrō, –ere, –currī, –cursūrus, run to help
Suēbī, –ōrum, *m. pl.*, the Suē´bans, *or* Suē´bī
sufficiō, –ere, –fēcī, –fectus, suffice
suffrāgium, –gī, *n.*, vote
suī, of himself, herself, itself, themselves
sum, esse, fuī, futūrus, be
summa, –ae, *f.*, sum; leadership; **summa imperī**, supreme command
summus, –a, –um, highest, most important, greatest; top of, surface of; **summum, –ī**, *n.*, top
sūmō, –ere, sūmpsī, sūmptus, take, assume
sūmptuōsē, *adv.*, extravagantly
sūmptuōsus, –a, –um, extravagant
super, *prep. w. acc.*, over, upon
superbē, *adv.*, arrogantly
superbus, –a, –um, haughty
superior, –ius, higher, upper, superior; previous
superō, 1, overcome, conquer; surpass; beat; defeat
supersum, –esse, –fuī, –futūrus, be left (over), remain, survive
superus, –a, –um, upper; *as noun, m. pl.*, gods (above)
supplex, *gen.* **supplicis**, begging
supplicātiō, –ōnis, *f.*, thanksgiving
supplicium, –cī, *n.*, thanksgiving; punishment
suprā, *adv. and prep. w. acc.*, above
suprēmus, –a, –um, highest, last
surgō, –ere, surrexi, surrecturus, rise
suscipiō, –ere, –cēpī, –ceptus, undertake, incur
suspendō, –ere, –pendī, –pēnsus, hang; **suspēnsus**, in suspense
suspīciō, –ōnis, *f.*, suspicion
suspicor, 1, suspect
sustineō, –ēre, –tinuī, –tentus, hold up, keep up *or* back; endure, withstand, hold out, check
sustulī, *see* **tollō**
suus, –a, –um, his, her, its, their; his own, her own, *etc.*
Syrācūsae, –ārum, *f. pl.*, Syracuse, *a city in Sicily*

T

T., *abbreviation for* **Titus**
taberna, –ae, *f.*, shop, tavern
tabula, –ae, *f.*, table, tablet (of the law); writing tablet
taceō, –ēre, tacuī, tacitus, be silent; **tacitus**, silent
taciturnitās, –tātis, *f.*, silence
tacitus, –a, –um, silent
tālis, –e, such
tam, *adv.*, so (*with adjectives and adverbs*)
tamen, *adv.*, still, nevertheless; however
tamquam, *adv.*, as if
tandem, *adv.*, at last, finally
tangō, –ere, tetigī, tāctus, touch
tantulus, –a, –um, so small

tantum, *adv.*, only
tantus, –a, –um, so great, so much, so large, such
tardē, slowly
tardō, 1, slow up
tardus, –a, –um, slow, late
Tarquinius, –nī, *m.*, Tarquin´ius, Tarquin
Tartarus, –ī, *m.*, Hades
taurus, –ī, *m.*, bull
tēctum, –ī, *n.*, roof, house
tegimentum, –ī, *n.*, cover
tegō, –ere, tēxī, tectus, cover
tellus, –ūris, *f.*, earth
tēlum, –ī, *n.*, weapon, missile
temere, *adv.*, rashly, without reason
temeritās, –tātis, *f.*, rashness
temperātus, –a, –um, temperate
tempestās, –tātis, *f.*, weather, storm
templum, –ī, *n.*, temple
temptō, 1, test, try, attempt, tempt
tempus, temporis, *n.*, time
tenāx, *gen.* **tenācis**, tenacious
tendō, –ere, tetendī, tentus, stretch, go
tenebrae, –ārum, *f. pl.*, darkness
teneō, –ēre, tenuī, tentus, hold, keep, possess; **memoriā teneō**, remember
tenuō, 1, make thin
tepeō, –ēre, —, —, be warm
ter, *adv.*, three times
tergum, –ī, *n.*, back
ternī, –ae, –a, three at a time
terra, –ae, *f.*, land, earth
terreō, –ēre, terruī, territus, scare, frighten, terrify
terribilis, –e, frightful
terror, –ōris, *m.*, terror
tertius, –a, –um, third
testāmentum, –ī, *n.*, will
testimōnium, –nī, *n.*, testimony, proof
testis, –is, *m.*, witness
testūdō, –dinis, *f.*, shed, turtle, testudo
Teutonī, –ōrum, *m. pl.*, the Teutons
theātrum, –ī, *n.*, theater
Thēbae, –ārum, *f. pl.*, Thebes, *a Greek city*
Thessalia, –ae, *f.*, Thessaly, *part of Greece*
Thrācia, –ae, *f.*, Thrace, *a country north of Greece*
Thrāx, –ācis, *m.*, a Thracian
thronus, –ī *m.*, throne
Tiberis, –is, *m.*, Tī´ber river
Tigurīnus, –ī, *m.*, Tīgurī´nus, *a Helvetian canton; pl.*, the Tīgurī´nī
timeō, –ēre, timuī, —, fear, be afraid
timidus, –a, –um, timid; **timidē**, *adv.*, timidly
timor, –ōris, *m.*, fear
titulus, –ī, *m.*, title, sign
toga, –ae, *f.*, toga (*cloak*)
tolerābilis, –e, endurable
tollō, –ere, sustulī, sublātus, raise, carry, remove, destroy
tormentum, –ī, *n.*, torture; artillery
torqueō, –ēre, torsī, tortus, twist, turn, torture
torreō, –ēre, torruī, tostus, roast, scorch
tot, *indeclinable adj.*, so many
totidem, *indeclinable adj.*, just as many, the same number
tōtus, –a, –um, whole, entire, all
trabs, trabis, *f.*, beam
trādō, –ere, –didī, –ditus, give *or* hand over, transmit, relate, surrender
trādūcō, –ere, –dūxī, –ductus, lead across, win over
trāgula, –ae, *f.*, javelin
trahō, –ere, trāxī, trāctus, draw, drag; take on
trāiciō, –ere, –iēcī, –iectus, strike through
trānō, 1, swim across
tranquillitās, –tātis, *f.*, calm
tranquillus, –a, –um, peaceful
trāns, *prep. w. acc.*, across
trānscendō, –ere, –cendī, —, board, climb over
trānscurrō, –ere, –currī, –cursūrus, traverse
trānseō, –īre, –iī, –itūrus, cross, pass, go
trānsferō, trānsferre, trānstulī, trānslātus, carry over
trānsfīgō, –ere, –fīxī, –fīxus, pierce through
trānsfodiō, –ere, –fōdī, –fossus, pierce through
trānsiliō, –īre, –siluī, —, jump across
trānsportō, 1, carry over, transport
trānsversus, –a, –um, cross
trecentī, –ae, –a, three hundred
tremor, –ōris, *m.*, shaking
trēs, tria, three
tribūnus, –ī, *m.*, tribune
tribuō, –ere, tribuī, tribūtus, bestow, grant, assign
tribūtum, –ī, *n.*, tax, tribute
trīclīnium, –nī, *n.*, dining room
trīduum, –ī, *n.*, three days
trīgintā, thirty
triplex, *gen.* **triplicis**, threefold, triple
tristis, –e, sad, severe
tristitia, –ae, *f.*, sadness
Troia, –ae, *f.*, Troy, *a city in Asia Minor*
Troiānus, –a, –um, Trojan; *as noun, m. pl.*, the Trojans
tū, tuī, you, yourself
tuba, –ae, *f.*, trumpet
tueor, tuērī, tūtus, look, guard
tulī, *see* **ferō**
tum, *adv.*, then
tumultus, –ūs, *m.*, uproar
tunc, *adv.*, then
tunica, –ae, *f.*, tunic
turbō, 1, roughen
turbulentus, –a, –um, muddy
turma, –ae, *f.*, troop (*of cavalry*)
turpis, –e, disgraceful, ugly
turpitūdō, –dinis, *f.*, disgrace
turris, –is, *f.*, tower
Tusculānī, –ōrum, *m. pl.*, the Tus´culans, people of Tusculum, *a town in Italy*
tūtus, –a, –um, safe
tuūs, –a, –um, your, yours (*referring to one person*)
tyrannus, –ī, *m.*, tyrant

U

ubi, *adv.,* where; when
ubicumque, *adv.,* wherever
ulcīscor, ulcīscī, ultus, avenge
ūllus, –a, –um, any, anyone
ulterior, –ius, farther
ultimus, –a, –um, last, farthest
ultrīx, *gen.* **ultrīcis,** avenging
ultrō, *adv.,* voluntarily, actually
ultus, *part. of* **ulcīscor**
umbra, –ae, *f.,* shade, shadow
umquam, *adv.,* ever, at any time
ūnā, *adv.,* at the same time, along
ūnanimus, –a, –um, of one mind, sympathetic
unda, –ae, *f.,* wave
unde, *adv.,* from which (place), by which
undique, *adv.,* from *or* on all sides
unguentum, –i, *n.,* ointment, salve
ūniversus, –a, –um, all (together)
ūnus, –a, –um, one, alone
urbs, urbis, *f.,* city
urgeō, urgēre, ursī, —, press hard
urna, –ae, *f.,* urn
ūrō, –ere, ussī, ustus, burn
usque, *adv.,* up to, continuously, still
ūsus, –ūs, *m.,* use, practice, experience
ut, *conj.,* (in order) that, to, so that; as (to), when; **ut... non,** that . . . not
uter, utra, utrum, which (of two); whichever
uterque, utraque, utrumque, each (of two), both
utī = ut
ūtilis, –e, useful
ūtilitās, –tātis, *f.,* usefulness
ūtor, ūtī, ūsus, use, make use of (*w. abl.*), enjoy
utrimque, *adv.,* on both sides
uxor, –ōris, *f.,* wife

V

vacō, 1, be uninhabited, have leisure
vacuus, –a, –um, empty, free
vādō, –ere, —, —, go
vadum, –ī, *n.,* ford, shallow place
vagor, 1, wander
valeō, –ēre, valuī, valitūrus, be strong, be well, be powerful, prevail; *imper.,* **valē, valēte,** farewell
valētūdō, –dinis, *f.,* health; illness
vallēs, –is, *f.,* valley
vāllum, –ī, *n.,* rampart, wall, barricade
vānus, –a, –um, empty, false
varius, –a, –um, changing, varying, various
vās, vāsis, *n.,* kettle, pot, vessel
vāstō, 1, destroy, ruin
vāstus, –a, –um, huge
vehemēns, *gen.* **vehementis,** vigorous
vehiculum, –ī, *n.,* carriage
vehō, –ere, vexī, vectus, carry; *passive,* sail, ride
Veiī, –ōrum, *m. pl.,* Vē´iī, *a town in Italy*
vel, *conj.,* or; **vel... vel,** either . . . or
vellus, –eris, *n.,* fleece, wool
vēlō, 1, cover
vēlōcitās, –tātis, *f.,* swiftness
vēlum, –ī, *n.,* sail
velut, velutī, *adv.,* just as, as
vēna, –ae, *f.,* vein
vēnātiō, –ōnis, *f.,* hunting, hunt
vēndō, –ere, –didī, –ditus, sell
venēnum, –ī, *n.,* poison
Venetī, –ōrum, *m. pl.,* the Vĕn´etī
veniō, –īre, vēnī, ventūrus, come
venter, –tris, *m.,* belly, stomach
ventus, –ī, *m.,* wind
Venus, –eris, *f.,* Vēnus, *goddess of love and beauty*
verberō, 1, beat, strike
verbum, –ī, *n.,* word; **verba faciō,** speak, make a speech
Vercingetorīx, –īgis, *m.,* Vercingetorix (Versinjet´orix)
vērē, *adv.,* truly
vereor, verērī, veritus, fear, respect
Vergilius, Vergilī, *m.,* Virgil
vergo, –ere, —, —, slope, lie
vēritās, –tātis, *f.,* truth
vērō, *adv.,* in truth, but, however
versicolor, *gen.* **–ōris,** of various colors
versō, 1, turn over; *passive,* live
versor, 1, move about, be engaged, live, be
versus, –ūs, *m.,* line, verse
vertō, –ere, vertī, versus, turn; *passive,* turn (oneself); *sometimes deponent*
vērus, –a, –um, true
Vespasiānus, –ī, *m.,* Vespasian (Vespā´zhian), *the emperor*
vesper, –erī, *m.,* evening; **vesperī,** in the evening
Vesta, –ae, *f.,* Vesta, *goddess of the hearth*
Vestālis, –e, Vestal, of Vesta
vester, –tra, –trum, your, yours (*referring to two or more persons*)
vēstibulum, –ī, *n.,* entrance
vēstīgium, –gī, *n.,* footprint, foot
vestiō, –īre, –īvī, –ītus, clothe
vestis, –is, *f.,* clothing, clothes, garment
vestītus, –ūs, *m.,* clothing
veterānus, –a, –um, veteran, experienced
vetō, –āre, vetuī, vetitus, forbid
vetus, *gen.* **veteris,** old
vetustus, –a, –um, old, ancient
vexō, 1, disturb
via, –ae, *f.,* way, road, street; journey
viātor, –ōris, *m.,* traveler
vīcēnī, –ae, –a, twenty (each)
vīciēs, *adv.,* twenty times
vīcīnus, –a, –um, neighboring; *as noun, m.,* neighbor
vicis, –is, *f.,* change; **in vicem,** in turn
victima, –ae, *f.,* victim

victor, –ōris, *m.,* victor; *adj.,* victorious
victōria, –ae, *f.,* victory
vīctus, –ūs, *m.,* living, food
vīcus, –ī, *m.,* village
videō, –ēre, vīdī, vīsus, see; *passive,* be seen, seem, seem best
videor, vidērī, vīsus, seem
vigil, *gen.* **vigilis,** wakeful
vigilia, –ae, *f.,* watchman, watch (*a fourth part of the night*)
vīgintī, *indeclinable,* twenty
vigor, –ōris, *m.,* vigor
vīlis, –e, cheap, worthless
vīlla, –ae, *f.,* farmhouse, villa
Vīminālis (mōns), –is, *m.,* the Vĭm´inal Hill
vincō, –ere, vīcī, victus, conquer, defeat, overcome, win
vinculum, –ī, *n.,* bond, chain
vindicō, 1, claim, appropriate
vīnea, –ae, *f.,* grape arbor, shed
vīnētum, –ī, *n.,* vineyard
vīnum, –ī, *n.,* wine
violō, 1, injure
vir, virī, *m.,* man, husband
virgō, –ginis, *f.,* virgin, maiden
virtūs, –tūtis, *f.,* manliness, courage, virtue
vīs, —, *f.,* force, power, violence; *pl.,* **vīrēs, –ium,** strength
vīta, –ae, *f.,* life
vitiōsus, –a, –um, full of faults
vitium, –tī, *n.,* fault
vītō, 1, avoid
vīvo, –ere, vixi, victus, live
vīvus, –a, –um, alive, living
vix, *adv.,* scarcely, with difficulty, hardly
vōbīscum = cum vōbīs
vocō, 1, call, summon, invite, invoke
volō, 1, fly
volō, velle, voluī, —, want, wish, be willing
Volscī, –ōrum, *m. pl.,* the Volscians (Vŏl´shians)
volucris, –ris, *f.,* bird
voluntās, –tātis, *f.,* wish, consent
voluptās, –tātis, *f.,* pleasure
volvō, –ere, volvī, volūtus, roll (up); turn over; *passive,* toss about
vōs, you, *pl. of* **tū**
voveō, –ēre, vōvī, vōtus, vow, promise
vōx, vōcis, *f.,* voice, word, remark, talk
Vulcānus, –ī, *m.,* Vulcan, *god of fire*
vulgus, –ī, *n.,* common people
vulnerō, 1, wound
vulnus, vulneris, *n.,* wound
vultus, –ūs, *m.,* expression, features

English–Latin

For proper nouns and proper adjectives not given in this vocabulary see the Latin-English Vocabulary or the text.

Verbs of the first conjugation whose parts are regular are indicated by the figure 1.

A

able (be), possum, posse, potuī, —
about, dē, *w. abl.*
accomplice, socius, –cī, *m.*
accomplish, cōnficiō, –ere, –fēcī, –fectus
account (on), *see* **on**
accustomed (be), cōnsuēscō, –ere, –suēvī, –suētus
achieve, efficiō, –ere, effēcī, effectus
across, trāns, *w. acc.*
add, adiciō, –ere, adiēcī, adiectus
admire, admīror, 1
adopt, adoptō, 1
adorn, ōrnō, 1
after (*conj.*), postquam; *use abl. abs.*
again, iterum
against, contrā, *w. acc.*
agree, cōnsentiō, –īre, –sēnsī, –sēnsus
aid, auxilium, –lī, *n.*
all, omnis, –e; tōtus, –a, –um; **all other,** cēterī, –ae, –a
allow, licet, –ēre, licuit *or* licitum est
almost, paene
alone, sōlus, –a, –um
already, iam
also, etiam
although, cum; quamquam; *use participle or abl. abs.*
always, semper
among, inter, *w. acc.*
and, et; –que
another, alius, alia, aliud
any(one), ūllus, –a, –um; quis, quid (*after* sī)
appear, appāreō, –ēre, appāruī, appāritūrus
approach (*noun*), adventus, –ūs, *m.;* (*verb*), accēdō, –ere, accessī, accessūrus (*w.* ad); adeō, adīre, adiī, aditūrus; appropinquō, 1 (*w. dat.*)
arena, arēna, –ae, *f.*
arise, orior, orīrī, ortus
arm, armō, 1
arms, arma, –ōrum, *n. pl.*
army, exercitus, –ūs, *m.*
arrival, adventus, –ūs, *m.*
arrive, perveniō, –īre, –vēnī, –ventūrus
art, ars, artis, *f.*
as... as possible, quam, *w. superl.;* **as soon as possible,** quam prīmum; **as to,** ut
ask, rogō, 1
at (near), ad, *w. acc.; abl. of time or place*
Athens, Athēnae, –ārum, *f. pl.*
attack, oppugnō, 1; aggredior, aggredī, aggressus
author, auctor, –ōris, *m.*
await, exspectō, 1
away (be), absum, –esse, āfuī, āfutūrus

B

bad, malus, –a, –um
baggage, impedīmenta, –ōrum, *n. pl.*
bandit, latrō, –ōnis, *m.*
banish, expellō, –ere, expulī, expulsus
battle line, aciēs, aciēī, *f.*
be, sum, esse, fuī, futūrus
bear, ferō, ferre, tulī, lātus
beat, superō, 1
beautiful, pulcher, –chra, –chrum
because, *use participle or abl. abs.;* quod, quoniam
become, fīō, fierī, (factus)
before (*adv. and prep.*), ante, *w. acc.*
beg, ōrō, 1; petō, –ere, petīvī, petītus
begin, incipiō, –ere, incēpī, inceptus; **began,** coepī, coeptus
believe, crēdō, –ere, crēdidī, crēditus (*w. dat.*)
besiege, obsideō, –ēre, obsēdī, obsessus
best, optimus, –a, –um
better, melior, melius
between, inter, *w. acc.*
blame, accūsō, 1
book, liber, librī, *m.*
boy, puer, puerī, *m.*
brave, fortis, –e; **bravely,** fortiter
bridge, pōns, pontis, *m.*
bring, ferō, ferre, tulī, lātus; īnferō, īnferre, intulī, illātus; **bring together,** condūcō, –ere, –dūxī, –ductus
Britons, Britannī, –ōrum, *m. pl.*
build, exstruō, –ere, exstrūxī, exstrūctus; aedificō, 1
building, aedificium, –cī, *n.*
burn, incendō, –ere, incendī, incensus
business, negōtium, –tī, *n.*
but, sed
buy, emō, –ere, –ēmī, emptus
by, ā, ab, *w. abl.; sometimes abl. alone*

C

call, appellō, 1
camp, castra, –ōrum, *n. pl.*
capture, expugnō, 1; capiō, –ere, cēpī, captus

carry, portō, 1; ferō, ferre, tulī, lātus; **carry on war**, bellum gerō; **carry back**, referō, referre, rettulī, relātus
cause, efficiō, –ere, effēcī, effectus (*w.* ut *and subjunct.*)
cavalry, equitātus, –ūs, *m.;* equitēs, –um, *m. pl.*
certain, a certain (one), quīdam, quaedam, quiddam; **certainly**, certē
chain, vinculum, –ī, *n.*
chance, cōpia, –ae, *f.*
check, sustineō, –ēre, –tinuī, –tentus
children, līberī, –ōrum, *m. pl.*
choose, ēligō, –ere, ēlēgī, ēlēctus; dēligō, –ere, dēlēgī, dēlēctus
circumstance, rēs, reī, *f.*
citadel, arx, arcis, *f.*
citizen, cīvis, –is, *m.*
city, urbs, urbis, *f.*
civil, cīvīlis, –e
client, cliēns, –entis, *m.*
close, claudō, –ere, clausī, clausus
collect, conferō, conferre, contulī, collātus
come, veniō, –īre, vēnī, ventūrus
command (be in), praesum, –esse, –fuī, –futūrus (*w. dat.*)
common people, plēbs, plēbis, *f.*
complete, cōnficiō, –ere, –fēcī, –fectus
conceal, cēlō, 1
concern, cūra, –ae, *f.*
condemn, damnō, 1
condition, condiciō, –ōnis, *f.*
conference, colloquium, –quī, *n.*
conquer, vincō, –ere, vīcī, victus; superō, 1
conspire, coniūrō, 1
consul, cōnsul, –ulis, *m.*
consult (for), cōnsulō, –ere, –suluī, –sultus
country, patria, –ae, *f.*
courage, virtūs, –tūtis, *f.*
cover, tegō, –ere, tēxī, tectus
creditor, crēditor, –ōris, *m.*
criticize, accūsō, 1
cross, trānseō, –īre, –iī, –itūrus
crowded together, cōnfertus, –a, –um
cruel, crūdēlis, –e
cruelty, crūdēlitās, –tātis, *f.*
custom, mōs, mōris, *m.*
cut off, interclūdō, –ere, –clūsī, –clūsus

D

daughter, fīlia, –ae, *f.*
day, diēs, diēī, *m. and f.*
dear, cārus, –a, –um
decided (be), placet, –ēre, placuit
decorated, adōrnātus, –a, –um
deed, factum, –ī, *n.*
defeat (*noun*), calamitās, –tātis, *f.;* (*verb*), superō, 1; pellō, –ere, pepulī, pulsus; vincō, –ere, vīcī, victus
defend, dēfendō, –ere, dēfendī, dēfēnsus
defenses, mūnītiō, –ōnis, *f.*
delay, mora, –ae, *f.*
demand, postulō, 1
depart, excēdō, –ere, excessī, excessūrus
departure, exitus, –ūs, *m.;* profectiō, –ōnis, *f.*
desire, cupiō, –ere, –īvī, –ītus
despair (of), dēspērō, 1
destroy, dēleō, –ēre, –ēvī, –ētus
determine, cōnstituō, –ere, –stituī, –stitūtus
die, morior, morī, mortuus
differ, differō, differre, distulī, dīlātus
difficult, difficilis, –e
dinner, cēna, –ae, *f.*
divide, dīvidō, –ere, dīvīsī, dīvīsus
do, faciō, –ere, fēcī, factus; agō, –ere, ēgī, āctus
draw up, īnstruō, –ere, īnstrūxī, īnstrūctus
drive out, expellō, –ere, expulī, expulsus
during, per, *w. acc.*
dutiful, pius, –a, –um
duty, officium, –cī, *n.*

E

each one, quisque, quidque
eager for (be), studeō, –ēre, studuī, — (*w. dat.*)
eagerness, studium, –dī, *n.*
earn, mereō, –ēre, meruī, meritus
earth, terra, –ae, *f.*
easy, facilis, –e; **easily**, facile
elect, creō, 1
elevated, ēditus, –a, –um
embassy, lēgātiō, –ōnis, *f.*
empire, imperium, –rī, *n.*
encourage, cōnfirmō, 1
endure, ferō, ferre, tulī, lātus
enemy (*personal*), inimīcus, –ī, *m.;* (*national*), hostis, –is, *m.*
enjoy, ūtor, ūtī, ūsus (*w. abl.*)
enter, ingredior, ingredī, ingressus
entire, tōtus, –a, –um
entrust, mandō, 1
envoy, lēgātus, –ī, *m.*
envy, invideō, –ēre, invīdī, invīsus (*w. dat.*)
erect, exstruō, –ere, exstrūxī, exstrūctus
escape, fugiō, –ere, fūgī, fugitūrus
establish, cōnstituō, –ere, –stituī, –stitūtus
everything, omne *or* omnia
example, exemplum, –ī, *n.*
excel, praestō, –āre, –stitī, –stitūrus (*w. dat.*)
exclaim, (ex)clāmō, 1

F

fame, fāma, –ae, *f.*,
family, familia, –ae, *f.*
famous, clārus, –a, –um
farm, ager, agrī, *m.*,
farmer, agricola, –ae, *m.*
farthest, extrēmus, –a, –um; ultimus, –a, –um
father, pater, patris, *m.*
fear, timeō, –ēre, timuī, —; vereor, verērī, veritus
feel, sentiō, –īre, sēnsī, sēnsus
few, paucī, –ae, –a
fierce, ferus, –a, –um
fight, pugnō, 1

find, inveniō, –īre, invēnī, inventus
first, prīmum; **at first**, prīmō
flame, flamma, –ae, *f.*
flee, fugiō, –ere, fūgī, fugitūrus
food, cibus, –ī, *m.*
for (*conj.*), nam; (*prep.*), ad, ob, *w. acc.;* prō, *w. abl.;* **for the purpose** *or* **sake of**, causā *or* grātiā (*preceded by gen.*); *sometimes not expressed*
forest, silva, –ae, *f.*
former (the), ille; **the former . . . the latter**, ille... hic
fortify, mūniō, –īre, –īvī, –ītus
fortune, fortūna, –ae, *f.*
free (*adj.*), līber, –era, –erum; (*verb*), līberō, 1
fresh, integer, –gra, –grum
friend, amīcus, –ī; *m.;* **(girl) friend**, amīca, –ae, *f.*
friendly, amīcus, –a, –um
frighten, terreō, –ēre, terruī, territus
frog, rāna, –ae, *f.*
from, ē, ex, ā, ab, dē, *w. abl.*; **from one another**, inter sē
furnish, praebeō, –ēre, –uī, –itus

G

gate, porta, –ae, *f.*
Gaul, Gallia, –ae, *f.;* **Gauls**, Gallī, –ōrum, *m. pl.*
general, dux, ducis, *m.;* lēgātus, –ī, *m.*
get, parō, 1; **get (possession of)**, potior, potiri, potītus (*w. abl.*)
girl, puella, –ae, *f.*
give, dō, dare, dedī, datus
gladiator, gladiātor, –ōris, *m.;* **gladiatorial**, gladiātōrius, –a, –um
go, eō, īre, iī, itūrus; **go out**, ēgredior, ēgredī, ēgressus; exeō, exīre, exiī, exitūrus
god, deus, –ī, *m.;* **goddess**, dea, –ae, *f.*
gold, aurum, –ī, *n.*
good, bonus, –a, –um
grain, frūmentum, –ī, *n.*
great, magnus, –a, –um; **greater**, maior, maius; **greatest**, maximus, –a, –um; summus, –a, –um; **great deal**, plūrimum; **so great**, tantus, –a, –um
Greece, Graecia, –ae, *f.*
Greek, Graecus, –a, –um
guard, praesidium, –dī, *n.*
guest-friend, hospes, –itis, *m.*

H

happen, accidō, –ere, accidī, —
harbor, portus, –ūs, *m.*
hardly, vix
harsh, dūrus, –a, –um
hasten, properō, 1; contendō, –ere, –tendī, –tentūrus
have, habeō, –ēre, habuī, habitus; **have to**, *use fut. pass. part.*
he, is; hic; ille; *often not expressed*
head, caput, capitis, *n.*
hear, audiō, –īre, –īvī, –ītus
help, auxilium, –lī
her (*poss.*), eius; (*reflex.*), suus, –a, –um; **herself** (*reflex.*), suī
high, altus, –a, –um
hill, mōns, montis, *m.;* collis, –is, *m.*
himself (*reflex.*), suī; (*intens.*), ipse
hinder, impediō, –īre, –īvī, –ītus
his (*poss.*), eius; **his own** (*reflex.*), suus, –a, –um
home, domus, –ūs, *f.*
Horace, Horātius, –tī, *m.*
horse, equus, –ī, *m.*
horseman, eques, equitis, *m.*
hostage, obses, obsidis, *m.*
hour, hōra, –ae, *f.*
house, domus, –ūs, *f.*
how, quō modō; **how much**, quantus, –a, –um
however, autem (*never first word*)
humble, humilis, –e
hurry (on), properō, 1

I

I, ego, meī; *often not expressed*
if, sī
immediately, statim
impel, impellō, –ere, impulī, impulsus
in, in, *w. abl.;* **in order to** *or* **that**, ut (*w. subjunctive*); **in order not to**, nē
influence (*verb*) addūcō, –ere, addūxī, adductus; (*noun*), auctōritās, –tātis, *f.*
inform, (eum) certiōrem faciō, –ere, fēcī, factus; *passive,* certior fīō, fierī
inhabit, incolō, –ere, incoluī, —
inspire, iniciō, –ere, iniēcī, iniectus
into, in, *w. acc.*
investigate, explōrō, 1
invite, vocō, 1
it, is, ea, id; hic, haec, hoc; ille, illa, illud; *often not expressed*

J

journey, iter, itineris, *n.*

K

keep, retineō, –ēre, retinuī, retentus; **keep from**, prohibeō, –ēre, –hibuī, –hibitus
kill, interficiō, –ere, –fēcī, –fectus; caedō, –ere, cecīdī, caesus; occīdo, –ere, occīdi, occīsus
kind, genus, generis, *n.*
kindness, beneficium, –cī, *n.*
king, rēx, rēgis, *m.*
know, sciō, scīre, scīvī, scītus; *perf. of* nōscō, –ere, nōvī, nōtus, *or of* cognōscō, –ere, –nōvī, –nitus

L

large, magnus, –a, –um; **so large**, tantus, –a, –um
later, posteā, post
latter, hic
law, lēx, lēgis, *f.*
lay aside, dēpōnō, –ere, dēposuī, dēpositus

lead, dūcō, –ere, dūxī, ductus; **lead a life,** vītam agō
leader, dux, ducis, *m.;* prīnceps, prīncipis, *m.*
learn, cognōscō, –ere, –nōvī, –nitus
leave (behind), relinquō, –ere, relīquī, relictus
legion, legiō, –ōnis, *f.*
letter (*epistle*), litterae, –ārum, *f.*
liberty, lībertās, –tātis, *f.*
life, vīta, –ae, *f.*
like, amō, 1
little later, paulō post
live (a life), agō, –ere, ēgī, āctus; (*dwell*), habitō, 1
long, longus, –a, –um; **long** (*adv.*), **(for) a long time,** diū
look at *or* **on,** spectō, 1
lose, āmittō, –ere, āmīsī, āmissus; perdō, –ere, –didī, –ditus
loss, dētrīmentum, –ī, *n.*
love, amor, amōris, *m.*
luxury, lūxuria, –ae, *f.*

M

make, faciō, –ere, fēcī, factus; **make war upon,** bellum īnferō (*w. dat.*)
man, vir, virī, *m.;* homō, hominis, *m.*
many, multī, –ae, –a; **so many,** tot; **very many,** plūrimī, –ae, –a
march, iter, itineris, *n.*
master, dominus, –ī, *m.*
matter, rēs, reī, *f.*
meanwhile, intereā, interim
meet (in battle), congredior, congredī, congressus
mercy, clēmentia, –ae, *f.*
messenger, nūntius, –tī, *m.*
mile, mīlle passūs; *pl.* mīlia passuum
molest, noceō, –ēre, nocuī, nocitūrus (*w. dat.*)
money, pecūnia, –ae, *f.*
month, mēnsis, –is *m.*
monument, monumentum, –ī, *n.*
more, magis, amplius; *use comparative*
mother, māter, mātris, *f.*
move, moveō, –ēre, mōvī, mōtus; afficiō, –ere, affēcī, affectus
much, multus, –a, –um
must, *use fut. pass. part.*
my, meus, –a, –um

N

name, nōmen, nōminis, *n.*
nature, nātūra, –ae, *f.*
near, ad *w. acc.;* (*adj.*), propinquus, –a, –um
necessary (it is), oportet, –ēre, oportuit; necesse est
neglect, neglegō, –ere, –lēxī, –lectus
neighbors, fīnitimī, –ōrum, *m.*
nevertheless, tamen
new, novus, –a, –um
next, proximus, –a, –um
night, nox, noctis, *f.*
no, nūllus, –a, –um; **no longer,** nōn iam
not, nōn, nē (*w. negative volitive and purpose clauses*)
noted, īnsignis, –e; nōtus, –a, –um
nothing, nihil
notice, animadvertō, –ere, –vertī, –versus
number, numerus, –ī, *m.*

O

obey, pāreō, –ēre, pāruī, pāritūrus (*w. dat.*)
obstruct, impediō, –īre, –īvī, –ītus
obtain (one's request), impetrō, 1
occur, intercēdō, –ere, –cessī, –cessus
often, saepe
old man, senex, senis, *m.*
omen, ōmen, ōminis, *n.*
on, in, *w. abl.;* **on account of,** ob *or* propter, *w. acc.*
one, ūnus, –a, –um
opinion, sententia, –ae, *f.*
oppress, opprimō, –ere, oppressī, oppressus
or, vel
oracle, ōrāculum, –ī, *n.*
order (*noun*), imperium, –rī, *n.,;* (*verb*), iubeō, –ēre, iussī, iussus; imperō, 1, *w. dat.;* **in order to** *or* **that,** ut; **in order not to** *or* **that,** nē
other, alius, alia, aliud; **the other,** alter, –a, –um; **others,** *see* **some; all other,** *see* **all**
ought, dēbeō, –ēre, dēbuī, dēbitus; oportet, –ēre, oportuit; *use fut. pass. part.*
our, noster, –tra, –trum
overcome, superō, 1; vincō, –ere, vīcī, victus

P

part, pars, partis, *f.*
pay, pendō, –ere, pependī, pēnsus; **pay the penalty,** poenam dō
peace, pāx, pācis, *f.*
people, populus, –ī, *m.*
permit, licet, –ēre, licuit *or* licitum est; permittō, –ere, –mīsī, –missus
persuade, persuādeo, –ēre, –suāsī, –suāsūrus (*w. dat.*)
place (*noun*), locus, –ī, *m.; pl.* loca, –ōrum, *n.;* (*verb*), pōnō, –ere, posuī, positus; **place in charge,** praeficiō, –ere, –fēcī, –fectus
plan (*noun*), consilium, –lī, *n.;* (*verb*), in animō habeō
please, be pleasing to, placeō, –ēre, placuī, placitūrus (*w. dat.*)
poem, carmen, carminis, *n.*
poet, poēta, –ae, *m.*
Pompey, Pompeius, –peī, *m.*
power, potestās, –tātis, *f.;* imperium, –rī, *n.*
praetor, praetor, –ōris, *m.*
praise, laudō, 1
prefer, mālō, mālle, māluī, —
prepare, parō, 1
prevent, prohibeō, –ēre, –hibuī, –hibitus
prisoner, captīvus, –ī, *m.*
proceed, prōcēdō, –ere, –cessī, –cessūrus
procession, pompa, –ae, *f.*

promise, polliceor, pollicērī, pollicitus
protection, praesidium, –dī, *n.*
pursue, īnsequor, īnsequī, īnsecūtus
put in charge of, praeficiō, –ere, –fēcī, –fectus

Q

queen, rēgīna, –ae, *f.*
quickly, celeriter

R

read, legō, –ere, lēgī, lēctus
ready, parātus, –a, –um
recall, revocō, 1
receive, accipiō, –ere, accēpī, acceptus; excipiō, –ere, excēpī, exceptus
recite, recitō, 1
reconnoiter, explōrō, 1
refrain, abstineō, –ēre, –tinuī, –tentus
region, regiō, –ōnis, *f.*
remain, maneō, –ēre, mānsī, mānsūrus
remember, memoriā teneō
repair, reficiō, –ere, refēcī, refectus
reply, respondeō, –ēre, respondī, respōnsus
report (*noun*), nūntius, –tī, *m.;* (*verb*), nūntiō, 1
reserve, reservō, 1
resist, resistō, –ere, restitī, — (*w. dat.*)
resources, opēs, –um, *f. pl.*
rest (of), reliquus, –a, –um; cēterī, –ae, –a
retire, mē recipiō
return (*verb*), redeō, –īre, rediī, reditūrus; (*noun*), reditus, –ūs, *m.*
revolution, novae rēs, novārum rērum, *f. pl.*
river, flūmen, flūminis, *n.*
road, via, –ae, *f.;* iter, itineris, *n.*
Roman, Rōmānus, –a, –um
rule, regō, –ere, rēxī, rēctus; imperō, 1 (*w. dat.*)

S

safety, salūs, –ūtis, *f.*
sail, nāvigō, 1
sailor, nauta, –ae, *m.*
sake of (for the), causā *or* grātiā (*w. gen. preceding*)
sally, ēruptiō, –ōnis, *f.*
same, īdem, eadem, idem
save, servō, 1
say, dīcō, –ere, dīxī, dictus; inquit (*w. direct quotations*)
scare, terreō, –ēre, terruī, territus
school, lūdus, –ī, *m.*
scout, explōrātor, –ōris, *m.*
sea, mare, maris, *n.*
see, videō, –ēre, vīdī, vīsus
seek, petō, –ere, petīvī, petītus
seem, videor, vidērī, vīsus
seize, capiō, –ere, cēpī, captus; occupō, 1; comprehendō, –ere, –hendī, –hēnsus
select, legō, –ere, lēgī, lēctus; dēligō, 1
senate, senātus, –ūs, *m.*
senator, senātor, –ōris, *m.*
send, mittō, –ere, mīsī, missus; **send out,** dīmittō, –ere, dīmīsī, dīmissus; **send ahead,** praemittō, –ere, –mīsī, missus; **send for,** arcesso, –ere, –īvī, –ītus
set out, proficīscor, proficīscī, profectus; **set on fire,** incendō, –ere, incendī, incensus
she, ea; haec; illa; *often not expressed*
shield, scūtum, –ī, *n.*
ship, nāvis, nāvis, *f.*
short, brevis, –e
show (*noun*), mūnus, –eris, *n.;* (*verb*), ostendō, –ere, ostendī, ostentus; dēmōnstrō, 1
sign, signal, signum, –ī, *n.*
sight, cōnspectus, –ūs, *m.*
since, quod, cum, quoniam; *use abl. abs.*
sing, cantō, 1
single one (not a), neque quisquam
sister, soror, –ōris, *f.*
six, sex; **sixty,** sexāgintā
size, magnitūdō, –dinis, *f.*
slave, servus, –ī, *m.*
slavery, servitūs, servitūtis, *f.*
small, parvus, –a, –um
sō, ita, tam; **so great** *or* **so large,** tantus, –a, –um; **so that,** ut; **so as not to, so that not,** nē
soldier, mīles, mīlitis, *m.*
some, nōn nūllī, –ae, –a; quīdam, quaedam, quiddam; **some . . . others,** aliī... aliī; **some (one),** aliquis
son, fīlius, –lī, *m.*
soon as possible (as), quam prīmum
speak, dīcō, –ere, dīxī, dictus; loquor, loquī, locūtus; verba faciō
spear, pīlum, –ī, *n.*
spectacle, spectāculum, –ī, *n.*
spend, cōnsūmō, –ere, –sūmpsī, –sūmptus; (*of time*), agō, –ere, ēgī, āctus; **spend the winter,** hiemō, 1
stand, stō, stāre, stetī, stātūrus
start, proficīscor, proficīscī, profectus
state (*noun*), cīvitās, –tātis, *f.;* (*verb*), dīcō, –ere, dīxī, dictus
station, collocō, 1
stop, cōnsistō, –ere, –stitī, –stitūrus
storm, tempestās, –tātis, *f.*
story, fābula, –ae, *f.*
strange, novus, –a, –um
strive, contendō, –ere, –tendī, –tentūrus
struggle, labōrō, 1
succeed, succēdō, –ere, –cessī, –cessus
such, tantus, –a, –um
summon, vocō, 1; convocō, 1
supplies, commeātus, –ūs, *m.*
surpass, superō, 1
surrender, trādō, –ere, –didī, –ditus
surround, circumsistō, –ere, –stetī, —
survive, supersum, –esse, –fuī, –futūrus
suspect, suspicor, 1
swiftly, celeriter

T

tablet (of the law), tabula, –ae, *f.*
talk, loquor, loquī, locūtus
teach, doceō, –ēre, docuī, doctus
teacher, magister, –trī, *m.*
tell, dīcō, –ere, dīxī, dictus
temple, templum, –ī, *n.*
tempt, temptō, 1
terrify, terreō, –ēre, terruī, territus
territory, fīnēs, –ium, *m. pl.*
terror, terror, –ōris, *m.*
than, quam
that (*dem. pron.*), ille, illa, illud; is, ea, id
that, in order that, so that (*conj.*), ut(ī); **that . . . not** (*purpose*), nē; (*result*), ut . . . nōn
their (*poss.*), eōrum, eārum, eōrum; (*reflex.*), suus, –a, –um
themselves (*reflex.*), suī; (*intens.*), ipsī, –ae, –a
then, tum
they, eī, eae, ea; illī, illae, illa; *often not expressed*
thing, rēs, reī, *f.; often not expressed*
think, putō, 1; existimō, 1; arbitror, 1
third, tertius, –a, –um
this, hic, haec, hoc; is, ea, id
thousand, mīlle; *pl.* mīlia
throw, iaciō, –ere, iēcī, iactus; coniciō, –ere, –iēcī, –iectus; **throw down,** dēiciō, –ere, dēiēcī, deiectus; prōiciō, –ere, –iēcī, –iectus
time, tempus, temporis, *n.*
to, ad, in, *w. acc.;* (*purpose*), ut
too, quoque; *use comparative*
top (of), summus, –a, –um
torture, cruciātus, –ūs, *m.*
toward, ad, *w. acc.*
tower, turris, –is, *f.*
town, oppidum, –ī, *n.*
train, instituō, –ere, instituī, institūtus
travel, iter faciō
traveler, viātor, –ōris, *m.*
tribe, gēns, gentis, *f.*
troops, cōpiae, –ārum, *f. pl.*
try, cōnor, 1
twenty, vīgintī
two, duo, duae, duo

U

under, sub, *w. abl.;* **under the direction of,** dux *or* prīnceps *in abl. abs.*
unfriendly, inimīcus, –a, –um
unharmed, incolumis, –e
unless, nisi
unlike, dissimilis, –e
until, dum
unwilling (be), nōlō, nōlle, nōluī, —
urge, hortor, 1; impellō, –ere, impulī, impulsus
use, ūtor, ūtī, ūsus (*w. abl.*)

V

very, *use superlative;* **very many,** plūrimī, –ae, –a
victory, victōria, –ae, *f.*
villa, vīlla, –ae, *f.*
village, vīcus, –ī, *m.*
Virgil, Vergilius, –lī, *m.*

W

wage war, bellum gerō
wait, exspectō, 1
war, bellum, –ī, *n.*
warn, moneō, –ēre, monuī, monitus
waste, cōnsūmō, –ere, –sūmpsī, –sūmptus
water, aqua, –ae, *f.*
wave, unda, –ae, *f.*
we, nōs; *often not expressed*
weapons, tēlā, –ōrum, *n. pl.*
wedding, nūptiae, –ārum, *f. pl.*
weep, fleō, flēre, flēvī, flētus
well, bene
what (*pron*), quis, quid; (*adj.*), quī, quae, quod
when, ubi; cum; *expressed by participle or abl. abs.*
which (*rel. pron.*), quī, quae, quod; **which (of two),** uter, utra, utrum
who (*rel. pron.*), quī, quae, quod; (*interrog. pron.*), quis, quid
whole, tōtus, –a, –um
wholesome, salūbris, –e
why, cūr
willing (be), volō, velle, voluī, —; **not be willing,** nōlō, nōlle, nōluī, —
win, mereō, –ēre, meruī, meritus
winter, hiems, hiemis, *f.*
wisely, sapienter
wish, cupiō, –ere, –īvī, –ītus; volō, velle, voluī, —; **wish not,** nōlō, nōlle, nōluī, —
with, cum, *w. abl.; sometimes abl. alone*
withdraw, concēdō, –ere, –cessī, –cessūrus; discēdō, –ere, –cessī, –cessūrus
without, sine, *w. abl.*
woman, mulier, –eris, *f.;* fēmina, –ae, *f.*
wonder, mīror, 1
word, verbum, –ī, *n.*
worship, colō, –ere, coluī, cultus
worthy, dignus, –a, –um
write, scrībō, –ere, scrīpsī, scrīptus

Y

year, annus, –ī, *m.*
yield, cēdō, –ere, cessī, cessūrus; concēdō, –ere, –cessī, –cessūrus
you, tū (*sing.*); vōs (*pl.*); *often not expressed*
young man, iuvenis, –is, *m.*
your, tuus, –a, –um; **yourself** (*reflex.*), tuī
youth, adulēscēns, –entis, *m.*

Subject Index

A

Academy, the, 125, 126
Achilles, *207*
Acropolis, *57, 79, 81,* 91, *92,* 95
Actium, Battle of, *179*
Adam of Bremen, 425
adopting children, *11*
Aeetes, King, 204, *216*
Aeneas, 446, 449-453
Aeneid, 22, *24,* 398, 446-453, *447*
Aesculapius, *76*
Aeson, King, 204, 206
Aesop, 413
agape, *201*
Agora, 79
Agricola, 419
Agrippa, Marcus, *35, 291*
Aisne River, 294
Albans, *145*
Alesia, 362, 363, *368,* 371, 375, *375*
  map of, *364*
Alexander, 234
Allobroges, *254,* 256
Ambiorix, 329, 338, 355, 357
America, discovery of, 425
amphitheater, Roman, *55, 316*
Anchises, 452
animals in Caesar's time, 354, *355*
Annals, 398, 419
antefix, *212*
Antiochus III, *193*
Antony, Mark, 125, *179,* 190, 192, 404
Apollo, *76, 99, 197*
  Temple of, 106, *109, 183*
Appia, Via, see Appian Way
Appian Way, 45, 64, *65, 74*
aqueduct, Roman, *241*
Aquitania, 296, 302
Arar River, 260
Arch of
  Septimius Severus, *30*
  Tiberius and Germanicus, *257*
  Titus, *322*
arch, Roman, *282*
architecture
  Greek, 138
  Roman, 138
arena, Roman, *279*
Argo, 208, *209, 220*
Argonauts, *203,* 204, *209, 220*
  map of their voyage, *205*
Argus, 204, 208
Ariovistus, 277, 280, 281, *283,* 285, 287, 289
Aristotle, *124*
Arles, France, *279*
armor, Roman, *174*
army, Caesar's, 236-239
Artotrogus, 400
Arvernians, 358, 359
Athena, *209, 435*
  Nike, Temple of, *92*
Athens, 57, 78, 80, 86, 91, *92,* 95, *112,* 138, 204
Atlas, 443
ātrium, *5*
Atrius, Quintus, 325
Atuatuci, 295-296, 329, 338
Augustine, 423
Augustus, Emperor, 2, 17, *20, 23,* 78, 120, 125, 126, 146, *147, 165, 179,* 190, *191,* 192, *231, 352, 370,* 374, 410, 413, 419
Aurelius, Marcus, *173*
Avaricum, 359, 360
Aventine, *154*
Avranches, Normandy, 300

B

barbarians, *272*
barges, Roman, *367*
Bath, England, *83*
baths, Roman, *83, 352*
Battle of Actium, *179*
Battle of Cannae, 178
Belgians, 240, 242, 294-296, 322
Bellovaci, 294
Bembo, Pietro, 433
Bias of Priene, 111
Bibracte, 267
Bibulus, 233
Bingen, Hildegard von, 426, *427*
biremes, **Roman,** *67, 298*
Bituriges, 358
Black Sea, 204, *209*
boats, Roman, *67*
books, Roman, *16, 22*
boxing, *116*
bridge, Roman, *307*
Britain, 303, *313,* 315, 324, *324,* 325
Britons, 186, 188, 321
Brittany, France, *299*
Brundisium, 73, *74*
Brutus, 125, 156, *235,* 296

C

Caecilia Metella, 64, *65,* 101-102, 104
Caesar, Augustus, *11*
Caesar, Julia, 186, *234*
Caesar, Julius, 11-12, 22, 48, *73,* 76, *84, 85, 98,* 120, 125, *165,* 186, 188, *189,* Units V-VII (pp. 230-379), 402, 407, 408
Caligula, *324, 370*
Calpurnius, 82, 84
camp, Roman, *365*
Cannae, Battle of, 178
Cape Cod, 425
Capitoline Hill, *172, 173*
Capua, 68, 71, *74*
Carmina Burana, *428*
Carnutes, 329, 338, 357
carriage, Roman travelling, *71*
Carthage, *158, 179, 180,* 423, 448, *448*
Carthaginians, 178
Caryatid, *81*
Cassius, 125, 190
Cassivellaunus, 325, 329
Catiline, 186, *187,* 188, *397,* 404, 407
Cato, 409
Catullus, 402
cavalry, Roman, *236*

celebrations, Roman, *41*
Celts, *342*
death masks, *268*
Cenabum, 357
censorship, Gallic, 349
centaur, 206, *207*
Cerinthus, 411
Cernunnos, *350*
Ceutrones, 256
Channel, English, 310
Chilon of Sparta, 111
Chiron, *76, 207*
Churchill, Winston, 234
Cicero, Marcus Tullius, 120, 186, *187*, 188, 290, 374, 382, *397*, 402, 404, 405, *405*, 406, 417, 431
Cicero, Quintus 329, 331, 333 (different than poet)
Cimbri, 290
Circus Maximus, 49
Cisalpine Gaul, 289
cithara, *90*
civilization
Greek, 138-140
Roman, 138-140
Claudian, 200
Claudius, Emperor, 324, *324*, *370*
Cleobulus of Rhodes, 111
Cleopatra, *189*, 190, 192
Cloaca Maxima, *155*
coinage, *98, 338*
Colchis, *203*, 204, 208
Collingwood, R.G., 324
Colosseum, Roman, *421*
comedy, Roman, 399
Comum, 382
Considius, 264-265
Constantine, *173, 238*
consuls, Roman, 84
Corinna, 412
Corinth, 182, *183*, 204, *227*
Isthmus of, 182
Corinthian columuns, *95*
Coronis, *76*
Costa, Lorenzo, *203*
Cotta, 329
Crassus, Publius, *65*, 232, *234*, 289, 296, 302
Creticus, Quintus Caeciliius Metellus, *65*
cubiculum, *385*
Cumae, 451
Curia, *30, 33, 231*
Curiatii, *145*
Cynthia, 412

D

David, Jacques-Louis, *145*
Deal, 324
decursio, *278*
del Sarto, *337*
Delia, 412
Delphi, *99*, 106, 109, *109*, 156, *157*
Delphic Oracle, *109*
Demosthenes, 120, *121*
Deucalion, 438-440, *439*
Dido, 448, *448*, 450, 451
Dioskorides of Samos, *133*
Discobolus, *123*
Dispater, *346*
Diviciacus, 264, 280
Domitian, 419
Doric
columns, *183*
temple, *140*
Dover, 324, *328*
drama, Roman, 132
Druids, *327*, 341, *342*, 344, *345*
Drusilla, Livia, 17, *20*
Dumnorix, 256, 264, 325

E

Eburones, 329
Echo, 441, *442*
Eclogues, *24*
education
Greek, 86
of children, early, *16, 21*
Roman, 86
Elaver River, 360
Elysian Fields, 412
Empire, Roman, 199-200
map of, 136-137
Ennius, 398
Epicureans, *401*
Epicurus, 400, *401*
Erechtheum, *81*
Ericson, Leif, 425
Etruscans, *14*, 138, *149, 158*
Euclid, 138
Euridice, *437*, 444, *445*
Eutropius, 146

F

Facilis, Marcus Favonius, *331*
family
matters, Gallic, 349
unit, Roman, *11*
festivals, Roman, *39*
fire brigade, Roman, 82
First Triumvirate, 232
Flamininus, 182
Fleece, Golden, *203*, 204, 208, 219, *220, 222*
food, Roman, 58
fortifications, Caesar's, *253*
Fortuna (goddess), 44, 48, *48*, *161*
Forum of Julius Caesar, *293*
Forum, Roman, *3, 30, 42, 233*, *293*
founding of Rome, *149*
freedoms, Roman, 200
Fulvia, 8, 32, 37
Fundanus, *388*
funeral rites, Roman, 82
funerals, Gallic, 349
Furianus, Unit I-II (pp. 1-143)

G

Galba, Servius, 296
Gallia, map of, 228-229
Garden, the (school), *401*
Gaul(s), 167, *168*, 171, *172*, 173, 186, 188, Units V-VII (pp. 230-379)
Gellius Aulus, 175, 420
Geneva, *254*
Georgics, *24*
Gergovia, 360, 362
Germanicus, *370*
Germans, Units V-VII (pp. 230-379)
Gesta Romanorum, 431
gladiators, 49, *53*, 54
Glauce, *227*
Golden Fleece, *203*, 204, 208, 219, *220, 222*
Gordiano, Emperor, *55*
Gorgon, *435*
government, Roman, 200
Great Fire of 1666, 324
Great St. Bernard Pass, 296
Greek civilization, 138-140

H

Hades, 444, 451, 452
Hadrian, Emperor, *95*
  Villa, *81*
Haeduan, 325
Haeduans, 260, *261*, 264, 285, 325, 361, 362
Hammer-God, *346*
Hannibal, 178, 234
Harpy, *212*
Helen of Troy, 450
Helvetians, Unit V (pp. 230-291)
Herculaneum, *216*, *382*, 383
Hercynian Forest, 354
Hermes, *445*
Hirtius, Aulus, 375
Histories, 419
holidays, Roman, 42
Holmes, T. Rice, 290
Homer, 120, *121*, 138
Horace, 22, *23*, 126, 410
Horatii, *145*, 148
Horatio, 138
House of the Moralist, *416*
houses, Roman, 58
hunting, Roman, *421*

I

Iacopone of Todi, 429
Iberian Peninsula, 290
Ides of March, 232
Ile de la Cité, *361*
Ile St. Louis, *361*
Illyricum, 233, 325
impluvium, *5*
ink, Roman, *69*
inkpot, Roman, *69*
invasions of Britain, Caesar's, 324, 325
Isthmus of Corinth, 182
Italy, map of, 194

J

Jason, Unit IV (pp. 202-229)
Julio-Claudian line, *23*
Junius, 156
Juno, *172*, 441, 448
Jupiter, *346*, 438, 443, 449, 450
Juvenal, 420

L

Labienus, 256, 257, 264-265, 295, 296, 322, 325, 329, 331, 338, 362, 371
Lambaesis, *262*
Laura, *432*
Laws of the Twelve Tables, 26-27, *27*, *30*, *45*
Libanius, 78
liberty, Roman political, 200
libraries, Roman, 22
Libya, 199
Liger River, 296
Lingones, 271
literature, Latin, 398
Liutprand, 424
Livius, Titus, *see* Livy
Livy, 146, *147*, 175, 409
Loire River, 296
Londinium, 324
Longinus, Cassius, *235*
Louvre, *91*, *286*, *445*
Lucius, *35*
Lucretia, *153*
Lucretius, 120, 400-401, 402
Lupercalia, *39*
Lutecia, 362
Lycurgus, 112, 114
Lyon, France, *261*

M

Maison Carée, *243*
Mandubii, 369
Manlius, 175
map of
  Gallia, 228-229
  Italy, 194
  Roman Empire, 136-137
  Rome, 197
  Siege of Alisia, *364*
  voyage of the Argonauts, *205*
marathon race, 116
Marcus, 11-12, 15
Marius, 120, 287, 290
Maro, Publius Vergilius, *see* Vergil
marriage ceremonies, Roman, 101, *103*
marriages, Gallic, 349
married women, Roman, *130*
Martial, 418
masks, theater, *291*
Mauritania, *324*
Maxentius, *233*
Maximus, Valerius, 414
meals, Roman, 58, *59*, *61*
Medea, 204, *216*, *224*, *227*
Medusa, *435*, 443
megalith, prehistoric, *327*
Menapii, 302, 304, 338
Menelaus, 450
Mercury, 450
Mérida, Spain, *291*
Messalla, 411
Metamorphoses, 438
Metella, Caecilia, 64, *65*
Metiosedum, 362
Michelangelo, *173*
Micon, *79*
Milton, *442*
Misenum, 383
Mithradates VI of Anatolia, *127*
Morini, 302, 310, 322
mosaic, Roman, *75*, *114*, *133*
Mucius, 159, 160
Myron, 116, *123*

N

Naples, 383
Napoleon, 234
Narbo, 358
Narcissus, 441, *442*
Naso, Publius Ovidius, *see* Ovid
navy, Roman, *179*
Nepos, Cornelius, 402
Neptune, Temple of, *140*
Nero, 195, *196*, 197, 382, 415, 416
Nervii, 294, 329, 338
New Year, Roman, *39*
Nike, *91*, *92*, *93*
Nile
  Mosaic, *161*
  River, *161*
Nîmes, France, *241*, *243*
Nine Lyric Poets, The, 111
Norsemen, 455
Notre Dame de Paris, *361*
Numa, 120
Numidia, 407

O

Ocelum, 256
Octavian, 11, 125, 190, 234, 374
Octodurus, 296
oculus, *35*
Oedipus, *109*
Olympeium, Temple of, *95*
Olympic Games, 116, *118*, 182
omens, 48
omphalos, *99*
oracles, 44, 106, 109, *109*, *157*, 204
Orange, France, *246*, *282*
oratory, art of, *111*
Orgetorix, 244, 245, 248, 249
Orpheus, 355, *437*, 444, *445*
Ostia, *41*
Ovid, 24, 82, 84, *84*, 85, 412, 435, 438, *439*

P

Paestum, *140*
Painted Stoa, *79*
Palmyra, Syria, *193*
Pantheon, *35*
Paris, 361, *361*
Parisii, *338*, *361*
Parnassus, Mt., 438
Parthenon, *57*, 91, 95, *112*
patricians, 133, 163
Pax Romana, *191*
peace, Roman, 200
Pelias, King, 204, 206, *207*, *222*, *224*
Periander of Corinth, 111
Pericles, *112*, 120, 234
peristylum, *5*
persecutions of Christians, 200
Perseus, *435*, 443
Petrarch, 431, *432*
Petronius, 415-416
Phaedrus, 413
Pharsalus, 234
Pheidippides, 116
Philip, 182
Phoenicia, 178, 448
Phoenicians, *158*
Phorcys, *435*
Pirustae, 325
Pittacus of Mytilene, 111
Pius, Antoninus, *278*
Plato, *87*, *124*
Plautus, *133*, 399, *399*
plebians, 133, 163
Pliny the Elder, 200, 382, 383
Pliny the Younger, 381, 382, 383, 384, *391*, 392, 420
Plutarch, 232
Pluto, 444
Poggio, 433
Pollians, *331*
Polygnotus, *79*
Pompeii, *1*, *381*, *382*, 383, *385*, *399*, *416*
Pompey, 73, 76, 120, 186, 188, 232, 234, *234*, 338
Pont du Gard, *241*
Porch of Maidens, *81*
Porsena, 159
Portus Itius, 325
Poussin, Nicolas, *437*, *442*
Praeneste, *161*
Praetorian Guard, *196*, *238*, *324*
Propertius, 412
prophecies, 44
prophesy, *99*, *157*
Propylaea, *57*, 91, *92*
Proserpina, 444
Provence, *268*
Publius Vergilius Maro, *see* Vergil
Publius, Unit I & II (pp. 1-143)
Punic Wars, 178, *179*
Pygmalion of Cyprus, 445-446
Pyrgopolinices, 400
Pyrrha, 438, *439*
Python, *99*

Q

Quintilian, 382, 417, 418
Quintus, 11-12

R

races, chariot, *395*
Raphael, *124*
Regulus, 178, 180
Remi, 294
Renaissance, 139, 431, *432*
rhetoric, art of, *87*
Rhine River, 290, 296, 304, 306, *307*, 338, *370*
Rhone River, 253, *254*, *261*
rights, Gallic, 349
Rome
  civilization, 138-140
  founding of, *149*
  map of, 197
Romulus, *149*, *164*
roof tiles, Roman, *319*
Rubicon River, 234, *337*
Rufus, Cornelius, *1*, 8
ruins, Roman, *199*, *227*, *258*, *262*, *316*

S

Sabines, *164*, 398
Sabinus, 300, 329
sacrifices, Roman, *409*
Sallust, 407
Samothrace, *93*
Santoni, *257*
Saône River, 261, *261*, 264
Saturnalia, *39*
Scaevola, 159
"School of Athens", *124*
schools, Roman, *424*
Scipio, 120
Secular Games, 22
Secular Hymn, The, 22
Secunda, 2, 26, 31, 32
Segusiavi, 256
Seine River, *361*
Senate, Roman, 32, *165*, *191*, *231*
  House, *30*, *231*
Senators, Roman, 32
Seneca, 415, 418
Senones, 338
Sequanians, *261*, 280
servants, Roman, *142*
Seven Wise Men, The, 111
Sextus, *153*
Shakespeare, 232
Shaw, George Bernard, 232
ships,
  Gallic, 297
  Roman, 297, *301*
Sibyl, 451, 452
Silvanus, *346*
slavery, Roman, 200
slaves,
  daily tasks of, *70*
  Roman, *394*
Socrates, *109*, 120
Solon, 111, 120
Sotiates, 302

spectacles, Roman, *55*
sports,
Olympic, *116*
Roman, *55, 116*
St. Albans, England, 316
statue of Victory, 91
Stonehenge, *327*
Sucellus, *346*
Suebi, 303, 304, *304,* 338, 355
Suessiones, 294
Suetonius, 232
Sulla, 126, *127, 165,* 232
Sulpicia, 411-412, *411*
Syria, *193*
Syrus, Publilius, 408

T

Tacitus, Cornelius, 290, 324, 383, 384, 419
Tamesis River, 329
Taranis, *346*
Tarquin, 152, *153, 157*
Tarquinia, *14, 139*
Tarquins, *155, 157*
Tasgetius, 329
Tatius, Titus, 398
taxes, 3
Temple of
Apollo, 106, *109, 183*
Athena Nike, *92*
Neptune, *140*
Olympeium, *95*
Venus and Rome, *42, 233*
Venus Genetrix, *293*
Ten Attic Orators, The, 111
Tencteri, 304
Terence, 399, *399*
Teutonic, 290
Teutons, 290
Thales of Miletus, 111
Thames River, 329
theater, Roman, *133, 246, 291*
Themistocles, 120
Theodosius I, *50*
Thermopylae, 112, 113, *193*
Thessaly, 204, 206, *222*
Thomas of Celano, 429, *430*
Thrace, *324*
Tiber
Arch, *155*
city of, 146
River, 159
Tiberius, *20*
and Germanicus, Arch of, *257*
Tibullus, 411, *411,* 412
Timgad, Algeria, *262*
Titus, Arch of, *322*
Tivoli, *81*
Tiziano, *153*
Torquatus, 175
Trajan, *269, 298*
Transalpine Gaul, 233, *246*
Treasury of the Athenians at Delphi, *107*
Treveri, 295, 296, 325, 331, 334, 338, *352*
Treverorum, Augusta, *352*
Trier, Germany, *352*
Trimalchio, 415-416
Trinovantes, 329
Trojan War, 450
Trojans, 448, 450
Troy, fall of, 450
Turner, William, *448*
Twelve Tables, Laws of the, 26-27, *27, 30, 45*
Tyre, 448, *448*

U

Usipetes, 304

V

values, Greek and Roman, 128
Veneti, 296, 300, 357
Venus, 232, *233,* 445, 449
and Rome, Temple of, *42, 233*
Genetrix, Temple of, *293*
Vercassivellaunus, 371
Vercingetorix, 357, *357,* 359-363, 371, *373,* 375, *375*
Vergil (Publius Vergilius Maro), 22, *23, 24,* 120, 138, 140, 398, 410, 435, 446-447, 453
Vergilius Maro, Publius *see* Vergil
Verona, Italy, *258*
verse, Latin, 436
Vesontio, 289
Vespasian, Emperor, 417
Vestal Virgins, *18,* 38, *42*
Vesuvius, Mt., *382,* 383
Via, Appia, see Appian Way
Vichy, 360
Victory, statue of, *91*
Virgins, Vestal, *18,* 38, *42*
Volubilis, Morocco, *199*
"vulgar" Latin, 290

W

Washington, George, 146, 234
water standards, *129*
weaponry, Roman, *174*
wedding customs, 101, *101*
well, community, *129*
Wheeler, Sir Mortimer, 324
women's responsibilities, Roman, *21*
writing implements, Roman, *69,* 97

Grammar/Vocabulary Index

A

ablative
absolute, 30, 53
of accompaniment, 14, 52
of agent, 30, 53
of comparison, 54
of degree of difference, 84, 192
of means, 20, 52
of *place where,* 7, 52
of respect, 41, 53-54
of separation, 188
of *time when,* 7, 52
uses of, 52
accusative, 6
active subjunctive, present, 60-61
adjectives
agreement of, 7
comparison of, 46, 47, 50-51
dative with, 48
first declension, 4
indefinite, 107-108
interrogative, 34
irregular, 39
second declension, 4
third declension, 13
adverbs, comparison of, 46, 47, 51
aliquis, 176
antecedent, 37
anticipatory clauses, subjunctive in, 262
apposition, 7
assimilation, 55
aviation terms from Latin, 177

C

cardinal numerals, Latin, 67
causal clauses with *quod* and *quoniam*, 268
commands, indirect, 117, 176
comparative, 47
comparison of
adjectives, 46, 47, 50-51
adverbs, 46, 47, 51
consonants
double (in Latin), 55
silent (in English), 162
cum, 88
clauses, 154, 169

D

dative
case, 14-15
of agent, 157
of possession, 261
of purpose, 134, 172
of reference, 134, 172
with adjectives, 48
with compounds, 149-150
with special verbs, 133-134
declension
first
adjectives, 4
nouns, 4
second
adjectives, 4
nouns, 4
third
adjectives, 13
nouns, 12
fourth, 59-60
fifth, 83
demonstratives, 40
deponent verbs, 98
derivatives from Latin, 16
description, 191
direct object, 6
double consonants, 55

E

eō, 108-109
etiam, 193

F

fīō, 126
ferō, 74-75
fifth declension, 83
first declension
adjectives, 4
nouns, 4, 83
fourth declension
nouns, 59-60
future
infinitive, 36
passive participle, 113, 122, 157
perfect tense, 23-24
tense, 5, 19

G

genitive of the whole, 168-169
geometrical terms from Latin, 166
gerund, 121-123, 157
gerundive, 122-123

H

hic, 40
hortatory subjunctive, 61-62

I

idem, 45-46
ille, 40
imperative, 183
imperfect
subjunctive, 69, 70
tense, 5, 19
impersonal verbs, 164-165
indefinite
adjectives, 107-108
pronouns, 107-108
indefinites *quis, aliquis,* and *quīdam,* 176
indirect
commands, 117, 176
object, 14-15
questions, 103-104
statement, 36
infinitives
active, 33-34
passive, 33-34
tenses of, 36
used as subject and object, 20
interrogative
adjectives, 34
pronouns, 34-35
ipse, 45-46
irregular adjectives, 39
is, 45-46
***i–stem* nouns,** 12

J

jussive subjunctive, 61-62

L

legal phrases from Latin, 111
locative case, 154

M

mālō, 153
mathematical terms from Latin, 166
medical terms from Latin, 77
milia, 41
mille, 41
mottos, state, 124, 270, 356
musical terms from Latin, 90

N

names in Latin, foreign, 243
nē, 65, 80
nōlō, 129-130
nominative, 4
  predicate, 6
  subject, 6
nouns
  clause of result, 117
  fifth declension, 83
  first declension, 4
  fourth declension, 59-60
  i–stem, 12
  second declension, 4
  third declension, 12
numerals
  cardinal, 67
  ordinal, 67

O

object
  direct, 6
  indirect, 14-15
ordinal numerals, Latin, 67

P

participles, 28-29
  agreement of, 29
  future passive, 113, 122, 157
  present, 105
  used as adjectives and nouns, perfect, 29
  used as clauses, 29
passive
  participle, future, 113, 122, 157
  subjunctive, present, 60-61
  voice, 27-28
perfect
  infinitive, 36
  participles used as adjectives and nouns, 29
  subjunctive, 92-93, 94
  tense, 23-24
personal pronouns, 102
place
  names from Latin, 273
  to which, 180
pluperfect
  active subjunctive, 87
  subjunctive, 92-93
  tense, 23-24
possum, 40, 84
postquam, 88
predicate nominative, 6
prefixes, Latin, 15, 21, 25, 31, 48, 55, 127, 155, 170, 198
present
  active subjunctive, 60-61
  infinitive, 36
  participle, 105
  passive subjunctive, 60-61
  stem of verbs, 5
  tense, 5, 19
pronouns
  indefinite, 107-108
  interrogative, 34-35
  personal, 102
  reflexive, 102
  relative, 34, 36-37
purpose clauses with *ut* and *nē*, 65, 80

Q

quīdam, 176
questions, indirect, 103-104
quidem, 193
quis, 176
quisquam, 184
quisque, 184
***quod,* causal clauses with**, 268
***quoniam,* causal clauses with**, 268
quoque, 193

R

reflexive pronouns, 102
relative
  as connective, 179
  pronouns, 34, 36-37
  purpose clauses, 196
result clauses, 184
  with *ut* and *ut nōn,* 79-80

S

scientific terms from Latin, 100
second declension
  adjectives, 4
  nouns, 4
sentence structure, Latin, 160
sequence of tenses, subjunctive, 94
Spanish, Latin influence in, 115, 185, 243
statement, indirect, 36
subject nominative, 6
subjunctive
  after verbs of fearing, 160
  hortatory, 61-62
  imperfect, 69, 70
  in anticipatory clauses, 262
  jussive, 61-62
  mood, 60-61
  possum, 84
  sum, 84
  pluperfect active, 87
  present active, 60-61
  present passive, 60-61
  sequence of tenses, 94
  sum, 84
  tense sequence in purpose clauses, 70-71
suffixes, Latin, 37, 43, 72, 119, 181
sum, 6, 40, 24, 70, 84
  omission of, 172
superlative, 47

T

third declension
  adjectives, 13
  nouns, 12
time clauses: *ubi, postquam, cum,* 88
translation hints, 205

U

ubi, 88, 104
ut, 65, 79-80
ut nōn, 65, 79-80

V

verbs
deponent, 98
future perfect tense, 23-24
future tense, 5, 19
imperfect tense, 5, 19
impersonal, 164-165
perfect tense, 23-24
pluperfect tense, 23-24
present stem, 5
present tense, 5, 19
vocative, 4
volō, 129-130